CERAMIC GLAZES

CERAMIC GLAZES

CULLEN W. PARMELEE
(1875 - 1947)

THIRD EDITION

Completely revised and enlarged by
CAMERON G. HARMAN, Ph.D.
Consulting Ceramic Technologist

Sponsoring Editor: J. J. Svec, Editor, *Ceramic Industry*

Ceramic Book and Literature Service (CBLS)
119, Brentwood Street
Marietta, OH 45750 USA
Tel: (614) 374-9458
Fax: (614) 373-2138

Library of Congress Catalog Card Number: 70-183371
ISBN: 1-878907-05-0

Reprinted in India in 1993 in limited quantity with permission from the copyright holder (Van Nostrand Reinhold) by:

Ceramic Book and Literature Service (CBLS)
119, Brentwood Street
Marietta, OH 45750 USA
Tel: (614) 374-9458
Fax: (614) 373-2138

Contents

Preface to the Third Edition

The first edition of *Ceramic Glazes* was prepared by Professor Parmelee during the late 30s and early 40s. Since that time, all branches of science and technology have advanced an almost unbelievable degree. The science and art of glazes and glazing also have advanced. The purpose of this edition is to bring this book more nearly in line with the present state of the art.

Because the art and technology of glazes date so far back, they were relatively well established at the time the first edition was prepared. So much intelligent effort went into empirical investigations that the art of glazes was much further advanced than related science. Much of the work done during the first 25 years of this century still forms the basis of current glaze technology.

Consequently, the classic works of the earlier investigators have more than historic significance. Some of the literature, in a sense, is basic. Because certain of the earlier contributions are as useful today as they were at the time of their original publication, such references in this edition have not been disturbed.

During the preceding quarter of a century, investigative effort has been primarily concerned with fields other than ceramic glazes. Some new and revolutionary developments have been made. Included in this category are improved ceramic pigments, which are typified by the zirconium-vanadium stains, and the classic developments in glass-ceramics. New materials have been introduced, as have new techniques such as automation and superfast firing. New uses for glazes have been opened, such as precision resistors, electrically conducting glazes, and glazes for sophisticated electronic components.

Things are possible now and for foreseeable developments that only a short time ago were regarded as forever impossible. These include glazes for low-, even negative-expansion ceramics, nucleated in situ opacification, and new colors.

Modern basic science has contributed much to the advancement and understanding of glaze technology. The ramifications of crystal structure, nucleation and crystallization of glazes, and materials science in general have been recognized and taken into account. These, per se, are not proper subjects for detailed treatment in this volume.

The second edition of *Ceramic Glazes* was edited and revised by E. D. Lynch, assistant professor in the Department of Ceramic Engineering, University of Illinois, and by A. L. Friedberg, a research fellow in the same department.

Cameron G. Harman, who completely revised and updated this new third edition, entered the University of Illinois the year following the appointment of Professor Parmelee as head of the Department of Ceramic Engineering. By 1939, he had earned his bachelor's, master's and doctor's degrees while engaging in a blend of academic and industrial activities. He served on the staff of the University during most of the period ending in late 1945, when he became permanently engaged in industrial and private enterprises. He was active in the American Ceramic Society and was elected a fellow in 1942.

His work continued to include the general field of ceramics, nonmetallics, silicate technology, and composite materials. It covered the field's entire spectrum from conventional ceramics, electronic components, glass, refractories, coatings, and nonmetallics through inorganic materials applicable to space, nuclear and defense programs. His experience has been about equally distributed among research, academic work and engineering. He has wide experience as a consultant and has directed more than 100 contract research projects during the last twenty years.

In addition to numerous classified and confidential reports, Dr. Harman has published over fifty technical papers and has been granted twenty-four patents. He is listed in *American Men of Science* and similar rosters.

Much of Dr. Harman's experience has been in the area of directing and supervising technical activities in research and in industrial practice, and in pyrochemical and pyrophysical problems. He has been continuously engaged in such work for about forty years. For much of that time, he has been a recognized leader in his field. He has made valuable contributions in the general fields of high temperature physiochemistry of nonmetallic inorganic materials, as well as in disperse systems of water—solids. He has extensive experience in interfacial reactions between metals and nonmetallic materials. He was responsible for early work on coatings for refractory and nuclear applications and specialties such as reinforced composites and the synthesis of ceramic fibers and whiskers.

Foreword

The art of making glazes may be traced back through six or seven millenniums. Notwithstanding the decay and disappearance of several successive civilizations, the knowledge of the art survived these catastrophes or was rediscovered by later generations of men. There is no reason to believe that any important body of glaze-making facts, possessed by the ancients, has been lost. Naturally, the potter of all ages has jealously guarded the secrets of the craft. These have been his means of livelihood, the tokens of his skill honored by fellow workers of the same guild. Unfortunately, the "secret formula" has too often been used to beguile the potter into the purchase of recipes having a dubious past history and an even less bright future.

While there is much yet to be learned regarding glazes, the introduction of the principles of chemistry, as well as expanding knowledge in that field, has marked the passing of the Dark Ages in the history of ceramic development. The great pioneers who strove during the nineteenth century to promote the change include the names of Brogniart, Salvetat, and especially Hermann Seger. They taught the younger generation a new knowledge and a new technique which have produced, during the past half century, the great volume of extremely valuable ceramic scientific literature.

This great accumulation of printed information has in fact proved to be an embarrassment of riches because of the time and the effort required to read, classify, digest, and analyze the data. Such a period of accumulation of information is a phase common to the history of any science. As soon as sufficient material has been gathered, there follows the coordination of the facts and the deduction of the basic principles.

These fundamentals are the elements from which the new knowledge may be created with greater surety and less time and effort. It is unfortunate, but understandable, that much published literature on glazes is lacking in essential and precise data. A description of a glaze is made more valuable and practicable if it is accompanied by full details as to the sources and the analyses of the constituent materials, the details of the preparation, application, and the firing. Such information is too frequently fragmentary or lacking. Another desirable goal is the inclusion in the discussions of data on operations made with precision apparatus and methods and fewer records that rely mainly on personal judgment. A very great improvement is observed in this respect at the present. A greater volume of very valuable physical data is now appearing in the literature.

The following book on glazes is an attempt to summarize information gathered from the extensive literature relating to this topic. In order to represent glaze compositions, the use of the convenient ceramic or Seger formulas has been employed. This practice is so widespread, so well established, and so easily learned that all who are interested in glazes, but unacquainted with the method, are urged to acquire the habit.

Unfortunately, the authors cannot personally vouch for the validity of all the statements presented. However, the data have been carefully gathered from reliable sources and any failures to obtain the desired results may honestly be attributed to a difference in materials. or their preparation, application, or firing. It is humbly requested that the experimenter who is guided by this book will accept his disappointments with charity and have abundant reason to rejoice over successes.

1

General Concepts

Definition of Glazes

Glazes are thin continuous coatings, usually prepared from fused silicate mixtures fusion-bonded to ceramic surfaces. Glazes are commonly applied on claywares or other ceramics for protective, marking, sealing, or decorative purposes. They are glasses in their physical and chemical nature: hard, slightly or completely insoluble, excepting in hydrofluoric acids or strong bases, and impermeable to gases and liquids. Like glasses, they are not definite chemical compounds but complex mixtures which sometimes are described as "undercooled solutions," since many of their properties are analogous to those observed in ordinary solutions. Glazes are more or less lustrous. Generally the surface is highly reflecting or glossy, but the matt glaze has a surface which has been compared, quite accurately, with the appearance of a glace kid, and all gradations of glossiness or mattness may be observed.

An absence of a visible structure is characteristic of glasses and glazes with the exceptions of the true matt, which contains great numbers of microscopic crystals, and those glazes in which the individual crystals are macroscopic and therefore easily distinguishable.

Glazes may be colored or colorless, transparent, translucent, or opaque. Whatever the appearance, the glaze or similar coating is used on ceramic wares to serve one or more of the following purposes: (1) to render the ware impermeable to liquids and gases, (2) to provide an aesthetically attractive coating which covers up blemishes and provides a decorative effect, (3) to provide readily cleanable surfaces, (4) as various functionally protective coatings, (5) to increase strength, and (6) for special effects, of which electrical, optical, and chemical are major examples.

A bright or "full" glaze is a glossy and generally a transparent coating. If coloring oxides are used in the compositions, they usually have the effect of obscuring the body underneath. Also, the glaze may contain an unimportant amount of undissolved material or scattered minute crystals, especially at the glaze-body interface, but such conditions should not prevent the use of the term "full" glaze.

The term enamel is given to a fused vitreous, superficial coating used on claywares, similar in its properties and use to the glaze, and differing only in the uniform opacity observed when one examines the surface of the fracture when the enamel layer is broken. The enamel may be white or otherwise colored. A distinction must be made between (a) the glaze enamel just described, (b) the vitreous or porcelain enamel used to coat metals, and (c) the easily fusible colored glass which is applied on glass or glaze surface for decorative pattern.

Another kind of superficial coating frequently used to coat claywares with or without the addition of a glaze coat is the slip, or engobe. If used under the glaze it also may be called an underslip. These coatings do not develop to the completely glassy character of the glaze but vary from the porcelaneous appearance of the vitreous slip to the semivitreous appearance of the ordinary slip.

The slip or engobe as usually employed is a coating on the body to cover minor defects of color or texture, and thereby furnish a better foundation for the glaze coat. The vitreous slip is frequently used without a glaze coating since slip of this sort may serve to decorate and protect the ware. Underslips are seldom vitrified.

The Antiquity of Glazing

With our present knowledge we now attribute the origin of the art of glazing to the Egyptians at least as early as the fifth millenium B.C., although Petrie[1] sets a much earlier date, namely, 12,000 B.C. The earliest objects were steatite, coated with a vitreous layer. The term faience, as generally used by the Egyptologist, refers to a body containing 85% or more of silica which was not bonded with clay, according to published analyses. In this respect it is distinct from the clayey body of the typical pottery faience. The term paste is used also by the archeologist to designate a similar composition. Glazed faience in the form of beads appeared among the relics of the fourth millenium and, later, as scarabs, amulets, and statuettes. Larger wares, such as steatite vases and statuettes, appeared about 2000 B.C.

The oldest dated glazed fragment (ca. 3300 B.C.) bears the name

King Mena and was done in polychrome in a complicated technique. The history of the development of bodies and glazes in India and Mesopotamia can be traced back to the third millenium B.C.; the composition of the body and the glaze were very similar to those used by the Egyptians.[2]

Glazed paste objects appear to have been introduced from Egypt into Crete and the islands of the Aegean during the third millenium B.C., and from thence the knowledge of the technique probably spread to Greece. Neither the Greeks nor the Romans manifested much interest in the Egyptian type of glaze but developed the very thin, varnishlike terra sigillata, which distinguished the Samian ware. Other peoples of the eastern Mediterranean and Asia Minor eventually achieved a more interesting and varied glaze technique for use on clay bodies.

The marked technical skill in the use of glazes in ancient times is clearly seen in the excellence of the craftsmanship of large objects as well as small, e.g., the elaborate, monumental embellishments of the great buildings erected by the Assyrians and the Babylonians. The marvelous palace of Sargon near Mosul, Iraq, built 722–705 B.C., was decorated with a profusion of figures of lions, bulls, ravens, and other animal life done on an heroic scale. These were constructed of molded paste and, later, clay brick coated with colored glaze. The equally imposing Ishtar Gate and Processional Road of Babylon is another noteworthy example. Fortunately, the library of Ashur-bani-pal, King of Assyria, 668–626 B.C., has been found and the clay tablets inscribed with cuneiform characters which describe in detail the compositions and procedures for glazing, and preparing pastes and, possibly, glass are being translated.[3]

The extremely siliceous faience or paste used in the East in early times required the glaze coating to be highly alkaline and siliceous and the product had a high gloss. The body had only a slight plasticity. To achieve similar results with a clay body, it had to be coated with a siliceous underslip as a foundation upon which the alkaline glaze was applied. This was the method which was ultimately transmitted to the Moors and introduced by them into northern Africa and thence into Europe. The early potters of the Iranian peninsula apparently learned the use of paste and the alkaline-siliceous glaze from Mesopotamia or even farther west.

When and where the use of lead in glazes was discovered is not known. If the Egyptians used it, the practice seems to have been introduced during the Ptolemaic period.[4] Opinions as to the antiquity of the use of lead in glazes in Egypt and the Middle East are at variance. The Greeks and Romans had some knowledge of its value. The latter are credited with introducing it into Gaul. It was established in France by the 12th century. Lead glazes continued to be the kind most generally in use in Europe until about the fifteenth century.

Lead glazes did not originate in any one country. The lead ore, galena (PbS) was widely employed by primitive people generally. The Chinese used it before authentic history. Galena still is used on crude pottery.

The development of tin enamel is another milestone in the technical progress of the potter. Metallic tin was used in the Middle East at a very early time and the Phoenicians imported tin ores from Cornwall. The properties of the metal were well known and it was widely used in the Mediterranean area in antiquity. Some of the glazed ware from Assyria and Babylonia has been mistakenly described as being coated with tin enamels because the brilliant white glossy coatings resembled them in appearance. The Moors are believed to have taken the knowledge with them to the island of Majorca and from thence to Italy. The earliest recorded reference to tin-enameled ware in Italy is about the year 1330 A.D. Another path of migration for the technique has been traced to Persia, at about 500 B.C., thence to Brusa in modern Turkey, where examples may be seen in the decoration of the "Green Mosque," which was built in 1423 A.D. Brogniart[5] was unable to find any tin in glazes on pottery made in Europe before the thirteenth century.

Hirschvogel of Germany visited Italy in 1503 A.D. and carried the secret of the preparation of white-enameled ware (majolica) back to the homeland. In France in 1542 A.D., Bernard Palissay perfected a white-enamel technique which is said to have been inspired by the inspection of a small sample imported from Italy. He is frequently credited with discovering the procedure through great personal effort and sacrifice. His notable success as an artist-potter created a great sensation at that time and stimulated the manufacture of fine ware which could be sold to the moderately prosperous citizenry of France and contiguous countries. The discovery of the use of frits in glazes can be definitely ascribed to the Egyptians or the Middle East, probably Egypt. Other types of glazes in modern use may be considered variants of those described above, i.e., from a historical point of view.

The appearance of the typical porcelain glaze was a logical consequence of the production of that ware in Europe early in the eighteenth century. Porcelain was made in Italy about a century earlier, but the credit for the establishment of an industry belongs to Saxony at the time mentioned. Such ware is fired at very high temperatures, and it was inevitable that the potter would observe and use the information gained from the results of the kiln operations. Further, information and even raw materials were brought to Europe by hardy explorers who had visited the Orient. It does not seem too reckless to point out the kinship, technically, of the porcelain glaze to the clay-slip glazes and, therefore, to the terra sigillata of the Greeks and the Romans.

Classification of Glazes

The classifications of glazes published in ceramic literature are generally very inadequate and are usually bare outlines based on a few properties. The older writers, for example, Kerl and Brogniart, dismissed the matter with scant attention. Thus, Kerl[6] divided glazes into these groups:

1. Lead glazes formed essentially from lead oxide, perhaps a part of the silica replaced by boric oxide or by tin oxide, and a part of the lead oxide by alkalies or alkaline earths
2. Earth glazes made from insoluble minerals
3. Salt glaze, the result of the action of the fumes of common salt

Between the first and second groups there are many variations.

Various methods have been used to characterize or describe individual glazes or groups of related compositions. Some of the terminology is based on characteristics indicated in the following list.

1. relative fusibility, e.g., "easily fusible," "difficultly fusible," and sometimes by cone maturing temperature or range
2. the use or absence of some important glaze ingredient, e.g., "salt glaze," "raw lead glaze," "leadless glaze," "tin enamel," and so on
3. the kind of wares upon which the glazes are used, e.g., whiteware glaze, porcelain glaze, majolica glaze, stoneware glaze, and others
4. the place of origin, such as Albany slip glazes, Bristol glazes, Rockingham glaze; or the name of the inventor, as, for example, Seger porcelain glaze
5. the method of preparation or application; that is, the glazes may be raw or fritted or applied by fuming

Such interesting properties as color and texture—gloss, mattness, opacity—in all degrees are not peculiar to any limited group of glazes and cannot be considered as adequate bases for classification; nor can we divide them into groups defined by the presence or absence of crystallization since that phenomenon may be developed in almost all kinds of compositions, depending in part on the concentration of particular components and the heat treatments. The separation of the glazes into groups according to the character of the bodies on which they are used has notable limitations, because a variety of basic types of glazes can be successfully applied to almost any type of body.

The absence of a unique crystalline structure in glazes makes the identification on the basis of any graphic pattern derived from X-ray studies impossible at the present time. As stated elsewhere, glazes, like glasses, are analogous to ordinary aqueous solutions in this respect. For many years we have known that glaze compositions must conform to certain limits for particular types of bodies and temperature conditions; for example, Funk[7] groups some types of glazes as shown in table 1.1.

Table 1.1. Silica to alumina ratio in some glazes[7]

Body	Mol. equiv. Silica	Mol. equiv. Alumina	Approximate maturing cone temps.
Common earthenware	0.8 -2	0 -0.3	010–06
Steingut (Common whiteware)	0.8 -2	0.1–0.5	4
Stoneware	1.25–2	0.1–0.8	4–9
Porcelain	2.00–2.6	0.5–1.25	10 and above

During the last half of the preceding century, Schumacher[8] presented the concept of glazes being constituted of norms, or molecular groups. The idea was again introduced in the U.S. early in this century. The idea is neither theoretically nor experimentally sound. A chemical classification was proposed by Parmelee as follows:

A. Raw glazes
- I. Containing lead
  - a. No alumina present
    - 1. Lead the only base
    - 2. With other bases
  - b. Containing alumina and various bases
    - 1. High lead, 0.5 mol. equivalent or more
    - 2. Low lead, less than 0.5 mol. equivalent
    - 3. Containing boric oxide (not fritted)
    - 4. No alkali present, containing boric oxide (not fritted)
- II. Leadless, containing alumina, with various bases
  - a. Containing alkaline earths, but no alkalies
  - b. Containing alkalies and alkaline earths
    - 1. Natural clay slips
    - 2. Synthetic mixtures of minerals
  - c. Containing alkalies, alkaline earths, and zinc oxide
  - d. Containing boric oxide
  - e. Salt glazes

B. Fritted glazes
- I. Containing lead in addition to other bases
  - a. Without alumina or boric oxide
  - b. With alumina and boric oxide
    - 1. Without alkali
    - 2. With alkali
- II. Leadless
  - a. Without boric oxide
  - b. With boric oxide

1. Alkalies, the only bases present
2. Alkalies, alkaline earths, with or without zinc present

c. Containing important amounts of barium

It is not an ideal classification but, if taken in the spirit in which it is offered, can be of some use. It deals only with conventional and classical glazes and does not attempt to cover some of the more recent and unconventional glazes and coatings.

Opaque Glazes

Opaque glazes are those sufficiently low in light transparency as to effectively hide the body from view. They usually are white, but this is not a requirement. The more opaque the glaze, the greater the hiding power per unit of glaze thickness.

The term "enamel" sometimes is used to describe a white, densely opaque glaze, usually used over colored bodies; it may be applied to glazes that are to be used in a relatively thin layer to effectively hide the substrate from the observer.

In glass, the terms "alabaster," "opal," and "milk" are applied to white products of low or reduced light transmissions; more simply, to those having a pronounced degree of opacity. Usually, alabaster refers to glass products of moderate to dense opacity that weakly transmit white light in thinner sections. The term opal refers to a glass of moderate to weak opacity that appears white, as in alabaster, but has in addition a fiery appearance similar to opal. It is slightly less white in reflected light than alabaster but less dense in transmitted light, and the diffracted or fiery appearance is evident.

Theoretical Considerations

Opacity in glazes is due to the reflection and refraction of light by phases and particles suspended in the clear matrix. To be opaque, the glaze layer must contain materials in a fine state of subdivision that have refractive indices different from that of the matrix glass. The degree of opacity depends on several factors. These are summarized as follows:

a. The difference in refractive index between the transparent matrix and the dispersed opacity-causing particles.

b. The size of the dispersed particles or, more specifically, the degree of dispersion. In general, the smaller the particles, the more effective is the opacity. The effective size, however, ultimately is limited by the wavelength of the light. The "fire" of opal and the opallike effects result from internal reflections by particles too small to effectively reflect light from the longer wavelength while still reflecting light of shorter rays.

c. Opacity increases as the number of times a light beam is reflected during the passage through the medium. This is tantamount to saying that, for a given thickness, opacity increases as the number of reflecting particles per unit volume increases. Thus, opacity increases as the concentration of opacifier increases, but the rate of increase decreases. The absorption coefficient of the various media will of course have their influence.

d. The character of the boundary zone between opacifier particles and the transparent matrix has a modifying influence. The sharper the boundary, the more effective the opacifier. A solution-rim or a diffusion zone impairs the sharpness and consequently the effectiveness. Thus, the greater the solubility of the opacifier or the more corrosive the matrix, the less the opacity.

Crystals precipitated in place could, on this basis, be of maximum effectiveness in regard to sharpness of interface boundaries. Intensification of opacification for the purpose of reducing the quantity of opacifier to save cost or to improve coverage might be achieved on the basis of several approaches. Some examples are:

a. Select fine-grained, high-index opacifiers for mill-adding; then develop by experiment minor additives to function as high temperature dispersing agents. These would be among those that would ionize in the melt, and become weakly adsorbed by the opacifier particles. The ideal degree of adsorption would be such as to cause particles of opacifier to become dynamically dispersed, analagous to deflocculation in aqueous systems.

b. Utilization of liquid-liquid phase separation by a combination of glaze composition and heat treatment. Thus, emulsions of glasses would be formed instead of dispersed crystals or crystal aggregates.

c. Precipitation in situ of high index or low index crystals during the cooling of the glazes. The glazes might be formulated so that, during the cooling, a high index crystal of very small size would separate. To operate at maximum efficiency, nucleating agents may be required as with gold ruby. Good opacification might be achieved and high gloss still be retained with surfaces that would not be subject to metal marking.

d. Existing compositions could be modified to furnish base glazes that yield greater opacification without changing opacifiers.

e. Crystal phases should be as fine as possible and as uniformly dispersed as possible. There should be as much difference in refractive index of crystal and glass as possible. Where the opacifier is of high index, a reduction of index of base glass can be considered. A remarkable increase in opacity can be achieved by optimum control of particle size and distribution.

f. Some opacity results when indices of refraction of the parent glass and

Table 1.2. Refractive indices of some materials[10]

Material	*Mean index*	*Difference in N_d between glaze and opacifier*
Tin oxide	2.04	0.49
Cerium oxide	2.33	0.78
Zirconium dioxide	2.40	0.85
Titanium dioxide	2.50	0.95
Antimony trioxide	2.60	1.05
Zirconium silicate	2.05	0.50
Calcium fluoride	1.43	0.12
Zinc oxide	2.10	0.55
Air	1.00	0.55
Glaze	1.55	0.00

the dispersed phase differ by as little as 0.04. Some opacity develops when cristobalite ($n = 1.486$) is dispersed in glass of index of 1.51. Most opacifiers in glazes have indices in the range of 2.1 to 2.4 and are, of course, much more effective than low index fluorides, but could be even more so if they could be precipitated in situ in very small crystallites and well dispersed.

The intensity of opacification is related to the difference between the index of refraction of the opacifier and the glass matrix. This has been described by Kerstan[9] as:

$$I_r = \frac{I_e(n_2 - n_1)^2}{(n_2 + n_1)^2}$$

where,

I_r = intensity of diffuse reflected light
I_e = incident light
n_1 = index of refraction of glass matrix
n_2 = index of refraction of the opacifier

Some typical materials and their refractive indices are listed in table 1.2. According to Larson and Berman,[10] Gladstone and Dale (cited by reference 10) showed that all liquids (and glasses) have specific refractive energies that are the sum of the refractive energies of their components. This was indicated as:

$$\frac{n - 1}{d} = K, \qquad \text{and} \qquad K = k_1 \frac{P_1}{100} + k_2 \frac{P_2}{100} + \text{etc.}$$

where K is the specific refractive energy of any substance, and n and d are its index of refraction and density, respectively. The terms P_1, P_2 and k_1, k_2, etc., are weight percentages and specific refractive energies, respec-

Table 1.3. Specific refractive energies ($\frac{n-1}{d} = K$) of oxide components of glazes and opacifiers[10]

Component	*K*	*Component*	*K*	*Component*	*K*
H_2O	0.340	CuO	0.191,0.253	SnO_2	0.145
Li_2O	0.31	ZnO	0.153,0.183	SbO_2	0.198
$(NH_4)_2O$	0.503	HgO	0.18	TeO_2	0.200
Na_2O	0.181	PbO	0.137,0.175	ThO_2	0.12
K_2O	0.189	B_2O_3	0.220	N_2O_5	0.240
Cu_2O	0.250	C_2O_3	0.265	P_2O_5	0.190
Rb_2O	0.129	Al_2O_3	0.193,0.214	Cl_2O_5	0.218
Ag_2O	0.154	Cr_2O_3	0.27	V_2O_5	0.43
Cs_2O	0.124	Mn_2O_3	0.300	As_2O_5	0.169
Hg_2O	0.169	Fe_2O_3	0.308,0.36	Br_2O_5	0.183
Tl_2O	0.120	As_2O_3	0.202,0.225	Cb_2O_5	0.295
BeO	0.220	Y_2O_3	0.144	Sb_2O_5	0.152,0.222
MgO	0.200	Sb_2O_3	0.209,0.232	I_2O_5	0.177
CaO	0.225	La_2O_3	0.149	Ta_2O_5	0.133
MnO	0.224	Ce_2O_3	0.16	SO_3	0.177
FeO	0.187	Bi_2O_3	0.163	CrO_3	0.36
NiO	0.184	CO_2	0.217	SeO_3	0.165
CoO	0.184	SiO_2	0.207	MoO_3	0.241
CdO	0.134	TiO_2	0.397	TeO_3	0.607
BaO	0.127	SeO_2	0.147	WO_3	0.133
SrO	0.143	ZrO_2	0.201	UO_3	0.134

ely, of the components of that substance. The law applies fairly well the crystalline as well as to the amorphous or glassy states. For anisopic substances, the mean index is taken as

$$\frac{2\omega + \epsilon}{3} \quad \text{or} \quad \frac{\alpha + \beta + \gamma}{3}$$

where ω, ϵ, β and γ are refractive indices in the directions of the principal crystallographic directions. Because the specific refractive energies of oxides can be used to estimate the refractive indices of glasses, glazes, and crystalline species, the values in table 1.3 are of interest.

Possibly the first theoretical work on the scattering of light by very small particles was done by Lord Rayleigh.[11] He showed that the blue color of the sky is a light-scattering phenomenon. Subsequent studies have been conducted concerning the scattering of light by particles of various sizes. In fact, light scattering is used analytically as the basis of one method for evaluating the size of colloidal particles.[12]

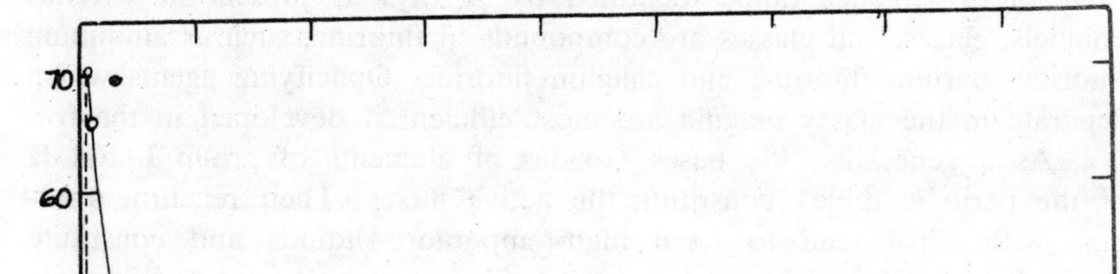

Figure 1.1. Change in reflectance with particle size for a 5-mil layer of 95% glycerine and 5% opacifier, by volume.[13]

The effect of particle size and index of refraction on reflected light from opaque enamels and glazes was studied by King.[13] His results are summarized in fig. 1.1. The maximum opacity was achieved with particles of about $\frac{1}{4}$ (0.24) micron in diameter. Lower reflectance values were achieved with particle sizes greater or less than this value. For the larger particles, the scattering power varied as the total surface of the opacifier. According to Rayleigh's law, the scattering coefficient for extremely small particles should vary as the fourth power of the particle diameter.

Opacifiers

Opacifiers that function because of their insolubility in the glaze melt are advantageously added to the mill batch. A mill batch is the raw material ingredients used in the glaze recipe to make the charge for the processing mill. Examples of mill batch opacifiers are zirconium silicate, tin oxide, and zirconium oxide. A second type separates as crystals or coagulations of dispersoids. Some identified by X rays as present in vitreous enamels, glazes, and glasses are compounds of fluorine, such as aluminum fluoride, barium fluoride, and calcium fluoride. Opacifying agents which separate in the glassy magma are most efficient if developed in the frit.

As a generality, the bases (oxides of elements of group I and II of the periodic table) constitute the active fluxes. Their reaction products with silica tend to form high-temperaure liquids and constitute the general basis for glaze formation. Acid oxides, such as listed in table 1.4, tend to have low rates of solubility in silicate melts, as do their salts

Table 1.4. Acid oxides that would cause opacity in glazes

Oxide	*Refractive indices*	*Melting temp.,°C*	*Coefficient of expansion ×10⁷/°C**
Al_2O_3	1.760–1.768	2,050	70–80
$3Al_2O_3 \cdot 2SiO_2$	1.638–1.653	1,850	54
Sb_2O_3	2.18 –2.35	655	–
As_2O_3	1.871–2.01	312	–
CeO_2	high	>2,600	86
P_2O_5	1.54 –1.59	570	–
SiO_2	1.54 –1.55	1,713	high
ThO_2	2.20	3,050	90
SnO_2	2.00 –2.09	1,625	41
TiO_2	2.585–2.67	1,830	88
MoO_3	–	795	–
ZrO_2	2.19 –2.20	2,715	65–75
$ZrO_2 \cdot SiO_2$	1.923–1.960	2,430	41

*Correct thermal expansion coefficients are to be obtained by multiplying the tabulated numbers by 10^{-7}.

or reaction products. In a general discussion of opacifiers, therefore, substances such as alkalies, alkaline earths, etc., while contributing somewhat to opacity, function primarily as fluxes. Opacifiers are mainly among the acid constituents illustrated in table 1.4 and the insoluble fluorides and phosphates.

With the exception of fluorides, which under proper circumstances serve as useful and effective opacifiers, major reliance is placed on a few stable acid oxides. In good bright glazes, Al_2O_3 is in solution and becomes a part of the glass, forming no opacity. When it is present in excess of that, opacity results, along with a reduction of gloss. Mullite falls in about the same class, and probably is the source of opacity due to high concentration of mill-added clay in some types of glazes.

The oldest opacifier and still an excellent one, is tin oxide. During the past century other reagents have been extensively studied so that at present the list includes additional materials such as zirconium compounds, ceria, some phosphates, arsenic trioxide, antimony oxide, certain spinels, and some compounds which function under special and narrowly limited conditions, such as zinc oxide, alumina, magnesia, calcia, titania, and others. Irrespective of the opacifying agent, its efficiency will be dependent upon composition, firing conditions, and possibly the method of preparing the glaze. In some cases the presence of microcrystals, as in true matts, or the development of macrocrystals, or the insolubility of a chromophore, may be responsible for the phenomenon.

Bone ash and some other phosphates will give opacity up to cone 11 (see table 1.6) and possibly higher. Their use is frequently accompanied by defects associated with the decomposition of these compounds, as well as crawling and beading. Earhart[14] studied the effects of various opacifiers when introduced in leadless-boric oxide glazes applied on a sanitary ware body, and fired at cone 11 in a commercial kiln. The results obtained with phosphates were comparable to those with tin oxide in respect to the color, texture, brilliance, and opacity. Naturally, such effects depend in some degree upon the compositions of the glazes and the temperature of the firing.

The use of arsenic oxide is objectionable because of its toxic character, and it is suitable only for low temperatures, such as with vitreous enamels applied on metals for jewelry or art objects.

Antimony oxide may be used as an opacifier at somewhat higher temperatures than arsenic oxide. It will usually give a yellowish color if the glaze contains lead, due to the precipitation of yellow lead antimonate.

Cerium oxides[15,16] may develop opacity at high temperatures under suitable conditions with respect to the glaze composition and firing, but may act as a coloring agent and also cause a vesicular structure mainly due to the dissociation:

$$2CeO_2 \rightarrow Ce_2O_3 + \frac{1}{2}O_2$$

Silica acts as an opacifier only when it is present in excess in undissolved form, or as a product of crystallization or devitrification in an excessively siliceous glaze. Molybdic oxide also is of low solubility and will produce opacity in low-fired glazes and enamels. But it tends to be bluish, to sublime, and generally is not reliable as an opacifier.

Thorium oxide would make an excellent opacifier, but it is expensive and is not readily available in a controlled opacifier grade, and it tends to be radioactive.

Titanium oxide may act as a white opacifier at low temperatures and with other favorable conditions, but its performance within the usual commercial range of compositions and thermal treatment is not always satisfactory, since the color is likely to be cream to yellowish.

Zinc oxide, alumina, and some spinels are serviceable as opacifiers for appropriate glaze compositions within the range of cones 4 to 10 and probably higher; yet zinc oxide may be satisfactory as low as 1,000° C if used in the presence of a relatively high alumina content.

TIN OXIDE. Tin oxide is useful and dependable for producing a superior white opacity and gloss. Its solubility in glaze melts is low, depending upon the melt compositions. This has been estimated as approximating 0.01 molecular equivalent in a typical borosilicate lead-containing whiteware glaze, or possibly 10% of the amount of the oxide used. Observation[17] has shown that the solution and dissolution of tin oxide is a reversible process in lead-containing frits, but in alkali-rich frits tin oxide may remain in solution, separating later in the glaze; hence the advisibility of adding the tin oxide to the mill batch rather than the frit.

Systematic work with earthenware and related types of glazes by Panickar[18] established that the solubility of SnO_2 in the glaze was increased by Na_2O, K_2O, and B_2O_3. Calcia, BaO, ZnO, Al_2O_3, and to limited extent, PbO reduce the solubility of SnO_2; to that extent the amount of SnO_2 required for opacification was reduced. The amount of SnO_2 required also was reduced by small additions of fluorides or phosphates; but these could lead to glaze defects. Four to ten percent of tin oxide was used.

Tin putty or tin ash is an efficient form in which to add the oxide, in some cases, because of the very fine state of subdivision. According to Stuckert,[17] relatively high calcia, high alumina and silica are required in compositions intended for use at low temperatures—cones 08 to 02—since tin can react with the bases and form stannates, which, presumably, are more soluble in such fusions. The presence of boric oxide does not lessen the opacity. Potassia is preferred to soda in glazes containing lead and boric oxide. In a series of glazes containing the bases PbO, Na_2O,

BaO, CaO, and ZnO, Stuckert found that the opacity increased in the sequence of BaO, CaO, ZnO when substituted in triad groups of which the other members were lead oxide and alkali.

The substitution of zirconia for a small part of the silica in tin-containing glazes increased the opacity and improved the gloss, even excelling that had with tin alone. Also, the presence of fluorspar in tin-containing glazes definitely promoted opacity, which is true also of small increments of bone ash, although the latter impaired the luster in some degree. These ingredients should not be introduced into the mill batch, and caution must be exercised in the use of the last named two materials.

The presence of tin oxide has been found to increase the modulus of elasticity slightly. The lesser tendency to craze, however, is due to the fact that the coefficient of thermal expansion of SnO_2 is low (about $41 \times 10^{-7}/°C$) and it therefore lowers the expansion of glazes containing it.

The amount of the tin oxide required for colored glazes will depend upon the opacifying property of the chromophore chosen and the intensity of the color desired. If high color intensity is required, less opacifier will be needed than in the pastel shades.

ZIRCONIUM. Zirconium compounds are comparatively recent additions to the list of opacifiers and their use has been rapidly extended. Considerable data have been published regarding their employment in all types of glazes, and on the effects of other oxides upon the development of opacity with zirconia in lead-oxide-borosilicate whiteware glaze for cone 3.[19] Alkalies do not seem to exert any appreciable effect when used in amounts up to 10%. Zinc oxide is desirable, when possible; since the opacity and texture of the glazes are more readily controlled with it, the opacity is more dense and the gloss is improved. About 5% is sufficient for most glazes.

The same investigators[20] reported the results had with a leadless borosilicate glaze containing also calcium fluoride and zinc oxide. The glazes were matured at cones 3 and 5. It was found that the particular form in which the zirconium was added, i.e., spinel, silicate, zirconate, or oxide, had a specific effect upn the opacity, gloss, and texture. Satisfactory results have been reported[21] as obtained in a cone 11 Bristol-type glaze containing zirconia.

Zirconium compounds now are the most widely employed opacifiers. The most popular of these is zirconium silicate (zircon or $ZrO_2 \cdot SiO_2$) However, in the fired glaze, the zirconium-bearing crystal responsible for the opacity in glazes usually is zirconium silicate, regardless of the starting material. With ZrO_2 as the opacifier used, $ZrO_2 \cdot SiO_2$ is formed during firing, resulting in a corresponding reduction of the silica content in the vitreous portion of the glaze This is a possible explanation of the poor texture of some glazes containing more than 5% or 6% of ZrO_2. When ZrO_2 is added, the silica should be increased by almost an identical molar amount.

Even though the final opacifying phase in glazes resulting from all types of zirconium opacifiers is zircon, direct use of zirconium silicate as an opacifier does not always yield the best glazes[23] The use of double silicates makes slips with better working properties than with zircon or with ZrO_2. The slips are of lower thixotropy and characteristically impart smooth uniform surfaces and result in less opacifier segregation than zircon or ZrO_2. The commonly employed zirconoium-bearing opacifiers for glazes[22] are:

zircon	$ZrO_2 \cdot SiO_2$
zirconia	ZrO_2
barium zirconium silicate	$BaZrSiO_5$
zinc zirconium silicate	$ZnZrSiO_5$
calcium zirconium silicate	$CaZrSiO_5$
magnesium zirconium silicate	$MgZrSiO_5$

These may be of different particle size and purity grades and sold under different trade names by various suppliers.

For zirconium-bâse opacifiers the alkalies have little influence when used in amounts up to 10%. In early work on these opacifiers Commons[19] found that although dense opacity can be achieved in zincless glazes, the presence of zinc makes it easier to control opacity, texture, and gloss. He found that calcium contributes somewhat to zirconium opacity and that 4% to 5% seems useful. Barium is in about the same category. Commons found it advantageous to keep Al_2O_3 to less than 10%, but the effectiveness of ZrO_2 was reduced when Al_2O_3 fell below about 6%.

ZrO_2 functions as an opacifier in amounts from 3% to 15%. Pure white glazes are produced with zirconium opacifiers under the same conditions that produce various tints of pink with tin. The portion of the ZrO_2 that goes into glaze solution increases the chemical resistance, and raises the strength.

Commercial zircon opacifiers having a mean particle size of 15 microns to 20 microns are widely used in one-fire sanitary ware glazes. They are used in proportions of 6% to 18% and reduce the thermal expansion of the glazes, thereby increasing glaze compression. It is said that additions of zircon opacifiers up to 10% increase abrasion resistance of the glaze.

TITANIUM. Attempts to opacify ceramic glazes with TiO_2 were initiated by Rieke[24] in 1936. He obtained dense opacity but with a yellow tone. Later, with Boncke[25,26] and with Pralow,[27] he was able to develop several white opaque glazes based on TiO_2 employing the recrystallization mechanism. These workers reported that the solubility and recrystallization of TiO_2 in their glazes were controlled to a predominant degree by the Al_2O_3 content. These glazes, however, did have a yellowish cast according to subsequent reports,[28,29] but further work by Claudet[30] made some progress with specific glaze compositions. The whole subject was reviewed by Biogiotti[31] in 1951.

Glass technologists long have realized that alumina is an important ingredient in producing fluoride opals. Investigators have shown that even though it is desirable to have Al_2O_3 in the glaze, aluminum fluoride is not present in the opacifying phase. Perhaps a similar auxiliary role of alumina also is effective in titania-opacified glazes.

More recent work by Styrh and Beals[32] developed white glazes by crystallization of TiO_2 from clear frit during the firing of glazes. Some glazes developed by them are given in table 1.5. These authors concluded that yellowing was due to grain-growth of the titania. Excessive fluidity appeared to lead to coarse grains of TiO_2 and an accompanying yellowing. They concluded that to prevent this the flux content should not exceed 18% and where the more active fluxes were used, this limit was 10 mole % to 12 mole %, depending on content of silica and alumina. A total of at least eight mole % of fluxes was required to produce good gloss and sufficiently low viscosity to permit precipitation of the TiO_2.

The titanium oxide separated in the form of anatase in the more simple compositions. As the complexity of the glasses increased, there was an increased tendency toward rutile. It appears that higher viscosity favors anatase and lower viscosity favors rutile, whether this is achieved by temperatures alone or by composition. Other things being equal, the higher firing temperatures would favor rutile formation. There has been an increase in rutile noted with increased firing temperature. Glazes fired at the lower temperature, where anatase is predominant, have relatively high reflection in the blue, which is considerably repressed when fired higher.

The color and opacity of the fired glazes is influenced not only by the relative proportions of anatase and rutile, but also by their particle size. The concentration of TiO_2 in the frit exercises a strong influence on the size of the precipitate. An amount of 3 mole % to 5 mole % of TiO_2 will cause opacity, but a larger percentage of particles in the preferred range (0.2 micron to 0.4 micron) results from higher concentrations (7 mole % to 9 mole %) with a corresponding improvement in opacity.

Table 1.5. Self-opacified titanium glazes[32]

No.	Composition, in mole equivalents												Temp., °C	Color	Fit*	Gloss
	SiO_2	B_2O_3	Al_2O_3	TiO_2	Na_2O	K_2O	CaO	MgO	BaO	ZnO	PbO	P_2O_5				
1	5.23	0.700	0.700	0.700	1.000	–	–	–	–	–	–	–	925–1100	Blue wht	OK	Good
2	3.25	0.434	0.434	0.434	1.000	–	–	–	–	–	–	–	850–950	Ivory	Craze	Poor
3	3.75	0.500	0.500	0.500	0.500	–	–	0.500	–	–	–	–	1000–1075	White	Good	Good
4	3.75	0.500	0.500	0.500	0.313	0.125	0.125	0.313	0.125	–	–	–	950–1050	White	Good	Good
5	6.42	0.860	0.860	0.860	1.000	–	–	–	–	–	–	–	975–1125	Blue wht	Good	Good
6	4.40	0.586	0.586	0.586	0.429	–	–	0.571	–	–	–	–	975–1100	White	Good	Good
7	5.23	0.700	0.700	0.700	0.500	–	–	–	0.500	–	–	–	Same	Off wht	Good	Good
8	4.38	0.585	0.585	0.585	0.527	0.214	0.214	–	–	–	–	–	925–1050	Off wht	Good	Good
9	4.38	0.585	0.585	0.585	0.286	–	–	0.357	0.357	–	–	–	Same	Off wht	Good	Good
10	4.79	0.639	0.639	0.639	0.231	0.154	0.154	0.308	0.154	–	–	–	950–1050	White	Good	Good
11	6.42	0.860	0.860	0.860	0.600	0.400	–	–	–	–	–	0.1975	875–1025	Blue wht	Good	Excell.
12	3.86	0.547	0.653	0.330	1.000	–	–	–	–	0.333	–	–	925–975	White	Good	Excell.
13	5.23	0.700	0.700	0.700	0.667	–	–	–	–	–	–	CdO	900–1075	White	Good	Excell.
14	5.23	0.700	0.700	0.700	0.667	–	–	–	–	–	–	0.333	900–1000	White	Good	Good
15	5.23	0.700	0.700	0.700	0.333	–	–	–	–	0.333	–	–	900–1050	White	Good	Good
16	5.23	0.700	0.700	0.700	0.333	–	–	–	–	0.667	0.333	–	Same	White	Good	Excell.
17	5.23	0.700	0.700	0.700	0.333	–	–	0.333	–	0.333	–	–	Same	White	Good	Good
18	4.07	0.725	0.725	0.700	0.333	–	–	0.333	–	–	0.334	–	875–925	White	Good	Good
19	6.42	0.860	0.860	0.700	0.600	0.400	–	–	–	–	–	–	875–1025	Blue wht	Good	Excell.
20	5.30	0.710	0.710	0.505	0.339	–	–	0.165	0.165	0.165	0.165	–	925–1050	White	Good	Good
21	5.23	0.700	0.700	0.700	1.000	–	–	–	–	–	–	–	915–1100	Blue wht	Good	Good

*The specimens were fired o[illegible] body with a mean coefficient of linear thermal expansion of 68×10^{-7} / °C (30–600°C).

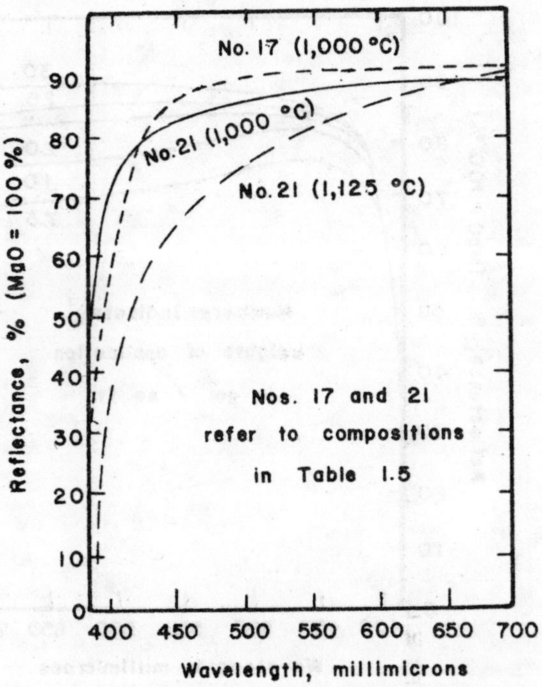

Figure 1.2. Reflectance curves for self-opacified titania-basis glazes, showing an example of a good white glaze, no. 17; and the effect of firing temperature on glaze no. 21.[32]

Higher firing temperatures tend to produce coarser TiO_2 crystals and account for the yellow cast and for reduced opacity. The purity of raw materials is of very considerable importance. Even small proportions of iron or chromium (or other transition elements) tend to cause yellowish tones in the fired glazes. The formation of rutile as opposed to anatase is favored by multiple species in the RO group. For a full discussion of RO, see chapter 3.

Curves of reflectance versus wavelength are shown in figure 1.2 for glaze no. 17 fired at 1,000° C and glaze 21 (table 1.5) fired at 1,000° C and 1,125° C. The covering power of such glazes is illustrated in figure 1.3 with data obtained by Styrh and Beals.[32]

SELF-OPACIFIED GLAZES. Self-opacified glazes can be prepared in which the opacifying phase that separates is a titania compound other than the simple rutile or anatase. This might have some advantage in stability of color and opacity, control, and cost. Some work toward this end was

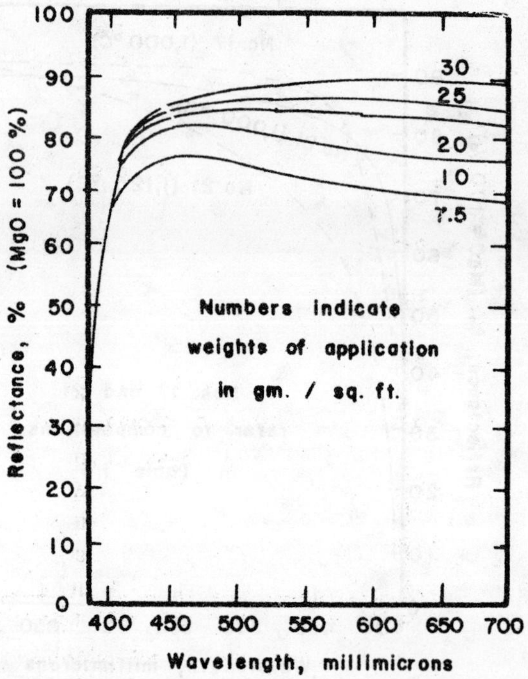

Figure 1.3. Illustration of covering power of glaze no. 5 (table 1.5) applied over a dark red body in various thicknesses and fired at 1,000°C.[32]

reported by Geiss and Beals.[33] This work was of interest and the results encouraging, although much remains to be done. Good white glazes firing in the range 1,050° C to 1,150° C were obtained using:

$0.409Na_2O$		
$0.288K_2O$	$0.465Al_2O_3$	$2.63SiO_2$
$0.363CaO$*		

PROPERTIES OF TITANIA CRYSTALS. The four major oxides of titania, on the basis of their oxygen content, are TiO, Ti_2O_3 TiO_2, and TiO_3. Each of these may have variable oxygen content. For example, it is very easy for the TiO_2 to lose some oxygen and become $TiO_{1.995}$ or TiO_{2-x} where x is a small number. The color darkens when the oxygen is less than $TiO_{2.0000}$. There are three allotropic forms of TiO_2: brookite, anatase, and rutile. Only the last two have been found in glaze frits

* MgO, BaO, or SrO may be substituted partially or completely for CaO. The color depends some on the nature of the RO elements and on firing temperature. For example, the substitution of all BaO for all of the CaO leads to an off-white glaze. The above form of writing a glaze formula is discussed in detail in chapter 3.

The size of the crystals separating from a given composition depends upon the nucleation, concentration of TiO_2 in the glass, and the time-temperature circumstances. All of these parameters have different values depending on the base composition of the glaze. The crystal phase, the polymorphic form, and the crystal size and shape control the color and opacity characteristics. Rutile has a higher refractive index than anatase. The maximum absorption of anatase is more toward the violet than the red, so anatase opacifiers are characteristically blue white. This is contrasted with the yellow white or rutile opacification.

According to Shannon,[34] the presence of high field-strength ions in a glass solution (N^{+5}, P^{+5}, or S^{+6}) favors the formation and precipitation of anatase but large weak ions such as Cl would cause the rutile form to prevail.

Gas Opacifiers. The presence of very small gas bubbles evenly distributed in a glassy fusion will cause opacity. There are so many disadvantages and limitations associated with this type of opacity development that it is not used much as a practical procedure. It is mentioned here mainly because it is an inadvertent opacifying variable and can be a source of some opacity when none is sought or expected.

However, a method of controlled gaseous opacifications was advocated by Kreidl[35] in a French patent. Their method was based on mill additions* of finely porous absorbent material that would release small gas bubbles and effectively produce opacity. Silica gel in which the pores do not exceed one micron diameter but in which the total pore volume was around 80% was effective. The pores of these gels were saturated with organic fillers such as solutions of coal tar in benzene. They recommended mill-additions of about 3% of these special powdered aerogels.

Liquid-liquid Separation. Glaze opacification by inclusion of liquid particles in the vitreous matrix is technically possible but has not been explored or developed to any great extent. The primary reason for this may be partly a lack of information on liquid immiscible systems. The limited appreciation of the principles involved and of the potentialities of this approach also are partly responsible for lack of development of this type of glaze opacification. Liquid opacification not only would not develop a market for new opacifiers but would reduce the necessity for the use of mill-added crystalline particles. Thus, the developments would be left to

* **Mill addition.** Any ingredient other than frit that is a part of a proportioned mixture of materials to form a charge for a ball mill or other mixing equipment.

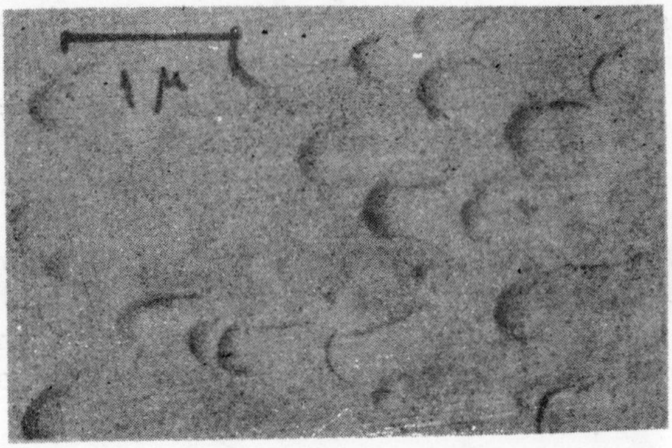

Figure 1.4. Electron micrograph of liquid immiscibility in a composition containing $65SiO_2$, $20TiO_2$, 5CaO, and $10Li_2O$ (×18,800).[38]

Figure 1.5. Electron micrograph of liquid immiscibility in a composition containing $65SiO_2$, $20TiO_2$, 5CaCO, and $10Li_2O$ after holding at 1,200° C for 48 hours (×18,800).[38]

users of glazes or to the suppliers of materials critical to the development of appropriate liquid-liquid immiscibility.

Two-liquid separation has been found and reported in several simple systems. In the system Li_2O–SiO_2–TiO_2, two liquids separate: a low index, high silica glass, and high index titania-rich glasses.[36] This would be of academic interest only, since well-balanced glaze compositions would not be expected. The system CaO–SiO_2–TiO_2 contains a two-liquid region yielding enamellike opaque glasses and has been fully described by DeVries, Roy, and Osborn.[37] Continuing from these simple systems, Hummel, Tien, and Kim[38] investigated more complicated multicomponent systems. They concluded that the probabilities for developing practical glazes based on CaO, Li_2O, TiO_2, and SiO_2 or Na_2O, Li_2O, CaO, BaO, SiO_2 and TiO_2 are extremely promising. These glasses when cooled to room temperature contained small glass spheres dispersed in the matrix glass. Examples of the structures obtained are shown in the electron micrographs of figures 1.4 and 1.5. The dispersed spherical particles responsible for the opacity had particle sizes in the range of 0.1 micron to 0.5 micron. Furthermore, when reheated, these compositions precipitate extremely fine crystals that still further increase opacity.

In the fields investigated by Hummel[38] it was necessary to include at least 10% of TiO_2 to achieve the two-liquid separation. The thermal expansion was 80×10^{-7} or higher, consequently not suited for most bodies. It seems likely that future work can develop large fields of glaze composition suited to fit a wide range of body types.

NONHOMOGENEITY. Another source of mild opacity or for variations in opacity, is that of nonhomogeneity in the fused coating. Microscopic or even macroscopic areas of compositional variation in the fused layer will have corresponding variations in refractive index, hence show some opacity. These can be created as a result of areas of concentration residual from dissolved but not thoroughly diffused particles of mill-added ingredients. An example would be a siliceous residue from a newly dissolved quartz grain. The mixture of two frits, if not thoroughly interdiffused and homogenized, could be another example. Because PbO and B_2O_3 tend to lower surface tension in glasses, cords tend to diffuse more rapidly when they are present. For that purpose, the more the better.

References

1. Petrie, W. M. E. 1926. Glass in the early ages. *J. Soc. Glass Tech.* 10:226.
2. Debevoise, N. C. 1934. The history of glaze and its place in the ceramic technique of ancient Seleucia on the Tigris. *Bull. Am. Cer. Soc.* 13:293.
3. Ibid.
4. Lucas, A. 1936. Glazed ware in Egypt, India, and Mesopotamia. *J. Egyptian Archaeology* 22, pt. 2:150.
5. Brogniart, A. 1877. *Traits des arts ceramiques.* 3d ed. Vol. 1. Paris, p 16.
6. Kerl, B. 1907. *Handbuch der gesammten Thonwarenindustrie.* Braunschweig, p 329.
7. Funk, Wm. 1933. *Rohstoffe der Feinkeramik.* Berlin, p 239.
8. Schumacher, W. 1876. Glasurstudien. *Sprech.* 9:103.

Table 1.6. Temperature equivalents Orton Standard Pyrometric Cones[39]

Cone Number	Large Cones (1) 60°C	Large Cones 108°F	Large Cones 150°C	Large Cones 270°F	Small Cones 300°C	Small Cones 540°F
022	585°C.	1085°F.	600°C.	1112°F.		
021	602	1116	614	1137	643°C.	1189°F.
020	625	1157	635	1175	666	1231
019	668	1234	683	1261	723	1333
018	696	1285	717	1323	752	1386
017	727	1341	747	1377	784	1443
016	767	1407	792	1458	825	1517
015	790	1464	804	1479	843	1549
014.	834	1533	838	1540		
013	869	1596	852	1566		
012	866	1591	884	1623		
011	886	1627	894	1641		
010	887	1629	894	1641	919	1686
09	915	1679	923	1693	955	1751
08	945	1733	955	1751	983	1801
07	973	1783	984	1803	1008	1846
06	991	1816	999	1830	1023	1873
05	1031	1888	1046	1915	1062	1944
04	1050	1922	1060	1940	1098	2008
03	1086	1987	1101	2014	1131	2068
02	1101	2014	1120	2048	1148	2098
01	1117	2043	1137	2079	1178	2152
1	1136	2077	1154	2109	1179	2154
2	1142	2088	1162	2124	1179	2154
3	1152	2106	1168	2134	1196	2185
4	1168	2134	1186	2167	1209	2208
5	1177	2151	1196	2185	1221	2230
6	1201	2194	1222	2232	1255	2291
7	1215	2219	1240	2264	1264	2307
8	1236	2257	1263	2305	1300	2372

Cone Number	P.C.E. Cones 150°C	P.C.E. Cones 270°F
12	1337°C.	2439°F.
13	1349	2460
14	1398	2548
15	1430	2606
16	1491	2716
17	1512	2754
18	1522	2772
19	1541	2806
20	1564	2847
23	1605	2921
26	1621	2950
27	1640	2984
28	1646	2995
29	1659	3018
30	1665	3029
31	1683	3061
31½	1699	3090
32	1717	3123
32½	1724	3135
33	1743	3169
34	1763	3205
35	1785	3245
36	1804	3279
37	1820	3308
38	1850*	3362
39	1865*	3389
40	1885*	3425
41	1970*	3578
42	2015*	3659

9	1260	2300	1280	2336	1317	2403
10	1285	2345	1305	2381	1330	2426
11	1294	2361	1315	2399	1336	2437
12	1306	2383	1326	2419	1355	2471
13	1321	2410	1346	2455		
14	1388	2530	1366	2491		
15	1424	2595	1431	2608		
16	1455	2651	1473	2683		
17	1477	2691	1485	2705		
18	1500	2732	1506	2743		
19	1520	2768	1528	2782		
20	1542	2808	1549	2820		
23	1586	2887	1590	2894		
26	1589	2892	1605	2921		
27	1614	2937	1627	2961		
28	1614	2937	1633	2971		
29	1624	2955	1645	2993		
30	1636	2977	1654	3009		
31	1661	3022	1679	3054		
32	1706	3103	1717	3123		
32½	1718	3124	1730	3146		
33	1732	3150	1741	3166		
34	1757	3195	1759	3198		
35	1784	3243	1784	3243		
36	1798	3268	1796	3265		

(1) The rate of heating up the cones during the last several hundred degrees of the tests.

Note 1. All temperature equivalent values given in °C are average values as determined at the National Bureau of Standards and were measured at the time that the tip of the cone touched the plaque. All temperatures given in °F were calculated by the use of the following equation: °F=1.8×°C+32. Temperature equivalents were not determined for Small Cones Nos. 022, 014, 013, 012, and 011. The temperature equivalent values in °C shown in the table (except as noted) were determined by Henry P. Beerman, Research Associate, at the National Bureau of Standards for The Edward Orton Jr. Ceramic Foundation.

Note No. 2. The temperature equivalent values given in this table apply only to Orton Standard Pyrometric Cones when heated in an air atmosphere at the rate of heating shown. The temperature equivalent values are furnished for information purposes only. They are not necessarily the temperature actually in a furnace at the time when the cone goes down.

*See Fairchild and Peters, "Characteristics of Pyrometric Cones," Jour. Amer. Cer. Soc., Vol. 9, No. 11 p. 700 (1926) Cones Nos. 39–42, incl. were heated at a rate of 600 deg. C. per hour.

Courtesy, Edward Orton Jr. Ceramic Foundation

9. Kerstan, W. 1954. White opacification of ceramic glazes. *Euro-Ceram.* 4(5):134–35.
10. Larsen, Esper S. and Berman, Harry. 1934. The microscopic determination of the nonopaque minerals. *U.S. Dept. of the Interior, U.S. Geological Survey Bull.* 848:30.
11. Rayleigh, Lord. 1871. On the light from the sky, its polarization and color. *Phil. Mag.* 41:107.
12. Ryde, J. W. and Cooper, B. S. 1931. Scattering of light by turbid media. *Proc. Roy. Soc. (London)* A131:451.
13. King, Burnham W., Jr. 1940. Effect of particle size and index of refraction on reflectance. *J. Am. Ceram. Soc.* 23(8):221–25.
14. Earhart, W. H. 1941. Use of phosphate opacifying agents in sanitary ware glazes. *Bull. Am. Ceram. Soc.* 20:312.
15. Steger, W. 1936. Opaque hard porcelain glazes. *Ber. Deut. Ker. Ges.* 17:484.
16. Steger, W. 1939. Action of tin oxide and cerium oxide as opacifying agents. *Ber. Deut. Ker. Ges.* 20:310.
17. Stuckert, L. 1940. Tin oxide in ceramic glazes. *Sprech.* 73:13, 21, 29, 37, 45.
18. Panickar, K. N. Madhava, 1948. Note on compounding opaque glazes with tin oxide. *Trans. Indian Ceram. Soc.* 7(1):32–33.
19. Kinzie, C. J. and Commons, C. H. 1934. The effect of zirconium oxide in glasses, glazes and enamels. *J. Am. Ceram. Soc.* 17:283.
20. Kinzie, C. J. and Commons, C. H. 1937. The effect of various zirconium and titanium compounds on a glaze. *Bull Am. Ceram. Soc.* 16:1.
21. Danielson, R. R. 1946. Effect of composition on properties of cone 11 zirconium-silicate–opacified glazes. *J. Am. Ceram. Soc.* 29:282.
22. Jacobs, C. W. F. and Baldwin, W. J. 1954. Effects of zirconium-type opacifiers on properties of glazes. *J. Am. Ceram. Soc.* 37(6):258–66.
23. Jacobs, C. W. F. 1954. Opacifying crystalline phases present in zirconium-type glazes. *J. Am. Ceram. Soc.* 37(5):216–20.
24. Rieke, R. 1936. Zur Frage des Ersatzes von Zinnoxyd in Schmelzglasuren (The problem of replacing tin oxide in fused glazes). *Ber. Deut. Keram. Ges.* 17(4):182–92.
25. Dietzel, Adolph and Boncke, Richard. *Process for the preparation of enamels, glazes, or glass fluxes which have been white-opacified with titanium dioxide.* German Patent 688,787, Feb 15, 1940.
26. Dietzel, Adolph and Boncke, Richard. *Black enamels and glazes.* Ger. Patent 702,057, Jan 2, 1941.
27. Dietzel, A., Boncke, R., and Pralow, W. 1941. Titanium dioxide and its effects in enamels, glazes, and glasses, pts. 1, 2, and 3. *Sprechsaal* 74:295–97, 303–04, 311–12, 372–76, 463–65, 477–79; 1942. 75:342–46, 365–68.
28. Busch, Werner and Struman-Bolenbach, Hilde. Titanium compounds in the ceramic industry. *Ber. Deut. Keram. Ges.* 1943. 24(10/11):335–39.

29. Busch, Werner and Struman-Bolenbach, Hilde. 1944. Opaqueness of boron and lead-free glazes. *Ber. Deut. Keram. Ges.* 25(1):17–27.
30. Claudet, A. F. M. *Process for glazing earthenware and glaze therefor.* U.S. Patent 2,498,912 Feb 28, 1950.
31. Biogiotti, E. 1951. Ceramic titanium glazes. *Ind. Cerrm. Silicate* 4(4):22–30.
32. Styrh, K. H., Jr., and Beals, M. D. 1958. Use of titanium dioxide in self-opacifying glazes. *Bull. Am. Ceram. Soc.* 37(11):480–85.
33. Geiss, E. A. and Beals, M. D. 1959. Boron-free opaque white glazes containing titanium dioxide. *Bull. Am. Ceram. Soc.* 38(2):54–60.
34. Shannon, Robert D. 1959. Study of the polymorphic forms of titania in porcelain enamels. *Bull. Am. Ceram. Soc.* 38(3):110–16.
35. Kreidl, I. and Kreidl, W. *Gaseous opacifiers for enamels and glazes.* French Patent 922,524, June 11, 1946.
36. Kim, K. H. and Hummel, F. A. 1959. Studies in titanium oxide systems; 6, Progress report on the system Li_2O–SiO_2–TiO_2. *J. Am. Ceram. Soc.* 42(6):286–91.
37. DeVries, R. C., Roy, R., and Osborn, E. F. 1955. Phase equilbria in the system CaO-TiO_2-SiO_2. *J. Am. Ceram. Soc.* 38(5):158–71.
38. Hummel, F. A., Tien, T. Y., and Kim, K. H. 1960. Studies in lithium oxide systems; VII, Application of silicate liquid immiscibility to development opaque glazes. *J. Am. Ceram. Soc.* 43(4):192–97.
39. 1958–59. Ceramic Data Book, page 529, Industrial Publications.

2

Glaze Materials

The materials used in the compounding of glaze batches are classified chemically as follows:

1. Bases, the conspicuously fluxing agents, which are of the form represented by the RO and the R_2O classification (explained in chapter 3) in the ceramic formula and include the alkalies, the alkaline earths and zinc oxide, lead oxide, and many of the coloring oxides or chromophores
2. Intermediates, which include amphoteric oxides, the R_2O_3 classification, a group from which alumina is the common example and to which ferric, chromic, manganic, and other oxides are sometimes assigned
3. Acids, which are represented by the RO_2 classification, of which silica is the type and to which phosphoric oxide, zirconia, and fluorine also belong

Boric acid is frequently placed in the acid group because of its well-known conduct in fusions, but there are valid reasons for considering it as functioning sometimes as an intermediate; and American ceramists have very generally placed it in the R_2O_3 group. Tin oxide and some other oxides, which have only a very limited solubility in glaze fusions and whose usefulness depends chiefly upon their segregation as opacifying agents, are written in the graphic formula following the acid group.

The Alkalies

The alkalies used by the ceramist are compounds of sodium, potassium, and lithium. These are widely distributed in nature, chiefly (with exceptions to be mentioned) as water-insoluble compounds or associated with other bases in complex insoluble silicates. The chlorides, carbonates, and nitrates occurring naturally or prepared industrially are readily soluble and must be incorporated in frits to permit their use in the usual glaze slip. However, relatively small amounts of some of the soluble alkali salts are sometimes introduced as such for specific purposes.

The alkalies are strong fluxes. They increase the fluidity of the molten glaze and have important influences upon the development of color, varying each from the other and depending upon the chromophore used. They increase the refractive indices of the melt, and therefore the brilliancy and, within certain limits, have a direct bearing on the resistance to water solution and, consequently, to weathering. Because their influence upon the thermal expansion properties is considerable, the kind and the content of the alkali bases used in a glaze have a direct bearing upon crazing.

Mixed Alkali Effect

It has long been recognized that variations in physical and chemical properties occur with variations in the ratio of the alkali species to each other. There commonly can be found a ratio that is optimum. This behavior is termed the *mixed alkali effect*.

Many workers have observed and reported this from Gehlhoff and Thomas[1] in 1925 to Charles[2] in 1965 and others. Charles reported optima in electrical resistivity values in glasses as follows:

$$\frac{Na}{Li + Na} = 0.33, \qquad \frac{K}{Li + K} = 0.33, \qquad \text{and } \frac{Cs}{Li + Cs} = 0.30$$

He ascribed these effects to liquid-liquid phase separation.

There seems to be no doubt but that as far as the chemical durability of glasses is concerned, those containing K_2O and Na_2O are better than those with K_2O or Na_2O alone. Morey[3] reports data on glasses showing optimum chemical durability where, in weight percentage, the ratio is:

$$\frac{Na_2O}{Na_2O + K_2O} = \frac{6}{20} = 0.3$$

Sodium

Sodium imparts the highest coefficient of expansion of all of the bases in silicate fusions. It decreases the tensile strength and the elasticity as compared with the action of the other bases commonly used. Although closely resembling potassia in many chemical characteristics, the substitution of one for the other in glaze compositions is inadvisable unless the amounts are quite small.

SODIUM CHLORIDE. This is the sodium salt (NaCl), common salt, ound most abundantly in nature. It has been used in large tonnage for the purpose of vapor glazing certain types of structural wares—sewer pipe, building brick, etc. Small amounts of sodium chloride are sometimes introduced into a frit to bleach the color by causing the vaporization of some iron oxide which is practically always present as an impurity of many glaze materials, notably the clays. A little salt is sometimes employed in the preparation of certain color compounds.

SODIUM CARBONATE. This compound (Na_2CO_3) is known in the trade as soda ash, which can be had in ample quantity and at a relatively high degree of purity for a low price. Made generally by the ammonia-carbon dioxide process, the compound contains negligible amounts of foreign matter and is, with the exception of borax, the chief source of sodium used by the potter.

SODIUM NITRATE. This compound ($NaNO_3$), sometimes called soda niter, is too expensive for use as a major source of sodium. Its special value lies in its action as a powerful oxidizing agent, sometimes required in the preparation of frits.

BORAX. The composition of this compound, called sodium tetraborate ($Na_2O \cdot 2B_2O_3 \cdot 10H_2O$), is: Sodium oxide, 16.3%; boric oxide, 36.5%; water of crystallization, 47.2%.

Because the water of crystallization content is susceptible to variations due to local storage conditions, care should be taken to store the material in a place where the conditions do not fluctuate much. Where precision is required in the use of the substance, the water content should be determined carefully. The total water content may be expelled at a low temperature (735° C), and this product is known as fused borax. Fifty-three pounds of this is equivalent to 100 pounds of the hydrated salt. One of the advantages of the use of the dehydrated compound is the avoidance of intumescence, i.e., the swelling of borax during the fritting. It is claimed that the use of the fused salt lessens the need for greater space for storage of the raw material as well as in the crucibles or furnaces required for the melting of large frit batches.

Borax is a very strong flux and a solvent for all the materials used in glaze batches. It has specific action on color oxides, making possible the preparation of certain colors and shades. It reduces the viscosity and surface tension, thus assisting in the healing of defects due to the formation of scratches, cracks, or pitting in the glaze surface prior to the maturity. This useful remedial action, due to the increase of the fluidity of the glaze melt, is sometimes induced by adding very small amounts of borax—about 10%—to the very viscous, high-fire glazes, e.g., the porcelain type. An excess may cause the formation of pinholes and blisters.

CULLET. This is a common bottle or window glass which is crushed to a suitable fineness. It has the approximate composition, $0.5Na_2O \cdot 0.5CaO \cdot SiO_2$. The compositions of the different types of glasses differ importantly according to the product or, more particularly, the process of forming employed in making the ware. Modern glass batches are subject to very careful chemical control in order to insure that the physical properties of the molten mass may be precisely suited to the automatic forming processes so commonly used. Cullet is raw material which has been found useful as well as cheap, but it is a frit having sufficient water solubility to cause trouble in the mill or storage tank, if left undisturbed for a few hours, by settling to form a rather dense cement. This fault may be avoided by the careful correction of excessive alkalinity through the addition of the necessary amount of acid—acetic, for example.

SODA FELDSPAR. The mineralogical name of soda feldspar ($Na_2O \cdot Al_2O_3 \cdot 6SiO_2$) is albite. It is doubtful that it is ever found pure excepting as very carefully selected hand specimens. It is present in greater or less proportions with the other types of feldspar where it may be associated with free silica, ferric oxide (0.04% to 0.15%), and traces of calcia and magnesia. The theoretical composition, by percentage, of the albite is: Silica, 68.7; alumina, 19.5; soda, 11.8.

The analysis of the particular soda feldspar to be used may be had from the supplier and should be used by the ceramist in his calculations. Feldspar acts either as a flux or as a refractory, depending upon the other batch constituents and the maturing temperature of the glaze. It has important effects upon the glaze consistency as it can contribute some soluble alkali if the milling is very fine and prolonged, particularly if the glaze storage period is for several hours. In the fusion and the maturity of the glaze, the alkali, alumina, and silica play their accustomed parts in developing the chemical and mechanical properties. Because of the somewhat lower fusibility imparted to the glaze batches by soda feldspar, it is the preferred form of the mineral used by the glaze maker. A representative analysis of a soda feldspar is shown as follows, by percentage: SiO_2, 66.22; Al_2O_3, 21.76; Fe_2O_3, 0.04; CaO, 2.06; MgO, tr.; K_2O, 0.41; Na_2O, 9.37; Li_2O, 0.00; ignition loss 0.16.

CRYOLITE. Cryolite (Na_3AlF_6) is a mineral obtained in Greenland. It and the synthetic preparation are largely used by the makers of vitreous enamels but rarely by the glaze maker. It is a powerful flux and an opacifier.

Potassium

The compounds of potassium of importance to the ceramist correspond closely in chemical form and behavior to those of sodium, but their effects during fusion and upon the chemical and mechanical properties of the glaze are sufficiently dissimilar so that the substitution of one for the other, excepting in small equivalents, is often inadvisable. This is conspicuously true in the preparation of colored glazes. The substitution of potassium for sodium in sufficient quantity in glazes increases the expense; may give a more brilliant product; decreases the fluidity; increases the scratch hardness; increases the resistance to solution by water; and decreases the coefficient of expansion.

POTASSIUM CARBONATE. This is known to the glaze maker as pearl ash (K_2CO_3). It is somewhat delinquescent, very soluble in water, and may contain small amounts of potassium chloride and the sulfate.

POTASSIUM NITRATE. This (KNO_3) is known as saltpeter and niter. Its use is primarily as an oxidizing agent for which sodium nitrate may be substituted satisfactorily at less cost, unless the introduction of the sodium is objectionable.

POTASH FELDSPAR. The mineralogical name for potash feldspar ($K_2O \cdot Al_2O_3 \cdot 6SiO_2$) is orthoclase or microcline, depending upon the crystalline form. The latter is more common. This mineral, like the soda feldspar, is never found pure except as small handpicked specimens. The theoretical composition, in weight %, is: Silica, 65.7; alumina, 18.4; potassa, 16.9.

Cornwall Stone

Cornwall stone is also called Cornish stone, stone, or China stone. It is an altered pegmatite or granite rock whose constituent minerals are pale or smokey brown quartz, white feldspar frequently more or less decomposed, usually other minerals, lepidolite (a lithia mica) and tourmaline (a silicate containing alumina, lime, magnesia, alkalies, and sometimes fluoride and boron in small quantities). It also contains some quantities of fluorspar, which gives the rock its purplish or bluish color and a greater fusibility. The presence of tourmaline is objectionable. The average analysis of twelve samples of Cornwall stone, as found by Coulter[4], in 1905, closely resembles contemporary analysis shown as follows:

Analysis (%)		Ceramic formula	
SiO_2, 71.10	$0.493K_2O$	$1.163Al_2O_3$	$8.35SiO_2$
Al_2O_3, 16.82	$0.261Na_2O$	$0.067Fe_2O_3$	$0.045F_2$
Fe_2O_3, 0.16	$0.238CaO$		$0.494H_2O$
CaO, 1.60	$0.008MgO$		
MgO, 0.05			
K_2O, 6.57			
Na_2O, 2.29			
CaF_2, 0.50			
L.O.I., 1.25			

Formulas given by Jackson and Richardson[5] are as follows:

$$RO:1.05R_2O_3:7.73\ SiO_2$$
$$RO:1.20R_2O_3:7.98\ SiO_2:0.02F_2$$
$$RO:1.45R_2O_3:9.40\ SiO_2:0.03F_2$$
$$RO:1.88R_2O_3:13.20\ SiO_2$$

Cornish stone is a material of the first importance to the English potter because it is his chief source of the alkali. It was once used to a considerable extent in the U.S., although all must be imported since we do not know of any domestic supply unless it is the Carolina stone. It is used in the preparation of glazes and bodies. Cornish stone is a mixture of minerals and consequently, as will be seen in the above analyses, has no constant composition. According to Ashley[6], American potters who have occasion to use a formula calling for Cornish stone usually make mixtures to suit the purpose, such as the following: feldspar, 67%; flint, 22%; china clay, 11%. The contention is sometimes made that such mixtures have not the same fluxing action as the real mineral. The explanation may probably be found in the fact that the rock is a more intimate mixture than can be made by the ordinary processes and further that the presence of the fluoride in the rock naturally makes it more readily fusible.

Cornish stone should vitrify in the biscuit kiln of white earthenware and, if fired in a hard place, should have the glassy appearance of a white enamel, but the trials should not lose their shape. The mass should not be scoriaceous or bubbly, but should be dense. Cornish stone which swells or becomes puffy at this temperature is likely to give rise to the formation of blisters or pinholes in the glaze. Because of the high silica in the Cornish stone, its addition increases the viscosity and the fusing temperature. Hence glazes intended for use over underglaze prints usually contain much of this ingredient, i.e., according to the English practice.

Coulter has given the following conclusions regarding the use of Cornwall stone and feldspar: (1) When Cornwall stone is used, the shrinkage of the unfired glaze is less owing to the smaller clay content required; (2) the Cornwall stone gives a more fusible glaze for the same molecular equivalent of KNaO, if the feldspar is low; (3) there is less tendency for the glaze to bead, owing to the smaller shrinkage during burning. In glazes where the alkali is low, stone is never the best flux to use; but where the alkali is high, it does not matter which flux is used.

Carolina stone is a domestic material having a chemical and mineral composition similar to Cornwall stone. It is proposed as a substitute for the imported material since it is said to be possible to match any variety of the Cornwall stone by small additions of feldspar, kaolin, and fluorspar. Cornwall stone is often used in engobes and may be a useful corrective for crazing and crawling of glazes.

Lithium

At the present time, lithium is coming into more general use in glazes where its presence is supposed to be sufficiently advantageous to compensate for its cost. It is a strong alkali and has chemical properties similar to sodium and potassium. The atomic weight is only 6.94 against 23 for sodium and 39 for potassium. This, theoretically, permits the substitution of 1 pound of lithium carbonate for 3 to 5 pounds of the other alkali carbonates without changing the volume percentage of the total alkali present. Such a reduction in alkali content has the effect, theoretically, of reducing the expansion and increasing the durability of the glass. Usually only a small substitution of LiO_2 for KNaO is effective.

Table 2.1. Typical analyses of lithium ores

	Amblygonite[7] %	*Spodumene*[7] %	*Lepidolite*[7] %	*Petalite* %
Li_2O	8.48	6.78	4.65	4.3
K_2O	0.30	0.69	10.33	N.D.
Na_2O	1.63	0.46	0.13	N.D.
SiO_2	5.16	62.91	52.89	77.0
Al_2O_3	22.96	28.42	26.77	17.5
Fe_2O_3 or FeO	0.019	0.53	0.19	N.D.
MgO	Tr.	0.13	0.31	N.D.
CaO	0.15	0.11	0.92	N.D.
P_2O_5	54.42	N.D.	N.D.	N.D.
MnO_2	None	N.D.	N.D.	N.D.
F_2	2.67	N.D.	0.59	N.D.
Loss on ignition	4.80	0.28	0.66	N.D.

LEPIDOLITE. The theoretical lithium content of lepidolite ($LiF \cdot KF \cdot Al_2O_3 \cdot 3SiO_2$), commonly called lithium mica, is 6%, but the guaranteed minimum of commercial grades is 3%. It is used in the manufacture of glass.

AMBLYGONITE. The amount of lithium present in the commercial material is about 8%. The mineral ($LiAlFPO_4$) promotes rapid fluxing and high gloss. Because of the large content of fluoride and phosphoric oxide it is particularly useful in opaque glazes. The ceramic formula of a commercial sample is given as follows:

$0.065K_2O$		$0.155SiO_2$
$0.203Na_2O$	$0.784Al_2O_3$	$0.372P_2O_5$
$0.092CaO$	$0.001Fe_2O_3$	$0.625F_2$
$0.639Li_2O$		

SPODUMENE. The pure mineral has the formula ($Li_2O \cdot Al_2O_3 \cdot 4SiO_2$). Commercial samples contain about 6% of lithia. Soda and potash frequently replace part of the lithia in the native mineral. Because of its relatively high alumina content it is quite refractory.

LITHIUM CARBONATE. This is an anhydrous, white crystalline substance (Li_2CO_3) which is sparingly soluble in water, the solubility decreasing as the temperature rises. It is used in the preparation of colors, melts more rapidly than the corresponding sodium or potassium salts, and forms eutectics with both.

COMMERCIAL MATERIALS. Lithium raw materials and chemicals are relatively expensive, but not because of scarity of ores. It is partly because of the low content of lithia in them. The highest Li_2O content of ores is less than 10%. The analyses of important beneficiated and concentrated raw materials are shown in table 2.1. Some of the more popular commercial lithium chemicals used in glazes are listed in table 2.2.

FUNCTION IN GLAZES. The advantages claimed for lithium compounds in glazes of the better sorts are numerous and may be briefly listed as follows: the addition of 1% of the carbonate to glazes for dinnerware, electrical porcelain, and sanitary ware increases the gloss; mechanical strength of electrical porcelain glazes and resistance to weathering are greater; the stronger fluxing action of the base permits the use of larger amounts of calcia, alumina, and silica in the raw alkaline glazes, thus promoting stability as well as facilitating the production of more beautiful

Table 2.2 Commercial lithium-bearing materials[8]

Product	*Properties*	*Application*
Lithium aluminate	Insoluble in water; M.P. 1,625°C	Source for Li_2O and Al_2O_3
Lithium carbonate	Water solubility, 1.3% to 0.7% between 25°C and 100°C; M.P. 735°C	Source for Li_2O
Lithium metasilicate	M.P. 1,201°C; insoluble in water	Mill-addition; smelter-addition
Lithium metatitanate	Insoluble in water; M.P. 1,250°C	Mill-addition in titania-bearing glazes
Lithium zirconate	Insoluble in water	Mill-addition flux and opacifier
Lithium zirconium silicate	Insoluble in water	Flux-bearing opacifier; mill-addition to increase gloss and eliminate surface defects

blues with copper and better colors with some chromophores. As little as 0.5% of Li_2O is said to improve glaze surfaces in some compositions.

Lithia in higher concentrations tends to promote crystallization in glazes far more than the other alkalies. It is, therefore, particularly useful in crystal glazes. Lithium ions have a very high diffusion coefficient. When used in a one-fire porcelain glaze, some lithium has been found to migrate several inches into the porcelain body. This unusually high capacity for diffusion is one reason for some of its beneficial effects in glazes. It tends to promote homogeneization by reducing cords or fine-grained compositional irregularities.

Eiduks and Vaivads[9] substituted Li_2O for Na_2O, K_2O, CaO, and MgO in the following glaze:

$0.434Na_2O$		
$0.325K_2O$	$0.397Al_2O_3$	$4.17SiO_2$
$0.135CaO$		
$0.106MgO$		

Substitutions of Li_2O for Na_2O, up to 0.14 mole, decreased the softening temperature, but larger amounts raised it. Glaze softening temperatures were lowered by substituting Li_2O for CaO, MgO, Al_2O_3, or SiO_2. Molar substitutions of Li_2O for K_2O first decreased the thermal expansion but continued substitutions reversed the effect. Expansion was increased by the substitution of Li_2O for CaO. Crystallization was intensified when Li_2O exceeded about 1%.

The Alkaline Earths

Calcium

Calcium compounds are constituents of practically all kinds of glazes. As a constituent component, calcium oxide contributes these properties to the mature glaze: (*a*) increases the hardness, i.e., resistance to abrasion; (*b*) increases the resistance to weathering and the solvent action of water, and to dilute solutions of the ordinary inorganic acids; (*c*) increases the tensile strength and lowers the coefficient of thermal expansion greatly as compared with the action of the alkalies.

In the glaze batch, within certain composition limits, it vigorously attacks clay and silica at temperatures of about red heat, but its fluxing action is best shown at the higher temperatures—cone 4 and above. The rate of change in viscosity of the melt is variable and the increase in fluidity, in passing from the lower to the higher temperatures, is very rapid. If calcia is present in excess of certain stability relations, the refractoriness of the glaze is increased and devitrification with the separation of microcrystalline structures is frequently observed in glazes of widely different types. This is one of the most commonly used methods of forming the matt texture. The crystals have been identified as anorthite, which is a calcium feldspar, and also wollastonite ($CaO \cdot SiO_2$).

Calcium is an important component of almost all kinds of glazes fired above cone 010. It is usually the predominating base in compositions fired at very high temperatures, such as some of the porcelain type. The calcium compounds most frequently used are abundant, cheap, and relatively pure. The carbonate, the form most commonly employed, has a low specific gravity and readily remains in suspension in the glaze slip, assisting in floating the heavier materials. Calcia does not increase the refractive index and, therefore, the brilliancy or the fusibility, as some of the other bases do.

CALCIUM CARBONATE ($CaCO_3$) occurs in nature in several forms that are of importance to the ceramist, such as: (*a*) Limestone, a massive form of the mineral calcite; (*b*) marble, a metamorphosed limestone which is frequently found very pure; (*c*) chalk, a fine, earthy material, which is a marine deposit formed by the accumulation of the remains of minute organisms; (*d*) English cliffstone, a very pure chalk containing some colloidal material, according to Ashley.[10] (It has this analysis, by percentage: moisture, 0.10; silica, 1.06; alumina, 1.28; ferric oxide, trace; calcium carbonate, 97.20; magnesium carbonate, 0.61; sulphate should not be present and magnesia should be less than 1%.); (*e*) Paris white, originally a washed and purified form of chalk, still used to some extent in England.

PRECIPITATED CALCIUM CARBONATE, a by-product of several industries, is important because of its uniformity, purity, and fineness.

WHITING is a finely ground form of calcium carbonate graded as to size and named as follows: (arranged according to grain size, the coarsest being first) Paris white, commercial whiting, American Paris white, English cliffstone, and fine grade Paris white. The "special potter's whiting" is of an indefinite size.

SPECIFICATIONS OF WHITING. Specifications for whiting are proposed by the Bureau of Standards in Circular 152 and state, in part, the requisites that follow.

Definitions. Ceramic whiting is a finely ground powder composed of nearly pure calcium carbonate or calcium carbonate and magnesium carbonate obtained from pulverizing and sizing of chalk, marble, or limestone, or as a chemically precipitated product.

Packing. Whiting is packed and shipped in barrels holding not more than 325 pounds or bags holding not more than 125 pounds.

Quality. Whiting shall be uniform in quality both as to fineness of grain and composition. The calcium, magnesium, or total carbonates shall not vary more than 1 percent and silica not more than one-half of one percent from a figure set by contract within the limits of the composition shown in Class 1 or Class 2. It should be practically free from particles of pyrites, iron-bearing silicates, metallic iron, and gypsum.

Composition. Whiting can be divided into two classes, based on chemical analysis, as shown in table 2.3.

MARL. Marl is an earthy form of natural calcium carbonate of sedimentary origin. It grades from mainly calcium carbonate to calcareous clays.

Table 2.3. Examples of two classes of whiting based on their chemical compositions.

	Class 1		*Class 2*	
Constituents	*Maximum* %	*Minimum* %	*Maximum* %	*Minimum* %
Total carbonates	–	97	–	97
$CaCO_3$	–	96	–	89
$MgCO_3$	2.0	–	8	–
Fe_2O_3	0.25	–	0.25	–
SiO_2	2.0	–	2	–
Total S computed to SO_3	0.1	–	0.1	–

Table 2.4. Fluorspar specifications

	Special	*No. 1 Standard*	*No. 1 Special*
CaF_2	95.5% min.	95.0% min.	95.0% min.
SiO_2	1.0% max.	3.0% max.	3.0% max.
Fe_2O_3	0.1% max.	0.1% max.	0.25% max.
PbO	none	trace	trace
ZnO	none	trace	trace
S	trace	trace	trace

DOLOMITE. Dolomite is a natural mineral having a nominal composition of $CaMg(CO_3)_2$, or a sedimentary rock composed mainly of that mineral. It is a magnesia-bearing limestone, and is discussed under the heading of "Magnesium."

CALCIUM PHOSPHATE. Calcium phosphate is used to some extent. It is the chief component of bone ash. It also occurs in the natural mineral apatite. It is available as a refined chemical.

CALCIUM FLUORIDE. Calcium fluoride (CaF_2) occurs in nature as the mineral fluorspar or fluorite. It is carefully selected for various uses. The purest grade contains over 98% of CaF_2 and is used in the manufacture of hydrofluoric acid. The next grade contains from 85% to 98% of CaF_2. The specifications for fluorspar, as set forth by one producer, are as listed in table 2.4. The Special is used in glazes and enamels and is ground so that 70% passes through 200 mesh and 93% through 100 mesh. The No. 1 Standard is employed for glasses and enamels, and the No. 1 Special in vitreous or glassware batches.

Fluorspar is a very powerful flux and makes glasses and enamels opaque when properly used. Also, it has an important effect upon the development of certain colors, particularly greens. It is rarely used in glazes, and usually at low heats, because it combines with some silica to form SiF_4 and volatilizes as SiF_4 causing bubbling. On the other hand, fluorspar imparts to the glazes a higher gloss and a greater fusibility than is had with a molecular equivalent of calcium as the carbonate and dissolves the coloring oxides better. Saggers are not attacked by the fluorine. It is not surprising that there are differences of opinion regarding the action of fluorspar since the type of glaze used, temperature, and the amount of fluorspar will all influence the results. Recent studies have demonstrated the usefulness of the fluoride with strontium oxide in the preparation of leadless glazes.

CALCIUM CHLORIDE. This chemical ($CaCl_2$) is sometimes used as an electrolyte to flocculate glaze slips. The purpose is to "set-up" glazes by thickening the consistency to facilitate the application to the ware. It acts much in the same fashion as other flocculents such as acids, magnesium sulfate, or sodium chloride. It may be useful in preventing "curtaining" in dipped ware.

CALCIUM SILICATE. This is the natural mineral wollastonite ($CaO \cdot SiO_2$). Some slags are composed predominantly of calcium silicates. Wollastonite is available commercially in several grades at a low price. When used in raw glazes it has the effect of fritted $CaCO_3 + SiO_2$. The most actively mined deposit is near Willsboro, New York, but other deposits also are worked, notably some in California.

A typical analysis[11] of a commercial product is: 50.90 SiO_2, 46.90 CaO, 0.55 FeO, 0.25 Al_2O_3, 0.10 MnO, 0.10 MgO, 0.05 TiO_2, and 0.90 L.O.I. percent, respectively. The material has a true specific gravity of 2.9 and its solubility in water is about 0.01 g per 100cc. The solubility is such that a 10% slurry develops a pH of 9.9 due to Ca^{++} ions in solution. For most applications this is not deleterious but it would flocculate a slip. Wollastonite has been credited with producing smoother and brighter glazes than does $CaCO_3$.

Strontium

The use of strontium in glazes has been practiced in a small way for many years. Within the last few decades the matter has been more systematically and vigorously investigated with encouraging results. Clark's[12] summary of the state of the art some time ago is still applicable. This was as follows:

a. When replacing calcia in a dinnerware glaze on a molecular basis, strontia is a more active flux, increases fluidity, the softening temperature and solubility, and slightly raises the thermal expansion of the glaze.
b. When replacing an equal weight of calcia in the glaze, strontia increases fluidity and lowers the softening temperature but does not seem to alter the thermal expansion. Good glaze frit was obtained in all calcia replacements and, though desirable advantages are derived from the use of strontia in mill additions, results showed that the maximum effect of increased fluidity and lowered softening temperature was obtained by including the strontia in the frit.
c. When replacing zinc oxide in a dinnerware glaze on a molecular basis, strontia increases fluidity, lowers the solubility, and slightly raises the thermal expansion but does not seem to affect the softening temperature.
d. When replacing lead oxide in a dinnerware glaze on a molecular basis,

strontia decreases fluidity, increases the softening temperature, and slightly increases the thermal expansion. Satisfactory lead glazes can be obtained through additional soaking during the firing of this type of glaze (a lead borosilicate tableware glaze).

Clark concluded that superior glazes could be had by using strontia for replacing some of the other bases, that satisfactory leadless glazes may be had in better colors than with high calcia-containing compositions, and that the greater fluidity accompanying the use of strontia facilities the formation of smoother surfaces on glazes containing zirconia. The opinion is expressed that the use of strontia as a replacement for calcia and baria will promote a more satisfactory interfacial reaction with a resulting better glaze frit. It is expected that there will be a greater scratch resistance and lower solubility in water and other fluids commonly brought in contact with tableware.

Harman and Swift[13] studied the effect of strontia in raw glazes free from lead and boric ozide and fired through a wide range of temperatures. They found the oxide essential because it increased the fusibility when the ratios of CaO to MgO to SrO were properly adjusted.

The acid resistance of an uranium red glaze was found by Thiemecke[14] to be increased by the substitution of strontia for calcia. This permitted the reduction of the amount of lead and a greater firing range.

STRONTIUM CARBONATE. This is the form employed by the glaze maker. The mineral form, strontianite ($SrCO_3$), is mined in some areas, but most of the domestic supply is prepared from celestite ($SrSO_4$). The carbonate has a slight solubility in water, particularly in the presence of carbon dioxide. The technical grade is approximately 99% pure, with calcium carbonate the principal foreign material, but usually containing also some baria.

Magnesium

Magnesium is commonly distributed in nature and is a frequent constituent of limestone and some of the other materials used in glaze batches. It is found, therefore, in many types of glazes but rarely in amounts comparable with calcia. At the lower temperature levels it acts as a refractory, but in the higher ranges it becomes a very vigorous flux, strongly increasing fluidity. It lowers the coefficient of expansion of the melt to a much greater degree than other base and, in general, compares favorably with other alkalies and alkaline bases in its influence upon the other mechanical properties of the glaze containing it.

Magnesia, like the other alkaline earths, has its own specific action in the development of colored glazes. Under some conditions it promotes a certain degree of opacity in glazes. This has been observed in such diverse types as the Bristol and lead borosilicate tableware and sanitary glazes. This opacity cannot be compared with the effect obtained with tin or zirconia but it is useful. A definite increase in glossiness accompanies the balanced use of magnesia in some glazes, and because of its refractoriness it is given as a constituent of some low temperature matts. The amount of magnesia present in different types of glazes is quite variable. In the Bristol type, the amount can be up to 0.2–0.3 molar equivalent. The usual lead borosilicate tableware glaze may contain 0.1–0.15 molar equivalent and sometimes a little more. In the leadless-borosilicate type, particularly those containing strontia, it is used sparingly. In porcelain glazes for the higher temperatures the amount is frequently as great as 0.3 mol. equiv., but in special porcelain glazes the amount may reach 1.0 mole.

MAGNESIUM CARBONATE. This compound ($MgCO_3$) has a slight but notable solubility in water. The specific gravity is relatively high, approximately 3. The light magnesium carbonate is the basic form with the formula $3MgO \cdot Mg(OH)_2 \cdot H_2O$. It is sufficiently soluble to be effective as a flocculant for the clay content of the glaze slip.

The precipitated grades of $MgCO_3$ and of the basic carbonates are readily available and have an extremely low bulk specific gravity. These fluffy products are the only readily available commercial magnesium carbonates. When used as mill-additions, they require excessive water for preparing slips. The resulting high drying and firing shrinkages lead to cracking and crawling during the drying and firing of the glaze. The fluffy grades are satisfactory in compositions to be fritted. Dense grades of magnesium carbonate, derived by grinding natural magnesite ($MgCO_3$), are not generally available. When available, however, they could be used as mill-additions without encountering disasterous consistency effects with resulting crawling. Magnesite formerly was quarried in the state of Washington and in California. Russia, Austria, Manchuria, Greece, and Czechoslovakia are active producers of magnesite.

SEAWATER MAGNESITE (MgO) is produced in large tonnages from seawater by precipitation of $MgCO_3$ followed by calcination at high temperature. The resulting MgO is hard and reasonably low in water solubility when finely ground, but is not considered useful as a mill-addition in glazes. It is satisfactory as an ingredient in batches to be fritted. The MgO content is in excess of 98%, but the product is available in various degrees of purity.

Table 2.5. Typical dolomites (wt %)*

Oxide	California	England	N.W. Ohio
CaO	30.60	31.15	30.48
MgO	21.52	20.57	21.77
Al_2O_3	0.28	0.15	0.02
Fe_2O_3	trace	0.16	0.04
L.O.I.	47.70	47.08	47.54

**Ceramic Industry* magazine, January 1968, p. 77.

DOLOMITE OR $(Ca,Mg)CO_3$. Because MgO seldom is to be used in glazes except in conjunction with an equal or greater quantity of CaO, dolomite, $(Ca,Mg)O \cdot CO_2$, which is readily available commercially, is used as the source for MgO, along with some of the CaO requirements. The true mineral, dolomite, is equivalent to 56% of calcium carbonate and 44% of magnesium carbonate; commercial deposits of dolomite are widely distributed and it is mined in several states. Typical analyses of some dolomites are given in table 2.5.

STEATITE AND TALC. The mineral $(3MgO \cdot 4SiO_2 \cdot H_2O)$ is talc, and the rock in which the mineral is the chief component is called steatite. It has not been widely used in glazes. It should be quite useful when modern materials of a high degree of reliability in chemical and physical compositions are employed. The analysis would need to be known and the batch composition calculated to utilize it.

Beryllium

Berillia is an uncommon component in glazes, although it has been used with success. When added to a lead borosilicate hotel china glaze, it increases the Knoop hardness,[15] but is less effective in this regard than ZnO or Li_2O. It also is reputed to aid in the production of excellent high-temperature chrome greens. Beryllium compounds should be used with caution. Vapors containing it are extremely toxic, leading to beryllosis.

The natural mineral $3BeO \cdot Al_2O_3 \cdot 6SiO_2$ is the main ore from which beryllium chemicals are derived. It is a very hard mineral and has been used as an ingredient in glazes to a limited extent. It is used to introduce BeO, the lightest member of the alkaline earth group, and would be shown as such in the glaze formula.

Barium

Under favorable circumstances, barium is a more vigorous flux than other alkaline earths. It produces glasses having higher indices of refraction, therefore, more brilliancy, than other alkaline earths, but not equal to that to be had with lead. According to Hall,[16] in comparison with CaO and ZnO it gives a lower elastic constant in all proportions used. This is true only to a limited degree when compared with PbO and Na_2O. With respect to the influence upon the coefficient of thermal expansion, baryta is similar to PbO and less effective than the alkalies and calcia. Baryta is not susceptible to action of reduction which is a defect of lead and zinc oxide. Nor does it have their high vapor pressures. It does have, however, a degree of toxicity.

Barium Carbonate. This occurs in nature as the mineral witherite ($BaCO_3$), which is prepared for industrial use. Most commercial barium carbonate is prepared by reducing the mineral barite ($BaSO_4$) to the sulfide and precipitating the carbonate with carbon dioxide. The product may contain some sulfur. The use of air-floated witherite is said to be less likely to cause the crawling which may accompany the addition of a light grade of the chemical. The use of barium carbonate in the glaze batch is generally limited because it reacts slowly and acts generally as a refractory, often producing dull or matt textures. If fritted or fired at the higher temperatures it becomes a vigorous flux, and is most effective. Barium carbonate, per se, has a decomposition temperature of 1,421° C and when used raw in a glaze batch, some of it may persist during and even after the maturing of the glaze.

Barium Sulfate. This is the form known as barytes ($BaSO_4$). Seger demonstrated that it is feasible to use this abundant, cheap mineral as a glaze component, providing that it is mixed with carbon in a mass which is carefully fired and ultimately fritted. Generally speaking, it is never used as a glaze ingredient.

Zinc

Zinc oxide is an important constituent of several types of glazes, functioning as a flux, improving the gloss, modifying the action of chromophores, sometimes drastically, and sometimes contributing to opacity. Excessive amounts will render the melt too refractory, i.e., too viscous, without greatly lessening the glossiness. As is usual in glazes the effects obtained will be dependent in some degree upon the character and amount of the other bases present, as well as upon the content of silica and alumina. For example, in the Bristol type of glaze, the replacement of part of the calcia with zinc oxide is said to give a greater fusibility than that had with either constituent used alone. Zinc oxide has the greatest effect of any of the bases—excepting calcia and magnesia, according to Hall[16]—in increasing the elasticity. It is second only to magnesia in its power to lower the coefficient of expansion, but Hall rates it as a little lower than calcia. With the exception of calcia it ranks first in increasing the strength. Judging from its valuable conduct in making glass more resistant to attack by water, we may assume that this is probably true of glaze melts.

Zinc oxide (ZnO) is practically the only compound of the element used in ceramics. It sublimes at 1,800° C and is readily reduced to the metal. There are several grades, depending upon the purity which in turn depends upon the method of preparation. The best grade is prepared by the volatilization of metallic zinc and the oxidation of the vapors which are classified into various size groups during the process of condensation. The cheaper grades, prepared from the ores by a simpler process, may be contaminated with the oxides of iron, cadmium, and lead. Inferior grades may contain considerable lead sulfate. Calcination of zinc oxide has long been practiced to minimize shrinkage during the firing of the glaze and the consequent tendency to crawl and bead.

CRAWLING. Crawling of glazes high in zinc oxide frequently has been attributed to its allegedly developing fusions of high surface tension. There is no data to indicate that ZnO raises the surface tension of molten glazes or that it would cause crawling if it did.

Zinc oxide can cause crawling but this mainly is due to physical factors associated with glaze slips and with shrinkage and vitrification behavior during firing.

ZINC OXIDE OF VARIOUS GRADES. Different grades of zinc oxides perform differently in glaze slips and during firing. Reising[17] selected four types of zinc oxides and prepared slurries of them. The viscosities of the slips after successive periods of milling gave results as shown in table 2.6. Each of the slips developed a peak viscosity, then tended to stabilize. It

Table 2.6. Viscosities of ZnO-water slurries[17]

ZnO sample no.	1	2	3	4
Particle size, micron	0.20	0.28	0.37	0.65
Surface, sq. m./gram	10.91	5.27	3.82	1.7
Calcination	none	none	med.	hard
Viscosity*, cps, after 0 hrs. milling	235	265	205	200
after ½ hrs. milling	500	655	255	200
after 1 hrs. milling	765	670	250	240
after 2 hrs. milling	1340	660	240	130
after 4 hrs. milling	1340	630	240	200
after 8 hrs. milling	1435	625	255	190

*75 wt.% water, 25% ZnO, ball milled

was also noted that ZnO tends to react with water to form a gelatinous zinc hydroxide.

Highly calcined, low-surface ZnO limits the formation of zinc hydroxide sufficiently to almost eliminate the increase in viscosity with milling time. Glaze slips were prepared from each of these zinc oxides and applied as glaze deposits. Zinc oxides no. 1, 2, and 3 of table 2.6 all were cracked severely during drying, but the hard calcine, no. 4, dried without developing cracking. It was concluded that the degree of reaction of ZnO with water and the shrinkage characteristics are directly related to the specific surface of the ZnO powder. It further was noted that crawling was directly related to the shrinkage of the glaze slip during its drying or firing. Difficulties due to crawling in zinc glazes are minimized by using dead-calcined ZnO.

Zinc oxide is used to some extent for whiteware and raw lead glazes. However, it rarely is used in high-fire porcelain glazes. Small amounts introduced into high-fire porcelain glazes are useful in starting fusion and forming a more perfect surface.

When the amount of zinc oxide added to a glaze is excessive, the oxide acts as a refractory and imparts whiteness. This whiteness is not of the same excellent value as that due to the more conventional opacifiers, but, on the contrary, usually bestows a slightly pinkish tone. The zinc oxide necessary to produce opacity, in general, becomes less as the Al_2O_3 and alkaline bases are increased. The use of zinc oxide in whiteware glazes seems to be a peculiarly American practice.

Zinc oxide has some effect on colors, assisting in spreading a few and modifying others. For example, it benefits blues and tends to prevent the formation of greens with chromium oxide. It has been found that zinc oxide imparts to glazes a greater brilliancy, and also that it is a valuable constituent in correcting crazing.

The saturation of a glaze with zinc oxide is a method frequently used for obtaining a crystalline texture. If large fan-shaped crystals are to be produced, the glaze must first be heated above the crystallization range and then cooled down to the crystallization range again and held there for at least 3 hours. An excessive soaking period (10 hours and over) will cause the crystals to stand out above the surface of the glaze and give the appearance of roughness. The following glaze composition had a crystallization range, i.e., the only temperatures at which crystals will form, of from 750° C to 1,050° C.

$0.65ZnO$		
$0.30Na_2O$	$0.05Al_2O_3$	$1.8SiO_2$
$0.05CoO$		$0.3B_2O_3$

Zinc is oftentimes used in face brick manufacture to obtain green surfaces on otherwise red burning clays. The process is called zinc flashing and consists of throwing lumps of metallic zinc into the fireboxes at the finish of the burn. The dampers are then nearly closed and the whole kiln allowed to soak in the zinc vapors for about 20 minutes. To obtain the best results sometimes 3 or 4 flashings are necessary. As the zinc has a tendency to burn off while the kiln is cooling, it is the customary practice either to cool rapidly or close the damper and fireboxes completely for the first 24 hours in order to keep the flash on the brick.

Lead*

Because of the cheapness of the oxides and carbonates of lead and the ease with which these enter into combination with silica and boric oxide and because of the perfect miscibility of these compounds in the glasses which are readily formed, lead finds a large use in the preparation of glazes. Its addition to a batch in appreciable quantities affects a silicate melt as follows:

a. It gives a high brilliancy due to the high index of refraction.
b. It lowers the coefficient of expansion as compared to the alkalies.
c. It increases the "stretching ability" or, in other words, it lowers the modulus of elasticity.
d. It decreases the viscosity of the melt.
e. It makes the melt less likely to devitrify.
f. Lead glazes have longer maturing ranges than leadless ones. In some high lead formulas the maturing range may exceed 5 cones.
g. PbO lowers the surface tension of molten glazes containing it, thus helping to homogenize and create surface smoothness.

The use of lead compounds in glazes has some disadvantages, such as: (1) the poisonous nature of many of the forms used by the ceramist, which serious fault may be minimized or avoided by incorporating the lead into a frit; (2) improperly constituted glazes may be dangerously susceptible to attack and solution by fruit juices and other foodstuffs; (3) some lead glazes show the formation of a film, dimming the brilliance after a prolonged exposure to gases commonly present in the atmosphere; (4) raw lead glazes are very easily reduced by careless firing operations, giving grayish to blackish color; (5) the abrasion resistance of the glaze is decreased importantly as the content of lead rises; (6) the strength of the

* Refer to section on lead glazes for full discussion of controls on lead content of glazes.

lead-containing glaze is usually decreased as the alkaline earth members decrease; (7) it should not be used above cone 6 to 7, because of its volatility.

GALENA. This is a widely distributed and cheap lead mineral of theoretical composition PbS. It has been extensively used in the glazing of the cruder forms of pottery for many centuries, even during quite recent times in this country. It is not currently used in the U.S.

LITHARGE. Litharge (PbO) is made by spraying molten metallic lead in the presence of air. It is also obtained as a by-product of the separation of silver from lead. If PbO is fused and allowed to cool rapidly, reddish yellow crystals are formed which are called yellow litharge. The amorphous product formed upon the surfaces of molten lead is yellow and is called massicot. Impurities in excess of the following percentages render litharge unsuitable for use in colorless glazes: Copper, 0.0041; antimony, 0.0050; bismuth, 0.0050 to 0.0075.

A simple chemical test for the purity of litharge is to dissolve the sample in a concentrated solution of lead acetate. Collect the residue which should be the red lead present and, after washing and drying, weigh.

RED LEAD OR MINIUM. Red lead is Pb_3O_4, and may be considered as a mixture of $2PbO$ and PbO_2. It is prepared by roasting litharge; the commercial product usually consists of 75% "true red lead" and 25% litharge. A good quality of red lead will contain 28% to 29% of the lead dioxide and the iron oxide content should not exceed 0.01%, nor the copper oxide be greater than 0.005%. A simple test for insoluble impurities is made by placing a 5-gram sample in a solution of 25 cc of a 1:1 dilution of nitric acid. This is heated carefully and 10 cc of hydrogen perioxide are added gradually. All of the red lead should dissolve and any residue may be examined. Red lead is esteemed for silicate melts because of its high oxygen content and the consequent lesser likelihood of reduction.

WHITE LEAD. The basic lead carbonate $[2PbCO_3 \cdot Pb(OH)_2]$ is the form sometimes preferred by ceramists for introducing lead into a glaze slip because it is a relatively pure compound. In former years it had a definite advantage in this particular over other compounds of lead then available. Other advantages are the smaller size of the individual particle and the specific gravity, which is less than those of the oxides. These two important characteristics permit the carbonate to remain in suspension more completely than the oxides. It decomposes at about 400° C and the evolution of the water and carbon dioxide in the glaze layer has a valuable function of making it more porous and reactive to oxygen in the kiln gases. Pure white lead should dissolve completely in dilute CP nitric acid. Adulterants which have been used in white lead intended for use in paint are barytes, calcium carbonate, and lead silicate. White lead is unsuited for use in frit batches because of the higher cost and inferior oxidizing properties as compared to the cheaper red lead

LEAD SILICATES. These are frits of different compositions which may be as simple as the eutectic mixture, 16% SiO_2, 84% PbO (approximately), that forms liquid at a little below 730° C. This mixture is known in the trade as "lead monosilicate." There are other eutectic mixtures having low fusion temperatures. The so-called "lead bisilicate" has the approximate composition of 65% PbO, 33% SiO_2, 2% Al_2O_3 with a fusion temperature of about 900° C. The costs are said to be sufficiently low so as to make them competitive with the other forms of lead ordinarily used by the ceramist; also there are such important advantages as freedom from dust, less loss of lead by volatilization, and minimizing the danger of lead poisoning.

Lead is one of the most important of the bases available for potters' use and is an ingredient of several types of glazes used throughout a wide range of temperatures, from cone 022 to cone 6. It is the only base that may be used alone with silica or silica and clay to give practical, low to moderate maturing-temperature glazes. This has a yellowish color peculiar to such silicates. Lead glazes are brilliant and easily scratched unless the silica content is high. Lead glazes dissolve almost all color oxides easily and the shades obtained are influenced strongly by the lead content.

The solubility of lead glazes used on culinary wares is a matter of great importance and is safeguarded by legislation in many countries. The chemical test adopted officially by the pre-war German government prescribed that the glaze must not be so soluble in the presence of a 4% solution of glacial acetic acid, at the boiling point for one-half hour, as to yield a solution which may be precipitated by hydrogen sulfide. Thrope[18] has proposed the following ratio as showing the relative solubility of glazes containing lead:

$$\frac{\text{Sum of the bases including alumina} \times 223}{\text{Sum of the acids} \times 60}$$

should be less than 2. Mellor[19] proposed that, since 223/60 is the constant, the same results may be given in the following manner:

$$\frac{\text{Sum of the bases including alumina}}{\text{Sum of the acids}}$$

should be less than 0.5.

All of the common raw materials containing lead are potentially dangerous to the health of the workmen inasmuch as repeated and frequent contact with the raw lead compounds might produce lead poisoning unless the greatest care is exercised. To lessen this danger, all lead for glazes or enamels should be fritted and not put into the raw batch. This procedure converts the lead to an insoluble form which is not nearly so dangerous to the health of the workers.

Aluminum

Alumina is rarely absent from glaze compositions and its presence and quantity make, perhaps, the most conspicuous difference between glasses and glazes. The small percentages of alumina used in special glass compositions—representing the extreme practice—are insignificant as compared with the much greater quantities required in all types of important commercial glazes. This is significant of the very important role the element plays in glaze construction and properties. The notable exception is the relatively low alumina content found in crystalline glazes, because alumina strongly increases the viscosity of the fusion and retards or prevents the growth of the macrocrystalline structure. On the other hand, a relatively high amount of alumina is useful in promoting the formation of the microcrystalline growth, which distinguishes the best type of matt texture. It is needed, in the latter case, to facilite the growth of the desired crystallites.

In the glassy type of glazes the alumina content regulates the degree of fluidity of the molten mass and gives it the stability needed at the temperatures required for maturity. Otherwise, the glaze would not cover the ware evenly and, in many instances, would flow to the lowest level. A glaze that is too fluid at maturity will damage an underglaze pattern.

The alumina content affects refractoriness and hence the maturity of the glaze. Glazes intended for the low cone temperatures will have as little as 0.05 mol. equiv. and a cone 14 glaze may have as much as 0.9 mol. equiv. The amounts are quite variable because they are conditioned, in part, by the nature and amount of the bases used. Alumina increases the hardness and other mechanical properties of a glaze, also its resistance to chemical action, including weathering. It has been found useful for correcting crazing in improperly balanced glazes. The ratio of the molecular equivalents of alumina to silica varies between 1:4 and 1:20, depending upon the type of glaze composition and the maturing temperature. The best ratio for the glossy glazes is usually 1:7 to 1:10. The ratios for matt textures show notably lower amounts of silica; for example, the alumina-silica ratio for bright (i.e., glossy) porcelain glazes at cones 10–12 is about

1:7 or 1:8, where the matt glazes of the same RO composition will be 1:3.2 to 1:3.8.

Alumina in the glaze may influence the kind and quality of the colors to be had with many of the chromophores customarily used; for example, in the absence of alumina, cobalt oxide may be used, in appropriate compositions, to make rose-pink glazes. In the usual type of composition, cobalt furnishes some shade of blue. Chromia and alumina if calcined together furnish a pink-colored pigment; for this reason alumina frequently causes the appearance of reddish or rusty colors in glazes containing chromium introduced with the expectation of forming a green color. Numerous other instances of the influence of alumina in the development of color will be encountered in the description of glaze composition. The mineral or industrial chemicals used for the introduction of aluminum in glaze batch are numerous and only the more commonly employed are to be mentioned here.

ALUMINA. Aluminum oxide (Al_2O_2) is the calcined form of the hydrate, $Al(OH)_3$. Both of these compounds may be had in quite a pure state. The hydrate sometimes is used because its physical condition is suited for suspension in the glaze slip; it has good adhesive properties; and it is reactive during the early stages of the fusion. It has been reported that aluminum hydrates tend to promote the formation of dull and matt textures more than equivalent amounts of alumina introduced in the form of clay or feldspar. This could be due to incomplete homogenization and composition leveling at the cites of dissolved Al_2O_3.

FELDSPAR AND CORNWALL STONE. The properties of these materials are described elsewhere.

CRYOLITE. Reference to this mineral has already been made.

CLAY. This is almost indispensable as a glaze material because: (1) it assists in keeping other glaze materials in suspension in the slip; (2) it is largely responsible for causing adhesion of the unfired slip to the ware, and (3) it is a medium for control of the shrinkage of the unfired slip applied upon unfired ware.

Clays suitable for colorless or transparent glazes should contain a minimum of the oxides of iron and titanium; therefore, china clays (and kaolins) are preferred. If a more highly dispersed, i.e., colloidal type, is desired because of its flotative and adhesive properties, one of the superior secondary kaolina may be used, but some sacrifice of the purity of color may be expected. Certain ball clays may be needed in slips applied on unfired bodies, particularily those in a leather-hard condition. These are permissible also in the batches of many colored glazes, notably with the darker colors.

The amount of clay used in a slip applied on a nonporous body may be as low as 0.05 mol. equiv. and does not usually exceed 0.15 mol. equiv. on an absorbent biscuit. The amount used on a bone-dry body will vary from 0.10 to 0.30 molecular equivalent; whereas the leather-hard body will require 0.20 mol. equiv. and upwards. If all of the alumina-silica required cannot be safely added to the batch as raw clay because of the consequent shrinkage and accompanying defects, a portion of the clay should be calcined. The conduct of the clay in the slip batch, with respect to the flotative and adhesive properties, is susceptible to control by the addition of electrolytes. This varies greatly with the selection of the clay used.

Antimony

Antimony may perform two important functions in silicate fusions such as glazes: it can act both as an opacifier and as a coloring agent. When used alone, it does not appear to be capable of yielding colored melts. The yellow ascribed to it is caused either by the presence of the oxides of lead or iron.

The maximum effect of antimony as an opacifier is limited to such low temperatures as are required for glazes which mature below cone 1. Because there are cheaper and better opacifiers, it is seldom used in glazes for that purpose.

ANTIMONY OXIDE. Antimonious oxide (Sb_2O_3) or antimony trioxide, is referred to as the "oxide of antimony." It is prepared by roasting the mineral stibnite in a controlled atmosphere. Its impurities may consist of small particles of the sulphide or metallic antimony. Analysis of the product, in percentages, is: Water, 0.75; antimonious oxide, 91.30; ferric oxide, 1.15; arsenic trioxide, 5.25; silica, 1.60. It is poisonous and slightly soluble in water.

NAPLES YELLOW. The basic antimonate of lead $Pb_3(SbO_4)_2$, is a paint pigment that can be used by the ceramist as a low-temperature yellow stain.

SODIUM ANTIMONATE. This compound, $2NaSbO_3 \cdot 7H_2O$, contains 84% to 87% of the sodium meta-antimonate and is used successfully as an opacifier for enamels. It does not function well in glazes having firing temperatures higher than 1,000° C.

Reference has been made to antimony as an opacifier in low temperature glazes, and to its use in developing yellow and orange colors for underglaze, inglaze, and overglaze decoration. It has also been employed to produce greens for roofing tile by mixing cobalt oxide and antimony sulfate with the glaze

A mixture, known as "yellow base," suitable as a ceramic color, has the following composition, expressed as percent by weight: Red lead, 52; antimony oxide, 34; tin oxide, 14. This is prepared by calcining the mixture at about cone 09, grinding, and then washing. It is used for inglaze color.

Chambers and Rigg[20] have reported that 60% red lead and 40% antimony oxide was the only one of several binary mixtures which gave a good yellow color. These mixtures were calcined to cone 09a (920° C) in a muffle kiln, ground, and washed. The addition of 20% of potassium nitrate improved the colors of some of these mixtures, while the addition of tin oxide made still further improvement. The addition of ferric oxide improved the color but equal amounts of iron oxide introduced directly into the frit were not as effective.

Salvetat[21] prepared a yellow color of the following percentage composition for porcelain: Red lead, 42 parts; boric acid, 9 parts; sand, 12 parts; potassium antimonate, 12 parts; zinc oxide, 3 parts

Silicon

With the exception of oxygen, silicon is the predominating element in all glazes because the oxide, silica (SiO_2), combines freely with many other oxides, notably bases, to form an extensive variety of complex silicates. These silicates possess the following significant properties:

a. In general, they are macroscopically miscible at all temperatures.
b. They can be made to exist at ordinary temperatures as undercooled solutions that possess optical and mechanical properties desired in glazes.
c. They may be prepared so as to have a high resistance to attack by gases, water, and most alkali and acid solutions.
d They can, by proper additions, form colored or opaque undercooled solutions.

In most glassy compositions, the SiO_2 content will constitute over 50% of the batch. As a general rule, increasing the silica content in glaze will: (1) raise the melting temperature, i.e., make the melt more refractory; (2) decrease the fluidity of the melt; (3) stabilize the resistance of the matured glaze against solution by water and to chemical attack; (4) lower the coefficient of thermal expansion; and (5) increase the hardness and strength. It should be kept in mind, however, that these effects are modified by the amount and character of the other elements present and whether the silica is in the limits of well balanced glaze formulations.

The normal limits of the silica used in all types of glazes lie between 1 and 12 molecular equivalents. If the silica is too low, the glaze will be unstable, e.g., too soluble. If the silica is too high, the glaze becomes excessively refractory.

SILICA. Although there are several crystal modifications of the compound SiO_2, quartz is the form stable at ordinary temperatures and most uncombined SiO_2 used as a ceramic raw material can be shown to have quartz as its major crystalline phase. Silica may be obtained as sand and in high purity from a variety of sources, the chief of which are sandstone, rock crystal, and flint or chert.

The sands and sandstones consist of particles of quartz crystals which, in the former, are loose, while, in the latter, they are more or less firmly bound together. These materials represent the ultimate product of the decomposition of igneous rocks that have weathered and gradually lost the associated bases by solution. The most important commercial sources of sands or sandstone in the United States are situated in Pennsylvania, West Virginia, and Illinois. The material is prepared for use by crushing, washing, screening, and grinding in either ball or tube mills. Most of the powdered silica called "potters flint" used in the U.S. for glazes is from these sources. The term *flint* is a carry-over from the popular flint from France and England.

Quartz crystal is obtained from veins, dykes, or masses of siliceous rock and is more costly to prepare for market than the sands or sandstone. Ground quartz derived from either source is, as a rule, very pure, containing 99.7% or 99.8% SiO_2.

Flint is a microcrystalline variety of silica obtained chiefly from France and England, but very general in its occurrence. It is prepared for use by calcination and grinding. The grinding is done coarsly on a chaser mill after which it is completed in cylinder mills. The impurities are small amounts of alumina, calcia, and iron. Flint is the term commonly used by the American ceramist to designate the raw material used to introduce free silica in glaze batches, irrespective of the mineralogical nature of the raw material. However, discrimination should be made between flint prepared from cryptocrystalline material, i.e., *pebble flint* and the crystalline quartzy sands or rocks. The calcined pebble flint has specific gravity of approximately 2.33 whereas the quartz flint is much higher (about 2.65). This difference is of much importance if substitutions are made of one for the other in slips. If suitable corrections are not made it may be a subtle but possible cause of crazing. Another difference between the two types of materials is the greater chemical reactivity of the pebble flint because of its cryptocrystalline character.

Microcrystalline silica also is abundant in the U.S. in several locations. It generally is mined and processed for applications other than glazes. It is, however, available and useful. The domestic cherts, novaculites, ganisters, and flints are ground without having been calcined and quenched. A good grade of potters' flint, when burned to cone 8, should be a pure white color and easily friable. A material of this type may have the following chemical composition (by percentage): Silica—minimum, 99.60; potash and soda—maximum, 0.15; oxides of iron—maximum, 0.05; lime—maximum, 0.10; magnesia—maximum, 0.10; alumina—maximum, 0.10.

The fineness of flint is an important factor and two popular grades, based on screen analysis are shown in table 2.7. Finely ground, free, and uncombined silica if continually taken into the lungs as dust will eventually lead to a disease called *silicosis*. Tuberculosis practically always accompanies the final stages of the disease. To properly protect laborers from this danger, provisions should be made to keep the silica dust content of the air below certain maximum limits over all parts of the plant in which men are continually working.

NATURAL SILICATES. These include clays, feldspars, and some other kinds of ordinary glaze materials. They are described elsewhere.

SILICATES OF SODA. A number of compositions varying in the relative proportions of the soda and silica are available. The term is quite indefinite so analyses of particular lots or brands should be had. They are all alike in being readily soluble in water. Aside from the possibility of using these silicates in a frit batch, which would be pointless, the unique use in ceramic glazes is as an adhesive medium. The colors and other glaze ingredients needed may be mixed in the water solution of silicate. This is applied to

Table 2.7. Two grades of potter's flint, based on fineness of grind.

Grade	Mesh					
	On 100	On 140	On 200	On 270	On 325	Thru 325
1	0.10%	0.20%	1.50%	2.00%	5.00%	91.20%
2	0.50	1.00	2.50	3.50	6.50	86.00

the ware by painting or dipping and, after drying, the ware is fired. The glaze coat will swell somewhat but should settle back smoothly. A 47° Bé silicate with a Na_2O to SiO_2 ratio of 1 to 2.9 reportedly has been so used.

Boron

Boron is used in several very important types of glazes because it:

a. forms easily fusible silicate fusions of interest to the glaze ceramist
b. has a strong solvent action on color oxides
c. appreciably lowers the thermal expansion in amounts up to about 12%, but further additions reverse this effect
d. increases the gloss or brillance of the melt but does not increase refractive index
e. aids in the formation of glasses that are viscous at lower temperatures, but which are disproportionately more fluid at the higher temperatures; this is an advantage in the flowing of glazes
f. does not crystallize from fusions and also tends to hinder the crystallization of other phases
g. is an acid and usually forms a part of the silica network
h. lowers surface tension
i. properly used, can greatly improve chemical durability
j. when present in high concentrations in a frit, has a tendency to dissolve some in water to yield complex hydrated sodium borates or boric acid.

Compared with silica, the introduction of boric oxide increases elasticity, decreases the tensile strength, and, within certain limits as to quantity, lowers the coefficient of thermal expansion.

FUNCTION OF BORIC OXIDE IN GLAZES. Binns[22] suggested that B_2O_3 should be placed in the R_2O_3 column with the alumina in the formula because all of the sesquioxides may function either as acids or bases. Although it is a matter of little or no importance, B_2O_3 should be treated mainly as an acid along with silica.

Bleininger and Teetor[23] examined the reaction of boric oxide and silica and concluded that such mixtures are typical glasses without definite deformation points. Binns' convictions have been supported by others, including Singer.[24] Stull and Radcliffe[25] reported the results of experiments on the use of boric acid in certain glazes and concluded that its action will depend upon the ratio of bases to silica (expressed as an oxide ratio) existing in the glaze before the addition of the boric oxide. If this ratio is not greater than 1:2 the glazes will be clear and will not craze; otherwise, opalescence due to immiscibility and crazing tendencies will be observed.

ANHYDROUS BORIC OXIDE. Fused B_2O_3 in tiny glass pellets resembling powder is commercially available. It has an application in many frit-batch formulations. It is fairly stable, perhaps more so than the hydrated boric acid.

BORIC ACID. This is a soft flaky substance (H_3BO_3 or $B_2O_3 \cdot 3H_2O$) readily soluble in water. The hydrated acid loses water partially at 100° C and fuses at red heat to form the anhydride (B_2O_3). Care should be taken to store the hydrated form in a place of moderate temperatures if the moisture content is to be held constant.

Some frits, being temporary or expedient intermediate processing products, may have appreciable water solubility, especially when in powdered form. From some of these, it is possible that hydrated boric oxide or other borates could be leached from the powder during grinding, or in situ in a glaze slip. It is important to realize that hydrated boric oxide or boric acid when heated has a strong tendency to vaporize or sublime as shown in figure 2.1. Through this process, boric oxide in variable amounts can be lost during the initial firing stages of glazes from some frits from which boric acid has been leached. This may be minimized or even eliminated by causing the boric acid to react with an alkali or alkaline earth to form their borates which do not sublime.

Boric acid may be obtained in either refined or crude grades. The refined material analyzes 99% H_3BO_3, while the crude material will run from 80% to 90%. The impurities are traces of sulphates and chlorides, as well as some insoluble matter. Only traces of iron oxide are present.

According to Guertler[26] the oxides of the following elements are either insoluble or sparingly soluble in molten boric acid: beryllium, aluminum, chromium, silicon, thorium, tin, molybdenum, and uranium. These matters are shown precisely by phase equilibrium diagrams for the binary systems of B_2O_3 with Al_2O_3, BaO, Bi_2O_3, CaO, CdO, CoO, Cs_2O, H_2O, K_2O, La_2O_3, Li_2O, MgO, MnO, Na_2O, PbO, ThO_2 and ZnO, respectively, as published by Levin, Robbins, and McMurdie.[27] The same publication also contains several ternary systems having B_2O_3 as one of the components.

BORAX. The compound $Na_2B_4O_7 \cdot 10H_2O$ is a common form of sodium borate and crystallizes in the prismatic form, while $Na_2B_4O_7 \cdot 5H_2O$ crystallizes in octahedrons. The octahedral form passes slowly into the prismatic upon standing for some time in moist air. The purity of the com-

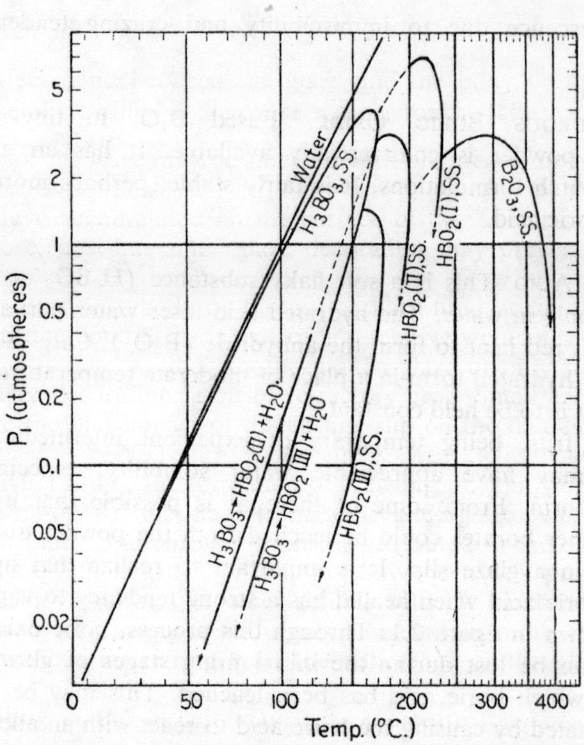

Figure 2.1. System H_2O–B_2O_3: pressure-temperature diagram for vapor pressures of saturated solutions. (F. C. Kracek, Morey, G. W., and Merwin, H. E. (1938). *Am. J. Sci.* 35A, 162. This figure was taken from Levin, Ernest M., McMurdie, Howard F., and Hall, F. P. 1956. *Phase diagrams for ceramists*. Columbus, Ohio: American Ceramic Society, Inc., p. 248.)

mercial borax is guaranteed to be over 99.5%. Dehydrated or fused borax ($Na_2O \cdot 2B_2O_3$) may be substituted for the hydrated form in the ratio of 53 parts of the former for 100 parts of the latter. The advantages of its use have been previously explained (under Sodium). Borax is generally available in three grades: granular, fine granular, and powdered. It comes as pentahydrate, decahydrate, borax glass, and annhydrous forms. All grades are said by the suppliers to approach optimum analysis.

COLEMANITE. This is a natural hydrated calcium borate ($2CaO \cdot 3B_2O_3 \cdot 5H_2O$) formerly found in commercial quantities in California and Oregon, but it is now scarce or unavailable. It fuses at about 900° C and is slightly soluble in water. By its use raw leadless glazes may be had to mature as low as cone 04 if cryolite is added to the batch.[28]

Titanium

Titania acts pyrochemically as an acid, as does SiO_2 and is added to glazes for its influence on color, its tendency to produce opacity, and to promote crystallization. It is only slightly soluble in the melt. The coefficient of the thermal expansion factor of the oxide (TiO_2) is about midway in the list of common oxides.

RUTILE. Natural rutile usually is associated with 1% to 25% of FeO in solid solution in the crystal, as well as lesser amounts of silica, chromium, and vanadium oxides. Titanium oxide pigments in the form of milled rutile are used extensively. These pigments are not pure titanium dioxide, but the natural rutile contains a significant proportion of iron oxide.

TITANIUM DIOXIDE. Pure titania (TiO_2) is manufactured in large tonnages as a white pigment for paints, paper, and general use. It is scarcely used in glazes for that purpose. It has extensive use in glazes, however, for other purposes.

Titania is used in glazes to increase acid resistance and to produce color and texture. It has been used in cone 2 glazes to secure textured finishes, especially for flooring tile. These effects are due to the formation of sphene ($CaO \cdot TiO_2 \cdot SiO_2$) formed in the glaze by pyrochemical reactions. There is considerable potential and some active interest in the development of clear frits that yield self-opacified glazes. Titania also has potential special application as an ingredient to effect nucleation in the now-developing "glass-ceramic" type of glazes, discussed in another chapter.

Titanium oxide has been used in the preparation of underglaze colors. Pure titania added to a frit and applied as an underglaze color on a calcareous body, under a lead glaze, gives a reddish yellow. Using rutile, a dark yellow has been obtained because of the small content of iron present. Titania, substituted for tin oxide in pink salts (chrome-tin pink), gives a useful yellowish-reddish-brown underglaze color. Ashley[29] obtained a ruby color. Titanium oxide has a strong influence on the color obtained with iron in certain cone-6 Bristol glazes, since the addition of 0.10 molecular equivalent has been found to change the color of a glaze containing 0.09 molecular equivalent of iron from an intense brown to an intense green. With no iron present the titania addition merely produced a whitish blue tone.

Titanium dioxide is susceptible to reduction by carbon monoxide and other reducing agents yielding the sesquioxide Ti_2O_3, which is a copper-red compound. Intense blues are sometimes obtained by reduction.

Table 2.8. Effects of elemental magnesium and antimony as in-batch reducing agents in a glass containing dissolved titania[30]

Additive	*Modifier*	*Proportions*	*Color*
Magnesium	–	lesser	black
Magnesium	–	lesser	yellow
Antimony	$Na_2S_2O_3$	–	yellow
Antimony	$Na_2S_2O_3$	–	red

Unusual colors may be achieved in glazes containing titanium oxide and a reducing agent. For example,[30] in a base glass containing Na_2O, K_2O, SiO_2, Al_2O_3, and TiO_2 plus metallic particles of Mg, Al or Zn as in-batch reducing agent and melted at 1,400° C the colors in table 2.8 were obtained. When rutile and cobalt are present together, green may result because of the optical blending of the yellow and blue colors.

Phototrophy (sensitivity to light) of glazes has been attributed to the action of titania.

Phosphorus

When phosphates are introduced into a glaze, they tend to cause opacity and to slightly increase the index of refraction. It is used to a very limited extent.

CALCIUM PHOSPHATE, $Ca_3(PO_4)_2$. There are two forms of calcium phosphate of interest to the ceramist: the mineral apatite and bone ash. Bone ash does not have a constant composition, but the following analysis in weight percent is indicative: Phosphate of lime, 85.9; carbonate of lime, 5.9; phosphate of magnesia, 3.80; chloride of sodium and potash, 5.15; fluoride of calcium, trace. This corresponds to $4Ca_3(PO_4)_2 \cdot 2CaCO_3$. The material is prepared by the calcination of selected animal bones and subsequent grinding. It is used as an opacifier.

Table 2.9. Apatite and bone ash analyses, weight %.

Component	*Apatite*	*Bone ash*
Silica	0.06%	1.80%
Alumina and ferric oxide	0.72	1.30
Lime	55.70	53.30
Magnesia	0.20	0.30
Alkalies	0.80	0.64
Water	0.28	–
Fluoride	3.10	3.20
Phosphorus pentoxide	39.24	40.15

Apatite, $CaF \cdot Ca_4(PO_4)_3$, is found in large deposits in eastern Canada. An approximate analysis is: Tri-calcium phosphate, 67.85%; calcium carbonate, 3.10%; calcium fluoride, 4%. Ultimate analyses of both apatite and bone ash are given in table 2.9.

As a glaze material, bone ash is used to a limited extent as an opacifier at low temperatures. If used in excessive amounts or at too high a temperature it causes dullness, pinholes, and blistering. The presence of small amounts of phosphoric oxide has been reported in the analyses of some Chinese and Japanese glazes.

Laboratory experiments have disclosed that as much as 0.15 molecular equivalent of P_2O_3 may be present in a typical cone 02 raw lead glaze with safety if the glaze is applied thinly. Too heavy an application is likely to cause crawling, beading, or blistering. The texture will vary from glossy to matt and the glaze will be semi-opaque, depending upon the amount of phosphoric acid used. Brown craze lines observed in a green-gray glaze of a certain type of old Chinese ware of the Sung Dynasty (960–1270 A.D.) have been attributed[31] to the oxidation of the ferrous phosphate in the glaze composition exposed by the fissuring of the protective skin. This oxidation phenomenon is known to occur in bone china.

Arsenic

Arsenic is only occasionally used in glazes. Its compounds are very poisonous.

ARSENIC OXIDE. Arsenous oxide is a white powder and the As_2O_3 is the form of arsenic practically always added to silicate batches. Arsenic pentoxide, As_2O_5, decomposes to $As_2O_3 + O_2$ at 400° C and thus may act as a low temperature oxidizing agent. It also would act as an opacifier. Fused As_2O_3, when quenched, can exist as an amorphous glass.

ZIRCONIUM ARSENATES. It is notable that some zirconium arsenates that might be useful in glazes were described by Peyronel.[32] These act as oxidation, firing, or frothing agents, depending upon viscosity characteristics of the glaze. The residual arsenic and zirconium oxides would act as opacifiers. It is possible that analogous compounds with corresponding dissociation products would be found in zirconium antimoniates. The decomposition behavior of the zirconium arsenates is:

$$2(ZrO_2 \cdot As_2O_5) \xrightarrow{900^\circ C} 2ZrO_2 \cdot As_2O_5 + As_2O_3 + O_2$$
$$3(2ZrO_2 \cdot As_2O_5) \xrightarrow{950^\circ C} 2(3ZrO_2 \cdot As_2O_5) + As_2O_3 + O_2$$
$$3ZrO_2 \cdot As_2O_5 \xrightarrow{1{,}000^\circ C} 3ZrO_2 + As_2O_3 + O_2$$

Tin

The chief use of tin oxide in glazes is as an opacifier. Because of its low solubility in silicate melts, its high covering power, and superior white color, it will continue in wide use notwithstanding its high price. It is important, also, for production of certain very desirable colors for inglaze, underglaze, and overglaze decoration.

TIN OXIDE, which is the chemist's stannic oxide (SnO_2), is prepared from the ore cassiterite obtained chiefly in the Malay States and Bolivia. A simple test formerly used for the quality of the commercial tin oxide was the levigation, i.e., washing, of about 10 grams of the oxide in water. The operation was the repetition of stirring the sample with water, allowing it to stand for 10 seconds, and decanting the supernatant water. Gradually the lighter portion was separated from the heavier residue of metallic tin, chips of metallic iron from machinery, particles of firebrick from the furnaces, etc., which remained in the beaker used in the washing process. Modern grades, however, are sufficiently reliable as to render such tests generally needless.

RECOVERED TIN OXIDE is oxide salvaged from tin plate and other suitable sources by an intricate chemical process. A possible contamination is the black stannous oxide, which is objectionable. These grades are inferior for ceramic use.

TIN ASH is a mixture of the oxides of lead and tin formed by the calcination of the two metals on a hearth while being stirred frequently. After calcination, the product is crushed and levigated to separate the lighter ash from the heavier unoxidized or partially oxidized particles. This glaze material is seldom encountered in modern recipes. The proportions of lead are about 80–60 to 20–40 tin.

Very little tin oxide is used in a glaze batch—6% to 10%—and only a small fraction of this is dissolved in the melt, less than 0.05 mol. equiv. according to some observers. The amount in any case will depend upon the type of glaze and the maturing temperature. The maximum opacifying effect is said to be had if the tin oxide is used with a frit containing boric oxide. Excessive amounts of the oxide produce a dull or even a matt texture. The presence of even traces of Cr_2O_3 or its vapors in glaze compositions containing tin oxide will produce pink to maroon colors. Tin-containing glazes set in close proximity to chromium colors will be affected by the fumes, producing pink discolorations or shades.

Zirconium

Zirconium compounds are used in glazes chiefly as opacifiers and as major ingredients to form the base of modern ceramic pigments. Of major interest are the oxide (ZrO_2), the silicate ($ZrO_2 \cdot SiO_2$), and some binary zirconium salts. The oxide used is a chemically prepared product of various grades of purity running from extremely pure to grades of practical purity for the purposes intended. The silicate is finely ground purified grades of natural zircon sands. They are used as opacifiers in glazes for temperature ranges of cones 04 to 14 and above. Opacification begins at 4% or 5% and 10%–15% yields excellent opacification and covering power. In some glazes satisfactory opacification has been achieved with as little as 3% of ZrO_2.

This subject is covered in greater detail in the sections on opacifiers and ceramic stains.

Bismuth

Bismuth oxide, Bi_2O_3, is a strong flux, and behaves in glazes in a manner similar to PbO. It has been used experimentally in amounts up to 50% and showed a higher degree of durability, higher density, and higher index of refraction than corresponding glasses containing PbO. There may be a tendency for bismuth glasses or glazes to have a gray color, but this is counteracted by small additions of As_2O_5—or other effective oxidizing agents.

GLAZES. Bismuth glazes have a longer firing range[33] than lead glazes and are more craze-resistant. They also are completely nontoxic.[33] Yellows, yellow-green, and grays may result from the presence of Bi_2O_3. The yellow color is stable at high temperatures. Good semimatt finishes are readily obtained with bismuth fluxes. Bierbreuer[33] obtained good yellows at 1,200° C under reducing conditions with a glaze of the following empirical formula:

$$\left.\begin{cases} 0.2K_2O \\ 0.1Na_2O \\ 0.1CaO \\ 0.3BaO \\ 0.3ZnO \end{cases} \quad 0.26Al_2O_3 \qquad 2.26SiO_2 \right\} + 15\% \text{ of } Bi_2O_3$$

Bismuth-bearing frits are not altered in color due to oxides of iron, copper, and manganese.

Bismuth Oxide. This material (Bi_2O_3) is readily available and is insoluble in water but soluble in acids. It is prepared by the calcination of bismuth nitrate. It is used as a fluxing ingredient in some fired-on silver paints. It also has been used to bond silver flake to ceramic bodies.

Bismuth Subnitrate. This material ($BiONO_3 \cdot H_2O$) is insoluble in water but soluble in acids. It decomposes to Bi_2O_3 at 260° C. It is used to make pearly lusters on glazes. It has been used experimentally to prepare low-temperature lead-free glazes.

Cadmium

Cadmium oxide behaves in glazes something like a poor substitute for ZnO. It is used only in low-temperature pigments. Cadmium, when used with sulfur and selenium, makes important red and orange pigments for low-temperature glazes and enamels. It is discussed in some detail in another section.

Chromium

The sole use of chromium in glazes is as coloring agent. Cr_2O_3 is a bright green compound, completely insoluble in water and almost completely insoluble in molten silicates. When present as Cr_2O_3 it makes the well-known chrome green. This probably has the lowest solubility in silicate melts of any oxide and perhaps is the most powerful of chromophores. In the presence of zinc oxide, brown colors result due to the formation of zinc chromate. High-lead glazes form yellow lead chromate and different shades of orange will form in some low-temperature glazes of very low silica. These are high in lead, low in alumina, low in silica, and fire around cone 010 and produce the well-known Chinese reds. They usually develop a somewhat crystalline texture.

Chromium oxide is used with tin oxide to form chrome-tin pinks. Iron chromate, the natural mineral, is pulverized to a very fine size and employed as a satisfactory black ceramic pigment. Chromium oxide is a constituent of almost all black ceramic stains. It runs up to 65% in copper-chrome blacks and from 12% to 40% in chrome-cobalt-iron black pigments.

Cerium

CeO_2 or Ce_2O_3 when added to a glaze in high enough concentration is an opacifier. It is never used for this purpose, however, because there are other materials that are better and cheaper. When a small amount of Ce_2O_3 is fritted into a glaze it fluoresces when exposed to ultraviolet light.

Copper

Copper oxides sometimes are used in glazes for their coloring power. The color of the glaze depends upon the following:

1. the concentration of copper in the glaze
2. whether the atmosphere is oxidizing or reducing
3. the nature of the RO constituent
4. the degree of acidity of the glaze, i.e., the ratio of $Na_2O:SiO_2$

When reducing conditions prevail, red or ruby colors are obtained. Normally a green color results from copper, but in excessively high soda glazes, you get turquoise blue. Copper oxide is useful in that it is the only commonly available oxide that produces clear green glazes under all circumstances of composition and processing except the extremes required to obtain copper ruby and to obtain the turquoise blue. The turquoise is obtained in combination with SnO_2 and an extreme degree of alkalinity.

Light shades of green are obtained with 0.03 to 0.06 molecular equivalents of CuO and darker shades of green when it is 0.06 to 0.10 molecular equivalents.

CuO is properly a member of the RO group. It is a strong and efficient flux, although never used specifically for that purpose. Being a strong flux the CuO soon reacts with the silicate complex and Cu^{++} ions form a part of the glass structure, producing green color. There are two mechanisms for color development: (1) colored ions in solution and (2) insoluble dispersed pigments. CuO goes into solution, making a "soluble" color with no dispersed, suspended, colored pigment particle. The precipitation of Cu_2O crystals, if and when it occurs, would be of the insoluble-particle type. There are two stable oxides of copper, Cu_2O (red) and CuO (black). Cu_2O may be precipitated as such in reduced glazes. The phase fields of the oxides were described by Prantis.[34] Thermal expansion coefficients of the oxides are:

$$Cu_2O\ (20°\text{–}700°\ C),\quad \alpha = 3.5 \times 10^{-6}/°\ C$$

$$CuO\ (20°\text{–}700°\ C),\quad \alpha = 6.5 \times 10^{-6}/°\ C$$

Cobalt

The sole function of cobalt in glazes is as a coloring agent. It is the most widely used color oxide. Cobalt oxide is a base, and CoO is a member of RO group. Being an effective flux, it dissolves in the glaze glass complex as cobalt ions. Usually the ion is divalent, with the same valence as alkaline earths. The trivalent state also is possible and the color imparted depends upon the valence and coordination of the dissolved ion. The color, however, is the characteristic cobalt blue, except under unusual and special circumstances.

Being a solution color, the glaze glass containing cobalt is transparent to light except for the band of blue absorbed by the Co^{++} ions. Thus, even though cobalt is a strong and dependable coloring agent, it can spread, due to displacement or flow of the glaze and to some extent by ion diffusion.

It is one of the most powerful of coloring agents. As little as 2 parts of CoO per million parts of silica glass produces a recognizable tint. For most glazed ware a sufficiently intense blue is obtained with 0.02 parts of CoO per 100 parts of base glaze.

The fine blue is obtained with all furnace conditions, either reducing or oxidizing, and will not burn out, as can, for example, copper. Cobalt is used to obtain blue and various shades of blue colors in decals, in-glaze, on-glaze, and stains. Strong blues in porcelain glazes are obtained with as little as 0.025 mole and as much as 0.10 mole of CoO.

Calcines of alumina with a cobalt compound produce especially stable and satisfactory stains or insoluble pigments. Stains based on alumina with ZnO and cobalt are used at all practical firing temperatures. Lighter, but strong, blues are obtained with the alumina base.

In proper combination with MgO, SiO_2, and B_2O_3, violet, red, pink, and lavender shades of stains or pigments develop. Black stains can be prepared in combination with manganese oxide.

Cobalt Oxide. This material ($Co_2O_3 \cdot CoO$ or Co_3O_4) is the usual commercial source for cobalt in glazes. It is insoluble in water and in most acids and is obtained by roasting purified cobalt ores.

Cobalt Carbonate ($CoCO_3$), is a stable commercial product, insoluble in water and soluble in acids. It decomposes readily to CoO and CO_2 when heated. It is an excellent reagent for introducing cobalt into frit or glaze batches.

Cobalt Chromate. This material ($CoCrO_4$) is a chemically prepared product and is used with Al_2O_3 and ZnO to produce light-blue stains for low-firing glazes.

COBALT NITRATE. This water-soluble cobalt compound $Co(NO_3)_2$ sometimes is used as a source of cobalt in the preparation of colors and stains.

COBALT SULFATE. Cobalt sulfate ($CoSO_4 \cdot 7H_2O$) sometimes is used where a soluble cobalt reagent is required for the preparation of stains. It is sometimes used on art pottery where soluble compounds are needed for spray work. For most glaze applications, sulfates of all kinds are avoided because of the possibility of defects arising from high temperature gaseous evolutions.

Gold

GOLD. This element (Au) is the most widely used metallic decoration on ceramic ware. It is extremely inert chemically, being highly resistant to higher-temperature oxidation and almost chemically inert at room temperature.

Gold ruby colors in glazes, glasses, and ceramic stains once formed the only good sources of red and pink colors for glazes. Now there are others, but it still is used where that distinctive tint is desired.

Several preparations are available from which the decorator can choose for applying metallic gold films. These include liquid bright golds, liquid burnish golds, brown powder golds, and paste golds. There are various types and grades among each of these, as regards their chemical compositions and also their working properties. Each gold has its own set of circumstances where it will yield satisfactory results.

Gold in powder form has been used to prepare surface coatings and decorations for many centuries. Powdered gold may be put into slip slurry or paint form using an appropriate liquid vehicle, and fired. After fusing or suitable sintering the coating or deposit must be smoothed and polished. This is an expensive process, and effort was directed toward developing a cheaper way to decorate with gold as far back as 1800. This seems to have been achieved in Germany about 1830 at the Meissen porcelain factory. A French patent issued in 1851 introduced the idea of using an organic gold compound. This was dissolved in an organic solvent, applied to the ceramic surface, and thermally decomposed in place by firing in air.

LIQUID BRIGHT GOLD. This is a soluble form of the metal in a well-balanced flux in liquid form. These usually contain a little more than 10% of gold in the form of gold resinate. A good product can be worked in the temperature range of 60° to 100° F with good flow and spread. This type of gold is applied in very thin layers, only about 5 millionths of an inch thick. Firing is done slowly, 12 hours to 24 hours to a maturing temperature in the range of 1,400° to 1,500° F. Good ventilation and draft during firing is absolutely essential.

PRECIPITATED OR BROWN POWDERED GOLD. This form of gold has almost completely displaced the older pure gold leaf. In use it is mixed with a suitable flux, which may be a frit of satisfactory thermal expansion and chemical durability that will fire-out at the decorating temperature. These fluxes may or may not be rich in Bi_2O_3.

PURPLE OF CASSIUS. Purple of Cassius is prepared from a mixture of stannic and gold chlorides. Mixtures in the range of 10:1 yield a maroon color; 5:1, rose; and 4:1, a light purple. When calcined it makes a color stable to cone 16.

Platinum

This metal is almost inert chemically at room temperature and even at very high temperature in air. It melts at 1,755° C and does not oxidize. It is sometimes used in glazes to obtain luster and metallic effects. Liquid bright platinum, as does palladium, produces a better, more stable silver finish than silver and does not tarnish. Platinum as an in-glaze colorant yields a gray glaze, but it is not used because there are cheaper and better ways to get gray colors.

Silver

Silver is fairly resistant chemically, has a melting point of 960° C, but can tarnish by forming silver sulfide. It is resistant to oxidation at high temperature. Metallic silver is used in the decoration of glazes. The forms used are powdered (precipitated), fluxed, paste, and white-gold paste silvers.

PRECIPITATED SILVER. This is analogous to precipitated or powdered brown gold. Decorations made by it are rather easily altered by oxidation or tarnishing. Practically all of the powdered silver is in the form of a mixture of flux and silver powder that can be applied to the glaze and matured by firing. The silver preparation cannot be fired as high as gold, and must be burnished to bring out the characteristic silver color and luster. There is no liquid bright silver.

Silver Oxide. This material (Ag_2O) decomposes to silver and oxygen when heated above 300° C. It is soluble in ammonia and in acids. It is used some to produce a yellow color in low-temperature glazes. When so used, CaO and ZnO must be avoided because these components could, and usually do, result in a brownish color. Silver oxide coatings on glazes fired in a reducing atmosphere produce a metallic luster. The oxide per se usually is not used as such, the preference being other silver compounds.

Silver Carbonate. Silver carbonate ($AgCO_3$) is used to produce iridescent sheens and stains on glazes. The processing is done above 300° C and up to 700° C. An example of a silver luster is made by adding 1% or 2% of $AgCO_3$ or Ag_2O to a transparent colorless low-maturing glaze (even a lead glaze) and firing in a slightly reducing atmosphere.

Silver Chloride. This compound (AgCl) sometimes is used in low percentages in a low-firing glaze to produce lusters. It also is added to glazes to produce a yellow color. To produce a yellowish silver luster, 30% of silver chloride is mixed with 70% of clay and enough water to form a paste. This is applied to the glaze surface, dried, and fired to 700° C.

Lusters. Lusters of varied metallic appearance and coloring are made from a mixture of lead borate, bismuth oxide, and silver chloride, or silver carbonate, and fired at 700° C in a reducing atmosphere. Lusters also are obtained by mixing the AgCl with an ethereal oil and honey or molasses and firing at 700° C. These lusters have a gold tarnish with a greenish tint.

Organosilver Salts. Preparations for silver coatings fired to ceramic bodies or on ceramic glazes may be prepared[35] by using a mixture of organosilver salts, and organic solvents and vehicles. Silver salts of racemic or tartaric acids may be mixed with organic solvents such as glycols, alcohols, acetates, or esters in vehicles such as cellulose derivative or celluloid and thoroughly milled to yield a liquid preparation. More specifically, 97 grams of racemic silver is ground with 3 grams of bismuth nitrate in a ball mill; this powder then is mixed with an ethyl glycol solution with 5% of celluloid to produce a spreadable mass. These preparations yield silver coatings when fired to 400° to 600° C.

Striking Silver Glasses With Ultraviolet Light. Clear glasses containing a small amount of silver, when exposed to ultraviolet light, will cause the silver to precipitate when heated at about 400° C.[36] The colloidal silver so produced makes an amber color. The same glasses that have not been irradiated require considerably higher heat-treatment temperatures to cause the color to "strike."

Manganese

Manganese behaves as a member of the RO group in glazes, being a relatively active flux. Its sole function in glazes is as a colorant. In this respect it is mild in intensity. As a colorant, when it is in a form to function as a base or RO member, it enters into the glass structure as a divalent or a trivalent ion, hence is a "solution" color. When combined with other components it can form compounds or phases that are of low solubility in the melt, forming pigments or stains.

When in solution in the vitreous matrix the characteristic color may be amethyst, reddish violet, or pink, or sometimes brown. Purple or plum-colored glazes, based on manganese, once were popular. It is better to use manganese colorants as mill-additions rather than to fuse them with the frit. Better and more reliable colors are achieved from mill-additions than when fritted.

Many stains contain manganese as an essential ingredient. When calcined with alumina, dark brown spinels are formed. Black, brown, purple, and reddish stains containing manganese also are common.

MANGANESE DIOXIDE. (MnO_2) is the most common form of manganese as used by the glaze ceramist. It is insoluble in water. When heated, $MnO_2 \rightarrow MnO + \frac{1}{2}O_2$ at 535° C. To that extent it is an oxidizing agent. Manganese dioxide occurs in nature as a blue-black mineral called pyrolusite. For some of the less-demanding glaze applications, the powdered natural mineral is used.

Molybdenum

Molybdenum oxides, or chemicals that decompose to yield them, may be added to glazes on rare occasions for special effects. The trioxide, MoO_3 has a vapor pressure of 760 mm at 2,111° F and is sparingly soluble in cold water. In glazes, MoO_3 can be precipitated in the melt as alkaline earth molybdates and thus be responsible for some opacity. The color of glazes containing MoO_3 are likely to have a characteristic smokey blue cast. MoO_3 forms a continuous series of solid solutions with Bi_2O_3 and raises the fusion temperature upwards from 825° C. The pyrochemical equilibria of MoO_3 with silicates have not been reported.

MoO_3 is one of the few materials that causes significant lowering of surface tension in silicate melts. In amounts of 0.1% to 0.2% it is effective in this regard and acts as a high-temperature wetting agent. Molybdenum salts are used in glazes only in rare instances, such as to achieve the characteristic coloring or opacity or to utilize the high temperature wetting agent effect.

Iron

Compounds of iron are present in all natural raw materials running from a trace in rare instances to several percent in others. It is one of the elements to guard against in selecting and using raw materials for glazes. The effect of iron compounds in glazes is mainly a matter of color. Various colors are imparted to glazes by iron, depending upon the components of the glaze, the firing atmosphere, the concentration or proportions, and upon the valence of the iron in the glaze.

Iron compounds impart green, yellow, red, buff, brown or black, depending on glaze composition, iron concentration, and degree of oxidation or reduction. The colors of glass characteristic of various concentrations of dissolved Fe_2O_3 were summarized by Searle and Grimshaw[37] as shown in table 2.10. These are various shades of green, which tend to hold for glazes also.

Theoretically, ferrous iron in solution in glass or glazes makes a very intense blue and ferric ions yield a reddish color. Because almost certainly the glaze contains an equilibrium mixture of ferric and ferrous ions, the color in a glaze results from a mixture of ferric and ferrous ions.

In addition to "solution" colors, insoluble or pigment stains are com-

Table 2.10. Colors imparted to glass by various concentrations of ferric oxide[37]

Color of glass	*Ferric oxide added (%)*
Colorless	less than 0.02
Nearly colorless	0.02–0.05
Faintly green	0.05–0.10
Yellowish green	0.1 –0.3
Green	0.3 –1.0
Dark green	1 –2

mon. A common black glaze stain is powdered iron chromate ($FeO \cdot Cr_2O_3$). Magnetite ($FeO \cdot Fe_2O_3$) also makes a black stain. Iron oxides are commonly used in a variety of glaze stains. Iron oxide is probably most frequently used to alter shades or tones produced by other colorants such as oxides of Cu, Cr, Co, Ni, etc.

Ferrous oxide is a fairly strong flux and is a member of the RO group. Ferric oxide, per se, is not so strong a flux and its solubility in the glaze is moderate to low. Iron aventurines are possible because of the limited solubility of Fe_2O_3 in the glaze.

Nickel

The one function of nickel oxide in glazes is that of a colorant. Although there are two nickel oxides, Ni_2O_3 goes to $2NiO + \frac{1}{2}O_2$ at 600° C. Thus, nickel functions only as a member of the RO but the color imparted depends upon the kind and amount of other RO members. It can be used to produce blues, grays, greens, browns, and yellows.

A blue glaze[38] develops by using 0.15NiO in the following glaze at cone 5:

$0.25K_2O$		
$0.14CaO$	$0.3Al_2O_3$	$2.0SiO_2$
$0.21BaO$		
$0.40ZnO$		

A purple glaze is obtained with 0.15 molecular equivalent of NiO from the following slightly modified formula:[38]

$0.25K_2O$		
$0.20CaO$	$0.3Al_2O_3$	$2.0SiO_2$
$0.30BaO$		
$0.25ZnO$		

In the same glaze with the NiO still at 0.15 mole equivalents, but with varying concentrations of ZnO, the resulting colors are brown with 0.15ZnO, reddish purple with ZnO = 0.25, and a dark blue when the ZnO reaches 0.35 mole equivalents.

Two forms of nickel oxide are available, green NiO or black Ni_2O_3. The direct use of nickel oxide as coloring agent has largely been replaced by more stable ceramic stains and pigments.

Vanadium

Vanadium pentoxide produces color in glazes, where various tints of yellow, greenish yellow, and reddish brown may be obtained. An emerald green has been produced under reducing conditions. The presence of high alkali tends to bleach and weaken the colors. These are the solution colors, the vanadium being in solution. An excess of vanadium can lead to some precipitation and the development of irregular surface coloration.

Vanadium ions in solution in the molten glaze matrix reduces the surface tension, making it an effective high temperature wetting agent. It is a strong flux.

Vanadium also is the essential ingredient in a number of new stable and popular ceramic stains such as vanadium-zirconium yellows, tin-vanadium yellows, zirconium-vanadium blues and turquoise, etc.

It appears that surface tensions of glazes will be markedly lowered by additions of 1% or 2% of either V_2O_5 or MoO_3. Other oxides tried by Amberg[39] did not demonstrate dramatic lowerings.

VANADIUM PENTOXIDE (V_2O_5) is only slightly soluble in water, melts at 690° C, is reddish brown in color, and has a negative thermal expansion. It is a strong flux in glazes, but is never used for that purpose. Some material classified as vanadium pentoxide contains an appreciable content of sodium vanadate.

AMMONIUM METAVANADATE. This compound (NH_4VO_3) is prepared from alkaline vanadate solutions by ammonium chloride. It decomposes into V_2O_5 at 210° C. Where good purity is required, this chemical may be the best choice for the starting material.

Raw Materials Control

It is important to have definite knowledge as to how each lot of each glaze material will perform in a glaze. The usual materials tests—chemical analysis, screen tests, subsieve particle size determinations, fusibility tests, shrinkage, color, and contamination checks—do not tell us that. These data tell only how the stuff compares with previous shipments.

To tell how a material will behave in a glaze, it is best to check it in a base-glaze formulation and observe the results. Such tests will tell whether the subject lots can be used in the usual manner in the usual proportions; or whether some adjustments must be made. Good practice is to get a preshipment sample of each new lot and run a base-glaze check. When the new shipment arrives, the test is repeated from samples selected from it.

The matter of sample selection presents a problem. A procedure as good as any is to select one bag from the car or truckload and test it. If this random sample gives results that agree with previous lots, accept the shipment. If the grab sample differs, repeat with another sample until you can establish acceptance or rejection.

References

1. Gehlhoff, G. and Thomas, M. 1925. Physical properties of glass in relation to its compositions. *Z. Tech. Physik.* 6:544–54.
2. Charles, R. J. 1965. The mixed alkali effect in glasses. *J. Am. Ceram. Soc.* 48(8):432–34.
3. Morey, G. W. 1954. *The properties of glass.* 2d ed. New York: Reinhold Publishing Corp., p 122.
4. Coulter, L. B. 1905. A comparative study of Cornwall stone and feldspar in raw lead glazes. *Trans. Am. Cer. Soc.* 7:356.
5. Jackson, W. and Richardson, A. G. 1903. Visit to the clay deposit of Cornwall and Devon. *Trans. Engl. Ceram. Soc.* 3:58.
6. Ashley, H. E. 1905. Some evidence that bodies high in silica craze by overfire. *Trans. Am. Ceram. Soc.* 7:69.
7. Betz, Geo. C. 1938. Lithium minerals and compounds in ceramics. *J. Am. Ceram. Soc.* 21:189.
8. Lithium Corporation of America Inc., Minneapolis, Minn. Trade pamphlet.
9. Eiduks, J. and Vaivads, A. 1954. Influence of lithium on physiochemical characteristics of low-melting glazes. *Latvijas PSR Zinatnu Akad. Vestis* 11:115–29.
10. Ashley, H. E. 1910. Requirements of pottery materials. *Trans. Am. Ceram. Soc.* 12:433.
11. 1968. Materials for ceramic processing. *Ceram. Ind.* 90(1):137.
12. Clark, N. D. 1944. Strontia as a ceramic glaze oxide. *Foote Prints* 16:9.
13. Harman, C. G. and Swift, H. R. 1945. Raw leadless whiteware glazes. *J. Am. Ceram. Soc.* 28:48.
14. Thiemecke, H. W. Communicated to Clark (see reference 12), p. 11.
15. Koch, W. J., Harman, C. G., and O'Bannon, L. S. 1950. *J. Am. Ceram. Soc.* 33(1):1–8.
16. Hall, F. P. 1930. Influence of the chemical composition on the physical properties of glazes. *J. Am. Ceram. Soc.* 13:182.
17. Reising, J. A. 1962. Zinc oxide and crawling of glazes. *Bull. Am. Ceram. Soc.* 41(8):497–99.
18. Thrope, T. E. 1935. Employment of lead compounds in pottery. Report of the Government laboratory, London, 1901. Reference cited by Mellor, J. W. in *Trans. Engl. Ceram. Soc.* 34:123.

19. Mellor, J. W. 1935. Durability of pottery frits, glazes, glasses, and enamels in service. *Trans. Engl. Ceram. Soc.* 34:113.
20. Chambers, A. and Rigg, J. F. 1925. Notes on antimony yellows, pt. 1. *Trans. Engl. Ceram. Soc.* 25:101.
21. Salvetat, A. 1871. *Decorations of earthenware.* Vienna.
22. Binns, C. F. 1964. The function of boron in the glaze formula. *Trans. Am. Ceram. Soc.* 40:225.
23. Bleininger, A. V. and Teetor, P. A. 1912. A thermal study of boric acid-silica mixtures. *Trans. Am. Ceram. Soc.* 14:210.
24. Singer, F. G. 1910. Position of boron in the glaze formula. *Trans. Am. Ceram. Soc.* 12:676.
25. Stull, R. T. and Radcliffe, B. S. 1910. Opalescence and the function of B_2O_3 in the glaze. *Trans. Am. Ceram. Soc.* 12:129.
26. Guertler, W. 1904. Miscibility of anhydrous boric acid and borates. *Z. Anorg. Chem.* 40:225.
27. Levin, Earnest M., Robbins, Carl R., and McMurdie, Howard F. 1964. *Phase diagrams for ceramists.* Ed. and published by the American Ceramic Soc., Inc.
28. French, M. M. 1931. Colemanite as glaze material. *J. Am. Ceram. Soc.* 14(10):139.
29. Ashley, H. E. 1909. Discussion on paper by A. Henbach, (Production of ceramic red colors.) *Trans. Am. Ceram. Soc.* 11:58.
30. Beyersdorfer. 1941. Titanium oxide colored glasses. *Glastech. Ber.* 19(11):349–53.
31. Hetherington, A. L. 1937. *Chinese ceramic glazes.* Cambridge. p 45
32. Peyronel, Giorgio. 1943. Arsenates of zirconium; 1, existence of the arsenates $ZrO_2 \cdot As_2O_5 \cdot H_2O$ and $ZrO_2(As_2O_3)_2$; 2, Thermal decomposition of $ZrO(AsO_3)_2$ and the existence of $(ZrO)_2As_2O_7$ and of $(ZrO)_3(AsO_4)_2$. *Chem. Abs.* 7:573.
33. Bierbrauer, Gebhard. 1954. Bismuth oxide as a glaze and color ingredient. *Keram. Z.* 6(6):275–76.
34. Prantis, A. L. 1968. Phase fields and thermal cxpansion of oxides of copper. *J. Am. Ceram. Soc.* 51(3):182.
35. Durrwachter, Eugen. Manufacture of Ag preparations of low firing temperature for ceramic objects. German Patent 741,762, 1943.
36. Badger, A. E. and Hummel, F. A. 1945. Effect of ultraviolet light on glass containing silver. *Phys. Rev.* 68(9 and 10):231.
37. Searle, Alfred B. and Grimshaw, Rex W. 1960. *The chemistry and physics of clays, and other ceramic materials.* 3d ed. London: Ernest Benn Ltd. p 314.
38. 1968. Materials for ceramic processing. *Ceram. Ind.* 90(1):114.
39. Amberg, C. R. 1946. The effect of molybdenum and other oxides on surface tension of silicate to melts and on properties of refractories abrasives. *J. Am. Ceram. Soc.* 29(4):87–93.

3

Calculations

The Empirical Formula

The glaze ceramist has developed a unique system for organizing, correlating, collating, representing, and expressing composition and formulations. It makes it possible to deal effectively with the highly complex inherent relationships. Seldom does the ultimate composition of a glaze involve as few as three oxide components. The ultimate analysis of fairly simple glazes would consist of six oxides, eight to ten being common; even more are not unusual. Now, the ultimate components alone would describe a glass fairly well; but a glaze is not a homogeneous thing and may contain one or more dispersed undissolved phases. Even crystal or liquid phases may not be uncommon.

In addition, the batch ingredients are usually not simple one-component materials. For example, a glaze batch may contain feldspar, clay, frit, and other materials. Each of these may be not only multicomponent, but multiphase as well. It is essential that the glaze be so compounded as to fulfill, exactly, the required ultimate melted analysis. In addition, there are important physical requirements with respect to the handling, mixing, and working properties of the glaze slip. The applied glaze film must be of the right thickness, smoothness, and bondability. The film, once applied, must go through numerous pyrochemical and pyrophysical changes during firing.

Anything that can be done to help the glaze ceramist to comprehend and control these complex matters, even though he may not be able to quantitatively predict their behavior, is essential. One could learn, by experience, the behavior of a single glaze and a batch for its preparation. But when it comes to comprehending and effectively working with the entire spectrum of glazes, something better than a collection of recipes is necessary.

The Oxide Concept

The raw materials nearly always are oxides or compounds that can be expressed as oxides. Ceramic glazes and ceramic products also can be so regarded. By expressing the components in such a manner that the phase compositions of the materials are comprehensible, a step toward simplification is achieved. For example, if ceramic materials are expressed as phases, possibly having known characteristics, there are obvious advantages. The analysis of a clay may contain half a dozen elements, the precise significance of which may not be immediately obvious. If represented in terms of, say, kaolin, feldspar, muscovite, limonite, and quartz, its pyrochemical and pyrophysical behavior begins to be clear. Thus, there are a rational reason and some advantages to the system of expressing compositions as oxides in terms of molar proportions, i.e. molecular equivalents.

Development of the Formula

It is customary for chemists to express chemical formulae in terms of individual elements as, for example, tricalcium phosphate, $Ca_3P_2O_8$; willemite, Zn_2SiO_4; and muscovite, $H_4K_2Al_6Si_6O_{24}$. On the rational oxide or ceramic empirical formula basis these would be respectively: $3CaO \cdot P_2O_5$, $2ZnO \cdot SiO_2$, and $K_2O \cdot 3Al_2O_3 \cdot 6SiO_2 \cdot H_2O$. Ceramic materials, however, are seldom in the proportion of simple stoichiometric ratios. For example, a commercial lead bisilicate has a nominal composition of 65% of PbO, 34% of SiO_2 and 1% of Al_2O_3. The empirical formula would be:

$$PbO \cdot 0.0336Al_2O_3 \cdot 1.95SiO_2 \qquad \text{example 1}$$

This conversion was accomplished by the process shown in table 3.1, as example 2.

Table 3.1. Calculation of the empirical oxide formula of a lead bisilicate from its chemical analysis: Example No. 2.

Chemical analysis				*Empirical formula*
Oxide	*Weight %*	*Molecular weight*	$\left(\frac{\text{Moles}}{}\right)$ *weight / molecular wt*	*Divide each oxide by sum of moles of RO*
PbO	65	223	0.291	1.000
Al_2O_3	1	102	0.0098	0.0336
SiO_2	34	60	0.567	1.950

Table 3.2. Classification of the more common oxides as RO (bases), R_2O_3 (amphoterics), and RO_2 (acids), as required for the empirical ceramic formula

RO group (basic)	R_2O_3 (intermediate)	RO_2 *(acid)*	R_2O_5* *(acid)*
Li_2O, Na_2O, K_2O, BeO, MgO, CaO, BaO, SrO, PbO, ZnO, FeO, MnO, CdO, CuO, NiO, CoO	Al_2O_3, B_2O_3, Fe_2O_3, Cr_2O_3, Bi_2O_3	SiO_2 SnO_2 ZrO_2 TiO_2 CeO_2 ThO_2	P_2O_5 V_2O_5 Ta_2O_5

*R_2O_5 oxides usually are grouped with RO_2 oxides

Concept of RO, R_2O_3, and RO_2

A possibly confusing detail in table 3:1 is the meaning of the term *RO* in the fifth column. This is standard terminology for glaze oxides classified as bases, such as oxides of alkalies or alkaline earths. To be more explicit, for purposes of the ceramic formula, all oxides are to be classified as basic, "neutral" (amphoteric), or acid. This classification is rigidly required by the structure of the empirical formula, which is consistently expressed in the following form:

RO	R_2O_3	RO_2
moles of bases = 1.00	moles of "neutral or amphoteric oxides	moles of acid oxide

To further illustrate, some of the more common oxides are listed as RO, R_2O_3, and RO_2 in table 3.2. Note that these groupings correspond in a way to periodic table classifications in that the proportion of oxygen atoms to metallic atoms is consistent in each of the group classifications. Because of this, the convention has developed where R is the general symbol for the metallic atoms and O for oxygen. This leads to the generalized notation of RO or R_2O, R_2O_3, and RO_2 as shown and as used throughout this book.

Terminology

The composition of chemical compounds and of molecules is accurately indicated by defining the chemical elements present and the proportions in which they occur. A molecule has been described as the smallest particle of a substance that is capable of independent existence while still retaining its chemical properties. The molecular weight is the number, in grams, corresponding to the sum of the atomic weights of all of the atoms comprising the formula of the molecule. Glazes and similar materials are not chemical compounds; so we do not use the term molecular weight—instead, the term *formula weight.* Formula weights are calculated in precisely the same manner as are molecular weights.

The *equivalent weight* is the weight equivalent to one formula weight of the substance. A formula weight is the "molecular weight" of the empirical formula.

An *equivalent,* as used in glaze terminology, is the number of moles of an oxide contained in a specific empirical formula. A *batch* is a mixture of raw materials such that, when fused, the composition would correspond to the empirical formula from which it was or could be calculated. The *formula batch weight* is the equivalent weight of the batch corresponding to the equivalent (or formula) weight of the empirical formula.

Batch weights and formula weights of materials that lose weight when heated may be those for the raw (as received) condition or the condition after removal of the volatiles. For example, the formula weight of calcium carbonate ($CaCO_3$) is 100.1. During the firing process, CO_2 is lost: $CaCO_3 \rightarrow CaO + CO_2\uparrow$, leaving only CaO having a weight of 56.1. Many things lose some weight when heated, and a determination may be made of the amount of loss due to heating. The volatiles so lost are reported as *loss on ignition,* L.O.I. for short. Thus, some materials may have two formula weights, one of them being for *ignited-basis* material, the other for raw unheated material.

Moles and *equivalents* numerically are the same. When dealing not with molecules but with units analogous to and equivalent in value to moles, the more exact terminology is molar equivalents, equivalent weights, or, in short, equivalents. Throughout this presentation, the terms moles, molecular equivalents, and equivalents may be used interchangeably. Chemists and chemical engineers are familiar with the meaning of *moles;* many ceramists have been trained to use *molecular equivalents* or *equivalents.* In some cases, no units are mentioned, the units in the ceramic empirical formula being implied as molar equivalents.

Calculation of an Empirical Formula of a Raw Material from Its Chemical Analysis

Chemical Analysis

As a demonstration, the empirical formula of a nepheline syenite will be computed from its chemical analysis. The composition to be converted is a typical chemical analysis[1] given as SiO_2, 60.4; Al_2O_3, 23.6; Fe_2O_3, 0.08; CaO, 0.7; MgO, 0.1; Na_2O, 9.8; K_2O, 4.6; L.O.I., 0.7 and total, 99.98, weight percent respectively.

Conversion of Chemical Analysis into Empirical Formula

The first step in the calculation is to consider the numbers in the analysis as being units of weight (grams or pounds) instead of percentages. The analysis includes 0.7 gram of volatile matter for each 100 grams of raw nepheline syenite. This is mostly water and possibly some CO_2. The procedure is to ignore this 0.7 gram; calculate the formula for the remaining 99.3 grams. After the formula has been computed on that basis, the formula weight can be corrected to include the 0.7-gram loss. Raw formula weight

$$= \frac{100}{99.3} \times \text{formula weight as calculated (on ignited basis)} \qquad \text{example 3}$$

The second step is to convert the grams of each oxide of the analysis into moles. To do this we need to know only that weight divided by molecular weight equals moles, or moles =

$$\frac{\text{weight}}{\text{molecular weight}} \qquad \text{example 4}$$

Proceed to convert the analysis into moles as in example 5, which is presented in table 3.3.

In establishing the empirical formulas for glazes, the RO group of oxides always is established as unity. The moles calculated directly from the analysis as shown in example 5 are then adjusted so that the total molar equivalents of RO and R_2O are brought to unity and equal one. This is example 6. For the example of nepheline syenite under consideration here, the number of molar equivalents in the RO groups are: CaO, 0.0125; MgO, 0.0025; Na_2O, 0.1580; K_2O, 0.0488; total RO = 0.2218.

Table 3.3. Example 5: conversion of compositions in terms of weight to respective moles

Oxide	*Weight**	*Molecular weight*	*Moles*
SiO_2	60.4	60	1.005
Al_2O_3	23.6	102	0.231
Fe_2O_3	0.08	160	0.0005
CaO	0.7	56	0.0125
MgO	0.1	40.3	0.0025
Na_2O	9.8	62	0.158
K_2O	4.6	94.2	0.0488

*Or chemical analysis

After separating the various oxides into their proper groups we can apply example 6 by dividing each of the moles obtained in example 5 directly from the chemical analysis, by 0.2218. The formula for the nepheline syenite then is written:

$0.056CaO$			
$0.011MgO$	$1.04Al_2O_3$	$4.54SiO_2$	example 7
$0.713Na_2O$	$0.0025Fe_2O_3$		
$0.220K_2O$			

Formula Weight, Ignited-Basis Material

The formula weight, analogous to molecular weight, would be computed (see table 3.4) on the basis that

$$\text{moles} \times \text{molar weight} = \text{weight} \qquad \text{example 8}$$

Formula Weight, As-received Basis

The chemical analysis of the nepheline syenite included 0.7% of volatile matter. This is not represented in the formula weight of 444.5. The conversion of formula weight from fired basis to as-received basis can be done by employing example 9 which follows:

weight (as received)

$$= \left(\frac{100}{100 - \text{ignition loss}}\right) \times \text{calcined wt}$$

$$= \left(\frac{100}{100 - 0.7}\right) \text{ or } 1.007 \times \text{calcined wt} \qquad \text{example 9}$$

Table 3.4. Formula weight calculation: Example 8

Oxide	Molar equivalents*	Molecular weight**	Molar equivalents × molecular (or equivalent) weight (col 2 × col 3)
Na_2O	0.713	62	44.3
K_2O	0.220	94.2	20.7
CaO	0.056	56	3.13
MgO	0.011	40.3	.44
Al_2O_3	1.04	102	106.1
Fe_2O_3	0.0025	160	0.4
SiO_2	4.54	60	272.4
Total			444.47 = Formula wt†

*From example 7.

**Corresponds exactly to the oxide expressed in example 7.

†Formula weights, excluding ignition loss = 444.5

Table 3.5. Conversion of a glaze composition from percent by weight into moles of its constituent oxides: Example 11.

Oxide	*Weight*		*Molecular weights*		*Moles (unadjusted)*
SiO_2	61.00	÷	60	=	1.02
Al_2O_3	8.24	÷	102	=	0.08
CaO	8.60	÷	56	=	0.15
K_2O	4.96	÷	94	=	0.05
Na_2O	2.83	÷	62	=	0.05
PbO	11.00	÷	223	=	0.05
B_2O_3	3.37	÷	70	=	0.05

formula weight (as-received basis)

$$= \mathbf{1.007 \times 444.5 = 447.6} \quad \text{example 10}$$

Empirical Glaze Formula from Chemical Analysis

The empirical formula of a glaze may be determined in a manner similar to that used in the calculation of the formula for nepheline syenite as was expressed in example 7. Assume the composition of the glaze,[2] in percentage figures, to be as follows: Silica, 61.00; alumina, 8.24; calcia, 8.60; potash, 4.96; soda, 2.83; lead oxide, 11.00; boric oxide, 3.37; total, 100.00.

Divide the percentage of each ingredient by its molecular weight as in example 11 in table 3.5. From all of the moles calculated in example 11, select those of the RO members and find the total moles of the entire RO group.

Table 3.6. Final empirical glaze formula derived from results in table 3.5 by making Σ RO=unity: Example 13.

Oxide	*Moles from table 3.5*		*Total RO*		*Empirical formula, molecular equivalents*
SiO_2	1.02	÷	0.30	=	3.40
Al_2O_3	0.08	÷	0.30	=	0.27
CaO	0.15*	÷	0.30	=	0.50
K_2O	0.05*	÷	0.30	=	0.17
Na_2O	0.05*	÷	0.30	=	0.17
PbO	0.05*	÷	0.30	=	0.17
B_2O_3	0.05	÷	0.30	=	0.17

*Σ=0.30

$CaO, 0.15 + K_2O, 0.05 + Na_2O, 0.05 + PbO, 0.05 = \text{total RO}, 0.30.$ example 12

To bring the RO group to unity and adjust the whole formula to that basis, divide each oxide by the total of the RO obtained by example 12, as shown in example 13 which is given as table 3.6: The empirical formula then is written:

$0.50CaO$			
$0.17K_2O$	$0.27Al_2O_3$	$3.40SiO_2$	example 14
$0.17Na_2O$	$0.17B_2O_3$		
$0.17PbO$			

Percent Composition of a Glaze from Empirical Formula

For this demonstration, assume the following empirical glaze formula:

$0.40K_2O$			
$0.40CaO$	$0.50Al_2O_3$		
$0.10BaO$	$1.25B_2O_3$	$3.50SiO_2$	example 15
$0.05MgO$			
$0.05SrO$			

The process to follow is the reverse of that described for the calculation of the empirical formula from the percentage composition. The example used here was taken from the *Ceramic Data Book*.[2] The first step is to convert the molecular equivalents into weights, as follows:

Weight = moles × molecular weight example 16

Table 3.7. Conversion of equivalents (moles) contained in an empirical formula of a glaze into weights of the respective oxides: Example 17.

Oxide	*Moles**		*Molecular weight*		*Weight*
K_2O	0.40	×	94.2	=	37.7
CaO	0.40	×	56.1	=	22.4
BaO	0.10	×	153.0	=	15.3
MgO	0.05	×	40.3	=	2.0
SrO	0.05	×	103.6	=	5.2
Al_2O_3	0.50	×	101.9	=	50.9
B_2O_3	1.25	×	69.6	=	87.0
SiO_2	3.50	×	60.1	=	210.4
Total formula weight				=	430.9

*From example 15

Table 3.8. Conversion of formula weights of table 3.7 into percentages of oxides corresponding to a chemical analysis: Example 18

Oxide	*Weight*							%
K_2O	37.7	÷	430.9	×	100	=		8.8
CaO	22.4	÷	430.9	×	100	=		5.2
BaO	15.3	÷	430.9	×	100	=		3.6
MgO	2.0	÷	430.9	×	100	=		0.4
SrO	5.2	÷	430.9	×	100	=		1.2
Al_2O_3	50.9	÷	430.9	×	100	=		11.8
B_2O_3	87.0	÷	430.9	×	100	=		20.2
SiO_2	216.4	÷	430.9	×	100	=		48.8
Total						=		100.0

This calculation is performed with each oxide component from example 15 as detailed in example 17 shown in table 3.7.

To change the weights in the right-hand column of example 17 into percentages to correspond to a chemical analysis, divide the weight of each oxide by the total of all of the weights, in this case 430.9, and multiply each by 100, as shown in example 18 detailed in table 3.8.

Compounding of Glazes

Glaze Batch Weights

The calculation of "batch weights" of the glaze from the formula becomes necessary when the mixture is to be made. The various oxides called for by the formula must be supplied by raw materials. In some cases it is impossible to fulfill all the requirements of the glaze formula by natural insoluble materials. It then becomes necessary to use soluble substances which, with a portion of the other ingredients, are melted to form an insoluble glass or "frit" which is then used as a glaze ingredient.

The necessity of having only insoluble ingredients in the raw glaze mixture is due to several factors. Dry or biscuit wares absorb water from the glaze coating when applied and soluble matter would be removed from the glaze and carried into the body, a detriment to both glaze and body. In drying out the ware the water moving to the surface carries soluble substances and leaves them there upon evaporation. The soluble ingredients are thus concentrated at the surfaces where evaporation has taken place most rapidly. In the suspended glaze mixture it is impossible to keep a uniform relation between soluble and insoluble matter as one is likely to be used more rapidly than the other.

Selection of Glaze Ingredients

Glazes containing frits are known as fritted glazes as distinguished from unfritted or "raw" glazes. The proper selection of ingredients for a glaze requires some experience in glaze making. This is especially true of fritted glazes. They will be taken up later. For the present only raw or unfritted glazes will be considered and these will contain nothing but insoluble ingredients. Reference to the list of materials below will show the source of various oxides appearing in the glaze formula and some practice will be necessary before the best selection can be made. The most common oxides in glaze formulas and the materials usually used to supply them are as follows:

K_2O	Feldspar, nepheline syenite, K_2CO_3
Na_2O	Feldspar, nepheline syenite, Na_2CO_3, borax
CaO	Whiting, $CaCO_3$, wollastonite
MgO	Magnesium carbonate, dolomite, talc
ZnO	Zinc oxide
BaO	$BaCO_3$
PbO	Red lead, white lead, lead silicates
Al_2O_3	Feldspar, clay, alumina, $Al_2O_3 \cdot 3H_2O$
Li_2O	Li_2CO_3, spodumene, petalite
B_2O_3	Borax, boric acid, frit
ZrO_2	Zirconia, zircon
SiO_2	Feldspar, clay, flint, frit

It will be noted that some of these materials furnish more than one oxide. Feldspar furnishes nominally $1K_2O$, $1Al_2O_3$, and $6SiO_2$ and clays furnish $1Al_2O_3$ and $2SiO_2$. If one of these oxides is to be added to the glaze by use of feldspar or clay, care must be taken not to use so much that it will furnish more than the requirement of one of the others. So far as possible K_2O is generally introduced into a glaze by means of feldspar but an allowance of 0.05 to 0.10 molecular equivalents Al_2O_3 is usually left to be provided by ball clay or kaolin. The raw clay acts as a suspending and bonding agent for the glaze mixture and makes it adhere to the body. Some clays also introduce several associated oxides.

If, after adding feldspar or nepheline syenite to provide the necessary K_2O and raw clay to furnish 0.05 to 0.10 Al_2O_3, there remains some Al_2O_3 to be provided, it may be added as calcined clay. An excess of raw clay causes cracking of the glaze on the ware in drying and early stages of burning, which is overcome by use of some calcined clay. The introduction of Al_2O_3 by use of $Al_2O_3 \cdot 3H_2O$ is not common since it is more expensive than clay and more refractory. It also may cause cracking of the drying glaze.

All SiO_2 not provided by feldspar and clay or other silicates is added as ground quartz, commercially known as potter's flint.

Commercial glaze materials are by no means so pure as to conform exactly to theoretical mineral compositions. It will be necessary to analyze materials and determine their proper formula. More often these variations are not of enough importance to demand exact analyses except as a means of keeping track of the uniformity of successive shipments of a given material at the plant where the glaze mixture has been tried and adopted. With our present knowledge of silicates and their behavior in fusion and in mixtures it is impossible to predict the exact result to be obtained from a certain glaze formula or from use of a certain ingredient. The empirical formula is a serviceable guide but not an exact one.

In his experiments, the ceramic chemist does not attempt to depend on a single glaze mixture for a given set of conditions, but prepares a group of glazes having variations in certain constituents so that among the number he somewhere obtains a composition to fit his needs. For the present exercise on calculations, only a single glaze will be calculated from its formula. The method is best illustrated by an example.

Raw Glaze Recipe from Empirical Formula

The following example will illustrate a procedure for converting the empirical formula[2] of a glaze into batch weights. Assume the following glaze formula:

$0.23Na_2O$			
$0.07K_2O$			
$0.50CaO$	$0.40Al_2O_3$	$3.85SiO_2$	example 19
$0.10MgO$			
$0.10BaO$			

The next step is to set up a tabular scheme to serve as a work-form to assist in organizing the calculations. Table 3.9 was arranged as example 20. This table contains both horizontal and vertical tabulations. The horizontal tabulations are identified as lines no. 1, 2, 3, etc.

Line 1 tabulates the oxide species in glaze formula of example 19.

Line 2 tabulates the number of moles of each oxide species from example 19.

Line 3 starts the actual calculations for the glaze recipe. Nepheline syenite can be selected as the component to introduce Na_2O, K_2O, some CaO and MgO, Al_2O_3 and SiO_2. By inspection, it can be seen that all of the Na_2O and possibly all of the K_2O can be introduced as nepheline

Table 3.9. Tabular work-form for establishing glaze recipe from an empirical glaze formula: Example 20

Line no.	*Raw materials selection*			*Molecular equivalents*						
1	Components in glaze from example 19			Na_2O	K_2O	CaO	MgO	BaO	Al_2O_3	SiO_2
2	Moles of each component in glaze formula			0.23	0.07	0.50	0.10	0.10	0.40	3.85
	Raw material	Moles	Limiting factor							
3	Nepheline syenite (ex.7)	0.323	$Na_2O + K_2O$ requirements	0.23	0.07	0.018	0.004	–	0.335	1.465
4			Remainder	0.0	0.0	0.482	0.096	0.10	0.065	2.385
5	Dolomite	0.096	MgO	–	–	0.096	0.096	–	–	–
6			Remainder	–	–	0.386	0.0	0.10	0.065	2.385
7	Whiting	0.386	Remaining CaO	–	–	0.386	–	–	–	–
8			Remainder	–	–	0.0	–	0.10	0.065	2.385
9	$BaCO_3$	0.10	All of the BaO	–	–	–	–	0.10	–	–
10			Remainder	–	–	–	–	0.0	0.065	2.385
11	Kaolin	0.065	The remaining Al_2O_3	–	–	–	–	–	0.065	0.130
12			Remainder	–	–	–	–	–	0.0	2.255
13	Silica	2.255	Remaining SiO_2	–	–	–	–	–	–	2.255
14			Remainder	–	–	–	–	–	–	0.0

syenite, without exceeding the molar requirements of anything else. To find the amount of nepheline syenite to use, calculate as follows:

$$\frac{\text{moles } Na_2O}{\text{moles of syenite}} \times \text{moles of syenite} = \text{moles } Na_2O \qquad \text{example 20}$$

From example 7 the moles of Na_2O per mole of syenite = 0.713. The moles of Na_2O required by the glaze formula are 0.23 Na_2O from example 19. By substituting these in example 20, we get:

$$0.713 \times \text{moles of syenite} = 0.23 \text{ moles of } Na_2O \qquad \text{example 21}$$

Thus, the moles of nepheline syenite required =

$$\frac{0.23}{0.713} = 0.323 \qquad \text{example 22}$$

This number will be listed in table 3.9 under moles of nepheline syenite.

The next step is to log into tables 3.9, under the respective oxide species, the number of moles of each introduced by 0.323 moles of nepheline syenite. To obtain this information, perform these operations:

$$\text{Moles of } Na_2O = \frac{0.713 \text{ moles } Na_2O^*}{\text{mole of neph syenite}} \times 0.323 \text{ moles syenite} = 0.23 \qquad \text{example 23}$$

$$\text{Moles of } K_2O = \frac{0.220 \text{ moles } K_2O^*}{\text{mole of neph syenite}} \times 0.323 \text{ moles syenite} = 0.07 \qquad \text{example 24}$$

$$\text{Moles of } CaO = \frac{0.056 \text{ moles } CaO^*}{\text{mole of neph syenite}} \times 0.323 \text{ moles of syenite} = 0.018 \qquad \text{example 25}$$

$$\text{Moles of } MgO = \frac{0.011 \text{ moles of } MgO^*}{\text{mole of neph syenite}} \times 0.323 \text{ moles of syenite} = 0.004 \qquad \text{example 26}$$

$$\text{Moles of } Al_2O_3 = \frac{1.04 \text{ moles of } Al_2O_3^*}{\text{mole of neph syenite}} \times 0.323 \text{ moles of syenite} = 0.335 \qquad \text{example 27}$$

$$\text{Moles of } SiO_2 = \frac{4.54 \text{ moles of } SiO_2^*}{\text{mole of neph syenite}} \times 0.323 \text{ moles of syenite} = 1.465 \qquad \text{example 28}$$

* Values from example 7.

Line 4 is the following step: by substracting the equivalents of each oxide introduced with the nepheline syenite and entered on line 3 from the original formula on line 2, the batch components remaining to be included are given in line 4.

example 29

Line 5 shows introduction of MgO. This can best be done with dolomite ($CaO \cdot MgO \cdot 2CO_2$). It should be noted that the formula as written will have a molecular weight of $56 + 40.3 + (2 \times 44) = 184.3$. In accordance with this formula:

$$\frac{\text{moles of MgO}}{\text{moles of dolomite}} = 1.0$$

example 30

$$\frac{\text{moles of CaO}}{\text{moles of dolomite}} = 1.0$$

example 31

$$\text{required moles of dolomite} = \frac{\text{moles of MgO (line 4)}}{\dfrac{\text{moles of MgO}}{\text{moles of dolomite}}}$$

example 32

$$\text{Required moles of dolomite} = \frac{0.096 \text{ (line 4)}}{1.0 \text{ (example 30)}}$$

example 33

Moles of CaO introduced with dolomite

$$= 0.096 \text{ moles dolomite} \times \frac{1.0 \text{ moles CaO}}{\text{mole dolomite}} = 0.096$$

example 34

Line 6 gives the components remaining to be added. *Line 7* shows 0.386 moles of remaining CaO to be supplied with whiting ($CaO \cdot CO_3$) which contains 1.0 mole of CaO per mole of whiting.

$$\text{Moles of whiting} = 0.386 \text{ (from line 6)} \times 1.0 = 0.386$$

example 35

Should the whiting deviate much from $CaCO_3$ an empirical formula for it would need to be developed and the impurities accounted for in the formulation. *Line 8* shows the oxide components still to be supplied.

Line 9. The BaO can be introduced as $BaCO_3$. This could contain 1.0 mole of BaO per mole of $BaCO_3$. In that case, the number of moles of $BaCO_3$ required is equal to the number of moles of BaO in line 8, or 0.10. *Line 10* shows that there are 0.065 moles of Al_2O_3 and 2.385 moles of silica remaining to be supplied. *Line 11*. The clay needed for floating

Table 3.10. Glaze recipe

Material	Mole	Line no. in table 3.9	Mol. weights Weight	Example no.	Parts by weight. col 2 × col 4	Percent
Nepheline syenite	0.323	3	447.6	10	144.5	38.8
Dolomite	0.096	5	184.3		17.7	4.7
Whiting	0.386	7	100	–	38.6	10.4
$BaCO_3$	0.100	9	197.4	–	19.7	5.3
Kaolin	0.065	11	258	37	16.8	4.5
Silica	2.255	13	60		135.0	36.3
Totals					372.3	100.0

the slip can be supplied with kaolin that would introduce 0.065 moles of Al_2O_3. The formula for the kaolin is taken as

$$Al_2O_3{\cdot}2SiO_2{\cdot}2H_2O \qquad \text{example 36}$$

with molecular weight of 258 example 37

If the clay deviated much from this theoretical composition, a formula for it would be developed as was the formula for nepheline syenite (example 7). Its introduction into the recipe formula would be developed then as was done with nepheline syenite, discussed in this section under line 3. In that case, its introduction would necessarily be done early in the process, very likely as the first step even before the nepheline syenite, as follows:

$$\text{moles of kaolin required} = \frac{\text{moles of } Al_2O_3 \text{ required}}{\dfrac{\text{moles of } Al_2O_3}{\text{moles of kaolin}}} \qquad \text{example 38}$$

$$\text{moles of kaolin required} = \frac{0.065 \text{ moles of } Al_2O_3 \text{ (line 10)}}{\dfrac{1.0 \text{ moles of } Al_2O_3}{\text{moles of kaolin}} \text{(example 36)}} = 0.065 \qquad \text{example 39}$$

moles of SiO_2 in 0.065 moles of kaolin =

$$0.065 \text{ moles of kaolin} \times \frac{2.0 \text{ moles of } SiO_2}{\text{moles of kaolin}} = 0.130SiO_2 \qquad \text{example 40}$$

Line 12 indicates that all that remains to be added is 2.255 moles of silica (SiO_2). *Line 13*. The recipe is completed by adding 2.255 moles of powdered silica or potter's flint. *Line 14* shows a remainder of zero, indicating that the formulation is complete.

Glaze Recipe

The glaze recipe is calculated from the information contained in table 3.9. The glaze batch recipe is developed in table 3.10 from the information in table 3.9. The chemical constants of ceramic raw materials and oxides needed for calculations are listed, for convenience, in table 3.11. These include chemical formula, molecular weights, equivalent weights, and conversion factors. It may be less confusing and lead to fewer errors if the worker selects the composition or chemical formula he is going to use, and computes his own formula weight from that. Conversion factors are good when you can be sure what it is you are converting.

Bristol Glaze

The empirical formula of a typical Bristol glaze is as follows:

0.35KNaO		
0.35CaO	$0.60Al_2O_3$	$3.50SiO_2$
0.30ZnO		

These unfritted glazes usually are applied to raw or unfired bodies. Because the glaze is applied directly to the green body, the glaze should contain a high content of raw clay. For this exercise we will use 0.15 equivalents of raw clay. The KNaO requirements can be met with feldspar, which, with the clay, will fulfill the Al_2O_3 conditions of the empirical formula of the glaze. For this exercise, a Keystone feldspar having the following empirical formula was used:

$0.751K_2O$	$1.130Al_2O_3$	$6.23SiO_2$
$0.251Na_2O$	$0.0015Fe_2O_3$	$0.112H_2O$
0.018CaO		

Referring to the empirical formula of the feldspar, it is shown that 0.982 represents the total of the KNaO supplied by one mole of it. The empirical formula of the glaze calls for 0.35 equivalents of KNaO, and in order to supply that, it is necessary to introduce 0.35/0.982 or 0.357 equivalents of the feldspar. The 0.357 equivalent is then multiplied by the equivalents of each of the other oxides in the empirical feldspar formula. This and the remaining calculations are fully illustrated in table 3.12.

In this example, the remaining components of the empirical formula of the glaze can be satisfied by the following equivalents of the following materials: 0.344 whiting; 0.30 calcined zinc oxide; 0.15 raw clay; 0.046 calcined clay and 0.888 flint. On the basis of this, the formula weight now may be calculated. This calculation is performed in table 3.13. The number of equivalents of each raw material necessary to furnish the molecular por-

Table 3.11. Chemical constants for ceramic raw materials

Name of Material	Formula	Mol. Wt.	Equiv Wt.		Oxides Entering Fusion	Molecular Weights of Oxides	Conversion Factor
			RO		Na_2O	62	.118
Albite	$Na_2O \cdot Al_2O_3 \cdot 6SiO_2$	524	R_2O_3	524	Al_2O_3	102	.195
			$6RO_2$		$6SiO_2$	60	.687
Alumina	Al_2O_3	102			Al_2O_3	102	1.0
Aluminum hydroxide	$Al_2(OH)_6$	156			Al_2O_3	102	.654
Aluminum sulphate	$Al_2(SO_4)_3$	342			Al_2O_3	102	.298
Antimony oxide	Sb_2O_3	292			Sb_2O_3	292	1.0
Arsenic oxide	As_2O_3	198			As_2O_3	198	1.0
Barium carbonate	$BaCO_3$	197			BaO	153	.777
Barium chloride	$BaCl_2$	208			BaO	153	.736
Barium chromate	$BaCrO_4$	253	2RO	506	BaO	153	.605
			R_2O_3		Cr_2O_3	152	.30
Barium hydroxide	$Ba(OH)_2$	171			BaO	153	.895
Barium oxide	BaO	153			BaO	153	1.0
			RO		BaO	153	.577
Barium selenite	$BaSeO_3$	265	R	265	Se	79	.298
Barjum sulphate	$BaSO_4$	233			BaO	153	.658
Baryta	$BaSO_4$	233			BaO	153	.658
Barytes	$BaSO_4$	233			BaO	153	.658
Bismuth oxide	Bi_2O_3	464			Bi_2O_3	464	1.0
					3CaO	56	.542
Bone ash	$Ca_3(PO_4)_2$	310	RO	103	P_2O_5	142	.458
Boracic acid	$B_2O_3 \cdot 3H_2O$	124	R_2O_3	124	B_2O_3	70	.565
			RO		Na_2O	62	.162
Borax	$Na_2O \cdot 2B_2O_3 \cdot 10H_2O$	382	$2R_2O_3$	382	$2B_2O_3$	70	.366
					Na_2O	62	.307
Borax (melted)	$Na_2O \cdot 2B_2O_3$	202			$2B_2O_3$	70	.693
Boric oxide	B_2O_3	70			B_2O_3	70	1.0
Cadmium sulphide	CdS	144					
			RO		2CaO	56	.272
Calcium borate	$2CaO \cdot 3B_2O_3 \cdot 5H_2O$	412	$1.5R_2O_3$	206	$3B_2O_3$	70	.51
Calcium carbonate	$CaCO_3$	100			CaO	56	.56
Calcium chloride	$CaCl_2$	111					

Calcium fluoride	CaF_2	78					
Calcium hydroxide	$Ca(OH)_2$	74			CaO	56	.758
Calcium oxide	CaO	56			CaO	56	1.0
					3CaO	56	.542
Calcium phosphate	$Ca_3(PO_4)_2$	310	RO	103	P_2O_5	142	.458
Calcium sulphate	$CaSO_4$	136			CaO	56	.412
Celestite	$SrSO_4$	183			SrO	104	.57
Cerium oxide	CeO_2	176			CeO_2	176	1.0
			R_2O_3		Al_2O_3	102	.395
China clay	$Al_2O_3 \cdot 2SiO_2 \cdot 2H_2O$	258	$2RO_2$	258	$2SiO_2$	60	.465
Chromium oxide	Cr_2O_3	152			Cr_2O_3	152	1.0
Chromium sulphate	$Cr_2(SO_4)_3 \cdot 15H_2O$	662			Cr_2O_3	152	.23
Cobalt chloride	$CoCl_2 6H_2O$	238			CoO	75	.316
Cobalt oxide (cobaltic)	Co_2O_3	166	RO	83	CoO	75	.903
Cobalt (black) oxide	Co_3O_4	241	RO	80	CoO	75	.934
Cobalt (cobaltous) oxide	CoO	75			CoO	75	1.0
Cobalt nitrate	$Co(NO_3)_2 \cdot 6H_2O$	291			CoO	75	.256
Cobalt sulphate	$CoSO_4 \cdot 7H_2O$	280			CoO	75	.268
			RO	278			
Copperas	$FeSO_4 \cdot 7H_2O$	278	R_2O_3	556	Fe_2O_3	160	.288
Copper carbonate	$CuCO_3$	124			CuO	80	.645
Copper chloride	$CuCl_2 \cdot 2H_2O$	171			CuO	80	.468
Copper oxide (cupric) (green)	CuO	80			CuO	80	1.0
Copper oxide (cuprous) (red)	Cu_2O	144			CuO	80	1.11
Copper sulphate	$CuSO_4$	160			CuO	80	.50
			RO		RO		
Cornish stone (cornwall)	$1RO \cdot 2.5Al_2O_3 \cdot 20SiO_2$	1550	$2.5R_2O_3$	1550	Al_2O_3	102	.164
			$20RO_2$		SiO_2	60	.775
			3RO		Na_2O	62	.443
Cryolite	$3NaF \cdot AlF_6$	210	R_2O_3	420	Al_2O_3	102	.243
					CaO	56	.304
Dolomite	$CaCO_3 \cdot MgCO_3$	184	RO	92	MgO	40	.218
			RO		K_2O	90	.169
Feldspar (potash)	$K_2O \cdot Al_2O_3 \cdot 6SiO_2$	556	R_2O_3	556	Al_2O_3	102	.183
			$6RO_2$		SiO_2	60	.648
			RO		Na_2O	62	.119
Feldspar (soda)	$Na_2O \cdot Al_2O_3 \cdot 6SiO_2$	524	R_2O_3	524	Al_2O_3	102	.195
			$6RO_2$		SiO_2	60	.686
			RO		CaO	56	.205
Feldspar (lime)	$CaO \cdot Al_2O_3 \cdot 2SiO_2$	278	R_2O_3	278	Al_2O_3	102	.365
			$2RO_2$		SiO_2	60	.431

Table 3.11. Continued

Name of Material	Formula	Mol. Wt.	Equiv. Wt.		Oxides Entering Fusion	Molecular Weights of Oxides	Conversion Factor
Ferric chloride	$FeCl_3 \cdot 6H_2O$	270.5			Fe_2O_3	160	.296
Ferric hydroxide	$Fe(OH)_3$	107			Fe_2O_3	160	.747
Ferric oxide	Fe_2O_3	160			Fe_2O_3	160	1.0
Ferric sulphate	$Fe_2(SO_4)_3$	400			Fe_2O_3	160	.40
Ferrous carbonate	$FeCO_3$	116			Fe_2O_3	160	.69
Ferrous oxide	FeO	72			Fe_2O_3	160	1.13
Ferrous sulphate	$FeSO_4 \cdot 7H_2O$	278			Fe_2O_3	160	.288
Ferroso-ferric oxide	Fe_3O_4	232	R_2O_3 RO	155 78	Fe_2O_3	160	1.035
Flint	SiO_2	60			SiO_2	60	1.0
Fluorspar	CaF_2	78			CaO	56	.718
Gold chloride	$AuCl_3$	303.5					
Gypsum	$CaSO_4 \cdot 2H_2O$	172			CaO	56	.326
Heavy spar	$BaSO_4$	233			BaO	153	.655
Kaolin (ite)	$Al_2O_3 \cdot 2SiO_2 \cdot 2H_2O$	258	R_2O_3 $2SiO_2$	258	Al_2O_3 SiO_2	102 60	.396 .47
Lead carbonate	$PbCO_3$	267			PbO	223	.835
Lead carbonate (basic) (white lead)	$2PbCO_3 \cdot Pb(OH)_2$	775	RO	258	PbO	223	.863
Lead chloride	$PbCl_2$	278			PbO	223	.800
Lead chromate	$PbCrO_4$	323	2RO R_2O_3	646	PbO Cr_2O_3	223 152	.69 .235
Lead oxide (plumbic) (litharge)	PbO	223			PbO	223	1.0
Lead oxide (red) (minium)	Pb_3O_4	685	RO	228	PbO	223	.975
Lime	CaO	56			CaO	56	1.0
Lithium carbonate	Li_2CO_3	74			Li_2O	30	.405
Lithium oxide	Li_2O	30			Li_2O	30	1.0
Magnesium carbonate	$MgCO_3$	84			MgO	40	.476
Magnesium chloride	$MgCl_2 \cdot 6H_2O$	203			MgO	40	.197
Magnesium hydroxide	$Mg(OH)_2$	58			MgO	40	.69
Magnesium oxide	MgO	40			MgO	40	1.0
Magnesium sulphate	$MgSO_4 \cdot 7H_2O$	246			MgO	40	.162
Manganese carbonate	$MnCO_3$	115	RO		MnO	71	.61
Manganese oxide (greenish)	MnO	71			MnO	71	1.0

Manganese dioxide (black)	MnO_2	87			MnO	71	.817
Manganese oxide (brownish-black)	Mn_2O_3	158	RO=79		MnO	71	.90
Manganese oxide (red)	Mn_3O_4	229	RO=76 1/3		MnO	71	.955
Minium	Pb_3O_4	685	RO=228		PbO	233	.975
Nickel carbonate	$NiCO_3$	119	RO	119	NiC	75	.630
Nickel oxide (nickelous) (green)	NiO	75			NiC	75	1.0
Nickel oxide (nickelic) (black)	Ni_2O_3	166	RO=83		NiO	75	.903
Paris white	$CaCO_3$	100			CaO	56	.56
Pearl ash	K_2CO_3	138			K_2O	94	.68
Plaster of paris	$CaSO_4 \cdot ½H_2O$	145			CaO	56	.387
			RO	220	K_2O	94	.472
Potassium silico fluoride	K_2SiF_6	220	RO_2	220	SiO_2	60	.273
Pyrolusite	MnO_2	87			MnO	71	.817
					K_2C	94	.32
Potassium dichromate	$K_2Cr_2O_7$	294	RO,R_2O_3		$Cr_2($	152	.517
Potassium carbonate	K_2CO_3	138			K_2O	94	.68
Potassium chromate	K_2CrO_4	246	$RO½R_2O_3$		K_2O	94	.382
					Cr_2O_3	152	.308
Potassium nitrate	KNO_3	101	RO	202	K_2O	94	.465
Potassium oxide	K_2O	94			K_2O	94	1.0
Selenium	Se	79					
			R_2O		Na_2O	62	.160
Sodium antimonate	$Na_2O \cdot Sb_2O_5$	386	R_2O_3	386	Sb_2O_3	292	.757
					Na_2O	62	.162
Sodium biborate	$Na_2O \cdot 2B_2O_3 \cdot 10H_2O$	382	$RO.2B_2O_3$		B_2O_3	70	.366
Sodium bicarbonate	$NaHCO_3$	84	RO=168		Na_2O	62	.37
Sodium carbonate (crystal)	$Na_2CO_3 \cdot 10H_2O$	286			Na_2O	62	.217
Sodium carbonate (fused)	Na_2CO_3	106			Na_2O	62	.585
Sodium chloride	NaCl	58	RO	116	Na_2O	62	.535
Sodium nitrate	$NaNO_3$	85			Na_2O	62	.272
Sodium oxide	Na_2O	62			Na_2O	62	1.0
			RO	322	Na_2O	62	.193
Sodium phosphate	$Na_2HPO_4 \cdot 10H_2O$	322	P_2O_5	44	P_2O_5	142	.220
			R_2O		Na_2O	62	.359
Sodium selenite	Na_2SeO_3	173	R	173	Se	79	.457
			RO	188	Na_2O	62	.33
Sodium silico fluoride	Na_2SiF_6	188	RO_2	188	SiO_2	60	.32
Sodium sulphate	Na_2SO_4	142	RO	142	Na_2O	62	.436
			RO	745	Na_2O	62	.083
Sodium uranate (uranium yellow)	$Na_2U_2O_7 \cdot 6H_2O$	745	R_3O_8	1117	U_3O_8	842	.755

Table 3.11. Continued

Name of Material	*Formula*	*Mol. Wt.*	*Equiv. Wt.*		*Oxides Entering Fusion*	*Molecular Weights of Oxides*	*Conversion Factor*
Strontium carbonate	$SrCO_3$	148			SrO	104	.703
Strontium oxide	SrO	104			SrO	104	1.0
Silica	SiO_2	60			SiO_2	60	1.0
Tin oxide (stannous)	SnO	135	RO_2	135	SnO_2	151	1.12
Tin oxide (stannic)	SnO_2	151			SnO_2	151	1.0
Titanium oxide	TiO_2	80			TiO_2	80	1.0
Uranium oxide	U_2O_3	525			U_3O_8	842	1.07
Uranyl sodium carbonate	$UO_2CO_3 \cdot 2Na_2CO_3$	542	R_2O	271	Na_2O	62	.144
			R_3O_8	1626	U_3O_8	842	.517
Witherite	$BaCO_3$	197			BaO	153	.777
Whiting	$CaCO_3$	100			CaO	56	.56
Zinc carbonate	$ZnCO_3$	125			ZnO	81	.647
Zinc oxide	ZnO	81			ZnO	81	1.0
Zirconium oxide	ZrO_2	123			ZrO_2	123	1.0

Table 3.12. Example of procedure for converting empirical formula of a Bristol glaze into corresponding batch materials. The final step is shown in table 3.13.

Derived batch		*Empirical equivalents*				
Moles raw material		*KNaO*	*CaO*	*ZnO*	Al_2O_3	SiO_2
		0.35	0.350	0.30	0.600	3.50
0.357	Keystone feldspar	−0.35	−0.006		−0.404	−2.20
		0.00	0.344		0.196	1.28
0.344	Whiting		−0.344			
			0.000			
0.30	Calcined zinc oxide			−0.30		
				0.00		
0.15	Raw clay				−0.15	−0.30
					0.046	0.980
0.046	Calcined clay				−0.046	−0.092
					0.000	0.888
0.888	Flint					−0.888
						0.000

tion called for in the empirical glaze formula is used. These equivalents are multiplied by the respective molecular or equivalent weight to give the products shown in table 3.13. The percentage composition can be derived from these numbers in an obvious manner.

Raw Lead Glaze

Conversion of the empirical formula for a raw lead glaze into the batch is accomplished by employing the same procedure as for the Bristol glaze. As an illustration, the following raw lead glaze formula was used:

Table 3.13. Second step in the conversion of a Bristol glaze from empirical formula to batch weights: calculation of formula batch weight and percentage composition

Raw materials	*Equivalents*		*Molecular weight*		*Weight*	*Percentage composition*
Keystone feldspar	0.357	×	577.72	=	206.3	56.2
Whiting	0.344	×	100.1	=	34.6	9.4
Calcined zinc oxide	0.30	×	81.4	=	24.4	6.6
Raw clay	0.15	×	258.1	=	38.7	10.5
Calcined clay	0.046	×	222.1	=	10.2	2.8
Flint	0.888	×	60.1	=	53.9	14.5
Formula batch weight					376.6	100.0

Table 3.14. First step in the conversion of a raw lead glaze from the empirical formula to a batch formulation. See table 3.15 for final steps.

Batch materials		*Oxide equivalents in empirical formula*				
Amount, Moles	*Raw material*	PbO	ZnO	MgO	Al_2O_3	SiO_2
		0.70	0.20	0.10	0.20	2.00
0.2333	Red lead	0.70				
		−0.70				
		0.00				
0.20	Calcined zinc oxide		−0.20			
			0.00			
0.10	Magnesium carbonate			−0.10		
				0.00		
0.10	Raw clay				−0.10	−0.20
					0.10	1.80
0.10	Calcined clay				−0.10	−0.20
					0.00	1.60
1.60	Flint					−1.60
						0.00

$$\begin{matrix} 0.7PbO \\ 0.2ZnO \\ 0.1MgO \end{matrix} \quad 0.2Al_2O_3 \quad 2.0SiO_2$$

The glaze and calculation parameters are arranged as shown previously and as arranged in table 3.14. The formula for red lead is Pb_3O_4; thus, one molecular equivalent of red lead will furnish 3 equivalents of PbO. In this specific example, 0.70 equivalent of PbO is required; therefore, 0.70 divided by 3 is equal to 0.2333, the number of equivalents of red lead which are necessary. The other components are determined as before.

Table 3.15. Second step in the conversion of a raw lead glaze from the empirical formula to batch weights. See table 3.14 for first step.

Composition	*Equivalents*		*Molecular weight*		*Weight ratio*	*Percentage composition*
Red lead	0.2333	×	685.6	=	159.95	48.6
Calcined zinc oxide	0.20	×	81.4	=	16.28	4.9
Magnesite	0.10	×	84.3	=	8.43	2.6
Raw clay	0.10	×	258.1	=	25.81	7.9
Calcined clay	0.10	×	222.1	=	22.21	6.7
Flint	1.60	×	60.1	=	96.16	29.3
Formula batch weight					328.84	100.0

The formula batch weight and percentage composition are calculated from table 3.14 by the same processes as were used in the example for a Bristol glaze. The computation used for the raw lead glaze is in table 3.15.

Fritted Glaze

Purpose of Fritting

It has been shown that soluble materials are not suitable for direct addition in the glaze mixture but must be rendered insoluble by incorporating them in an insoluble glass or frit. This is merely an artificial glaze ingredient which is treated in the calculations of the glaze batch like any other ingredient, introducing several of the required oxides. The whiteware glazes are characteristically fritted glazes because they require considerable amounts of Na_2O and B_2O_3. For the latter oxide the available materials are borax and boracic acid, both of which are soluble. The Na_2O is usually introduced by borax or soda ash (Na_2CO_3). To incorporate these soluble materials in a frit, portions of the other glaze constituents are selected in such amounts that the required additions of Na_2O and B_2O_3 may be made in the glaze without introducing an excess of any other constituent.

One purpose of fritting is to convert soluble glaze materials into a relatively insoluble form. In addition it is frequently desirable to frit certain constituents for one or more other reasons. The incorporation of the lead oxide into a well balanced frit makes it much less toxic and minimizes any danger of lead poisoning. With certain materials which are of a very fine particle size or are quite bulky, such as magnesium carbonate or zinc oxide, the excessive shrinkage of the glaze can be eliminated by the inclusion of these materials in the frit batch. In the preparation of many of the colored glazes employing the "solution colors" better and more uniform colors are obtained if the coloring oxides are incorporated in the frit. This is particularly true with cobalt oxide or with other strong colorants. Even when the strong colorants are ground very fine, they may appear as specks if added to the raw glaze; but when taken into solution in a frit and then added to the glaze a good uniform color is obtained. Prepared stains, however, must be added to the mill batch. Finally, by fritting a portion of the glaze batch the interreactions among the glaze materials have an opportunity to reach partial completion before the glaze is applied to the body. In recent years, there has been a trend towards the use of a greater proportion of frit in the glaze batch as in this way it is frequently possible to obtain a better and smoother glaze surface.

Fritting rules

As an aid in the proper compounding of frits certain empirical rules have been derived which are helpful in the proportioning of the glaze ingredients. It must be pointed out that the rules should serve only as a guide, as it is possible to prepare satisfactory frits which violate one or more of the empirically derived fritting rules. The necessary fritting rules may be briefly stated as follows:

1. The ratio of the RO group to the RO_2 group should be between 1:1 and 1:3.
2. The ratio of the alkalies in the RO group to the rest of the members in the RO group should not be more than 1:1.
3. The ratio of the B_2O_3 to the SiO_2 should be no greater than 1:2.
4. The Al_2O_3 content of the frit should not exceed 0.2 equivalents.

The first rule is designed to assure the ready fusion of the frit. Simply stated, it means that if the total sum of the various oxides composing the RO group of the frit is equal to 0.8 equivalents, at least 0.8 equivalents and not more than 2.4 equivalents of SiO_2 should be added to the frit. The second rule is designed to make certain that the frit will be insoluble. If the alkali content of the frit were allowed to become too high the resulting frit would approach the solubility of sodium silicate. The third rule is also designed to assure that the frit will be insoluble. Since boric acid is soluble, at least twice the amount of silica should be included in the frit as there is boric oxide to make the frit relatively insoluble. The fourth rule is also designed to aid in the ready fusion of the frit. If the alumina content of the frit is too high, the frit will become very viscous and will be very refractory. In most frits it is desirable to have at least 0.05 equivalents of alumina as it usually brings about a better balanced frit.

The proper compounding of frits and the successful application of the fritting rules will require some practice and experience. It must be remembered that the fritting rules have been derived empirically. In some cases every fritting rule can be adhered to, and still it is impossible to make a frit. On the other hand many useful frits can be made and used successfully which do not meet the requirements of the fritting rules.

Frit Calculation

From this empirical glaze formula the frit batch and the mill batch of the glaze are calculated in a manner similar to that used for the raw glazes and demonstrated in table 3.16.

The calculation of a fritted glaze and the application and use of the fritting rules are illustrated in the following example, using this empirical formula of a glaze:

$0.05K_2O$		
$0.10Na_2O$		
$0.30CaO$	$0.25Al_2O_3$	$2.50SiO_2$
$0.35PbO$	$0.30B_2O_3$	
$0.10MgO$		
$0.10ZnO$		

Feldspar is used as an economical source of the potash. Referring to the empirical formula of the feldspar (p 91), it is shown that 0.751 equivalents of K_2O are available. Therefore, to find the amount of feldspar necessary to supply 0.05 equivalents of K_2O, the 0.05 is divided by 0.751, which is equal to 0.0665, the amount of feldspar required. The equivalent of feldspar required, 0.0665, is multiplied by 0.231, the amount of soda in the feldspar, to obtain 0.015, the amount of soda added by the feldspar. The 0.0665 is multiplied by 1.13 to give 0.075, the amount of alumina; 0.0665×0.018 to give 0.001, the amount of lime; and 0.0665×6.23 to give 0.425, the increment of silica. Next, the 0.10 equivalents of included raw clay are added for keeping the glaze batch in suspension. When soda and boric oxide are necessary, they can be most economically supplied by borax. The 0.085 equivalents of borax will furnish 0.085 equivalents of Na_2O and 2×0.085 or 0.17 equivalents of B_2O_3. When the lead oxide is added to the frit batch it is usually preferable to add it as red lead, as the extra oxygen helps to assure oxidizing conditions in fritting. The other raw materials may be added as indicated.

The next step is to select the appropriate frit and mill batch. Since the borax and the boric oxide are water soluble, they must be included in the frit. It would be desirable to frit the lead and thus put it into a less toxic form. Because it is a potent flux, lead oxide would help the fusion of the frit. A portion of the whiting could be added to avoid an excessive amount in the mill batch. If the light, precipitated magnesium carbonate is used instead of the magnesite it would be desirable to add it to the frit. Because calcined clay is more difficult to take in solution than feldspar, a better glaze can be made by adding the calcined clay to the frit batch and including the feldspar in the mill batch. The selected frit batch and the mill batch are as follows:

Frit batch		Mill batch	
moles	materials	moles	materials
0.085	Borax	0.684	Frit
0.130	Boric acid	0.10	Raw clay
0.1166	Red lead	0.0665	Keystone feldspar
0.149	Whiting	0.15	Whiting
0.10	Magnesium carbonate	0.10	Zinc oxide

Table 3.16. Initial step in converting the empirical formula of a fritted glaze into appropriate mill batch and frit batch.

Batch materials		*Oxide equivalents in empirical formula*								
Moles	*Raw material*	K_2O	Na_2O	PbO	CaO	MgO	ZnO	B_2O_3	Al_2O_3	SiO_2
		0.05	0.100	0.35	0.30	0.10	0.10	0.30	0.25	2.50
0.0665	Keystone feldspar	-0.05	-0.015		-0.001				-0.075	-0.425
		0.00	.085		0.299				0.175	2.075
0.10	Raw clay								-0.10	-0.20
									0.075	1.875
0.085	Borax		-0.085					-0.17		
			0.00					0.13		
0.1166	Red lead			-0.35						
				0.00						
0.299	Whiting				-0.299					
					0.000					
0.10	$MgCO_3$					-0.10				
						0.00				
0.10	Zinc oxide						-0.10			
							0.00			
0.13	Boric acid							-0.13		
								0.00		
0.075	Calcined clay								-0.075	-0.150
									0.000	1.725
1.725	Flint									-1.725
										0.000

0.075	Calc. clay	0.725	Flint
1.0	Flint		

The formula batch weight of the frit is calculated from the above frit batch in table 3.17. To establish the amount of frit necessary for the mill batch, determine the proportion of each oxide added to the frit and group together as follows:

	RO	R_2O_3	RO_2
	0.35PbO		
	$0.085Na_2O$	$0.075Al_2O_3$	$1.15SiO_2$
	0.149CaO	$0.30B_2O_3$	
	0.10MgO		
total	0.684		

Next convert the RO group to units by dividing 0.684, giving the empirical frit formula:

0.512PbO		
$0.124Na_2O$	$0.109Al_2O_3$	$1.68SiO_2$
0.218CaO	$0.438B_2O_3$	
0.146MgO		

The empirical frit formula is checked to see that the fritting rules are satisfied. The corresponding weight or the equivalent weight is determined by multiplying the number of equivalents by the molecular weight of each oxide, as done in table 3.18.

Because 0.684 equivalents of the RO group of the glaze were included in the frit batch, 0.684 equivalents of the frit are added to the mill batch. The calculation of the mill batch appears in table 3.19.

One other calculation frequently useful is to determine the weight of frit theoretically obtained from a given raw frit batch. This can be done

Table 3.17. Calculation of the formula batch weight and the percent composition of the fritted glaze started in table 3.16.

Batch materials								
Moles	*Materials*		*Molecular weight*		*Weight*		*Percent composition*
0.085	Borax	×	381.4	=	32.42	=	14.2
0.130	Boric acid	×	123.7	=	16.08	=	7.0
0.1166	Red lead	×	685.6	=	79.94	=	35.0
0.149	Whiting	×	100.1	=	14.91	=	6.5
0.10	Magnesium carbonate	×	84.3	=	8.43	=	3.7
0.075	Calcined clay	×	222.1	=	16.66	=	7.3
1.0	Flint	×	60.1	=	60.10	=	26.3
Formula batch weight of the frit					228.54		100.0

Table 3.18. Determination of the equivalent weight of the empirical formula of the frit.

Oxide	*Equivalents*		*Molecular weight*		*Weight ratio*
PbO	0.512	×	223.2	=	113.30
Na_2O	0.124	×	62.0	=	7.69
CaO	0.218	×	56.1	=	12.24
MgO	0.146	×	40.3	=	5.59
Al_2O_3	0.109	×	101.97	=	11.12
B_2O_3	0.438	×	69.6	=	30.48
SiO_2	1.68	×	60.1	=	100.97
Equivalent weight					281.39

by multiplying the equivalents of each oxide by the molecular weight of the oxide in the empirical frit formula, before it is converted to unity, and adding them together. The resulting weight would equal the melted weight of the frit, exclusive of the volatile components. Since the equivalent weight of the frit was obtained by dividing the equivalents of each oxide in the frit by the summation of the equivalents in the RO group, the equivalent weight of the frit multiplied by the number of equivalents of frit used in the mill batch will give the same value. In the example just cited the ratio of the formula batch weight of the frit, 228.54, to the weight ratio, 192.47 (obtained by multiplying 0.684 × 281.39), represents the theoretical loss in fritting. In the fritting of small batches it is usually necessary to include 25% additional loss to take care of the frit that adheres to the smelter. Therefore, if one wished to make a 1,000-gram glaze batch, it would be necessary to have 1,000 × 0.595 or 595 grams of frit. In order to obtain 595 grams of frit it would be necessary to make a raw frit batch of 595 × 228.5/192.5 × 1.25 or 880 grams.

In many cases it is not desired to make a specific frit for the proposed glaze formula, but instead to use one of the commercially available frits. A frit must be selected which has the proper balance between the alkalies and the boric oxide to meet the requirements. The following calculation

Table 3.19. Calculation of mill batch of example fritted glaze.

Batch materials							
Moles	*Material*		*Molecular weight*		*Weight ratio*		*Percent composition*
0.684	Frit	×	281.39	=	192.47	=	59.5
0.10	Raw clay	×	258.1	=	25.81	=	8.0
0.0665	Keystone feldspar	×	577.72	=	38.42	=	11.9
0.15	Whiting	×	100.1	=	15.01	=	4.7
0.10	Calc. zinc oxide	×	81.4	=	8.14	=	2.5
0.725	Flint	×	60.1	=	43.57	=	13.4
Total					323.42		100.0

Table 3.20. First step in the conversion of the empirical formula of a selected fritted glaze to a batch formula using a commercial frit

Moles	Materials	Oxides and equivalents in empirical formulas							
		PbO	Na_2O	K_2O	CaO	MgO	B_2O_3	Al_2O_3	SiO_2
Empirical glaze formula		0.40	0.05	0.05	0.50	0.10	0.20	0.20	2.25
0.555	Commercial frit	-0.13	-0.05	-0.05	-0.32		-0.20	-0.10	-1.62
		0.27	0.00	0.00	0.08		0.00	0.10	0.63
0.10	Raw clay							-0.10	-0.20
								0.00	0.43
0.09	White lead	-0.27							
		0.00							
0.08	Whiting				-0.08				
					0.00				
0.10	Magnesite					-0.10			
						0.00			
0.43	Flint								-0.43
									0.00

Table 3.21. Calculation of formula batch weights and glaze recipe, in percent, of the fritted glaze of table 3.20 employing a commercial frit

Moles	*Materials*		*Molecular weight*		*Weight ratio*	*Percentage composition*
0.555	Commercial frit	×	309.5	=	171.8	55.7
0.10	Raw clay	×	258.2	=	25.8	8.3
0.09	White lead	×	775.6	=	69.8	22.5
0.08	Whiting	×	100.1	=	8.0	2.5
0.10	Magnesite	×	84.3	=	8.4	2.7
0.43	Flint	×	60.1	=	25.8	8.3
Total					309.6	100.0

will serve to illustrate the use of a commercial frit. If the empirical formula of the desired glaze is:

$$\begin{matrix} 0.40PbO & & \\ 0.05Na_2O & 0.20Al_2O_3 & 2.25SiO_2 \\ 0.05K_2O & 0.20B_2O_3 & \\ 0.40CaO & & \\ 0.10MgO & & \end{matrix}$$

and a certain commercial frit of the following composition is available:

$$\begin{matrix} 0.09K_2O & & \\ 0.09Na_2O & 0.18Al_2O_3 & 2.91SiO_2 \\ 0.58CaO & 0.36B_2O_3 & \\ 0.24PbO & & \end{matrix}$$

Equivalent weight 309.5

an example of its use is illustrated in table 3.20 and table 3.21. In this case the required boric oxide (0.20) is divided by the boric oxide available (0.36) to obtain the number of equivalents of commercial frit required. The 0.555 equivalents of frit is then multiplied by equivalents of each oxide in the frit and subtracted from the original glaze formula. The rest of the calculation is carried out as before.

The calculation of the empirical formula for a fritted glaze can be made if the percentage composition or weight ratio of both the frit and the complete glaze batch are available. It is calculated in the same way as outlined for the raw glazes.

References

1. 1968. Materials for ceramic processing. *Cer. Ind.* 90(1):112.
2. 1959–60. *Ceramic data book.* Chicago, Ill.: Industrial Publications, Inc., p 624.

4

Mixing and Milling

Basic Requirements

No step in the preparation of glazes is more important than the operations designed to give a homogeneous mixture ready for application to the ware. Except for methods of applying the glaze in the form of a dry powder, rarely employed nowadays, and glazing by exposure of the ware to the vapors of volatile salts during the firing period, the universal method is to mix the glaze ingredients with water to form a liquid suspension or slip. It is therefore necessary to use such methods and apparatus as will insure the preparation of a homogeneous mixture of the glaze constituents and water, free from coarse particles and lumps. This glaze slip must be of such composition and consistency that it will not show undesirable settling or separation in a reasonable time of standing; that it will not contain soluble salts of such a quantity or character as to be objectionable; that the consistency of the slip will be suited to the method of application and the nature of the body upon which it is to be applied; and, finally, that there will not be any particles of the constituents which may cause specks or other defects.

Essential conditions in the preparation of glazes are cleanliness and systematic order in the care and use of materials and equipment; thereby loss of time, labor, and materials may be avoided. Further there is the psychological effect of spurring the workers to be vigilant, which is a prime requisite in the production of good ware.

Quality of Water

One of the important conditions commonly disregarded in arrangements for the preparation of glazes is the quality of the water employed.

Chemically pure water is not difficult to prepare, but it is too costly for use in glazes. Water available for industrial use almost invariably contains carbonates, chlorides, and sulfates of the alkalies, alkaline earths, iron, and alumina, and less frequently other bases. The carbonates, acid carbonates, sulfates, and chlorides of the alkaline earths, lime, and magnesia are most commonly the salts present in and responsibile for "hard water." "Soft water" contains little or none of these objectionable compounds but may contain excessive amounts of other trouble-making substances, e.g., free sulfuric acid, organic wastes (sewage, refinery wastes, etc.), brines, or other substances. The water supply of some areas is naturally high in salts of the alkalies, making them very alkaline.

Information regarding the chemical nature of a municipal water supply may be had, ordinarily from those distributing the same. Data regarding the nature of the regional supplies are usually to be had from the proper state bureau. Commercial chemical laboratories specializing in analyses and furnishing advice regarding the proper methods for treatment to correct its faults are to be found in most cities. The correction of hardness or other faults of water cannot be discussed here. It is sufficient to say that the amount and character of the dissolved and suspended matter may have a profound effect upon the glaze during preparation and application and certain defects that appear during firing.

An impressive example of the harmful effect of pollution of a water supply was reported from an important pottery district in Ohio some years ago. Some of the factories of the district drew the water from the neighboring Ohio River which gathers the waste waters from the great industrial area of which Pittsburgh is the center. During a prolonged summer drought, the volume of the flow fell far below normal, but the volume of waste discharged remained the same and, consequently, the concentration of harmful substances in the river water distributed to the potteries caused serious difficulties in manufacture and created defects in the ware.

Water distilled under proper conditions is the best and most expensive for industrial uses. Because of the expense it usually may be excluded from consideration in ceramics except in the laboratory. Rainwater gathered and stored under proper conditions has been substituted for distilled water, but the quality had in industrial or largely populated areas may be suspected of containing more or less dust and gases common to such areas. Water softening processes are used successfully by many industries and the treated water may be recommended for many ceramic operations, providing carefully supervised control is maintained.

The most widely used process is that of base exchange by employment of an alumino-silicate, or zeolite. The sodium which this substance contains may be replaced by the calcium present in hard water, converting it into soft water. The reaction is reversible so the calcium-containing zeolite may be reconverted to the sodium zeolite reagent, and the cycle repeated many times. However, the soft water will contain a proportionate amount of sodium and the other inorganic and organic substances originally present. Deionized water is the product of a new process.

The principle of ion exchange or base exchange is employed in organic exchangers to supplement or replace the sodium zeolite. The resinous zeolites retain the bases of organic salts and release hydrogen to form the corresponding acids, e.g., bicarbonates yield carbonic acid, sulfates yield sulfuric acid, and chlorides liberate hydrochloric acid. The freed base is retained by the exchanger. The acid formed may be absorbed by an anionic absorber and the water is then comparable, it is claimed, to distilled water for some ceramic uses.

The weighing of the glaze batches should be done on scales of good construction, sufficiently sensitive and precise for the smallest quantities required. Due allowance must be made for the water present in the materials other than that recognized as normally part of their composition.

Same plants have gone to using deionized water, a special form of ion exchange process that can deliver the equivalent of distilled water.

Dry Grinding

The glaze batch is usually mixed or ground in the presence of a large excess of water. If it is desirable to mix the batch dry, as for example the frit batch, machines of widely varying capacities for this purpose are available. These range in sizes from hand-operated units to those, designed for the glass industry, which will handle a ton or more at a charge. Walker[1] suggested the use of the following simple device from small batches if other means are not at hand. In an empty ball mill place two or three boards about four inches wide so that they span the distance between the heads and are set so that their widths are radially disposed with respect to the periphery of the cylinder. The edge of each board nearest the lining is separated from it by the space of about an inch. The boards, if there are only two, are set so as to be on opposite sides of the cylinder. When more than two are used they are equally spaced. The purpose of this device is to cause the charge to cascade over the board flights and to prevent the charge from sliding on the mill lining, thus ensuring thorough mixing.

Particle Size Distribution

A well-prepared glaze slip, the so-called "well-ground slip," is considered by many operators to be one which passes readily through a lawn of a specified mesh with a minimum amount of coarser material retained on the lawn. This kind of specification, or rather, description, neglects entirely the consideration of the distribution of particle size, i.e., the percentage proportion of the different degrees of fineness. The significance of the fineness and especially of the distribution of the particle sizes has not been appreciated by the glaze maker as it deserves. The vitreous enamelers have studied the matter and have demonstrated that careful control yields real advantages in quality of the finished enamel and in the time and cost of production.

Schramm and Sherwood[2] found that fine grinding is an important factor in determining the properties of the glaze slip and furnishing a better fired glaze. Table 4.1 makes a comparison of two glazes of the same chemical composition but differing slightly in particle size distribution. The matured glazes differed significantly.

Grinding Equipment

When the raw materials for glazes are not obtainable in finely ground condition, or when powdered materials need further size reduction, and when well-mixed ingredients are desired, it is necessary to suitably process the slip batch. The usual and recommended practice is to mix and grind the glaze in an appropriate mill.

Because it now is convenient to purchase preground materials, there are those who prepare glaze slips in a high-speed blender or a blunger without any grinding action. There are numerous reasons why glazes usually are prepared in a ball mill. This usually is done wet, ending up with a slurry or slip.

Ball Mill

A mill, generally speaking, is a ball mill or a pebble mill, the terms being used interchangeably. In some chemical engineering terminology, a ball mill uses steel balls and a pebble mill is one that employs flint pebbles or manufactured ceramic grinding media.

Table 4.1. Particle size distribution of two glazes[2]

Radii	*New glaze*	*Old glaze*
Over 8.3 microns*	12.3%	13.3%
8.3 to 2.5 microns	35.3%	43.1%
Below 2.5 microns	52.4%	43.6%

*Micron = 0.000,001 meter, or 10^{-4} centimeter.

A ball mill (or pebble mill) is a cylindrical container, charged with grinding media (balls or pebbles) and the mill charge, that is rotated about its cylindrical axis. The smaller, laboratory or jar mills are usually ceramic cylinders, made in one piece and with up to 60 gallons' capacity. There are three-piece ceramic cylinders with up to 120 gallons' capacity. Larger mills usually are of steel, lined with porcelain, quartz blocks, or sometimes rubber. The capacities and dimensions of ball mills are given in table 4.2.

Mill Linings

Porcelain brick linings are popular since these can be made of a very strong body, resistant to abrasion and impact, exact in dimensions, and of the desired curvature required for any particular mill. The exactness of size and shape permits the replacements to be made with very thin joints and a minimum of cementing bond.

Silex, chert, flint, and jasper are natural silica rock of very fine crystalline texture. Because these are prepared by splitting and breaking from the massive rock, the blocks are only approximately regular in size and shape. This irregularity and the variable width of joint requires the use of greater amounts of the cement, consequently the probably of contamination of the mill batch by the cementing material is greater. These linings are very durable and the irregularity of the blocks increases the efficiency of the grinding operation.[3] Linings of rubber have been tried successfully, providing that the temperature of the interior of the mill does not increase above 150° F. Synthetic organic linings other than rubber are available for higher operating temperatures. Such linings are available in low-ash quality on special request. Such linings have been more satisfactory for small laboratory mills than for the larger sizes. In the latter case the linings must be made considerably thicker in order to withstand the wear due to great impact of the large balls.

Grinding Media

The grinding action of the mill is done by the abrasrve action of a charge of pebbles or balls sliding and tumbling as the mill rotates. There are various kinds and sizes of balls and each has its own advantages. Those commonly employed are flint pebbles, metal balls, regular porcelain, special porcelain, and high density and special balls made of appropriate materials.

FLINT PEBBLES. Flint pebbles of great toughness and durability are imported from Europe where they are gathered from certain areas of the

Table 4.2. Capacities and dimensions of ball mills

Buhrstone (Silex) Lined Pebble Mills										
	Total Capacity		Wet Grinding				Dry Grinding			
Mill Size	U.S. gal	cu ft	Ball or Pebble Charge lbs	Batch Size U.S. gal	Approximate Motor Horsepower	Mill Speed rpm	Ball or Pebble Charge lbs	Operating Cap. Based on lbs of Dry Sand (at 100 lbs per cu ft)	Approximate Motor Horsepower
15″ × 21″	–	–	–	–	–	–	–	–	–
21″ × 28″	–	–	–	–	–	–	–	–	–
24″ × 36″	38	5	253	23	1½	36	253	127	3
2′ 6″ × 3′ 6″	78	10	524	47	3	30	524	262	5
3′ 0″ × 4′ 0″	140	19	939	84	5	26	939	469	7½
3′ 6″ × 4′ 0″	200	27	1335	120	5	25	1335	667	7½
4′ 0″ × 5′ 0″	346	46	2310	207	7½	23	2310	1155	10
4′ 6″ × 3′ 6″	302	40	2018	181	7½	22	2018	1009	10
4′ 6″ × 4′ 6″	400	53	2673	240	7½	22	2673	1336	15
5′ 0″ × 4′ 0″	442	59	2954	265	10	21	2954	1477	15
5′ 0″ × 6′ 0″	689	92	4603	413	15	21	4603	2302	25
6′ 0″ × 5′ 0″	839	112	5610	504	15	19	5610	2805	25
6′ 0″ × 8′ 0″	1383	185	9248	830	20	19	9248	4624	40
6′ 0″ × 10′ 0″	1748	234	11687	1049	25	19	11687	5843	50
8′ 0″ × 8′ 0″	2576	344	17218	1545	40	17	17218	8609	75
8′ 0″ × 10′ 0″	3246	434	21701	1948	50	17	21701	10851	100
8′ 0″ × 12′ 0″	3913	523	26155	2348	60	17	26155	13078	125
9′ 6″ × 8′ 0″	3684	493	24623	2210	60	15	24623	12311	125
9′ 6″ × 10′ 0″	4645	621	31050	2787	90	15	31050	15525	150
9′ 6″ × 12′ 0″	5601	749	37443	3361	100	15	37443	18722	200

Porox Lined Pebble Mills

15″ × 21″	9.8	1.3	59	6	¾	42	59	33	1
21″ × 28″	27	3.5	162	16	1	40	162	90	1½
24″ × 36″	43	6	261	26	1½	36	261	145	3
2′ 6″ × 3′ 6″	87	12	524	52	3	30	524	291	5
3′ 0″ × 4′ 0″	153	20	921	92	5	26	921	512	7½
3′ 6″ × 4′ 0″	216	29	1298	129	5	25	1298	721	7½
4′ 0″ × 5′ 0″	368	49	2215	221	7½	23	2215	1231	10
4′ 6″ × 3′ 6″	323	43	1942	194	7½	22	1942	1079	10
4′ 6″ × 4′ 6″	425	57	2556	255	7½	22	2556	1420	15
5′ 0″ × 4′ 0″	469	63	2822	281	10	21	2822	1568	15
5′ 0″ × 6′ 0″	725	97	4361	435	15	21	4361	2423	25
6′ 0″ × 5′ 0″	880	118	5296	528	15	19	5296	2942	25
6′ 0″ × 8′ 0″	1440	192	8666	864	20	19	8666	4815	40
6′ 0″ × 10′ 0″	1816	243	10927	1090	25	19	10927	6071	50
8′ 0″ × 8′ 0″	2661	356	16011	1597	40	17	16011	8895	75
8′ 0″ × 10′ 0″	3346	447	20132	2008	50	17	20132	11184	100
8′ 0″ × 12′ 0″	4028	538	24234	2417	60	17	24234	13463	125
9′ 6″ × 8′ 0″	3793	507	22818	2275	60	15	22818	12677	125
9′ 6″ × 10′ 0″	4772	638	28458	2863	90	15	28458	15948	150
9′ 6″ × 12′ 0″	5746	768	34566	3447	100	15	34566	19204	200

coast of France and Denmark. They are had also from Greenland and some areas in the United States. The grading of the sizes of the pebbles is as follows: French no. 1 (1½–2 in.) and no. 2 (2–3¼ in.); Danish no. 1 (1–1½ in.) and no. 2 (1½–2 in.).

Flint pebbles are either black or cream color. The former have been found responsible, by enamelers, for contaminating the finished product with small black specks due to chips breaking off during the milling and mixing of the batch. This is infrequent, of course, but troublesome. The products obtained by grinding the same batch in a buhr mill and in a ball mill are not the same in physical character, differing in the percentage distribution of the particle sizes and the shapes of the particles.

Natural flint or chert pebbles have a density of 2.6. They are tough and very resistant to wear. Formerly they were universally employed for milling glazes and still are in quite common use. The irregular shape and the possible presence of surface flaws and crevasses make them troublesome to thoroughly cleanse.

METAL BALLS. These are seldom used for grinding glazes, but might have limited, highly specialized application. Because of their high density, milling time can be reduced to 30% of the time that would be required using flint pebbles. This is not of much concern in glazes because the problem is usually one of mixing rather than size-reduction.

PORCELAIN MEDIA, REGULAR DENSITY. These have compositions resembling electrical porcelain and a density of about 2.4. They are uniform in size, white in color, and easily cleaned. They do not grind quite as effectively nor wear quite so long as flint pebbles.[4]

HIGH DENSITY PORCELAIN. The usual high density grinding media are of high alumina porcelain. Among the media most commonly available, the density is in the range of 3 to 3.6, with some being higher. The balls or media having the higher density result in faster and finer grinding than is accomplished with the lighter balls. They outwear regular-density porcelain and some of them, but not all, outwear flint.

It has been advocated[4] that when using high density media, it is well, when possible, to employ higher viscosity slip than with the lighter media. Perkins recommended a viscosity of 21 or higher for most efficient grinding.

It should be kept in mind that high density balls not only grind faster than do the lighter media, but they also overgrind more quickly, and the slip is likely to heat up more than with lighter pebbles. The best results as regard grinding efficiency have been obtained by having a sufficient charge of slip in the mill to cover the balls by one or two inches.

Grinding with high density media generally is more effective using heavy balls than lighter. The advantages of milling with high density media as compared to regular porcelain media were tabulated by Perkins[4] as follows:

"1. Mill time was reduced an average of 45% when no increase was made in the mill charge. The average time reduction was 38% when the mill charge was increased by 46%.
2. Grinding media and power costs were reduced.
3. Cleaner enamel was obtained.
4. Grinding results were more uniform.
5. Less media had to be replaced following mill dumping, sorting and inspection.
6. Media wear-off was more uniform.
7. Smaller amounts of grinding media had to be regularly added to maintain the normal charge volume."

The disadvantages were:

"1. More wear on gears and mill linings.
2. Increased set of enamel.
3. Increased slip temperature."

SIZE OF MEDIA. More efficient grinding is done by the rubbing action between adjacent balls so the larger the number of contacts per cubic foot of charge, the more grinding, providing the balls are large enough to do the job. For example, there might be about one two-inch ball per pound compared to six one-inch balls per pound.

The influence of the shape of the media on grinding has been much discussed. Media have been produced in the shape of spheres, cylinders, oblate spheroids and irregular shapes. Davis[5] concluded that cylindrical media had a slight advantage over spherical media.

Establishment of Mill Practice

Each glaze slip requires an appropriate milling treatment which should be found by careful trial and thereafter observed. The factors which influence the results vary with the amount, solubility, and hardness of the frit used; the amount and kind of clay used; the size of the mill; and the number of sizes of the balls.

PRECRUSHING. Precrushing the dry mill batch to pass freely through a 16-mesh screen is desirable because dry milling requires less reduction of particle size by impact of the balls with each other and the mill lining

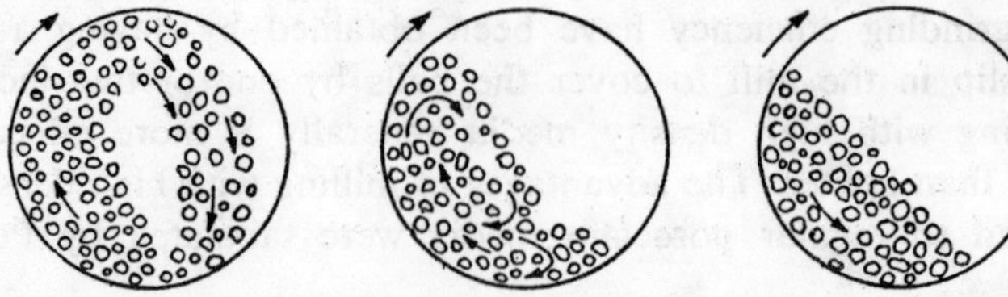

Figure 4.1. Varying effects of mill speeds on pebble movement: *c.* rapid speed, *b.* normal speed, *a.* slow speed.

and because wear and noise are reduced. In other words, the milling depends more upon the attrition of the moving balls and very little upon the crushing action. If the charge is to be wet ground, the best results may be had by a ratio of solids to water which will maintain a suitable slip coating on each ball. If the ratio of water is too low, the pasty layer will interfere with the free movement of the balls; if too high, the balls will splash about, doing little grinding.

Theory of the Ball Mill

The operation of ball mills has been carefully observed and analyzed and the principles are well understood. When an experimental ball mill, having one end covered with glass, is partially filled with small balls and rotated at a very slow speed, the balls will merely slide on the moving inner mill surface, wearing the same rather than grinding the batch (fig. 4.1*a*). If the mill with its charge is rotated at high speed, the centrifugal force will distribute the whole charge of balls uniformly over the entire inner surface of the mill just so long as the speed is sufficiently high (fig. 4.1*c*). If this high speed be slowly reduced, the centrifugal force will also decrease and presently will be unable to maintain a continuous layer of balls. The balls will then rise to a maximum height and cascade in a loose stream, striking the layer of moving balls underneath (fig. 4.1*b*). The crushing of particles is done between the falling balls and the sliding balls. This heavy impact causes excessive wear and cracks in the mill lining, breakage of the balls, and is very noisy.

Formerly the ball mill grinding operation was considered to be done chiefly by the action just described. It is now recognized that more efficient grinding action is had by rotating the mill at a sufficient speed to cause a churning of the balls throughout the whole charge and with the maximum effect exerted by bringing the greatest number of moving surfaces into action.

The work done by a ball mill grinding unit is dependent upon many factors: the size of the mill, the size and number of the balls, the weight and volume of the ball charge, the particle size of batch, the amount of water used, the viscosity of the batch, the duration of the grind, and the temperature.

ORDER OF GRINDING. Since the soft materials require little grinding, and because the glaze materials are generally sufficiently fine as purchased, the portion which requires particular consideration is the frit. Commercial frits now are conventionally furnished in ground or powdered form. Crude, unground frit and all other coarse hard material, such as flint and color oxides, should be placed in the mill with enough clay to keep the ingredients from settling out and with all but 10% to 30% of the required water. There should be enough of the latter to form a thick cream. This is important because the viscosity of the slip has an important influence upon the efficiency of the grinding operation. Too much water gives too thin a slip and the heavier particles will separate. Too little water yields a thick, sticky paste which coats the balls and retards the grinding action.

If the frit is notably soluble—as was, for example, the flint-boric acid fusion formerly extensively used, or the feldspar is more soluble than usual—or the grinding is unduly prolonged, or the amount of water is excessive, the glaze becomes ropey or liverlike in consistency and develops "curtains," that is, heavy streaks form on the ware during the dipping.

DURATION. The time required to reduce the harder materials to suitable fineness will depend upon: size of the mill; sizes, weight and number of the balls; quantity of the charge; diameter and speed of rotation of the mill.

When the harder portion of the charge has been satisfactorily ground, the softer materials (excepting the portion of the clay already introduced) are added and the operation completed by continuing the rotation of the mill just long enough to effect a complete mixing. The total time required by this method is actually less than if the whole batch is introduced in the mill at the beginning, since the division of the charge as described accelerates the real grinding operation. The latter part is merely a mixing process which is quickly completed. The glazes thus prepared possess a very low viscosity at the dipping tub although the weight per pint may be quite high.

Sechrist,[6] using $1\frac{1}{2}$-in. balls in the charge, found the milling time was reduced 67%, as compared with that required by the 3-in. balls, but 1%–2% unground frit remained. Fellows[7] reported that the smaller the size of the ball, the faster the grinding. Many papers have been published with valuable data relating to the operation of ball mills in grinding frits and vitreous enamel batches, wet and dry. While the batches are notably different from practically all types of glazes, other than some kinds of fritted compositions for low temperatures, the principles have a wide application. Some of these have been summarized in a report[7] describing the practice of thirty enamel plants. This is briefly summarized below.

SPEED OF THE MILL. The 31-inch (inside diameter) mills operated satisfactorily at 87% of the critical speed. The critical speed is determined as the lowest speed at which a ball will just ride with the mill lining. This may be calculated from the relation

$$\text{Critical speed (r.p.m.)} = 54.9/\sqrt{R}$$

where R is the radius of the mill in feet. The larger size mills—39- and 44-inch diameters—operated at about 64% of the critical speed.

SIZE OF BALLS. Two-inch balls are the maximum size recommended for large mills and they may be allowed to wear down to an inch or even less in diameter before they are removed from the mill. A gradation to the smaller sizes in the charge promotes more efficient milling. The larger sizes are useful only when coarser and tougher particles of frit are present. The smaller the balls, the more quickly the grinding is done.

CHARGE OF BALLS. It is recommended that the ball charge be maintained at 55% to 62.5% of the mill volume and that the wear of the balls be compensated by adding the requisite amount of the largest balls with each charge of frit. Usually 5 to 10 pounds of balls are consumed in milling 1,000 pounds of frit. Both flint pebbles and porcelain balls are used, the former frequently with the harder batches and the latter with the less resistant mixtures.

The fineness of the enamel may be controlled with greater ease in a mill with a large frit charge than the small mill with a small frit charge. When a smaller frit charge is used, the milling is more rapid and the danger of overmilling is greater. According to Andrews[8] a deviation from size of the usual charge will result in a different distribution of the particle size of the frit being ground. Small batches mill rapidly and the wear of the mill will be greater because the cushioning effect of the charge will be less. An undercharged mill wears rapidly and a mill containing only water and the charge of balls deteriorates rapidly if run for only a few revolutions. The authors agree that the batch should be 45% of the volume of the mill. The frit should be 21%.

WATER CONTENT. Lowering the water content lowers the effect of the milling and may be compensated by increasing the weight of the balls or flints used. A certain amount of water is required for each batch formula for the minimum amount of milling time, but no variations in the fineness of grinding have been noted as accompanying variation in the amount of water.

TEMPERATURE. The prolonged rotation of a ball mill loaded with balls will develop internal heat which will generate steam from moisture or water present in the batch. In several known instances this condition has resulted in the blowing out of the head of the mill which contained a "dry" charge of batch since the small amount of water present was sufficient to produce the necessary pressure. A rise of temperature during milling need not be very great to increase importantly the amount of solution taking place in a wet batch, and this may result in significant changes in the conduct of the finished slip. Ceramists[9] engaged in the preparation of batches used in making vitreous enamels have noted an increase of the solubility of a frit resulting in a change in the ratio of the soda to the boric oxide and a consequent alteration in the setting conduct of the slip.

A simple expedient used by Burnham and Sechrist[10] to prevent or, at least, moderate the rise of temperature was the flow of water from a perforated pipe over the rotating mill. A more elaborate device is a water jacket for the mill through which water flows continuously during the grinding operation. Fellows[11] was unable to discover any significant difference accompanying the variation of temperatures between 88° F and 138° F.

Spurrier[12] found that prolonged stirring or agitation of a slip may change the hydrometer reading but not the weight per pint, or other unit of volume. Also, he cites the case of a slip which remained at a constant specific gravity for several days, but the comparative viscosities as measured by the rate of flow of a unit volume were those in table 4.3. The hydrometer specific gravities of glazes often reported as used in potteries

Table 4.3. Influence of aging on the relative viscosity of a glaze slip

Period of standing, days	*Rate of flow, seconds per 100 cc*
0	18.0
15	18.4
30	25.2
34	27.6
43	24.4

Table 4.4. Specific gravities of pottery glaze slips for bodies of different absorptivities

Type of body	*Specific gravity*
Soft-burned biscuit and raw bodies	1.430 to 1.470
Medium hard biscuit	1.500 to 1.600
Hard biscuit	1.600 to 1.700
Medium soft biscuit	1.460 to 1.500

are as given in table 4.4. The weights of glaze slips per pint as reported in use in potteries appear in table 4.5.

Spurrier[12] found the following procedure useful in maintaining uniform consistency in a glaze to be sprayed on architectural terra cotta: the slip should be adjusted to a desirable specific gravity, the viscosity determined with suitable apparatus and thereafter maintained by the addition of small amounts of sulfur dioxide gas to increase the viscosity, or alkali to lessen it.

Consistency

The consistency of a glaze slip is the result of a complex of physical properties which gives it the characteristics required for successful application to ware by dipping, spraying, painting, or other analogous operation. The parameters involved and their interrelationship are shown in figure 4.11. It cannot be correctly described as viscosity since that term is restricted properly to true fluids; whereas the so-called consistency of glazes displays the characteristics of plasticity. The typical curve of viscosity of a true fluid, when rate of flow is plotted against force, is a straight line (*a* in Fig. 4.2), starting from the zero zero point. The corresponding curve (*b* in Fig. 4.2) for the plastic state is rectilinear and its intercept with the

Table 4.5. Weight per pint of glaze slips used in potteries for various types of bodies and glazes

Type of glaze	*Type of body*	*Weight per pint, oz.*
One-fire raw lead	Plastic	24 to 28
One-fire leadless	Plastic	22 to 24
One-fire raw lead	Red-burning	24
One-fire leadless	Red-burning	21 to 23
Leadless	Vitreous bisque	24 to 26
Stoneware (Bristol)	Green stoneware	23 to 25
Albany slip	Not stated	24 to 25

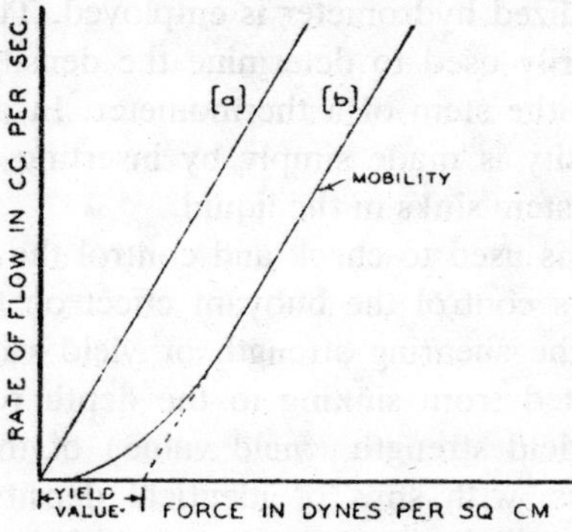

Figure 4.2. Yield value and mobility of glaze.

line of force is not at the zero zero point but at a distance denoting that an appreciable amount of energy is required to initiate a plastic flow. Plastic flow, by definition, is initiated by a minimal force.

Thin suspensions of solids in liquids may have flow characteristics similar to liquids. With each increase in concentration a greater force is required to move the slip. The items in figure 4.2 which are of particular significance to the glaze maker are the intercept on the base line, formed by the prolongation of line, and its slope. The intercept is called the yield value and the slope is known as the index of mobility.

The former indicates amount of shearing stress required for the movement of the suspended particles in any layer upon an adjacent layer. The mobility is comparable to fluidity and it determines the manner and the rate at which a freshly applied glaze slip will form a coating of the desired uniformity and thickness upon a piece of pottery. The yield value indicates the ability of the glaze slip coating to maintain the correct thickness and distribution unaltered by gravity, minor shocks, inertia, and slight centrifugal force. It is obvious that the glaze slip successful for a specific use must conform, in both of these properties, to the requirements of the ware to be coated, the method of application, the temperatures of the ware and the glazing room, and possibly to the humidity conditions.

Testing

Many methods of testing consistency have been used during the centuries, ranging from dipping a finger in the slip and judging the condition from the manner in which it flows off, or dipping a piece of ware and observing the same phenomenon. It is obvious that this method is suited only for an approximation of the condition.

One method used in some shops is the hydrometer or *Baumé* test.

In this test, a standardized hydrometer is employed. The kind of hydrometer is the type ordinarily used to determine the density of a liquid; it has a calibrated stem like the stem of a thermometer. In a liquid, an accurate determination of density is made simply by inserting the hydrometer and observing how far the stem sinks in the liquid.

A similar device is used to check and control the consistency of slips. With slips, two factors control the buoyant effect on the hydrometer: the density, per se, and the shearing strength or yield value of the slip. The hydrometer is prevented from sinking to the depth required by the fluid density because the yield strength (yield value) of the slip also is active in supporting it. Thus, with slips of identical density, but progressively higher yield values, the hydrometer readings will be progressively greater. Obviously, variation in shapes of the hydrometers that would not influence readings in true liquids would do so for this application.

To apply this test, two things are required: (1) hydrometers are selected by comparison against a standard reference hydrometer by trial, rejecting those that give readings differing from the standard, and (2) all tests are made on slips previously adjusted to a prescribed fixed value of true density by an independent test such as with a pycnometer.

Density or specific gravity measurements have long been used as more exact methods of batch control but they fail to furnish information regarding the two essential properties, yield value and mobility. There are two methods generally used for determination of density (or specific gravity): the weight of a measured volume of the glaze, for example, the "weight per pint" as so frequently recorded in some literature; the weight of an exactly measured volume at a known temperature.

The second method for this purpose is the use of a hydrometer for reading the specific gravity directly by partial immersion of this instrument in the slip. The objections to the use of this method are many, as Spurrier[12] has stated:

> "The method is applicable only in liquids, whereas the slip is not a solution but a suspension of colloids and crystalloids in a liquid; the viscous properties of the slip falsify the readings of the instrument; changes in the physical conduct of the glaze due to solution, growth of algae, bacteria, chemical reactions, and temperature changes accompanying a period of aging, may be of very great importance. Within narrow limits of a specific glaze, plant operation for a given glaze composition, and with reasonable control of the temperature of the slip, the method offers a simple and convenient means for checking the correctness and the uniformity of the batch weighing."

During the second decade of this century, attention was directed in this country to the method of studying slip consistency by measuring the rate of flow from a tube of small diameter attached to the end of a larger tube supported in a vertical position to act as the reservoir of the material. The early efforts failed to give desired information until the principles of Bingham's study of plastic flow were applied. He introduced the conceptions and terms yield value and mobility. Apparatuses which have been designed and used to measure consistency in the factory for control purposes are known as the flux type as described by Bleininger[13] and more precise modifications devised by Shearer,[14] Cooke,[15] Harrison,[16] and others. In the apparatus used by the last named, special care was given to the control of the temperature of the slip and the length and the internal diameter of the small tube through which the slip flows from the larger tube. Figure 4.3 shows the consistometer used by Harrison.

Some of the other devices which have been used for research purposes include:

1. The rotation of a paddle wheel in a cup containing the slip, such as the Stormer[17] and the MacMichael[18] apparatuses.
2. The penetration of a slip by a plunger impelled by gravity to sink in the mixture, such as the Gardner mobilometer used by McIntyre and Irwin.[19]
3. The dipping plate method. An evaluation system employing this concept was developed and studied extensively by Harman[20] and associates.

The third method is based on the measurement and correlation of three quantities: coherence value, receptivity, and pickup. Coherence value is defined as the weight of slip adhering to a unit area of a glass plate when withdrawn from a reservoir of slip at one centimeter per second. A second parameter, receptivity (R value), is the weight of water picked up, per square centimeter of contact area of a sample of the substrate body, due to contact with water under controlled conditions. This is a measure of the surface and capillary nature of the body. The third quantity, pickup, is a measure of the combined capillary properties of the substrate body and the depositing layer of glaze. It was defined as the weight of solids in grams, deposited per square centimeter of area of a test sample of the ware to be glazed, after contact with the test slip under standard conditions.

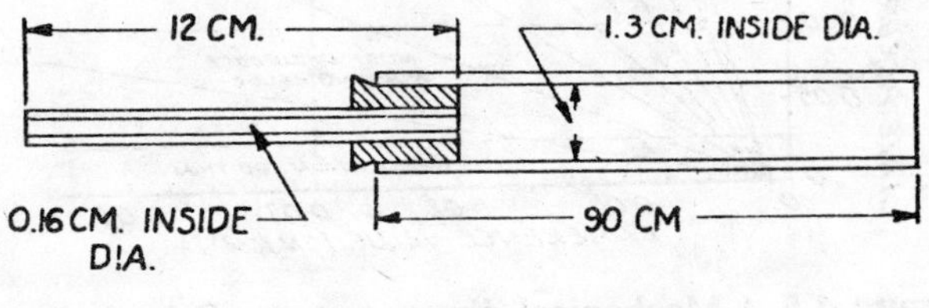

Figure 4.3. Consistometer used by Harrison.[16]

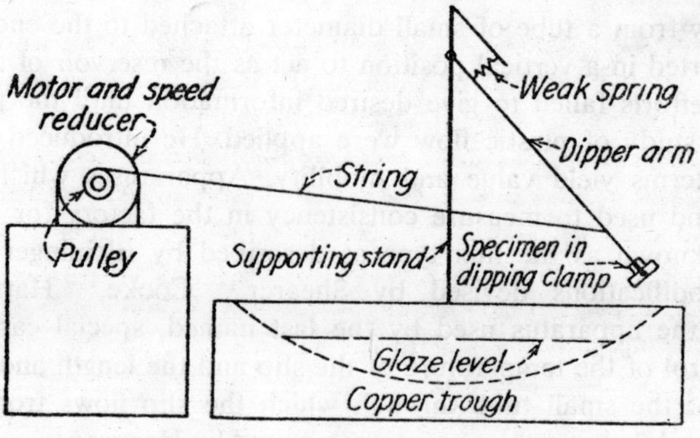

Figure 4.4. Mechanical dipper for measuring glaze values.[20]

The correlation between these factors can be represented by a simple first-order equation as follows: $P = K(R/100)(C - 0.001)$, wherein P = pickup, K = deposition constant, R = receptivity, and C = coherence value. The method is applicable to all types of slips and can be used as well to check incoming raw materials; as a basis for selection of raw materials; as a control test for slip consistency; and as an aid in control at various steps in manufacturing.

The measuring apparatus was designed to permit a careful regulation of the time of contact of the test piece with the slip. The mechanical dipper portion of the apparatus is shown schematically in figure 4.4. Some results obtained from tests with slips of Bristol and fritted glazes of varying consistencies are shown in figures 4.5 and 4.6, respectively. These graphs show typical relations between coherence values and pickup. Typical plots of R values versus pickup are illustrated in figure 4.7 and 4.8.

Three fundamentals that influence the consistency of the glaze slip are:

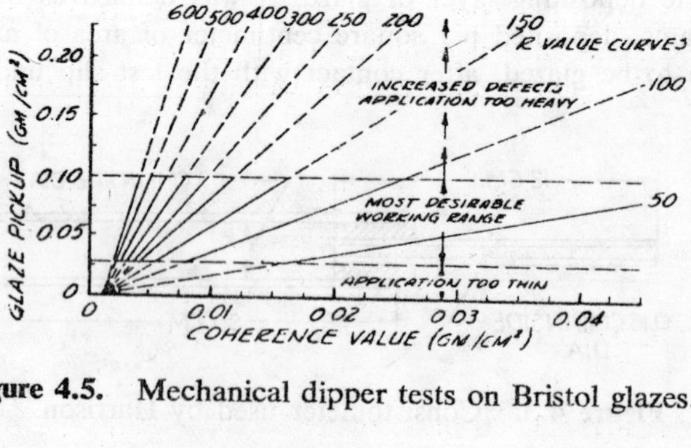

Figure 4.5. Mechanical dipper tests on Bristol glazes.[20]

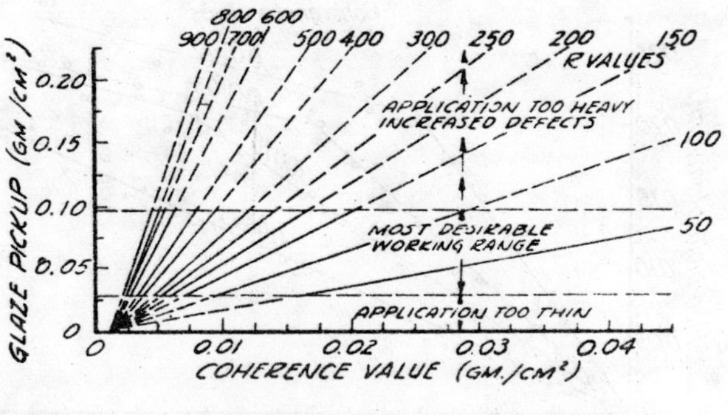

Figure 4.6. Mechanical dipper tests on fritted glazes.[20]

1. The amount and character of the colloidal dispersions.
2. The amount and the physical characteristics of the noncolloidal materials, e.g., size, shape, and specific gravity.
3. The amount of water.

The methods of control which are available for altering any slip batch of a given glaze composition are: (1) grinding; (2) heating; (3) aging; and (4) using electrolytes.

Importance of Clays

The clays used in a glaze batch are not the only colloidally dispersed materials, but, because of the relatively large amounts and activity, they are most important. If any single clay is used, it obviously must be chosen with care so as to satisfy the requirements as to color, floating, and

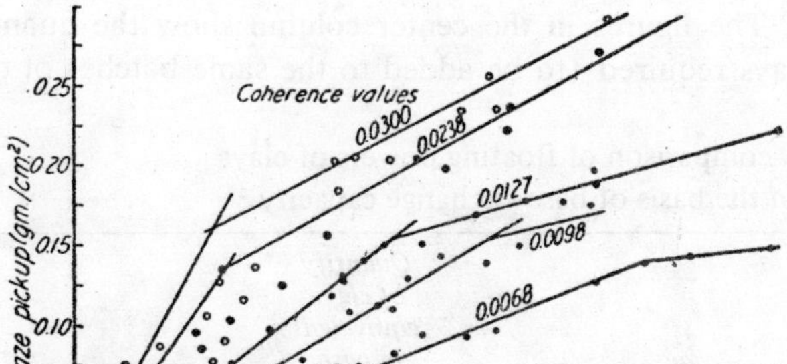

Figure 4.7. Receptive value of glaze.

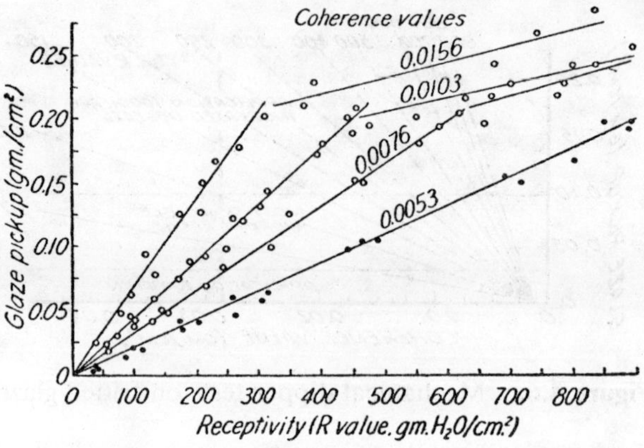

Figure 4.8. Receptive value of glaze.[20]

adhesive properties. It is possible to obtain widely different consistency values for the slip by the judicious choice of clay. If ball clay is the only clay used, the slip will have relatively low viscosity; Florida kaolin will give a medium viscosity and North Carolina kaolin gives a high viscosity.[21] By the judicious choice of clays the use of electrolytes may be minimized or eliminated and certain defects, such as cracking, peeling, and dusting, avoided.

It is extremely important to have a dependable guide for selecting a clay best suited for use in a slip or glaze. In addition to the necessary prerequisites of suitable color, freedom from objectionable impurities, and proper degree of fineness, it has been proposed[22] that the flocculating or deflocculating, as well as other important physical properties of clays, may be rated on base exchange capacities. The author illustrates his proposal in table 4.6. The figures in the center column show the quantities of the respective clays required (to be added to the same batches of the same in-

Table 4.6. A comparison of floating powers of clays on the basis of base exchange capacity.[22]

Kind of clay	*Quantity of clays equivalent in base exchange capacity*	*Exchange capacity M.E./100 gm clay*
Florida	12 parts	8
Valendar	7 parts	14
X-Clay	3 parts	33
Bentonite	1.2 parts	80

gredients) to yield slips having the same dipping consistencies—assuming that the conditions of grinding, the time and temperature of aging, and the quantities of water are alike and from the same source.

Mobility and Yield Value

The degree of flocculation of the colloids in the slip is subject to control by the amount and character of the electrolytes present or added. Any condition which promotes solution in the slip—such as standing for several hours, days, or weeks, finer grinding, heating, fermentation, chemical action of low forms of vegetable life, chemical action induced by the action of light—will influence the development and conduct of the dispersoids. In general, an increase of flocculation either by the amount or kind of clay added, or the effect of suitable electrolytes, will increase the yield value.

Mobility may be increased by an increase in the water content (fig. 4.9), by the use of suitable electrolytes, i.e., those which cause deflocculation, and by heating, aging, and by finer grinding. Fetterolf[23] found that aging increased the alkalinity and thereby the degree of flocculation, altering the yield value and mobility (fig. 4.10). The conduct of a glaze composition will generally display peculiarities which are attributable to the choice of the raw materials, method of preparation, and even the water supply.

Schramm[24] summarizes the conduct of a particular glaze slip in this way:

"An acid like acetic or an acid salt like aluminum sulfate caused a setting-up (i.e., a flocculation) chiefly through lowering the mobility with little or no effect on yield value; borax, and especially calcium hydrate, increased the yield value and mobility. With a reagent of

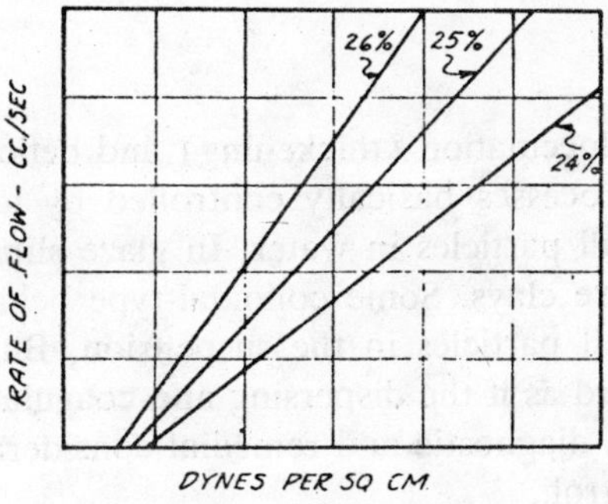

Figure 4.9. Effect of increase in water content.[23]

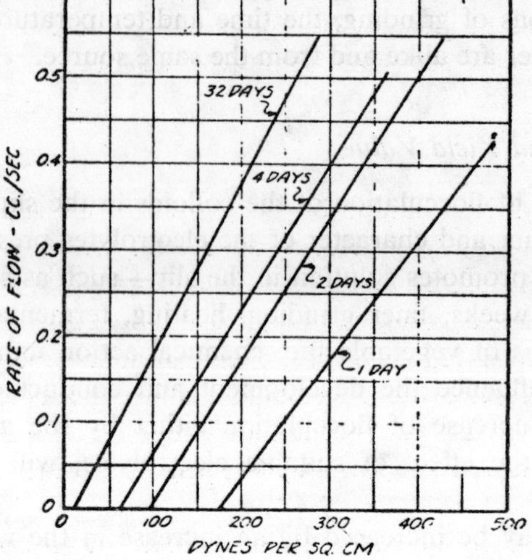

Figure 4.10. Effect of aging on relative viscosity and surface tension of a selected terra cotta glaze slip.[23]

the former type, the glaze does not flow readily because of the low mobility, but neither does it adhere tenaciously to the ware, owing to its low yield value. Glazes of low yield value can be applied only at higher specific gravity. The effect produced by borax or lime is more favorable because the high mobility promotes the necessary flow of the excess glaze, whereas the high yield value gives a tenaciously adherent thin layer. These reagents must be ground in the charge to obtain the full effect. If used in an excessive amount, the glaze may set up to a paste entirely unfit for use. Something of this nature has been observed with the first charge from a newly lined mill, the glaze taking up lime from the cement used in setting the blocks. The addition of a little water glass is effective in counteracting excessive gelation."

Electrolytes

MECHANISM. Flocculation (thickening) and deflocculation (thinning) of glaze slips are processes basically controlled by ion adsorption at the surfaces of very small particles in water. In glaze slips, the predominantly active constituents are clays. Some colloidal-type behavior is exercised by other extremely small particles in the suspension. But by considering the behavior in this regard as if the dispersing and coagulating properties were the same as for clay, diagnostic and remedial considerations can be simplified for practical control.

Clay may be regarded as a surface-active colloid or suspensoid. Because of the structural constitution of clay, surface charges exist in clay due to partially unused negative charges on the very last oxygen in the silicate particle. This leaves clays negatively charged.

These negative residual structural charges in the surfaces of clay attract positively charged ions (cations) from the aqueous environment. Clay, being cationic-active, attracts and adsorbs cations. The cations most likely to be of importance in flocculation and deflocculation in glaze slips are: H^+, Na^+, K^+, Mg^{++}, Ca^{++}, Ba^{++}, and Al^{+++}. Other ions and molecular groups also are of importance.

In simplified terms, when the charges on the adsorbed ions become exactly neutralized, an isoelectric point is reached and maximum flocculation or coagulation would occur. When the adsorbed ion retains a high charge, even after being adsorbed, a deflocculation state is created in the slip. When the degree of adsorption is so high as to tend to neutralize the charge on the adsorbed ion, flocculation occurs.

These behaviors are indirect. The adsorbed ions attract and orient a swarm of water molecules about them. The oxygen ends of the water molecules point toward the adsorbed cations. The positive end of the water dipole, the position of the two hydrogens, is oriented away from the point of adsorption. The two hydrogens in the solvated water molecules form the sites for a secondary water molecule attraction, and so on. This is a simplified picture of solvation.

The field strengths about ions are to a great extent related to the valence of the ions divided by their ionic radii. Thus, large monovalent ions, such as sodium, have a relatively weak field strength and are weakly adsorbed, retaining much of their charge even after being adsorbed. The small ions are more strongly adsorbed than the large ones. For example, a hydrogen ion may be adsorbed with 93% of its field strength, leaving 7% of its charge for solvation and the like. This is compared with 80% for sodium, leaving it 20% ionized after adsorption.

So, in general, large monovalent ions like NH_4^+, K^+, and Na^+ cause deflocculation. The strong ions like H^+, Mg^{++}, Ca^{++}, Al^{3+}, etc., cause flocculation.

For many purposes, it is convenient to consider surface-active particles as polyvalent acids in which the surface-sensitive particle is a large anion surrounded by a swarm of adsorbed cations. The large ions are not so strongly attracted and so form thin suspensions, unless the large ions are in great excess. The only ions like this are Na^+, K^+, Li^+, and NH_4^+.

All other ions, such as H^+, Ca^{++}, Mg^{++}, Al^{3+}, Fe^{3+}, etc., characteristically "set up" or thicken the slips. Apparently the main effect of the anions (OH^-, Cl^-, SO_4^{--}, etc.) seems to be that of influencing the general ionization equilibrium in the aqueous medium.

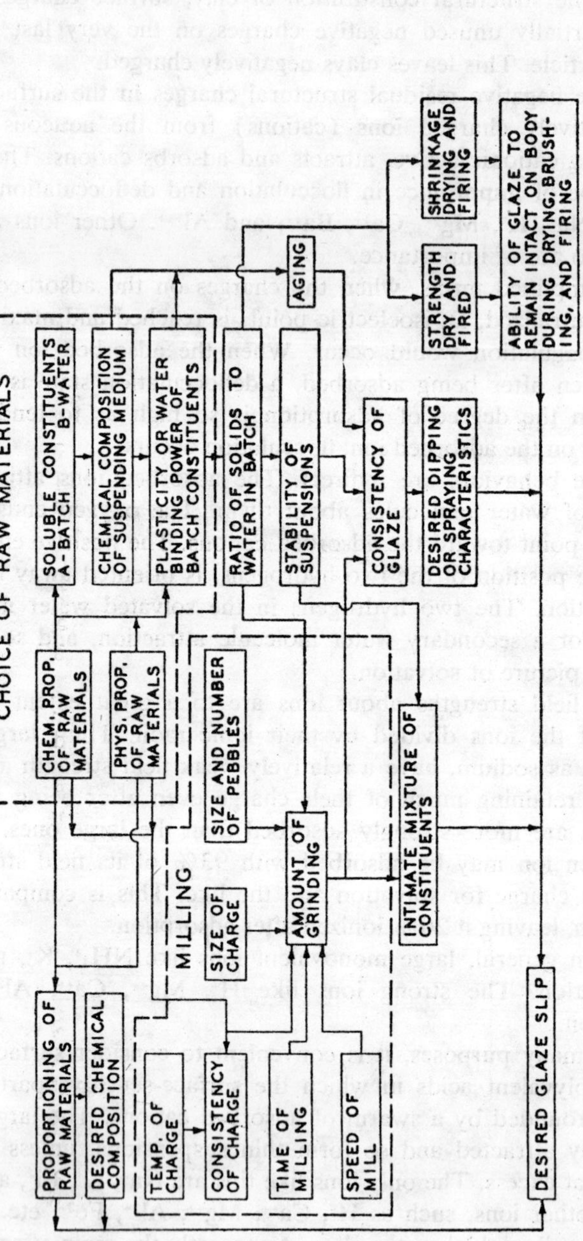

Figure 4.11. Control of glaze consistency.

The addition of NaCl to water ionizes to give equal amounts of $Na^+ + OH^-$ and $H^+ + Cl^-$. This is tantamount to an addition of HCl because the degree of adsorption of H^+ is so very much stronger than that of Na^+ that the effect is about the same as if the Na were not there. Hence, NaCl is a strong flocculant.

The salt of any strong acid and an alkali cation cause flocculation. Deflocculation occurs in basic solutions, usually best at pH values of around 8–9, provided the solution is not rich in divalent and trivalent cations. For example, an alkaline solution of $Ca(OH)_2$ has strong flocculating action, in spite of the high pH.

DEFLOCCULANTS. The effects produced by the presence of electrolytes in a glaze will vary according to the amount and kind of the reagents used, the clays in the slip, the fineness of the grinding, and the duration of the aging, if any. Among the deflocculants which have been used we find water solutions of gum arabic, sodium silicate, soda ash, the carbonate of potassium, the sodium and potassium hydroxides, and sodium phosphates.

Fetterolf[23] found that gum arabic used in amounts ranging from 0.1% to 0.3% of the dry weight of the glaze acted like a deflocculant in decreasing the yield value of a glaze but unlike it in decreasing the mobility, which he suggests is due to the increase in viscosity attributable to the addition of the gum. The gum dispersoid suspended in water carries a negative charge and acts as a "protective colloid which either nullifies the effect of increasing alkalinity of the glaze or, by adsorption on the surfaces of the particles of solids, prevents the solution of salts soluble in water."

Other organic substances may have important effects upon the colloids as deflocculants. Some of these are tannic acid and tannates, gallic acid, the water extract of some dark ball clays, glue and gums and the products of organic fermentation, solution of soap, feldspar, glass, frits and sodium carboxymethylcellulose.

FLOCCULANTS. The flocculating reagents commonly used are acetic acid and acid salts, magnesium oxide and certain carbonates, lime, calcium borate, plaster of Paris, phenol (carbolic acid), the water extracts of some clays, sodium chloride, calcium chloride, complex organic polyelectrolytes, and magnesium sulfate, to mention a few.

In general, mobility decreases and yield value increases with finer grinding[25]; however, the solubility of a frit will increase as the individual particle is reduced in size, and a contrary effect may be observed as noted by Schramm and Sherwood[2] who report that, when a certain frit was ground first alone, the unfritted portion of the batch being added toward the end of the operation, the glaze was found more fluid than if the whole had been ground together. They suggest that a considerable amount (relatively) of alkali has been dissolved from the finer frit which produces a greater degree of deflocculation. Apparently the clay and other raw ingredients added later do not absorb this alkali to counteract the effect, although when added in the beginning they do.

Cooke[15] has reported the following effects of chemically equivalent quantities of inorganic salts upon the mobility and yield value of enamel slips:

Salts which increase the yield value slightly without changing the mobility: sodium chloride, sodium carbonate, sodium acetate, sodium thiosulfate, ammonium chloride, and ammonium carbonate
Salts which increase the yield value without changing the mobility: borax, acetic acids, and aluminum chloride
Salts which increase the yield value enormously and reduce the mobility: magnesium sulfate, barium chloride, and calcium chloride
Sodium silicate reduced the yield value to zero and decreased the mobility; sodium phosphate does likewise

These results were had with vitreous enamel slip compositions and are assumed to be true, in a greater or less degree, of glaze compositions.

The selection of a correct consistency for a glaze will depend upon the method of application and the condition of the ware. The procedure to be used may be either of two possible methods:[26] (*a*) the glaze may be heated and its thinning out thus completed at once, after which the viscosity can be brought up to gage by the addition of electrolyte, or (*b*) the glaze may be made several days in advance of its use and then treated with electrolyte.

Adhesives and Suspension Agents

The suspension of the glaze ingredients in the glaze slip for several hours or even days is a highly important objective usually attained more or less perfectly: (1) by the kind and amount of clay used—ball clay will be more effective than kaolin; and (2) the physical form and fineness of the other ingredients, e.g., zinc oxide is a good flotative agent.

Sometimes the limitations of the composition prevent the use of the obviously desirable materials and resort must be made to the use of substances which are particularly serviceable for this purpose. Aside from the highly colloidal clays, such as ball clay, bentonite, and the less efficient secondary kaolins, also some of the inorganic glaze ingredients, e.g., magnesium carbonate, the most successful reagents for promoting suspension and adhesion are organic colloids. The list is quite long and includes the gums, starch and associated materials, glue and gelatin, sodium alginate, polyvinyl alcohol, the white of an egg, a decoction of quince pips, glucose, sugar syrups, blood, and probably other organic substances less generally known.

Common Gums

The gums most commonly used in glazes are gum arabic, gum tragacanth, and gum karaya. The first named is the most expensive and differs from the others in being readily soluble in water, whereas the others dissolve less completely but swell very greatly. Gum arabic dissolves slowly in twice its weight of water, and precipitates separate and settle, if solutions of certain salts of metal bases are added. A recommended method for the preparation of the gum for use in glaze slips is 3% of gum based on weight of the glaze batch soaked in cold water for several hours, brought to a boil, and passed through a coarse lawn (e.g., 40-mesh). The direct introduction of the gum into the glaze slip is impracticable, since it will form separations of sticky masses.

There are many gums and several grades and variations of each. Some of them are shown in figure 4.12 in a comparison of the viscosities of their water solutions. A considerable background of up-to-date information concerning natural and synthetic gums and polymers is to be had from commercial suppliers.

GUM ARABIC. The deflocculating action of gum arabic has been noted and is said to increase slightly with time. Brown[28] recommends from 0.02% to 0.3% as usually being effective in preventing wall-splitting. On the other hand Fetterolf,[23] studying a terra cotta glaze, found that gum arabic apparently gave protection against deflocculation by moderate amounts of alkaline salts, and stabilized the consistency. The gum arabic acted similarly to alkaline deflocculants only insofar as it affected yield value. Gum glazes were less susceptible to flocculation than were gumless glazes. Under some circumstances gum arabic and dextrin act as flocculants.

GUM TRAGACANTH is prepared for use by soaking in water for several hours or until it has ceased swelling. It is then boiled for a few minutes and passed through a 40-mesh sieve. Specific directions are as follows:[29] Six grams of the gum are added to 500 cc of cold water, soaked overnight, boiled 15 min., made up to 1,000 cc, poured through a 40-mesh sieve, and cooled before using. For 1 unit of dry weight of the glaze, 1 unit to 1½ units of gum solution should be put in the mill and ground with the

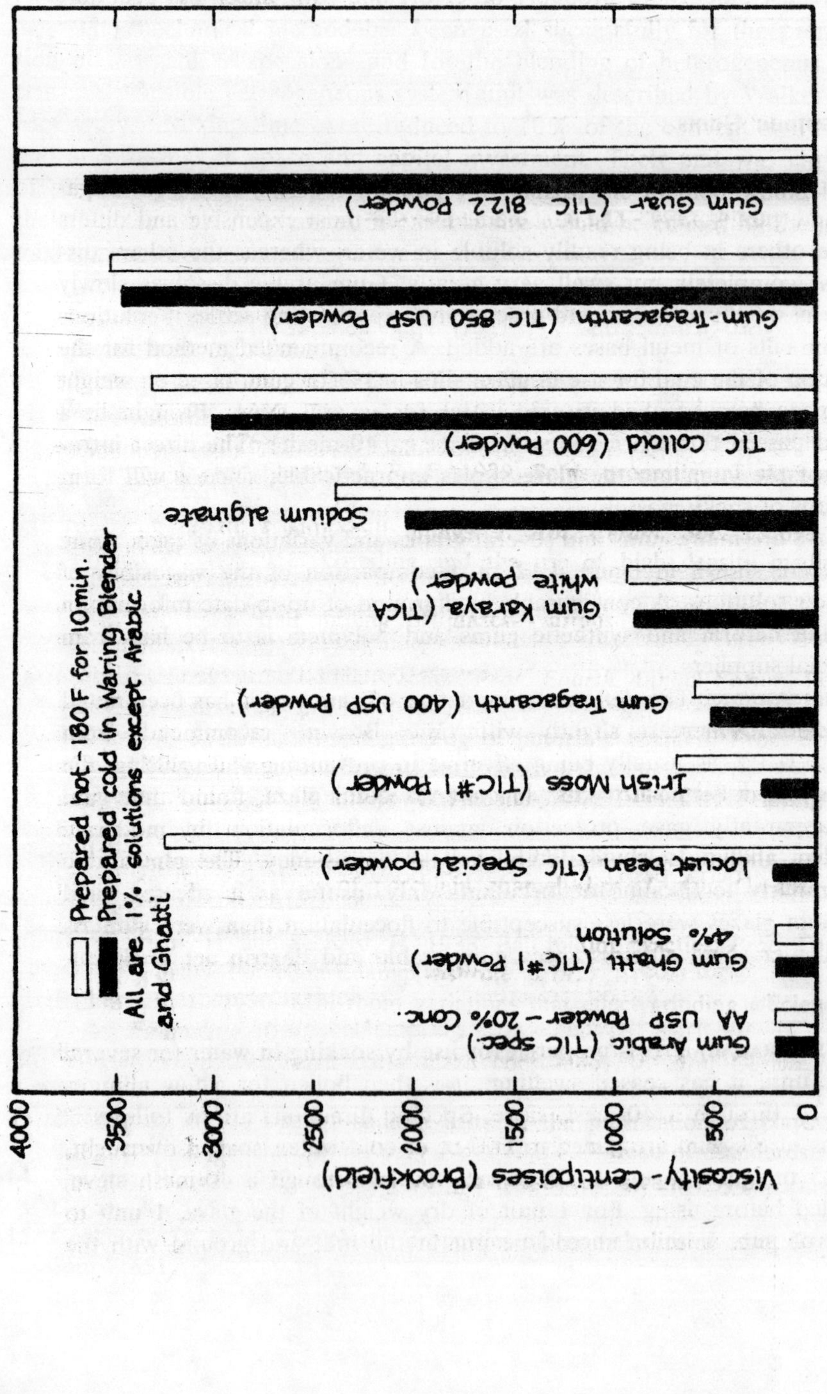

Figure 4.12. Comparison of viscosities of solutions of water soluble gums.[21] *Note:* TIC designation refers to Tragacanth Importing Corp.

glaze. (A portion of the gum solution may be reserved for the washing of the balls and the mill after the grinding operation.)

The gums which swell to considerable bulk, such as tragacanth and karaya, increase the bulk and promote suspension but may reduce the specific gravity of the slip.

GUM KARAYA acts like gum tragacanth and may be substituted for the same. The preparation is similar both as to the proportions of gum and water, and the soaking and heating, but the karaya yields a stringy suspension. The addition of a small amount of gum arabic is said to improve the adhesive properties.

DEXTRIN is made by roasting flour or starch and is completely soluble in water, forming a neutral solution. It is cheaper than the gums previously mentioned and is described by Foster[29] as a fair suspension and adhesive agent. The addition of about 3% of dextrin to the glaze batch is usually sufficient.

GELATIN is a product obtained by refining the glue rendered from bones and skins of animals. It is completely soluble in relatively small amounts of water. An important use of the material is in the compositions of glazes which are to be applied by painting large surfaces. Also gelatin is a very desirable addition to glazes which are to be applied on a fired glaze or similar vitreous surface. Each separate coating should be permitted to dry before another coat is applied. A light coat of glaze containing gelatin may be spread over the ware by brushing and, after drying, a heavy coat of the glaze, without gelatin, may be sprayed onto this. There is sometimes an advantage in applying a coating of gelatin, dextrin, or starch to the surface of green or highly porous ware before the application of the glaze. Foster's[29] directions for preparation are: 1 part of gelatin is dissolved in 4 parts of water, and added 1 part by volume to 6 parts by volume of the glaze which had previously been ground and set at 58 oz to 60 oz weight per quart.

CORN STARCH is available in several forms, each of which has some unique applications.

Ultrasonic Processing

Ultrasonic energy may be considered as a possible means for the agitation of glaze slips instead of the usual ball mill. In this type of system the ultrasonic energy is generated through transduced piezoelectric crystal vibrations.[30] There are other techniques in which the ultrasonic vibrations can be generated mechanically.[31]

The mechanical method has been used successfully for the preparation of inorganic suspensions and for the blending of heterogeneous systems. A plausible heterogeneous system unit was described by Walker and McCarthy.[32] Mixing times were reduced to 10% of the conventional times and at a savings in space and capital investment. Their unit was capable of processing 50 gallons per minute. For glazes, the method would have the advantage that no changes in particle size would be caused by the glaze mixing process.

References

1. Walker, F. W. 1900. The mechanical preparation of glazes. *Trans. Am. Ceram. Soc.* 2:126.
2. Schramm, E. and Sherwood, R. F. 1929. Some properties of glaze slips. *J. Am. Ceram. Soc.* 12:270.
3. Twells, R. 1930. Pebble mill linings. *J. Am. Ceram. Soc.* 13:699.
4. Perkins, W. W. 1956. Grinding and the use of high density media. *J. Can. Ceram. Soc.*, 25:7–17.
5. Davis, H. 1953. Ball milling of glazes—various grinding media. *Bull. Am. Ceram. Soc.* 32(6):209.
6. Sechrist, H. 1939. Ball Mill Practice. *Proc. Fourth Annual Forum,* Porcelain Enamel Institute, p 136.
7. Fellows, R. L. Ball mill wet grinding of porcelain enamels. Proc. Fourth Annual Forum, Porcelain Enamel Institute, p 147.
8. Andrews, A. I. 1935. *Enamels.* Champaign, Ill.: Twin City Printing Co. p 230.
9. Fellows, R. L. and McLaughlin, J. L. 1939. Study of milling and its effects on the properties of porcelain enamel slips. *J. Am. Ceram. Soc.* 22:260.
10. Burnham, A. H. and Sechrist, H. 1938. Ball milling practice, *Proc. Fourth Annual Forum,* Porcelain Enamel Institute, p 79.
11. Fellows, R. L. 1930. Mill room variations that effect grinding efficiencies. *Better Enameling* 10:9.
12. Spurrier, H. 1929. Terra cotta glaze consistency. *J. Am. Ceram. Soc.* 12:577.
13. Bleininger, A. V. Use of sodium salts in the purification of clays and in the casting process. *Tech. Paper No. 51,* U.S. Bureau of Standards.
14. Shearer, Walter 1922. Control of plasticities of ceramic slips. *J. Am. Ceram. Soc.* 15:622.
15. Cooke, R. D. 1924. The plastic properties of enamel slips. *J. Am. Ceram. Soc.* 7:651.

16. Harrison, W. N. 1927. Controlling the consistency of enamel slips. Tech. paper no. 356, U.S. Bureau of Standards. Also, *J. Am. Ceram. Soc.* 10:970.
17. Bleininger, A. V. and Brown, G. H. 1908. Note on the viscosity of clay slips (Stormer viscosimeter). *Trans. Am. Ceram. Soc.* 11:596.
18. MacMichael, R. F. 1915. Testing of clay. *Trans. Am. Ceram. Soc.* 17:639.
19. McIntyre, G. H. and Irwin, J. T. 1932. Application of the Gardner mobilometer to enamel slip consistency studies and controls. *J. Am. Ceram. Soc.* 15:433.
20. Harman, C. G., Schaefer, C. F., Blanchard, M. K., and Johnson, H. C. 1944. Study of factors involved in glaze-slip control, 1–4. *J. Am. Ceram. Soc.* 27:202.
21. Twells, Robert 1924. Preparing and spraying a glaze glip with especial reference to the control of the various operations. *J. Am. Ceram. Soc.* 7:465.
22. Harman, C. G. 1939. Concept of unit clay as an aid to glaze slip control. *Bull. Am. Ceram. Soc.* 18:332.
23. Fetteroff, L. D. 1930. A study of the consistencies of raw terra cotta glazes. *J. Am. Ceram. Soc.* 13:675.
24. Schramm, Edward 1938. Problems in whiteware glazes. *Bull. Am. Ceram. Soc.* 17:436.
25. Harrison, W. N. 1927. Vitreous enamel slips and their control. *J. Am. Ceram. Soc.* 10:970.
26. Bowman, Jas. R. 1927. Studies of the changes in the viscosity of clay slips and glaze suspensions on ageing and by treatment with electrolytes. *J. Am. Ceram. Soc.* 10:508.
27. Tragacanth Importing Corp. *Water soluble gums.* New York, N.Y., p. 24.
28. Brown, Lawrence H. 1934. Preparing of slips and glazes for the best results. *Ceramic Industry* 22:376.
29. Foster, E. S. 1929. Organic agents as aids to the adhesion and suspension of glazes. *J. Am. Ceram. Soc.* 12:264.
30. Hueter, T. F. and Bolt, R. H. 1955. *Sonics: Techniques for the use of sound and ultrasound in engineering and science.* New York: John Wiley & Sons, Inc.
31. Jacobs, J. 1958. Ultrasonic processing. In Clark, G. L. and Hawley, G. G. eds. *Encyclopedia of chemistry supplement.* New York: Reinhold Pub. Corp., p 300.
32. Walker, N. H. and McCarthy, W. W. 1967. Ultrasonic, dispersion of clay bodies. *Bull. Am. Ceram. Soc.* 46(2):188–90.

5

Application

The methods used for the application of glazes to ware may be grouped under three general heads—wet, powder, and gaseous. The first includes all methods by which the solid suspension of the glaze materials in water (or other fluids) is applied on the ware. The powder process is carried out by dusting the dry glaze on the slightly damp ware or rolling the damp piece in contact with dry powder. The powder methods are very old and little used at this time. The gaseous process is accomplished by exposing the ware to an atmosphere of volatile substances during the firing process. The most familiar example is the salt glazing process.

Another instance is the fuming of lead from the interior walls of saggers washed with a lead-containing composition. By using this expedient the ware, coated with a lead-containing glaze slip and placed in the sagger, is surrounded during firing by an atmosphere of lead fumes contributed in part by the wash and, therefore, the glaze is not robbed of its gloss. Numerous examples of this important phenomenon and its harmful or beneficial effects may be observed by the ceramist.

Mention should be made of the self-glazing of certain clays which may be traced to the presence of soluble salts drawn to the surface by capillary action during the drying and in the early stages of firing. If the deposit is in sufficient quantity and of a suitable character a glassy film or sheen appears on the surface.

The wet processes are those most widely used and most dependable, producing the desired thickness and uniformity of the completed coating. The various methods employed are: (*a*) painting, (*b*) pouring, (*c*) immersion, (*d*) spraying, and (*e*) contact transfer.

Painting

The technique of painting glazes on ware does not differ essentially from that commonly employed on other materials. It is an ancient process still widely employed by primitive artists. Craftsmen and artists of the more advanced cultures use the method to produce special effects, or to meet some special need; e.g., large, cumbersome pieces of ware cannot be immersed as small pieces are commonly treated. Bathtubs and similar wares were formerly painted. Spraying has very generally superseded painting for many such operations.

Pouring

Pouring is also an old and obsolete practice of the ceramic industry. Prior to the beginning of this century, it was the custom in the wall-tile industry to place several wall tiles in a shallow tray and pour the glaze over the exposed faces. After the glaze had become firm; the individual tiles were carefully separated and the edges trimmed, i.e., fettled. This was slow and costly. The method is sometimes necessary in order to coat large interior surfaces not otherwise readily accessible. Flow coating of tile is an accepted method today. Tile is conveyed through a waterfall of glaze on a continuous belt. Edges are automatically brushed of excess glaze if necessary.

Immersion or Dipping

Immersion or dipping is the method which has been most commonly used particularly for pieces which are of a size and shape which can be manipulated with one or two hands. Pieces as large as closet bowls and tanks are about the limiting sizes for the operation. The simplicity of the necessary apparatus and the ease and convenience of moving it about as necessary have tended to perpetuate the practice. However, spraying is being substituted in many plants in all branches of the industry where there is a sufficient production of pieces of a similar size, shape, and condition. Continuous, automatic dipping is practiced in Europe. Several machines have been perfected to do this.

Success in dipping depends upon experience, judgment, and good timing in the operation since the consistency of the slip must be regulated according to the condition of the ware, i.e., whether unfired, porous, or vitreous; the shape and size of the ware; and the duration of immersion. Porous wares differing in thickness must be treated differently. These conditions should be studied by the use of representative trial pieces dipped to different thicknesses in different consistencies and fired at the widest variations of the kiln temperatures which may be expected. Records should be made of the densities and the consistencies found permissible. Frequent stirring and occasional testing of the density of the glaze slip must be done during the dipping, although the potter is inclined to rely upon his observation as to whether the slip adheres to his fingers or flows off.

Porous Ware

The capillary structure, which is characteristic of the porous ware, acts like a piece of wicking absorbing water when the ware is immersed in the slip, the solid material being retained on the surface. Therefore, the density of the slip should be relatively low (about 1.40 sp. gr.) and the fluidity high. In all cases, the part of the porous ware which first comes in contact with the glaze slip should be the first to emerge. Too long contact between the glaze and the ware results in an unduly thick coating, and too short a dipping time yields too thin a layer.

Too prolonged a contact of the ware and slip in the dipping tub may be followed by a softening of the deposited layer and an uneven coat. Since there is a certain proportion between the thickness of the piece and the thickness of coating deposited in a given time, a thin piece will absorb less water than a thick one and the deposit of glaze material will be less; therefore, very thin, porous ware should be dipped in thicker glaze than ordinary. Inequalities of thickness of the ware, or of the porosity, may cause differences in the thickness of the matured glaze. The thickness of the glaze on the edges will be less than elsewhere and care should be taken to prevent thicker accumulation by drainage of the glaze to the depressed center of flat pieces.

Very soft biscuit which has been fired at a low temperature will be very absorbent, and the consistency of the glaze should be chosen to prevent the formation of an excessively thick glaze layer, or the biscuit may be saturated with water before dipping. Pinholes and blisters are less likely to occur on wares having a high permeability because the pores have sufficiently large diameters to permit the ready displacement of the air contained therein. The harder fired ware with the smaller capillaries shows these faults much more frequently.

Green, i.e., unfired, ware cannot be successfully dipped unless it is thick walled and the density of the glaze is relatively high. Shearer[1] states that the glaze should have a low plasticity, and the more nearly deflocculated it is, the more smoothly it dips and the less frequently crawling occurs. He reports that glaze specific gravities of approximately 1.62 were used satisfactorily in coating electrical porcelain and dry-pressed specialties.

Vitreous Ware

Vitreous, i.e., nonabsorbent, ware retains the glaze coating by surface adhesion, and thick slips having high specific gravities are necessary. Two examples of many which have been cited in literature are 1.63 for vitreous sanitary ware and 1.74 for vitreous tableware. It is obvious that the nature and the proportions of the glaze components, as well as the methods of preparation and control of consistency, will be responsible for considerable variations in the specific gravities of glazes applied on wares which are vitrified or even of low but similar porosities.

In general, it may be stated that the consistency of the glaze must be chosen after trial, since the results will be dependent upon the variables mentioned. Glazes prepared for dipping are neither completely dispersed nor completely deflocculated. Uniformity of coverage is of first importance so the degree of mobility (fluidity) is chosen with respect to the size and design of the ware; i.e., cups and hollow ware require a thinner glaze layer, therefore a slip having a lower specific gravity is employed and additional flocculating agents are added to regulate the running off. Glazes used on flat ware must have considerable fluidity to insure even distribution, but the tendency to run off is less.[2]

The glaze used in coating hollow ware is somewhat thinner and must be emptied out of the piece promptly as soon as the inside is uniformly coated. An extra thick accumulation may be the cause of crazing at that particular place. Also, such irregularities are harmful to the decorations where they are thus covered. In emptying the piece the dipper must shake the piece well when it is inverted to get rid of drops which otherwise will cling to the rim. The contact of the fingers of the dipper with the surface of the piece must be manipulated so that no part of the surface to be glazed is thus continuously covered, but every part has a fair opportunity to be brought in contact with the slip. Dippers of flat pieces use a thumb-stall terminating in a hooked piece of wire to slip over the rim of the piece which is supported also by the fingers on the opposite side. The piece is then dexterously passed through the slip and the excess thrown off the edges. Automatic dipping is not practiced with vitreous wares where speed of production is necessary. However, in large pieces specially devised jigs which rotate ware properly to get even glaze application are in use.

Spraying

The principle of the process of applying glazes by spraying is the mechanical atomization of the glaze slip and its impingement upon the surface of the ware. The Chinese are said to have obtained similar results on a small scale by blowing glaze slip through a tube covered at one end by cloth of fine mesh. The outstanding advantages of the simplicity and portability of the modern apparatus, the speed of operation, the easy control and regulation of the distribution have resulted in the wide application of this method where the size and shape of the wares permit the operation to be made automatic, e.g., to spark plugs, brick, and much pottery. Spraying is the most practicable manner of applying glazes to architectural terra cotta.

The equipment required is a spray gun or sprayer, a reservoir for the glaze slip, a support for the piece of ware, and usually a booth or hood for drawing off the unused atomized spray and thus protecting the operator.

Spray Guns

Spray guns, sprayers, atomizers, or airbrushes, as the smaller sizes are called by the decorators, vary widely in size and design, but they all operate according to the same simple principle, namely the rapid flow, at high pressure, of a stream of gas across the open end of a tube through which a liquid may be fed that will disperse the latter and eject it as a fine spray. The glaze slip may be supplied to the spray head by gravity, or, in small atomizers, by suction through the tube which dips below the level of the liquid in the container used for the supply. The design of the sprayer or spray head provides a central opening through which the glaze is fed with an annular opening surrounding this orifice to permit the passage of the high-pressure airstream.

The desirable characteristics of a spray-gun head are simplicity of design, ease in cleaning, convenience in making adjustments and replacement of worn parts, and high resistance to wear. Figure 5.1 is an illustration of the assembly of a spray-gun head on which the several parts are named.

Spray Patterns

The normal pattern formed by the impact of the cone of spray issuing from such a head is a circular area. If a flat spray is desired it may be

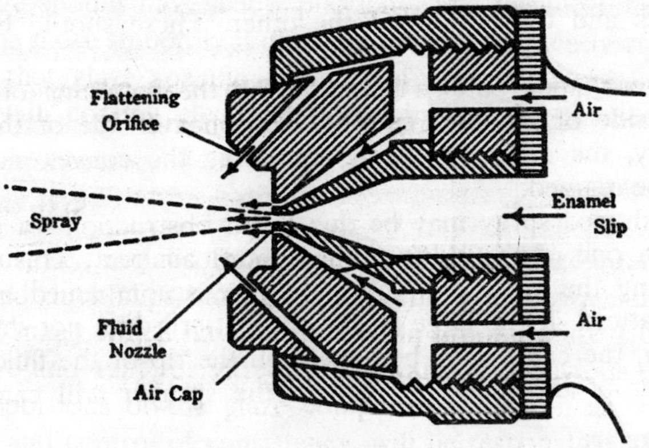

Figure 5.1. Spray gun head.[3]

had by regulating the air gap so that streams of air are directed through the orifices on two sides of the cone, causing the flattening of the slip stream. Various patterns which may be had by design or accident are shown in figure 5.2. Andrews[3] has listed some of the causes of these patterns as follows:

1. An elliptical pattern may be due to the wear of the atomizing port, and a new fluid nozzle and air cap will be needed.
2. A split spray may be due to defects on the atomizing port which should be reamed to a perfect circle. The enlargement of the flattening ports by wear will cause the same defect.
3. An S-shaped pattern is caused by a burr on the top of one of the flatten-

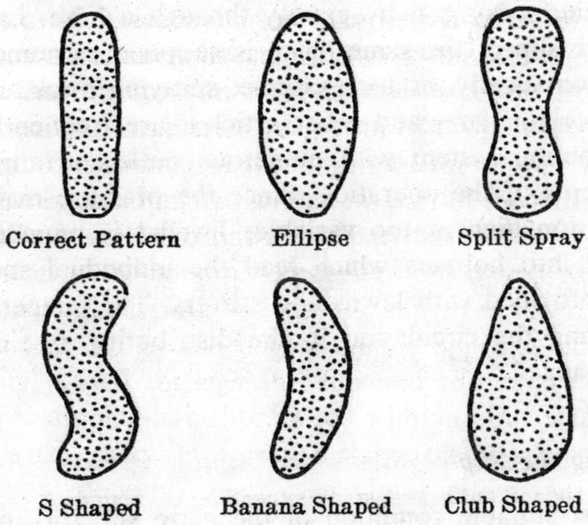

Figure 5.2. Spray gun patterns.[3]

ing ports and the bottom of the other. These should be removed by reaming.

4. A banana-shaped pattern is caused by the flattening of the air ports. The outside of the port causing the concave side of the bow and, if necessary, the inside of the port causing the convex side of the bow should be reamed.
5. A club-shaped spray may be due to an obstruction—a burr or a particle—on one of the sides of the central air port. This may be tested by turning the air cap which should be accompanied by the rotation of the pattern. If the large end of the pattern does not shift in the same direction, the cause may be a burr on the tip of the fluid nozzle. Poor alignment of the fluid nozzle with the sprayer will cause the defect.

Other defects are:

1. Spattering may be caused by an improperly secured nozzle or air cap, a hose connection, or a loose needle valve.
2. Spitting may be due to any of the causes listed for spattering as well as defective packing, loose packing nuts, or coarse or foreign particles in the slip.
3. Insufficient pressure on the air or feed line will give a ragged spray pattern.

Reservoirs

The reservoirs from which the slip is supplied to the spray guns are of different types according to the needs of the installation. The simplest form is a small container which is an integral part of the sprayer. For larger volume the reservoir may be a tank or hopper suspended overhead and feeding the spray gun by gravity through a hose. Large installations in which glaze slip of the same batch is supplied to numerous spray guns operating automatically, as for example, spraying brick, spark-plug cores, electrical porcelain parts and other articles, are frequently provided with a pipe distributing system with numerous outlets arranged according to the requirements of the operation. Since the pressure maintained in these lines may be too high or too variable, Twells[4] recommends that the slip be drawn off into hoppers which feed the individual spray guns. These hoppers are provided with lawns and stirrers. The temperature of the slip may rise during the circulation in the distributing system, and the consistency be changed.

Balancing the Slip

The most suitable condition of the glaze slip for application on the body should be determined by trial which will include the appearance of the glaze after firing. After satisfactory results have been obtained, these data should be recorded and, thereafter, the slip should be maintained at the specific gravity determined, altering the consistency if necessary by the addition of electrolytes. The yield values of the slip will be high. A slip which is too "heavy" does not contain enough water, or the amount of acid electrolyte present is too high. Such a glaze slip will show a tendency to settle in the hoppers and form a heavy spray coating which will dust when dry and the coat will be rough and spongy.

The inevitable loss by evaporation from the slip before application is usually safely compensated by direct addition of water. Slip which contains too much water or too much alkali electrolyte will flow irregularly and bead. It should be noted that variations in consistency may be due sometimes to variations in the blunging conditions, kind of clay, or some other materials substituted without adequate preliminary testing. A decrease may be traceable, in some cases, to aging which may be corrected by the use of electrolytes, but the results will not be as satisfactory, according to Twells.

A freshly made slip will not give as good results as one properly aged. This may be due in part, in his opinion, to the presence of air. Fermentation and the consequent chemical changes are always an important factor in the consistency conditions. Wilson[5] has reported that a glaze containing low clay, high carbonates of the alkaline earths, zinc oxide, and feldspar is more easily altered in viscosity by addition of electrolytes than one containing high clay.

Dextrin, gum arabic, gum tragacanth, and some other organic substances are useful additions to the glaze to promote adhesion in the dry state and prevent dusting, but the consistency of the slip will not be as readily altered then by the introduction of electrolytes. These substances act as stabilizers of the colloids or suspensoids. It is much better to develop the desired consistency by correct procedure in the process of preparation than to be obliged to resort to the use of electrolytes at a later stage.

The pieces of ware are variously supported during the spraying, depending upon kind and size. Large, heavy pieces such as architectural terra cotta are supported on platforms which may be rotated. Sometimes these units are mounted on turntables. This latter device is also suited for small pieces of ware. Bricks may be carried by a conveying belt passing through the zone where the spray impinges on the individual pieces.

Wet and Dry Spraying

The techniques of "wet spraying" and "dry spraying" are described in the chapter on engobes. Wilson[5] summarized the relative advantages and disadvantages of the two systems, as related to their use with the highly viscous type of glazes applied on architectural terra cotta, briefly as follows:

1. Dry spraying is slower than wet spraying.
2. It takes a little practice and is not foolproof.
3. It gives excellent results in filling angles with heavy glaze without cracking. The glaze is added in a firm powder form to the dry underslip which has developed its drying cracks. This powder, containing so little water, will not crack on drying and is in a position to melt and fill up all the underslip and body cracks.
4. It requires a glaze which will develop and melt several cones below the finishing temperature; otherwise it may be dry and rough.
5. It is not applicable or necessary with those glazes whose viscosity is low during firing and which heal imperfections well.

A simple process frequently used in the stoneware industry to apply glazes on the interior of crocks is a hose nozzle outlet terminating a pressure line fed, usually, by a pump. The crock is inverted over the nozzle and the spray gushing from the nozzle as the pump is operated washes the interior walls of the ware. This same device is used in automatic spraying of hollow ware in the dinnerware industry. Hollow ware is inverted. Waterfall glaze coats the outside and the fountain spray coats the inside.

Mechanized Spraying

Automatic spraying of glazes is standard practice in large plants and for most high production. Of course, anything could be glazed by automatic or mechanized methods, but it is not always desirable to do so. In the first place, there may be technical reasons for not spraying; it may be desirable or necessary to dip, dust, paint, flame-spray, or some other process. In addition, certain other variables may be controlling, such as production rate, and cost of equipment. The entire subject was well summarized by Verba.[6] Much of the information immediately following was taken from his review.

TYPES OF MECHANIZED SPRAYING APPARATUS. In general there are four types of mechanized glazing concepts: (1) circular spindle type; (2) straight line spindle type; (3) straight line nonspindle type; and (4) the single or double spindle, nonconveyor type. There are supplementary devices that can go with or supplement the glazing machine to more fully mechanize the glazing system. These include preheating and after-heating facilities; a system for reclaiming and recirculating the glaze, wash units, moving guns, and other mechanical or electrical controls. Glaze recovery and reuse systems may or may not be desirable, depending on factors characteristic of the particular ware being processed. Machines would be equipped with either a washing or reclaiming system or even a dry type spray booth.

Usually the spray guns would be so mounted as to make them either stationary, oscillating, or reciprocating. The machines may contain multiple guns instead of one or two.

Machines are designed to glaze automatically any type of ware, vitreous, semivitreous, or unfired. In some cases, an engobe, undercoat, or preliminary coat may be applied before the final glaze. For glazing dinnerware, the circular type with revolving spindles is popular because of its flexibility and adaptability. Straight-line machines of the nonspindle type are preferred for flat ware such as wall tile.

Waterfall, airless spray, and electrostatic applications are also used, depending on the ware to be coated.

RECLAIMING GLAZE. With ware such as bisque dinnerware the system is commonly equipped for glaze reclaiming.

It may not be desirable to reclaim glazes in some cases. For example, in the spraying of some unfired ware such as porcelain insulators, fragments or pieces of broken porcelain may find their way into the overspray and thus contaminate the glazes. Whether or not to reclaim glazes depends upon the degree to which reclaiming can be done without contaminating the glaze with body or with other glazes.

PREHEATING. When practical, the ware is heated before reaching the spray guns so that the proper glaze layer can be applied without difficulty from glaze-runs, nonuniform application, crawling, or take-off. Direct flame application is popular, and so is separate heating before the ware reaches the spray booth.

SANITARY WARE. Sanitary ware is glazed automatically. Single or double automatic spindles with moving guns are used. Pieces are placed on the machine and removed manually. Some shops are fitted with conveyorized units.

WALL TILE. Tiles usually are conveyed through one or more booths on chains or belts. The edges of the tile are kept absolutely clean with proper adjustment of the guns or by cleaning belt devices.

Most machines have an off-bearing belt that runs faster than the conveyor through the booth to facilitate ware removal.

STRUCTURAL CLAY WARES. Glazed brick and hollow tile are glazed automatically. Glaze can be applied directly to a wet column immediately after cutting; or it can be applied to dried ware before firing.

In some installations, a hopper is situated directly above the die of the auger machine and feeds the glaze to a roller riding on the column before being cut.

Many brick and hollow tile plants spray three faces of the ware simultaneously. Some machines are equipped with special attachments to produce mottled and spotted effects.

Usually a circulating feed is used for glazed brick. The booths preferred are of the dry type and the overspray is immediately reclaimed.

ELECTRICAL PORCELAIN. Automatic glazing of electrical porcelain resembles that used in dinnerware. The work holder may contain a shield to prevent application of glaze to selected areas. Instead of, or in addition to, the work holder mask, portions of the ware may be precoated with wax.

ARTWARE. Some artware also is automatically glazed. Small pieces such as spark plugs conventionally are automatically glazed.

VITREOUS CHINAWARE. Some problems in connection with the use of mechanized spraying of vitreous chinaware have been discussed by Christensen and Schramm.[7] To start with, the wet glaze must be caused to cover, wet, and bond to the ware. Adequate adhesion is easily obtained using heavy slips. But these glazes could lack the flow properties required to distribute the deposit in a uniform layer. It is important to obtain uniform thickness on inside and outside surfaces without run-down in hollow pieces and thin zones on top edges.

To assist in overcoming this problem, ware is heated before the sprayed slip hits. It then remains on the dry side until the appropriate thickness is achieved. The ware should be dry enough to remove from the machine shortly after being sprayed. The combination of preheating, slip consistency, gun settings, and machine speed should be so adjusted that the glaze does not dry as soon as it hits. There must be some time for the glaze to smooth out by flowing.

The ideal glaze would contain a hardening agent and a deflocculant. The deflocculated slip is likely to settle out in the recovery tank. This must not be allowed. The slip must be so constituted that it will not settle out, but will yield a wet, flowed-out layer during spraying. This calls for a minimum degree of deflocculation and a moderate-to-light preheat temperature. Schramm and Christensen[7] advocate an additive based on methyl cellulose.

They report that glaze slips can be prepared that make it possible to operate the machine with results equivalent to dipping.

Electrostatic Spraying

Electrostatic spraying of glazes is accomplished by electrically grounding[8] the ware and spraying the slip in a polarizing electric field. Electromagnetic attraction causes all surfaces directly in the path of spray particles to be coated.

Waterfall Glazing

Waterfall glazing was developed in Europe in the tile industry and is now widely used. Tiles are placed on a conveyor, generally of two metal ribbons, and passed under the waterfall machine. Two layers of glaze are applied. Silk screening of patterns on the tile with up to three colors (at three consecutive stations) is practiced in Europe. Each color is dried between applications and the final station applies the glaze by waterfall. Most of the continuous decorating and glazing lines operate on bisque tile at the rate of 35–60 per minute. One-fire tile is decorated in the same manner, both underglaze and overglaze.

Airless Spray

Artware factories in Italy have developed an airless spray. A mist of glaze is created in an enclosure. Glaze is under pressure and forced through fine nozzles only via the pressure. The ware passing through the mist is glazed.

Silk-Screen Process

The silk-screen process is extensively employed for decorating glazed articles. It can be either manual or mechanized. The simplest setup consists of a frame, usually wood or aluminum, over which bolting cloth or fine wire gauze is stretched. The screen usually is 125 to 150 mesh.

A stencil is then placed on the screen and held taut by the frame; and varnish is applied to fill the area not covered by the design to be printed.

The color or colored glaze prepared to suitable paste consistency is pressed through the open parts of the screen by a roller or squeegee. The paste is called squeegee paste and the vehicle called squeegee oil. The pattern thus is stenciled onto the ware.

The stencil can be made by hand or photographically. An aid to this type of process is the collodion-film transfer and similar innovations.

A silk-screen process has been used with success to apply platinum decorations.[9] The paste used was prepared from platinum powder, a mercury salt, an organic vehicle, a low melting ceramic flux, and an organic solid (such as biphenol) that will volatilize during firing without carbonizing (cracking).

A gold silk-screening paste has been described in another patent.[10] This gold silk-screen printing paste contained a volatilizable solid that is insoluble in the medium carrying it. Basically the paste consists of a mixture of gold powder, a ceramic flux (lead borosilicate), Bi_2O_3 as $BiOCl$, and an organic vehicle; Hg_2Cl_2 also may be present.

Xerography

Decoration of ceramics by xerography[11] involves the following steps:

1. sensitizing the xerographic plate
2. exposing the plate to a light image
3. developing the image with the decorating powder and
4. transferring the powder image to the article

The process is based on the formation of a latent electrostatic image on a photoconductive insulating material and the building on the latent electrostatic image of an adherent decorating powder by electrostatic attraction.

For a ceramic decoration, ceramic stains and a flux are admixed with the usual types of organic electrostatically sensitive powdered resin. The xerographic developers contain carrier powders along with the ceramic color.

The deposition and formation of the image with the powders depend upon their having the proper triboelectric properties. Only one color can be printed at a time by xerography.

Decalcomania

A general definition of a decal is that it is printing of designs, pictures, or type on a specially prepared surface such as a gummed paper. This printing is subsequently transferred to a surface which is often difficult to decorate directly, due to curvature or complexity of contour. The decal is flexible and will conform to the surface applied to.

A ceramic decal is printed with specially formulated inorganic oxides, which will fuse or melt at high temperatures into a glassy formation on the surface they have been applied to. Inorganic stains are printed on specially treated paper and the final step is an overprinting of a protective layer of varnish, lacquer, or some similar material. This layer also serves to support the decal and to protect it during the transferring process. The substrate can be glass, china, vitreous or earthenware, tile or porcelain enamel coatings on steel or aluminum. The firing temperature of the decal is primarily determined by the ability of the substrate to maintain its shape and composition while exposed to elevated temperatures. The colors or oxides used in the decal must fuse at temperatures below which the substrate or ceramic ware is distorted or undergoes an undesirable change. This may be a change in color, glaze texture, or shape caused by slumping or melting or deformation from a desired contour.

The resultant fired appearance is an attractive and colorful enhancement of the ware which makes it more appealing and desirable to the consumer.

Decal can be applied over or under the glaze.

Two basic printing methods are used in the manufacture of ceramic decal. These are the offset lithography technique and the screen printing technique, two distinctly different methods.

Offset Lithography

Traditionally, limestones from a certain area in Bavaria were used in the litho system of printing. The surface of the stones was highly polished and milled flat. In the early days the artist worked directly on the stones, using a grease or wax crayon. After the advent of photographic techniques, the surface was coated with a special photosensitive emulsion upon which the artwork was positioned. The exposure of the emulsion to strong actinic light resulted in a water insoluble impression of the artwork on the stone. The artwork was transparent, permitting a hardening and solidification of the area, while the covered background areas washed out. Each color used in the printing of the decal had its own printing stone.

The actual printing was carried out by the coating of the surface with water to make it nonreceptive to the varnish used in the printing. The raised surface of emulsion was coated with varnish which was then deposited onto the surface of the decal paper. The colorant or the inorganic oxide was then dusted onto the varnish and worked into the varnish. The excess or undesirable color on the surface of the printing sheet was removed by brushing with flour. The process was repeated for each color until the complete pattern was printed. The final step was to print a varnish over the pattern to permit transfer of the decal from the tissue-bearing paper. After the tissue was stripped from the surface the decal was rubbed down into a tacky varnish with soap and brush, and the tissue was washed off with water.

This traditional method of printing was exacting and required considerable skill. The introduction of metal printing plates, such as aluminum or zinc, made the preparation of the printing mechanism much simpler. Instead of the cumbersome stone, a thin sheet of metal, chemically and mechanically treated so that its surface will retain a thin film of water, is used as the printing plate. The same procedure of coating and exposing the photosensitive emulsion is carried out. The printing plate is then installed on a high speed printing press where the plate is fastened to the surface of a drum or cylinder. The plate is moistened with water and then comes in contact with the varnish rollers. Because oil and water do not mix, the varnish adheres to the raised portion of the artwork only and is transferred to the printing sheet. The paper is then conveyed to another station and rotated on a drum, thus coming in contact with the dry color contained in a fountain. Here dry color is applied to the varnish and dusted in by lamb's wool pads.

The sheets are then set aside to dry overnight and then a separate machine is used to apply flour to the surface of the sheet. The purpose of this operation is to remove all loose color clinging to both top and bottom surfaces of the sheet by a static-electrical charge.

The following day, the printing plate for the second color in the sequence is installed on the printing press and the procedure is repeated. The usual sequence of color rotation is to start with the strongest color, chromatically speaking, and work down to the weakest. There is another consideration, the factor of pick-up by one color of another. Therefore, the colors less likely to be changed in shade by other stains are printed first, with more susceptible colors being printed later in the sequence. Since the advent of the simplified slide-off decal most of the printing is done on a gummed paper and after the last color has dried, and the sheet has undergone its final inspection, a lacquer or slide-off coating is registered over the decal.

Screen Printing Process

The screen process is a practical method for printing ceramic decals. The shop practices of the litho printer are used in this process as well. The control of temperature and humidity is a major factor in assuring quality of printing and the best results in registration. The screen printer, as does his counterpart in the litho printing industry, stores the paper he will use in the controlled atmosphere in order to "age" it, or allow it to come to equilibrium.

The mechanism of printing in the screen process is naturally the screen itself. Early screens used for the printing of decals were composed of silk fibers. The abrasiveness of the ceramic powders used in the printing necessitated frequent changes of the screen. As synthetic fibers came into being, the screen printer adapted these to his use, and now screens are made of nylon, dacron, and other polyesters. Where extremely heavy deposits are desired, woven wire screen cloth is used. The mesh sizes of the screens vary from coarse for heavy deposits to very fine, such as 325 mesh, for thin deposits. Thus the printer can make use of the screen to control the amount of the ceramic color that is deposited.

The screen is prepared in the same fashion as is the litho printing plate. The mesh is coated with the photosensitive emulsion, the artwork positioned, and the assembly exposed to strong light. The areas covered by the artwork wash out, while the exposed portions have been rendered insoluble by the photochemical reaction. It is through these open areas in the screen that the color is pushed by the squeegee and applied to the paper.

Again, the colors of the artwork have been separated and each color is printed separately. Modern high speed printing presses have created a necessity for quick drying printing vehicles, and the use of massive wicket dryers. The dryers permit the more rapid printing of a decal edition with the application of more than one color possible in a single work day.

When all the colors have been applied to the paper, the layer of varnish or lacquer is then printed over the colors to permit the transfer from the paper.

Control System of Decal Printing Techniques

In both types of printing, maximum use of the printing sheet is ensured by the skill of the personnel involved in "layout" and "paste-up" operations.

The preparation of the ceramic powders for the printing operations is a very critical operation, which requires close control. The selection of the colors, the "matching" of colors to artwork, and obtaining the desired results after exposure to the firing operation have often been likened to Russian roulette. Few people possess a knowledge of this art and, once the color palette has been established, careful attention must be given to the proper implementation of the required procedures.

The mixing of the color in the vehicles is closely controlled and often specially ground stains are obtained from color suppliers. Color blocks are prepared, applied, and fired for comparison with standards and proof blocks to ensure uniformity. Firings at intervals during the printing sequence are also carried out to ensure that the proper shades are obtained. Final checks and production firings of advance shipment by the customer are the final steps in the control system.

Decal Application

Once the decal has been printed, its function as a decoration is carried out by application to the product. There are two basic techniques now commonly used for transferring decal to porcelain enamel, the water-mount slide-off method and the heat release method.

WATER-MOUNT SLIDEOFF METHOD. As the name implies, this method is a wet hand application in which the decal has been printed on gummed paper. The decal also has a lacquer coating which serves to hold the decal together during transfer. Immersion of the decal in water results in a dissolving of the gum and a release of the decal for transfer. The usual indicator of readiness for transfer is the uncurling of the decal paper after the initial curling into a roll. The decal is slid off the paper, face up, and positioned on the ware. The decal is squeegeed down with a rubber squeegee and excess water and air bubbles are removed. The decal is then allowed to air dry for several hours to ensure tight adhesion by elimination of excess moisture and air.

It should be noted that this technique is a hand application. As such it is best suited for applications on complex shapes and contours.

HEAT-RELEASE METHOD. This decal differs from the water-mount slide-off type in its composition. Heat-sensitive coatings sandwich the ceramic colors and are printed on a wax coating in place of gummed coating.

The ware to be decorated is heated to a temperature ranging between 250° to 300° F. The decal is placed face down on the ware and, by a combination of temperature and pressure, is released. The paper can be removed by an air jet or by hand, unlike the slide-off. No drying is required and the ware can be immediately fired.

This technique lends itself to a straight-line production system where the ware may retain residual heat from the firing process. Also, the process can be adapted to mechanical motions for handling, applying, pressing, and removing of the paper. Production speeds are much greater and labor costs can be materially reduced. The decal is usually die-cut in shapes for magazine loading and handling is made easier.

Selection of Decal Application Method

The decorator has a choice between the hand-applied water-mount slide-off system and the machine appliable heat-release system. Each system offers advantages which can be used to solve decorating problems.

Where the volume of the production is nigh, the best technique to utilize is the heat-release method. Production speeds of 40–50 pieces per minute are attainable where the decoration is limited to a panel type of decoration. Recent development of a unique decorating device permits mechanical decoration, of full wrap-around proportions. The decoration can be applied around handles and spouts on cookware. Also, wrap-arounds can be applied to cylindrical shapes without handles, and joined accurately for exact fit. Tapered contours can be decorated by this technique, as well as concave and convex contours. The key component of the mechanism is the permeable decal holder, which can be shaped to fit the exact contours of the ware and is the exact size of the decorated area. The decal can be fed out of a hopper by the motion of the decorating head. In the case of longer sections of decal for larger diameter ware, the decal is top-fed onto the decorating stage by means of an adjustable vacuum bar. A single decorating head is capable of fully decorating ware at a rate of 10–20 pieces per minute. The rate of productivity will be dependent on the size of the ware, which determines the length of the decal being applied.

The chief advantage of the slide-off water-mount is the ability to conform the decoration to any contour. The flexibility of the lacquer film permits the decal to adhere to a complexity of concave and convex surfaces. This type of decal is also suited to production of smaller quantities of a variety of items and does not require setting up of complicated machinery.

Effective production lines of skilled decal applicators have been set up in many porcelain enamel manufacturing operations. Excellent use has been made of imaginative time and motion techniques and production scheduling to make these operations quite efficient. For instance, the people applying the slide-off decal of wrap-around proportions on cookware have devised ingenious techniques for using sponges as well as squeegees for removing the water from under the decal films.

Both varnish mounts and later slide-off decals were hardened onto biscuit ware with a nardening-on fire. But now most patterns are non-hardening-on decals. Both slide-off and heat release techniques are used, onto which a clear glaze can be directly applied by hand dipping or by spray. Where opaque glazes are used, the decal can be applied over the unfired "green" glaze and fired with excellent results.

Production rates for slide-off applications vary from 25 doz to 200 doz per girl per shift depending on size of the decal, numbers of strikes, etc.

Heat-release applications can be applied mechanically at the rate of over 100 dozen per hour. Firing cycle time has been reduced in some cases by 30 minutes to one hour.

Decorating Unfired Ware

One of the modern innovations with decorated ware is the development of processes for once-firing the ware, including bisque, glost, and decoration, all in one fire. The decoration may be either under the glaze or over it as desired. Max Compton[12] and his associates have been among the leaders in these developments.

Unfired china can be decorated, glazed, and the whole operation matured in a single firing. Decoration can be applied to unfired ware or to bisque ware but the glaze does not need to be prefired before decorating. The dry unfired ware is sprayed or coated with glaze and dried. This dried glaze coating then is brushed with a synthetic resin, preferably an emulsion or dispersion of 20%–35% of methacrylate in water. The resin must be sufficiently high in molecular weight to prevent it from being absorbed into the pores of the green ware. The trick is to prevent the polymer from entering the pores where it would crack to carbon during firing. After the emulsion has dried thoroughly to form a continuous resilient film, the ware can be decorated with decals, transfers, hand brushing, or silk screen in the usual manner.

Gold Etching

Gold etching is a process in which a design is etched into the glaze to create a relief design that then is gold-lined to produce the illusion of deep gold patterns. The etched surface is coated with a gold paste by hand with a brush and fired.

The ware must be fired in a strictly dust-free environment in a well-ventilated oxidizing atmosphere. The temperature should be controlled within ±5° F.

Contact Transfer

The principle of contact transfer for coating tile has been widely employed but is now about entirely abandoned. The essential parts of the apparatus are:

1. a large reservoir containing the glaze slip
2. a drum rotating in the large reservoir so as to gather a small quantity of the slip which is transferred, by contact, to
3. a perforated surface across which the tile is made to travel from
4. one section of a moving belt to the opposite section, which conveys it away for inspection and placing in setters

Control of Glaze Consistency

This subject was considered in chapter 4 in the section on "Consistency."

For Spraying

The same general principles apply to the control of the consistencies of glazes for spraying on bodies in different physical conditions—unfired, porous, and vitreous—as are true for the process of dipping. In general, the more porous wares require the thinner slips. If too heavy air pressure is used with thin slips, the glaze coating will increase in thickness too rapidly, with the resulting formation of a ripple or "orange peel" effect. This is quite certain to occur if the work is too close to the spray head. The ideal conditions for the best results on a vitrified body are had by the use of a heavy slip finely atomized by the lowest practical air pressure.[2] Vitreous wares are sometimes heated before spraying to facilitate the formation of a more uniform and thicker coating.

For One-fire Glazes

For the glazing of one-fire ware, the primary objectives of control are: (1) development of satisfactory uniform defect-free glaze coverage; (2) proper glaze thickness; (3) prevention of soaking and cracking; (4) prevention of crawling and pinholing; and (5) proper drain-off.

Much of this is controlled by the consistency of the glaze slip. Pinnow and Merwin[13] determined this by dipping (or spraying) a number of samples with varying parameters such as specific gravity, dipping rate, consistency, set, thickness, etc. The kind and amount of clay are of paramount importance. Ball clays contribute to the fluidity of the slip. China clays contribute to the set. A proper ratio of the two is desired.

Milling is another factor that can change the consistency. Split grinding often is helpful—grinding hard materials first and later adding soft stuff like whiting, opacifiers, etc.

The use of electrolytes is critical. They have a profound influence both on a spurious and on a intentional basis. The Brookfield viscometer is preferred to the Mariotte tube because it is rapid reproducible, accurate, simple, and versatile.

Binders

Binders are used in glazes to produce tough dry glaze coatings that will not be easily scuffed or skinned due to normal handling from the spray machine to the glost kiln. The toughness and strength resulting from clay alone is not sufficient for many products. An effective binder can greatly reduce refires and cut the cost of refiring ware by several hundred dollars a day.

Factors to consider in the selection of binders have been discussed by Knapp.[14] Does it foam? clog the lawns? interfere with settling, either by delaying it or throwing down the nonplastics? affect specific gravity? permit dipping as well as spraying? Does the plant have adequate washing facilities for spindles, guns, lines, etc.? Is it stable indefinitely at 100° F? Will it fire out, leaving no residue or defects? Knapp[14] classified glaze binders into four groups: (a) alcohols and cellulose derivatives; (b) sugars, starches, and flours; (c) gums; and (d) wax emulsions.

Alcohols and Cellulose Derivatives

These are effective at low concentrations, as low as 0.5% or less, but they tend to foam. The addition of an antifoam agent such as polyglycol can remedy this. Some of these binders have a tendency to deflocculate the slips and render them less sensitive to the usual flocculating agents. But they do not deteriorate with time. Many of these additives are difficult to put into water solution. Some of them have such powerful thickening tendencies that too much water must be added to produce workable viscosities, thus reducing the specific gravity of the slips.

Sugars, Starches, and Flours

Some of these are of good binding power and some are poor. Many will thicken the glaze too much, making it difficult or impossible to process slips through screening equipment. They decompose or "sour" unless an effective germicide is used.

Gums

The shelf life of glaze slips containing gums is short. Where the glaze is to be used in a short time and if it is not to be recycled or reclaimed, gum binders are satisfactory. They are likely to sour quickly, but they do develop very good strength.

Wax Emulsions

Generally the wax from the emulsions remains with the solids and has but little tendency to concentrate in the supernatant liquid when the glaze solids settle. At least 2% of wax emulsion usually is required. It is not good practice to add a wax emulsion prior to ball milling; the emulsion can be broken during the ball-milling action. In some cases, waxes have caused difficulty in screening through 200 mesh.

Summary of Binders

Sugar is cheap and can develop a tough coating with 0.5% additions. It has no effect on viscosity, providing fermentation is avoided. Sugar does not cause foaming or interfere with lawning or handling. It does not ionize and cannot cause flocculation or deflocculation.

Commercial preservatives are available to prevent souring. Some popular preservatives are formaldehyde, Dowicide, and sodium benzoate. None of these can be effective permanently.

A number of binders were checked by Treischel and Emrich[15] for their strength development properties. The materials used and the strengths developed when 3% of each were added to talc are summarized in table 5.1. This table is useful in that it tabulates the strength-development potentials of six groups of binders.

Carboxymethylcellulose is formed by the reaction of monochloracetic acid with alkali[16] cellulose. This yields the sodium salt, the most commonly applied derivative. This salt is readily soluble or dispersible in water to yield solutions of high viscosity. The material primarily is used for its

Table 5.1. Strengths of extruded talc specimens prepared with 3% of various binders[15]

Kind of binder	*M. of R.* in psi*	*How added*	*Source*
Flours, Starches, and Dextrins			
Cere-Amic	940	Dry powder	Ill. Cereal Mills
Wheat flour	110	Dry powder	Conventional
Potato starch	920	30% paste	Conventional
Cornstarch	760	Cooked paste	Conventional
Borated cornstarch	960	Cooked paste	Staley Co.
Eclipse K	1050	Cooked paste	Staley Co.
Flocgel	1680	Dry powder	A.S. Meincke & Co.
Amijel	1960	Dry powder	Corn Products Refin. Co.
Dextrin	600	Cooked paste	Conventional
Gums			
Gum arabic	720	Dry powder	
Gum tragacanth	1490	Dry powder	
Gum ghatti	2070	Dry powder	
Locust seed gum	1130	Dry powder	
Acacia gum	1220	Dry powder	
Karaya gum	1340	Dry powder	
Alcohols and Cellulose Derivatives			
Methocel	1230	1% solution	Dow Chemical Co.
Polyvinyl alcohol	2120	3% solution	
Sodium carboxy methyl cellulose	1800	3% solution	Herculese Powder Co.
Hydroxy ethyl cellulose	2260	3% solution	Union Carbide Corp.
Collocel S	1900	3% solution	Dow Chemical Co.
Wood Extracts			
Plasticade	170	Dry powder	Mead Corp.
Goulac	510	Dry powder	Robinson Process Co.
Alginates			
Algin HV	1580	Dry powder	Innis Spieden Co.
Ammonium alginate	1110	Dry powder	Kelco Mfg. Co.
Inorganic			
Vee-gum	840	Dry powder	R.T. Vanderbilt Co.

*Modulus of rupture or flexure strength.

thickening properties to aid in the suspension of finely divided solids and to control some of their rheological properties.

The Dow Chemical Company[17] has patented a glaze slip using methyl cellulose for a binder and consistency-control agent. There are several grades of methyl cellulose. Many of them are recommended and useful in glaze slips for tile, sanitary ware, dinnerware, electrical porcelain, and others. They have applications for spray as well as dip coatings.

Methyl cellulose can minimize glazing defects due to damage from handling dried glazed ware as well as from running and beading. It also slows the drying rate. It aids in producing smooth, uniform glaze coatings and promotes scuff-resistance of dried glaze films. Fundamentally, methyl cellulose is a film former, binder, hardener and adhesive, as well as a plasticizer, suspending agent, and leveler. Polyglycol P1 200 has been recommended for glazes. The amounts of methyl cellulose recommended are $\frac{1}{4}\%$ to $\frac{1}{2}\%$ of the solids content of the glaze batch.

References

1. Shearer, W. L. 1932. Control of plasticities of ceramic slips. *J. Amer. Ceram. Soc.* 15:622.
2. Schramm, Edward. 1938. Problems in whiteware glazes. *Bull. Am. Ceram. Soc.* 17:436.
3. Andrews, A. I. 1935. *Enamels.* Champaign, Ill.: Twin City Printing Co., p 276.
4. Twells, Robt. 1924. Preparing and spraying a glaze slip with special reference to the control of the various operations. *J. Am. Ceram. Soc.* 7:465.
5. Wilson, Hewitt. 1926. Monograph and bibliography on terra cotta. *J. Amer. Ceram. Soc.* 9:104.
6. Verba, R. S. 1954. Automatic spraying of glazes. *Bull. Am. Ceram. Soc.* 33:307–8.
7. Christensen, P. L. and Schramm, Edward. 1952. Application of the Schweitzer spray machine to the glazing of vitreous ware. *Bull. Amer. Ceram. Soc.* 31(10):384–85.
8. Dickson, Thomas A. 1949. Electrostatic glazing. *Ceram. Age* 54(1):28.
9. Johnson, Matthey and Co., Ltd., Kerridge, F. E., and Couper, C. S. British Patent 641,205, June 21, 1950.
10. British patent no. 641,525, June 28, 1960.
11. Oughton, C. D. 1949. Decoration of glass and ceramic articles by xerography. *Glass Ind.* 30(12):662–64, 684.
12. Compton, Max De Forest and Ragan, Randall C. Manufacture of decorated china. U.S. Patent 2,700,008, Jan 18, 1955.
13. Pinnow, H. R. and Merwin, B. W. 1952. Control methods for the consistency of one-fire glazes. *Bull. Amer. Ceram. Soc.* 31(9):332–33.
14. Knapp, Thomas. 1954. Glaze binders. *Bull. Amer. Ceram. Soc.* 33(1):11–12.
15. Treischel, C. C. and Emrich, E. W. 1946. Study of several groups of organic binders under low-pressure extrusion. *J. Am. Ceram. Soc.* 29(5):124–32.
16. Hallabaugh, C. B., Burt, Leland, and Welsh, Anna Peterson. 1945. Carboxymethylcellulose, uses and applications. *Ind. Eng. Chem.* 37(10):943–47.
17. 1950. Methyl cellulose in ceramic glazes. *Chem. Ind.* 66(2):244, 246.

6

Conversion of the Batch to the Glaze

The conversion of a glaze batch to a glaze is a complicated process not well understood in detail. It involves the use of high temperatures acting during intervals of time, both of which factors are vital in producing useful results. This is also true of the preparation of frits, which are glasses prepared for use as constituents of the glaze batch. In spite of the selection of a suitable glaze composition, carefully chosen raw materials, proper grinding, mixing, and application, the labor of many hours may be nullified by poor firing conditions.

The various stages through which the glaze composition passes on its way to the finished glassy coat may be briefly enumerated: (1) dissociation of the original components, (2) chemical combinations, (3) sintering, (4) fusion, and (5) crystallization. These operations are well defined but frequently overlap and may be repeated in some degree as the temperature rises and new compounds appear and disappear.

Basic Processes Involved

Dissociation

Dissociation may be defined for our use as the disintegration of a substance into two or more substances solely through the action of heat. It includes such examples as dehydration of the clays, and the dissociation of the carbonates, sulfates, nitrates, and oxides. Some examples with temperatures of dissociation are given in table 6.1.

A somewhat more detailed example of dissociation, showing the influ-

Table 6.1. Decomposition of materials due to heat alone: solid → solid + gas

Formula	Material	Type of Trans-formation	°C	Transformation	Source
$Al_2(SO_4)_3$	Aluminum sulfate	Decomp.	757	$Al_2O_3+3SO_3$	–
Sb_2O_5	Antimony pentoxide	Decomp.	450	$Sb_2O_3+O_2$	*
$Sb_2O_3 \cdot Sb_2O_5$	Cervantite	Decomp.	>1060	$2Sb_2O_3+O_2$	*
As_2O_5	Arsenic pentoxide	Decomp.	400	$As_2O_3+O_2$	*
$BaCO_3$	Witherite	Decomp.	1421	$BaO+CO_2$	*
$BaNO_3$	Barium nitrate	Decomp.	664	$BaO+NO_2$	*
$CaCO_3$	Calcite	Decomp.	894	$CaO+CO_2$	*
$Ca(OH)_2$	Calcium hydroxide	Decomp.	525	$CaO+H_2O$	*
$CaMg(CO_3)_2$	Dolomite	Decomp.	800	$CaCO_3+MgO+CO_2$	**
$CaCO_3+MgO+CO_2$	Decomposing stage	Decomp.	950	$CaO+MgO+2CO_2$	–
CeO_2	Ceric oxide	Decomp.	?	$\frac{1}{2}Ce_2O_3+\frac{1}{4}O_2$	–
$4Mg(CO_3)_3(OH)_2 \cdot 3H_2O$	Basic magnesium carbonate	Decomp.	250	$4Mg(CO_3)_3(OH)_2+H_2O$	**
$4Mg(CO_3)_3(OH)_2$	Basic carbonate H_2O	Decomp.	~ 450	$3MgCO_3+MgO+4H_2O$	**
$3MgCO_3$	Decomposing stage	Decomp.	535	$3MgO+3CO_2$	**
$MgCO_3$	Magnesite	Decomp.	750	$MgO+CO_2$	**
K_2CO_3	Potassium carbonate	Melt	895	Melt	*
K_2SO_4	Potassium sulfate	Melt	1069	Melt	*
Na_2CO_3	Sodium carbonate	Melt	851	Melt	*
Na_2SO_4	Sodium sulfate	Melt	884	Melt	*
Li_2CO_3	Lithium carbonate	Melt	735	Melt	*
$SrCO_3$	Strontianite	Decomp.	1289	$SrO+CO_2$	*
$Pb_3(OH)_2(CO_3)_2$	Hydrocerussite	Decomp.	400	?	*
$PbCO_3$	Cerussite	Decomp.	~ 400	$PbO+CO_2$	**
$ZnCO_3$	Smithsonite	Decomp.	296	$ZnO+CO_2$	*
$ZnSO_4$	Zincosite	Decomp.	740	$ZnO+SO_3$	*

**Data on chemicals for ceramic use.* Bulletin of the National Research Council No. 118, June, 1949. Comp. by Herbert Insley, George W. Morey, Frederick D. Rossini, and Alexander Silverman.

**R. M. Gruver, Differential thermal analysis studies of ceramic materials: 1, Characteristic heat effects of some carbonates. *J. Am. Ceram. Soc.* 33[3]: 96–101 (1950).

ence of the presence of even small amounts of other phases, may be instructive. For pure dolomite, the structure is stable to 770° C. At 780° C, energetic dissociation begins; it proceeds in 2 steps as follows:

$$CaCO_3 \cdot MgCO_3 \rightarrow CaCO_3 + MgO + CO_2$$

dissociation reaches the following stage at 900° C:

$$CaCO_3 \rightarrow CaO + CO_2$$

The presence of impurities changes the equilibrium entirely. The 780° C reaction is shifted by 5% of Na_2CO_3 or K_2CO_3 to 630° C. A small addition of an alkali carbonate causes a premature decomposition[1] as follows:

$$CaCO_3 \cdot MgCO_3 \rightarrow CaCO_3 + MgCO_3 + 4500 \text{ calories}$$

One percent of NaF or NaCl reduces the 780° C reaction by 100° C.

A few sulfates decompose spontaneously when heated. Most of them having possible interest in glazes are given, with their published dissociation temperatures, in table 6.2. The others, which is most of them, decompose slowly and incompletely, or not at all, when heated. For example, $CaSO_4$ slowly and continually evolves SO_3 upon prolonged heating in air at high temperature. It seems that no matter how long the heating is continued, some SO_3 continues to be evolved. Some sulfates, notably alkali sulfates, are rather stable in the molten condition.

It is well to regard the sulfates as being only partially decomposable and as being troublemakers. Even those that spontaneously and readily decompose, such as $Al_2(SO_4)_3$, evolve SO_3 that can react with other glaze components to form more stable sulfates. Sulfates, in general, are not decomposed effectively by heat alone, but must be decomposed chemically as outlined in another section.

Pyrochemical Decomposition

Of greater importance in glazes than outright dissociation is the conversion of solid materials into a new solid, plus a gas phase through chemical reaction. An example is the reaction, due to heat, of Na_2CO_3 with SiO_2 to yield sodium silicate and CO_2 gas. In a similar reaction $CaCO_3$ reacts with SiO_2 to form calcium silicates plus CO_2 or with kaolin to form calcium aluminum silicate plus H_2O and CO_2.

Sulfates are most effectively broken down in this manner. For example, $CaSO_4$ plus silica when heated tends to form calcium silicate plus SO_3.

Table 6.2. Sulfates that readily decompose by heat alone: solid → solid + gas

Sulfate		*Dissociation products*	*Dissociation pressure mm of Hg*	*Dissociation temperature (°C)*
$Al_2(SO_4)_3$	→	$Al_2O_3+SO_3$	760	757
$Bi_2(SO_4)_3$	→	$Bi_2O_3+3SO_3$	760	773
$FeSO_4$	→	$FeO+SO_3$	760	665
$Fe_2(SO_4)_3$	→	$Fe_2O_3+3SO_3$	760	707
$MnSO_4$	→	$MnO+SO_3$	296	1,110
$ZnSO_4$	→	$ZnO+SO_3$	760	740

Sodium sulfate would tend to do the same thing except that molten sodium sulfate, being immiscible in molten silicates, tends to separate as do oil and water.

Sulfates are more effectively decomposed by reducing the sulfate to the less stable sulfite or sulfide with carbon or another of the reducing agents. The sulfides or sulfites then can be converted into an active RO oxide and SO_2 or SO_3 gas by continued heating in air.

Too little is known about the chemical combinations which do or may take place in glaze making except for a few examples of the simplest sort, involving two or three components, as in the preparation of commercial glasses. The complexity of all kinds of glazes and enamels is so great that the details of the reactions, except during dehydration and dissociation, are generally beyond our present knowledge.

According to Turner,[2] sodium carbonate and silica will react completely in the solid state (i.e., in the absence of the liquid phase) at temperatures below 700° C and the mass is only slightly sintered up to 800° C. Lea and Desch[3] suggest a "somewhat idealized" program for the reactions between clay and calcium carbonate, as follows:

below 800° C, $CaO \cdot Al_2O_3$ is formed and probably $CaO \cdot Fe_2O_3$
between 800° and 900° C, $CaO \cdot SiO_2$ is formed
between 900° and 950° C, $5CaO \cdot SiO_2$ is formed
between 950° and 1,200° C, $2CaO \cdot SiO_2$ is formed

Lead oxide (PbO) reacts with silica to form $PbSiO_3$ at about 580° C and there is a marked thermal acceleration between 670° C and 730° C.[4]

An oxidizing condition is normal for the firing of glazes. Therefore the carbon in the clays used, or accidentally present, is removed at temperatures between 500° and 800° C. This is important in avoiding seeds and pinholes. Ferrous iron is rapidly oxidized at 900° C.

Solid State Reactions

Substances, when intimately mixed, will react chemically at surprisingly low temperatures to form new compounds even in the absence of a liquid phase. For example, silica reacts with alkaline earth oxides or carbonates at temperatures as low as 400° C. Lime reacts with clay at about 530° C. These temperatures are far below the melting points of the individual constituents.

Such reactions and their products are of very great interest to the ceramist in all departments of his work at high temperatures: The preparation of glasses, glazes and enamels, bodies, colors, refractories, cements, etc. These reactions furnish a means for preparing many materials which cannot be obtained otherwise because they are either unstable at their melting points or the viscosity of the melt prevents crystallization. For example, lime and magnesia will react with clay at about 800° C, forming alkaline earth silicates many hundreds of degrees below the liquidus temperatures.

Solid state reactions are initiated and promoted by conditions which weaken the interatomic forces or strain and loosen lattice structure, decrease its rigidity, and increase its interior mobility. Such agents or conditions are: thermal activity, inversions, ionic deformations, mechanical deformation, association of materials having different lattice structures, mechanical and electrical stresses, polarization, and exposure to radiations of certain wavelengths.

The velocity of the reaction is determined by the "heat of activation" which is a measure of the amount of energy necessary to produce the atomic vibration large enough to accomplish the exchange of the ion or atom in the structure.

The manner in which a solid state reaction may proceed is probably typified by the stages observed when sodium carbonate is heated in contact with silica grains.[5] As the temperature rises, the thermal activity loosens the lattice bonds of the silica and sodium ions penetrate the surface, causing first a cloudiness and then an opalescence. This is not a combination in definite proportions but a result of absorption, an ionic diffusion. Littleton[6] suggests that there may be also an absorption of the silica by the soda analogous to the absorption of silica by boric oxide or phosphorus pentoxide.

One of the reactions of interest occurring in the solid state is that calcium carbonate and silica react to form calcium metasilicate. It is expressed in this way: $CaCO_3 + SiO_2 \rightarrow CaSiO_3 + CO_2$. This can be detected as low as 610° C if the heating has been maintained for a very long period. If heated at 1,100° C, about 19% of calcium silicate will be formed in one hour.[2] Sodium carbonate and silica begin to react as low as 390° C, doing so completely and giving powdered products at temperatures below 700° C; these are only slightly sintered up to 800° C. Barium carbonate and silica react to form barium metasilicate ($BaCO_3 + SiO_2 \rightarrow BaSiO_3 + CO_2$). The reaction will occur between 700° and 750° C, depending upon the proportions used, and is complete at 1,155° C. Lead oxide reacts with silica to form lead metasilicate ($PbO + SiO_2 \rightarrow PbSiO_3$). This reaction occurs at about 580° C. Long[4] states that the reaction begins at between 670° and 730° C. The oxide of lead (PbO) begins to liquefy at 835° C.[4]

Keppeller[7] has suggested the usefulness of preheating the glass batch to promote solid state reactions as a means of preventing the segregation of classes of particle sizes in the handling of the batch after mixing.

Sintering

Sintering is a process whereby heat converts a powder into a cohesive mass without developing much glassy phase. The necessary temperature can be far below the melting point of a pure substance or the fusion temperature of a mixture. Naturally, the mass will lack strength and is usually in a friable condition. Powdered feldspar will form a compact but friable mass if heated for a short time at a temperature far below any evidence of vitrification. The strength and durability of pottery and brick fired at the customarily low temperatures used by primitive as well as more skilled clayworkers are due to the sintering of the mass.

Conditions promoting sintering are:

a. the presence of fine particles which have relatively large surfaces, higher surface energy
b. the constant operation of diffusion at suitable temperatures to repair defects in the lattice structure with the result that the edges of the fractures are affected
c. the constant migration from the smaller to the larger particles because of the higher surface energy of the former and the gradual disappearance of the small particles and increase in size of the large

Bancroft[8] has indicated, theoretically, that finely divided particles will behave like liquids. Two drops of the same liquid but of different sizes, if contiguous, cannot exist long separately as is shown in the equation:

$$\text{vapor pressure} = (\text{surface tension})/(\text{radius of the drop}).$$

Some physical effects of sintering are shown in figure 6.1. The shrinkage in a powdered glass due to heating corresponds to the reduction in pore spores between constituent particles. The original powder (—325 mesh) was less densely packed and shrank more than an identical, but coarser-grained (—150 mesh) glass powder.

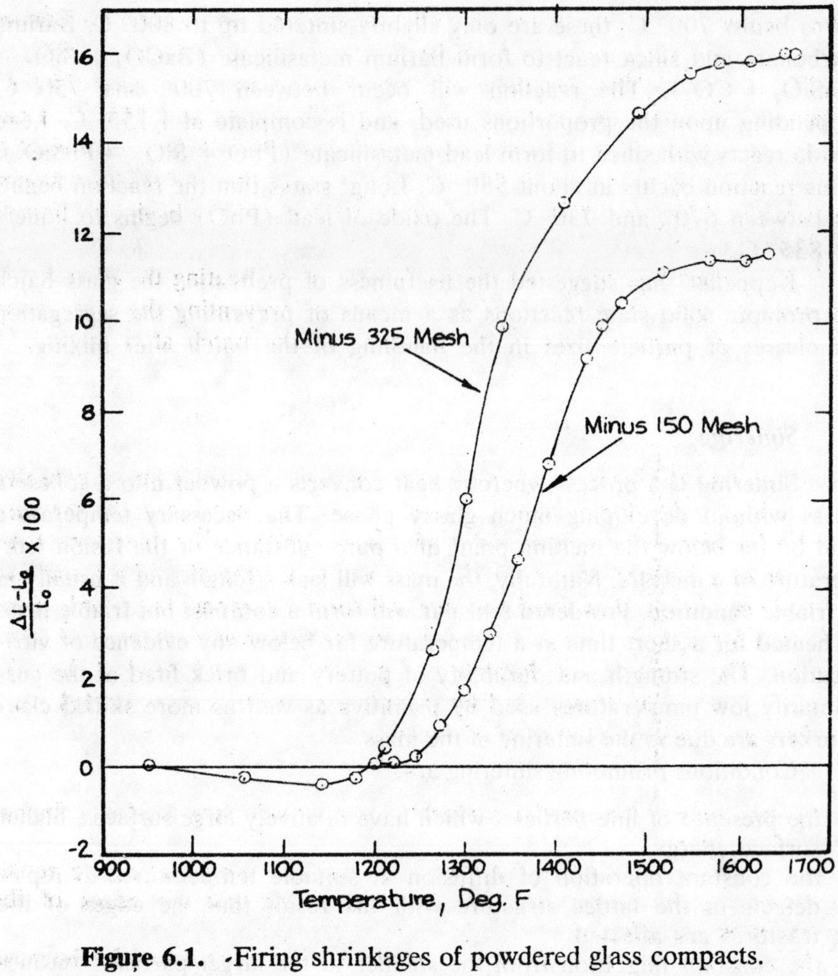

Figure 6.1. Firing shrinkages of powdered glass compacts.

Brown[9] presented a lucid illustration, shown here as figure 6.2, of the simultaneous sintering and solid state reaction of powders of ZnO and SiO_2 to yield a sintered product of $2ZnO \cdot SiO_2$. The zinc oxide particles react not only among themselves (sintering) but also with the silica, resulting in sintered $2ZnO \cdot SiO_2$.

Fusion and Melting

Melting is a thermal process whereby a solid is converted to the liquid phase. The melting point is the temperature at which the two phases are in equilibrium.

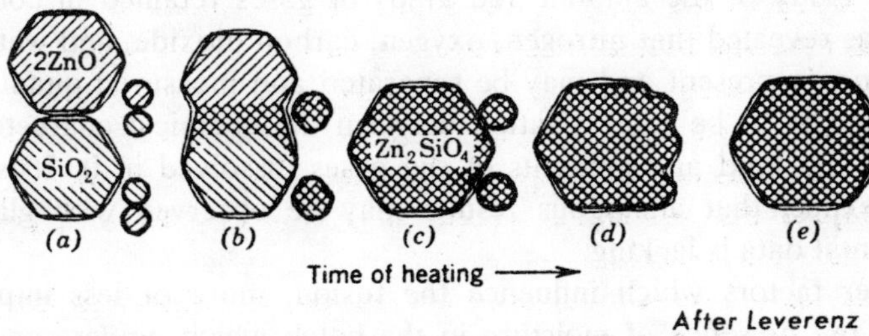

Figure 6.2. Schematic description of the solid state reaction of ZnO with SiO_2 and the growth by sintering of the resulting $2ZnO \cdot SiO_2$.[9]

The term solid as used above implies crystalline matter having an internal geometrical arrangement of atoms or ions in a lattice structure as contrasted with liquid where such an arrangement is lacking or quite imperfect.

Fusion is the ultimate result of several conditions operating in sequence, or simultaneously, to produce a mobile melt at a higher temperature. Besides high temperature, the conditions bringing about fusion are: (1) chemical decomposition and combination, (2) diffusion, and (3) solution. Sintering plays an important part initially as already explained. As the lattice structure is loosened by heat some inversions may occur leading to a metastable condition. Stresses, developed by thermal expansion, especially if these vary according to the axial directions, cause minute fractures, reducing the sizes of grains and increasing the surfaces. Crushing and abrading expose the edges and corners to attack. Eutectics develop a liquid phase and the more refractory particles gradually go into solution.

During the early stages, the most effective stirring agent is the action of the escaping gases. This proceeds slowly throughout the low temperatures when the viscosity of the melt is high, but it is accelerated as the viscosity decreases with the higher temperatures. More rapid diffusion and chemical action accompany the lower viscosity and promote more complete homogeneity.

The primary source of gases is that gas occupying the pore spaces between solids in the original glaze layer; that which fails to be expelled during sintering and early stages of fusion becomes permanently occluded as bubbles in the final glaze. A secondary source is from the incomplete elimination of decomposable and gas-forming materials such as sulfates, carbonates, organic matter, and the like. A tertiary source of gases is that adsorbed on the surfaces of and dissolved within batch particles. Other possible sources of gases are those absorbed from the kiln atmosphere and those liberated from the body on which the glaze is being fired.

The study of the amount and kinds of gases retained in commercial glasses has revealed that nitrogen, oxygen, carbon dioxide, and water vapor are commonly present and may be separated and measured quantitatively. There appears to be some relation between the chemical character of the glass and the kind and amounts of the gases dissolved in it. It is reasonable to expect that analogous results may be observed with glazes, but experimental data is lacking.

Other factors which influence the fusion, more or less importantly, are: (1) the presence of moisture in the batch which, under some conditions, has been found useful in lowering the melting temperature of glass batches and (2) the size of the batch particles, for the reasons stated with respect to the surface energy, etc. In general, the advantages gained by the fine grinding of the glaze batch, with respect to the maturing of the glaze, may be summarized as follows: a lower fusion temperature; a shorter time for fusion; a better homogeneity of the melt; a greater fluidity while maturing; and consequently the development of a smoother surface more free from defects, mechanically stronger, and hence less readily scratched. However, it is to be noted that the escape of the maximum amount of the gases adsorbed on the surface of the batch particles is sometimes best insured by the avoidance of too early fusion of part or all of the glaze batch. For that reason a certain proportion of the relatively coarse refractory ingredients may be used.

Heat exchanges during fusion are generally endothermic for evaporation, volatilization, dissociation, inversions, and melting; and exothermic, generally, for the formation of new compounds. The relative quantities of the reacting substances have an important influence upon the extent to which the reactions proceed, according to the principles of the mass law. Silicates as a class are believed to be more strongly dissociated in the melt than metals, i.e., metals may be separated from basic slags more readily than less basic silicate. It is to be expected that the effect of the common ion in melts should be comparable to that in aqueous solutions.

COMPOSITION. Probably the ultimate composition of glazes is more important in the process of conversion of the batch into the glaze than any other single factor. The matter of composition is so complicated and varied that it cannot adequately be generalized.

The best information available with respect to the pyrochemistry involved is in the form of phase equilibrium data. Equilibrium diagrams of many pertinent two and three component systems have been published. Existing equilibrium diagrams have been compiled and published by Levin, Robbins and McMurdie[10] and work is in progress to update these at practical future intervals. The glaze ceramist should be familiar with pertinent

Table 6.3. Scale of acidity and basicity of oxides in glass forming[11]

	*M-O**	*Coordination number of M***	*Arbitrary scale (M-O bond strength)*
↑	Glass formers		
	B_2O_3	3	119
	SiO_2	4	106
	P_2O_5	4	88-111
	Al_2O_3	4	79-101
	B_2O_3	4	89
A	Sb_2O_3	4	68-85
C	ZrO_2	6	81
I			
D	Intermediates		
I	TiO_2	6	73
C	Al_2O_3	6	53-67
	ZrO_2	8	61
B			
A	Modifiers		
S	SnO_2	6	46
I	PbO	6	39
C	MgO	6	37
	PbO	4	36
	ZnO	4	36
	CaO	8	32
	BaO	8	33
	CdO	4	30
	Na_2O	6	20
	CdO	6	20
↓	K_2O	9	13

*Metal to oxygen bond

**Metal ion

Table taken from Brown, Harvey E. 1957. *Zinc oxide rediscovered;* New York, N.Y.: Market Development Div., New Jersey Zinc Co.

equilibrium diagrams since this is the only source he has for systematic high temperature silicate chemistry. None of his information can be applied to the practical development, formulation, and control of glazes. It does, however, furnish a sound basis for understanding the pyrochemical problems relating to the maturing of glazes.

In a step toward the condensation of this vast and complex field of chemistry, Sun[11] created the concept shown in table 6.3. He classified the oxides that may be components of glass (or glazes) on the basis of an arbitrary scale. He based this scale on the calculated bond strength between the metal ions and an oxygen ion. The oxides were grouped into three categories: acid, intermediate, and basic. In table 6.3, the most acid oxides are at the top of the table and the basic oxides are at the bottom, leaving the amphoteric oxides in the middle.

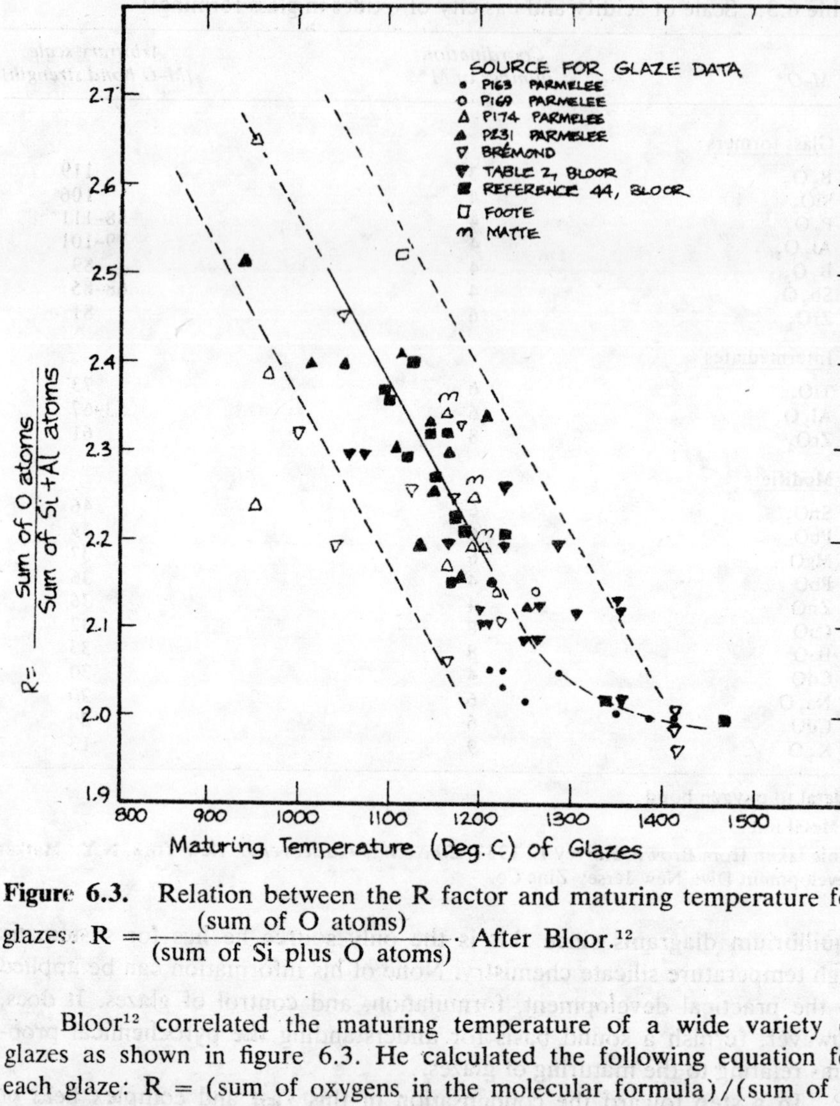

Figure 6.3. Relation between the R factor and maturing temperature for glazes. $R = \frac{\text{(sum of O atoms)}}{\text{(sum of Si plus O atoms)}}$. After Bloor.[12]

Bloor[12] correlated the maturing temperature of a wide variety of glazes as shown in figure 6.3. He calculated the following equation for each glaze: R = (sum of oxygens in the molecular formula)/(sum of Si and Al and B in the glaze). Although the points are widely scattered, the general trend is unmistakable. Bloor said that R is a measure of the number of single-bonded oxygen (R_2O). When R = 4, all of the oxygens in an all-silica (no B_2O_3) network would be single-bonded. The limit in practical glazes is about R = 2.5 in which $\frac{1}{4}$ of the oxygen in an all-silica network would be single-bonded; the rest would be attached to silicon by 2 bonds.

Solution and Miscibility

The matrix of a glaze is glass and, according to the generally accepted viewpoint, a solution. A solution is a homogeneous phase, the composition of which varies between wide limits. Gases, liquids, and solids may be mutually soluble, and examples of most of these conditions may be observed in the preparation of glasses and glazes. The solution consists of the solvent, the dissolving agent, and the solute, the substance which is dissolved. Since it may be difficult to distinguish between the two, the solvent is conventionally the reagent present in the larger quantity.

All gases are soluble in all liquids and in solids, in amounts determined by the temperature and the pressure. In cases where chemical reactions take place, the original components cannot be wholly separated by mechanical means and therefore it is not an example of true solution and is only a solution in proportion to the successful recovery of the gases. According to Henry's law the maximum volume of gas dissolved by a specified quantity of liquid is the same at all pressures. When several gases are present in a mixture each constituent gas is dissolved as though the other gases were not present, i.e., it is absorbed proportionally to its partial pressure in the mixture. The gases so absorbed diffuse freely through the liquid in the same manner as the other solutes.

Binary systems of silica and soda, potassa, baria, and alumina are miscible; silica and lime, strontia, magnesia, and ferrous oxide are partially immiscible. The ternary systems, silica-lime-magnesia, silica-lime-strontia, silica-lime-ferrous oxide, silica-alumina-magnesia, silica-alumina-lime, and silica-magnesia-soda, show some immiscibility.

The solution of liquids in liquids is more limited and varies greatly according to their nature and the temperature. There are numerous examples of perfect miscibility, in fact that seems to be the general rule in the silicates and in commercial glasses and glazes. Melts which are miscible at high temperatures may be immiscible at low temperatures and vice versa. However, immiscibility is not unknown, as Greig[13] and others have reported.

Le Chatelier[14] found that the binary system, boric oxide and zinc oxide, gave immiscibility when the basicity or acidity fell outside of certain limits; i.e., the continued addition of boric acid to a glassy transparent melt of a metallic-borate will be accompanied by the separation into two layers—the excess of the boric oxide will float on top of the clear glass. The easy mutual solubility in glass and glaze melts, generally observed, is a happy circumstance inasmuch as it facilitates the production of desirable results otherwise difficult and costly to obtain.

Immiscibility is common also in $RO–B_2O_3$ and $RO–SiO_2–B_2O_3$ systems. Examples are: B_2O_3–BaO, Bi_2O_3, CaO, CeO, MgO, PbO, ThO_2, and ZnO, respectively; and Al_2O_3–SiO_2, BaO–SiO_2, CaO–SiO_2, PbO–SiO_2, ZnO–SiO_2, and B_2O_3–SiO_2, respectively. Detailed information on immiscibility in oxide systems was collected and published by Levin, Robbins and McMurdie.[10]

A false immiscibility may be caused sometimes by the separation of the more fusible and fluid portion of the glaze, which is absorbed by the porous body, or it forms a glassy magma surrounding the partially fused and undissolved portions. A more careful selection of the raw materials or the incorporation of the troublesome portion in a frit, as a part of the glaze batch, will remedy the difficulty.

Hummel[15] quoted Kracek as having summarized liquid immiscibility in binary silicate systems in a comprehensive diagram involving RO–SiO_2 and R_2O–SiO_2 systems, including the 'S-shaped' liquidus curves of some of them. He also discussed the "tendency to immiscibility" in some systems like the RO–SiO_2. These references were to the most familiar type of immiscibility in which two liquids remain side by side without mixing. An example of analogy would be a layer of oil on water. Other extreme examples would be mercury and water or a layer of molten sodium sulfate floating on molten glass.

The two-liquid regions might not be so strikingly obvious. The separation might be on a fine-grained, but macroscopic scale; or on a microscopic scale.

There is another type, now becoming commonly recognized in silicate technology, where the cooled melt or glass appears to be one homogeneous liquid. It may even be optically transparent and homogeneous even under high-power optical microscopy. However, when examined by electron microscopy, it will be disclosed that one liquid phase, usually minute spheres, is dispersed in a glass matrix of different composition. An example is shown in figure 6.4.

Similar fine-structure immiscibility is observed in which the glass as originally cooled appears to be one homogeneous amorphous phase even under the highest electron microscopic magnification. But when heat treated in an appropriate manner, liquid–liquid separation occurs.

Sometimes glasses having fine structure immiscibility are optically clear and transparent; sometimes they are opaque. Often, as the original melt cools, it will be clear and transparent but upon further cooling the formation of two liquids will occur and cause light scattering. The electron microscope is extremely useful, if not indispensable in observing and identifying fine-structure immiscibility.

Hummel[16,17] has investigated immiscibility in several systems of interest to ceramists. This type of system can be of interest in the creation

Figure 6.4. Electron micrograph showing liquid–liquid immiscibility in a $PbO–B_2O_3–SiO_2$ glass.[16]

of a new and sorely needed glaze. For example, to fit low expansion bodies. The glaze would be caused to have liquid–liquid separation and the two separated phases crystallized to produce glass ceramic-type coatings of extraordinary low expansion coefficients. Hummel was interested in the development of opaque glazes by the application of silicate liquid immiscibility. Opaque glasses and frits have been prepared based on two liquid phases of differing refractive indices. Work has so far been very limited, but future developments in this area are to be expected.

Induced liquid–liquid immiscibility is of possible value in glaze development. It possibly is of even more importance to be aware of the possible appearance of liquid–liquid separations that might occur unintentionally.

Fluid State

Inorganic as well as organic substances may be produced in the glassy condition but the term glass, in its most widely used meaning, is a product formed from silica, the silicates, or a mixture of the same. Inorganic glasses are relatively rare since the number of glass-forming elements is narrowly limited by the chemico-physical peculiarities of the essential lattice structure.

Glass made from silica, the silicates, or analogous glass forming compounds—boric oxide, phosphoric oxide, etc.—possesses physical properties in the rigid state which are continuous with those in the fluid state; in other words, glass is a supercooled or undercooled melt or solution. Its viscosity, which is one of its characteristic and most important properties, varies from that of a thin fluid at a high temperature (ca. 1,300° C upwards) to a rigid condition at room temperature. This property permits the shaping of the mass to form wares and also the removal of strains, which otherwise might be disruptive. Also, strains may be developed and maintained in the ware to increase its mechanical strength.

When the melt of a pure substance or the saturated solution of a salt is slowly cooled, crystallization will take place. Crystals may be macrocrystalline, i.e., large and easily visible; microcrystalline, i.e., microscopic in size; or sub-microscopic, i.e., distinguishable or identifiable only with the most refined methods such as the X-ray diffraction pattern or with the use of the electron microscope. Only recently these newer techniques have given a hint of the probable structure of liquids, including glasses.

The terms supercooled and undercooled, which have long been applied to glasses, are not explanations but merely descriptions and not helpful until the structure of liquids is understood. In fact, the rapidly expanding knowledge of the structure of glass will probably give us a better understanding of all liquids. However, the comparison of glass with undercooled liquids is helpful. When a conventional liquid melts, or the hot saturated solution of a salt is gradually cooled, a temperature will finally be reached at which crystals will appear and no further decline in temperature will be observed until this stage is completed.

This lag or terrace in the cooling curve, figure 6.5, is due to the compensating effect of the heat which is liberated by crystallization. A similar effect will be observed in the melting of a crystal due to the conversion of heat to the work of fusion. These lags usually coincide, but high viscosity of the melt may interfere. If the cooling process is done with caution,

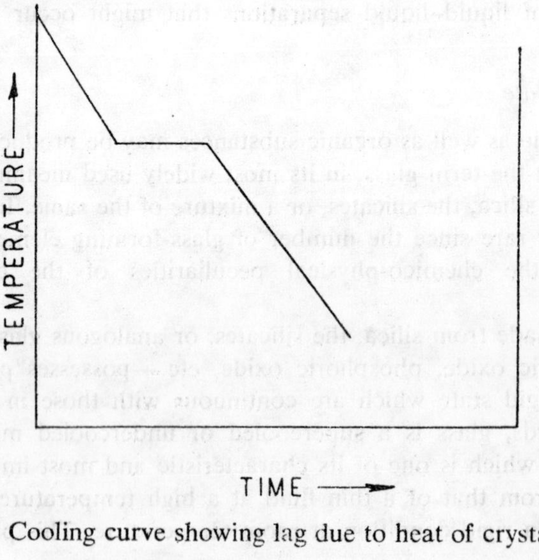

Figure 6.5. Cooling curve showing lag due to heat of crystallization.

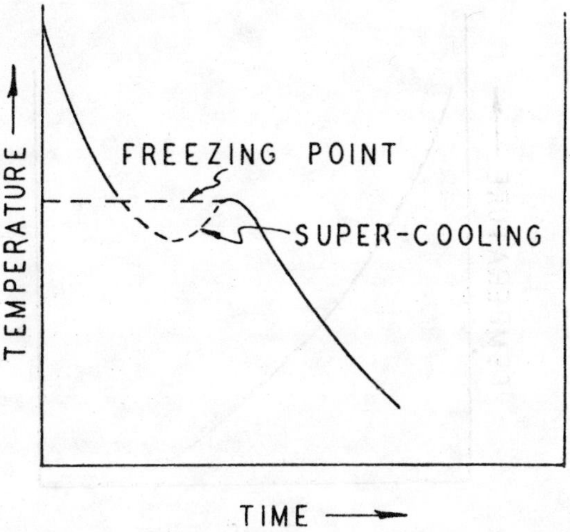

Figure 6.6. Supercooled liquids may restore temperature to freezing point on crystallization.

especially with very viscous melts, it is possible to pass the freezing point for several degrees, i.e., supercool, before crystallization begins. When crystallization does occur, the evolution of heat may proceed so rapidly as to restore the temperature of the system to that of the proper freezing point, figure 6.6. A corresponding superheating has been observed in the case of microcline.

The cooling curve (or the fusion curve) of an amorphous material, such as a glass, is smooth as shown in figure 6.7. If crystallization occurs to a very limited amount in a mixture, such as ordinary glasses, the thermal effect just described may be too small to appear on the cooling curve.

In the present state of knowledge of the nature of silicate solutions, such as glass, at high temperature, it is generally assumed that the component oxides are present as such or in simple combinations of a fugitive nature. These groupings have been described as dynamic, not static. There is a temporary sharing of the binding forces with the adjacent atoms to satisfy the immediate and temporary needs. As the thermal excitation decreases with the falling temperature, the coherence may result in all possible molecular groupings in proportions dependent upon the conditions tending constantly toward the more complex or permanent molecular species. The appearance of certain crystalline groups is evidence only of the orientation of the components under suitable time-temperature-viscosity conditions and not of their presence under other less favorable conditions.

Discontinuities or lags in the cooling and the heating curves are generally associated with internal structural orientations, and in the more sig-

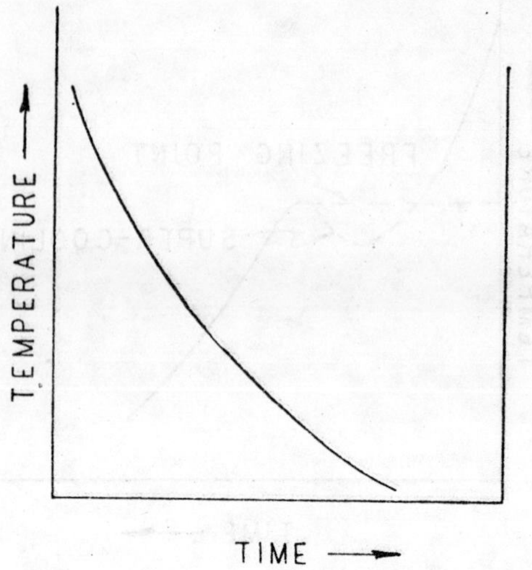

Figure 6.7. Cooling curve of amorphous material.

nificant cases are found to be indicators of important changes in the physical properties, such as volume (or density), thermal, optical, electrical, and mechanical.

Tammann and Hesse[18] have shown a curve for a cooling melt in figure 6.8, indicating empirically three characteristic zones. Zone 3 is the fluid state at high temperatures, that is ca. 1,350° to 1,400° C, when the glass can be drawn as a thread; the viscosity will be of the order of 10^2 poises and less. (This term is defined later in the chapter.) Zone 2 includes the glassy range suitable for many kinds of working operations depending upon its mobility at particular temperatures. The maximum viscosity at the minimum working temperature will be of the order of 10^7 to 10^{10} poises. The viscosity at T_a, the lower end of zone 2, will be of the order of 10^{13} poises in the annealing range, or a temperature of about 500° to 600° C. The above correlation of properties and temperatures is only approximate since these are dependent upon the composition of the glass.

Zones 1 and 3 of the curve are virtually straight lines, and in zone 2 there is a gentle curve joining the other segments. Tammann names this the "transformation interval" and it may be of the magnitude of 20° to 30° C. The curve of the first derivative, dP/dT, figure 6.9, shows the presence of an inflection point at T_w. Some observers have sought to interpret inflection or transformation points as indications of the presence of definite compounds. On the other hand, it has been shown that the previous thermal treatment of the glass may be the cause.

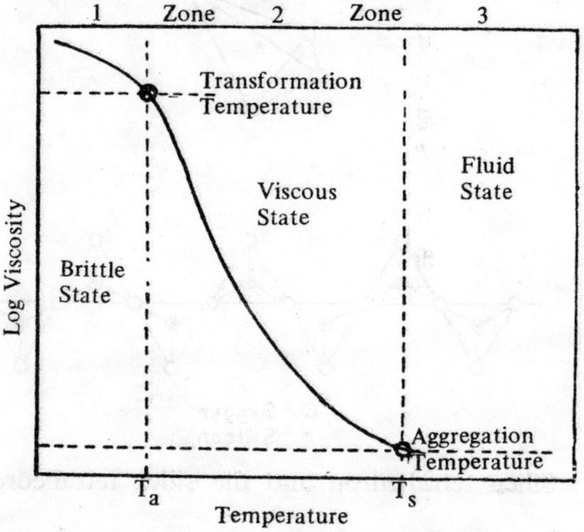

Figure 6.8. Three stages in the cooling of glass melts.[18]

THE STRUCTURE OF GLASS. As stated previously, the use of the X-ray diffraction technique has been invaluable in furnishing data useful for the understanding of the forces governing the structure of glass and its properties. Briefly reviewing the elementary facts, we start with the generally accepted theory that the "lattice" structure, deduced from the diffraction pattern of a crystal, is due to the geometric arrangement of the constituent atoms or ions of the composition and that the crystal is an exemplification of the molecular structure. Glass does not give a comparable crystal pattern but one which is highly diffused, similar to liquids in general, which is in keeping with the widely held opinion that the glassy condition is coextensive with the liquid condition at high temperature and lacking in the

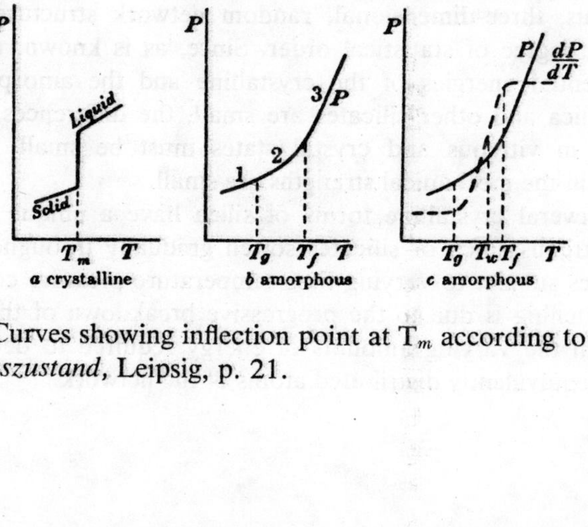

Figure 6.9. Curves showing inflection point at T_m according to Tamman.[18] 1933. *Der Glaszustand*, Leipsig, p. 21.

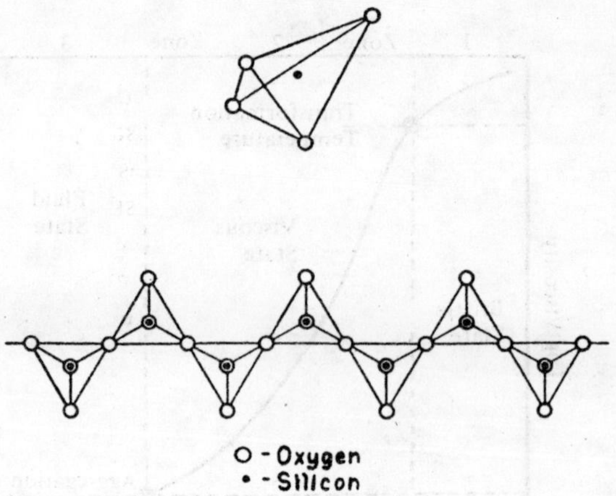

Figure 6.10. Silica tetrahedron and the silica tetrahedron in a chain.[19]

presence of definite, well-organized compounds (excluding devitrification products, of course). However, the diffused pattern which may be obtained is susceptible of the following explanation, proposed by Zachariesen.[19]

The unit basis of structure in silica and the silicates is a tetrahedron formed by a silicon atom linked by primary bonds to four atoms of oxygen (fig. 6.10). The tetrahedra are joined by a bond from a corner oxygen to a corner oxygen in an adjacent tetrahedron, and thus a three-dimensional arrangement is formed. The chemical and physical properties of a compound will depend upon (1) space relationships, which determine the density, volume changes, etc.; and (2) electric charges or valencies which determine the strength, hardness, refractoriness, etc. In the crystalline silica and silicates there is a periodic and symmetrical distribution of these tetrahedra. This conception is shown in a two-dimensional plan of the arrangement representing crystal silica, figure 6.11. On the other hand, the glassy (vitreous) silica (fig. 6.11) is assumed by Zachariesen and others to have a continuous, three-dimensional, random network structure which, however, has a degree of statistical order. Since, as is known, the differences in the potential energies of the crystalline and the amorphous (glassy) forms of silica and other silicates are small, the differences in the atomic differences in vitreous and crystal states must be small; therefore, the differences in the mechanical strengths are small.

The several crystalline forms of silica have a unique melting point, whereas vitreous silica or silicates soften gradually throughout a range of temperatures subject to varying time-temperature-pressure conditions. This gradual softening is due to the progressive breakdown of the structure resulting from the varying amounts of energy required to detach the structurally nonequivalently distributed atoms of the network.

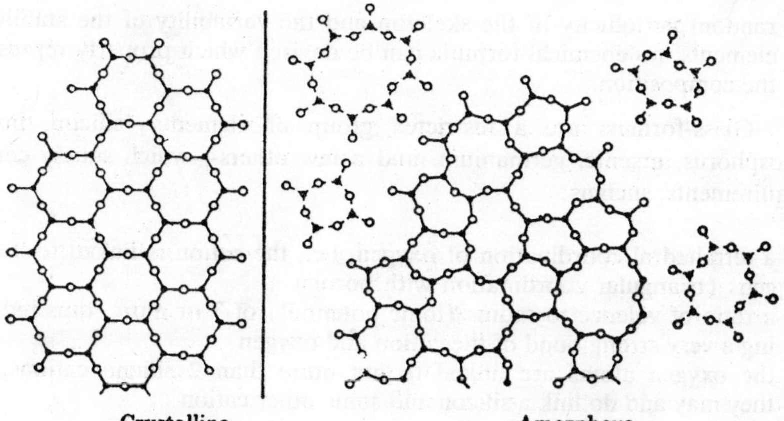

Crystalline. **Amorphous.**

• = silicon atom; O = oxygen atom; - - - = "liquid"

Figure 6.11. *Left:* crystal silica lattice; *right:* fused silica lattice.

Viscosity is due to the internal friction of the atoms or aggregation of atoms. The less the bonds between the silica tetrahedra are disrupted and the larger and more complex the associations of the silicates, the greater will be the impedance to movement of the groups and the greater the viscosity. High viscosity is due to uniformity and strength of bond linkages which must be broken or extended, and therefore weakened, in order to permit flow. Also, we may assume that a wide range of groupings exists at any moment, varying from the simple to the complex, and there is much entanglement of the groups. Supercooling is the consequence of this confused and viscous condition at the freezing temperature.

The high bond strength existing in the silica structure is manifest in its mechanical strength, its hardness, and its resistance to the action of most solvents. The low thermal expansion of fused silica is due to the random arrangement of the internal structure, permitting some freedom of adjustment with small volume change and with minimum effect upon the bonding strength.

The present conception of the structure of glass may be stated briefly as follows:

1. It is a product having a random or noncrystalline network in which there is a definite scheme of coordination with definite interatomic distances, but in which no unit repeats itself at regular intervals in three dimensions.[20] The skeletal unit is a tetrahedral of triangular coordination of a glass former with oxygen.
2. The interstices of this network are more or less filled by stabilizing elements which profoundly modify the physical properties. Because of the

random periodicity of the skeleton and the variability of the stabilizing elements, no chemical formula can be devised which properly represents the composition.

Glass-formers are a restricted group of elements—silicon, boron, phosphorus, arsenic, germanium, and a few others—which satisfy certain requirements, such as:

1. a tetrahedral coordination of oxygen, i.e., the cation is linked to 4 oxygens (triangular coordination with boron)
2. a ratio of valence to radius (ionic potential) of 7 or more, thus indicating a very strong bond of the cation and oxygen
3. the oxygen atoms are linked to not more than 2 silicon cations, but they may and do link a silicon and some other cation

The stabilizers are elements possessing an ionic potential less than 7. Those ordinarily used in commercial glasses are: sodium, potassium, calcium, magnesium, barium, lead, and aluminum. Other elements, exclusive of coloring agents, opacifiers, decolorizers, etc., and less frequently used are zinc and lithium. This list is constantly being extended to meet scientific and industrial requirements.

These stabilizers occupy the spaces in the silica network; consequently their size, or ionic radius, and their bond strength, or valency, are of great importance. Reference to table 6.4 shows that the stabilizers are relatively large as compared with the glass formers.

A comparison of the ionic potentials of these stabilizers with the experimental results of substitutions in glass compositions illustrates the value of a knowledge of the above data and offers a rational explanation of the results. For example: the substitution of alkaline earths for alkalies in glasses increases the strength, durability, and refractoriness by increasing the strength of the structure as indicated by the higher ionic potentials. The optical and electrical properties can also be conditioned. Beryllium increases the electrical resistivity of glasses if substituted for alkali or the other alkaline earths. Bivalent lead and barium have similar effects in fusions and in mechanical, electrical, and optical properties.

Aluminum is of special interest because it can coordinate either 6 or 4 oxygens, which explains the double role it plays in glass. The substitution of small amounts for soda or lime improves the working properties of the hot glass and the hardness, mechanical strength, elasticity, and resistance to chemical attack. This is explained by the assumption that small amounts of the aluminum may act as a substitution for the sodium, and the higher bonding power (trivalency) of the former increases the strength of the structure. However, the introduction of the larger amounts of alumi-

Table 6.4. Some cations used in glass and their ionic potentials

Cations	*Valency*	*Ionic radius (Å)*	*Ionic potential valence/radius*
Lithium	1	0.68	1.5
Sodium	1	0.98	1.0
Potassium	1	1.33	0.75
Beryllium	2	0.31	6.5
Magnesium	2	0.71	2.8
Calcium	2	0.99	2.0
Strontium	2	1.13	1.8
Barium	2	1.35	1.4
Zinc	2	0.74	2.7
Lead	2	1.21	1.17
Boron	3	0.20	15.0
Aluminum	3	0.50	6.0
Silicon	4	0.41	9.8
Titanium	4	0.68	5.9
Zirconium	4	0.80	5.0
Tin	4	0.71	5.6
Lead	4	0.84	4.8
Phosphorus	5	0.34	14.7
Arsenic	5	0.47	10.6

num (ionic potential, 6) for silicon (ionic potential, 9.8) obviously weakens the structure.

Attention should be paid to the very large ionic radius of oxygen (1.40) as contrasted with the radii of the common elements used in glass. Since the volume composition of common glass is 92% oxygen ions, 5% sodium ions, 2% calcium ions, and only 1% of silicon ions, it is quite clear that such a glass volume is predominately an oxygen structure to which the glass formers (and stabilizers) have given form.

VISCOSITY. Viscosity is a property of fluids, is due to internal friction, and is manifest in the rate of flow. It is of very great importance at all stages in the preparation and use of glassy melts at high temperatures. Only a brief summary can be made here of its influence on melting, fining, application, crystallization, decoration, and annealing.

The rate and the uniformity of the melting operation will depend upon the easier melting and more mobile portion surrounding, penetrating, and dissolving the refractory grains. Diffusion during and after this state will be hastened by the increasing mobility and chemical changes accompanying the rising temperature. Solution and diffusion are accelerated by the agitation caused by the gases set free; therefore, homogeneity will be attained as the time, temperature, and viscosity permit.

While the escape of the gases plays a very important role in the preliminary stage—the advanced sintering and prefusing stage of a glaze—their retention beyond that point would yield a product marred by blisters, bubbles, blebs, seeds and pinholes. A similar condition in glass manufacture is corrected by a prolonged "fining period," that is, maintaining the melt at a high temperature for a sufficiently long time to permit the fining reagents to complete the task of "sweeping" out the bubbles. Since the layer of glaze on the ware is very thin, there is no recognized "fining" period; but a proper regulation of the composition and temperature, hence viscosity, accomplishes the same purpose. Naturally the expansion, and consequently the increased buoyancy, of the bubbles at the higher temperatures is an equally important factor.

Viscosity is the property which controls the thickness uniformity of the matured glaze. If the glaze is too mobile, it will drain off vertical or inclined surfaces and form a puddle about the foot of the piece, "freezing" it to its support; or it will result in an objectionable accumulation on an edge or rim or at a low spot. If such a fluid glaze covers a colored decoration, the movement of the molten glaze often causes a smearing or even the displacement of the pattern, or at least the marring of the details.

Glazes which are very mobile cannot be used satisfactorily on highly porous bodies, whether previously fired or unfired, because they penetrate too far and too readily below the surface, initiating physical and chemical effects not only in the body but in the finished glaze coat. In fact, the porous body may soak up the more fusible portion of the glaze as it forms during the initial stages of the glaze fusion, leaving the more refractory portions of the composition isolated on the surface as an immature or semi-vitreous coating.

The high viscosity of the glaze is the indispensible restraining influence operating to limit or prevent the formation of crystals. Without this restraint on the formation and growth of crystals, the defect of devitrification probably would be inescapable, and the lustrous, glassy, or transparent glazes would be rarities.

The unit of viscosity is named the *poise* after Poisseule, a French physicist who studied this property. This unit has been defined by Maxwell as "the tangential force per square centimeter of area of either of two horizontal planes, one centimeter apart, one of which is fixed, while the other moves with a unit velocity, the space between being filled with a liquid empirically selected as having a unit viscosity." Water at 20° C has a viscosity of 0.010 poise. Castor oil at the standard temperature has a viscosity of 10 poises, and commercial glass ranges from about 10^{13} poises at 500° C to 10^{2} poises at 1,400° C. The conventional symbol of the poise is the Greek letter eta (η), and for convenience in expressing the rather

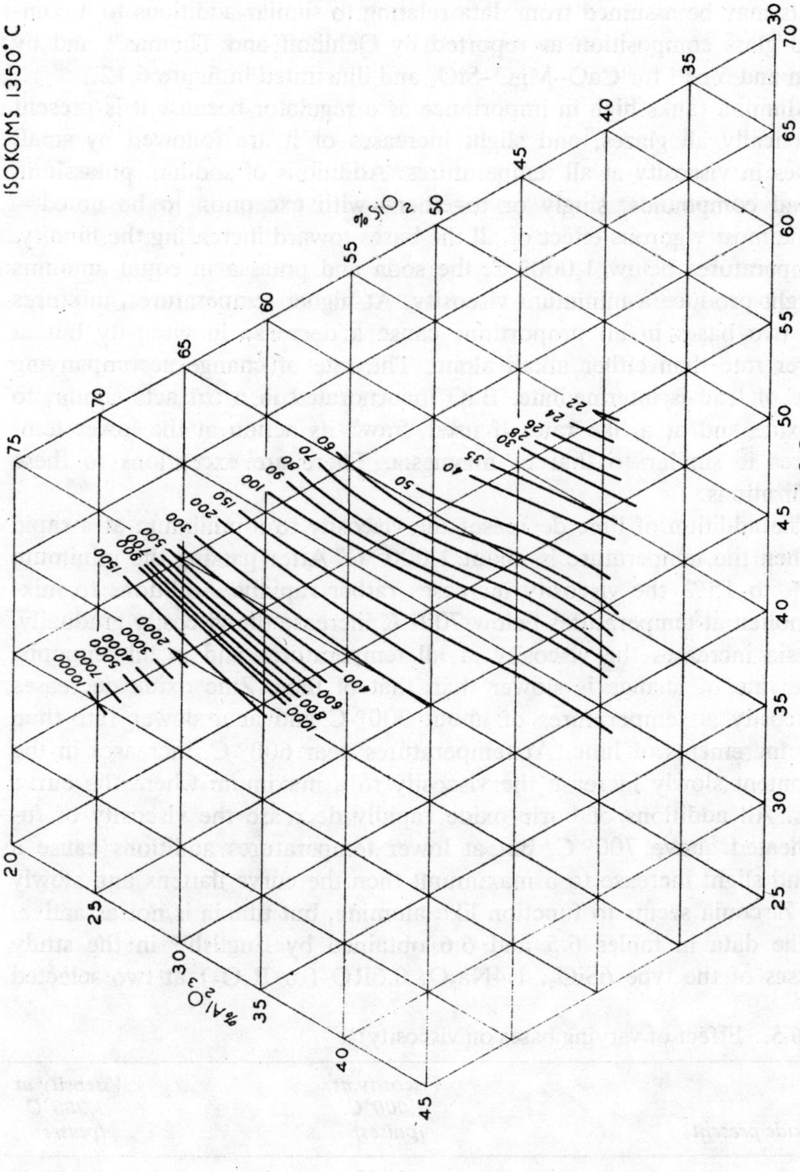

Figure 6.12. Viscosity of melts in the systems $CaO-Al_2O_3-SiO_2$. After Machin and Yee.[22]

cumbersome values of eta, frequently encountered, the logarithm of the unit is represented by the Greek letter zeta (ζ).

The effects of alterations in the amounts of the more usual glaze constituents may be assumed from data relating to similar additions to a commercial glass composition as reported by Gehlhoff and Thomas[21] and by Machin and Yee[22] for CaO–MgO–SiO_2 and illustrated in figure 6.12.

Alumina ranks high in importance as a regulator because it is present in practically all glazes, and slight increases of it are followed by small increases in viscosity at all temperatures. Additions of sodium, potassium, and lead compounds, singly or together—with exception to be noted—have the most vigorous effect of all the bases toward increasing the fluidity. At temperatures below 1,000° C, the soda and potassa in equal amounts by weight produce a minimum viscosity. At higher temperatures, mixtures of the two bases in all proportions cause a decrease in viscosity but at a slower rate than either alkali alone. The rate of change accompanying the use of lead is intermediate. BaO incorporated in a frit acts similar to lead oxide and at a like rate. If used "raw" its action at the lower temperatures is similar to that of magnesia. There are exceptions to these generalizations.

The addition of lime decreases the viscosity to a minimum at a rapid rate when the temperature is about 1,000° C. After passing the minimum at 10% to 15% the viscosity increases rather rapidly. Additions to mixtures molten at temperatures below 700° C increase the viscosity gradually. Magnesia increases the viscosity at all temperatures and in all amounts, but the rate of change is slower than that of lime. Zinc oxide decreases the viscosity at temperatures of about 900° C and at a slower rate than similar increments of lime. At temperatures near 600° C, increases in the zinc content slowly increase the viscosity to a maximum where the curve flattens. All additions of boric oxide rapidly decrease the viscosity of fusions heated above 700° C, but at lower temperatures additions cause a slow and slight increase to a maximum; then the curve flattens and slowly drops. Zirconia seems to function like alumina, but titania is not as active.

The data in tables 6.5 and 6.6 obtained by English[23] in the study of glasses of the type $6SiO_2$, $1.4Na_2O$, $0.6RO$ (or R_2O_3) at two selected

Table 6.5. Effect of varying bases on viscosity[23]

Basic oxide present	*Viscosity at 1,000° C (poises)*	*Viscosity at 1,200° C (poises)*
Lime	5,500	457
Magnesia	11,200	933
Alumina	43,600	3,980

Table 6.6. Comparison of the influence of CaO, MgO and Al_2O_3 in silicate glasses on high temperature viscosity.[23]

Variable oxide species	*Range of viscosity, poises*	*Temperature range (°C)*
Lime	141 to 7.26 × 10^6	749 to 1385
Magnesia	109 to 1.17 × 10^7	748 to 1410
Alumina	627 to 5.56 × 10^6	797 to 1390

temperatures are of interest in showing the relative effects of three bases after equivalent substitutions.

The viscosity of fired or matured glazes in the temperature range of 500° to 800° C has some importance. This primarily is in connection with the firing of decorations on glazed ware in a special firing to 600° to 800° C. During this decorating fire, bubbles in the glaze can form or grow and perhaps burst and leave unhealed craters. The texture of the glazed surfaces and even the number of bubbles have been shown[24] to be associated with the viscosity of the glaze at the decorating temperature. Bubbles will expand and grow in glazes having low viscosities at decorating temperature but none will develop in the rigid glaze. The low temperature viscosity also defines the temperature at which the glaze becomes sufficiently rigid to develop stress due to thermal expansion when cooled; or released when heated.

James and Norris[24] ran low-temperature viscosities on thirty different pottery glazes with results as summarized in table 6.7. These values were determined by the application of a bending-beam method.

Although viscosity data on glazes in the low-temperature range are rare, results of measurements in the high temperature range (800° to 1,350° C) are even more so. This property is, as has been mentioned, important in the maturing of glazes. High temperature viscosities of pottery

Table 6.7. Low-temperature viscosities of some pottery glazes[24]

	Log$_{10}$ of viscosity, η			
	Lead bearing		*Leadless*	
Temp. °C	*No.**	*Range*	*No.**	*Range*
600	7	9.6–11.4	–	–
650	19	8.3–10.8	–	–
700	19	7.2– 9.2	10	9.2–10.9
750	10	7.1– 8.1	11	7.9– 9.1
800	–	–	14	7.3– 8.0

*Identifying numbers used by James and Norris.[24]

Table 6.8. Examples of viscosities of pottery glazes for the temperature range 800° to 1,300° C[24]

Glaze No.	Type of glaze	Log_{10} of viscosities at designated temp., °C 800	900	1,000	1,100	1,200	1,300
1	Leadless	–	–	5.3	4.3	3.7	3.4
2	Leadless	–	5.7	4.5	3.8	3.3	3.1
3	Leadless	–	–	4.4	3.8	3.3	2.9
4	Leadless	6.8	5.4	4.5	3.9	3.3	–
5	Low-solubility	5.6	4.4	2.6	3.0	–	–

glazes were measured at the British Ceramic Research Association and reported by James and Norris.[24] Some of their data are summarized in table 6.8.

These authors presented considerable data showing that glazes conformed to the laws for viscous flow of a Newtonian liquid. Glazes containing 5% of suspended tin oxide, and opacified thereby, still behaved as a true liquid. Two viscosity-temperature curves from James and Norris are shown in figure 6.13. The forms of the viscosity-temperature curves were found to be identical with those obtained on commercial glasses. The glazes tested behaved in accordance with theories on glass viscosity.

A fairly good correlation exists between the flow of a glaze down an inclined plane and the measured viscosity of bulk glaze in a crucible. This conclusion has been supported by Lehmann, Engell and Hellbrugge.[25]

Due to the many complex factors involved, it is not possible to deal quantitatively with the relation between glaze composition and viscosity. Some generalizations can be made. Glass technologists know that viscosities calculated in accordance with additive relationships are extremely limited in their applications and validity. Bremond,[26,26a] after extensive investigations, found that increasing SiO_2 and Al_2O_3 was accompanied by increasing viscosities measured at 1,200° C.

Bremond concluded that at the maturing temperature, the viscosity of glazes is in the range of log viscosity equal to 2.5 to 4.3. The glazes at log viscosity 5 would be immature; at log η equal to 4, matt, and at log η equal to 2.6 it would be too fluid, overfired, and very bubbly. He concluded that the ideal viscosity is around 2,400 poises (log viscosity of about 3.38, but always in the range of η equal to 2.5 to 4.3).

Diffusion

Diffusion is the phenomenon of the migration of ions, atoms, or molecules in a gas, liquid, or solid from a high to a lower concentration. Some examples of diffusion which are of ceramic interest follow.

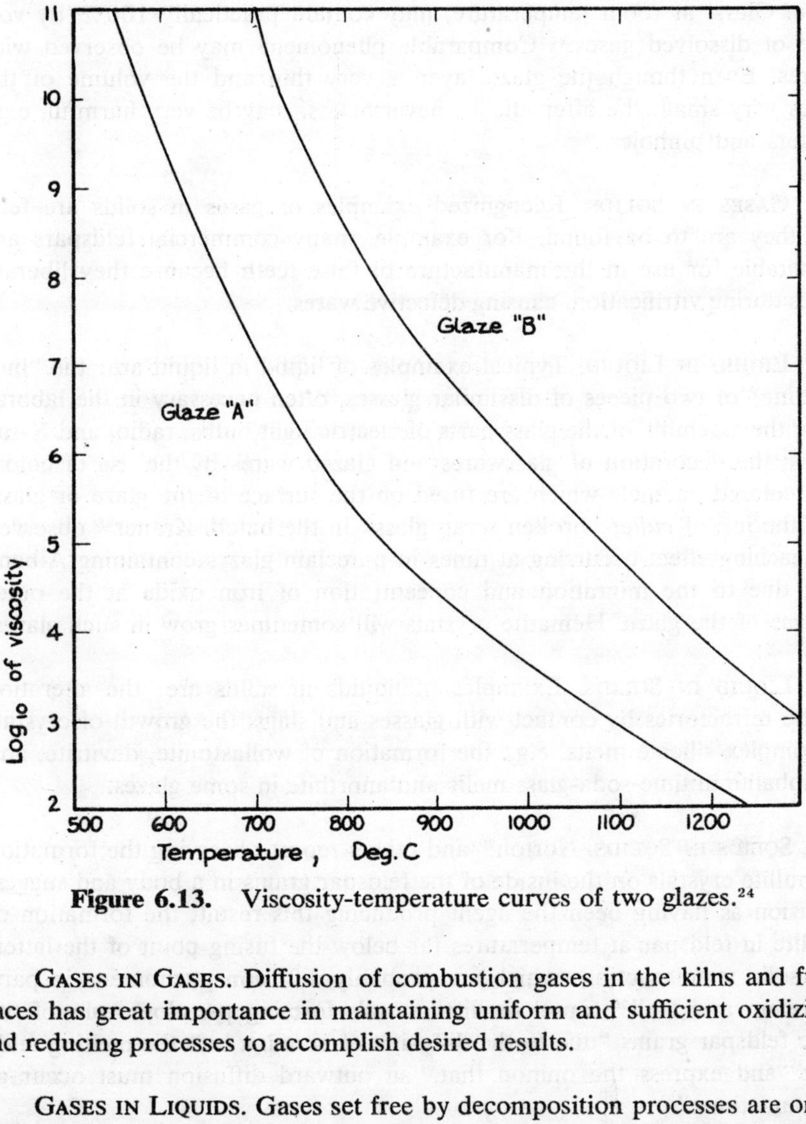

Figure 6.13. Viscosity-temperature curves of two glazes.[24]

Gases in Gases. Diffusion of combustion gases in the kilns and furnaces has great importance in maintaining uniform and sufficient oxidizing and reducing processes to accomplish desired results.

Gases in Liquids. Gases set free by decomposition processes are only slowly and partially liberated from the molten glasses and glazes; therefore, a fining period is necessary during which high temperatures and chemical and mechanical methods are employed to expell the maximum volume of these gases and thus prevent the appearance of seeds and bubbles in the finished product. The sources of these gases are not limited to decomposable salts but include atmospheric gases retained between the fine particles of the batch as well as those adsorbed on surfaces of the individual grains; also the combustion gases ad- or absorbed by the batch in the furnace. Glass, at room temperature, may contain practically 100% by volume of dissolved gases.[27] Comparable phenomena may be observed with glazes. Even though the glaze layer is very thin and the volume of the gases very small, the after effects, nevertheless, may be very harmful, e.g., blisters and pinholes.

GASES IN SOLIDS. Recognized examples of gases in solids are few, but they are to be found. For example, many commercial feldspars are unsuitable for use in the manufacture of false teeth because they liberate gases during vitrification, causing defective wares.

LIQUID IN LIQUID. Typical examples of liquid in liquid are: the "butt welding" of two pieces of dissimilar glasses, often necessary in the laboratory; the assembly of the glass parts of electric light bulbs, radio, and X-ray tubes; the decoration of glasswares and glazed wares by the use of colors and colored enamels which are fused on the surface of the glaze or glass; and the use of *cullet* (broken scrap glass) in the batch. Kraner[28] observed a bleaching effect occurring at times in porcelain glazes containing Albany slip, due to the migration and concentration of iron oxide at the outer surface of the glaze. Hematite crystals will sometimes grow in such glazes.

LIQUID IN SOLIDS. Examples of liquids in solids are: the alteration of the refractories by contact with glasses and slags; the growth of crystals in complex silicate melts, e.g., the formation of wollastonite, devitrite, and cristobalite in lime-soda-glass melts and anorthite in some glazes.

SOLIDS IN SOLIDS. Norton[29] and others report observing the formation of mullite crystals on the inside of the feldspar grains in a body and suggest diffusion as having been the agent producing this result; the formation of mullite in feldspar at temperatures far below the fusing point of the latter; and solid state reactions which are probably diffusion phenomena in part. Schramm and Hall[30] found mullite crystals forming pseudomorphs of the large feldspar grains "due to the diffusion of alumina into the melting feldspar" and express the opinon that "an outward diffusion must occur at the same time."

Sintering and pyrochemical reactions of finely divided material depend primarily on diffusion dynamics. The transport of ion species into, out of, and through batch grains and surrounding reaction rims is accomplished by means of diffusion. The microstructure of a matured feldspathic porcelain affords an excellent example of diffusion. Microscopic examination of thin sections of matured porcelains shows the larger grains of feldspar to contain growths of mullite needles in their central parts. Reference to the K_2O–Al_2O_3–SiO_2 equilibrium diagram shows that mullite cannot exist at equilibrium in feldspar. It shows, also, the areas of composition in which mullite could develop. Simple arithmetic then tells how much K_2O would have to be diffused out of $K_2O \cdot Al_2O_3 \cdot 6SiO_2$ to reach compositions where mullite is a stable phase.

To carry this thought one step further, what happens to the K_2O that leaves the feldspar grains? It diffuses into the surrounding areas, rich in clay and in silica, and poor in alkali. By and large, this is the only mechanism for the development of pyrochemical reactions in the earliest stages of firing, and is an important factor even at high temperatures.

Fick, in 1855, discovered the law governing the rate of diffusion, which is:

$$\frac{dm}{dz} = -Dq\frac{dc}{dx}$$

when *dm* is the mass, *dz* is the time, *dc* is the concentration, *dx* is the distance, *q* is the cross sectional area, and *D* is the coefficient (sometimes constant). The law states that the quantity of material *dm* which passes in the time *dz* through a cross-section *q* in cm^2 is proportional dc/dx. The dc/dx is the driving force.

"The quantity diffusing through a given area is proportional to the difference between the concentrations of two areas infinitely near one another, or is proportional to differences of concentration." The law is modified for high concentrations since diffusion rates decrease gradually as concentration increases. It does not apply in those cases in which there are molecular changes in the condition of the dissolved substance, e.g., ionization or dilution.

According to Tammann,[31] the value of *D*, the diffusion coefficient of Fick's law, is a periodic function of the atomic weight. Cations having large atomic volumes have the smaller *D* values. Therefore, the alkali and alkali earth elements have smaller *D* values than zinc, cadmium, tin, gold, and lead. There is a close parallelism between the rates of diffusion and the electrical conductivities of the elements.[32] When several substances diffuse from a mixture, each substance diffuses almost independently of the others, each at its own specific rate. The order of the diffusion-coefficients in aqueous solutions is as follows:

$$H > K > NH_4 > Ag > Na > Ca, Sr, Ba, Pb, Hg > Mn, Mg, Zn > Cu > Al$$

Since the osmotic pressure increases in proportion to the absolute temperature, diffusion must occur from the warmer to the cooler parts until the osmotic pressure has become the same in both and, therefore, concentrations must vary inversely as the absolute temperature. In the more concentrated solutions the ratio between concentration and absolute temperature is somewhat modified.

Mellor[33] reported that a glaze fired on a biscuit containing cobalt stain will sometimes show a blue coloration.

Surface Tension

The forces which cause small quantities of liquids at room temperature to form globular drops on horizontal surfaces operate in molten glazes, and the results are similar insofar as the temperature, composition, and viscosity of a molten mass will permit. The phenomenon observed at the liquid-solid contact is known as interfacial tension. If the phenomenon occurs when a liquid phase is in contact with its vapor or a mixture of air and its vapor, it is then described as surface tension.

The internal forces of the liquid function as an inward attraction exerting a pull on the surface as though the liquid drop were inclosed in a tough, elastic membrane under uniform tension. If the mass of the liquid is small, it will assume a globular form, since the sphere has the minimum surface area. As the mass is increased, gravity will distort the sphere, altering its shape to that of a flattened globule, a rounded disc, or simply a flat, thin layer with a slightly thickened edge.

In all cases of vitrified wares and glassy melts the surface skin will be found denser, harder, more lustrous, and more free from blebs than the interior. Such results are natural consequences of the forces of tension operating within the more fusible and more fluid compositions. The maximum effect in such a case will be attained under static surface tension conditions when sufficient time has elapsed and the temperature and viscosity permit an approach to equilibrium.

The work of some investigators has shown that orientation accompanies migration in some liquids and this may be the case in glass. Little is known about the surface tensions of solids. Bancroft[34] suggested that the melting point of a solid may be defined as that temperature at which surface tension overcomes the crystalline forces. Also Mellor and associates[35] said that "the softening temperature measures the temperature at which the inward surface pressure of the substance becomes greater than the intermolecular forces which hinder the molecules taking up the position of stable equilibrium—the minimum surface area."

There is an intimate relation between surface tension and vapor tension as is clearly shown in the phenomenon of capillarity. Hence the penetration of a porous body by a molten glaze will be controlled by the viscosity of the glaze, the size and character of the pores, and the interfacial surface tension of the glaze. Of course the chemical reaction between the body and the glaze is always important and is frequently the most important condition.

Reference has already been made to the fact that powders sinter at lower temperatures than the softening or melting temperatures of the same compositions in the mass. That is, the surface energy increases as the small particle is subdivided. This relation may be represented by the expression, given by Morey,[36]

$$\gamma = \frac{\delta \epsilon}{\delta \varsigma}$$

where γ = surface tension, $\delta\epsilon$ = energy change, and $\delta\varsigma$ = surface area change. This is conditioned by the state of the neighboring masses. With the decreasing size of the particle and corresponding decrease in the radius of the curvature, the greater the inward surface pressure (tension) will be. As the temperature is raised, the inertia of the molecules in a glaze is gradually overcome and softening of the particle takes place, with perceptible rounding of the edges. If the temperature is sufficiently high and other conditions such as viscosity and surface tension permit, small masses of glazes will frequently separate in patches and even as small beads.

The ability of a glaze to "wet" the surface upon which it is applied determines, in part, its adherence. This phenomenon is completed by the chemical reactions between the body and the glaze which are much more pronounced in cases where the glaze and body are matured together at a high temperature. Low temperature glazes matured on a biscuit body are, comparatively, much less active. An examination under the microscope of a thin section cut at right angles to the interface of the body and glaze illustrates this condition very clearly.

The property of "wetting" is due to the relations between the three independent surface tensions which may exist at the contact surfaces. These are the liquid (molten glaze)-air contact, the solid (body)-air contact, and the solid-liquid contact. The surface tension of the body-air cannot be measured, but the adhesion tension may be computed at the difference between the interfacial tensions of the solid-liquid and solid-gas or the difference between the interfacial tension of the liquid-gas multiplied by the cosine of the angle of contact of the liquid and solid.

The angle of contact is the angle made by the tangent to the surface of the liquid and the surface of the solid at the point of contact of the two. This is illustrated in figure 6.14, showing the diagrams of the vertical cross sections. When the angle of contact is less than 90° the liquid will not wet the solid because the sum of the gas-liquid and solid-liquid interfacial tensions is greater than the gas-solid interfacial tension. The liquid takes the contour as shown. If the angle is greater than 90° (figure 6.15)

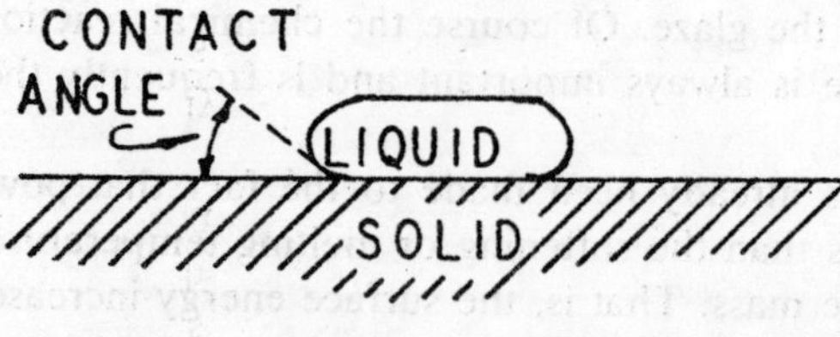

Figure 6.14. If angle of contact is less than 90°, liquid will not wet solid surface.

it wets the surface, because the sum of the gas-liquid and the liquid-solid interfacial tensions is less than the amount of the gas-solid tension. The liquid wets the surface and spreads over the solid because of the effect of gravity. If the adhesion tension is equal to or greater than the surface tension of the liquid, then the glaze will not wet and coat the surface upon which it is applied. Of course, the viscosity of the molten glaze, even the most mobile, is high and is an important factor in controlling the flow.

There is some published data on the surface tensions of molten glazes. Clark[37] used a method similar in principle to that devised by Quincke,[38] i.e., the formation by careful heating of a drop on the end of a fiber, then weighing the drop when it is melted off. He examined a composition corresponding to a typical Bristol glaze

$$0.34KNaO, 0.33CaO, 0.33ZnO, 0.5Al_2O_3, 3.0SiO_2$$

which is a very viscous type of melt at 1,360° C, the temperature of the experiment. The value obtained for the surface tension of the glaze was 252 dynes per cm. This may be compared with the surface tensions (obtained by another method) of six commercial glasses of widely varied compositions which ranged from 247 dynes per cm to 318 dynes/cm at 1,200° C and 245 dynes per cm to 315 dynes per cm at 1,350° C. A soft coat enamel having the batch composition: silica, 40.9%; boric oxide, 17.5%; soda, 4.5%; potassa, 15.3%; lime, 8.4%; alumina, 7.7%; man-

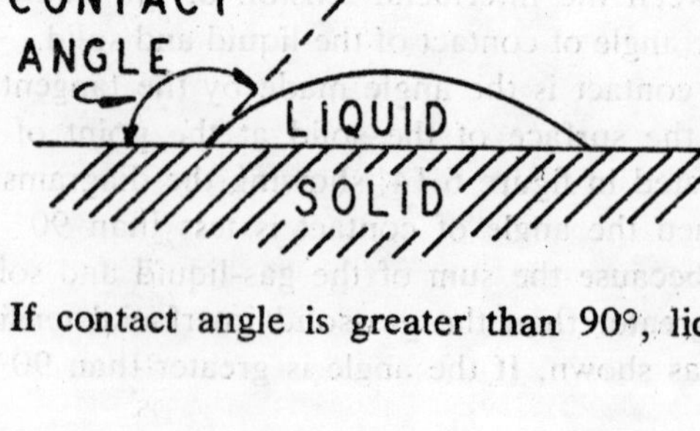

Figure 6.15. If contact angle is greater than 90°, liquid will wet solid surface.

ganese dioxide, 1.2%; nickel oxide, 0.5%; CoO, 0.6%; fluorine, 3.5%, differing much from any of the typical commercial glazes but essentially a fritted glaze maturing at a low temperature of 925° C, was found to have a surface tension (by the bubble method) of 244 dynes per cm.[43]

The penetration of the capillaries under the surface of a porous body is possible under favorable circumstances but is commonly avoided by proper control of the composition of the body, the firing conditions, and the viscosity and surface tension of the glaze. At the glaze-body interface there is a penetration to various degrees due to the processes of solution, diffusion, and crystallization. Since capillary flow is so intimately associated with interfacial tension, surface tension, and adhesion tension, consideration should be given to Washburn's statement[39] of the rate of penetration in a capillary system which is:

$$x^2 = \frac{\sigma \cos \theta}{2\eta} rt$$

Table 6.9. Changes in the surface tension of glasses, in dynes per cm, due to additions of 0.1 mole of each oxide per mole of base glass. After Bloor[12, 41, 42]

	Dietzel[41]	*Lyon,*[42] *for glasses in which SiO_2:Na_2O exceeds 3.25*	
Group	*At 900°C*	*At 1,200°C*	*At 1,400°C*
Li_2O	13.7	7.9	6.9
Na_2O	9.3	0.0*	-7.6*
K_2O	9.4	–	–
MgO	26.6	23.3	22.1
CaO	26.9	27.6	27.6
BaO	56.7	56.7*	58.3*
ZnO	38.2	–	–
B_2O_3	5.5	1.6	-1.6
Al_2O_3	63.2	61.0	59.6
SiO_2	20.4	19.5	19.5
TiO_2	23.0	–	–
ZrO_2	50.5	–	–
PbO	26.8	–	–
FeO	32.2	–	–
Fe_2O_3	–	71.9*	70.3
CoO	33.7	–	–
NiO	33.6	–	–
MnO	31.9	–	–

*Estimate only

when x = distance, σ = surface tension, cos θ = angle of contact, r = radius, t = time, and η = viscosity.

It is believed that low surface tension favors the elimination of gas bubbles during firing, as well as the wetting of the body by the liquid glaze. In the wetting of ceramic surfaces by glazes, it is obvious that the body is as important as the glaze. Some work was published by Lampman[40,40a] using these four methods: (1) inclined flow of glaze on body; (2) horizontal flow of glaze on body; (3) angle of contact of fused buttons of glaze; and (4) radius of curvature of fused buttons of glaze.

The most suitable method was found to be the angle of contact method. Among his results was the observation that, when the same glazes were fired on two different bodies (two different clays), maturing temperatures varied by 4 cones.

The degree to which surface tension is an additive quantity is indicated by data from Dietzel[41] in 1929 and in 1944 by Lyon.[42] Some of their results were summarized by Bloor.[12] His tabulations are given here in table 6.9.

Badger, Parmelee, and Williams[43] made molar additions to the following glass composition: $0.61Na_2O \cdot 0.39CaO \cdot 2.6SiO_2$. Their results showed these additions to lower the surface tension from the base glass in the following decreasing order: PbO, K_2O, B_2O_3, Na_2O, base glass, Li_2O, SiO_2, BaO, CaO, $0.5Al_2O_3$, ZnO, and MgO.

Table 6.10. Effects on surface tension of oxide additions to base glazes and enamels at 1,380° C[44]

Additive, wt %		*Surface tension, dynes per cm*	
Oxide	*%*	*Glaze*	*Enamel*
None	0	224	199
MoO_3	1	212	186
MoO_3	3	204	163
V_2O_5	1	220	195
V_2O_5	3	201	183
WO_3	1	214	194
WO_3	3	224	178
Sb_2O_3	1	215	195
Sb_2O_3	3	209	198
Ni_2O_3	1	214	194
Ni_2O_3	3	208	192
Co_3O_4	1	215	199
CO_3O_4	3	215	200
MnO_2	1	212	194
MnO_2	3	216	208
WO_2	1	216	197
WO_2	3	215	195
As_2O_3	1	218	196
As_2O_3	3	223	197

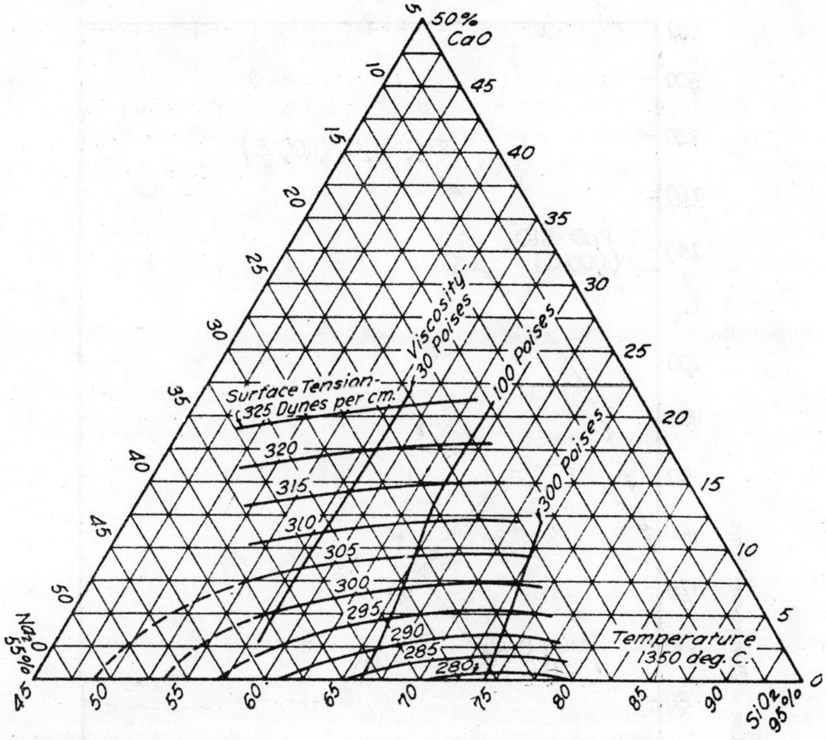

Figure 6.16. Comparison of the manner in which surface tension and viscosity vary with composition in the Na_2O–CaO–SiO_2 system.[15]

Some useful data were developed by Amberg[44] in the course of some work to find "high temperature wetting agents" for silicate fusions. Most of the oxides used were more or less effective in reducing surface tension, but MoO_3 and V_2O_5 produced the greatest reduction. The results are summarized in table 6.10.

Precision determination of surface tensions of melts in the ternary system Na_2O–CaO–SiO_2 was made by Parmelee and Harman.[45] The results for the temperature 1,350° C are shown in figure 6.16. Superimposed on this chart are viscosity data for the same glasses. It is interesting to compare the manner in which surface tension varies with composition as compared to that for viscosity. Lines for constant viscosity tend to parallel lines of constant silica, while the equisurface tension lines tend to parallel the lines of constant CaO.

Some surface tension data obtained at the National Bureau of Standards are useful in glazes. Because these data are useful in thinking processes, some are reported here. Shartsis, Spinner, and Smock[46] examined melts in the PbO–B_2O_3 and PbO–SiO_2 systems. Data from this work

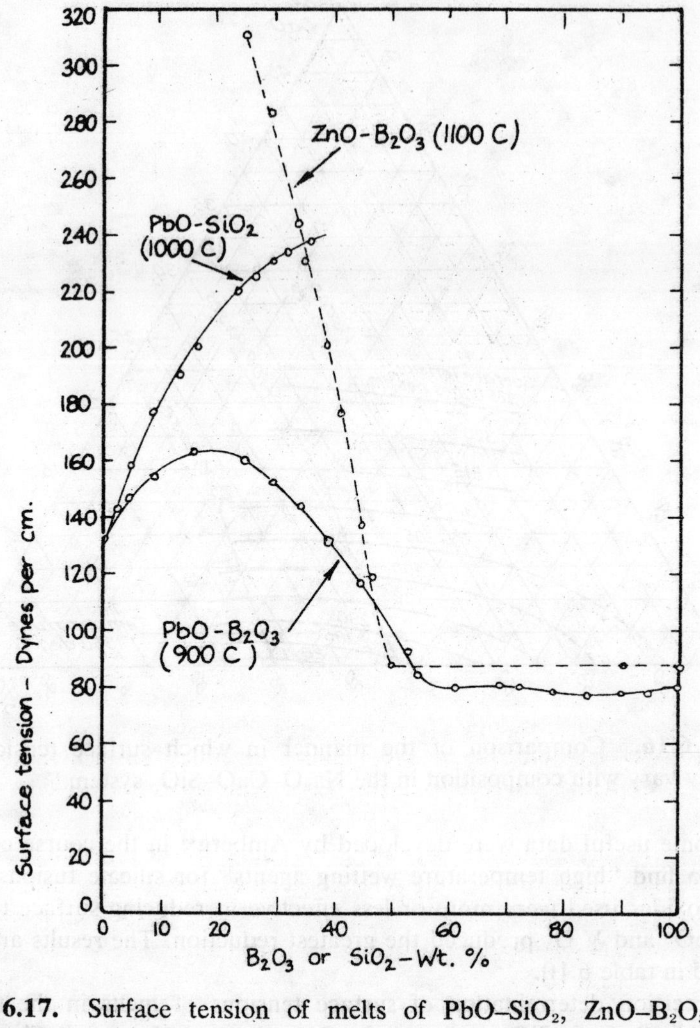

Figure 6.17. Surface tension of melts of $PbO–SiO_2$, $ZnO–B_2O_3$, and $PbO–B_2O_3$.[46]

are shown in figure 6.17 along with the surface tensions of melts of $ZnO–B_2O_3$. The surface tensions of molten borates of Li_2O, Na_2O, K_2O, PbO, and ZnO were shown by Shartsis and Capps[47] in mole percent. This comparison is given in figure 6.18.

These curves show that as B_2O_3 increases, surface tension sharply drops, attaining some very low values. In figure 6.17, the curve shows surface tensions of melts in the system $PbO–SiO_2$. As SiO_2 increases, or PbO decreases, surface tension rapidly increases.

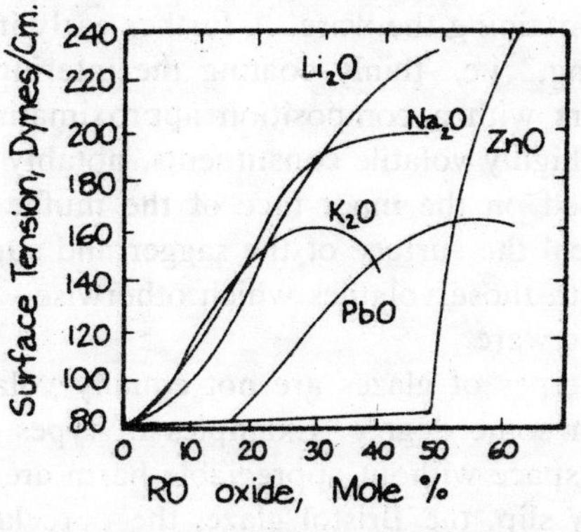

Figure 6.18. Surface tension of binary borate melts at 900° C. Note: The high B_2O_3 portions of the PbO and ZnO curves represent the B_2O_3-rich phase of the two-liquid systems.[47]

Gaseous atmospheres surrounding glasses, and presumably glazes, can significantly alter surface tension. Parikh[48] reported the following figures for a soda-lime glass at 700° C, in dynes per cm: vacuum, 310; dry air, 300; dry CO_2, 290; dry SO_2, 230; wet SO_2, 215; water vapor-12mm, 215; dry H_2, 309; dry HCl, 260; and dry NH_3, 230.

Frits, glazes, or melting-batch materials may contain areas of varying compositions. Localized nonhomogeneities due to localized residues from dissolving batch materials or incompletely diffused frit grains are common. These microirregularities influence glaze appearance as well as durabilities. Composites of glasses of differing compositions diffuse into each other depending upon their relative surface tensions. The glass with the lower surface tension shows a greater spreading tendency than those of higher values. Measurements[49] show a more rapid rate of spreading of the glass having the lower surface tension.

Volatilization

All constituents of a glaze coating are volatile in some degree according to the temperature, the vapor pressure of each constituent, the duration of the heating, and the atmosphere of the surrounding space. Early glaze makers observed that many glaze coatings, if exposed to contact with hot gases, ashes, and possibly flame, were harmed and some kind of protection for the ware had to be devised. This eventually led to the use of saggers, or clay boxes, into which the ware was placed and enclosed.

A later refinement was the construction and use of the muffle kiln. In this type, the hot flue gases pass outside of and around the wall enclosing the chamber containing the ware. A further early improvement was the practice of "washing," i.e., thinly coating the interior side walls and the cover of the saggers with a composition approximating that of the glaze with respect to its highly volatile constituents, notably lead. A "wash" has sometimes been used on the inner face of the muffle walls. The purpose of the wash is to seal the surface of the sagger and supply the atmosphere of the enclosure with those volatiles which otherwise would be stolen from the glaze coat on the ware.

However, all types of glazes are not equally volatile, although many components are, in some degree. Examples of types which may be fired in the "open" kiln space without appreciable harm are: natural slip glazes, such as the Albany slip, the Bristol glaze, the porcelain glaze, and modifications of the same. Protection of glazes containing certain colorants is generally necessary. Several coloring agents are very sensitive and will even "boil" out of the glaze at low or moderate temperatures, e.g., copper which escapes at about cone 6. Selenides are not good above cone 04.

Glazes containing notable amounts of lead must be protected in saggers washed with a composition high in lead in order to insure an atmosphere highly charged with lead fumes about the ware; otherwise the glaze would not have the desired gloss. It would be "sucked" or "dry." Some call this "glaze jumping." The same principle is used in the "fuming" of ware for decorative effects. In that case a saucer or other container filled with a rather volatile mixture of common salt, lead oxide, some inert material, and possibly a color oxide is placed in the sagger with the ware. After the firing the latter will be found to have a very thin varnish-like coating. It should be noted that leadless glazes should not be fired in saggers coated with a lead-containing wash, nor should matt texture glazes be exposed to such atmosphere, without some experimentation.

Observations made on losses by volatilization from lead-bearing silicates show that the volatilization of lead from a raw batch is greater than if the lead is introduced as a frit constituent. Hilpert's experiments[50] showed that the volatilization of lead from a lead-silica mixture is least when the silica content is highest. For example, the volatilization from $2PbO \cdot 3SiO_2$ is negligible up to 1,000° C; the loss from $PbO \cdot SiO_2$ is very small up to 930° C; the loss from $2PbO \cdot SiO_2$ is 3% when heated for 1 hour.

Anderson[51] found that a mixture of PbO and SiO_2 containing 85% of the former showed an initial loss at a temperature as low as 900° C, while a mixture containing 60% of PbO did not lose lead before 1,100° C. Experience with optical glass has shown that the amount of the loss is influenced by the area and the amount of agitation at the molten surface. The loss of PbO from a melt has been found[52] to vary between 0.5%

and 5%. Other losses from glass batches which have been reported are: boric oxide, from 1% to 5%; and the alkalies, soda and potash up to 5%. It is not surprising to learn that the surfaces of such molten batches are reported to show an enrichment of silica.

Harrison and associates,[53] using a sensitive technique, found the following oxides begin to volatilize from a cone 04 glaze in this order: boron, 450°; lead, 850°; and chromium, 1,000° C. An increase in the silica content of the glaze increased the volatilization temperature of these oxides. A soaking heat increased the amount of volatilization. In a glaze containing a high calcium content and a frit introducing the boric oxide and part of the lead oxide, the boric oxide loss was less at all temperatures than when it was introduced raw in the batch, as in the form of colemanite (calcium borate), and the volatilization of the lead oxide was lowered.

Hall,[54] comparing the analyses of glaze flakes stripped from fired ware and the same batches fused on platinum, found that loss by volatilization and by exchange with body was greatest whenever the ware had been fired in a large free space, at the higher temperatures, and from the thickest applications. A thin layer might even show an actual gain. The loss amounted to 0.5% to 2.5% of the glaze weight which, however, did not fully account for the changes in the composition. The analysis of the dust collected in the end of a saggerless glost muffle kiln gave 90% lead and boric oxides.

An impressive illustration of the volatility of an extremely refractory oxide and its effect upon nearby glazes is afforded by the pinkish discolora-

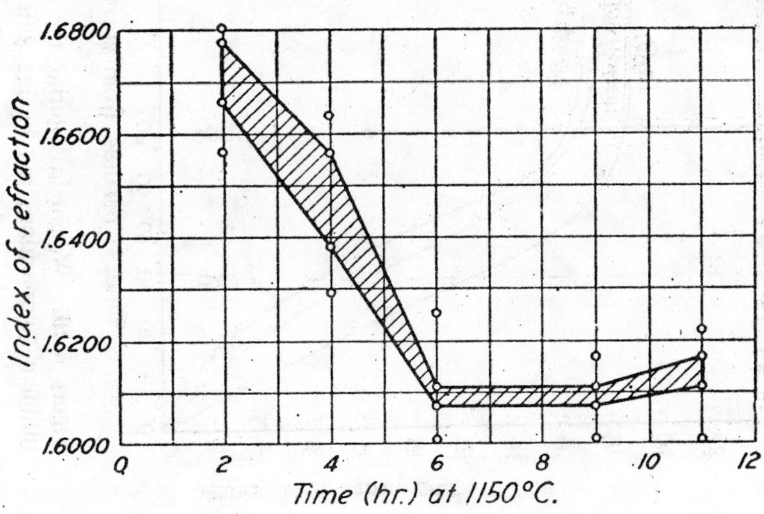

Figure 6.19. Change of index of a glaze with firing time at 1,150° C.[55]

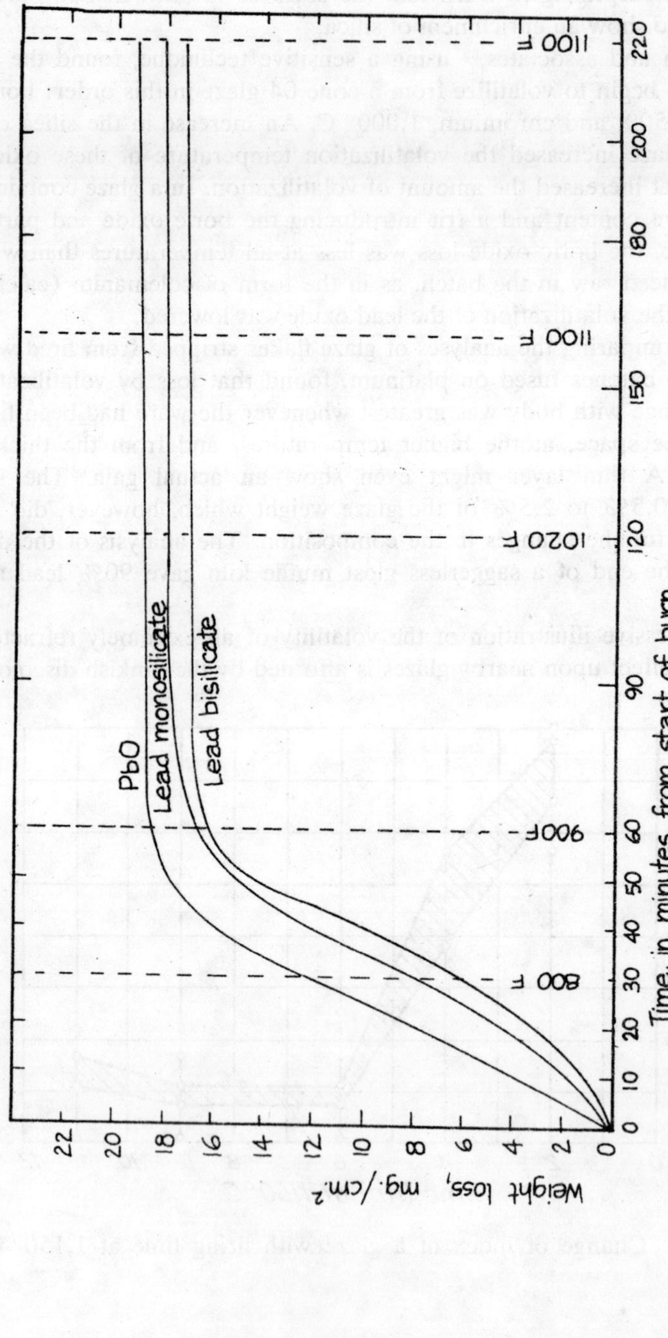

Figure 6.20. Weight loss during the heating, in platinum crucibles, of glaze batches of identical ultimate compositions but having differing sources for PbO.[56]

tion of a tin-containing, white-firing glaze if the same is matured in the immediate neighborhood of a glaze containing chromium oxide. This characteristic may be used for the creation of special effects. The fuming of color oxides and compounds in a kiln chamber is commercially employed to alter the natural color of structural clay products.

The change of the index of refraction of a homogeneous melt, as the result of prolonged heating or heating at a higher temperature, is partly a result of the loss of the volatile solids (chiefly alkalies), lead and boric oxide. Figure 6.19 shows[55] such changes observed when, compared to a normal glaze, portions of the same glaze batch were placed on platinum foil enclosed in a glazed crucible and heated for varying periods of time. This technique was used as an indicator of the rate and magnitude of changes proceeding under thermal treatment. However, the composition, and therefore the optical properties of a glaze, matured on a body are profoundly affected by their mutual interractions.

Hallse and Cook[56] published some results of volatilization losses from the following lead glaze:

0.7PbO		
0.2CaO	$0.2Al_2O_3$	$7.5SiO_2$
0.1ZnO		

This composition was prepared using the following sources for PbO: litharge, lead monosilicate, and lead bisilicate. The curious results shown in figure 6.20 were obtained. The entire weight loss occurred by the time 1,100° F was reached, in 150 minutes. No appreciable loss occurred after that. Apparently the major loss occurred from the surface of the powder before and during sintering. After fusion, in the crucible, there was very small exposed surface per unit weight of lead.

This was different from the results from firing the same glazes on a body under actual ceramic firing conditions. These results are summarized in table 6.11, they differ markedly from those shown in figure 6.20. It appears that the volatibility of PbO can be reduced in the smelting operation by using lead in the more stable combined frit. The weight loss

Table 6.11. Effect of source for PbO on volatilization due to firing of glazes on bodies

Lead source	*Average weight loss (mg^8/cm^2)*
Litharge	11.5
Lead monosilicate	7.3
Lead bisilicate	5.1

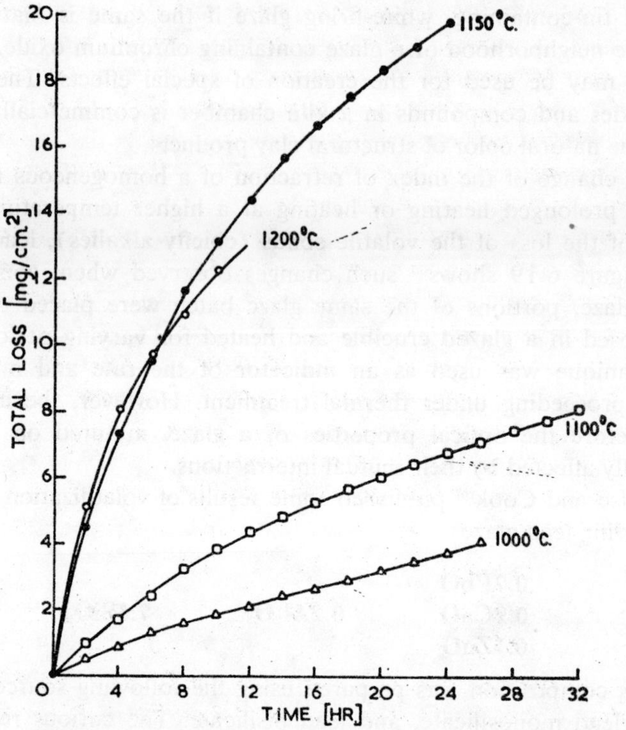

Figure 6.21. Volatilization loss of a leadless glaze, expressed as weight-loss per unit area.[57]

per unit area when fired on a body is lower than when melted in crucibles. Part of the difference is due to lead diffusion into the body.

Quite different results were found by Norris[57] for a leadless earthenware glaze fired on a platinum strip. Typical weight losses for this system are shown in figure 6.21. Norris found these losses to follow the same law as that relating to vapor pressure, log (loss) $= A - B/T$.

Loss during the smelting of frits is likely to be of considerable importance because of the relatively long period of time the batch is subjected to high temperature in an atmosphere which is changing rapidly, thus constantly carrying off the gaseous and powdered products losses. Poste and Rice[58] report that the compositions of the frit and the batch may differ importantly; in the frit the silica content was materially higher; the alumina, lime, and potassa were slightly higher; and the soda and boric oxide were very much less. Continued heating increased the silica and decreased the soda and the boric oxide contents relatively.

The salt glaze, which has been used during the past 700 or 800 years, is an excellent example of the use of the principle of volatilization for the development of a durable, glassy coating on clay ware. The process is the simplest conceivable. When the kiln of ware has reached a suitable temperature, quantities of common salt are introduced in the fireboxes or the kiln chamber, filling the same with dense fumes, and this condition is maintained until test pieces drawn from the kiln show that a good glaze has developed. The sodium vapors react with the clay to form a complex insoluble alkali silicate, or alkali-alumina-silicate.

Common salt in small quantities is sometimes added to the batch of a frit in order to bleach the same by reacting with some of the iron content of the raw materials; when heated, the iron forms the very volatile ferric chloride, is quickly driven out.

Maturing Glaze

Crystallization

As a strongly heated fusion of a silicate or mixture of silicates cools, the thermal motion of their atoms, molecules, or aggregations will diminish and, because of the crowding together of these units and the strengthening of the bonds between them, thermal contraction and an increase in viscosity ensue. It is inevitable that, at many places in the melt, unit lattice cells will form as a result of the attractive forces and will disintegrate continuously because of the thermal agitation. There will be a constant tendency for the molecular species present to become more complex. At some temperatures the rate of rupture will diminish so that, according to the laws of chance, the perfect cell will find itself able to become associated with other cells in its vicinity or to attract to itself the proper ions to build up a crystal of sufficient size to be identifiable.

Tammann[59] has shown that the formation of visible crystals depends upon three conditions: the number of nuclei formed, the rate of growth of the crystals, and the viscosity of the melt. These conditions and their relation to each other are shown in figure 6.22.

Changes of temperature are represented on the base line beginning with temperature t_1 at the left and decreasing to t_2 at the right. Curve 2 represents the rate of formation of the nuclei. Curve 1 is the rate of crystal growth. Curve 3 is the viscosity curve. These properties are measured on the ordinate. The narrower the temperature range between the peak of the nuclei curve and the peak of the crystal growth curve, the more abun-

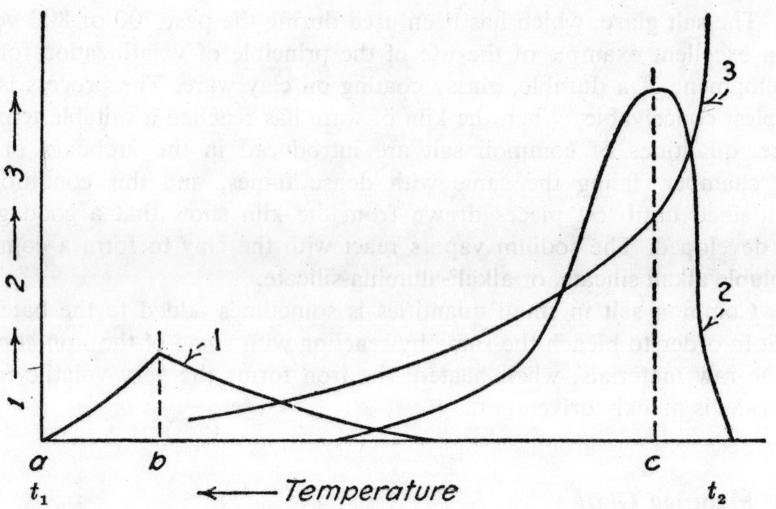

Figure 6.22. Relative relationship between: 1, rate of crystal growth; 2, number of nuclei; and 3, viscosity.[59]

dant and the larger the individual crystals will be, providing the increase of the viscosity permits.

The typical curve obtained by plotting the observations of the time-temperature changes during cooling the melt of a pure substance will show a uniformly smooth path until crystallization begins; then a "lag" in the temperature drop is shown by a discontinuity or "break" in the curve. Following this lag and the separation of crystals, the curve continues to fall smoothly until room temperature is reached. The lag is due to the evolution of the heat of crystallization (or heat of fusion), which temporarily compensates for decrease in temperature of the system. (See figure 6.23, also figures 6.5 and 6.6.)

A corresponding lag, due to the conversion of heat to work (i.e., heat of fusion), is observed during the melting process. The heat of fusion is a specific property of each crystalline pure substance. On the other hand, fusions of pure substances, which are too viscous to permit crystallization except after a prolonged slow cooling interval, of impure substances and of complex mixtures give smooth time-temperature cooling curves (fig. 6.7). This is characteristic of glasses, glazes, and enamels of silica, boric oxide, and other glass formers and of certain pure organic glass-forming compounds such as glycerine.

Supercooled or undercooled melts will have cooling curves as in figure 6.6. In such cases the cooling may be carried below the freezing point, but when the crystallization begins, the evolution of heat restores the temperature of the mass to its proper level, where the characteristic lag or

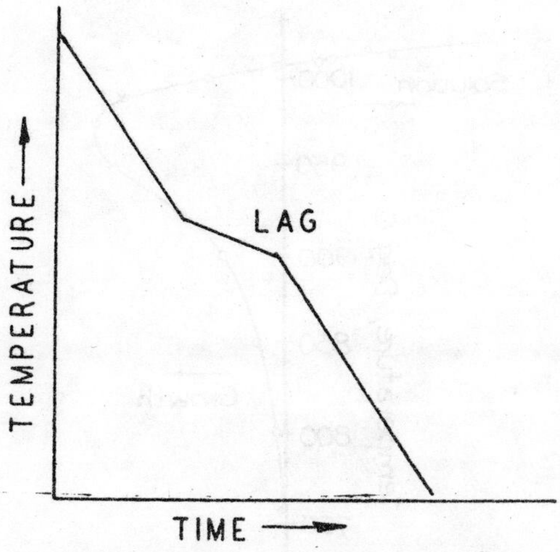

Figure 6.23. Lag in cooling curve indicates crystal formation.

terrace appears and continues until the stage is completed and the temperature falls as is normal. This may be demonstrated experimentally by cautiously cooling a supersaturated solution of sodium sulfate. By careful manipulation this may be kept liquid below its freezing point, but the introduction of a minute particle of the sodium sulfate crystal, or even some foreign substance, will be accompanied by instant solidification. Although

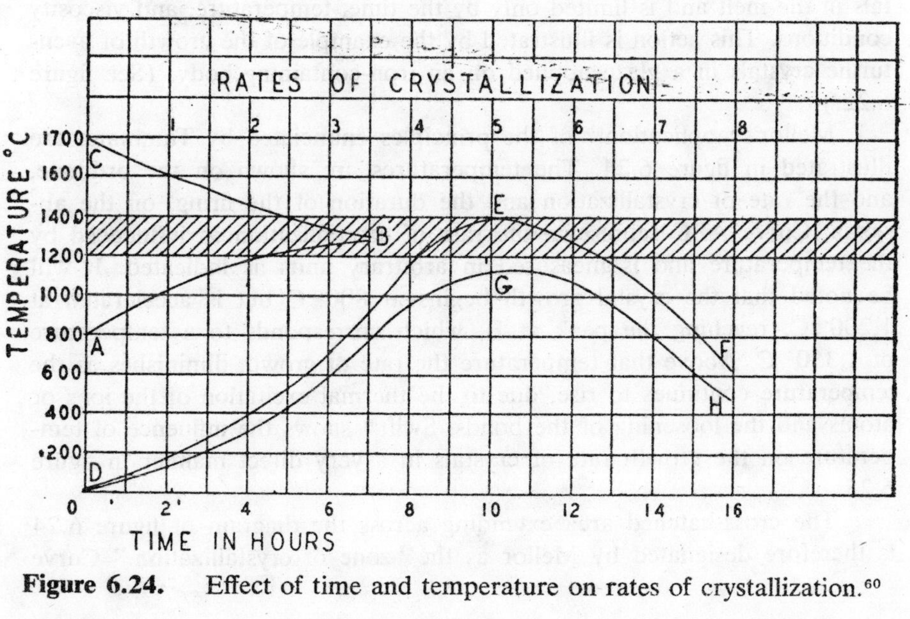

Figure 6.24. Effect of time and temperature on rates of crystallization.[60]

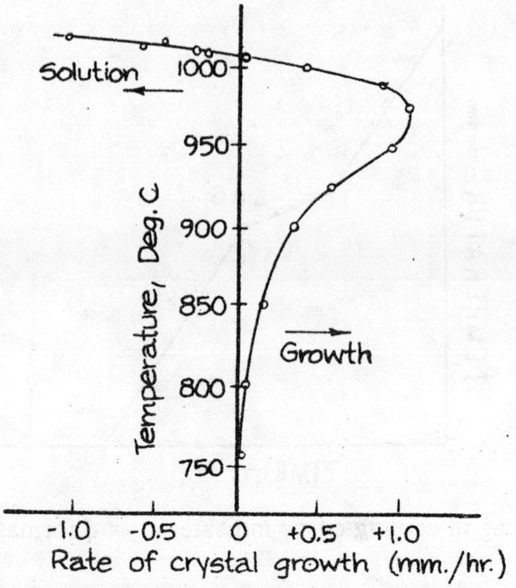

Figure 6.25. Rate of growth of crystals in a soda-lime-silica glass as influenced by temperateure.[61]

the analogy is not entirely satisfactory, commercial glasses and glazes are sometimes described as or compared with "undercooled solutions."

Diffusion plays an important role in the formation of individual crystals in the melt and is limited only by the time, temperature, and viscosity conditions. This action is illustrated by the example of the growth of aventurine crystals in a glaze applied on an iron-containing body. (See figure 6.22.)

Mellor's application[60] of the principles enunciated by Tammann are illustrated in figure 6.24. The temperatures are shown on the ordinate, and the rate of crystallization and the duration of the firing, on the abscissa. Curve ABC represents the rate of crystallization as influenced by the temperature and is measured in arbitrary units as indicated. It will be noted that the crystal growth begins at 800° C but is accelerated at 1,200° C, reaching the peak at B, which corresponds to a temperature of 1,350° C. Above that temperature the rate of growth diminishes as the temperature continues to rise, due to the thermal excitation of the ions or atoms and the loosening of the bonds. Swift[61] shows the influence of temperature on the growth rate of crystals in a very direct manner in figure 6.25.

The cross-hatched area extending across the diagram of figure 6.24 is therefore designated by Mellor as the "zone of crystallization." Curve

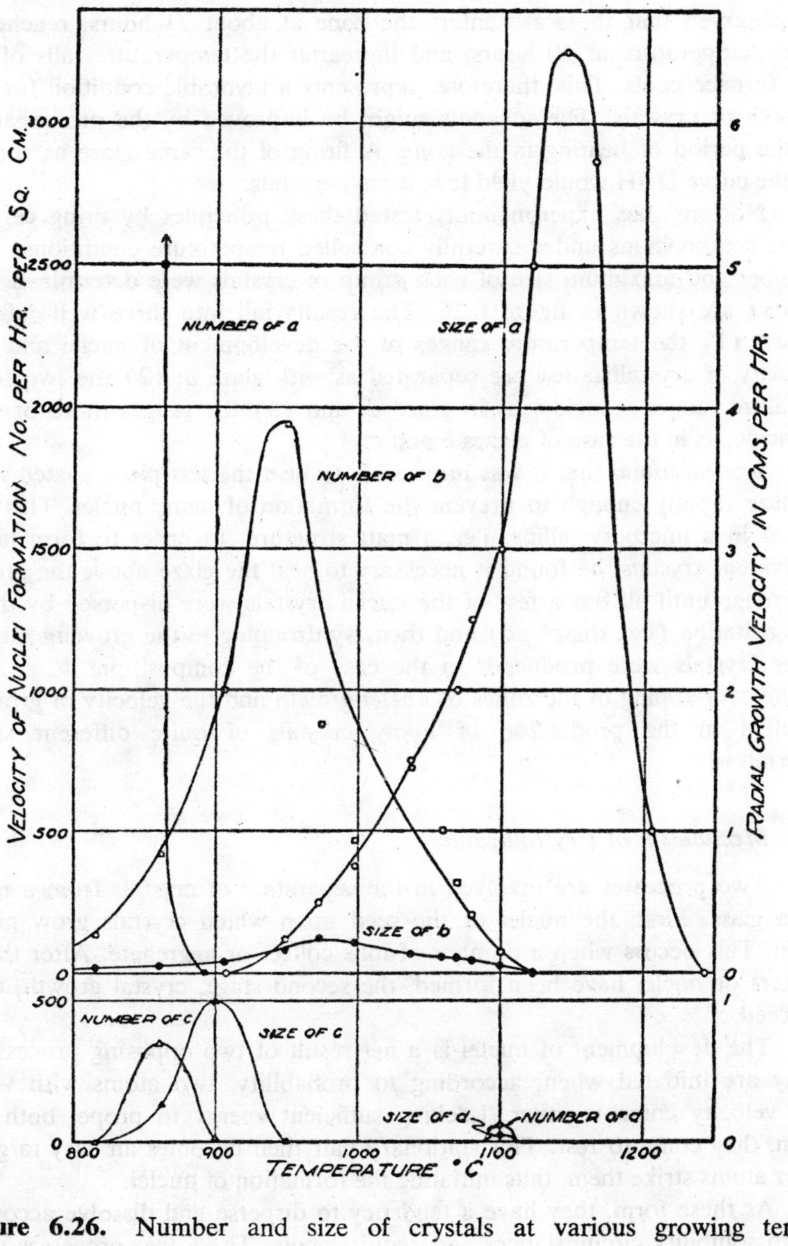

Figure 6.26. Number and size of crystals at various growing temperatures.[62]

DEF represents the firing curve used for a piece of glazed ware. It will be observed that the ware enters the zone at about 7½ hours, reaches a peak temperature at 10 hours, and thereafter the temperature falls off as the furnace cools. This, therefore, represents a favorable condition for the growth of crystals. The schedule might be improved by the prolongation of the period of heating in the zone. A firing of the same glaze as shown by the curve DGH would yield few, if any, crystals.

Norton[62] has experimentally tested these principles by firing certain glaze compositions under carefully controlled temperature conditions. The number and maximum size of each group of crystals were determined and plotted are shown in figure 6.26. The results fall into three well-defined types: (1) the temperature ranges of the development of nuclei and the velocity of crystallization are separated as with glaze *a*; (2) the two temperature ranges coincide, as in glaze *d*; and (3) the ranges more or less coincide, as in the case of glazes *b* and *c*.

Norton found that it was impossible to heat the test piece coated with a glaze rapidly enough to prevent the formation of many nuclei. This resulted in a microcrystalline, i.e., a matt structure. In order to form large individual crystals, he found it necessary to heat the glaze above the growing range until all but a few of the nuclei crystals were dispersed by thermal agitation (i.e., dissolved) and then, by dropping to the growing range, large crystals were produced. In the case of the compositions *b*, *c*, and *d*, the overlapping of the zones of nuclei growth and the velocity of growth resulted in the production of many crystals of quite different sizes intermixed.

Mechanism of Crystallization

Two processes are involved in the separation of crystals from a melt or a glass. First, the nuclei or the seed upon which crystals grow must form. This occurs when a number of ions collect or aggregate. After these centers or nuclei have been formed, the second stage, crystal growth, can proceed.

The development of nuclei is a net result of two opposing processes. They are initiated when, according to probability, two atoms with very low velocity come together. Lacking sufficient energy to propel both of them, they come to rest. This stationary pair then becomes an easy target; other atoms strike them, thus initiating the formation of nuclei.

As these form, they have a tendency to disperse and dissolve according to solubility circumstances and requirements. These two processes depend upon the solubility of the crystal in the liquid and upon temperature-viscosity relations. As the temperature drops, solubility of the crystal

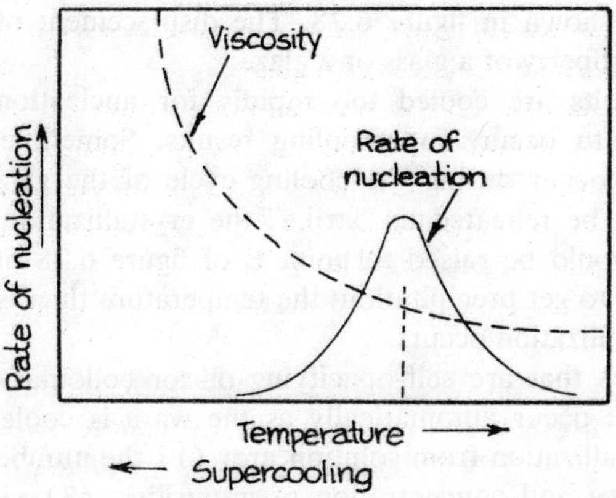

Figure 6.27. Diagram showing the relation between temperature, viscosity, rate of nucleation, and supercooling.

decreases and viscosity increases. The relation of nuclei formation to temperature is shown schematically in figure 6.27. As a melt begins to cool, the number and rate of nuclei formation increases until a maximum is reached. After this there is a rapid decline in rate. A rule of thumb is that this peak may be around 100 degrees below that at which crystallization can occur.

Nuclei are very small, being the order of 5 to 10×10^{-3} microns. The size range is near the limit for the electron microscope. As the nuclei grow they become crystallites and their rate of growth is the rate of crystallization. The peak rate for crystallization is displaced from the peak of

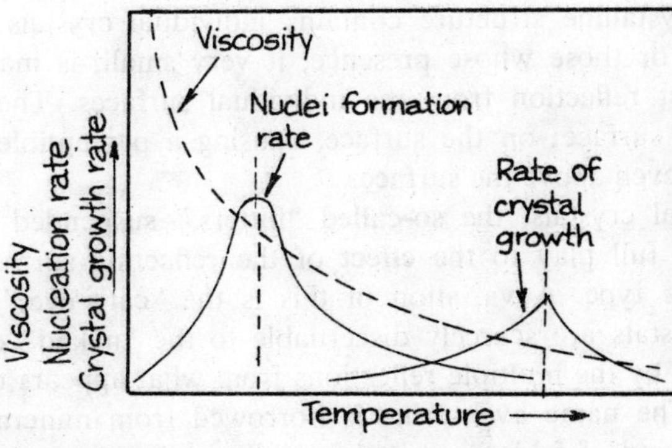

Figure 6.28. Schematic of relation between temperature favoring nucleation and crystallization in glazes.

nucleation as shown in figure 6.28. The displacement of these two peaks is a primary property of a glass or a glaze.

When melts are cooled too rapidly for nucleation and subsequent crystallization to occur, supercooling results. Sometimes nucleation and crystallization occur during the cooling cycle of the glaze. In other cases the ware must be reheated to "strike" the crystallization. In this case the temperature would be raised to point B of figure 6.28 and given time for nuclei to form to get precipitation; the temperature then is lowered to point A where crystallization occurs.

For glazes that are self-opacifying or for colloidal colors, these two processes must occur automatically as the ware is cooled. Factors which influence crystallization from solution are: (1) the number of phases separating, (2) type and concentration of impurities, (3) viscosity, (4) type of nuclei, (5) diffusion coefficients, and (6) time-temperature relations.

Foreign substances and inert suspended particles are known to exert tremendous influences on nucleation and on crystallization. The scientific basis for this has not been thoroughly established.

The sizes and the types of crystals formed in glassy fusions differ widely, ranging from spherulites to coarse projections above the surface. In general it may be stated that the thickness of the matured glaze coat imposes a limit on one dimension, and crystals of the hexagonal system predominate. More than one type of crystal may separate in a fusion of different temperature levels.

Crystallization appears in glazes either as macrocrystalline or microcrystalline types, if we disregard the accidental presence of undissolved particles of crystalline silica or some other batch constituent. The term devitrification may properly cover the occurrence of crystals as well as dull or matt-like glaze surfaces due to the presence of undissolved particles. The macrocrystalline structure contains individual crystals visible to the unaided eye, or those whose presence, if very small, is manifest because of the distinct reflection from the individual surfaces. The crystals may lie below the surface; on the surface, causing a perceptible roughness to the touch; or even above the surface.

Individual crystals, the so-called "flitters," suspended in the matrix so as to give full play to the effect of the reflecting surfaces, belong to the aventurine type. A variation of this is the "cat's-eye," in which the individual crystals are scarcely discernable to the "naked" eye but reveal their presence by the multiple reflections from what appears to be a careful orientation. The name aventurine is borrowed from mineralogy where it designates a kind of feldspar containing "flitters" of hematite, so we have aventurine glazes containing iron oxide and, in addition, there are aventurines obtained with chromium and uranium oxides. Copper aventurines have long been made by the glass industry but as yet they do not seem to have been produced in glazes.

The true matt glaze owes its lusterless, silky surface to the refraction and diffusion of light by the innumerable facets of its microcrystalline or cryptocrystalline structure, and its appearance has been compared to that exhibited by a fine glacé kid glove. Matt glazes are opaque or translucent but never transparent, and a cross section will show that the crystallization is complete from the surface to the body contact except, perhaps, where a slight solution of the body silica has occurred. A matt of the best type is not soiled by wiping with the moist fingertips.

Binns,[63] who seems to have been the first to discuss the technical aspects of this kind of glaze, attributes to R. W. Binns, Director of the Royal Porcelain Works about 1860, the earliest recognition of the aesthetic importance of this texture which, however, was not generally accepted until fifteen years later. Since mattness of varying degrees may be observed, ranging from silkiness to semigloss, it is not surprising that the appearance may be produced, more or less satisfactorily, by other means than crystallization, for example:

1. abrasion by sandblasting the glossy glaze after firing
2. chemical attack by sulfur oxides or other corrosive gases in the kiln; or by acids subsequent to firing
3. immaturity due to insufficiently high temperature of firing or insufficient time to dissolve an excess of refractory batch constituents
4. the retention of some of the gases as minute vescicles in the glaze
5. crinkled skin due to the peculiar contraction of the glaze surface during cooling[64]

In his paper, Binns[65] states that in order to develop the texture at the lower cones (04 to 4 or 5), a complex RO group and an "excess" of alumina are necessary. In general, these conditions are requisite although numerous later investigators[66,67,68] proved that the alumina does not possess any inherent power. The character and the amounts of the bases and even the forms in which they are introduced in the batches, the fineness of grind, the thickness of application, and the rate of cooling are all very important factors.

In the endeavor to rationalize the development of the texture, the conception of the separation of solids in the glassy matrix took form early. Purdy,[69] following the petrographer but without presenting microscopical evidence, assumed that certain norms—anorthite, wollastonite, leucite, and orthoclase—might be expected to occur. This was done later by several investigators[70,71] who identified the presence of most of these compounds as well as mullite and probably celsian (barium feldspar), depending upon the batch composition. Wilson[72] critically examined the data of several investigators and attempted to correlate it with the $CaO–Al_2O_3–SiO_2$ equilibria system. He concluded that "anorthite is the most common matt-forming compound; mullite is indicated in the low-lime and lime-free glazes. The role of wollastonite is less clear." Parmelee and Horak's findings included, among other items already mentioned, the following conclusions pertaining to raw lead glazes maturing at cones 03 to 6: (1) when zinc oxide is less than 0.3 equivalents, no zinc silicate separates but the element assists others in forming a more fluid matrix; (2) barium assists in forming matts by separating in a crystal believed to be celsian, i.e., barium feldspar.

Dispersoids or Colloids

A colloid or dispersoid is a particle or aggregate of matter—gaseous, liquid, or solid—larger than the molecule of the same chemical composition, and varying in size from those barely visible to the naked eye to those seen only with the aid of the ultramicroscope. Because of the very small size of the individual colloid particles they have a relatively large total surface and consequently possess distinctive physical properties, e.g.: (1) optical—diffusing light and producing opacity and colors; (2) electrical—the dispersoids are susceptible to the action of electrolytes; and (3) mechanical—remaining in suspension for indefinite lengths of time. Therefore, the presence or the addition of colloid materials to glasses or glazes enables the ceramist to produce interesting effects, and a knowledge of the characteristics and control of colloids may enable him to avoid certain faults.

Matter in its several forms (solid, liquid, and gaseous) may be dispersed as colloids in solids, liquids, and gases. Examples of these cases may be found in glasses and glazes, undoubtedly, but only a few of the more common types will be mentioned here. For example:

State of matter	*Examples of dispersion*
Gas in liquid (glaze)	Opacity due to the presence of minute bubbles of some gas; also foams
Gas in solid	Minute gaseous inclusions in crystals
Solid in liquid (glaze)	Metals diffused in the melt to form a decoration, e.g., silver
Solid in liquid (glaze)	Copper red or ruby glass or glaze, gold ruby glass
Solid in liquid (glaze)	Opalescence due to the separation of silica or phosphates, fluorides, etc

Colloids dispersed in an aqueous medium are said to be in stable suspension and, by analogy, the same term can be applied to similar conditions in a glaze.

Many of the elements which are known to yield colloidal dispersions in glasses and other fusions are named pyrosols. Some of these are gold, silver, copper, sulphur, and selenium, which are used as agents in silicate fusions furnishing colors similar to those had in aqueous suspensions. The classic example is the element gold, which Zsigmondy[73] demonstrated would yield colorless, red, rose, blue, or violet solutions depending upon the size of the dispersed particle. For this reason the color of a glass melt to which gold has been added will increase in intensity according to the heat treatment; the first gathering made by the glass blower is straw color. This is worked or blown into an approximate shape and then frequently reheated during subsequent operations until the color is satisfactorily developed by the increase in the sizes of the dispersed gold particles.

The tinctorial power of colloidal gold is extraordinary; one part in 50,000 is sufficient. Zsigmondy has reported that the size of the individual dispersed particle in ruby glass is of the order of 10×10^{-6} to 20×10^{-6} mm. Copper red glazes, such as the sang de boeuf and rouge flambé, owe their color to similar phenomena. The color is now generally believed to be due to the presence of highly dispersed metallic copper obtained by the use of copper oxide in the batch together with reducing agents such as stannous oxide or potassium bitartrate, and subjecting the ware to reducing conditions and suitable heat treatment. In this case, also, the amount of copper required is small, depending upon the composition of the glaze, varying from 0.02% to 2%.

One kind of the opal glass may be considered as due to the presence of solid particles having diameters of the order of 1.3 microns; the average being very much less. The size will depend on the cooling rate and the viscosity of the glass. According to one investigator, opals are transparent to the wavelengths of light of the order of 2 microns and the scattering power is proportional to the square of the wavelength. Since the size of the suspended particles is the criterion, it is conceivable that the particles may be nuclei of crystals, crystallites, or irregular insoluble particles. Sodium and calcium fluorides, sodium chloride, and sodium sulfate have been reported as functioning in the development and the destruction of opalescence. Silverman[74] explained a case of the latter occurring in a glass by the assumption that colloidal alumina is negatively charged in the melt, and the addition of the chloride or the sulfate caused the flocculation and the precipitation of the same. Wright[75] reports an example of turbidity in optical glass due to the presence of very small amounts of potassium and sodium chlorides and potassium sulfates as impurities in the potassium carbonate used in the batch for a light flint glass.

Glaze Body Interface

Evidence of the attack of the glaze upon the body during the firing is readily seen by magnification of a cross section of the contact of the two. Occasionally it is visible to the unaided vision as a serrated edge of a tile, or the corroded surface of the body underneath the glaze. The microsections, referred to above, commonly contain crystals which seem to have originated in the body and to have grown across the interface, although it is possible that the process may have been in the reverse.

The axiom that "the glaze feeds upon the body" describes the condition which prevails, depending upon (1) the nature and condition of the body, i.e., whether it is porous or nonporous, biscuit or unfired; (2) the temperature and the duration of the firing; (3) whether the glaze is fritted and to what extent; (4) the composition of the glaze, i.e., whether it contains much of the very active solvent components, such as lead, barium, alkalies, boric oxide, or lime; (5) the thickness of the glaze application; (6) the viscosity of the molten glaze; and (7) the mutual diffusibility of body and glaze components.

The most common evidence of the "feeding of the glaze" is the influence of body impurities upon the color. A raw lead glaze matured on a fireclay body (which, of course, contains enough iron oxide to give the body a cream color) will furnish a ware strongly colored yellow, and it is so named in the trade. The color is due, in a slight degree, to the faintly yellow color of the glaze alone which is characteristic of the type, but it is the solution of more iron oxide from the body which intensifies the hue.

Accidental impurities, whether minute particles of pyrites, oxides, or metal which have become incorporated in the surface of the body, are causes of specked glazes. Sometimes the specks are surrounded by halos or aureoles of color. Aventurine glazes, which are distinguished by the presence of hematite crystals suspended in a glassy magma saturated with iron oxide, give the best results when applied on red-firing bodies, since the latter are cheap, convenient sources of the oxide and furnish a suitable dark surface for the maximum aesthetic effect.

Mellor[76] cites the experiment of fusing soda ash in the bottom of a biscuit piece as a method for detecting the presence of cobalt stain in the body. In such a case the fusion will have a blue color. It is quite obvious that very chemically active glazes may be susceptible to similar results. Naturally the degree of vitrification of the body must be an important factor since the relative absorbency must have a large role in the mechanics and the extent of the attack; therefore, the same glaze may yield different results when used on the same body composition biscuited at different temperatures.[77]

Excluding, for the moment, the effect of the degree of vitrification upon the thermal expansion of a body, the mutual interaction is an explanation of why refiring the ware or firing it harder sometimes cures crazing. This procedure promotes a more homogeneous bond between the body and glaze; consequently the stresses and strains are decreased or dissipated. Fired wares which have a strongly marked line of demarcation between the body and glaze are much more likely to craze or shiver than those having no well-defined interface but rather an indefinitely developed zone. This latter condition is to be observed in the hard porcelains, the former in low-fire lead glazes.

The former condition is conspicuous on all types of bodies bearing low-fire glazes; also it may be observed with vitreous bodies coated with medium-fire glazes. Both of these types are likely to craze. The appearance of the interfacial zone indicates that the reaction of body and glaze is mutual and not limited solely to solution by the glaze. The use of a light wash or thin coating of flint, clays, and feldspar, alone or as a mixture and different from the body upon which it is applied, has been found to improve the glaze by "feeding" upon the underslip to its enrichment with some chemical constituent. Schramm[78] has pointed out that "Bodies of a highly absorptive nature, e.g., those with much free aluminum oxide, may take up most of the glaze in the course of the firing when the latter fuses at a temperature at which the body is still porous. To obtain a good glaze on bodies of this type, the composition of the glaze must be so refractory that fusion is delayed until the body approaches vitrification."

This is more especially true in the case of one-fire ware. High mechanical strength is required of certain wares, notably high tension electrical insulators, and it is known that the glaze coat plays an important role in the development of this property. It is clear that the nature, the extent, and the time-temperature schedule of the interfacial reaction must be properly adjusted in order to insure the maximum benefits. The manner in which the body and glaze should adjust themselves for the best results may be stated briefly as follows: After maturity, the body and glaze undergo a thermal contraction when the temperature falls. The body is rigid in contrast to the glaze coat which is viscous and able to follow the body changes until the temperature becomes so low the viscosity merges into plasticity and finally settles into rigidity. With continued decrease of temperature, the glaze coat is frequently under tension inasmuch as its coefficient of expansion is usually higher than that of the body and, according to Kraner,[79] the strength of the ware is thereby increased, because it is put under compression. In the case of the same body coated with a glaze having a low coefficient, the latter would be under compression (which is normally the desired condition in order to avoid crazing) and presum-

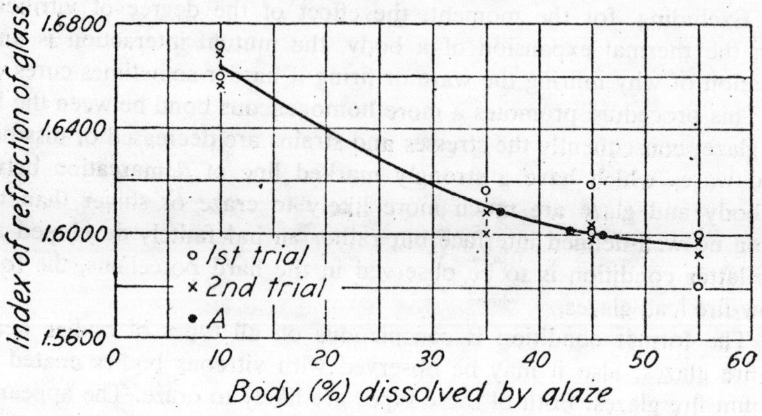

Figure 6.29. Solubility of body in a lead glaze; *A* shows indices of refraction of the glaze when fired on the body.[80]

ably the ware will be stronger. Kraner recommends that a glaze intended for spark plugs and chemical ware should have a high temperature of initial melting rather than be soft at the range at which it is to be used.

Attempts to determine the solvent action of glaze upon the body have been attended by many difficulties. Parmelee and Buckles[80] found that a comparison of the indices of refraction of a glaze fused alone and on the body indicated that 37% to 47% of the body could be dissolved, possibly even 55% (fig. 6.29). Shaw[81] found that the coating, when matured on the body at 1,000° C for a few hours, had a silica content which was 90% to 252% greater than the batch composition. The author doubts that this increase is to be explained by volatilization.

Hall[82] studied the interaction of a vitreous and a lead-borosilicate glaze applied on the biscuit and fired at cone 6. The silica and the alumina contents of the glazes increased, the latter more than the former. The potassa content was not appreciably altered, probably due to an approximately equal content of the same in the body and therefore no diffusion. The lime content decreased 1%, which it was assumed had been taken up by the body inasmuch as lime is nonvolatile and "no lime has been reported as present in the condensate from the flue gases." The observed loss of the lead oxide was attributed to volatilization and absorption by the body. Ninety percent of the dust gathered at the exit end of a saggerless glost muffle kiln consisted of lead and boric oxides.

It is a common assumption that the interfacial layer has a coefficient of expansion which is intermediate between that of the body and the average of the glaze coat. Naturally this becomes probable when the kind of bases used is the same and the proportioning of the other glaze components approaches that of the body; also, it is dependent upon the thermal treatment. For these reasons a porcelain glaze is less likely to craze than one containing soft fluxes in quantity and maturing at a low temperature as contrasted to the body. Another important reason for the latter type crazing is the chemical and physical heterogeneity of the interfacial layer as compared with the body, and more so when contrasted with the glaze. The frequent presence of crystal growths in the interface is evidence of inhomogeneity and of the presence of strains thereby created.

Changes occur in glasses when fired as glaze-layers onto a ceramic body. Kriedl and Weyl[83] found that some water-soluble glasses became chemically resistant when fired as glazes on bodies. Reactions between bodies and both leadless and lead-bearing glazes were examined by Norris[57] and by Smith[84] and others. They all observed the formation of interfacial reaction layers of glass and/or of crystals, depending on the compositions.

Reactions between body and glaze at the interface always occur. Usually these are minor or the reaction products are not radically different in their mean thermal expansion coefficients from that of the bulk of the body of the glaze. There are notable exceptions. The possible individual circumstances are extensive. The potential pyrochemistry and resulting pyrophysical properties of the reaction layers at the interface of each system must be considered.

For example, a wide variety of talcs are available for the preparation of tile bodies. Some relatively pure talcs, very low in CaO, might react with glaze materials to form a high concentration of forsterite, $2MgO \cdot SiO_2$, or even MgO, at the interface. These phases are of high thermal expansion and could cause the tile to have convex warpage. In this case, the cause of the warpage would be the glaze-body interfacial layer which is covered by a well-fitting glaze and no crazing would occur in spite of convex warpage.

Interfacial reaction influences glaze fit.[85] Not much has been published on this aspect. Webb and Ratcliffe[86] observed that crazing in clay-silica-feldspar bodies sometimes was influenced by the formation of cristobalite in the body. Their attention was mainly on the body as a whole and not so much with the interface.

The interfacial zone frequently may be higher or lower in expansion than the body or glaze and by no means always intermediate.

Numerous investigators have been concerned with glaze penetration into bodies and in general to glaze-attack on bodies. Schramm,[87] by applying various surface washes to the body under the glaze, found the glaze definitely to be influenced by the material at the glaze interface.

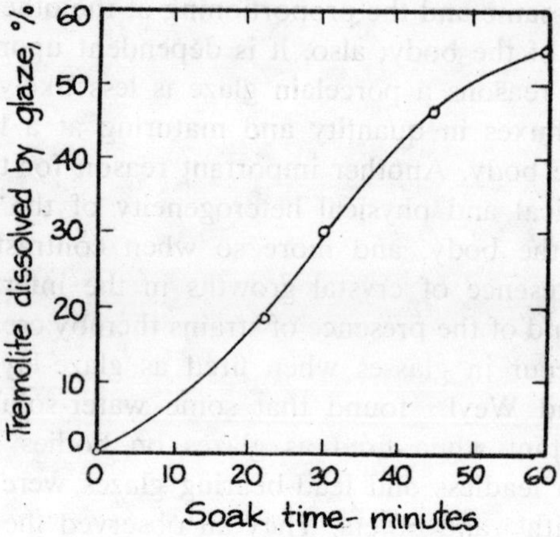

Figure 6.30. Rate of solution of a single crystal of tremolite in a lead glaze at 2,030° F.[85]

A major concern is with porous bodies such as wall tile or semi-vitreous ware and with one-fire ware. In these cases, the fine-grained body ingredients readily become surrounded by liquid phases from the glaze. In such cases, the behavior of the initial body ingredients in contact with liquid glaze reagents becomes of fundamental and basic concern.

Thermal decomposition of talc yields enstatite or clinoenstatite. The decomposition of magnesium silicate by ceramic fluxes can yield forsterite or even MgO. Dolomite plus a ceramic flux yields MgO plus a calcium-enriched flux. A lime-bearing talc will yield a different residue than a lime-poor or lime-free talc.

The amount of talc dissolved by the glaze varies considerably with

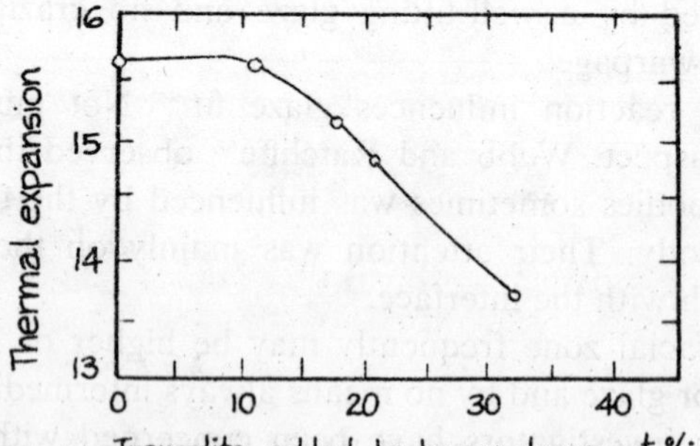

Figure 6.31. Effect of additions of tremolite to a base glaze on the thermal expansion of the resulting fusion.[85]

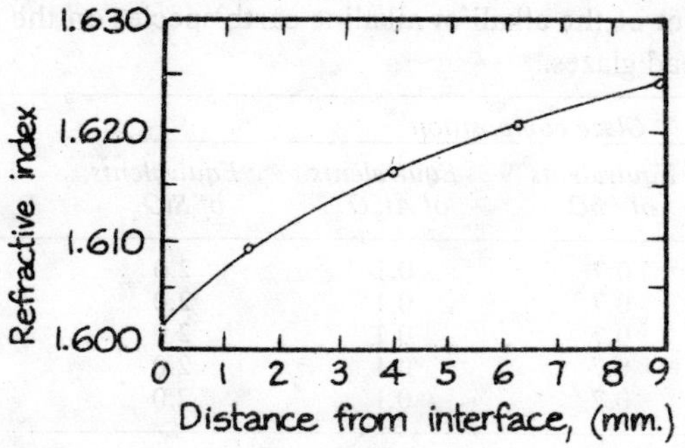

Figure 6.32. Index of refraction of glaze at various distances from a tremolite substrate.[85]

glaze composition. The corrosive influence varies not only with the kind of RO species, but also with the SiO_2/Al_2O_3 ratio. Some laboratory observations by Stone[85] are summarized in figures 6.30, 6.31, and 6.32.

Maturing the Glaze

The maturing temperature of a glaze is dependent upon these conditions: (1) fineness of the batch particles; (2) uniformity of the batch; (3) duration of the firing; and (4), most important, the kind and amounts of the fluxes.

The R_2O members include soda, potassa, and lithia. These, together with lead oxide (PbO), constitute the so-called "soft" fluxes; while calcia, strontia, magnesia, and zinc oxide of the RO group constitute the "hard" fluxes. Raw baryta logically belongs with these and is so used, but when introduced as a member of a frit, it is as powerful as lead oxide in its action. The use of the terms "hard" and "soft" refers to their relative effect upon the fluxing action. The soft fluxes are essential in the compositions maturing at the lower temperatures; while the hard fluxes dominate in those employed for the higher temperatures. It is true, however, that the hard fluxes contribute to the development of abrasion-resisting glazes. Likewise, the soft glazes are likely to be more readily attacked by water and acids.

The relative effects upon the fusibility of equimolecular substitutions of alkali and alkaline earths in a simple silico-alumino mixture, having a constant lead content, is shown in table 6.12.[88]

Increasing the number of the different bases employed in the glaze will generally lower the maturing temperature and extend the range

Table 6.12. Effect of the alkali or alkaline earth species on the fusibility of lead glazes.[88]

Glaze composition					
Equivalents	*Oxide species*	*Equivalents of PbO*	*Equivalents of Al_2O_3*	*Equivalents of SiO_2*	*Fusing temperature (cone)**
0.3	Na_2O	0.7	0.1	2.0	019
0.3	K_2O	0.7	0.1	2.0	016 to 017
0.3	BaO	0.7	0.1	2.0	015 to 016
0.3	CaO	0.7	0.1	2.0	015
0.3	MgO	0.7	0.1	2.0	013 to 014

*For temperature equivalents, see table 1.6.

throughout which it will be serviceable. Since these characteristics are the resultants of the presence of eutectics as well as other chemical and physical conditions, the above mentioned effects are not necessarily present in all cases. Barrett[89] makes the following comparison of the relative fluxing values of certain bases in porcelain glaze compositions:

1 equiv. CaO equals $\frac{1}{6}$ equiv. K_2O 1 equiv. CaO equals $\frac{1}{2}$ equiv. Na_2O
1 equiv. CaO equals $\frac{1}{2}$ equiv. ZnO 1 equiv. CaO equals 1 equiv. BaO

Alumina is the almost indispensable R_2O_3 or intermediate constituent. Ferric oxide, chromium oxide, and some others, including boric oxide, by analogy of composition and chemical conduct, may be classified in this group of amphoteric compounds. These oxides function importantly in the control of viscosity, color, durability, resistance to abrasion, and refractoriness. The amount of alumina used in a glaze designed for a specific cone temperature varies according to the amount and character of the bases, and the time, temperature, and conditions of firing. The order of magnitude of the molecular equivalents of alumina used in raw glazes for different cone maturity ranges is as given in table 6.13. Small increments of alumina have marked effects upon the maturity temperature and the viscosity of the glaze, increasing both.

Of the few elements which are capable of serving as glass formers, silica is preeminent. Amongst the many important functions which it

Table 6.13. The effect of the Al_2O_3 content on maturing temperature of glazes.[89]

Molecular equiv. of alumina	*Cone temperatures*
0 to 0.2	020 to 2
0.2 to 0.5	2 to 9
0.5 to 1.25	9 to 20

shares is the control of fusibility and of viscosity. Other oxides which are or may be substituted in some degree for the silica are boric oxide, phosphoric oxide, zirconia, titania, and germania; but because of the cost or the limitations peculiar to the materials or the products, these, excepting boric oxide, are either not used commercially or only in small amounts. Silica is the one constituent of any glaze batch which is used in the largest amount. The molecular equivalents of silica are normally 2 to 3 times the sum of the molecular equivalents of the bases plus the intermediates. If zirconia or phosphoric oxide is used it must be substituted for a molecular equivalent quantity of the silica in order to make the ratio of silica plus substitution conform to the bisilicate-trisilicate rule.

Boric oxide is frequently grouped with silica in the glaze formula, but there are reasons for considering this an anomaly, and in this country it is made a member of the intermediate group. In that case boric oxide-containing glazes conform to the above rule. Otherwise they may not. The amount of molecular equivalents of silica used in glazes ordinarily is 8 to 10 times the amount of the alumina. The higher the maturing temperature of the glaze, the greater must be the silica content. It is also true that too low a content of silica may likewise make the melt too refractory. The reason for this is found in the absence, under such conditions, of the formation of sufficiently fusible compounds or eutectics.

The principles stated above were summarized by Dr. Seger[90] many years ago as follows:

(1) The ratio (in molecular equivalents) between the fluxing bases, including the intermediates and the acid members, i.e., silica, etc., must lie between the bisilicate and the trisilicate. If it is too close to the former the glaze may be too fusible; if it exceeds the latter, the glaze will not mature properly or will be stringy.

(2) The kind and relative proportions of the fluxes present must be chosen carefully. To increase the fusibility, more of the soft fluxes should be used and in larger amounts, having due regard for proper durability, i.e., resistance to solution by acids and water and resistance to abrasion.

(3) An adequate content of alumina must be provided (*a*) to correct the tendency of the more active bases to lower the viscosity too much and (*b*) to maintain a satisfactory maturing temperature and heat range. Little alumina gives high mobility; too much alumina will yield a melt which is too viscous and will be matt, dull, or immature when cooled. Normally, the ratio of the alumina content to the silica content (for bright, i.e., glossy glazes) is 0.235 to 1.00.

(4) If boric oxide is substituted for molecular equivalents of the silica in order to decrease the maturing temperature or otherwise alter the physical properties of the glaze, the amount must not be so great as to

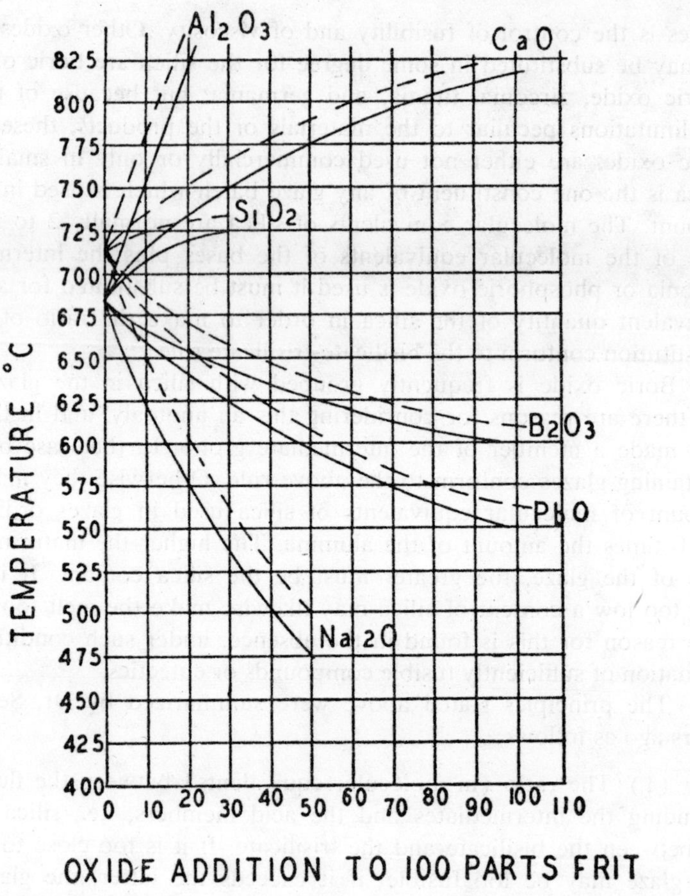

Figure 6.33. Effect of oxide additions to frit on softening point.[92]

increase the water solubility of the same. Ordinarily, the maximum substitution on a molar basis is one-half of the silica.

Zschimmer and his co-workers[91] studied the effects of adding certain oxides to a frit. Test pieces were formed as cones and heated at two different rates of temperature rise. The effects of oxide additions on the softening point of the frit are shown in figure 6.33.[92]

Blakely[93] described the progressive changes in the development of a fritted lead-boric acid glaze maturing at 1,150° C on a semivitreous body, as follows:

Below 550° C The glaze coat was too weak to permit sectioning for study.

600° C The frit content softened.
750° C The grains of quartz and feldspar may be observed
900° C A definite boundary exists between the glaze coat and the body.
1,025° C Little crystalline material is distinguished, the feldspar is dissolved.
1,095° C The melt is free from bubbles.
1,100° C The quartz is completely dissolved.
1,145° C The glaze-body interface shows erosion and solution of the body.
1,150° C The glaze is matured.

The gas bubbles first began to appear at 900° C and reached a maximum volume at 1,025° C, since few bubbles escaped below this temperature. This release is due to the combined effects of diminishing viscosity, less surface tension, decreased density of the melt, and expanded volume of the gas.

Bubbles in Glazes

Bubbles are to be found to some degree in all fired glazes. Their presence has a strong influence upon chemical and physical durabilities and on eye appeal. In high voltage electrical insulators, they influence the uniformity of the magnetic and dielectric fields about the surface. The presence of bubbles tends to reduce the physical strength of glazes and to render them more susceptible to physical damage by abrasion, impact, and the like in service. Bubbles also reduce the resistance of glazes to attack or corrosion by chemicals and detergents. To a surprising extent, they definitely reduce the brightness and brilliance of glazes.

Bubbles also are contributory to such undesirable phenomena in manufacture as, for example: (1) pinholing of glost ware; (2) blistering; (3) egg-shell effects; (4) spit-out; (5) a variety of surface texture due to unhealed craters from burst bubbles; and (6) variations in opacity.

There are a number of possible means for reducing the bubble population. Chief among these are: (1) physical and chemical constitution of the body, (2) firing of the body, (3) interfacial coating or wash, (4) glaze composition, (5) glaze fineness, (6) glaze thickness, and (7) glaze firing.

COMPOSITION OF BODY. It was found[94] that the substitution of alumina for silica in the body was an effective means for reducing the bubble count in fired glazes. The degree of reduction was proportional to the degree of substitution of alpha alumina for potters flint. In some instances, glazes on bodies containing 40% of free alpha alumina and nil quartz were almost free of bubbles. In separate trials, bodies to which lead silicate in very minor proportions had been added were of reduced bubble content.

FIRING OF BODY. With vitrified chinaware bodies, the effects of the degree of firing of the body on bubble population in glaze was minimal. This should not be construed as being the general case for all glazes and bodies.

INTERFACIAL COATING BETWEEN BODY AND GLAZE. When a wash of alumina was applied between body and glaze, the bubble count was reduced. The kind of wash that might be effective depends on body and glaze compositions.

GLAZE COMPOSITION. Bubble population is influenced by the glaze composition and by the choice of batch materials. By this means alone, it does not seem possible to essentially eliminate bubbles.

Best results have been achieved in fritted lead borosilicate glazes by using batches having a minimum of gas-producing constituents and using a blend of two frits, one being lead free and the other a more fusible lead-bearing frit. The clay content should be as low as possible. In laboratory trials, the best results were obtained when a high-purity kaolin was used that had previously been calcined at 800° C. Lead compounds should be fritted.

The addition of lithium compounds, powdered quartz, molybdenum compounds, feldspar, nepheline syenite, and some other mill additions tended to promote bubble formation.

GLAZE FINENESS. Glaze fineness has a slight modifying effect on bubble count. In general, the best results have been observed with glazes ground to 0.5% to 2.0% on a 325 mesh screen. Fair results have been achieved with coarser glazes.

GLAZE THICKNESS. The bubble count increases dramatically with glaze thickness. The best glazes are to be had with uniform coating firing out to 0.005 inch thick.

GLAZE FIRING. The overriding factor in the control of bubbles in glazes is through the glost firing technique. For cone 6 lead borosilicate glazes, the bubble count varies directly with the time between 1,750° F and finish.

In the firing of glazed ware, the heat must move from the glaze surface inward; for its temperature to rise, the glaze surface must be hotter than the interior of the glaze film. Consequently, there is the tendency for pores at the glaze surface to close and occlude gas-filled pores beneath the surface. To prevent this, the pores in a glaze must slowly close so as to squeeze occluded pore gas out as it sinters.

One of the effects of body composition on bubble concentration in fired glazes is that the interfacial zone becomes more refractory than the surface. Flux migration from the glaze into the body would tend to retard the fusion of the interfacial zone behind that of the surface.

Examination of a maturing glaze shows the layer to be very porous until it begins to sinter. It is during the sintering period that the bubble count goes from infinity to a discrete bubble population. In commercial practice, fewer bubbles result when the glaze is compounded and fired in such a manner as to aid in the exclusion of occluded gases from the glaze layer during its densification.

The Setting, Congealing, or Accommodating Period of the Glaze

The setting, congealing, or accommodating period of the glaze is the time-temperature interval during which the molten coating is: (1) cooling from a fluid condition of low viscosity, (2) passing with increasing viscosity into a so-called "plastic" condition, and, (3) finally, becoming hard or rigid at a few hundred degrees above room temperature. During the entire temperature range the volume of the body and of the glaze constantly change, and rarely at the same rate. It is obvious that an agreement is desirable, otherwise strains may, and commonly do, develop in either or both, which is serious when the glaze becomes too rigid to permit an equalization. In addition to the thermal contractions of the body and the glaze, volume changes due to the inversions of minerals in the body—notably of quartz (573° C) and cristobalite (230° C)—will cause strains if these changes occur after the glaze ceases to be mobile.

Thermal expansion curves showing the more important volume changes of quartz, cristobalite, and tridymite are shown in figure 6.34. The expansion curves of a highly vitrified body, i.e., porcelanic structure, and the same body fired at a lower temperature and possessing a semiporcelain structure are shown in figure 6.35. The presence of inflections on the expansion curve of the semiporcelain body at temperatures corresponding to the inversion of the quartz and of the cristobalite can be identified by comparing the two figures. In the case of the porcelanic body, the thermal treatment has been carried out at a sufficiently high temperature to complete the inversions and the solution of the free silica so that no inflection points are present.

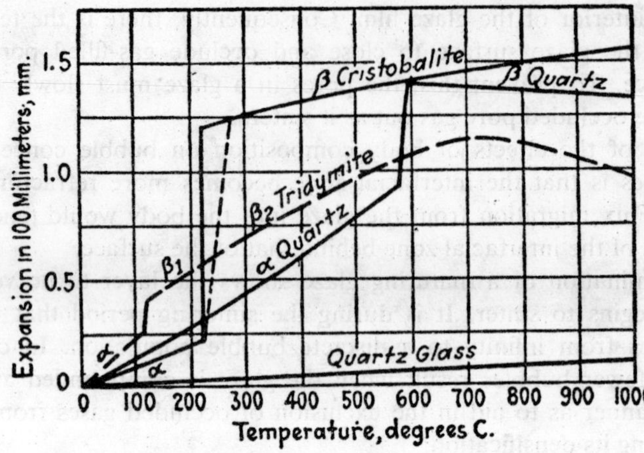

Figure 6.34. Thermal expansion of silica minerals.

The probability of silica inversions or the thermal contractions of the body and the glaze causing defects in glazes can be better understood if we examine in detail the nature of the changes accompanying the cooling of a glaze throughout its setting period. These can be traced by following the ideal curve representing the changes in viscosity as a molten glaze cools

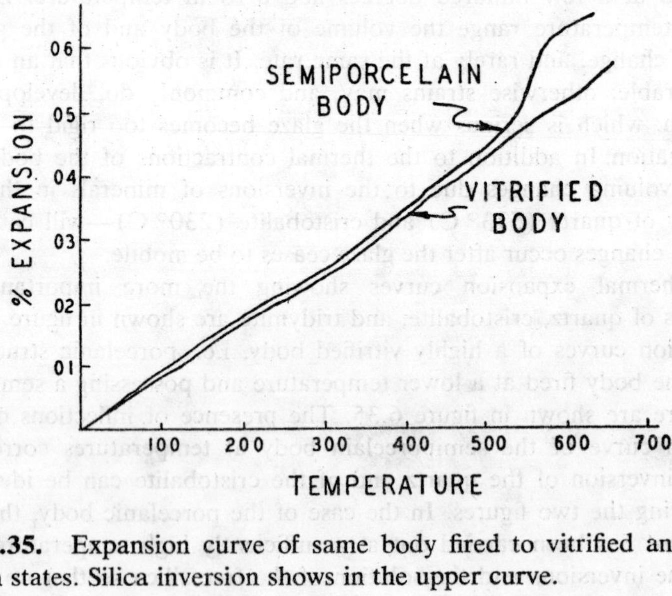

Figure 6.35. Expansion curve of same body fired to vitrified and semi-porcelain states. Silica inversion shows in the upper curve.

from a high temperature and a fluid state to room temperature and the rigid state.

Tammann and Hesse[95] suggested that this whole range of temperature and viscosity changes for glasses can be arbitrarily divided into three zones. Corresponding zones may be used in the case of glazes. These are shown in figure 6.8, beginning at a temperature at which the glass can de drawn as a fine filament, viscosity at about 2 poises—the condition above that temperature is that of a fluid and the temperature-viscosity curve is a straight line. This is within zone 3. The viscosity in the adjoining area, zone 2, follows a gentle curve as the temperature falls. This is the mobile glass (or glaze) zone which is empirically limited at the lowest temperature by a viscosity of 10^{13} poises, which marks the suitable condition for annealing commercial glasses. Below this point lies zone 1, the rigid state. Here the viscosity curve is again a straight path.

Zone 2, which has been called "transition range," "period of accomodation," and "critical zone,"[96] is spread over a range of 40°–80° C in temperature.[97] Within this whole range the glaze is sufficiently mobile to permit most of the strains which are present to be dissipated in a comparatively short time—rapidly at the higher temperatures and much more slowly at the lower. It is at the lower limit that the most suitable temperatures for the annealing of the glasses and glazes are found.

Thermal volume changes in the glaze should be closely adapted to

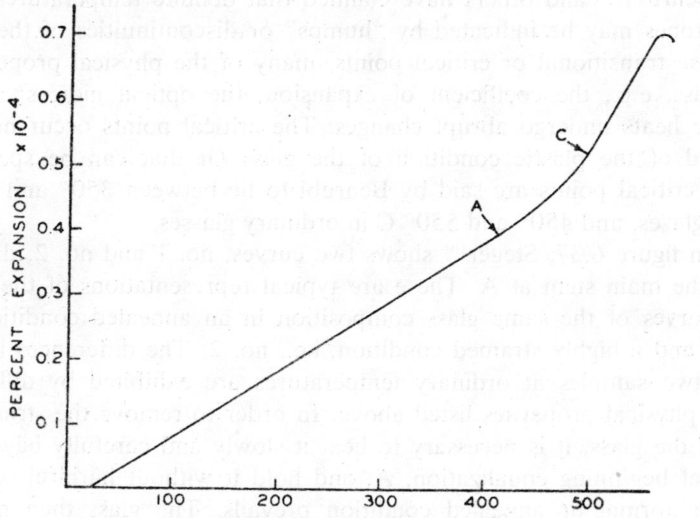

Figure 6.36. Thermal expansion of glaze.

those of the body so that a minimum of difference exists. This will be discussed in more detail in connection with the "Faults of Glazes." Mellor[98] has said: "The lower the congealing temperature and the longer the time occupied in the setting of the glaze the longer the period of accommodation, and the better the opportunity for the glaze to adjust itself to the contracting body in the glost oven."

Kohl[99] mentions a lead–boric oxide–silica glaze of the type used on a steingut (semiporcelain) body and fired at cone O1a. This glaze was still plastic at 560° C, although the deformation temperature was 400° C higher.

An examination of the thermal expansion curves of a typical glass or glaze is most useful in forming an understanding of the nature and the magnitude of the changes taking place at the lower temperature range of the mobile stages of the setting or congealing process. Such a typical curve is presented in figure 6.36. At the temperatures below A on this curve the glass or glaze will be so rigid that strains in the mass cannot be dissipated or only at an extremely slow rate. Between A and C the mobility of the mass increases as the temperature is raised. At the lower temperature near A, the strains can be removed in a reasonably short time, whereas at C they disappear quickly. The graph of the section A to C is gently curved, whereas below A and above C the paths are straight lines. The range A to C is the equalizing or relaxation zone (ausgleich zone). The location of this zone is peculiar to each glass or glaze composition.

Benrubi[100] and others have claimed that definite temperatures within these zones may be indicated by "humps" or discontinuities of the graph. At these transitional or critical points, many of the physical properties of the glass, e.g., the coefficient of expansion, the optical indices, and the specific heats undergo abrupt changes. The critical points occur nearly at the end of the plastic condition of the glass (if that can be specified). These critical points are said by Benrubi to lie between 350° and 450° C in his glazes, and 450° and 550° C in ordinary glasses.

In figure 6.37, Steger[101] shows two curves, no. 1 and no. 2, diverging from the main stem at A. These are typical representations of the expansion curves of the same glass composition in an annealed condition, i.e., no. 1, and a highly strained condition, i.e., no. 2. The differences between these two samples at ordinary temperatures are exhibited by differences in the physical properties listed above. In order to remove the strains, i.e., anneal the glass, it is necessary to heat it slowly and carefully beyond the point of beginning equalization, A, and hold it without harmful softening until a normal or annealed condition prevails. The glass then must be cooled without introducing a new strain gradient.

Tracing the course of the unannealed glass (no. 2) beyond point A,

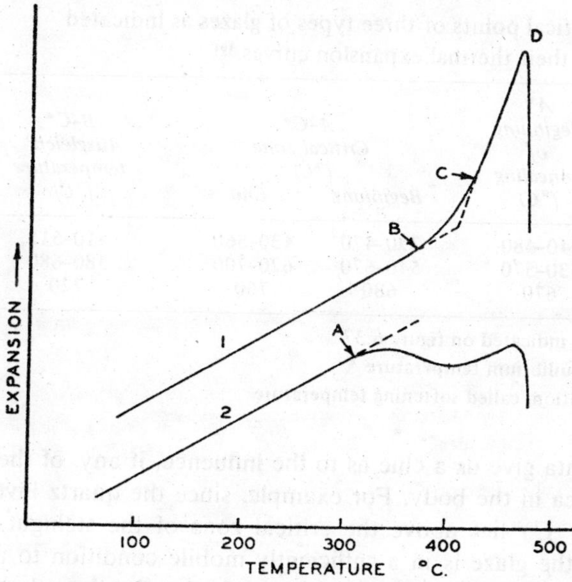

Figure 6.37. Expansion curves of glass: no. 1 for annealed glass, no. 2 for unannealed glass.[101]

one sees that the relaxation appears in the slow rise of the curve until it parallels the abscissa and drops to a minimum point. This decrease is obviously an indication of a shrinkage of the glass which can be demonstrated experimentally. After reaching a minimum, the expansion of the test piece rises, tending to parallel that of the annealed sample no. 1. This continues until sample no. 2 softens at a temperature corresponding to point D. The beginning of the critical zone is at point B, where the horizontal section starts to bend towards the abscissa. The end of this zone is the point on curve 2, opposite C. Beyond that temperature the path rises towards the deformation point which is at the same temperature as indicated by D on curve 1.

In this connection Steger[101] published data pertaining to three types of glazes: for semiporcelain, soft porcelain and hard porcelain. The critical points discussed in the preceding paragraph were determined and defined as to their temperatures in table 6.14. The critical points are identified in figure 6.37 and in table 6.14 as A, A-C, B-C, and D and the meaning of each noted and discussed.

The information in this table is of special importance in the understanding and prevention of defects of glazes caused by the presence of strains, e.g., crazing and shivering, which will be discussed in detail later.

Table 6.14. Critical points of three types of glazes as indicated by their thermal expansion curves.[101]

Type of glaze	*A** *Beginning of annealing (°C)*	*A–C** *Critical zone (°C)* *Beginning*	*End*	*B–C** *Ausgleich*[1] *temperature (°C)*	*D** *Beginning*[2] *softening (°C)*
Steingut	340–480	390–470	430–560	410–515	430–600
Soft porcelain	530–570	540–670	620–700	580–680	670–770
Hard porcelain	670	680	760	720	780

*Critical points as indicated on figure 6.37

[1] Relaxation or equilibrium temperature

[2] Notable deformation, called softening temperature

Further, the data give us a clue as to the influence, if any, of the inversions of the free silica in the body. For example, since the quartz inversion temperature (573° C) lies above the critical zone of the steingut glaze, it is apparent that the glaze is in a sufficiently mobile condition to adjust itself to the volume changes taking place in the body. On the other hand, this would not be true of the soft porcelain glaze and careful annealing would be necessary to remove the strains. It is obvious that the hard porcelain glaze would be a serious problem because it would be quite rigid at the inversion temperature. Fortunately the porcelain body is thoroughly vitrified and is free from uncombined silica.

A low annealing temperature is advantageous since the interval between that and the room temperature is short and strains are less likely to develop, are of smaller magnitude, and more easily corrected.

Gehlhoff and Thomas[102] could not find any linear relation existing between the chemical composition of the glasses they studied and the annealing temperature. They reported the influence of composition upon annealing as follows:

(1) The alkalies decrease the annealing temperature very strongly, the sodium more than the potash.

(2) The lime increases the temperature required very considerably, barium oxide less so; lead oxides, strongly; zinc oxide increases the temperature.

(3) Alumina requires a relatively high annealing temperature; the boric oxide has a very definite maximum in the composition-temperature annealing curve.

Valuable contributions to our knowledge of the conduct of congealing glazes have been made by the study of the nature of the stresses which develop during the cooling from the point of earliest deformation to room

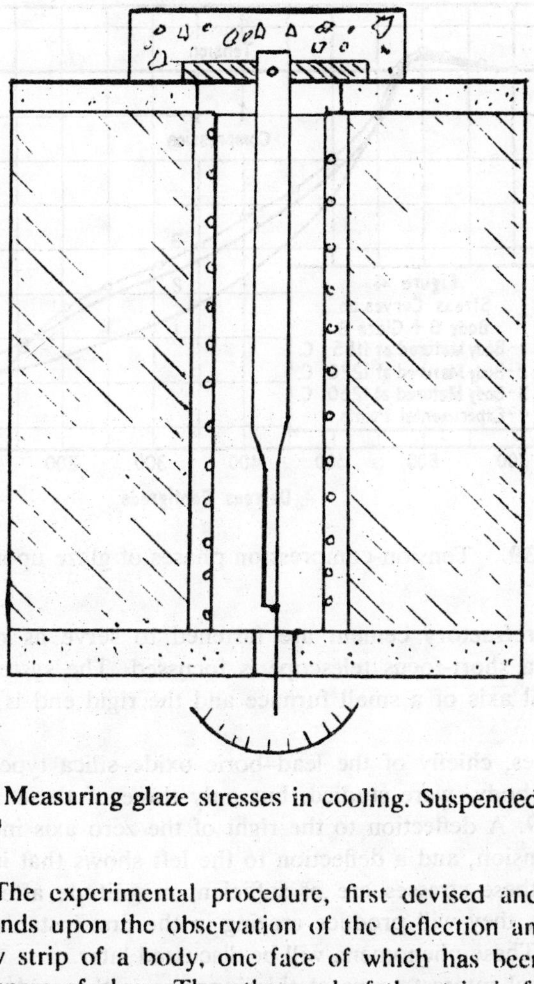

Figure 6.38. Measuring glaze stresses in cooling. Suspended bar is glazed on one side.[103]

temperature. The experimental procedure, first devised and reported by Steger,[103] depends upon the observation of the deflection and one end of a long, narrow strip of a body, one face of which has been coated with a normal thickness of glaze. The other end of the strip is fastened cantileverwise in a rigid clamp (fig. 6.38). The body strip is biscuited and the glaze is fired on the body before the system is placed axially at the core of a small horizontal furnace. When the furnace is heated an ink-fed pen point traces the path of the deflection of the free end. The movement is caused by the differential expansion of glaze and the body. Deflection in one direction indicates that the glaze is under tension; contrariwise, compression is indicated.

A modified and more refined device is that constructed by Blakely,[104] who used two long glazed strips separated by a short piece of the body inserted between them at one end and cemented to both. The assembly has the appearance of a tuning fork. On the free tips of the bars minute

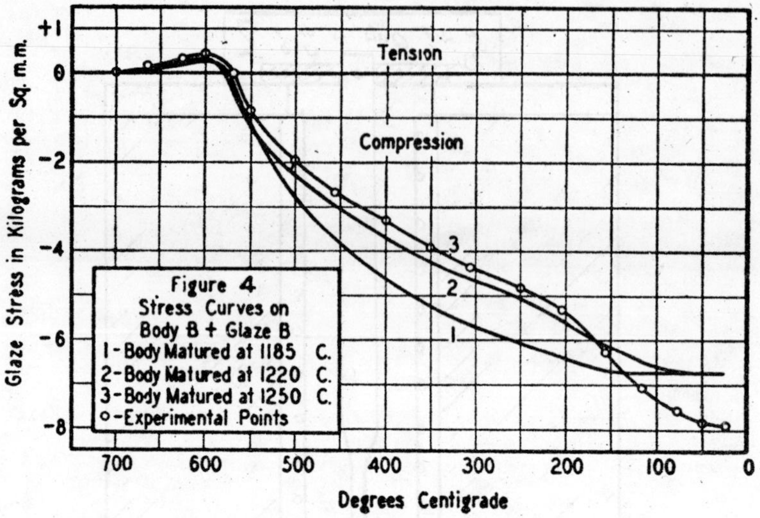

Figure 6.39. Tension-compression phases of glaze upon cooling.[104]

particles of refractory cement are fastened to serve as reference points upon which a short-focus telescope is focussed. The system is placed on the horizontal axis of a small furnace and the rigid end is firmly clamped to a support.

Six glazes, chiefly of the lead–boric oxide–silica type, suitable for a semivitreous body, were studied, but only three of these are shown here in figure 6.39. A deflection to the right of the zero axis indicates that the glaze is in tension, and a deflection to the left shows that it is under compression. If these stresses are of sufficient magnitude after the glaze has become rigid, they will produce crazing in the first instance and shivering in the latter. These phenomena will be discussed later.

Of special interest to us at this juncture is the evidence that strains develop in the glaze at temperatures far above the deformation range. Blakely suggested the location of the softening point as being the temperature at which the path of the curve in figure 6.39 crosses the zero axis.

References

1. Schwob, Yvan. 1947. Thermal dissociation of dolomite. Influence of small quantities of flux. *Compt. Rend.* 224(1):47–49.
2. Turner, W. E. S. 1934. Fundamental processes underlying glass melting. *J. Am. Ceram. Soc.* 17:21.

3. Lea, F. M. and Desch, C. H. 1937. *Chemistry of cement and concrete.* London: Edward Arnold and Co. p 104.
4. Long, Bernard. 1933. *Proprietes physiques et fusion due verre.* Paris, p 263.
5. Howarth, J. T., Maskill, W., and Turner, W. E. S. 1933. Rate of reaction between silica and sodium carbonate. *J. Soc. Glass Tech.* 17:25–49.
6. Littleton, J. T. 1934. Physical processes occurring in the melting and cooling of glass. *J. Am. Ceram. Soc.* 17:43–49.
7. In Long, op. cit., ref. 4, p 264.
8. Bancroft, W. D. 1921. *Applied colloid chemistry.* New York: McGraw-Hill Book Co., p 147.
9. Brown, Harvey E. c1957. *Zinc oxide rediscovered.* New York: Market Development Division, New Jersey Zinc Co. Harman's fig. 6.2 was taken by Brown from Leverenz, H. W. *Luminescence of solids.* 1950. New York: Wiley & Sons, p 49.
10. Levin, Ernest M., Robbins, Carl R., and McMurdie, Howard F. 1964. *Phase diagrams for ceramists,* Ed. and published by The American Ceramic Society, Inc.
11. Sun, K. H. Feb., 1948, *The glass industry,* p 78.
12. Bloor, E. C. 1956. Glaze composition, glass structural theory and its application to glazes. *Trans. Brit. Ceram. Soc.* 55(10):631–660.
13. Greig, J. W. 1927. Immiscibility in silicate melts. *Am. J. Science,* 13(5)1–44,132.
14. Le Chatelier, H. 1926. *J. Soc. Glass Tech.* 10:95.
15. Argyle, J. F. and Hummel, F. A. 1963. Liquid immiscibility in the system BaO-SiO_2. *Physics and chemistry of glasses* 4(3):103–5.
16. Johnson, David W. and Hummel, F. A. 1968. Phase equilibria and liquid immiscibility in the system PbO-B_2O_3-SiO_2. *J. Am. Ceram. Soc.* 51(4):196–201.
17. Hummel, F. A., Tien, T. Y., and Kim, K. H. 1960. Studies in lithium oxide systems: 7, Application of silicate liquid immiscibility to development of opaque glazes. *J. Am. Ceram. Soc.* 43(4):192–97.
18. Tammann, G. and Hesse, W. 1926. Relations of viscosity to temperature in supercooled liquids. *Z. Anorg. u. Allgem. Chem.* 156:254.
19. Zachariesen, W. H. 1932. Atomic arrangement in glass. *J. Am. Chem. Soc.* 54:3841.
20. Warren, B. E. and Biscoe, J. 1938. Fourier analysis of X-ray patterns of soda-silica glass. *J. Am. Ceram. Soc.* 21:259.
21. Gehlhoff, G. and Thomas, M. 1925. Electrical conductivity of glass. *Zeit. Tech. Physik* 6:544.
22. Machin, J. S. and Yee, Tin Boo. 1948. Viscosity studies of the system CaO–MgO–Al_2O_3–SiO_2:2, CaO–Al_2O_3–SiO_2. *J. Am. Ceram. Soc.* 31(7): 200–204.
23. English, S. 1924. Effect of composition on viscosity of glass, Part 2. *J. Soc. Glass Tech.* 8:205.
24. James, W. and Norris, A. N. 1956. Some physical properties of glazes. *Trans. Brit. Ceram. Soc.* 55(10):601–30.

25. Lehmann, H., Engell, K., and Hellbrugge, H. 1940. *Sprechsaal* 73:307, 321.
26. Bremond, P. 1951. *Bull. Soc. Franç. Ceram.* 11:4.
26a. Bremond, P. 1952. *Trans. 3rd Int. Ceram. Congr.* p 41.
27. Dalton, R. H. 1933. Gases in glass. *J. Am. Ceram. Soc.* 16:425.
28. Kraner, H. M. 1933. Microstructure of electrical porcelain glazes. *Ceram. Ind.* 21:73.
29. Norton, F. H. 1931. Influence of time on the maturing of white ware bodies. *J. Am. Ceram. Soc.* 14:205.
30. Schramm, E. and Hall, F. P. 1936. Fluxing effect of feldspar in white ware bodies. *J. Am. Ceram. Soc.* 19:159.
31. Tammann, G. 1925. *Textbook of metallography*. New York: Chemical Catalog Co., p 212.
32. Iddings, J. P. 1909. Igneous rocks. vol. 1. p 104, John Wiley and Sons, New York.
33. Mellor, J. W. 1912–13. The behavior of some glazes in the glost oven. *Trans. Engl. Ceram. Soc.* 12:11.
34. Bancroft, W. D. 1926. *Applied colloid chemistry*. 2d ed. New York: McGraw-Hill Book Co., p 159.
35. Mellor, J. W., Latimer, A., and Holdcroft, A. D. 1909–10. Softening temperatures of lead-silica glasses. *Trans Engl. Cer. Soc.* 9:133.
36. Morey, G. W. 1938. *Properties of glass*. New York: Reinhold Pub. Co., p 197.
37. Clark, C. B. 1936. Surface tension of Bristol glaze. Thesis, Univ. of Illinois.
38. Lecrenier and Gilard 1925. Mesure de la temperature superficielle du verre. *Revue universelle des mines* 6:186.
39. Washburn, E. W. 1921. The dynamics of capillary flow. *Phys. Rev.* 17:273.
40. Lampman, C. M. 1938. *J. Am. Ceram. Soc.* 21:252.
40a. Lampman, C. M. 1938. Flow of glazes on horizontal and inclined surfaces. *Bull. Am. Ceram. Soc.* 17:12.
41. Dietzel, A. *Sprechsaal* 1929 62:506, 524, 534, 562, 584, 603, 619, 638, 637.
42. Lyon, K. C. 1944. Calculation of surface tensions of glasses. *J. Am. Ceram. Soc.* 27:186.
43. Badger, A. E., Parmelee, C. W., and Williams, A. E. 1937. Surface tension of various molten glasses. *J. Am. Ceram. Soc.* 20:235.
44. Amberg, C. R. 1946. Effect of molybdenum and other oxides on surface tension of silicate melts and on properties of refractories and abrasives. *J. Am. Ceram. Soc.* 29(4):87–93.
45. Parmelee, Cullen W., Lyon, Kenneth C., and Harman, Cameron G. The surface tensions of molten glass. U. of Ill. Engineering Experiment Station, Bull. Ser. no. 311. Urbana: University of Illinois, June 6, 1939.
46. Shartsis, Leo, Spinner, Sam, and Smock, Alden W. 1948. Surface tension of compositions in the system $PbO–B_2O_3$ and $PbO–SiO_2$. *J. Res. Natl. Bur. Stad. (U.S.)* 40:61–66. R.P. 1855.

47. Shartsis, Leo and Capps, Webster. 1952. Surface tension of molten alkali borates. *J. Am. Ceram. Soc.* 35(7):169–72.
48. Parikh, N. M. 1958. Effect of atmosphere on surface tension of glass. *J. Am. Ceram. Soc.* 41(1):18–22.
49. Jebsen-Marwedel, H. 1943. Surface tension forces as an important factor in the disappearance of cords in melted glasses. *Glastech. Ber.*, 21(3):7–66.
50. Quoted by Mellor, J. W., Latimer, A., and Holdcroft, A. D., op. cit., ref. 35.
51. Anderson, O. 1919. The volatilization of lead oxide from lead silicate melts. *J. Am. Ceram. Soc.* 2:784.
52. Wright, F. E. 1921. *The manufacture of optical glass and optical systems.* Washington, D.C.: U.S. Printing Office, p 100.
53. Harrison, H. C., Lawrence, W. G., and Tucker, D. J. 1940. Volatility of glaze constituents, etc. *J. Am. Ceram. Soc.* 23:119–21.
54. Schramm, E. 1938. Problems in whiteware glazes. *Bull. Am. Ceram. Soc.* 17:436.
55. Parmelee, C. W. and Buckles, P. A. 1942. Study of glaze and body interface. *J. Am. Ceram. Soc.* 25:11.
56. Hallse, Robert and Cook, Ralph L. 1958. Volatility studies of lead silicate melts. *J. Am. Ceram. Soc.* 41(9):331–36.
57. Norris, A. W. 1956. Changes in a glass when used as a glaze. *Trans. Brit. Ceram. Soc.* 55(10):674–88.
58. Poste, E. P. and Rice, B. A. 1918. The effect of the degree of smelting on the properties of a frit. *J. Am. Ceram. Soc.* 1:221.
59. Tammann, G. 1925. Glasses as supercooled liquids. *J. Soc. Glass Tech.* 9:166.
60. Mellor, J. W. 1914. *Clay and pottery industry.*, London: Griffin and Co., p 49.
61. Swift, Howard R. 1947. Some experiments on crystal growth and solution in glass. *J. Am. Ceram. Soc.* 30(6):165–169.
62. Norton, F. H. 1937. The control of crystalline glazes. *J. Am. Ceram. Soc.* 20:217.
63. Binns, C. F. 1903. The development of the matt glaze. *Trans. Am. Ceram. Soc.* 5:50–57.
64. Staley, H. F. 1912. The microscopic examination of 12 matt glazes. *Trans. Am. Ceram. Soc.* 14:691.
65. Binns, op. cit., ref. 63.
66. Orton, E. A., Jr. 1908. A study of matt glazes maturing at cones 2–4. *Trans. Am. Ceram. Soc.* 10:547.
67. Parmelee, C. W., and Horak, W. 1934. Microstructure of some raw lead matt glazes. *J. Am. Ceram. Soc.* 17:67.
68. Wilson, H. E. 1922. Matt glazes and the lime-alumina-silica system. *Bull. Am. Ceram. Soc.* 1(18):447.
69. Purdy, R. C. 1912. Matt glazes. *Trans. Am. Ceram. Soc.* 14:671.
70. Thompson, C. L. 1931. The microstructure of some porcelain glazes. *U. of Illinois Eng. Expt. Station Bull.* 225:24.

71. Parmelee and Horak, op. cit., ref. 67.
72. Wilson, op. cit., ref. 68.
73. Zsigmondy, R. 1914. *Colloids and the ultramiscroscope*. Translated by J. Alexander. New York: Wiley.
74. Silverman, A. 1931. Colloids in glass, in *Colloid chemistry*, vol. 3. Edited by J. Alexander. New York: Chemical Catalog Co., p 286.
75. Wright, F. E. 1921. *The manufacture of optical glass and optical systems.* Washington, D.C.: U.S. Printing Office, p 85.
76. Mellor, J. W. 1912–13. The behavior of some glazes in the glost oven, pt 1. *Trans. Engl. Cer. Soc.* 12:11.
77. Norton, H. S. 1937. Control of crystalline glazes. *J. Am. Ceram. Soc.* 20:223.
78. Schramm, E. 1938. Problems in whiteware glazes. *Bull. Am. Ceram. Soc.* 17:437.
79. Kraner, H. M. 1926. Use of eutectics in glazes. *J. Am. Ceram. Soc.* 9:319.
80. Parmelee, C. W. and Buckles, P. A. 1942. Study of glaze and body interface. *J. Am. Ceram. Soc.* 25:11.
81. Shaw, D. T. 1932. Color formation in plumbic glazes. *J. Am. Ceram. Soc.* 15:37–58.
82. Schramm, op. cit., ref. 78.
83. Kried N. J., and Weyl, W. A. 1941. *J. Am. Ceram. Soc.* 24:372.
84. Smith, A. N. 1952. Some investigations on glaze body layers. *Trans. 3d Int. Ceram. Congress,* Paris, p 289.
85. Perricone, A. C. and Stone, Robert L. 1954. Interface reactions between glazes and the crystal phases in a high-talc body. *J. Am. Ceram. Soc.,* 37(2):33–38.
86. Webb, H. W. and Ratcliffe, S. W. 1939. Some observations on crazing: formation of cristobalite in earthenware and white tile bodies. *Trans. Brit. Ceram. Soc.* 38(1):100–105, *Ceram. Abstr.* 18(25):132.
87. Schramm, op. cit., ref. 78.
88. *Sprech. Kal. Ed.* 1916, p 34.
89. Barrett, M. 1909. A method for determining the melting points of glass and glaze silicates of the porcelain type, etc. *Trans. Am. Ceram. Soc.* 11:80.
90. Seger, H. A. 1902. *Collected writings,* vol. 2. New York: Chemical Publishing Co., p 566.
91. Leonhardt, E. and Zschimmer, E. 1928. Softening point of porcelain fritted glazes. *Sprechsaal* 61:763.
92. Salmang, H. 1933. Die physikalischen und chemischen Grundlagen der Keramik. Berlin, p 124.
93. Blakely, A. M. 1938. Life history of a glaze: 1. Maturing of a whiteware glaze. *J. Am. Ceram. Soc.* 21:239.
94. Personal files, 1969.
95. Tammann, G. and Hesse, W. 1926. Relation of viscosity to temperature in supercooled liquids. *Z. Anorg. u. Allgem. Chem.* 156:254.

96. Mellor, J. W. 1935. The crazing and peeling of glazes. *Trans. Engl. Cer. Soc.* 34:18.
97. Steger, W. 1927. Thermal expansion and annealing temperature of glazes. *Ber. deut. keram. Ges.* 8:24.
98. Mellor, J. W. op. cit. ref 96, p 24.
99. Kohl, H. 1922. The thermal expansion of semi-porcelain. *Ber. deut. keram. Ges.* 3:303.
100. Benrubi, J. A. 1936. Adherence of ceramic body and glaze. *Verre et silicates industriels.* 7:61, 73, 90.
101. Steger, W. 1930. *Ber. deut. keram. Ges.* 11:139.
102. Gehlhoff, G., and Thomas, M. 1925. Rapid cooling of glass. *Z. Tech. Physik.* 6:333.
103. Steger, W. 1928. Stresses in glazed ware. *Ber. deut. keram. Ges.* 9:203.
104. Blakely, A. M. 1938. Life history of a glaze. *J. Am. Ceram. Soc.* 21:243.

7

Physical Properties of Congealed Glazes

The Additive Law

Origin

Knowledge of the effects of the empirical use of raw materials constituted the art and the mystery of glassmaking for many centuries. More systematic methods had to await developments of science, the accumulation of a body of knowledge, and the perfection of the necessary physical techniques needed for the fundamental researches in a very difficult field of investigation. Faraday[1] seems to have been the earliest to have reported observations upon the relation of composition to the physical properties of glasses. It was a modest and limited contribution. The really epochal researches were the classic studies which Winkelmann and Schott of Jena made during the last decade of the nineteenth century. These beginnings have been largely supplemented in later years by numerous workers who have been studying glazes and vitreous enamels as well as glasses.

Winkelmann and Schott[2] proposed the "additive law," which states simply that the physical properties of glass may be systematically altered by the addition, subtraction, or substitution of specific elements to produce the desired changes. Within limits, this law has proven to be a logical and valued tool for use in the design or correction of compositions to meet particular needs.

Certain limitations in the use of such methods must be recognized. Some of these are as follows:

1. The data give only approximate, although useful, results.
2. The specific effect accompanying the use of any addition of an oxide

is influenced by the amount of, and the kind of the other oxides present.
3. The effects of the alteration of the amount of any oxide is not linear except to a limited degree; consequently the best results may be expected only from comparisons of similar systems prepared under like conditions.
4. The thermal treatment of the glaze during its maturing and the time-lag subsequent to coming out of the kiln have significant effects upon some and possibly all of the properties.
5. The composition of the matured glaze usually differs notably from the computation based upon the batch because of volatilization and the result of the chemical attack and solution of the body surface upon which it is applied.

Concept

The additive relationship of the composition to the physical properties of the glaze is a characteristic common to all liquids and is another illustration of the identity of the two.[3] On the basis of the dependence of the properties of glasses upon composition, it is possible to compute a specific property, e.g., density, thermal, mechanical, optical, and electrical, according to the general formula:

$$P = C_1x_1 + C_2x_2 + C_3x_3 + \cdots + C_nx_n$$

in which P is the property, C is the percentage weight of an oxide component, and x_1, x_2, x_3, and x_n are their appropriate factors. These factors have been computed from experimental data obtained by the investigation of glasses, vitreous enamels, and glazes. Notwithstanding the considerable differences between these three kinds of glassy fusions with respect to compositions, thermal treatment, and the bases upon which the latter two are applied, the use of the coefficients for the computations of properties of glazes has been helpful. Some progress has been made in the study of this special problem as will be noted in tables 7.1 and 7.2.

Calculations

COEFFICIENT OF THERMAL EXPANSION. The use of these factors in the calculation of the coefficient of thermal expansion of a glaze is shown in table 7.3.

The sum of the cubical coefficients is the cubical coefficient of the glaze. The linear coefficient is approximately one-third of the cubical, or 94.0×10^{-7}. Rieke[7] found that porcelain glazes vary from $(27 \text{ to } 42) \times 10^{-7}/^\circ C$, and stoneware (vitreous all-clay body) from $(57 \text{ to } 96) \times 10^{-7}$.

Table 7.1. Factors for computing some properties of glasses and enamels from composition

Composition	Thermal expansion W. & S.[2] × 10^{-7}	Thermal expansion E. & T.[4]	Density W. & S.[2] × 10^{-7}	Density Bailie	Tensile strength W. & S.[2] kg/sq mm	Crushing strength W. & S.[2] kg/sq mm	Elasticity C. & T.[5]
SiO_2	0.8	0.15	2.3	2.24	0.09	1.23	3.9
Al_2O_3	5.0	0.42	4.1	2.75	0.05	1.0	11.8
B_2O_3	0.1	-1.98	1.9	3.00	0.065	0.90	–
Na_2O	10.0	12.96	2.6	3.20	0.02	0.52	10.8
K_2O	8.5	11.7	2.8	3.20	0.01	0.05	–
PbO	3.0	3.18	9.6	10.30	0.025	0.48	–
ZnO	1.8	2.1	5.9	5.94	0.15	0.6	–
CaO	5.0	4.89	3.3	4.30	0.20	0.20	23.5
MgO	0.1	1.35	3.8	3.25	0.01	1.1	29.4
BaO	3.0	4.2	7.0	7.20	0.05	0.65	–
P_2O_5	2.0	–	2.55	–	0.075	0.76	–

Note: The tabulated numbers are to be multiplied by 10^{-7}. The units are per °C.

Table 7.2. Factors for transition element oxides for computing the thermal expansion of glasses containing them[6]

Composition	*Thermal expansion* × 10^{-7}
SnO_2	2.0
TiO_2	4.1
Cr_2O_3	5.1
CoO	4.4
CuO	2.2
Fe_2O_3	4.0
NiO	4.0
MnO_2	2.2

Note: The numbers in the table are to be multiplied by $10^{-7}/°C$

Danzin[8] calculated expansion coefficients from factors in table 7.4 from the relation:

$$\alpha_c = \Sigma p_i a_i$$

where α_c = cubic expansion; p_i = weight percent; and a_i = characteristic constants from table 7.4.

DENSITY. Because specific volume is the reciprocal of the density (1/D), density would be computed as follows:

$$1/D = \frac{P_1}{V_1} + \frac{P_2}{V_2} + \frac{P_3}{V_3} + \frac{P_4}{V_4} + \cdots + \frac{P_n}{V_n}$$

where P_1, P_2, P_3, P_4, P_n are the percentages of the component oxides and V_1, V_2, V_3, V_4, V_n are the densities of the component oxides.

Table 7.3. An example showing the application of factors for calculating thermal expansion from chemical composition

Glaze composition percentages		*Factor W. & S.*[2] × 10^{-7}		*Cubical coefficients* × 10^{-7}*
Silica	37.40	0.8	=	29.92
Alumina	4.17	5.0	=	20.85
Potassa	7.34	8.5	=	62.39
Soda	1.19	10.0	=	11.90
Lime	3.85	5.0	=	19.25
Lead oxide	45.92	3.0	=	137.76
Total	99.87			282.07

*The tabulated numbers are to be multiplied by $10^{-7}/°C$. The final value is 282.07 × $10^{-7}/°C$.

Table 7.4. Danzin factors for calculating thermal expansion[8]

Oxide	a_i	*Oxide*		a_i
SiO_2	0.20		PbO	2.5
B_2O_3	1.30	When low in heavy elements and $p_i = 0.1$ to 0.3		
Al_2O_3	1.65		Na_2O	17
MgO	0.20		K_2O	15
ZnO	1.6	When PbO + BaO exceed 18% and $p_i < 0.1$		
CaO	4.8		Na_2O	17
BaO	3.4		K_2O	15

ELASTICITY. Young's modulus of elasticity may be calculated from chemical analysis as follows:

$$E = p_1e_1 + p_2e_2 + p_3e_3 + \cdots + p_ne_n$$

where E is Young's modulus, p is the percentage of any oxide used, and e is the factor for that oxide from table 7.5.

Hall[9] investigated 118 glazes and 12 glasses and found that the moduli ranged between 5,500 and 10,000 kg per mm². Ricke[10] found the modulus of elasticity ranged from 5,700 to 6,800 kg per mm².

Table 7.5. Factors for calculating modulus of elasticity[9]

Group A			
	Factors		*Factors*
SiO_2	60	PbO	45–72*
Al_2O_3	100	ZnO	100
Na_2O	53	B_2O_3	40–160* if no PbO, MgO, or ZnO are present. Otherwise see below.
K_2O	43		
CaO	150		
Fe_2O_3	100		
MgO	190		
BaO	75		

Group A: B_2O_3 and PbO being present, but no MgO or ZnO; 20–187* for B_2O_3 factor; otherwise use factors as in Group A.

Group B: B_2O_3 and ZnO being present but no MgO or PbO. Other factors as in Group A. Factors for B_2O_3 are 80; for ZnO, 100.

Group C: B_2O_3 and MgO being present but no PbO or ZnO. Other factors as in Group A. Factors for B_2O_3 are 50; for MgO, 190.

Group D: B_2O_3, ZnO, and MgO being present but no PbO. Use the factors given for these in C and D and for the other oxides use factors in A.

Group E: B_2O_3, ZnO, MgO, and PbO being present. Use other factors as in Group A. Factors for B_2O_3 are 40; for ZnO, 100; for MgO, 190; for PbO, 72.

*Factors vary with composition in a way detailed in the original article.[9]

Table 7.6. Factors for estimating tensile strength of glass[9]

Group 1		*Group 2*		*Group 3*	
	Factors		*Factors*		*Factors*
SiO_2	0.07–0.15*	BaO	0.03	SiO_2	0.07
BaO	0.42–0.10*	ZnO	0.20	Al_2O_3	0.12
Na_2O	0.0 –1.00*	SiO_2	0.07	Na_2O	0.75
K_2O	0.0 –1.10*	Al_2O_3	0.12	K_2O	0.30
CaO	0.30–1.12*	Na_2O	0.20	PbO	0.20
MgO	0.80–1.00*	K_2O	0.40	B_2O_3	0.20
Al_2O_3	0.12	PbO	0.20		
ZnO	0.65	MgO	0.80		
B_2O_3	0.20	CaO	0.70		
PbO	0.20–0.57*	B_2O	0.20–0.67*		

*Factors vary with composition. For details consult original article.[9]

TENSILE STRENGTH. The general formula used is:

$$T = p_1t_1 + p_2t_2 + p_3t_3 + p_4t_4 + \cdots + p_nt_n$$

where T is tensile strength, p is percentage of any component oxide, and t is the tensile strength factor for the oxide used (table 7.6).

Hall found that the tensile strength in the series of glasses and glazes varied between 11 and 35 kg per mm². Rieke examined a few glazes and found that the tensile strength of the stoneware glazes investigated lay between 5 and 8 kg per mm² and might be as low as 3.5 kg per mm². Strength is more sensitive to textural and mechanical properties than to chemical composition. The factors may be indicative of comparative effects of various oxides.

COMPRESSIVE STRENGTH. The formula used for this purpose is similar to that used for tensile strength. This property has not been studied much, as it is less important than the tensile strength or the elasticity. It is probably of the order of 100 kg/mm² on the average. Gehlhoff and Thomas[11] have arranged the following series in decreasing order of influence of the individual oxides. Those underscored below have nearly the same values:

$$Al_2O_3 > \underline{SiO_2, MgO, ZnO,} > \underline{B_2O_3, Fe_2O_3,} > \underline{BaO, CaO, PbO} > Na_2O > K_2O$$

Many investigators have reported the influence of the composition upon the above mentioned and other mechanical properties, also thermal, electrical and optical properties of special and limited varieties of glasses

Table 7.7. Factors for the average coefficient of linear expansion over the range from room temperature to the lower critical temperature[9]

Oxides	*Factors* × 10^9*	*Oxides*	*Factors* × 10^9*
Na_2O	380	MgO	20
K_2O	300	PbO	75
CaO	150	Al_2O_3	50
BaO	120	SiO_2	5-50**
ZnO	100	B_2O_3	20

*The factors are in terms of 10^{-9}/°C and have been multiplied by 10^9 to tabulate.
**Factors are variable with composition.

and vitreous enamels. Glazes have been almost entirely neglected except for a few compositions used at very low temperatures. Recognizing the generally nonlinear relationship of composition and properties, Gehlhoff and Thomas[11] proposed that, if the composition and properties of a relatively simple glass are known, the changes in the properties accompanying the changes in a similar composition may be predicted by the use of suitable factors which have been determined experimentally. An excellent discussion of this method was published in 1937 in *Glass Industry* 18:227.

HALL'S FACTORS. Hall[9] published factors and methods—for the calculation of the tensile strength, Young's modulus of elasticity, and the coefficient of thermal expansion of glazes—which he considered reliable, providing "the composition of the new glaze does not vary too greatly from those considered" in the report. The glazes were divided into four groups: Group *A*, in which the members all contain soda, potassa, lime, and lead oxide (25% to 50%) and a few contain magnesia, baryta, zinc oxide, or boric oxide; Group *B*, in which all contain soda and potassa and a few, lime, lime and magnesia, baryta, or lead; Group *C*, in which all contain soda, lead oxide, and boric oxide, potassa (in all but two), and no alkaline earths; Group *D*, a miscellaneous collection of glaze and glass compositions with and without lead oxide, and with and without boric oxide.

Quoting the author: "In general, the glazes used in this investigation contained a greater percentage of basic oxides than those used in the industry in order to facilitate the liberation of gases during the melting of the batches." The compositions were not matured on bodies, but as glasses. His factors are listed in tables 7.5, 7.6, and 7.7.

Those factors in group 1 of table 7.6 should be used in all cases, with these exceptions: (*a*) If PbO and any or all of the following oxides—B_2O_3, MgO, CaO, ZnO and BaO—are present in amounts greater than 1%, use the factors given in group 2; (*b*) in case PbO and B_2O_3

are present and MgO, CaO, ZnO and BaO are absent, use factors in group 3.

TENSION DUE TO MOISTURE AND THERMAL EXPANSIONS. Expressions for calculating the tensions induced in glazes by the difference in thermal expansions between the body and the glaze and those due to moisture expansion were derived by Harkort.[12]

Tensile stress induced in the glaze by mismatch between the thermal expansion of body and glaze is as follows:

$$\sigma_z = \Delta\alpha \cdot \Delta t \cdot E$$

where σ_z is tensile stress in glaze in kg/mm²; $\Delta\alpha$ is the difference between the thermal expansions of body and glaze (per ° C); Δt is the difference, in degrees C, between the softening temperature (or other reference temperature) of the glaze and room temperature; and E is modulus of elasticity of glaze in kg/mm².

Tensile stress created in the glaze by moisture expansion in the body is expressed thus:

$$\sigma_z = \frac{\text{Moisture expansion, in } \% \times E}{100}$$

Crazing occurs when the tensile strength of the glaze is exceeded. This takes place commonly at tensile stresses in excess of 6.6 kg per mm². The autoclave test measures only moisture expansion. Not all crazing can be directly related to this test.

Thermal Expansion

Significant Points in the Thermal History of Glasses

At room temperature, the viscosity of silicate glasses is so high that they behave and function pretty much as a solid. When heated above room temperature several significant characterizations, with respect to temperature, develop consecutively. Several of these are most readily illustrated as points on the curve of thermal expansion vs. temperature. These are shown on figure 7.1.

Starting at room temperature, the thermal dilation is linear with temperature up to 300° C or so. This point is shown as t_{al} in figure 7.1 and may be considered as the lower annealing temperature or the strain release point. This segment of the curve will be only approximately straight for strained glass or for glasses containing some crystalline matter. As the tem-

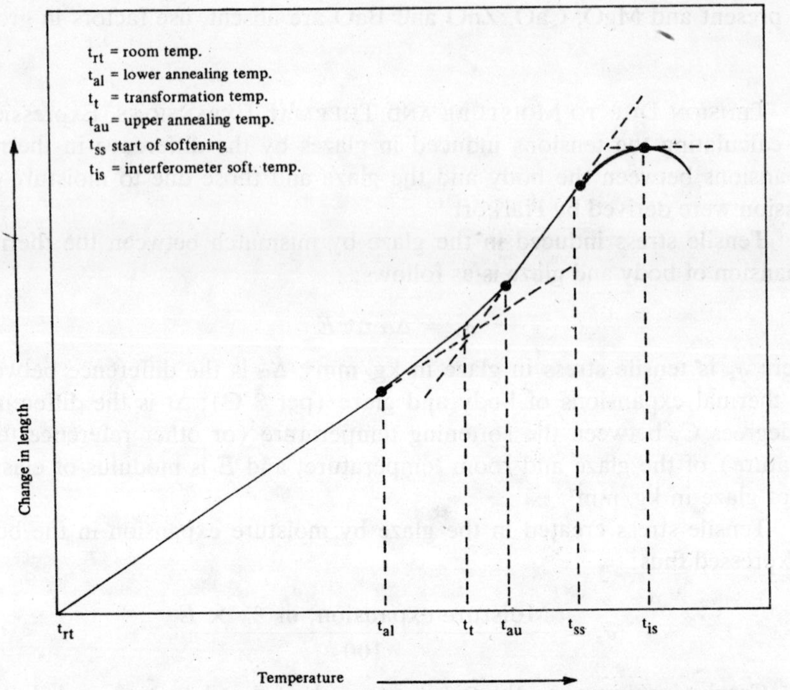

Figure 7.1. Elements of a thermal expansion curve of glass.

perature is raised from t_{al}, the rate of expansion increases very slightly as the temperature approaches and reaches t_t. This may be regarded as a transformation temperature and is thought of as a sort of breaking point between the rigid and plastic states. The viscosity still is very high.

The strain point, transformation temperature, upper annealing point,

Table 7.8. Significant terms and points in the thermal history of a glass

Symbol in fig. 7.1	*Stage or point*	*Viscosity, poises*
t_l	Strain point; lower annealing limit	$10^{14.5}$
t_t	Transformation temperature	$10^{13.3}$
t_{au}	Upper annealing point	10^{13}
t_{is}	Interferometer softening point	10^{11}
t_{ss}	Littleton softening point	$10^{7.6}$
none	Sintering temperature	10^6
none	Working point	10^4
none	Flow point for smooth glazes	$2–3 \times 10^3$

Table 7.9. Empirical formulas of some high-alumina glasses and glazes, and their respective thermal expansion coefficients

Oxide	*Molecular equivalents in ceramic formulas and respective coefficients of expansion*									
SiO_2	7.000[14]	5.42[14]	5.57[14]	2[15]	4[15]	6[15]	8[15]	4[16]	6[16]	10[16]
Al_2O_3	0.825	0.637	0.975	1	1	1	1	1	1	1
CaO	1.000	0.193	0.71	–	–	–	–	–	–	–
MgO	–	0.807	–	–	–	–	–	1	1	1
Na_2O	–	–	–	–	–	–	–	–	–	–
K_2O	–	–	0.29	–	–	–	–	–	–	–
Li_2O	–	–	–	1	1	1	1	–	–	–
$\alpha \times 10^7$ (expan coef.)*	30	25	43	76.0	66.6	52.5	43.6	33	27	20

*The tabulated coefficients of expansion are to be multiplied by 10^{-7}

and softening point all are shown on figure 7.1. The viscosity characteristic of these and other characteristic points are summarized in table 7.8.

Thermal Expansion Data

A very considerable volume of data exists on the thermal expansion of glazes, glasses, and related materials. A few expansion data are shown in table 7.9 for purposes of illustration. Control of thermal expansion of glazes is essential. However, this control in most cases is achieved by indirect methods or experience. For example, glaze fit may be estimated by such tests as an autoclave test, strength tests, or split ring test, to mention the most popular.

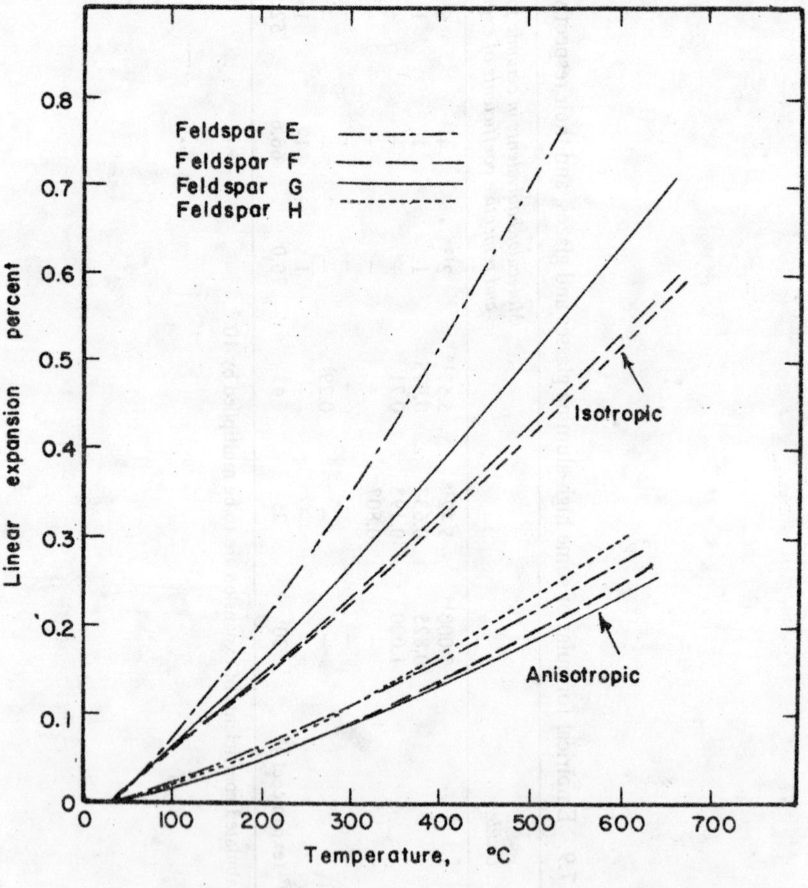

Figure 7.2. Thermal expansion of feldspar before and after firing.[13]

Table 7.10. Linear thermal expansion coefficients of feldspar glasses[17]

Material	*Na / (Na + k) molar ratio*	*Tg* °C*	*α** below Tg × 10⁷/°C*	*α above Tg × 10⁷/°C*
Pure potash feldspar	0	940	66	12
85–15 feldspar	0.15	905	70	12
Natural orthoclase	0.26	875	75	12
Amelia albite	0.96	815	74	20

*Transformation temperature
**Coefficient of linear thermal expansion
Note: The tabulated numbers for thermal expansion must be multiplied by 10^{-7}

Thermal expansion data[13] on four different feldspars, both before and after fusing, are shown in figure 7.2. The crystalline, unfused fledspars are designated as "anisotropic." The curves labeled "isotropic" show the respective materials after being converted to glass or to the isotropic state. This figure serves to illustrate the large differences in thermal expansions among different grades of feldspar. The differences in expansion between crystalline and fused feldspar are dramatic.

More detailed recent data as presented by Vergano, Hill and Uhlmann[17] on different kinds of feldspar completely converted to glass are shown in table 7.10. In this table are presented the basic parameters of the thermal expansion curves.

Glaze Fit

Glazes are vitreous layers fused to a ceramic underbody. The glaze, being basically glass, is a brittle material. And as is characteristic of brittle materials, while exceedingly strong under compression, they are subject to ready failure in tension. When a glaze is subjected to tensile stresses in excess of its ultimate tensile strength, it develops fractures, or crazing. The reverse case is that in which the glaze α is low and develops excessive compression, resulting in tensile or shear failure of the body or body-glaze interface, a condition called shivering, or peeling.

Satisfactory glazes must never craze, shiver, or peel under manufacturing or reasonable service conditions. Glazes meeting these requirements are said to fit.

Mechanism

As the glaze-body composite is cooled from high temperature the two components at the area of contact are firmly bonded to each other. The size of each at the area of contact must remain identical during cooling or something must give. This applies only to glaze temperature below the transformation point. If differences in volume or linear changes below that temperature are small, corresponding development of associated strains in the body and glaze would develop.

Characteristically, the body is much thicker than the glaze and consequently less likely to fail by rupture. Because the cross section of the body is so much greater than that of the glaze, the body usually is mechanically stable. Under certain circumstances, however, these applied stresses may cause body warpage or body failure near the interface.

Thermal Expansion Data

Stresses in the glaze layer will always result when the reversible thermal expansion of the glaze and body are not identical. If the coefficient of expansion of the glaze is greater than that of the body (below the softening temperature of the glaze) then, during initial cooling, the glaze layer will develop tensile stress. Because glazes are characteristically weak in tension, glaze layers subjected to tensile stress will rupture (craze).

Analytical Expressions

A cylinder is a model that can be subjected to simple analytical treatment and the effects of compression glazes on its cylindrical surfaces can be visualized. The schematic in figure 7.3 shows cylindrical surfaces under

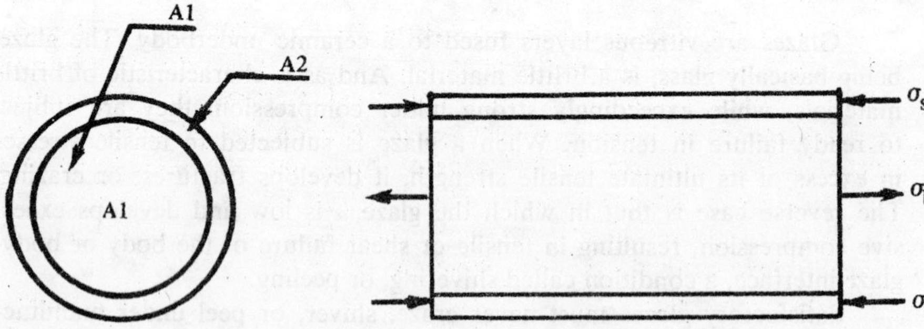

Figure 7.3. Schematic of stresses in a cylinder coated with a compression glaze.[18]

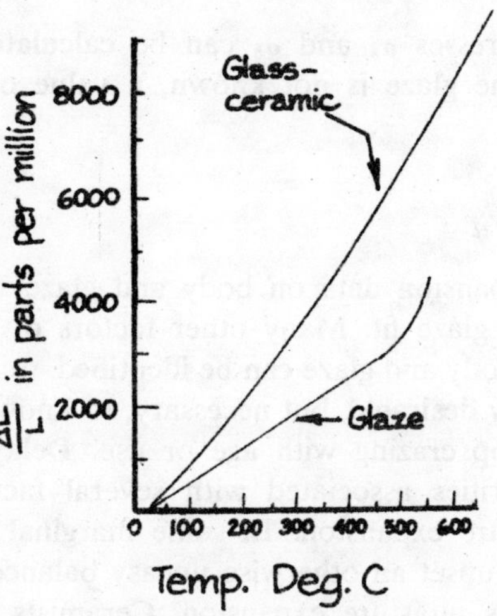

Figure 7.4. Thermal expansion of glass-ceramic and glaze.[18]

compression, while the interior portions are under reactive tensile stresses. Stresses in such a composite were analyzed by Duke, Megles, Macdowell and Bopp.[18] The assumptions were that (*a*) the surface compression zone and the interior volume both are isotropic and elastic, (*b*) the temperature distribution is uniform, (*c*) that the elastic moduli and Poisson's ratio of the body and glaze are equivalent, and (*d*) that the axial stresses are predominant and the radial and circumferential stresses are small and can be neglected. Then the following expression would apply:

$$\sigma_s = -(\alpha_1 - \alpha_2)\Delta T\left(\frac{E}{1-\nu}\right)\frac{A_1}{A}$$

and

$$\sigma_b = (\alpha_1 - \alpha_2)\Delta T\left(\frac{E}{1-\nu}\right)\frac{A_2}{A}$$

where σ_s and σ_b are compressive and tensile stresses, respectively, as in figure 7.3; α_1 and α_2 are linear coefficients of thermal expansion of body and glaze, respectively; ΔT = temperature difference between the setting point of the glaze and the temperature at which the stress is measured; E = Young's modulus; ν = Poisson's ratio; and A, A_1, and A_2 = cross-sectional area of cylinders, body, and glaze, respectively.

To obtain the total strain, $(\alpha_1 - \alpha_2)\Delta T$, it is convenient to plot the thermal expansion of body and glaze as in figure 7.4. When Young's modulus, Poisson's ratio, and A, A_1, A_2 can be measured for the body and glaze, the stresses σ_s and σ_b can be calculated. When the modulus of elasticity of the glaze is not known, a value of 10×10^6 psi can be assumed.

Estimating Fit

Thermal expansion data on body and glaze will not be sufficient to definitely predict glaze fit. Many other factors of isolated and separately fired samples of body and glaze can be identified.

It is not only desirable, but necessary, to know with certainty whether glazes will develop crazing with age or use. Delayed crazing can be the result of peculiarities associated with several factors, for example, fast cooling or moisture expansion. In some marginal cases, thermal stresses during use could upset an otherwise uneasy balance. A common cause for delayed crazing is moisture expansion. Ceramists, therefore, have developed more direct tests for glaze fit than thermal expansion.

The fundamental basis for glaze fit, or lack of it, is the degree and kind of stress in the glaze layer. Several tests are available for estimating fit.

FLAT PLATE TEST. Zane Schofield[19] used a flat plate test for wall tile. By measuring the warpage of tile before and after glost firing, glaze-induced warpage could be detected. With his device, concave warpage on the glazed side showed tension, convex warpage resulted from glaze under compression.

This method is applicable to two-fire ware that can be fabricated into large flat plates.

STRENGTH TEST. Flexural strength of ceramic bodies is greatly influenced by glaze coatings if the glaze is under stress. If the coating is in tension, the strength of the bodies can easily be reduced to less than 25% of that of unglazed bisque. Glazes under compression increase the strength as compression stresses increase until a broad plateau maximum is reached. Excessive compressive stresses lead to glaze failure by shivering or peeling. Numerous workers have used this test, starting with Gerold[20] in 1925, followed closely by Handrek[21] in 1926. Davage Rowland of Locke Insulator Co. was aware of the importance of glaze compression on the strength of electrical porcelain[20,21] and high voltage insulators have been manufactured on this basis for some time.

The authors in references 20, 21, 22, and 23 emphasized the importance of proper glaze fit but did not clearly show how glaze composition was involved. Thiess[24] published the results of some systematic work on

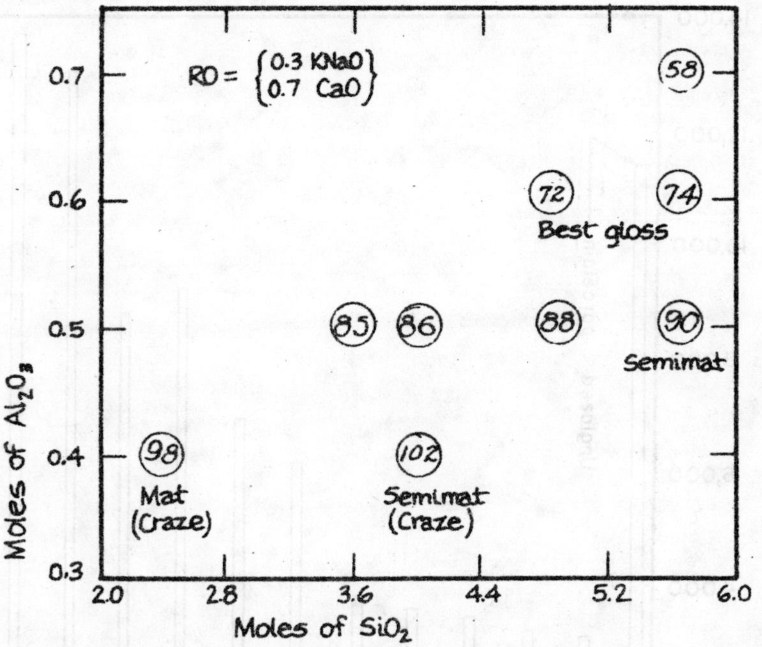

Figure 7.5. Glazes fired to cone 9½ on electrical porcelain bodies to evaluate the influence of glaze compression on strength.[24]

this. A summary of his findings is given in figures 7.5 and 7.6. In addition, single ingredients, such as opacifiers and colors, exert an influence on the strength of glazed ware. Kraner[25] observed that green-colored glazes with Cr_2O_3 were weaker than white opaque glazes.

The influence of glaze stress on strength was reported by Bettany and Webb[26] to be different for compressive strength than for modulus of rupture. They observed that the crushing strength of bodies was decreased as the compressive stress in the glaze increased. Conversely, they found compressive strength to increase as the coefficient of expansion of the glaze exceeded that of the body.

The effects of boric acid–sodium chloride mixtures on the strength of salt-glazed bodies containing various proportions of added quartz was evaluated by Schurecht.[27] The results are illustrated in figure 7.7.

The strength test method of fitting glazes to bodies is very reliable, but is slow and expensive to employ as a routine.

Steger Method. Steger[28,29] estimated glaze to body fit in a direct manner. This method was described on pages 233–34 of chapter 6.

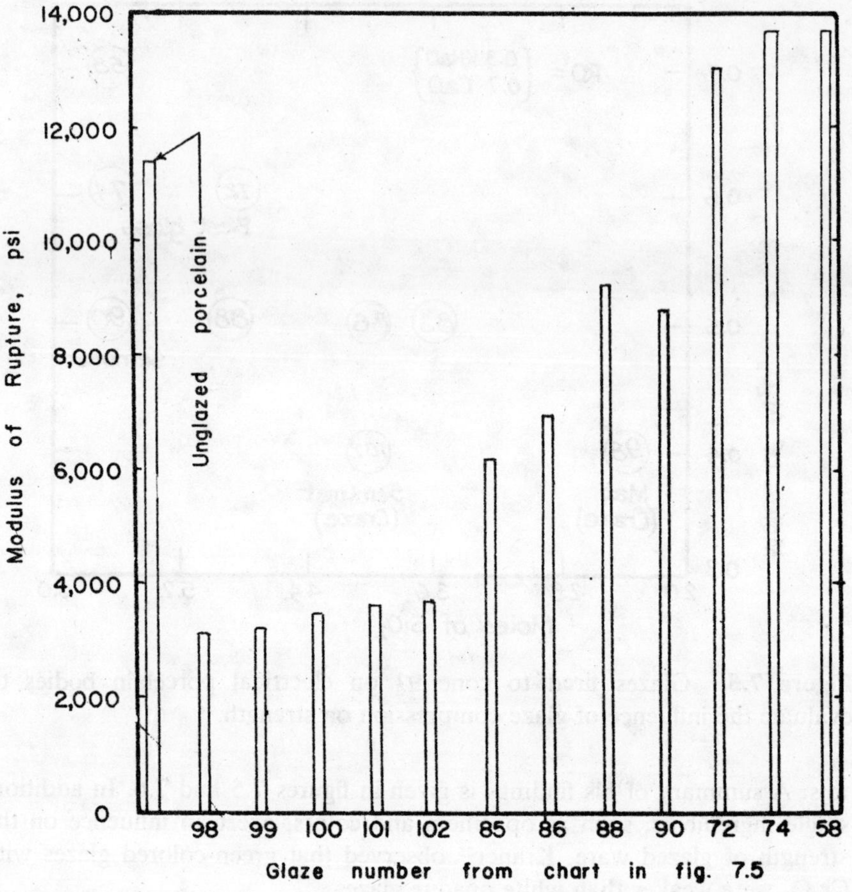

Figure 7.6. Influence of glaze compression on the strength of porcelain.[24]

A modification of this method was used by Blakely.[30] A sketch of the test specimen and the set-up as it was published by Schurecht[27] is shown in figure 7.8.

RING TEST. Another variation of the "bimetallic element" principle was used by Schurecht and Pole[30] and subsequently simplified by Davis[31] in the ring test. Rings of body are used that are 2 to 3 inches in diameter, $\frac{1}{2}$ to $\frac{3}{4}$ inches high and $\frac{1}{8}$ to $\frac{1}{4}$ inches in wall thickness. The thinner walled rings are used for the stronger, vitrified wares. The rings may be fabricated by any convenient or appropriate means.

Two small holes for markers about $\frac{1}{32}$ inch in diameter and $\frac{1}{16}$ inch deep are put in the upper rim of the ring at $\frac{1}{4}$ inch center to center. This

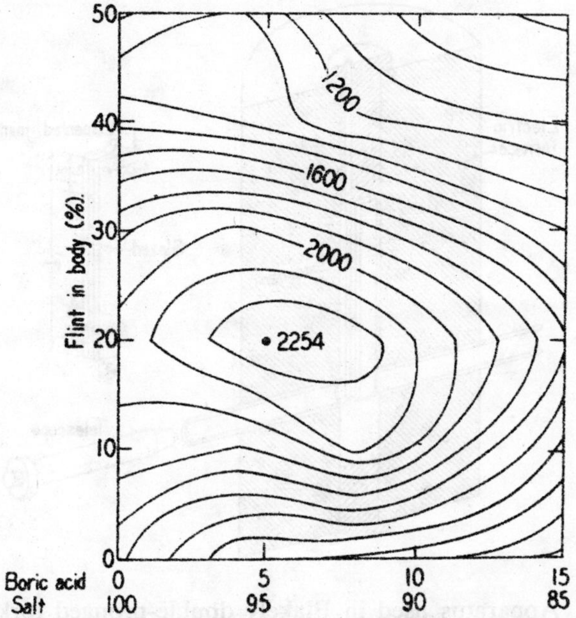

Figure 7.7. Influence of boric acid–salt mixtures on the modulus of rupture of salt-glazed bodies.[27]

may be done while the ware is plastic, using a pair of dividers, or the holes may be drilled in the dried unfired samples. Three rings are fired, then glazed on the outside circumference only; or, in case of one-fired ware, glazed, then fired. The fired rings then can be fitted with reference marks by sealing or cementing some suitable object in the previously prepared holes. Sometimes this might be pieces of capillary glass drawn down to a fine thread. Others prefer to seal pieces of shim stock on the rings and scratch reference marks on them.

The next step is to measure the distance between the reference marks with a micrometer microscope. Then the ring is to be severed between the reference marks with a silicon carbide or diamond saw, and the reference marks again measured. The contraction or expansion of the rings then can be calculated.

If there is a tendency for the glaze to craze, the ring expands. When the glaze is in compression the ring diameter and the distance between reference marks decrease. An extra large contraction is an indication of conditions favoring shivering or peeling. Usually the condition desired would be mild compression, leaving a reasonable factor of safety for the body to expand in service and still be craze-free.

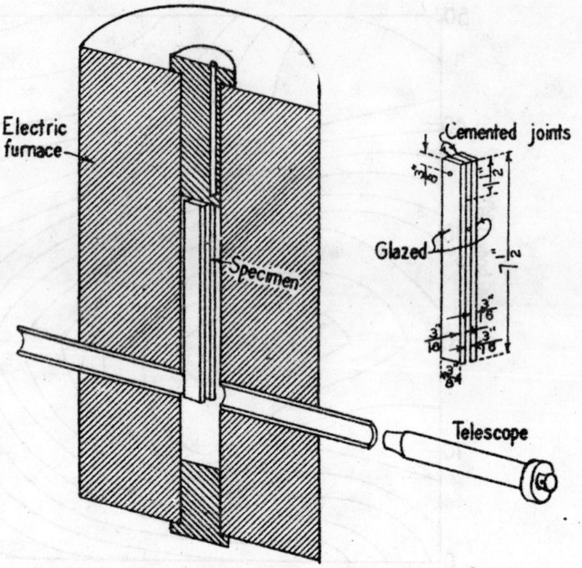

Figure 7.8. Apparatus used in Blakely double-pronged fork glaze stress test.[27]

This is a versatile method and has wide acceptance. The method even has been used with arrangements for self-recording.

Using the Steger test, the bars must be heated to a temperature at or above the stress-sustaining (annealing) temperature of the glaze to get a zero reading. With the ring test, this, of course, is unnecessary.

THERMAL SHOCK TEST. In this test method, the glazed sample is heated a few degrees, perhaps 50° C above ambient, and plunged into cold water, than examined for craze lines. When none is found, the temperature is raised another notch and requenched. The procedure is repeated until a temperature is found where the glaze crazes. The resistance to crazing then is reported as the maximum temperature from which the quench could be made without creating crazing.

BIREFRINGENCE METHOD. When glass is strained, it becomes birefringent. This fact has been made the basis for estimating stresses in glass. This might be referred to as the microscopic method. A section, perhaps 2 mm, is cut perpendicular to the glaze surface, both ends are polished and then it is mounted on a glass slide. The slide can be set on the stage of a petrographic microscope and both surfaces covered with an oil with a refractive index not too different from the glaze. The microscope should be fitted with a low-power objective and a gypsum plate and a Berek compensator.

A glaze free of strain is isotropic, while strained glaze is anisotropic. The tint plate should be so oriented that tension would show a blue color, then yellow would indicate compression. Details of the method have been described by Goranson and Adams,[32] among others. Using their system, the stress in the glaze can be calculated as follows:

$$F = \frac{\Delta}{2.6E}$$

where F = stress in kg per cm^2, E = thickness of sample in cm, and Δ = optical path difference in microns, as obtained with the compensator. This test obviously has its advantages and its limitations. It is not often used as a routine test.

AUTOCLAVE TEST. Ware having some porosity may be subject to moisture expansion. Such ware when exposed to weather or to moisture is likely to craze. To test for this type of crazing, the autoclave test is used. For testing, the specimen is placed in the autoclave out of contact with liquid water. The test has been used so much that there are specifications and standards for its use with some wares and under fixed circumstances. An example of how it could be operated would be to gradually, or in a controlled manner, increase the pressure to the preselected pressure, say, 150 psi. This pressure would be maintained for a specified period, say 1 hour, then released slowly, say over a period of from 10 to 30 minutes.

After removing the sample from the autoclave it should be cooled and wiped clean. Ink or dye can be applied to the surface to aid in detecting the presence, or absence, of craze lines.

A standard autoclave test has been in use in the wall tile industry for the last 30 years to evaluate the life expectancy of glazed tile in service. One of the standardized tests is ASTM C-424-58T, which employs steam pressure of 100 psi. Wall tile of bodies of extremely low moisture expansion covered with a good-fitting glaze can be treated repeatedly at 200 psi without crazing.[33]

Types of Crazing

THERMAL SHOCK CRAZING. Thermal shock crazing was discussed by Schurecht[34] at some length. He proposed that ware that would be subjected to thermal shock in service should pass a thermal shock crazing test. The suggestion was that the ware should not craze when cycled 10 times between 120° C dry air and water at 20° C.

STRESS CRAZING. It would be possible for glazed ware subjected to severe mechanical strain in service to craze due to applied stress. This does happen to tile and other types of ware. This sometimes would be caused by volume changes of the setting cement as well as mechanically applied stress or moisture expansion of the body. Schurecht and Pole[35] devised a test for this type of thing that loaded ware in compression to 1,000 psi and subjected the tile, while under this compression for 1 hour, to 150 psi autoclave pressure. The craze cracks that appear usually are parallel and it was called parallel crazing.

FROST CRAZING. Glazed ware can craze due to freezing and thawing. This type of crazing also was discussed by Schurecht.[35] It has usually been possible to select bodies and glazes that will not craze under repeated freezing and thawing.

MOISTURE CRAZING. This was discussed under the heading of "autoclave tests."

KILN CRAZING. Kiln crazing, why it develops, and how to detect it was reviewed by Schurecht.[36] This is a case of straight-forward poor glaze fit.

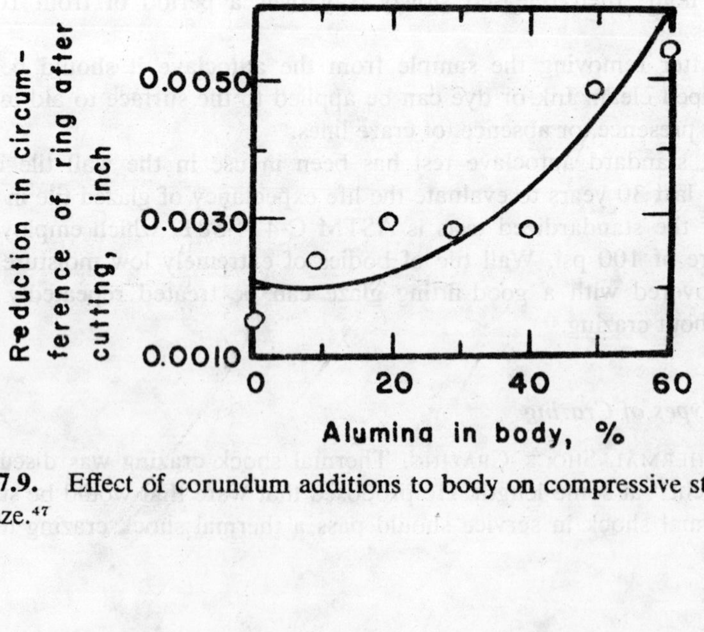

Figure 7.9. Effect of corundum additions to body on compressive stresses in a glaze.[47]

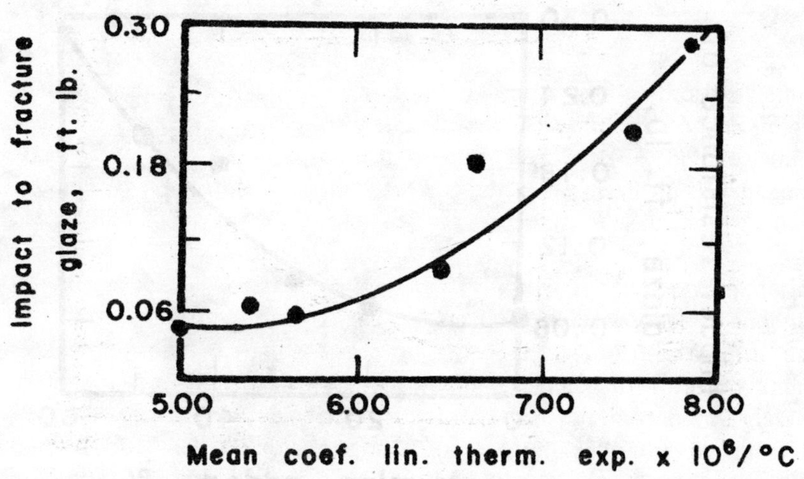

Figure 7.10. Effect of coefficient of expansion of chinaware body on resistance of glaze to impact damage.[47]

Fitting Glazes to the Body

According to Mellor,[37] crazing and shivering were recognized as due primarily to differences in thermal expansion between body and glaze by Seger and Schumacher in 1876. Griffin[38] was the first to discuss the influence of body-glaze reactions on glaze fit. Some of the later authors to confirm this are Merritt and Peters,[39] Johnson,[40] and Knecht.[41]

In 1911, Purdy[42] translated Seger's rules for correcting crazing, etc., by body or glaze formulations. Shortly thereafter, Stull and Howat[43] published an excellent paper on porcelain glazes from the point of view of controlling the properties of glazes on the basis of the molar proportions of silica and alumina.

A direct test for glaze fit based on the split ring concept was developed by Schurecht and Pole.[44] This was followed eight years later by Blakely[45] with a fork method for following the displacements as the glaze fork cooled. Two early papers summarized the work on glaze fit and glaze fit methods, one in 1935 by Mellor[37] and another in 1948 by Bell.[46]

INFLUENCE OF GLAZE COMPRESSION ON OTHER PROPERTIES. Several examples of the influence of the degree of glaze compression on physical and mechanical properties of glazes are given in figures 7.9, 7.10, 7.11, and 7.12.[47] The impact resistance and Knoop hardness (defined in following section) of glazes both increase with increasing compression in the glaze. The increase in Knoop hardness of the glaze is apparent, not real.

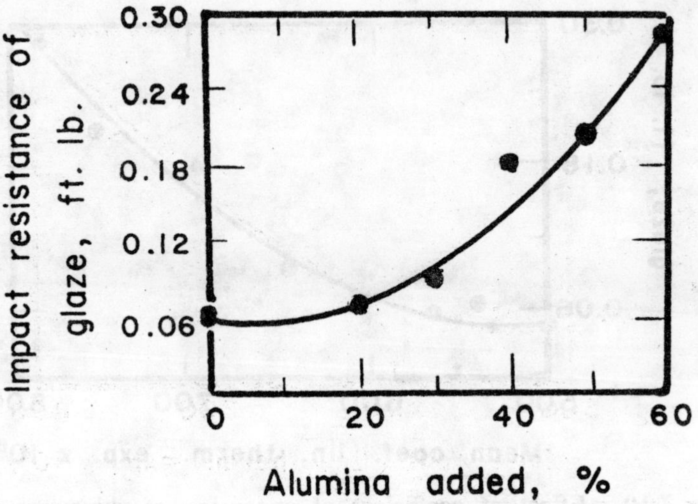

Figure 7.11. Effect of corundum additions to a vitreous china body on glaze impact resistance.[47]

In glazes under compression, the size of the indentation slowly closes some after the indentation has been made, due to the compressive forces surrounding the indentation. It appears from figure 7.10 that as the compressive forces in the glaze increase, the glaze becomes more resistant to damage by impact.

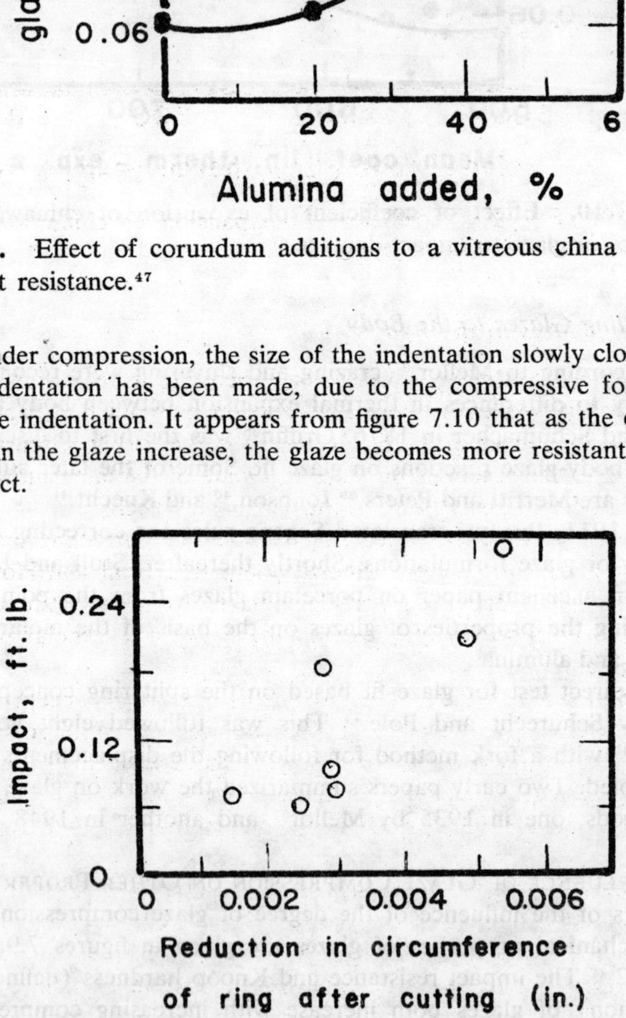

Figure 7.12. Effect of residual compressive stresses in glazes on their resistance to fracture due to impact, as measured by the split ring test.[47]

Hardness

The hardness of a substance is a relative term and cannot be defined or described except by comparison with standard materials. Mineralogists years ago introduced the concept of grading materials as to their resistance to scratching when rubbed hard against other minerals. For this purpose a series of minerals generally used for this purpose was selected as a basis for what is known as "Moh's scale."

Hardness usually is measured by observing the resistance of materials to (*a*) abrasion by other substances or (*b*) by their resistance to indentation. Glazes all rate about the same on Moh's scale and it is of little use. Other factors than hardness are involved in resistance to abrasion, therefore the scale does not serve as a satisfctory test for the hardness of glasses. Indentation tests are reliable and useful for comparing the hardness of glazes with other glazes and with other materials.

Diamond Pyramid Hardness

The size of the indentation varies some with the speed of indentation and with the time of contact. The test fundamentally is a measure of the yield in the glass structure and is in no way related to Griffiths flaws.[48]

The test is sensitive to glass composition, microscopic areas can be examined, and it is capable of a high degree of precision. If the load is applied at a reasonable rate and in an amount insufficient to cause fracture, the Knoop number (hardness value) is independent of the load. When load is applied to the diamond indenter, it causes plastic flow in the area of the diamond. The yield point of the glass structure is about 300,000 psi, compared to the ultimate breaking stress of 10,000 to 15,000 psi in tensile stresses. Glass, therefore, breaks before it flows.

Knoop Values of Glasses

Pavlish and Mockrin[49] prepared a number of glasses in a search for some sufficiently hard for "jewel" bearings in watches. Compositions in the Al_2O_3–CaO–B_2O_3–SiO_2 system in which the CaO was held at about 15% had Knoop values of 510 to 580. Various oxides were substituted for silica and hardness was increased only by BeO or MgO. A Knoop value of 690 was reached by substituting 6.9% of BeO for 6.9% of SiO_2. With MgO, a maximum reading of 640 was obtained by substituting 12.6% of MgO for 12.6% of SiO_2.

As an aid to putting hardness numbers into a comparative perspective, Knoop values of some selected typical materials are given in table

Table 7.11. Examples of Knoop hardness values of some selected materials

Materials	*Knoop values*
Soda-lime-silica glass	470
Soda-potash-lime-silica glass	440
Soda-boric-oxide-silica glass	495
Soda-lead-oside-silica glass	380
Calcite ($CaCO_3$)	100
Fluorite (CaF_2)	150
Magnetite (Fe_3O_4)	700
Corundum (Al_2O_3)	2,000
Silicon carbide (SiC)	3,000
Diamond	~8,000

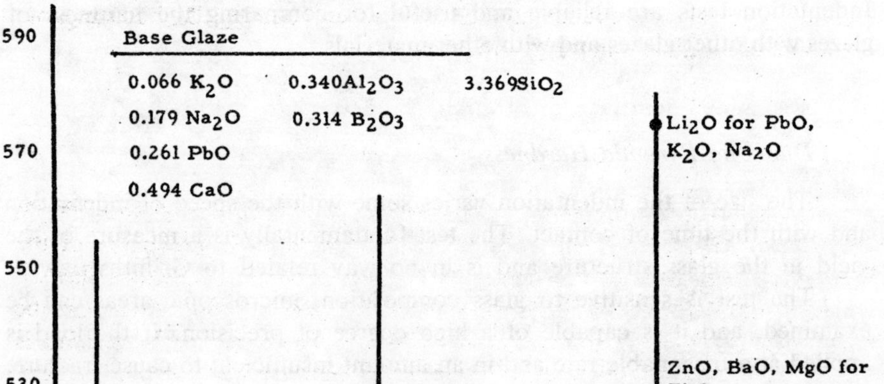

Figure 7.13. Knoop hardness of crucible-melted glaze compositions.[50]

Table 7.12. Composition and Knoop hardness of a family of vitrified hotel chinaware glazes[50]

Glaze no.	*Composition, molar equivalents*								
	Base	*1*	*2*	*3*	*4*	*5*	*6*	*7*	*8*
K_2O	0.122	0.122	0.122	0.122	0.110	0.047	0.045	–	0.132
Na_2O	0.123	0.123	0.123	0.123	0.110	0.048	0.050	–	0.036
Li_2O	–	–	–	–	–	0.150	0.150	0.245	–
PbO	0.261	0.261	0.261	0.261	0.235	0.261	–	–	–
CaO	0.494	0.494	0.494	0.294	0.445	0.494	0.605	0.605	0.403
ZnO	–	–	–	0.200	–	–	0.150	–	0.360
BeO	–	–	–	–	0.100	–	–	0.150	–
MgO	–	–	–	–	–	–	–	–	0.026
BaO	–	–	–	–	–	–	–	–	0.043
Al_2O_3	0.340	0.220	0.340	0.340	0.340	0.340	0.340	0.340	0.250
B_2O_3	0.314	0.314	0.250	0.314	0.314	0.314	0.340	0.340	0.105
SiO_2	3.369	3.369	3.369	3.369	3.369	3.369	3.369	3.000	3.380
ZrO_2	–	0.120	–	–	–	–	–	–	–
Knoop hardness	498	481	487	481	503	498	507	532	515

7.11. Among the glasses, note the low values for the lead-bearing glass. Potash seems to soften glasses more than soda.

Hardness of Glazes

The Knoop hardness of American vitrified hotel chinaware glazes, and of compositional variations thereon,[50] when melted and tested as glasses is shown in figure 7.13. With the base glaze as shown on the figure as the reference point, hardness is increased appreciably by decreasing the lead content. Hardness also is reduced by the partial or total replacement of lead by soda, potassia, lithia, or beryllia. Where CaO was added to the base glaze (fig. 7.13) hardness was increased but slightly. The substitution of ZrO_2 for Al_2O_3 has little influence. A melt having a Knoop value approximately 100 units greater than the base glaze was obtained when all of the PbO, K_2O and Na_2O was substituted by Li_2O.

The hardness values of glazes, per se, seem somewhat different than those obtained from polished sections of crucible melts. The hardness values of a family of glazes fired on hotel china plates are given in table 7.12. In glazes in which ions of large radii (lead, potassium and sodium) were replaced by those with smaller radii (beryllium, magnesium and lithium), hardness increased markedly.

The relation between hardness values and glaze compression (as inferred from the quantities plotted on the X-axis) for some lead-borosilicate glazes are shown in figure 7.14. The glaze applied was identical for all cases in this figure. Variations in compositions of the fired glazes, if any, were not investigated.

Gloss

Surface finishes have two main functions: surface preservation and control of appearance. By appearance is meant "that which is seen by the human eye." There are two major attributes of surface appearance: "color" and "gloss."

The property of surfaces that causes them to be highly reflective, mirror-like or shine is referred to as gloss. It cannot be measured, but specific reflective capacities can be.[51]

Characteristic capacities of surfaces to reflect light vary with angle of incidence and reflectance and the whole system becomes complex. Various gloss meters involve different geometric aspects of light reflectance and each provides numbers that have some relation to the glossy appearance of specific surfaces.

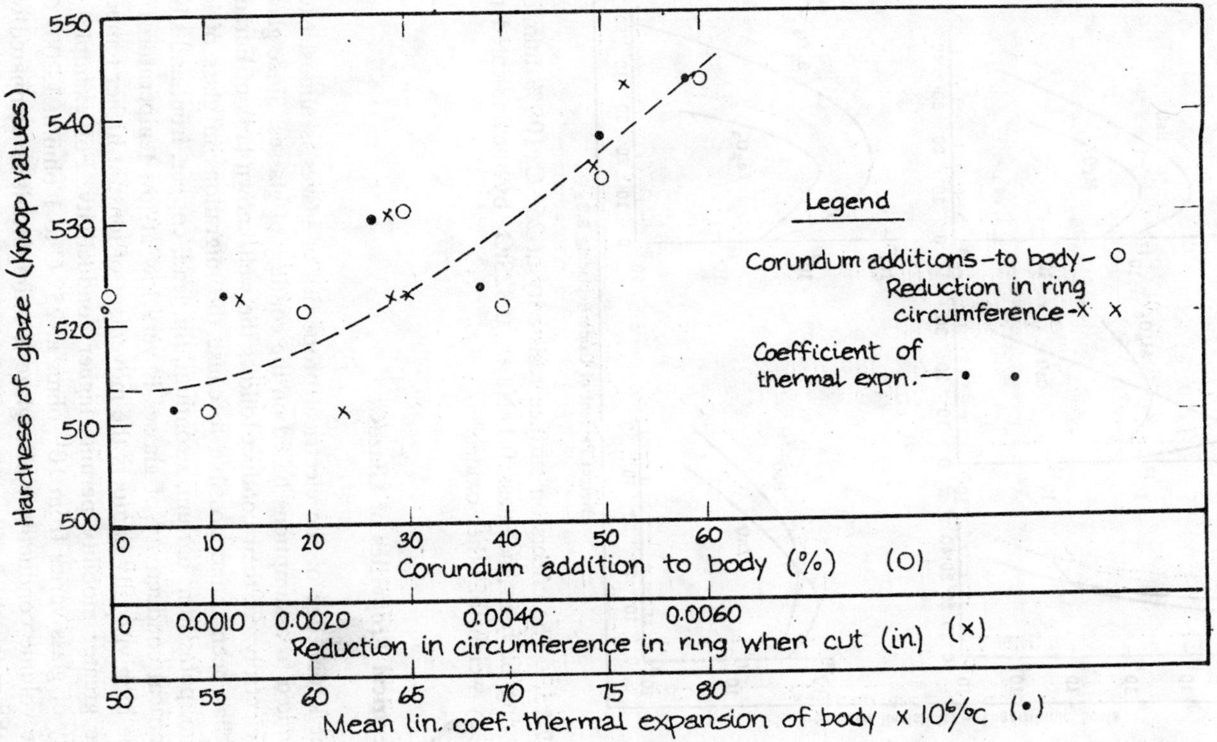

Figure 7.14. Knoop hardness values of a hotel china glaze as influenced by (*a*) body variations in alumina content, (*b*) glaze compression, and (*c*) thermal expansion of body.[50]

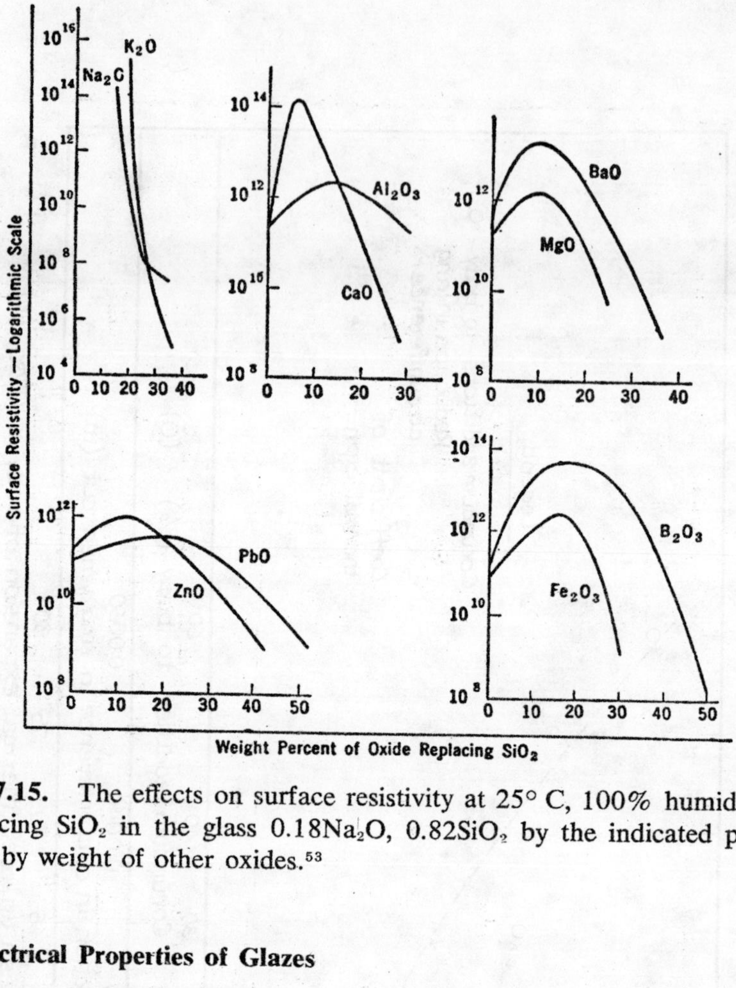

Figure 7.15. The effects on surface resistivity at 25° C, 100% humidity, of replacing SiO_2 in the glass $0.18Na_2O$, $0.82SiO_2$ by the indicated percentage by weight of other oxides.[53]

Electrical Properties of Glazes

Our knowledge of the electrical properties of glazes is almost exclusively limited to assumptions based on the conduct of glasses. Since glasses may be electrolyzed, their conduct follows the well-known laws of Faraday. Thus it has been found possible to cause the migrations in glass of ions of sodium, potassium, barium, strontium, tin, lead, copper, iron, and silver. The electrical conductivity of glasses is very low at low temperatures because the high viscosity hampers the movement of ions; at higher temperatures the greater mobility permits higher conductivity. For example, the resistivity of glass varies from 10^{19} ohms at 25° C to 1 ohm at 1,200° C.[52]

The volume conductivity of a glaze is unimportant as compared with that of the much thicker body upon which it is applied; but the surface conductivity of the glaze on a high tension insulator may have a special significance. Aside from the effects caused by the accumulation of atmospheric and industrial dusts on the surface of high tension insulators, the surface conductivity is due, primarily, to a layer of adsorbed water. Important factors influencing the degree of surface conductivity are: (*a*) the composition and characteristics of the mature glaze; (*b*) the temperature; (*c*) the humidity and amount and character of salts (such as seawater salts near the seashore) usually present in the surrounding atmosphere; (*d*) the perfection of the glaze surface; and (*e*) the degree of heterogeneity of the glaze, such as suspended bubbles and crystalline matter and their characteristics.

Electrical surface conductivity is defined as the amount of current conveyed by a surface of unit length and width. By analogy with the experimental results obtained in the study of the electrical surface conductivity of glasses by Fulda,[53] the effects of substitution of bases may be summarized as follows. The alkalies, soda and potassa, particularly the former, cause a rapid increase of conductivity. The introduction of the smaller amounts of lime causes a rapid decrease of conductivity which reaches a maximum and then increases rapidly. Similar conduct may be observed with magnesia and baryta with the latter showing a considerably greater conductivity than the former (the magnesia). Ferric oxide and boric oxide yield curves somewhat similar to the baria and the magnesia, but the alumina, zinc oxide, and lead oxide, although having maxima, have flatter curves. These are represented in figure 7.15 where the surface resistivities (the reciprocal of surface conductivities) are plotted against the weight percentage of oxide replacing silica.

Morey[54] has criticized the results reported above as not representing equilibrium conditions because of the insufficient testing time; and he advises caution in assuming that similar results may be had with other or more complex glasses.

Figure 7.16 shows the increase of the conductivity of two glasses and a glazed porcelain as influenced by increasing humidity, as reported by Curtis[55] who assumed the thickness of the adsorbed layer to be 6×10^{-6} mm.

Reversible Photosensitivity of Glazes

The first published report on the reversible photosensitivity of glazes was made by Parmelee and Badger in 1934.[56] They had observed that some glazes and bodies if partially protected from exposure to sunlight for a short time would exhibit notably lighter color than the unprotected

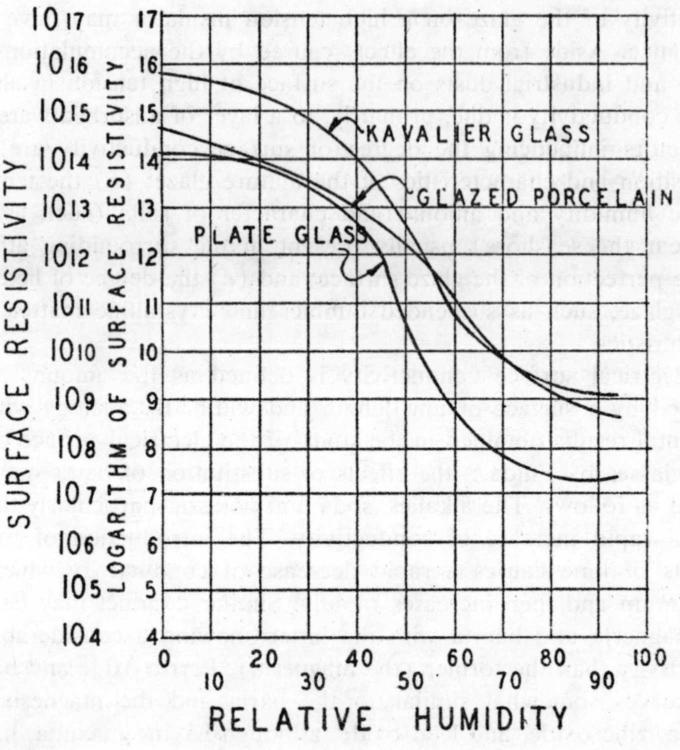

Figure 7.16. Relation of surface resistivity to relative humidity for three ceramic glasses. Kavalier glass is a very hard combustion tube composition, having a large K_2O and CaO content and a small amount of Na_2O.[55]

area; further, that the paler area would darken in color very rapidly, even during the brief period of examination. This reversible reaction could be repeated apparently without limit. A glaze containing titanium displayed this phenomenon conspicuously,[57] as did one without titanium but made with flint, whiting, barium carbonate, manganese carbonate, feldspar, zinc oxide, sodium uranate, and zirconium oxide. A similar glaze lacking zinc oxide, and one containing only flint, feldspar, clay, and whiting and also a considerable variety of commercial glazes darkened when exposed to ultraviolet radiation. Subsequently, others have observed the reversible darkening of glazes containing titania of laboratory grade as well as commercial qualities.

There are three polymorphic forms of TiO_2, rutile, anatase, and brookite. Commercial grades of titania usually are either rutile or anatase or a mixture of them. Williams[58] suggests the term "phototropy" for reversible photosensitivity of glazes containing rutile rather than the other polymorphs of titania. As a result of his study he concluded that the phenomenon cannot be traced to the glassy matrix of the glaze but, although apparently homogeneous, there are present microscopic crystalline particles which may be new or residual material. Glazes lacking suspended material fail. Sometimes anatase is of considerable purity, which is normally non-photosensitive, and produces phototropic glazes, but the property disappears if they are fired to higher temperatures.

Phototropy is dependent apparently, in some degree, upon the presence of very small amounts of impurities, e.g., 0.01% of ferric oxide derived either from the rutile or the glaze batch, also sodium compounds which are almost inseparable from many of the commercial grades of raw materials. Chromium compounds are said to inhibit the photosensitivity of titania. Not all glazes made with rutile are phototropic.

The use of reversible photosensitive glazes may be expected to be accompanied by some disadvantages, for example: (*a*) the color developed may be less pleasing, (*b*) sometimes unpleasant contrasts appear, (*c*) overheating or the presence of a small amount of lead oxide may yield an unsatisfactory white color, and (*d*) underfired leadless glazes give poor whites.

Much has been done and written concerning the influence of X rays in altering the color of glasses and minerals, including gems; and about the "fading" of glassware due to ultraviolet rays present in sunlight.[59] The oldest and most familiar of the examples of the latter phenomenon is the strong amethystine color exhibited by very old window glass after exposure to sunlight for many years.

Fluorescence in Glazes

Weyl[60] recognizes four classes of fluorescence, based on its general mechanism. These are: (1) glasses containing fluorescent crystals or crystal aggregates, (2) opal glasses in which the crystals are not fluorescent but the activator is contained in the glass phase, (3) glasses comprised of or containing energy-isolated atoms and molecules, and (4) glasses containing fluorescent ions. Examples of class 1 are those containing crystals such as zinc and tungstate phosphors in which the glass serves solely as a carrier. Class 2 examples are manganese activated zinc silicate opal glasses. Silver and cadmium sulfide activated glasses fall in this classification. True fluorescent glass falls in class 4, where ions forming an integral part of the glass are responsible for the fluorescence. This includes ions from dissolved manganese, uranium, the rare earths, copper, thallium, lead, tin, and vanadium.

Stability of Glazes and Colors

Stability of Glazes in Alkaline Detergents

The stability of chinaware glazes in alkaline detergent solutions is of practical interest. The relative resistance of glazes to attack by aqueous solutions of detergent materials has been estimated[61] by measuring the rate of decrease in the thickness of the glaze layer. A more common method has been by measuring weight loss due to boiling or refluxing specimens for 6 hours in 3.0% solutions of sodium carbonate or sodium phosphate. The weight-loss procedure, while informative, is not ideal. The chemical reaction involved may result in simultaneous weight gains and weight losses. For example, reaction products which remain a part of the glaze surface may contain hydrates, carbonates or other insoluble anions of the detergent such as phosphates. For example, a glaze surface after refluxing in a solution of sodium phosphate may contain small pits, each of which will be filled with a deposit of calcium phosphate. This, of course, is derived from a reaction of soluble sodium phosphate with glaze constituents.

INFLUENCE OF GLAZE COMPOSITION. The rate of solution or decomposition of glazes in alkaline aqueous solutions is related to chemical composition of the glaze. Some data[61] from a family of cone 4 vitreous hotel china glazes is shown in figure 7.17. As illustrated in this figure, the durability was improved by a substitution of some ZrO_2 for SiO_2 or when lithium was substituted for other alkalies. Improvement in durability also was achieved when lithium and beryllium were substituted for oxides of lead, potassium, and sodium.

These results indicate the direction and extent to which changes in RO in lead bisilicates might modify their chemical stability.

The attack on three different types of glass by solutions of potassium silicate is shown in figure 7.18. These data from Smith and Corbin[62] indicate that the composition of the corrosion agent may be more critical than the type of glass being attacked.

The results of attack of plate glass by alkaline solutions as determined by Tarnapol and Junge[63] are shown in figures 7.19, 7.20, and 7.21. This is typical of the effects to be expected on glazes. Many glazes have been designed to withstand attack by alkaline detergent solutions, so they would show far less attack. In some cases, the attack on glazes might be one

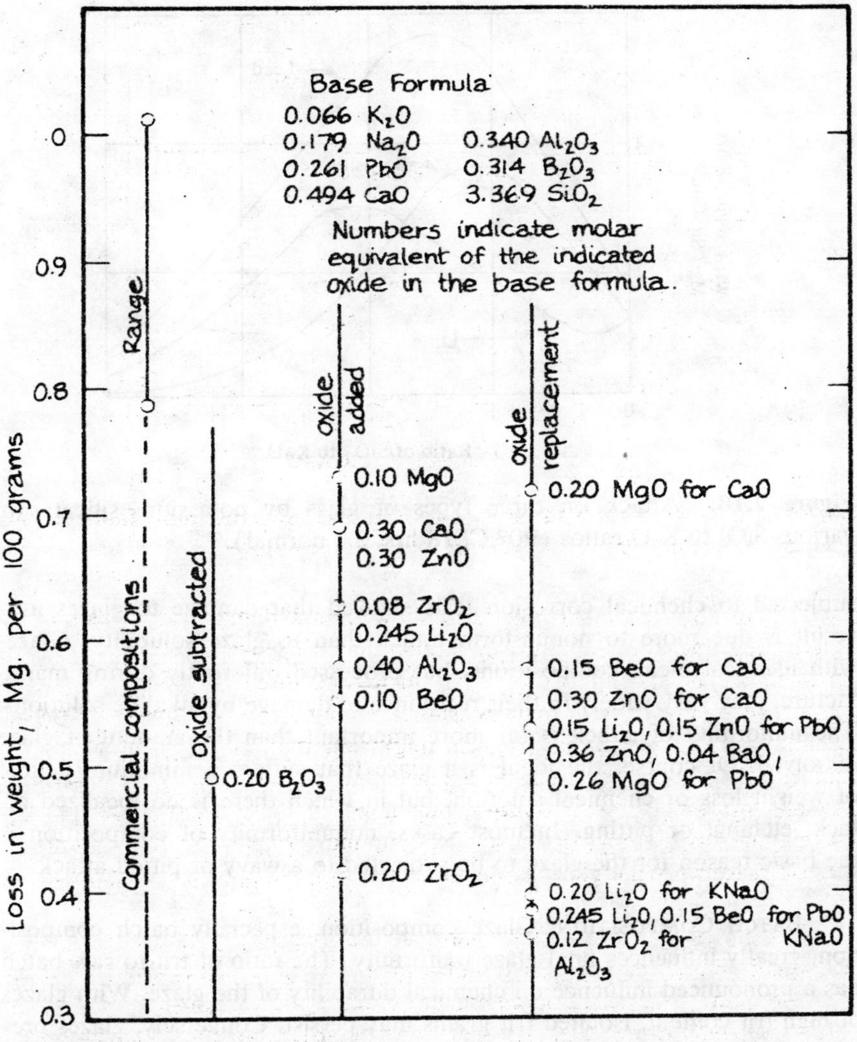

Figure 7.17. Resistance of powdered glazes (melted as glasses) to hot 3.0% sodium carbonate solutions.[61]

or two orders of magnitude less than that on plate glass. In other, less resistant glazes, it could be more.

INFLUENCE OF GLAZE HOMOGENEITY—PITTING. Although chemical durability of glazes is related to their chemical composition, other factors[61] may be of equal importance. Microscopic examination of glazes after being

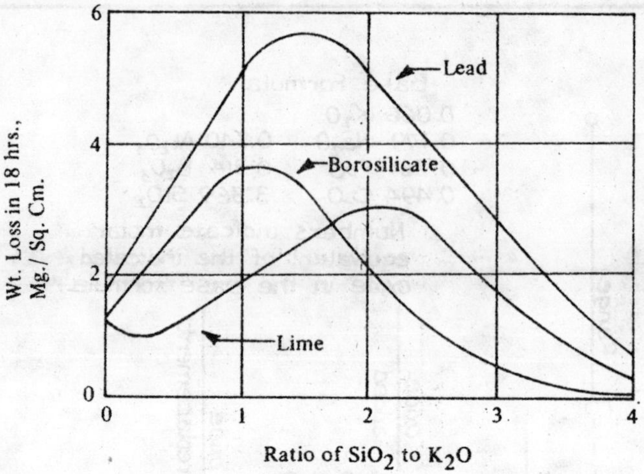

Figure 7.18. Attack on three types of glass by potassium silicates of various SiO_2 to K_2O ratios (90° C, 18 hrs, 2.0 normal).[62]

subjected to chemical corrosion tests showed that damage to glazes as a result is due more to nonuniform attack than to glaze solubility. Glazes with identical mean compositions, but processed differently during manufacture, may vary widely in their resistance to damage by alkaline solutions. The uniformity of attack is far more important than the amount of glaze dissolved. Of course, the ideal is a glaze that suffers a minimum degree of weight loss or chemical solution, but in which there is no localized attack, etching, or pitting. In most cases, nonuniformity of composition is the basic reason for the glaze to be subjected to a wavy or pitted attack.

Batch Composition. Glaze composition, especially batch composition, greatly influences final glaze uniformity. The ratio of frit to raw batch has a pronounced influence on chemical durability of the glaze. With glazes of high frit content, isolated frit grains may persist. Conversely, glazes prepared from a high percentage of raw batch may contain undissolved particles and localized residues from dissolved but not yet dispersed reaction products.

Nonhomogeneity would result in either case. Both types might be resistant to overall attack but both might have poor durability due to pitting and local attack sites.

It cannot be stated categorically that the more frit the better. The amount of frit is not alone a suitable criterion. It depends upon conditions at grain interfaces. A glaze prepared from 100% frit, which has a high surface tension and a low potential for ionic diffusion, grain to grain, will

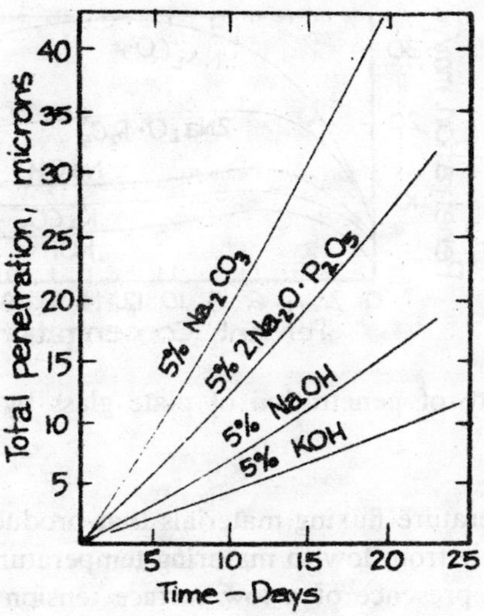

Figure 7.19. Rate of attack of alkaline solutions on plate glass at 150° F.[63]

show attack around or at frit grain boundaries. Thus, grain boundary attack by alkaline solutions can be as severe in raw glazes as in high frit glazes.

Turbulent or gassy conditions in the glaze during fusion tend to promote better homogeneity, in fluid glazes, than quiet fusion. Ideally, batch materials should be selected to promote ready solution of batch ingre-

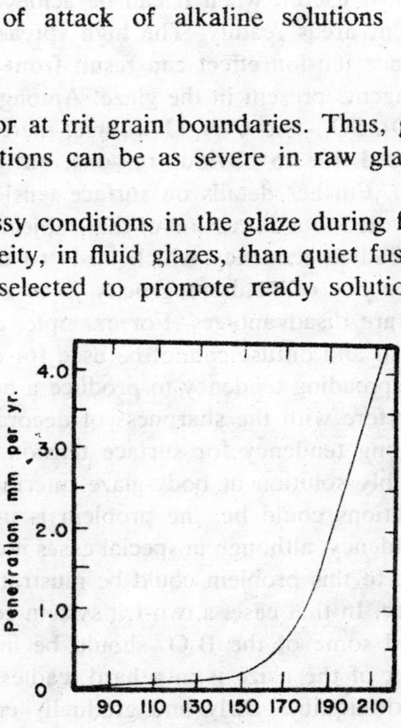

Figure 7.20. Penetration of plate glass by 30% NaOH as influenced by temperature.[63]

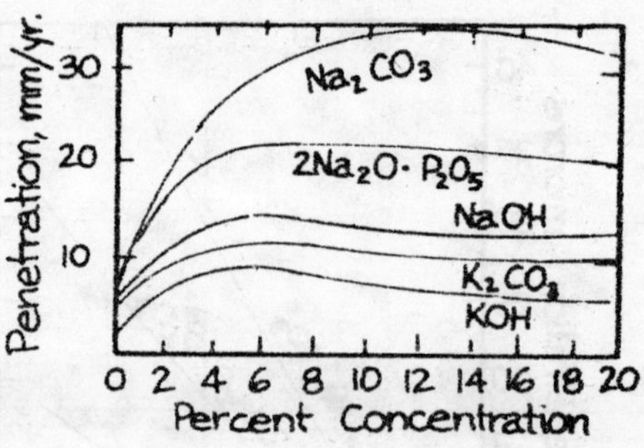

Figure 7.21. Rate of penetration of plate glass by alkaline solutions at 180° F.[63]

dients. Low temperature fluxing materials that produce fluid and corrosive liquids progressively from low to maturing temperatures contribute to good homogeneity. The presence of a low surface tension in part or all of the melting glaze is most useful, when it can be achieved. Such compositions diffuse into adjacent areas readily. The high spreading capacity resulting from the low surface tension effect can result from the presence of pyrochemical wetting agents present in the glaze. Among these are PbO, V_2O_5, MoO_3, Sb_2O_5, CrO_3, SO_3, and CO_2. Of course, there are cases where none of these can be used due to obvious reasons, but there are cases where some may be used. Further details on surface tension are to be found in another section devoted to a discussion of that subject.

The high spreading tendency which leads to the destruction of discontinuity and to zones of nonhomogeneity is to be desired in most instances, but there are disadvantages. For example, a glaze with too great a tendency to spread and diffuse cannot be used for overglaze work. There must be sufficient spreading tendency to produce a homogeneous glaze but not enough to interfere with the sharpness of decorations. Another disadvantage to too strong tendency for surface tension lowering is excessive diffusion and possibly solution at body-glaze interfaces. However, important as these conditions could be, the problem is usually not due to too much spreading tendency, although in special cases it could be.

One approach to this problem could be illustrated by a lead borosilicate chinaware glaze. In that case, a two-frit system could be advantageous. All of the lead and some of the B_2O_3 should be in one low-melting frit while the remainder of the glaze is in a hard leadless frit. The more fluid lead borosilicate frit liquifies early and gradually creates one final glaze by solution of the hard frit and the soft one.

Homogeneity development, while influenced by the chemical nature of the batch ingredients, also is very materially influenced by other factors.

Of primary importance is degree of dispersion, i.e., fineness and distribution of particles in the batch. Particle sizes and grinding is a primary variable also with regard to chemical durability of finished glazes. The glaze obviously should be as finely ground as possible, without encountering the problems due to excessive fineness. The technique of firing also is of importance. By increasing the time at about 1,700° F, and the temperature and time of soak at the finish, short of overfiring, improves durability greatly.

Stability of Glaze Decorations

Underglaze decalcomania used on commercial dinnerware can go off-color, called fading. The possible causes were classified by Donahey and Russell[64] as follows: (*a*) glaze attack on the color, (*b*) diffusion of color into glaze, (*c*) reaction of the color with body or with kiln atmosphere, and (*d*) diffusion of color into the body.

Fading of underglaze decalcomania colors can result in defective ware and in manufacturing losses. Much of the difficulty sometimes can be traced to the quality of the decalcomania employed and to workmanship in the shop. However, there are other factors, including glaze composition and the presence or absence of some critical constituents in the glaze. The firing practice also can be of importance.

Fundamentally, damage to underglaze colors can be caused by one or more of the following general factors: (1) composition and constitution of the color, (2) the character of the vehicles and carriers employed, (3) actual chemical decomposition of the color, (4) surface tension and diffusion effects at edges, and (5) chemical reaction of the color with glaze, body, flux, or kiln atmosphere.

METHOD FOR EVALUATING. Laboratory methods for evaluating the resistance of glazes and decorations to the action of dishwashing materials were discussed by Orthalek and Bacon.[65] A screening test for examining metal and color decorations, glazes, fluxes, etc., designated as FB–2C was recommended.

STANDARD PROCEDURE FB–2C: Accelerated test for the action of detergent solutions on overglaze decorations.

Principle. Deterioration is evaluated by exposing test subjects to static detergent solutions at 211° F and comparing the degree of fading with unexposed samples.

Table 7.13. Rating schedule for FB-2C[65]

Visual rating	*Color removal*	*Description of rating*
0	None	No pigment removed by rubbing, no fading, no loss of luster
2	Moderate	Traces of pigment on cloth; slight fading or dulling; first evidence of alteration
3	Considerable	Extensive pigment on cloth; extensive pigment removal (as judged by rubbed decoration)
4	Complete	Essentially complete pigment removal after rubbing

Apparatus. The test specimens are placed in 4 liter stainless steel vessels and immersed in the test solutions at 21½° F.

Test Apparatus. The test detergent is added to 3 liters of distilled water in amounts to yield 0.05%, 0.10%, 0.50%, and 1.0%.

Test Procedure. Place 3 test samples in the solution and remove one after 2, 4, and 6 hours of immersion. Immediately after removal, rub surface with clean white sheeting until no more of the decoration rubs off. Then rinse with water.

Evaluation. Test pieces are compared with new, unexposed pieces and each element of the decoration rated[65] in accordance with table 7.13.

LEACHING TEST. Lead-bearing colors on glazed porcelain were tested by Zapp[66] by treating them in 4% acetic acid solutions for 24 hours and analyzing the resulting acid solution for lead. The amount of lead dissolved was reduced as firing temperatures of the decorated glazes increased, except for selenium reds which showed no reduction of lead dissolved with high firing temperatures. Different glazes give different results, and those high in silica and low in fluxes allow PbO from the pigments to diffuse more thoroughly into and through the glaze, reducing the lead leachability.

GENERAL BACKGROUND ON UNDERGLAZED COLORS. A very successful glaze used on vitreous chinaware and published by Mayer[67] follows:

Glaze

$0.053K_2O$		
$0.203Na_2O$	$0.281Al_2O_3$	$2.807SiO_2$
$0.253PbO$	$0.335B_2O_3$	
$0.491CaO$		

Frit

$0.031K_2O$		
$0.273Na_2O$	$0.271Al_2O_3$	$2.547SiO_2$
$0.696CaO$	$0.546B_2O_3$	

This glaze, with minor modifications, has been used commercially for about a century and has given complete satisfaction with underglaze colors, fired at cone 3. Mayer used 60% of frit and was convinced that a part of the success with this glaze was due to the high frit content. He believed that by using even more frit, all loss of sharpness at color edges would disappear. But Svec[68] disputes this and said: "A glaze too high in frit tends to attack and run colors." He goes on to say:

> "Faded colors may be the result of an insufficient amount of color in the color-oil mix, fading because the glaze at high temperature will attack the color.
>
> "Colors which are compounded in such a manner that they contain too much flux will run. Some colors, such as cobalt, will not combine with the other ingredients of the color to form a permanent compound. Special firing care must be practiced in the use of cobalt containing colors.
>
> "Off-shade colors are due to reducing conditions or overfiring. Overfiring will cause running of colors since the glaze becomes too fluid and in flowing carries the color with it."

Resistance to Sandblast Test

There are a number of possible methods of testing glazes for their resistance to abrasion. In one,[61] the sandblast test, the specimen in the form of a plate or a tile is mounted at an angle of 70° and subjected to a blast of 80 mesh silica sand delivered under an air pressure of 10 psi. Fixed quantities of 800 grams per blast can be employed. A measure of the abrasion resistance is taken as the amount of glaze removed by the blast.

Factors Influencing Resistance to Abrasion. Using the sandblast test, the resistance of glazes to abrasion was found[61] to have some relation to the chemical composition of the glaze, but to a limited extent. Glazes with microscopic crystalline inclusion such as opacifiers, as zircon or zirconia, had high sandblast resistance. It appears that harder undissolved or crystalline inclusion reduced the percentage of area of the softer glazes available for abrading. The proportion of frit in the glaze influences the sandblast resistance. The amount of glaze abraded during the tests increased with increasing frit content, regardless of glaze composition, as

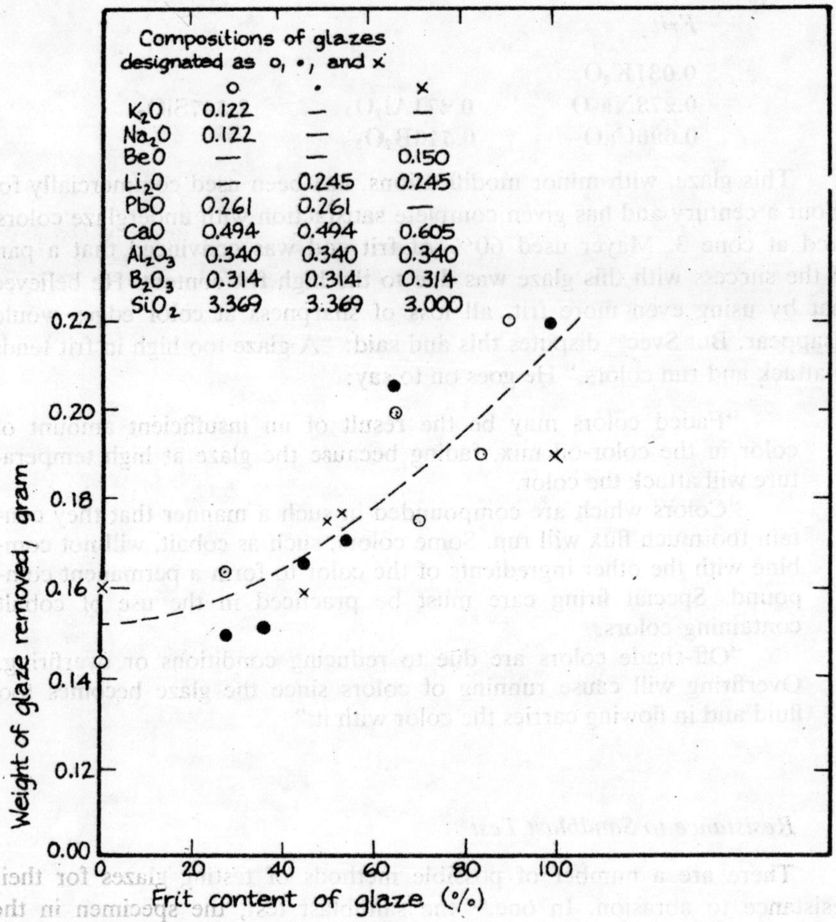

Figure 7.22. Relation between resistance of glazes to erosion in sandblast test and their frit content.[61]

illustrated in figure 7.22. This seems to be characteristic of the cases in which nonuniformity of the microstructure caused the glazes to be especially subject to abrasion. The nonhomogeneity was shown to be evident in chemical durability trials in which chemical attack occurred chiefly around isolated frit grains.

In general, the amount of glaze removed[61] in a sandblast test increased with the thickness of the glaze as shown in figure 7.23. This trend seemed to be due fundamentally to the same factors as those that function with increasing percentage of frit. It has been shown that glazes to which zirconia was added had notably high sandblast resistance. These glazes

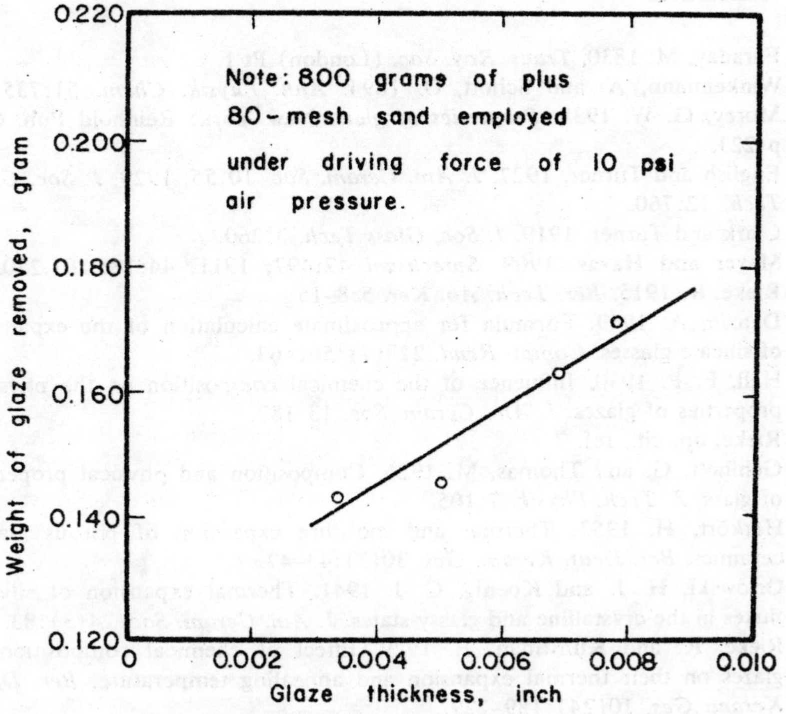

Figure 7.23. Effect of glaze thickness on rate of weight loss in a sandblast test of hotel chinaware.[61]

contained very fine zirconia-bearing hard crystals. This nonhomogeneity improved the sandblast resistance. In general, glazes with highly dispersed crystalline inclusions have greater sandblast resistance than the more homogeneous ones. Different types of inhomogeneities affected the physical durability in different manners. In general, the inhomogeneities that improved physical durability tended to diminish chemical resistance. Increasing the frit content of a glaze decreases its physical durability but increases its chemical durability.

Scuffing

Glazed ware, especially chinaware, is scuffed primarily due to "seizure"[69]—the rubbing of glaze over glaze. This is alleviated by putting different material on the foot of plates. High lead, soft glazes of low hardness are satisfactory. Stable organic polymers on the foot portion of plates and saucers are good.

References

1. Faraday, M. 1830. *Trans. Roy. Soc.* (London) Pt 1.
2. Winkelmann, A. and Schott, O. 1894. *Ann. Physik. Chem.* 51:735.
3. Morey, G. W. 1938. *Properties of glass.* New York: Reinhold Pub. Co., p 223.
4. English and Turner. 1927. *J. Am. Ceram. Soc.* 10:55; 1929. *J. Soc. Glass Tech.* 12:760.
5. Clark and Turner. 1919. *J. Soc. Glass Tech.* 3:260.
6. Mayer and Havas. 1909. *Sprechsaal* 42:497; 1911. 44:188,207,220.
7. Rieke, R. 1915. *Ber. Tech. Ab. Ker.* 5:8–15.
8. Danzin, A. 1949. Formula for approximate calculation of the expansion of silicate glasses. *Compt. Rend.* 228(7):561–63.
9. Hall, F. P. 1930. Influence of the chemical composition on the physical properties of glazes. *J. Am. Ceram. Soc.* 13:182.
10. Rieke, op. cit., ref. 7.
11. Gehlhoff, G. and Thomas, M. 1926. Composition and physical properties of glass. *Z. Tech. Physik.* 7:105.
12. Harkort, H. 1953. Thermal and moisture expansion of porous glazed ceramics. *Ber. Deut. Keram. Ges.* 30(3):43–47.
13. Orlowski, H. J. and Koenig, C. J. 1941. Thermal expansion of silicate fluxes in the crystalline and glassy states. *J. Am. Ceram. Soc.* 24(3):83.
14. Rieke, R. and Kunstman, E. 1929. Effect of chemical composition of glazes on their thermal expansion and annealing temperature. *Ber. Deut. Keram. Ges.* 10(24):189–229.
15. Brackbill, C. E., McKinstry, H. A., and Hummel, F. A. 1951. Thermal expansion of some glasses in the system Li_2O–Al_2O_3–SiO_2. *J. Am. Ceram. Soc.* 34(4):107–9.
16. Hummel, F. A. and Reid, H. W. 1951. Thermal expansion of some glasses in the system MgO–Al_2O_3–SiO_2. *J. Am. Ceram. Soc.* 34(10):319–21.
17. Vergano, P. J., Hill, D. C., and Uhlmann, D. R. 1967. Thermal expansion of feldspar glasses. *J. Am. Ceram. Soc.* 50(1):59.
18. Duke, D. A., Megles, J. E., Jr., Macdowell, J. F., and Bopp, H. F. 1968. Strengthening glass-ceramics by application of compressive glazes. *J. Am. Ceram. Soc.* 51(2):98–102.
19. Schofield, H. Z. 1937. Study of replacement of Cornwall stone by talc and feldspar in a wall tile body. *Bull. Am. Ceram. Soc.* 16(5):203–4.
20. Gerold, E. 1925. Influence of glaze on physical properties of porcelain. *Hermsdorf-Schomburg Mitt.* 15:395–497, *Keram. Rund.* 33:188–90; *Ceram. Abstr.* 4(6):169–70.
21. Handrek, H. 1926. Importance of glazes for safe porcelain insulators. *Hermsdorf-Schomburg Mitt.* 29–30:879–93; 1927. *Ceram. Abstr.* 6(9):392.
22. Rowland, D. H. 1929. Recent improvements in high voltage insulator design. *Gen. Elec. Rev.* 32:136–138; 1930. 33:384–87.
23. Rowland, D. H. Patent.

24. Thiess, L. E. 1936. Influence of glaze composition on the mechanical strength of electrical porcelain. *J. Am. Ceram. Soc.* 19(3):70–73.
25. Kraner, H. A. 1933. Microstructure of electrical porcelain glazes. *Ceram. Ind.* 21(2):73–75.
26. Bettany, C. and Webb, H. W. 1940. *Trans. Brit. Ceram. Soc.* 39:312.
27. Schurecht, H. G. 1943. Fitting glazes to ceramic bodies. *J. Am. Ceram. Soc.* 26(3):93–98.
28. Steger, W. 1928. Strain in glazed ware and its detection. *Ber. Deut. Keram. Ges.* 9(4):203–15.
29. Steger, W. 1930. Measuring tension in fired ceramic mixes. *Ber. Deut. Keram. Ges.* 11(3):124.
30. Schurecht, H. G. and Pole, G. R. 1930. Method of measuring strains between glaze and ceramic bodies. *J. Am. Ceram. Soc.* 13(6):639–75.
31. Davis, H. E. and Lenders, R. L. 1932. Simplification of ring method for determining glaze stresses *J. Am. Ceram. Soc.* 15(1):34–36.
32. Goranson, R. W. and Adams, L. H. 1933. Method for precise measurement of optical path difference, especially in stressed glasses. *J. Franklin Inst.* 216(4):475–504.
33. Bullin, L. and Green, K. 1954. Crazing of wall tile. *Trans. Brit. Ceram. Soc.* 53(1):39–66.
34. Schurecht, H. G. and Fuller, D. H. 1931. Some effects of thermal shock in causing crazing of glazed ceramic ware. *J. Amer. Ceram. Soc.* 14(8):565–71.
35. Schurecht, H. G. and Pole, G. R. 1932. Some special types of crazing. *J. Am. Ceram. Soc.* 15(11):623–37.
36. Schurecht, H. G. How to overcome crazing in ceramic glazes. *Ceramic Data Book, 1941–42*. Chicago, Ill.: Industrial Publications, Inc., pp 298–303.
37. Mellor, J. W. 1935. Crazing and peeling of glazes. *Trans. Ceram. Soc. (England)* 34(1):1–112. *Ceram. Abstr.* 14(9):233.
38. Griffin, H. R. 1900. Shivering and crazing. *Trans. Am. Ceram. Soc.* 2:135–38.
39. Merritt, G. E. and Peters, C. G. 1926. Interferometer measurements of thermal dilation of glazed ware. *J. Am. Ceram. Soc.* 9(6):327–42.
40. Johnson, A. L. 1939. Stresses in porcelain glaze. *J. Am. Ceram. Soc.* 22(11):363–66.
41. Knecht, A. O. 1940. Control of crazing in sanitary ware glazes by Mayer and Havas coefficient of expansion factors. *J. Am. Ceram. Soc.* 23(2):61–63.
42. Purdy, R. C. 1911. Segar's rules for correction of glaze defects by changing the body. *Trans. Am. Ceram. Soc.* 13:157–209.
43. Stull, R. T. and Howat, W. L. 1914. Deformation temperatures of some porcelain glazes. *Trans. Am. Ceram. Soc.* 16:454–60.
44. Schurecht, H. G. and Pole, G. R. 1930. Method of measuring strains between glazes and ceramic bodies. *J. Am. Ceram. Soc.* 13(6):369–75.

45. Blakely, A. M. 1938. Life history of a glaze: 2, Measurement of stress in a cooling glaze. *J. Am. Ceram. Soc.* 21(7):243–51.
46. Bell, W. C. 1940. Evaluation of glaze-fit test methods. *J. Am. Ceram. Soc.* 23(6):163–66.
47. Koch, W. J., Harman, C. G., and O'Bannon, L. S. 1952. Effect of residual compressive stress in hotel-china glaze on some physical durability properties of the glaze. *J. Am. Ceram. Soc.* 35(9):240–42.
48. Ainsworth, L. 1954. Diamond pyramid hardness of glass in relation to the strength and structure of glass: 1, Investigation of diamond pyramid hardness test applied to glass. *J. Soc. Glass Technol.* 38(184):479–500 T.
49. Pavlish, A. E. and Mockrin, I. 1947. Development of hard glasses. *J. Am. Ceram. Soc.* 30(2):54–61.
50. Koch, W. J., Harman, C. G., and O'Bannon, L. S. 1950. Some physical and chemical properties of experimental glazes for vitrified institutional whiteware. *J. Am. Ceram. Soc.* 33(1):1–8.
51. Hunter, Richard S. 1952. Gloss evaluation of materials. *A.S.T.M. Bull.* 186:TP190–97.
52. Morey, op. cit., ref. 3, p 44.
53. Fulda, M. 1927. Electrical conductivity of glass. *Sprechsaal* 60:769,789,810,953.
54. Morey, op. cit., ref. 3, p 453.
55. Curtis, H. L. 1914. Insulating properties of solid dielectrics. *Bull. Bur. Std.* 11:359.
56. Parmelee, C. W., and Badger, A. E. 1934. Coloration of glazes by light. *J. Am. Ceram. Soc.* 17:1.
57. Zwerman, C. H. Jr. Correspondence.
58. Williamson, W. O. 1940. The reversible darkening in daylight of some glazes containing titanium. *Trans. Brit. Ceram. Soc.* 39:345.
59. Badger, A. E. and Ottoson, A. C. 1942. Effect of light on color of glass. *J. Am. Ceram. Soc.* 25:104.
60. Weyl, W. A. 1946. Colored glasses: 5, Fluorescence and solarization of glass. *J. Soc. Glass Technol.* 30(138):90–172 T.
61. Koch, W. J., Harman, C. G., and O'Bannon, L. S. 1950. Some physical and chemical properties of glazes for vitrified institutional whiteware. *J. Am. Ceram. Soc.* 33(1):1–8.
62. Smith, Rowland D. and Corbin, Paul E. 1949. Attack of glasses by alkaline solutions. *J. Am. Ceram. Soc.* 32(6):195–98.
63. Tarnapol, M. S. and Junge, A. E. 1946. Resistance of plate glass to alkaline solutions. *J. Am. Ceram. Soc.* 29(2):36–39.
64. Donahey, John W. and Russell, Ralston, Jr. 1950. Color fading of underglaze decalcomania. *J. Am. Ceram. Soc.* 33(9):283–90.
65. Orthalek, Joseph Y. and Bacon, Leslie R. 1956. A method for testing the interaction of overglaze decorations with detergent solutions. *Bull. Am. Ceram. Soc.* 35(11):438–44.
66. Zapp, F. 1952. Improving the stability of glaze decorations on porcelain. *Ber. Deut. Keram. Ges. u. Ver. Deut. Emailfachleute* 29(9):297–301.

67. Mayer, Ernest. 1899. Notes on the production of underglaze colors. *Trans. Am. Ceram. Soc.* 1:56–61.
68. Svec, J. J. 1946. *Pottery production processes*. Chicago: Industrial Publications, Inc.
69. Harman, C. G., Koch, W. J., and Rice, H. H. *Ceramic ware*. U.S. Patent 2,690,065, Sept 28, 1954.

8

Leadless Glazes

Porcelain Glazes

The porcelain glaze derived its name from its association with and use on ware of that name. The two probably had their origins in the same region and at about the same time. There seems to be good reason to believe that the Chinese learned about the use of glazes from some nations in Western Asia, and that this, as Laufer[1] said, was a stimulus to their own accumulated experience; further, the "porcelaneous glaze of the post-Han times hardly offers any contemporaneous parallel in the West. From this time onward the Chinese exercise their own acumen in perfecting the process of glazing and multiplying the scale of beautiful color." The Han period can be placed as approximately 206 B.C. to A.D. 220. Laufer describes a specimen as having been manufactured during the latter part of the third century of this era. The grey colored, vitrified body is described as a "translucent . . . porcelain-like body." The chemical analysis of the glaze, table 8.1, is of particular interest, especially as compared with modern Chinese porcelain.

The glazes used on steatite in Egypt during the Badarian Period (ca. 5000 B.C.) and also on faience, which was made in India about 3000–2750 B.C. and somewhat later in Egypt, were alkali-alkaline earth-aluminuous silicates resembling, in a general way, the porcelain glaze type used during the past two hundred and fifty years by potters of the Western world. There is the possibility that the porcelain glaze technique originated in Mesopotamia or India and spread to Egypt and much later to the Far East.

Table 8.1. Porcelain glaze analyses[1]

	A	*B*	*C*
Silica	54.17	68	64.96
Alumina	14.16	12	12.74
Ferric oxide	4.38	Traces	0.80
Lime	19.05	14	8.78
Magnesia	2.04	Not deter.	Traces
Alkalies	5.49	6	4.25
Phosphoric acid	Not deter.	Not deter.	0.16

Notes: A. Analysis of the ancient glaze by H. W. Nichols.
B. Analysis of the modern Chinese porcelain glaze reported by A. Salvetat.
C. Analysis of modern Japanese glaze reported by Seger.

Faience, so-called, was a very highly siliceous fritted body quite distinct from the clay body used in Europe from the Middle Ages into the present time; this is used also in the Western world.

In Europe, the development of this type of glaze must have accompanied the invention of porcelain during the first decade of the eighteenth century. The better informed and more experienced potters of that period were familiar, in a general way, with the process of vitrification, since true stoneware was made in considerable quantity in the vicinity of Cologne, and the use of white engobes had been well known in some areas for many centuries. The chief problems in the production of true porcelain were sources of suitable clays, suitable fluxes, and the technique of forming and firing the wares.

Physical Characteristics

An examination of the analysis of the ancient Chinese porcelaneous ware shows that the fluxing agents were alkalies which might have been found, as they are now, in the partially disintegrated feldspathic rock from which the clay had been formed by weathering. The presence of the considerable amount of lime is due undoubtedly to the addition of crushed limestone or marble to the glaze batch as has been done in the Western world for many years.

The materials used in porcelain glazes, i.e., clay, alkaline earths (usually calcium and magnesium carbonates), and finely ground silica individually are extremely refractory. The alkali-alumina-silicates (feldspar, etc) which are added as fluxes require a minimum temperature of cone 4, usually higher, for deformation, and greater temperatures for fluidity. When these materials are mixed together and fused, the formation of eutectics lowers the temperature of fusions, but in any case the porcelain glazes

Figure 8.1. Electrical porcelain glazes are raw feldspathic type. For high tension work, special attention is given to coefficient of expansion, smoothness, and dielectric properties.

are the most refractory of all glazes. The approximate minimum cone maturing temperature is about cone 8 (1,250° C), although somewhat more fusible glazes are possible. Porcelain glazes are ideal for electrical porcelain (fig. 8.1).

The resultant glazes possess physical properties which compensate for the expense and the difficulties involved. They are insoluble in water and the usual solvents at all temperatures. They resist the action of all acids excepting hydrofluoric, phosphoric, and hot fuming sulfuric acids. They are also resistant to hot strong alkalies. The glazes are not easily scratched. They are mechanically strong and, under proper conditions, increase the strength of the body on which they are applied. Because they are composed largely of the same materials as the body, and fired at such high temperatures, the interface zone is formed by the mutual solution and diffusion of the two in which a certain degree of physical and chemical equilibrium is developed, thus minimizing strains and lessening the occurrence of crazing and shivering.

The volatilization of the glaze even at the high temperatures is slight because of the low vapor pressures of its components and the fused product; therefore the glazes may be fired in the kiln without being placed in a muffle or sagger, providing that they are properly protected from dust, soot, and contact with the flame and flying particles. The absence of reducible oxides (with exceptions to be noted) in the composition is one of the characteristics of the glaze and permits the use of firing methods that convert the traces of ferric oxide into the ferrous, which is strongly basic and dissolves readily in the glassy fusion, producing a very faint bluish or greenish blue color. The result is the enhancement of the purity of the white color of the ware for the same reason that the laundress uses bluing in order to whiten the color of the "wash." The porcelain glaze possesses high viscosity and surface tension, but the high temperatures of maturity allow its use on delicate artware as well as structural clay products. It may be clear, opaque, or colored. Texture may be varied from matt to glossy.

Components and Their Functions

The comparatively few chemical components employed to form the glazes distinguish them as very simple and easily prepared and applied. In an extreme case a single base may be adequate; for example, Kerl's[2] glaze was $CaO \cdot 1.16Al_2O_3 \cdot 8.98SiO_2$, while Riddle[3] specified the following composition as satisfactory for pyrometer tubes used up to the fusing temperature of cone 14: $CaO \cdot Al_2O_3 \cdot 4SiO_2$.

Berdel and Dannheim[4] examined several glaze compositions chosen from the area of the $CaO–Al_2O_3–SiO_2$ equilibrium system containing the eutectics detailed in table 8.2. A number of glossy and matt glaze compositions were had at cones 11 and 13 as shown in figure 8.2. The ranges of compositions were within limits outlined in table 8.3. Glazes having formulas of $CaO \cdot xAl_2O_3 \cdot ySiO_2$ can be prepared for maturing at cone 17. Two such glazes are shown in table 8.4 where they are compared in composition with the 4 $CaO–Al_2O_3–SiO_2$ eutectics having cone deformation points ranging from cone 4 to cone 13.

Batch compositions in table 8.5 are proposed as the most likely to prove satisfactory for industrial use. This conclusion is based on results obtained in ceramic plant kilns. The glazes are recommended for use on porcelain chemical and cooking ware, and on electrical insulators, chemical stoneware, and fireclay wares.

The low thermal expansions of the glazes make them virtually free

Table 8.2. Eutectics in the $CaO-Al_2O_3-SiO_2$ system used by Berdel[4] as a basis for developing porcelain glazes.

Oxide component	Weight percent: Eutectic A	Weight percent: Eutectic B
CaO	23.3	38
Al_2O_3	14.7	20
SiO_2	62.2	42

Note: Melting point of A is 1,170° C; of B is 1,265° C

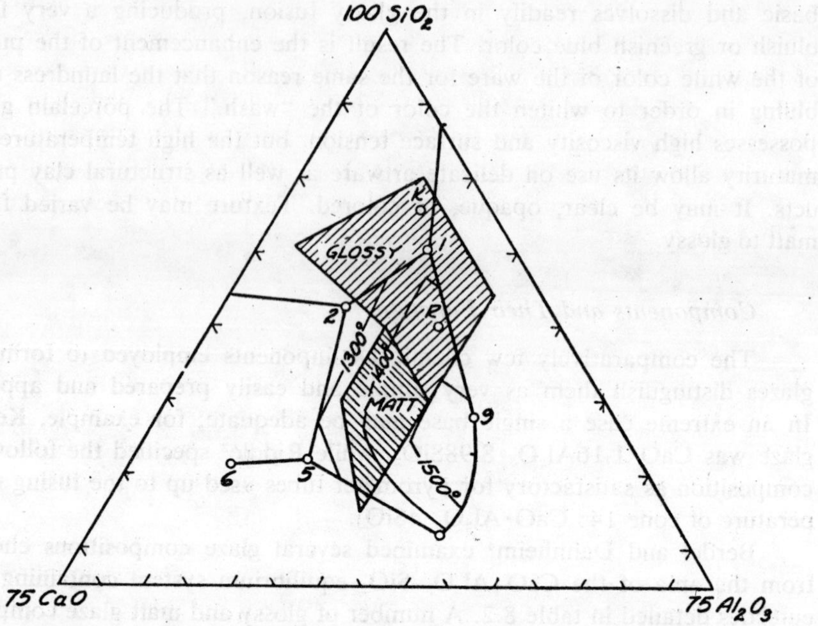

Figure 8.2. Ternary diagram $CaO–Al_2O_3–SiO_2$ and glaze compositions.[4]

from crazing. By substituting 27 parts, by weight, of borocalcite for 10 parts of the calcium carbonate (whiting) used, or 32 parts of calcium borate ($CaO \cdot B_2O_3 \cdot 2H_2O$) for 20 parts of the calcium carbonate, any crazing tendency may be further avoided. The conduct of the glazes with respect to production of colored melts or for use with overglaze or in-glaze colors was not materially different from the more common feldspathic type. These ceramists also recommended the following as satisfactory at cones 11–13 for insulators, laboratory ware, and tableware:

$$\begin{matrix} 0.22MgO & 0.3Al_2O_3 & 3.0SiO_2 \\ 0.78CaO & & \end{matrix}$$

Table 8.3. Range of compositions in the $CaO–Al_2O_3–SiO_2$ systems potentially suitable for porcelain glaze formulation[2,3]

Oxide components	Amounts, % by wt.	
	Glossy glazes	*Matt glazes*
Silica	80 to 50	60 to 35
Alumina	30 to 4	30 to 20
Lime	25 to 5	35 to 20

Table 8.4. Porcelain glazes of composition $CaO \cdot xAl_2O_3 \cdot ySiO_2$ for cone 17, compared with compositions and softening points of 4 eutectics[2,3]

Description	Composition, % by wt. CaO	Al_2O_3	SiO_2	Melting points, °C	Cone equivalents
Eutectic	9.8	19.8	70.4	1345	~13
Eutectic	23.3	14.7	62.2	1170	~ 4
Eutectic	38.0	20.0	42.0	1265	~10
Eutectic	47.2	11.8	41.0	1310	~12
Glaze, by Riddle	14.0	25.6	60.3		~17
Glaze, by Kerl	8.0	16.5	75.5		~17

During the last quarter of the previous century, Herman Seger[5] reported that he had found the most satisfactory choice of RO for a porcelain glaze to be:

$$0.3K_2O \quad \cdot \quad 0.7CaO$$

and his dictum still very largely influences the ceramist. A representative listing of the RO members with the customary molecular limits is:

0.1 to $0.3KNaO$
0.0 to $0.3MgO$
0.0 to $0.7BaO$
0.4 to $0.7CaO$
0.0 to $0.7SrO$

Alkalies are introduced in the form of a feldspathic mineral or a feldspathoid, such as nephelite. These are cheap, insoluble, and reasonably constant in composition. Soda strongly influences the coefficient of thermal expansion, increasing it greatly. It lowers the viscosity and, consequently, depresses the annealing and fusion temperatures. Potassa has similar effects in a less degree.

Table 8.5. Batch compositions for porcelain glazes for cones 11 and 13 composed solely of CaO, Al_2O_3, and SiO_2[4]

Maturing temp., cone	type of surface	Composition, parts by weight: Whiting	Raw kaolin	Calcined kaolin	Flint
11	Glossy	100	26	67	192
11	Matt	100	26	112	96
13	Glossy	100	26	245	396
13	Matt	100	26	290	198

Calcia, in the form of the ground marble, limestone, dolomite, or as the precipitated chemical by-product, is the chief component of the RO group. Used with feldspar in suitable amounts it constitutes the usual basis of this and many other types of glazes. The use of calcia as the sole member of the RO group has been mentioned, and Kraner's[6] proposed use of an eutectic of the CaO-Al_2O_3-SiO_2 system as a glaze maturing at cone 6 is noteworthy.

Glazes containing a high $CaO:Na_2O$ ratio, as compared to lower $CaO:Na_2O$ are more transparent and less viscous, therefore penetrate and react more completely with the body.[7] These calcareous melts should be applied less thickly to avoid the tendency of the fusion to develop a faintly unpleasant greenish color. The more calcareous glazes frequently are desirable to produce particular color effects when applied on certain underglaze compositions. The proper selection of the kind and the amounts of the RO members must be of prime importance in any case of this sort. When the alkaline members of the glaze predominate in the RO group, it will take on a milky translucency.

Calcium fluoride (fluorspar) is a useful minor addition to lower-fusion porcelain glazes because it facilitates the fusion process and it has a favorable effect upon the development of certain colors. The amount that may be used is limited to about 6% or 7%. Both components of CaF_2 can react with silica to form SiF_4 in addition to becoming a part of the complicated silicate network. SiF_4 is a gas and the evolution of it removes both silica and fluorine. Vogt[8] found that all of the 4.6% of fluorine introduced with the raw materials of a hard porcelain glaze disappeared from a sample of the glaze placed on platinum and fired at 1300° C under oxidizing conditions.

Magnesia is usually introduced as the dense form of the carbonate (magnesite), which has a slight water solubility. Dolomite, the double mineral carbonate of magnesia and calcia, is a cheap and satisfactory source. Talc, the hydrated silicate of magnesia ($3MgO \cdot 4SiO_2 \cdot H_2O$) is reported to produce lower fusibility and better gloss than are to be had with the same equivalents of calcium, i.e., on the basis of substitution, molecularly, of the one for the others.[9] In general the permissible amount of magnesia will be found to be less than the 0.3 equivalent shown above. Although it heightens the gloss, it is quite refractory.

Baria is introduced as the carbonate as witherite, or as the precipitated product which has the lower density. It requires a higher temperature to effect its decomposition than the two alkali-earth carbonates previously referred to, but it is a much more powerful flux, promoting the fusibility and transparency of the glaze. It is useful also in developing good matt textures.

Strontia has been used occasionally for many years, but the similarity in its conduct, as compared with calcium oxide, and its greater cost have caused neglect of the systematic study it deserves. It may be a useful material for the preparation of leadless raw glazes intended for vitreous and semivitreous whiteware bodies. A typical composition is given by Harman and Swift[10] as follows:

Emprical formula

0.2KNaO		
0.3SrO	$0.3Al_2O_3$	$3.0SiO_2$
0.1CaO		
0.4BaO		

Batch in wt. % was: barium carbonate, 22,1; calcium carbonate, 2.7; strontium carbonate, 11.6; nepheline syenite, 25.3; Tenn. ball clay no. 5, 2.2; pyrophyllite, 6.0; flint, 30.1.

In a laboratory firing, the glaze started to mature at cone 03 and was not overfired at cone 10. The surface of the glaze was smooth but not quite equal to a borosilicate glaze. The raw clay content had to be reduced to 0.03 equivalent to avoid application defects. A slight crazing tendency on some bodies was reduced by firing higher or by increasing the alumina to 0.4 equivalent and the silica to 4.0 equivalents. Superior results were had in using this glaze with ten underglaze colors as compared with a lead borosilicate glaze. The authors concluded that the strontia increases the fusibility of glaze and does not increase the thermal expansion as much as lime.

Rieke and Kunstman[11] have reported their study of effects produced by the substitution of various alkalies and alkaline earths in the base glaze, $CaO:0.83Al_2O_3:6.94SiO_2$. Lime was replaced successively by molecular equivalents of potassa, soda, magnesia, baryta, and zinc oxide. Although the experimental field was, in general, not representative of the present American industrial practice and therefore the conclusions may not be completely applicable, yet they furnish important basic information.

Some of the conclusions were:

a. The replacement of small amounts of the lime by magnesia was without effect upon the thermal expansion; but the first large substitution of magnesia lowered it. The replacement of a small amount of lime by magnesia decreased the annealing temperature, while a large substitution caused an increase. The thin fluidity of the base glaze at its softening temperature was decreased somewhat by the presence of a small amount of magnesia. A larger amount of magnesia reversed the effect.

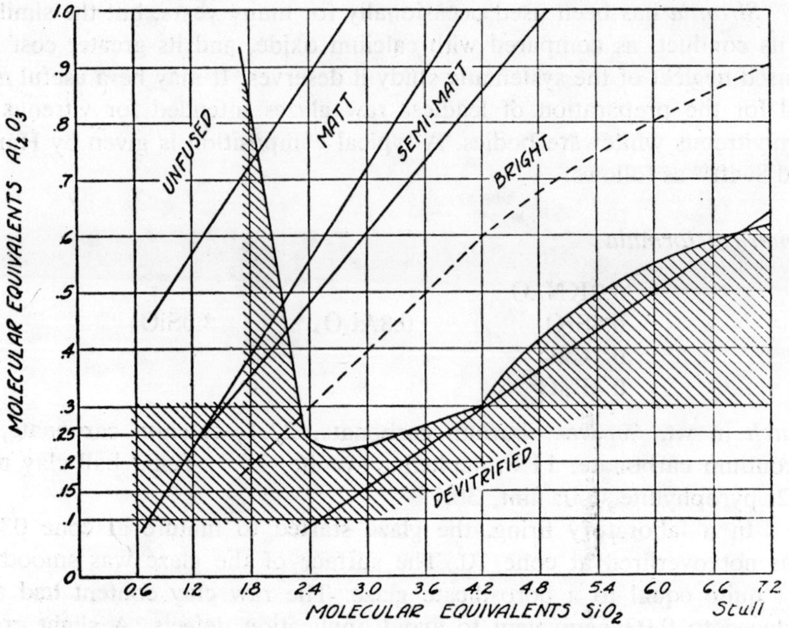

Figure 8.3. Porcelain glaze field having a constant RO and variable alumina and silica, fired at cone 11. Shaded area is crazed.[20]

b. The substitution of baryta for lime significantly decreased the thermal expansion, and the action was approximately as great as that of magnesia. The action of barium oxide in larger additions was to raise the annealing temperature. The action of baryta on the viscosity varied in an inverse manner: small increments increased it; further small additions had little effect, but large substitutions decreased the viscosity.

c. The investigators studied the effect of the replacement by cobalt and chromium oxides. Both decreased the expansions, the latter more than the former. The annealing temperatures were not perceptibly affected. The viscosities were strongly increased especially by the chromium oxide. These oxides made the glazes in which they were present more stable to resist the effects of temperature changes.

The following suggestions are useful in preparing glazes resistant to the effect of temperature changes:

a. Not more than 2.5% sodium oxide or more than 8% potassium oxide should be used. Considerable quantities of magnesium oxide may be introduced simultaneously with the potassa to the advantage of the thermal expansion and the gloss.

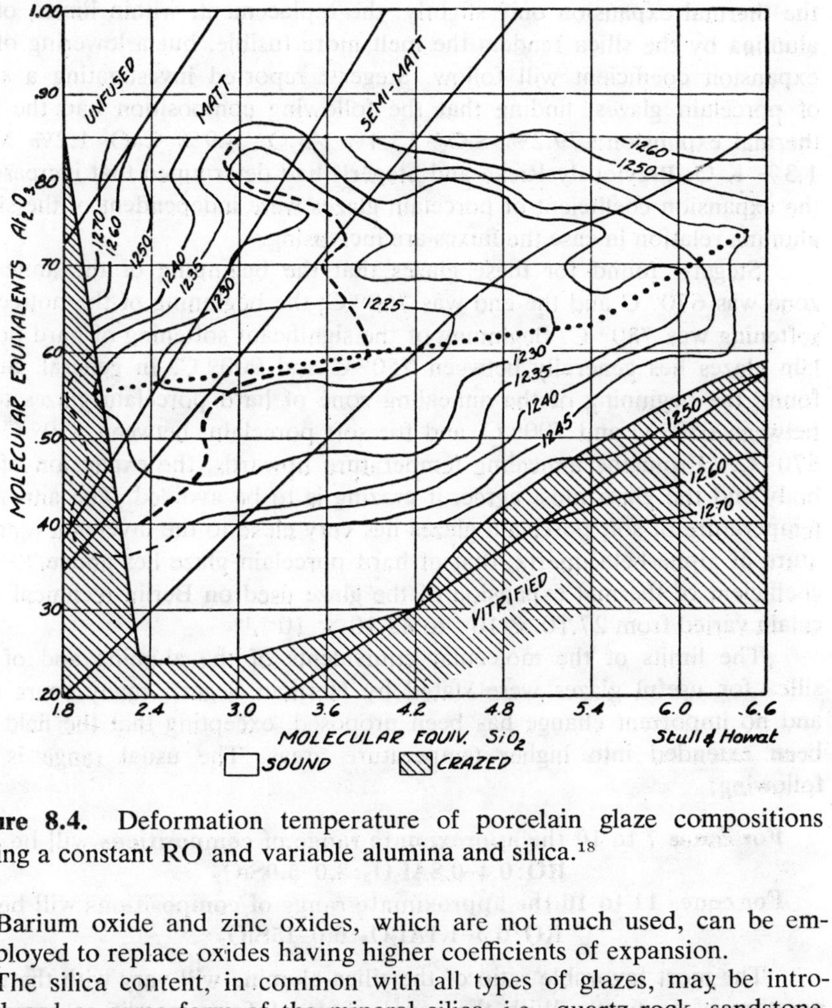

Figure 8.4. Deformation temperature of porcelain glaze compositions having a constant RO and variable alumina and silica.[18]

b. Barium oxide and zinc oxides, which are not much used, can be employed to replace oxides having higher coefficients of expansion.

c. The silica content, in common with all types of glazes, may be introduced as some form of the mineral silica, i.e., quartz rock, sandstone, unconsolidated sands, etc., very finely ground; or it may be introduced combined chemically in feldspar or feldspathic rock, in aluminous silicates; such as clay, or in other silicate minerals.

d. The alumina is introduced almost entirely in some silicate combination (clay, feldspar, etc.). The use of free alumina is infrequent.

The functions of alumina are varied and important. To a limited degree it is a glass former, but mainly a stabilizer, profoundly influencing the viscosity, fusibility, durability, annealing temperature, and many other physical properties. The replacement of part of the silica by alumina affects the thermal expansion only slightly; the replacement, within limits, of the alumina by the silica renders the melt more fusible, but a lowering of the expansion coefficient will follow. Steger[12] reported investigating a series of porcelain glazes, finding that the following composition had the least thermal expansion: 79.2% SiO_2, 13.4% Al_2O_3, 4.9% CaO, 1.2% MgO, 1.3% K_2O. Previously Rieke and Steger[13] had determined that increases in the expansion coefficient of porcelain glazes were independent of the silica-alumina relation in case the fluxes are increasing.

Steger[14] found for these glazes that the beginning of the annealing zone was 670° C and the end was 760° C; the beginning of the noticeable softening was 780° C. Beginning of the significant softening of hard porcelain glazes lies generally between 750° C and 900° C. In general, Steger found the beginning of the annealing zone of hard porcelain glazes to be between 650° C and 700° C, and for soft porcelain, between 530° C and 570° C. "From the annealing temperature upwards, the expansion of the body and the glaze must agree, if crazing is to be avoided. The annealing temperature of soft porcelain glazes lies very close to the inversion temperature of alpha-beta quartz; that of hard porcelain glaze lies above."[15] The coefficient of thermal expansion of the glaze used on Berlin technical porcelain varied from 27.10×10^{-7} to 42.10×10^{-7}.[16]

The limits of the molecular equivalents of the alumina and of the silica for useful glazes were stated by Herman Seger[17] many years ago, and no important change has been proposed, excepting that the field has been extended into higher temperature areas. The usual range is the following:

For cones 7 to 10 the approximate range of compositions will be

$$RO:0.4\text{–}0.8Al_2O_3:3.0\text{–}5.0SiO_2$$

For cones 11 to 16 the approximate range of compositions will be

$$RO:0.5\text{–}1.1Al_2O_3:6.0\text{–}15SiO_2$$

The most favorable ratio of the silica-alumina will vary with the temperature of maturity. With the usual range of firing conditions required for the ordinary types of porcelain wares it will fall within the general limits 7:1 to 10:1. Figure 8.3 represents very satisfactorily these relationships for a wide range of silica-alumina variations when the RO group was the constant, $0.3K_2O$ and 0.7CaO. The abscissa, or base line, is marked to show the variations in the molecular equivalents of the silica, and the ordinate shows the variations in the molecular equivalents of the alumina. The condition of the several glaze compositions, when matured at the same cone temperature, is shown by the boundaries and the descriptive terms, e.g., "unfused," "matt," etc. The axis of the compositions having highest gloss in figure 8.3 is the dotted line. In figure 8.4 the isotherms show the deformation temperatures of the glaze compositions. Stull and Howat[18] found a "group eutectic" which "lies near the center of the field of best glazes and the quality of the glazes decreases in all directions away from the eutectic point," i.e., the composition which is assumed to be located in the group. The general formulae of the best glazes are given as:

$RO:0.60Al_2O_3:4.0SiO_2$ Deform. temp. 1,220° C.
$RO:0.55Al_2O_3:3.5SiO_2$ Deform. temp. 1,227° C.
$RO:0.55Al_2O_3:4.0SiO_2$ Deform. temp. 1,230° C.
$RO:0.60Al_2O_3:3.5SiO_2$ Deform. temp. 1,222° C.

The difference between the deformation temperatures of these glazes and the temperature at which they were matured (cone 9, i.e., 1,250° C, at the rate of about 20° C per hour) is about one cone. This is subject in part to the rate of the kiln firing.

Stull and Howat observed that glazes whose formulae corresponded to the compositions of the cones 4, 5, and 6 (Orton, Standard) deformed at 1,228° C, 1,240° C, and 1,245° C, instead of 1,165° C, 1,180° C, and 1,245° C, which is attributable in part to difference in the firing conditions. Funk[19] stated that composition of the "Segerkegels" 4*a* to 6*a* are those of the typical porcelain glazes maturing at S.K. 8 to 11 (1,250° C to 1,320° C); compositions for S.K. 7 to 8 mature at S.K. 12 to 13 (1,350° C to 1,380° C); compositions of S.K. 9 to 11 mature at S.K. 14 to 16 (i.e. 15 to 17 of the Orton Standard Cones). S.K. 8 to 13 correspond to Orton Cones 9 to 14. He states further that one selects for the composition of a porcelain glaze that of the cone which deforms at one or two numbers lower.

Discussing the work of Stull,[20] Staley[21] suggested that a very simple rule can be devised for making a long series of good bright or matt porcelain glazes with this RO.

> "Any raw glaze should have at least 0.05 equivalent of clay for mechanical reasons, so we will start with 0.34 Al_2O_3 and 2.40 SiO_2. Now by adding Al_2O_3 and SiO_2 to this glaze in the proportion of 0.10 equivalent of Al_2O_3 to 0.8 equivalent of SiO_2, we can make a long series of glazes lying close to the line of best bright glazes free from crazing. In terms of batch weights, this means that we can start with a glaze of the following batch: 33 feldspar, 14 whiting, 2½ clay, and 6 flint. To this batch we add clay and flint in the proportion of 1 part clay to 1.4 parts flint. To get the longest possible series of matts we simply drop out the flint from the above base glaze and make successive additions of clay. The members lowest in clay of this series would be liable to craze."

The results of numerous investigations of the procelain type of glazes

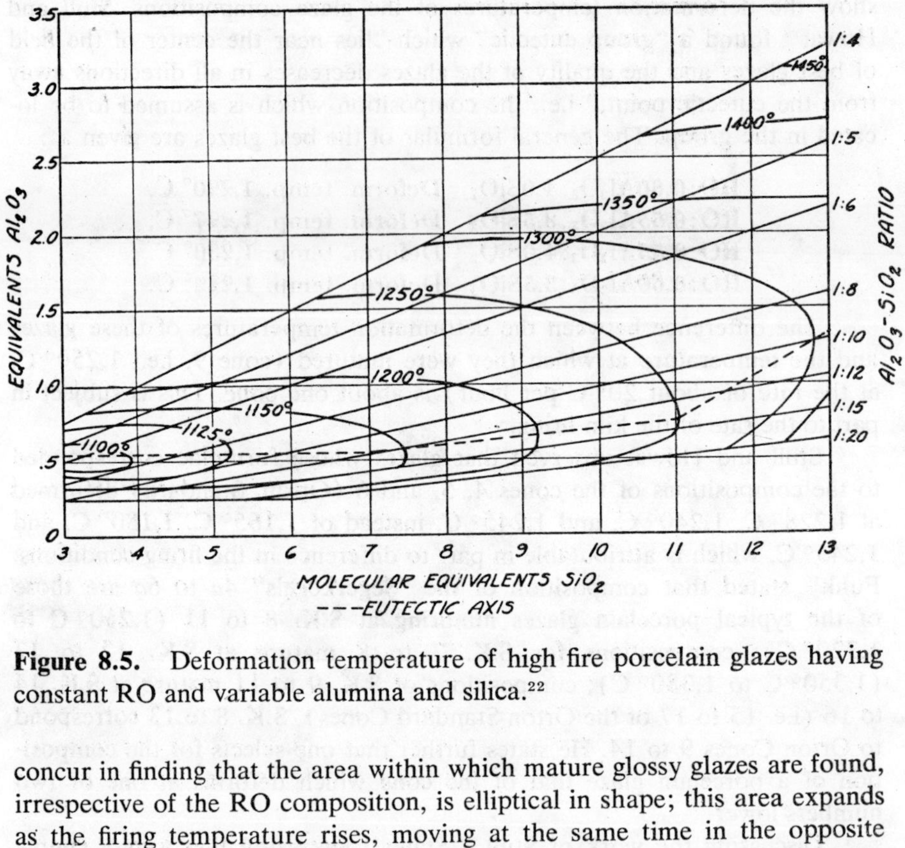

Figure 8.5. Deformation temperature of high fire porcelain glazes having constant RO and variable alumina and silica.[22]

concur in finding that the area within which mature glossy glazes are found, irrespective of the RO composition, is elliptical in shape; this area expands as the firing temperature rises, moving at the same time in the opposite direction to the origin of the coordinates; and the best are found in the approximate center.of the ellipsis.

High-temperature Glazes

Sortwell[22] and Twells,[23] using the same RO ($0.3K_2O$, $0.7CaO$), carried on their studies of porcelain glazes at higher temperatures than Stull and Howat. Sortwell varied the range of the alumina between 0.3 and 3.25, and that of silica from 3 to 13. The firing was done with gas under reducing conditions up to cone 8 and then neutral or slightly oxidizing conditions to the finish. The duration varied with the cone temperature desired as follows:

Cone 10 in 20 hours	Cone 14 in 22 hours
Cone 12 in 20 hours	Cone 16 in 24 hours

In figure 8.5 is shown the equal-deformation-temperature lines and

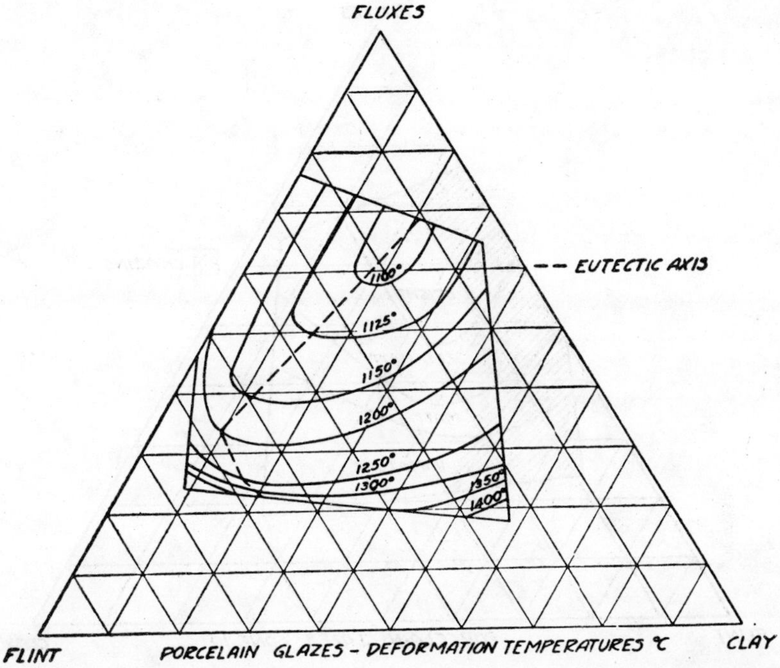

Figure 8.6. Deformation of high fire porcelain glazes as influenced by variable clay-flint-flux content.[22]

what Sortwell designates as the "eutectic axis" or, more appropriately, the deformation axis for the series which has a constant RO content of 0.3KNaO and 0.7CaO with variable silica-alumina content. In figure 8.6 are shown the isotherms for the deformations of this same system plotted with the variables, fluxes-silica-clay, on a ternary diagram. Results of firing these compositions at cones 10 and 16 are shown in figures 8.7 and 8.8 respectively. Twells used the alumina-silica ratio within the ranges 0.8–1.6Al_2O_3 and 6–16SiO_2. The firings to cones 17 to 19 were carried out in a Dressler tunnel kiln in 31 hours, and to cone 20 in a periodic kiln in 52 hours. The glazes were applied on porcelain trial pieces in an unfired condition. Sortwell concluded that the best glazes lie along a high gloss axis, practically a straight line, which may be represented approximately by the formula:

$$Al_2O_3 = 0.3 + \tfrac{1}{12}SiO_2$$

Twells and others have confirmed this, and at cone 20 this line passes through the location of the best composition. The range of the silica content for a given cone increases as the maturing temperature is raised; possi-

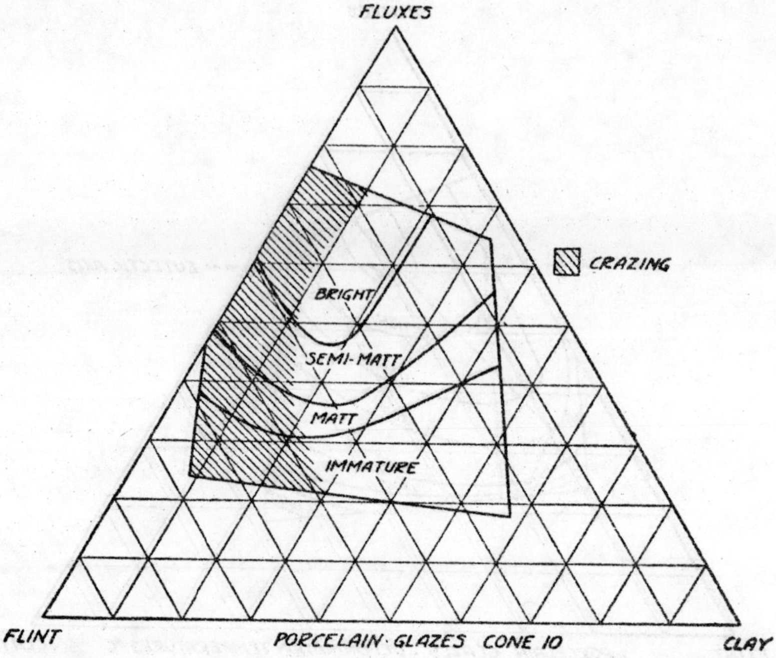

Figure 8.7. Field of porcelain glazes fired at cone 10 showing the effects of variable clay-flint-flux content.[22]

ble variations being from 3 to 13 equivalents. The range of the alumina is narrower. There is a deformation eutectic axis represented by Sortwell in figure 8.5. At any one temperature there were found areas of good mature glazes. Twells reports the best composition for the temperature range used in his experiments to lie within the following percentage limits: clay, 21.9 to 27.2; flint, 40.8 to 51.8; feldspar, 17.2 to 23.6; whiting, 7.2 to 10.0. Sortwell found that matt glazes could be had when "the alumina-silica ratio was 1:4 within the limits of 3 to 6 equivalents of silica and tapering down to 1:6 for 10 equivalents of silica." These are "aluminous matts" which do not become glossy with higher heat treatments.

Kitamura[24] has studied the effect of variations in the RO group with variations in the Al_2O_3 and SiO_2. The ranges of compositions are as follows:

0.1KNaO	0.9CaO	0.2 to 2.2Al_2O_3	4 to 26SiO_2
0.5KNaO	0.5CaO	0.2 to 2.2Al_2O_3	4 to 26SiO_2

The formulas of the best glazes for the cones indicated are given as in table 8.6. Along the "gloss axis" the silica varies with the alumina in

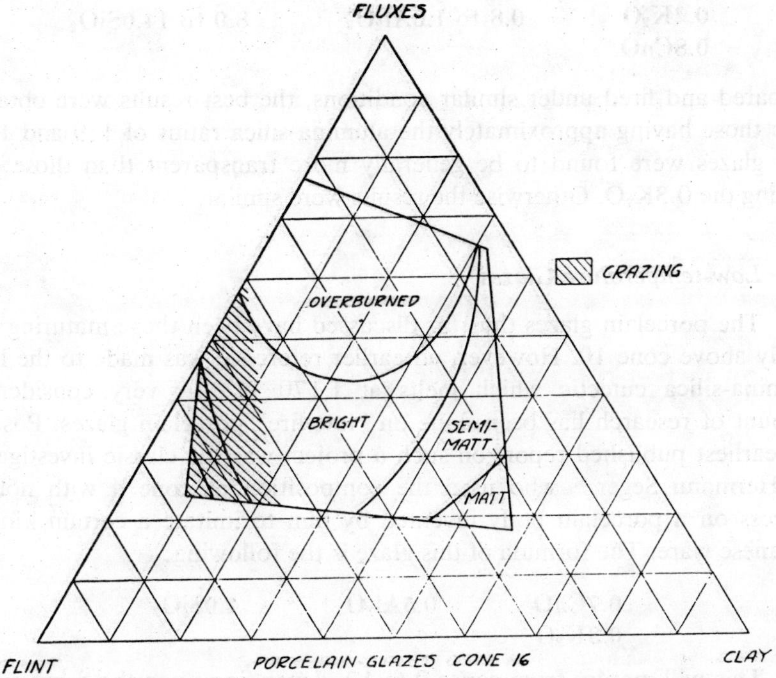

Figure 8.8. Field of porcelain glazes fired at cone 16, showing the effects of variable clay-flint-flux content.[22]

the ratio of 10 to 1, excepting in the case of the 0.1KNaO, 0.9CaO fired at cone 11; in this case the ratio is 8 to 1. The maximum amounts of alumina and silica in these glazes having high gloss are as given in table 8.7.

Twells[25] studied 21 glazes having the general formula $RO \cdot 1.3Al_2O_3 \cdot 11SiO_2$. The RO members and their limits in equivalents were found to be: 0.3 K_2O; 0.2 to 0.7 CaO; 0.0 to 0.5 BaO; 0.0 to 0.5 MgO. These glazes were applied on "green" porcelain trial pieces and fired in commercial periodic and tunnel kilns to temperatures between cones $16\frac{1}{2}$ and 19 flat. When fired in the periodic kilns for 24 hours, the transparency of all the glazes increased with the temperature. Those fired in the tunnel kiln to cone 19 flat in 31 hours were found to be more opaque and smoother than those fired in the periodic kilns at a temperature three cones lower. The replacement of the lime by magnesia and barium oxide had no important effect upon the appearance of the resulting glazes except for the greater number of smaller bubbles seen under low magnification near the apex of the high barium field.

In a series of glazes having the range of composition:

$$\begin{matrix} 0.2K_2O & 0.8 \text{ to } 1.6Al_2O_3 & 8.0 \text{ to } 14.0SiO_2 \\ 0.8CaO & & \end{matrix}$$

prepared and fired under similar conditions, the best results were obtained with those having approximately the alumina-silica ratios of 1:9 and 1:11. The glazes were found to be generally more transparent than those containing the $0.3K_2O$. Otherwise the results were similar.

Low-temperature Glazes

The porcelain glazes thus far discussed have been those maturing generally above cone 10. However, an earlier reference was made to the lime-alumina-silica eutectic which melts at 1,170° C.[26] A very considerable amount of research has been done on "low-fire" porcelain glazes. Possibly the earliest published report on such a project was the classic investigation by Hermann Seger,[27] who used the composition of cone 4 with notable success on a porcelain body invented by him to imitate a certain kind of Japanese ware. The formula of this glaze is the following:

$$\begin{matrix} 0.7CaO & 0.5Al_2O_3 & 4.0SiO_2 \\ 0.3K_2O & & \end{matrix}$$

This will mature from cones 9 to 12, depending upon the firing conditions, and has found extensive use on wares other than porcelain, e.g., architectural terra cotta and some other structural clay products, sanitary ware, etc. In these cases it has served as a base glaze modified to suit particular circumstances; for example, Montgomery and Kruson[28] added zinc oxide and boric oxide to eliminate seeds, i.e., fine bubbles. The staff of the laboratory of the National Manufactory at Sevres pottery, seeking the same objectives as Seger, produced a similar ware for which the glaze was, according to Bourry:[29]

$$\begin{matrix} 0.45CaO & 0.64Al_2O_3 & 6.77SiO_2 \\ 0.55K_2O + Na_2O & & \end{matrix}$$

It is interesting to compare this composition with that found by Hanna:[30]

$$\begin{matrix} 0.4CaO & 0.74Al_2O_3 & 4.83SiO_2 \\ 0.6K_2O & & \end{matrix}$$

The latter's deformation temperature was slightly below cone 3.

The empirical formulae of twelve low-maturing porcelain-type glazes are given in table 8.8. These compositions were taken from the literature, as indicated. All but two of these show potash but no soda. Undoubtedly

Table 8.6: Porcelain glazes based on KNaO, CaO, Al_2O_3 and SiO_2 for cones 11, 14 and 17[24]

Maturing temp., cone	Empirical formulas Molecular equivalents			
	KNaO	CaO	Al_2O_3	SiO_2
11	0.1	0.9	0.7	6.0
14	0.1	0.9	0.95	9.5
17	0.1	0.9	1.10	14.5
11	0.3	0.7	0.8	7.0
14	0.3	0.7	1.0	9.8
17	0.3	0.7	1.10	14.7
11	0.5	0.5	0.9	8.0
14	0.5	0.5	1.05	10.0
17	0.5	0.5	1.1	15.0

these were computed on the assumption that the high potash spar contained no soda, an invalid assumption. The practical significance of this is nominal.

Colored Porcelain Glazes

The color palette of porcelain glazes is limited as compared with those maturing at the lower temperatures. There is, indeed, a considerable difference between the "hard" and the "soft" porcelains, and cone 10 may be designated arbitrarily as the limit of usefulness of the more sensitive colors, for example, those prepared with iron and with copper. At the higher temperatures these colors either volatilize to such a degree that the color is impaired or bubbling and blistering injure the surface finish; or chemical changes occur in the colorant to its detriment. The choice of the kind and the amounts of the bases used is of very great importance, and in general

Table 8.7. Empirical formulas of some porcelain glazes in the KNaO-CaO-Al_2O_3-SiO_2 system[24]

Maturing temp., cone	Composition, molecular equivalents			
	KNaO	CaO	Al_2O_3	SiO_2
11	0.5	0.5	1.3	12
14	0.5	0.5	1.5	15
17	0.5	0.5	1.9	23
11	0.1	0.9	1.1	9
14	0.1	0.9	1.5	15
17	0.1	0.9	1.9	23

Table 8.8. Empirical formulas of some porcelain glazes maturing from cone 4 to cone 16

No.	K_2O	CaO	MgO	BaO	Na_2O	Al_2O_3	SiO_2	Cone
1[31]	0.30	0.50	0.10	0.10	–	0.40	3.85	4
2[31]	0.20	0.70	0.10	–	–	0.40	3.50	4
3[32]	0.20	0.70	0.38	–	–	0.40	3.50	7
4[31]	0.48	0.40	–	–	–	0.70	4.80	7
5[31]	0.25	0.37	0.10	–	–	0.75	7.10	7–9
6[33]	0.06	0.86	0.12	–	0.08	0.83	4.70	9
7[34]	0.20	0.70	–	–	–	0.65	5.50	11
8[35]	0.30	0.35	0.35	–	–	0.95	9.50	12–14
9[34]	0.20	0.70	0.22	–	–	0.85	7.50	13
10[36]	0.40	0.20	0.10	–	0.4	1.10	8.00	14
11[37]	0.11	0.67	0.10	–	–	1.00	10.00	15
12[34]	0.20	0.70	0.10	–	–	1.20	10.00	16

potassa has a more satisfactory effect upon color development than soda. Magnesia performs some special services in this respect. Otherwise it is undesirable. Pleasing effects are had most frequently by blending the stronger colorants, thus avoiding the harsh effects otherwise accompanying the sole use of primary colors. The oxide of iron and the oxide of nickel are sometimes employed as "shading" or "toning" colors for the same reason. Oxidizing condition during the firing is the normal practice since some colorants are injured by reduction, e.g., manganese may be made to yield a dirty grey under such condition. On the other hand, the typical green or greenish blue is furnished by copper oxide, if oxidized, but it gives interesting and even beautiful shades of red under the influence of reduction.

The color oxides suitable for the extreme temperatures and which have low volatility and high tinctorial power, thus limiting the amount required to small replacements of the more active bases, are: cobalt, manganese, chromium, nickel, iron, titanium, and uranium. Seger[38] recommends that oxides of the RO and R_2O types be introduced in place of molecular equivalents of the calcia of the formula and that the sesquioxides be substituted for molecular equivalents of the alumina. Hegemann[39] recommends that the following substitutions be made in calcareous glazes, in molecular equivalents per equivalent of CaO:

2 uranium nitrate
1 cobalt oxide
2 ferric oxide
2 manganese oxide
1 copper oxide

However, the substitutions should be governed by the nature of the other RO members and the color desired.

BLUES. Three to five percent of cobalt oxide (Co_3O_4), or 0.025 to 0.10 molecular equivalents of the CoO, introduced in the RO group, are the customary limits to produce the range of concentration of color from the light to the deep blue. Calcium has a beneficial effect; barium promotes the formation of the Turkish-blue; the presence of phosphoric acid yields a violet shade of color and a more luminous quality. The pleasing effect of some of the best Chinese blues is attributed to the presence of very small amounts of the oxides of iron or nickel.

GREENS. Only one or two percent of chrome oxide may be used because it is very refractory but, fortunately, a strong colorant. The maximum and the minimum molecular equivalents are 0.15 and 0.015. Between these limits are found the variations from light to dark green. The addition of a small amount of cobalt oxide is good practice, and a reducing atmosphere for the firing is beneficial providing that the lime content of the glaze is low. The presence of a small amount of calcium fluoride enlivens the color. An addition of barium with calcium intensifies the color. Baria with potassa yields a yellowish or hedge-apple green. Baria with magnesia and potassa gives greyish colors. Calcia and magnesia and potassa give brownish shades, but if the calcium is absent, the result is a faun color.[40] Small amounts of zinc oxide are said to be unobjectionable with chromium, although giving a greyish shade, but larger quantities give tans and browns. Alumina with chromium has the latter effect and tin oxide will produce useful pinks and maroons. Copper oxide may be used alone to produce bluish greens at temperatures below about cone 9. A high lime content is desirable in the glaze. The minimum and the maximum quantities used are 0.125 to 0.20 molecular equivalents. Volatilization weakens the color. Uranium yellow and cobalt blue, properly proportioned, will give greens, and praseodymium phosphate gives light and moss green colors.

BROWNS. Faintly violet to strong browns may be had by the use of manganese oxide if added within the minimum amount of 0.10 mol. equiv. and the maximum of 0.25 mol. equiv. Iron oxide will give light tan with the use of 0.025 mol. equiv., and a brown if the amount is increased to 0.10 mol. equiv. Nickel oxide will produce light to dark browns if used between the limits of 0.05 and 0.15 mol. equiv. Chromium is reported to furnish brownish shades if used with the bases: potassa, calcia, and magnesia in the same RO. Very strong browns may be had by using a mixture of equal proportions, in mol. equiv., of the oxides of manganese, chromium, and iron.

YELLOW AND CREAM. Uranium oxide will produce yellow glazes if they are fired under oxidizing conditions, otherwise they become greyish

Figure 8.9. Building tile are glazed with leadless, fritted glazes of the terra cotta or low-firing porcelain types.

to black. The addition of a small amount of calcium fluoride (fluorspar) will improve the yellow color. The minimum amount of the uranium oxide necessary for a faint yellow will be about 0.01 molecular equivalents. This must be considerably increased in order to intensify the color. Titanium oxide or rutile with only a slight amount of iron oxide will yield a cream color if used in quantities ranging from 1 to 3 percent. Oxidizing conditions must prevail in the kiln if rutile is used.

BLACK. This color may be had by the addition of 1 to 2 percent of cobalt oxide to a brown glaze or 2 to 4 percent manganese oxide to a blue glaze. In general, the principle is used of mixing two or more oxides of high tinctorial power in such a proportion as to produce an optical effect in which the action of any single component does not dominate. Iridium will produce a black but it is very expensive. Platinum produces a grey.

Uranium, as already stated, produces a black when fired under reducing conditions.

RED AND PINK. The chrome-tin pink calcine may be used for the low- and medium-fire porcelain glazes. Its preparation and use is described later. Some shade of red may be had without the use of a calcine, providing the essential constituent oxides, tin and chromium, are introduced in a glaze of a suitable chemical character.

The practical limit of the chrome-tin pink color is about cone 9. Iron oxide is unstable at high temperatures, giving greys and blackish colors, but fiery reds may be had, within the proper temperature limits, if alkalies are used as the bases to the exclusion of lime and probably the other alkaline earths. This will give a water soluble batch unless they are introduced as a frit. The following composition[41] has been reported as satisfactory at cone 8.

$0.80K_2O$	$1.17Al_2O_3$	$5.35SiO_2$
$0.20Na_2O$	$0.05Fe_2O_3$	

SPINELS. The introduction of colors in the form of spinels has been advocated by many ceramists because they are less subject to molecular changes during firing at high temperatures. The type formula of the spinel is $RO{:}R_2O_3$. The monoxide member may be any one of the following: MgO, ZnO, MnO, NiO, CoO, FeO, CdO. The sesquioxide member may be Al_2O_3, Cr_2O_3, Fe_2O_3, and others. The most resistant and beautiful colors are obtained by using these compounds.

Bristol Glaze

The Bristol glaze is a variant of the soft porcelain type, adapted to produce an opaque white coating on stoneware and similar colored clay bodies, maturing at temperatures generally lower than porcelaneous white bodies. The opacity and easier fusibility are in part attributable to considerable amounts of zinc oxide used in the glaze composition. While this oxide has been used occasionally and tentatively in small amounts in true porcelain glazes, sometimes with advantages, it cannot be considered as a typical ingredient of them, because of its relatively high volatility at porcelain heats. Typical applications are illustrated in figures 8.9 and 8.11.

Bristol glazes are not all opaque; they may be clear (colorless), opaque, colored, glossy, dull, or matt. They are most frequently applied on unfired clay bodies for which they are particularly suitable because of the considerable amount of raw clay necessary in the glaze batch. This

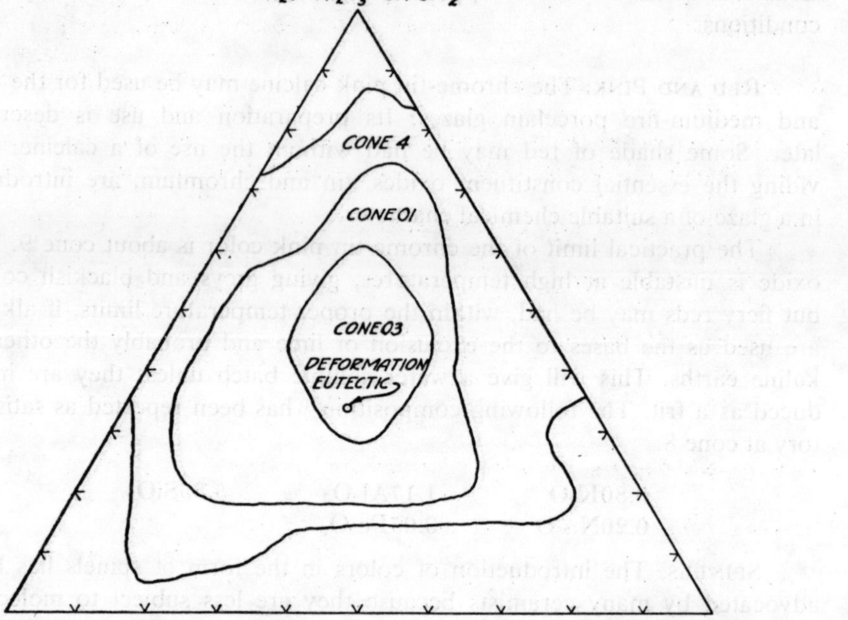

Figure 8.10. Cone deformation of ternary system.[44]

makes them practicable for use on unfired stoneware and structural clay products. On the other hand, they give excellent results on biscuited ware, providing proper adjustment is made of the raw clay content of the batch. This easy adjustment of the raw clay content and the absence of any high density ingredients in the batch minimize settling tendencies and simplify the application on the ware. No fritted additions are needed or made to the batch. Because of the low volatility of the batch ingredients at the temperatures used, the ware may be fired in the open without harm except for flying ash or dirt. The high viscosity of the melts permits the glazes to mature without running and consequent sticking of pieces of ware. On the other hand, the viscous coating conforms less satisfactorily to finely detailed decoration and will obscure the finer modelings. With proper adjustment, most of these difficulties may be overcome.

Chemically, the glaze may be described as the product of the fusion of alkalies, alkaline earths, zinc oxide, clay, and free silica. It is matured ordinarily between cones 5 and 9, but compositions have been proposed as satisfactory as low as cone 3. One of the characteristics of the glaze is its tolerance to prolonged duration of firing which is conducive to lower-

Figure 8.11. Bristol glazes, specially developed for terra cotta, are lead free.

ing the maturing temperature. The glaze is quite resistant to abrasion, weathering, and contact with the usual acid, alkalies, and cleaning reagents.

The origin of the name (Bristol) of the glaze is said to be traceable to that town in England where it is alleged it was invented for use on a body having a yellowish or cream color. However this may have been, its American origin seems attributable to the efforts of stoneware potters in Ohio to improve the appearance of their product. They seem to have proceeded by substituting zinc oxide in a yellow ware glaze, at the same time gradually omitting the lead and modifying its alumina silica content to withstand the higher kiln temperature. Whatever may have been the circumstances, we know that stoneware coated with Bristol glaze was exhibited at the Exposition held in New Orleans in 1884[42] and in 1902 Dr. Purdy[43] writes: "Bristol glaze is so recent that ceramists are not familiar with it." The superior attractiveness of the glaze speedily made it the standard commercial type for utility pottery for the household. Subsequently, it became the most widely used basic glaze for architectural and other structural clay products.

The type formula of a Bristol glaze for stoneware fired at cones 6–7 in 50–60 hours is:

0.35KNaO		
0.35CaO	$0.55Al_2O_3$	$3.30SiO_2$
0.30ZnO		

An important difference in the use of Bristol glaze on architectural terra cotta is its application on a white underslip, which is more favorable for the development of a white color than the practice followed in the stoneware industry of putting the glaze directly on the cream colored body; hence, opacity is a prime requisite in the latter case.

The range of the molecular compositions of terra cotta glazes is, approximately:

0.2 to 0.4KNaO		
0.1 to 0.5 CaO		
0.1 to 0.4ZnO		
0.0 to 0.2MgO	0.20 to $0.55Al_2O_3$	2.0 to $3.5SiO_2$
0.0 to 0.3BaO		
0.0 to 0.4SrO		

Terra cotta glazes are customarily fired to cones 3 to 6 in 50 to 70 hours. The Bristol glaze has been extensively studied and described. Because phase equilibria studies of such a complex multicomponent system have not been made owing to the evident difficulties, Watts[44] tried to simplify the problem by using these compositions as the apex members of a ternary field; orthoclase feldspar-quartz eutectic, $KNaO \cdot Al_2O_3 \cdot 6.4SiO_2$; the eutectic, $CaO \cdot 0.348Al_2O_3 \cdot 2.49SiO_2$; the deformation eutectic, $ZnO \cdot 0.318Al_2O_3 \cdot 0.81SiO_2$. This latter was determined by Watts to deform at cones 12–13. Hanna[45] found the orthoclase-feldspar eutectic mix-

Table 8.9. Glossy ZnO-bearing glazes maturing at cones 3, 4, and 5[46]

	Empirical formulas				
	molecular equivalents				
No.	K_2O	*CaO*	*ZnO*	Al_2O_3	SiO_2
1	0.4	0.25	0.35	0.600	3.47
2	0.35	0.20	0.45	0.565	3.10
3	0.3	0.3	0.4	0.534	3.00

ture deformed at cone 3. As shown in figure 8.10, Watts found a eutectic area of deformation at cone 03. The most fusible mixture had the following empirical formula:

$$\begin{matrix} 0.4KNaO & & \\ 0.3CaO & 0.6Al_2O_3 & 3.55SiO_2 \\ 0.3ZnO & & \end{matrix}$$

and was prepared from the following materials, in weight percent: Canadian feldspar, 59.62%; whiting, 8.03%; zinc oxide, 6.50%; Florida kaolin, 13.81%; and flint, 12.04%. This proved to be a good glossy glaze when fired in small experimental and large commercial kilns.

Other satisfactory compositions[46] closely related to the above, which were found good over a range from cone 3 to cone 14 were those given in Table 8.9. These were used with success on electrical porcelain fired at cones 12 and 14. "At cones 3, 4 and 5 they produced fine white smooth enamels suitable for novelty pottery and cooking ware. In no case was crazing noted. These glazes will not heal over if once their surfaces are broken, which is a frequent defect of such viscous fusions."[46] Hill[47] comments that

> "The fusible low-clay glazes area was not included in Watts' study since the mixtures with 0.10 equivalent clay or less contained 0.7 equivalent or more of feldspar. In the eutectic area the mixtures did not contain much more than 0.75 equivalent free silica. It is quite likely that in low-clay glazes, a further increase of SiO_2 would produce more fusible glazes."

Materials

With the exception of the zinc oxide, the materials used in compounding Bristol glazes are the same as those used in porcelain glazes and their functions are the same. The reason for using zinc oxide has been mentioned. Its fluxing action, in limited amounts, has been stated by Staley[48] to be equal (pound for pound) to that of lead oxide.

Fusibility

As already seen, fusibility is determined chiefly by the proper balance of the fluxes, the alumina, and the silica. A multiplicity of the RO members definitely contributes to increase in fusibility, which is axiomatic in glaze compositions; therefore, there is an advantage in using a number and variety of alkalies and alkaline earths.

The most favorable range of the KNaO is between 0.4 and 0.3 equivalents. Greater or smaller amounts are less fusible. With increase in the amount of alkalies there is an increase in glassy, transparent fusion, and a tendency to craze. It may be assumed that the glassy phase begins with the melting of the alkaline-alumina-silicates, accelerated by the presence of the alkaline earth, specifically calcium oxide. The effect on deformation temperatures of increasing the alkali at the expense of lime in the presence of a constant zinc oxide content is shown in figure 8.12, according to Purdy.[49] The potash (i.e., an alkali) is shown on the abscissa; the zinc oxide is constant at 0.4 equivalent; therefore, "the difference between the 0.4 equivalent ZnO and equivalent K_2O, as shown on the abscissa, and unity will equal the equivalents of calcia. The alumina in any mixture may be obtained by substituting the equivalent of K_2O (i.e., the alkalies) in the ratios which the curve represents and upon which the mixture is described, and computing the value of the alumina. The silica in all cases is 5.5 times the alumina."

The effect of the calcium content is evident from its powerful action in the $CaO–Al_2O_3–SiO_2$ system.[26] Its participation in the glaze fusion appears to be characterized by slower action than in the case of the alkalies, with a resultant creamy white opacity and a dull or matt texture if the amount is much increased. A definite tendency toward crazing will be observed if the lime content is high. The most fusible glazes were found by Hill[50] to be those in which there were equiequivalents of calcia and zinc oxides. This observation applied specifically to compositions having an alumina-silica ratio of 1:6. If either lime or zinc oxide were increased in amount beyond a ratio of 3:1, the glazes became more refractory. Calcium fluoride may be used to advantage in glazes up to about 0.05 equivalent for temperatures below cone 7.

Magnesium oxide is generally limited to amounts of about 0.2 or possibly 0.3 equivalent. Larger amounts increase the refractoriness and opacity, and produce stony rather than glassy fusions. Barium oxide may be used in somewhat larger quantities than magnesia, possibly up to 0.4 equivalent, without decreasing fusibility.[51] Hill[52] found that additions of BaO up to 0.40 equivalent produced white matts with sheen, progressively decreasing only slightly, but with fusibility decreasing also. Strontium oxide

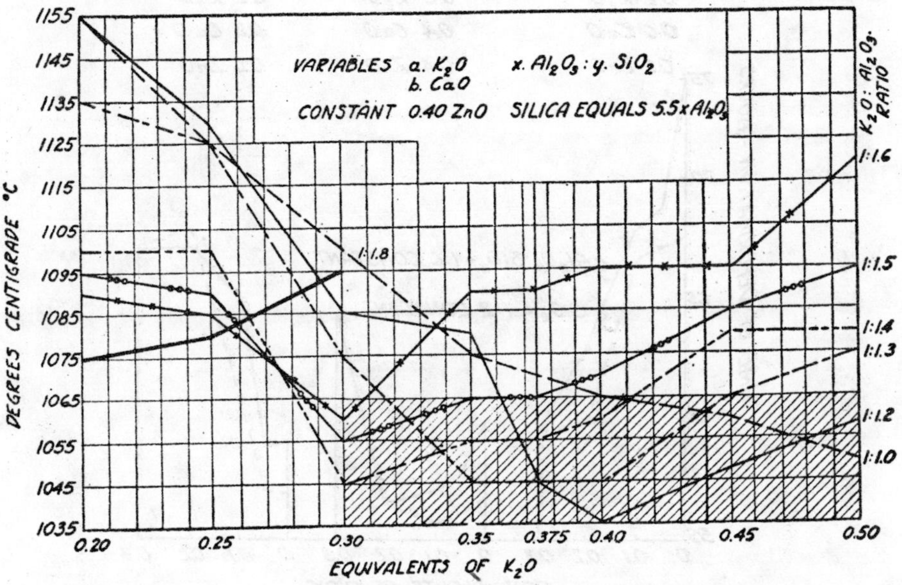

Figure 8.12. Deformation conduct of Bristol glaze compositions having constant content of zinc oxide; other components are variable. The shaded area represents the field of the most fusible compositions.[49]

added, according to Hill,[53] in increments of 0.05 to 0.40 equivalents decreases gloss and fusibility, giving matt texture. Harman and Swift[54] have reported some interesting results.

The most desirable contents of alumina and of silica may be inferred from the data on porcelain glazes reported by Stull and Howat[55] and the study of Bristol glazes on the eutectic basis. These studies clearly show, in a general manner, that increase of silica and alumina increases the refractoriness. It is also clearly evident that eutectic conditions do exist so that one must modify this general conclusion by examining the character and the amount of the bases present and the absolute amount and ratio of the alumina and the silica, which is 1:4 to 1:7 for the usual conditions and temperatures employed in the stoneware and the architectural terra cotta industries.

The influence of additions of clay upon the fusibility has been largely discussed by Purdy[56] and Hill.[57] The latter has found that, with a typical RO group and an Al_2O_3 to SiO_2 ratio of 1:6, the most fusible glazes contained 0.2 equivalent of clay. The most fusible glazes of the whole series were those having a comparatively high silica content and containing 0.05

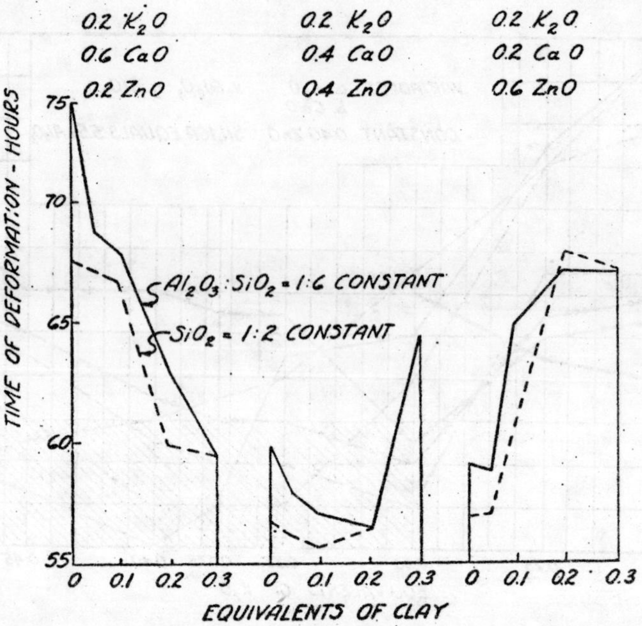

Figure 8.13. Effect of clay on fusibility of Bristol glazes.[57]

and 0.1 equivalent of clay, so that with higher silica contents, the clay content must be considerably lower to yield the most fusible glazes. The effects of varying the clay content of glazes having three different RO contents are illustrated by figure 8.13. Hill[58] says, "In high zinc Bristol glazes any increase of clay decreases the fusibility. It is evident that clay increases the fusibility of the mixtures only when CaO content is 0.40 equivalent or more." The deformation of glazes containing equimolecular quantities of SnO_2, MgO, SiO_2, and BaO was in that order in both high- and low-clay glaze. The BaO produced the least fusible composition.

Heat Range

The most fusible glazes were the least sensitive to firing temperatures. An example was given by Watts[59] that gave good results when fired any place in the range from cone 3 to cone 14.

Opacity and Gloss

Zinc oxide is the member of the RO which is primarily introduced because of its opacifying property. When used in excess of 0.3 equivalent,

Table 8.10. Empirical formulas of some terra cotta and stoneware glazes

No.	KNaO	CaO	ZnO	MgO	BaO	Al_2O_3	SiO_2	Cone	Texture
1	0.165	0.413	0.418	0.004	—	0.25	1.70	1	Matt
2	0.238	0.354	0.21	0.055	0.144	0.43	2.90	4–7	Bright
3	0.20	0.30	0.50	—	—	0.55	3.30	5	Bright
4	0.16	0.44	0.09	—	0.35	0.41	3.7	6	Bright
5	0.16	0.44	0.05	—	0.35	0.37	1.9	6	Matt
6	0.277	0.288	0.145	0.10	0.19	0.35	2.71	6–7	Satin matt enamel
7	0.40	0.20	0.40	—	—	0.47	2.96	6–8	Bright
8	0.3	0.6	0.10	—	—	0.4	3.8	10	Bright

the glaze gains in opacity, whiteness, and gloss but becomes more refractory and liable to "crawl," i.e., separate in patches more or less isolated. The lime content, if sufficiently high, dulls the gloss, gives a creamy white color and a limited degree of opacity. Equiequivalents of calcia and baryta substituted for the alkalies do not affect the gloss appreciably, but baryta substituted alone does. There is no difference in whiteness as the result of this replacement of calcia by baryta up to equiequivalent; beyond that, an increase of baryta produces greater whiteness.[60] At least one-half of the calcia may be replaced by zinc oxide and still produce the maximum gloss. If the calcia is less than required for a maximum gloss, additions of zinc oxide will increase the gloss but no more. If the glaze is overloaded with calcia or zinc oxide, substitutions of baryta will increase the gloss.[61]

If tin oxide replaces calcia, baryta, or zinc oxide, the whiteness increases up to a maximum. The effect of the tin oxides is about equal to baryta in producing a gloss, but if substituted for calcia or zinc oxide, the gloss is diminished. The best gloss was had with the lowest clay content when the alumina-silica ratio was 1:8 or 1:10. The lower feldspar glaze requires the higher ratios for maximum effect.[62]

Examples of several Bristol-type glaze compositions are given in table 8.10. These were used for stoneware and for terra cotta. Included among these are beautiful matt as well as glossy glazes. In general, these glazes were the base glaze for the addition of colorants of various tones. Other terra cotta and stoneware glaze compositions are to be found in references 28, 49, 64, 65, 66, 67, 68, and 69.

Colored Bristol Glazes

The colorants used and the effects produced in Bristol glazes are the same as those discussed under the topic, Porcelain Glazes, with a few notable exceptions. The most important of these is the zinc oxide, which is the most characteristic component of this variety of glaze. It lightens the shade of blue obtained with cobalt oxide.

With the use of the following compositions maturing at cone 5, Pence[63] obtained light browns with 0.005 equivalent of nickel oxide, purplish blues with intermediate amounts, and a light blue with the maximum, 0.02 equivalent:

$0.25K_2O$		
0.14 to $0.28CaO$	$0.30Al_2O_3$	$2.00SiO_2$
0.21 to $0.42BaO$		
0.05 to $0.40ZnO$		

As previously stated, a small amount of zinc oxide is permissible with the chromium oxide in compositions prepared to give greens, but larger amounts produce brownish yellows and further increases give red browns. The presence of magnesia with the zinc and chromium oxides gives pinkish shades in the lower concentrations of the colorant. Bright yellow buffs to brilliant yellows may be had by the proper selection of the amounts of color oxide, the lime, and the zinc oxide. Six percent of the commercial "uranium oxide" (sodium uranate) was used by Squier[20] for this purpose in the following composition: potash feldspar, 53.0%; flint, 18.5%; English ball clay, 4.5%; English china clay, 4.5%; whiting, 6.5% (zinc oxide in varying amounts was substituted for the whiting); and barium carbonate, 13.0% fired at cones 5 to 6 in a muffle kiln. The production of pinks or reds by the use of chromium and tin oxides of the chrome-tin stain cannot be done successfully in the presence of zinc.

Salt Glaze

The salt glaze is a vitreous coating formed on the surface of claywares by subjecting them to the action of an atmosphere of the fumes of common salt at a high temperature during the firing of the wares in the kiln. The method is generally believed to have originated in the vicinity of Cologne, Germany, during the 12th century from whence the ware was distributed under the name of Cologne Ware. About 1690 the Brothers Elers, who were of German origin, introduced the practice into England. Then it spread into the American colonies and became the usual method employed in the stoneware industries, gradually being superseded for household wares, about 1880, by the introduction of the Bristol glaze. However, it has continued to be of very great importance for a large variety of wares, notably chemical stoneware and structural clay products, such as conduits, sewer pipe, hollow building blocks, and other important items. During the 18th century salt glazing was rather extensively employed on whiteware, but the technique was difficult, and the introduction of Queensware displaced the older method.

From time to time potters have sought to improve the appearance of the salt glazed product by applying a slip containing white clay, flint, and feldspar on the surface of the ware before setting it in the kiln. Colors may be used in the slips.

Other salts of soda and related alkalies may be successfully employed in place of common salt, and certain advantages have been claimed in patents covering such practices, but the costs are much greater than for common salt, and it vaporizes at a lower point than any other which is available. Its melting point is 776° C, and it begins to vaporize at a little higher temperature. Cobb[71] has estimated that the rate of volatilization of salt at 800° C is about 6.9% per hour, under the particular conditions of his experiment.

The amount of salt volatilized depends upon its vapor pressure at the temperature used and the amount of air blown through the furnace. If the current of air-containing water vapor is brought into contact with molten salt, it will cause the latter to hydrolyze, and the products will recombine where the temperature is sufficiently low to permit. The reversal of the reaction is accelerated by rapid cooling and not retarded, as in the case of many gaseous systems. Experiments carried on by Thompson[72] showed that a current of dry air, at a temperature of 1,110.7° C, carried 0.0554 grams of salt per liter of air; while air saturated with water vapor at 21.7° C and heated to 1,114.6° C carried 0.078 grams of salt per liter. Hence one-gram molecule of water decomposes 0.37 gram molecule of salt at 1,130° C.

The amount of heat required for volatilization of salt has not been determined, but it has been estimated to be approximately 800–900 units per kilogram, which is considered sufficient to lower the temperature of a kiln by 200–300° C. Salt may be decomposed in the presence of silica without the aid of water vapor. A porous earthenware tube heated in an external atmosphere containing vaporized salt will gradually contain free chlorine in the interior of the tube, and the outer surface will be glazed by the combination of the sodium with the silica and alumina.

It seems to be clear that chlorine set free in the salting action combines partly with hydrogen of the water vapor and partly with iron in the body, as sometimes indicated by the reddish colored fumes escaping from the stack. Further, if a piece of white-burning clay is placed in the kiln, after the firing it will be found coated with a thin reddish glaze. Also, iron-stained sand used for setting of kilns is more or less bleached during the firing.

Glaze Composition

Because of the extreme thinness of the glaze coating formed by salting, it is extremely difficult to obtain a representative sample for chemical analysis. Barringer[73] used thick beads chipped from the edges of ware to determine the composition. On the basis of a study of a series of glazes which were systematic variations of the alkali-alumina-silica content of the analyzed sample, he concluded that the alumina-silica content of clays suited for salt glazing may be found within the range 1:4.6 to 1:12.5. These ratios correspond to the following approximate percentage compositions: silica, 62 to 77.5; alumina, 13 to 12.5; alkalies, etc., 15 to 12.0.

Various formulas have been suggested as representative of the composition of the salt glaze, but the practical difficulties of securing representative samples of such a thin coating from the ware and the acknowledged influence upon the composition by such variables as the wide differences in the chemical nature of the claywares, firing conditions, etc., have aroused much argument regarding the validity of the results. However, the following formulas[74,75,76] have some interest in defining the possible theoretical limits of molecular composition, assuming that soda is the dominant alkali and other bases are negligible, which is untenable. The molecular equivalents are:

Na_2O	$1.0Al_2O_3$	$5.5SiO_2$
Na_2O	$0.5Al_2O_3$	$2.8SiO_2$

Schurecht[77] summarized the benefits of the use of borax or boric acid with salt in the salt glazing process as applied to the manufacture of sewer pipe; it reduces glaze defects; increases the resistance of the glaze coat to gas leakage; increases the strength and therefore resistance to crazing; gives a better gloss; and makes possible the salt glazing of some clays which mature at a temperature too low for the ordinary salt glazing process. Another reagent recommended for the improvement of the glaze is the addition of 0.5 to 5% of zinc chloride, dissolved in water, used to wet the salt.

Salting Process

The process of salting is done by heating the kiln to the temperature necessary for beginning the vitrification of the wares, at which point salt is introduced at intervals in sufficient quantity to bring about the development of the glaze. The temperature range throughout which the salting is done is very wide, as low as cone 02 and as high as cone 12. The usual range is between cones 3 and 8, although the nature of the clay and its vitrification conduct are the determining factors. If salting is done before the clay is vitrified the vapors are absorbed by the body and, as the temperature is subsequently raised, the vapor in the body may expand in the lamination and cause bloating. At the period of salting the clay should still be sufficiently porous so that the salt vapor may penetrate a slight distance below the surface.

Salt is introduced either through openings in the crown of the kiln or, as is the usual practice, by throwing it into the fireboxes. The introduction of salt through the crown of the kiln has the disadvantage of causing suddenly violent vaporization of the salt whose vapors have only a short distance to travel before they escape through the stack. The introduction of salt at the firebox has the advantage of causing the vapors to travel a greater distance before they escape from the kiln, the volatilization is slower, and the salt vapor is brought into contact with any water vapor which is present in the products of combustion. The advantage of this latter condition is apparent from what has previously been stated. The salting process is repeated from time to time until draw trials show that the proper development of glazing has been attained. The frequency and number of saltings is dependent, in a measure, upon the character of the product; for example, sewer pipe, conduits, and similar wares require a much thicker glaze.

KILNS. Both the round and rectangular down-draft kilns, as well as continuous (chamber) and tunnel kilns are used. Important considerations are the construction of the kiln bottom of periodic kilns and the setting of the ware in them so as to have every part of the interior freely open to the salt vapors. Kilns with the well-hole type of flue system are said to be superior to the spider type for developing thick glaze coatings quickly. Uniform distribution of temperature and fumes is highly important.

COAL. A rapid burning fuel is preferred in order to complete the salting as quickly as possible. Coal, oil, and gas are used successfully. When oil or gas is used a few bricks are placed in the firebox so as to form a table upon which the salt is strewn. The use of steam to vaporize the oil is beneficial in developing a good glaze. A clean hot fire is absolutely necessary. Pyrometric cones are of no value as heat indicators after salting begins, since they are seriously affected by the alkaline vapors.

It is the practice in some factories to wet the salt with about 5% of water. This may be an advantage because (1) the small amount of water naturally present with the salt is driven off quite rapidly; (2) the water present or formed by combustion of the fuel is dissipated before the salting begins; and (3) the wetting retards the volatilization of the salt. The addition of a small (5%) amount of coal to the salt is said to promote its dissociation.

AMOUNT OF SALT REQUIRED. The amount of salt required for glazing will depend upon a number of factors, such as: Composition of the clay; kind of ware, since a conduit will present much more surface than a face brick; type of kiln used; method and temperature of firing, including the saltings. Some approximate data which have been published without adequate details of the operations are: 10 to 20 pounds of salt per 1,000 building bricks; 10 to 20 ounces of salt per cubic foot capacity of kiln capacity for fireclay wares; and 2 to 12 pounds of salt per cubic yard capacity of the kiln firing sewer pipe.

Colored Salt Glazes

The color obtained from salt glazing depends upon the character of the kiln atmosphere and the nature of the body. With an oxidizing fire the colors are lighter than with a reducing fire. If flashing is done it will darken the color. It is the practice in some factories to mix crude oil with the salt in order to intensify the color and even to produce a dull black. In this case the color is probably due in part to particles of carbon becoming entrapped in the glaze. A stoneware clay fired under oxidizing conditions will have a greyish color. Buff bodies give light yellow to dark brown; red bodies give dark brown to black. Flashed stoneware clay is reddish brown, increasing in intensity with the repetition of the flashing treatment. In general, reduction is used in developing commercial color, especially on light burning or buff color bodies used for sewer pipe and conduits. Green colors are sometimes obtained due to the presence of lime in such a form and of such a quantity as to produce that effect.

The addition of sand to clays which are deficient has been found to be of value in the development of a good salt glaze.

Schurecht[78] reported on the relations between the content of iron oxide, alumina, and silica in clays and their effect on the formation of color in a good salt glaze. He summarizes the relationship as follows:

White to tan, if the ferric oxide content is not above 1% and the silica is low; or up to 2.19% ferric oxide if the silica is high. (The ferric oxide content is calculated on the basis of calcined clay.)

Light brown, if the silica is low and the ferric oxide does not exceed 3.5%; or with ferric oxide 2.19% to 3.5%, if the silica is high. Brown, if the iron oxide lies between 3.5 to 4.75%. Mahogany, if the iron oxide exceeds 4.75% but is less than 8.2%. Black, if the content of iron oxide is greater than 8.2%.

Clays containing high ferric oxide should be salt glazed at a lower temperature than those low in the same. With the same content of ferric oxide, darker glazes are had with high alumina than with high silica.

The same investigator[79] discussed the effects of the presence of lime upon the color and brightness of the glaze and concluded: that even as little as 1% lime in the clay will prevent the formation of a bright glaze at low temperatures. They can be glazed best at temperatures above cone 5, providing that the content of ferric oxide is low. Clays containing much lime can be glazed at higher temperatures if the iron oxide is not too high (above 3.5%).

Soluble Salts

Clays containing more than 0.1% of soluble salts may be dull and thinly glazed. The more impure weathered clays are likely to show these faults whereas the purer clays may not. The corrective for the soluble salts is the addition of barium carbonate, or barium carbonate and barium chloride, or barium chloride and soda ash. The last named chemical is added after the clay has been pugged about half the usual time with the required amount of chloride, then $\frac{1}{8}$ to $\frac{1}{4}$ of this amount of soda ash is introduced. Black ash, an impure soda ash, is sometimes used together with the purified soda ash. Firing above 975° C under reducing conditions will decompose the harmful soluble salts.

Loam or Earth Glazes

Loam or earth glazes are naturally occurring clays or modifications of the same, which may be had by the addition of necessary fluxes, etc. In the natural form, the preparation for use may not be more extensive than slacking in water and passing through a lawn.

These materials are called "slip clays." They are of glacial origin and are fairly widespread. There is the clay from near Elkhart, Indiana that fuses to a straw-colored product at cone 3. Near Rowley, Michigan there is a similar product that yields a brown-colored glaze. The former Locke Insulator plant at Victor, New York, used one of these clays as a glaze years ago.

Albany slip, mined near Albany, New York, had a better color and a better firing range than these. It seems to have been derived from Ordovician shales rich in illite. The nominal composition[80] of Albany slip resembles the illitic shales from which it was derived. The use of Albany slip in glazes still continues on stoneware and structural clay products. It is low in cost and good.

The ceramic formula of Albany slip was given by Lagenbeck[81] as:

$0.195K_2O$		
$0.459CaO$	$0.608Al_2O_3$	$3.965SiO_2$
$0.345MgO$	$0.081Fe_2O_3$	

Albany slip has several unusual properties as a glaze: it is resistant to crazing and has been said by some never to craze or shiver; it has a very long heat range, it develops a dark glossy brown at about 1,170° C and a brilliant brownish black glaze at 1,210° C to 1,250° C, but at 1,290° C it makes a yellowish brown glaze. It is sensitive to the effect of sulfur oxides in kiln gases; they promote the formation of a film over the glaze surface that has frequently been employed as a coating on draw trials to indicate such contamination as well as to denote progress of the firing.

Stull and Johnson[82] made an interesting report on the methods they employed in utilizing three shales, three surface clays, and two fire clays in the preparation of glazes to be used on the product normally prepared from the respective clay or shale. The chemical analyses were the starting points for experimental procedure which consisted in adjusting the silica and alumina contents, after which the effects of the additions of various fluxes, whiting, and zinc oxide were tried in a systematic manner with satisfactory results. No specific rules can be presented but intelligent experimentation will yield interesting and worthwhile returns for the time spent.

A number of similar clays, have been used in Europe for centuries. Other domestic clays are available or may often be prepared from local materials by the addition of fluxes and coloring materials, carefully wet-grinding the batch, and lawning. Thus it may be possible for a brickmaker to utilize some of the brick clay, properly modified, as a glaze coating for his product. The use of glazes of this sort was very common in the oldtime stoneware industry and still continues for the coating of the interior of crocks, etc. For many years, Albany slip was used alone or in a modified form on electrical porcelain insulators for high voltage service. The following glaze batch, in weight % is reported by Montgomery and Kruson[83] as a typical composition for that purpose: Albany slip, 46.5; feldspar, 37.2; ferric oxide, 4.7; borax, 2.3.

Because Albany slip clay is mined by operators of small pits scattered over an extensive area of the Hudson River Valley between Albany and Catskill, New York, it shows a considerable variation in composition and properties. A chemical analysis, in percentage, which is representative of values commonly reported is shown in the following:[84] silica, 56.75; alumina, 15.47; ferric oxide, 5.73; lime, 5.78; magnesia, 3.23; titania, 1.00 ca.; alkalies, 3.25. Unreported are moisture, ignition loss, etc.

References

1. Laufer, B. 1917. *The beginnings of porcelain in China.* Chicago: Field Museum Publication No. 192.
2. Kerl, B. 1907. *Handbuch der gesammten Tonwaarenindustrie.* Braunchweig, p 1401.
3. Riddle, F. H. 1919. Porcelain for pyrometric purposes. *Bull. Am. Inst. of Min. and Met. Eng.* 153:227.
4. Berdel, E. and Dannheim, G. 1932. Alkali-free glazes. *Ber. Deut. Ker. Ges.* 13:20.

30. Hanna, H. H. 1915. A study of the most fusible mixtures of K_2O–CaO–Al_2O_3–SiO_2. *Trans. Am Ceram. Soc.* 17:672.
31. Funk, op. cit., ref. 15, p. 277.
32. Singer, F. 1923. *Die Keramik*. Braunschweig, p 177.
33. Vogt, G. 1901. *Tonind.-Zeit.* 25:789.
34. Singer, F. *Ceramic glazes*. Los Angeles: Pacific Coast Borax Co.
35. Gould et al. 1937. *J. Am. Ceram. Soc.* 20:195.
36. Greber, E. 1934. *Traite de ceramique*. Paris, p 330.
37. Funk, op. cit., ref. 15, p 306.
38. Seger, H. 1902. Decoration of Japanese and Seger porcelain. *Collected writings*. Vol. 2. New York: Chemical Publishing Co., p 729.
39. Hegemann, H. 1938. *Die Herstellung des porzellans*. 2d ed. rev. by F. Dettmer. Berlin, p 157.
40. Minton, R. H. 1914. Effects of the variation of RO elements upon chromium oxide as the coloring agent in a matt glaze. *Trans. Am. Ceram. Soc.* 16:248.
41. Geijsbeek, C. 1899. Red glazes at high temperatures. *Trans. Am. Ceram. Soc.* 1:62.
42. 1897. Ohio State Geological Survey Report. Vol. 7.
43. Purdy, R. C. 1902. Stoneware glazes. *Trans.. Am. Ceram. Soc.* 4:61.
44. Watts, A. S., 1916. Bristol glazes compounded on a eutectic basis. *Trans. Am. Ceram. Soc.* 18:631.
45. Hanna, H. H. 1915. Study of the most fusible mixtures of K_2O–CaO–Al_2O_3–SiO_2. *Trans. Am. Ceram. Soc.* 17:672.
46. Watts, A. S. 1917. The practical application of Bristol glazes compounded on the eutectic basis. *Trans. Am. Ceram. Soc.* 19:301.
47. Hill, E. C. 1920. Some data on the development of terra cotta glazes. *J. Am. Ceram. Soc.* 3:13.
48. Staley, H. F. 1908. The compounding of frits. *Trans. Am. Ceram. Soc.* 10:113.
49. Purdy, R. C. 1903. Further studies of white Bristol glazes. *Trans. Am. Ceram. Soc.* 5:136.
50. Hill, E. C. 1916. The effect of clay on the fusibility of Bristol glazes. *Trans. Am. Ceram. Soc.* 18:508.
51. Parmelee, C. W. and Heidingsfeld, R. 1912. Note on terra cotta glazes. *Trans. Am. Ceram. Soc.* 14:840.
52. Hill, E. C. 1920. Some data on the development of terra cotta glazes. *J. Am. Ceram. Soc.* 3:13.
53. Ibid.
54. Harman, C. G. and Swift, H. R. 1945. Raw leadless whiteware glazes. *J. Am. Ceram. Soc.* 28:48.
55. Stull, R. T. and Howat, W. L. 1914. Deformation temperatures of some porcelain glazes. *Trans. Am. Ceram. Soc.* 16:454.
56. Purdy, op. cit., ref. 49.
57 Hill. E. C. 1916. The effect of clay on the fusibility of Bristol glazes. *Ceram. Soc.* 18:508.

5. Seger, H. 1902. *Collected writings.* Vol. 2. New York: Chemical Publishing Co. p 708.
6. Kraner, H. M. 1926. Eutectics as glazes. *J. Am. Ceram. Soc.* 9:319.
7. Hainbach, R. 1924. *Pottery decorating.* 2d ed. London: Scott, Greenwood and Son, p 82.
8. Vogt, G. 1909. Function of fluorine in hard fire glazes. *Sprechsaal* 42:345.
9. Kanashima, S. 1917. The application of talc in porcelain glazing. *J. Chem. Ind. Tokyo* 20:850; 1918. *Chem. Abs.* 12:300.
10. Harman, C. G. and Swift, H. R. 1945. Raw leadless whiteware glazes. *J. Am. Ceram. Soc.* 28:48.
11. Rieke, R. and Kunstman, K. E. 1929. Relationship of thermal expansion and softening temperature of porcelain glazes. *Ber. Deut. Ker. Ges.* 10:189.
12. Steger, W. 1927. Heat expansion and annealing temperature of glazes. *Ber. Deut. Ker. Ges.* 8:40.
13. Rieke, R. and Steger, W. 1915. Influence of Al_2O_3-SiO_2 ratio on the properties of porcelain glazes. *Sprechsaal* 48:381.
14. Steger, op. cit., ref. 12.
15. Funk, W. 1933. *Rohstoffe der Feinkeramik.* Berlin, p 304.
16. Rieke, R. 1919. The physical properties of whiteware glazes. *Ber. Tech. Wiss. Abt. Verb. Keram. Gewerke* 5:8.
17. Seger, H. 1902. Defects of glazes and their causes. *Collected writings.* Vol. 2. New York: Chemical Publishing Co., p 557.
18. Stull, R. T. and Howat, W. L. 1914. Deformation temperatures of some porcelain glazes. *Trans. Am. Ceram. Soc.* 16:454.
19. Funk, op. cit., ref. 15, p 304.
20. Stull, R. T. 1912. Influence of silica and alumina on porcelain glazes of constant RO. *Trans. Am. Ceram. Soc.* 14:62.
21. Staley, H. F. Discussion on paper by Stull (ref. 20), p 69.
22. Sortwell, H. H. 1921. High fire porcelain glazes. *J. Am. Ceram. Soc.* 4:718.
23. Twells, R. 1922. The field of porcelain glazes maturing between cones 17 and 20. *J. Am. Ceram. Soc.* 5:430.
24. Kitamura, Y. 1921. Ratio of alumina and silica to RO in porcelain glazes fired at high temperatures. *J. Ind. Chem. Tokyo* 2:89; 1922. *Cer. Abs.*, 1:282.
25. Twells, R. 1923. Further studies of porcelain glazes maturing at high temperatures. *J. Am. Ceram. Soc.* 6:1113.
26. Levin, Ernest M., Robbins, Carl R., and McMurdie, Howard F. 1964. *Phase diagrams for ceramists.* Columbus, Ohio: American Ceramic Society, Inc., p 219.
27. Seger, H. 1902. *Collected writings.* Vol. 2. New York: Chemical Publishing Co. p 708.
28. Montgomery, E. T. and Kruson, I. A. 1914. Colored porcelain glazes at cone 10. *Trans. Am. Ceram. Soc.* 16:347.
29. Bourry, E. 1901. *Treatise on ceramic industries.* Translated by W. P. Rix. London: Scott, Greenwood and Co., p 735.

58. Ibid.
59. Watts, op. cit., ref. 46.
60. Hill, E. C. 1915. White terra cotta glazes at cones 6 and 7. *Trans. Am. Ceram. Soc.* 17:380.
61. Ibid.
62. Ibid.
63. Pence, F. K. 1912. Colors produced by nickel oxide in ceramic mixtures containing zinc. *Trans. Am. Ceram. Soc.* 14:143.
64. Larkin, P. G. 1918. Note on colors produced by the use of soluble metallic salts. *J. Am. Cer. Soc.* 1:429.
65. Wilson, H. 1918. Cobalt-uranium green glaze for terra cotta. *J. Am. Ceram. Soc.* 1:238.
66. Parmelee, C. W. 1907. Note on terra cotta glazes. *Trans. Am. Ceram. Soc.* 9:577.
67. Phillips, G. D. 1914. Terra cotta bodies, slips and glazes. *Trans. Am. Ceram. Soc.* 16:169.
68. Heubach, A. R. 1913. Notes on the cause of mattness in glazes. *Trans. Am. Ceram. Soc.* 15:591.
69. Davis, H. E. 1929. Lepidolite in cone 6 terra cotta glazes. *J. Am. Ceram. Soc.* 12:570.
70. Squier, L. R. 1928. Raw yellow glazes for terra cotta and development phenomena. *J. Am. Ceram. Soc.* 11:584.
71. Cobb, J. W. 1916. Refractory materials and salty coals. *Gas World* (Cooking Section) 64:11.
72. Thompson, M. A. 1917–1918. The dissociation of salt. *Trans. Engl. Cer. Soc.* 17:340.
73. Barringer, L. E. 1902. The relation between the constitution of a clay and its ability to take a good salt glaze. *Trans. Am. Ceram. Soc.* 4:211.
74. Mackler, H. 1905. The nature of salt glazes. *Tonind.-Zeit.* 251:440.
75. Neuman, B. and Fischer, W. 1927. Salt glaze. *Sprechsaal* 60:294, 314, 331, 349.
76. Neuman, B. 1929. Salt glaze. *Sprechsaal* 62:653, 673, 767, 787.
77. Schurecht, H. G. and Wood, K. T. 1942. *The use of borax and boric acid together with salt in salt glazing*. Bull. no. 2, Ceramic Experiment Station, New York State College of Ceramics.
78. Schurecht, H. G. 1923. Clay sewer-pipe manufacture. *J. Am. Ceram. Soc.* 6:717.
79. Schurecht, H. G. 1924. Influence of carrying lime content in clays upon some properties of salt glazes produced at different temperatures. *J. Am. Ceram. Soc.* 7:539.
80. Isaacs, Richard P. 1966. Albany slip clay—50 years later. *Bull. Am. Ceram. Soc.* 45(8):714–15.
81. Lagenbeck, K. 1895. *The chemistry of pottery*. Easton, Pa.: Chemical Publishing Co., p 84.
82. Stull, R. T. and Johnson, Paul V. 1942. Low cost glazes for structural clay products. *Nat. Bur. Std. (U.S.)* C. 436.
83. Montgomery and Kruson, op. cit., ref. 28.
84. Jones, R. W. 1916. Albany slip clay. *Trans. Am. Ceram. Soc.* 18:242.

9

Fritted Glazes

Functions

Fritted glazes constitute a distinct division because of (1) the special preparation due to the incorporation of the frit, (2) the use of water-soluble constituents incorporated in the frit, and (3) the wide choice of temperatures of maturity possible and, therefore, the kinds of wares upon which they may be applied.

Fritted glazes originally were mainly restricted to those maturing below cone 8. This limitation no longer prevails. They are used for their other advantages. Compared with raw glazes they promote: (1) better maturing, (2) more uniformity, (3) significantly less lead toxicity, (4) more uniform constitution, (5) reduction in number of items in storage, and (6) fewer defects, such as pinholes.

The frit is the prefused portion of the material, or a glass which is incorporated as such into the glaze batch. This procedure presents advantages as well as disadvantages. The former may be listed as follows:

1. Water-soluble materials, e.g., alkali carbonates, nitrates, borates, etc., which cannot be employed as such in the glaze slip, but which are converted, together with the other frit members, into an insoluble glass. Soluble salts in the glaze slip are objectionable because the porous biscuit will tend to absorb them, thus altering the composition of the glaze batch in the dipping tub. Also, the soluble salts taken up by the porous biscuit will tend to crystallize during drying upon the edges and raised ornaments, which will make these parts burn more densely and thus cause glaze troubles later. Further, these soluble salts when present will have a disturbing effect upon the colors used, tending to spread them unevenly.
2. Materials which are slow to react at low temperatures, such as barium

Figure 9.1. Fritted glaze for vitrified china over underglaze print decoration. Lead glazes are used.

compounds, become vigorous fluxes as components of the frit. The wider choice and larger amounts of powerful fluxes permissible through fritting permit a more extensive range of temperatures for maturity and a better choice of colors.

3. Glaze materials that may be objectionable, because contact with them

is harmful to some persons, may be safely used as members of properly constructed frits.

4. The frit is a highly concentrated portion of the glaze batch, less bulky than the corresponding portion of the raw materials, less active chemically because the thermal processes of dissociation and reaction have been completed; therefore, the attack on the body and the underglaze colors, if they be used, is minimized. Further, the fritted glaze is applied more thinly and, consequently, fits the contours of the ware more closely.
5. Homogeneity can be had by fritting, thus preventing the segregation of any batch constituents because of marked differences in density, size, shape, or hardness of the particle. This has a great importance in assuring a uniform distribution of colors by preventing specking, mottling, etc. It is said that greater brilliance of color is obtained.

An example of the difficulty experienced in the suspension of a glaze batch in water due to segregation is found in the use of lead compounds in raw glaze. Such mixtures must be well agitated before and during the application on the ware, otherwise the heavy ingredients will settle promptly. On the other hand, if the lead compounds and a suitable proportion of the other ingredients are fritted together, the resultant glass has less density and consequently remains in suspension with comparative ease. Satisfactory results cannot be had by casually mixing silica and alumina with the lead compounds and fritting. While the mixture may melt and flow readily at low temperatures, yet the frit may be so fluid as to be absorbed too easily by porous bodies upon which it is applied. Further, the progressive melting of the unfritted portions of the glaze will proceed with more uniformity and with better end results if there is a proper distribution in the quality of the frit and control of its temperature of melting as contrasted with the refractory members.

The elimination of a large portion of the gases evolved from the glaze materials by a premelting is a distinct gain, since thereby an important cause of bubbles and blisters is removed; but the presence of some raw clay in the batch permits the formation of seeds, i.e., fine bubbles.

Typical of the applications for fritted glazes are the manufacture of wall tile and decorative tile, such as shown in figure 9.1, and sanitary ware illustrated in figure 9.2. These glazes are likely to be lead-bearing and lead-free, respectively.

Rules Governing the Preparation of Frits

The two chief reasons for the use of frits are: (1) to permit the introduction of water-soluble materials into the glaze batch and (2) to render

Figure 9.2. Sanitary ware manufacturers now employ the one-fire technique, using a frit-bearing feldspathic type of glaze.

toxic materials harmless for the protection of persons engaged in using them in the preparation or the application of such glazes on wares.

Solubility

All materials having a notable solubility in water must be incorporated in the frit. These are the usual alkali salts, such as the carbonates, the nitrates, the chlorides (rarely used) of soda and potash, and the rarely used corresponding compounds of lithia as well as boric acid, and the alkali borates of which sodium borate, or borax, is customary. All these bases and the boric acid are powerful fluxes and have very important influences upon the physical properties of glazes. Calcium carbonate has an appreciable water solubility and magnesium oxide and carbonate have much more, but the inclusion of the first named in the frit is optional, while the effect of the latter in the raw batch is generally considered as insignificant insofar as the viscosity of the completed glaze in the dipping tub is concerned.

Solubility of Alkaline Silicates

Since the compounds formed by the reaction of silica and the alkali bases are readily soluble, it is imperative that there be present, in addition to the alkalies, one or more bases which by themselves form insoluble silicates. Such bases are the alkaline earths: calcium, magnesium, strontium, and barium. Either alone or with the alkaline earths the oxides of lead, zinc, etc. may be employed with the alkalies for the same purpose.

Aluminum Oxide

Aluminum oxide may be used with the alkalies in amounts not exceeding 0.1 or 0.2 molecular equivalents because it strongly increases the refractoriness and viscosity.

Ratio of Alkalies to the Other RO Members

In order to insure a low solubility, the total molecular amount of alkalies in the frit should not much exceed 50% of the total RO. Their molecular ratio to the other members should not be greater than in the completed glaze; otherwise some other insoluble form of the alkalies must be added to the latter, for example, feldspar.

Ratio of the Alkalies to the Boric Acid

Since borax ($Na_2B_4O_7 \cdot 10H_2O$) is the borate generally used, it is most practical to have the ratio of soda to boric oxide the same in the frit as in the glaze; otherwise some other insoluble compounds of these oxides must be found for use in the mill batch, which, in all probability, will require another frit or, possibly, the use of certain commercial glasses. This is a general principle applicable to other possible like situations.

Acid Members of the Frit

According to present day practice, silica is the indispensable acid member of the frit, boric oxide is commonly present, and there are a few

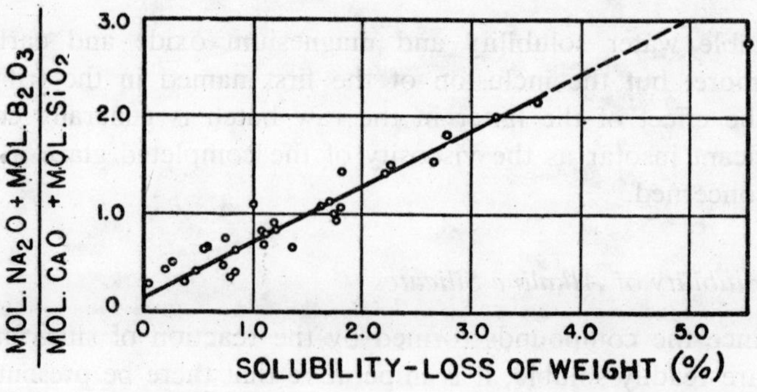

Figure 9.3. Solubility and composition $Na_2O–CaO–B_2O_3–SiO_2$.[1]

other oxides which conceivably might be used. The silica promotes water insolubility, but, for a fusion to have a practicable fluidity and a relatively low melting point, the molecular equivalents of silica should not fall below a ratio of 1:1.5 and should not exceed 1:3 with respect to the bases. The presence of boric acid will markedly increase the fusibility and the fluidity. It need not exceed 0.8 molecular equivalents for ordinary requirements,

Table 9.1. Results of water solubility and pH determinations[1]

Frit No.	*Solubility (%)*	*pH*	*Frit No.*	*Solubility (%)*	*pH*	*Frit No.*	*Solubility (%)*	*pH*
12	0.05	7.7	30	1.27	10.8	17a	0.16	8.4
13	0.38	9.0	31	0.74	9.0	18a	0.17	8.4
14	0.19	8.1	32	1.11	8.9	19a	0.43	9.6
15	0.50	9.1	33	1.06	8.9	20a	0.56	9.4
17	0.51	8.7	34	1.16	9.1	21a	0.84	9.5
18	0.29	8.7	35	1.78	9.6	24a	0.29	8.4
19	0.90	9.2	36	2.21	9.2	31a	1.24	9.0
20	1.42	9.5	37	1.59	9.1	33a	0.96	8.9
21	1.73	9.4	38	2.62	9.2	34a	0.91	9.4
23	0.78	8.9	39	3.55	9.2	35a	1.04	9.2
24	0.54	8.6	40	1.68	9.0	36a	1.69	9.2
	0.56		41	1.81	9.1	37a	1.18	9.6
25	0.86	9.1	42	2.80	9.1	40a	1.55	9.1
26	0.84	9.7	43	2.30	8.9	43a	0.08	9.0
27	1.23	9.2	44	3.20	9.0	45a	2.70	9.1
28	1.10	10.1	45	5.51	9.1	43b	0.19	8.9
29	1.72	10.3	12a	0.08	7.7	45b	2.71	9.1
	1.71	10.3	13a	0.29	8.7	43c	0.99	8.8
30	1.23		14a	0.15	8.5	45c	1.95	9.0
	1.24	11.0	15a	0.12	8.4	–	–	–

Notes: Check values are recorded in a few cases. It is thought that these results are fairly reliable. Those from nos. 13, 17, 23, and 25 seem to be in error but these were some of the glasses showing the presence of undissolved material.

and, in order to keep the water solubility low, the ratio of the boric oxide to the silica should not be more than 1:2.

Solubility Ratio

According to published data[1] assembled from experimental study of 75 frits, the water solubility of a frit is roughly proportional to the molecular ratio:

$$\frac{\text{moles of } Na_2O + \text{moles of } B_2O_3}{\text{moles of } CaO + \text{moles of } SiO_2}$$

This relationship is shown graphically in figure 9.3. In this series, the results are shown by the diagonal line representing the focus of points on the graph. The percent water solubilities are expressed in the equation:

$$\text{Solubility } (\%) = -0.23 + 1.703\left(\frac{\text{moles of } Na_2O + \text{moles of } B_2O_3}{\text{moles of } CaO + \text{moles of } SiO_2}\right)$$

In view of the results of the studies of some investigators who have reported on glasses of other compositions, the conclusions given above may have only a limited application. Further studies are needed.

A comparison of the water solubilities of the frits shown in table 9.1 and their molecular compositions may be had by reference to figure 9.4.

Small additions of alumina (in the order of 0.1 equiv.) may be ex-

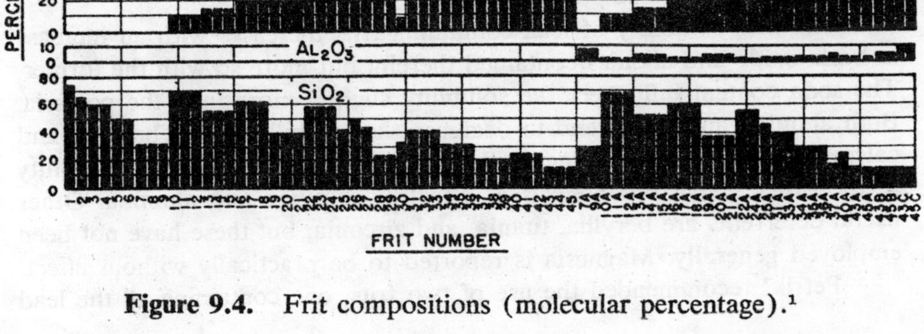

Figure 9.4. Frit compositions (molecular percentage).[1]

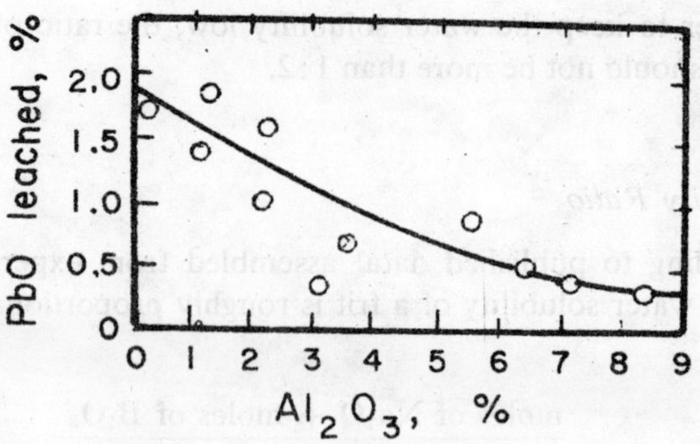

Figure 9.5. Leachability of lead from $PbO–Al_2O_3–SiO_2$ frits.[5]

pected to reduce the solubility about one-half. A frit of low solubility can be produced without the introduction of alumina.

Solubility of Lead-containing Frits

The toxic effects of soluble lead compounds and the sensitivity of some persons to contact with them has been widely discussed by writers on industrial or occupational diseases. Recognition of the serious nature of the problem is common in the ceramic industry; the generally practiced method of dealing with the glaze phase aspect is to introduce the element as a component of a frit having a negligible water solubility, in which case the completed glaze will presumably, also be nontoxic. In the latter case, resistance of the glaze to attack by weak organic acids, e.g., the acids encountered in fruits and vegetables, is more important. However, there is a fairly close parallelism between water and acid solubility, with the latter being of a greater order of magnitude. The topic of glaze and frit solubility has been discussed frequently in technical literature. A paper by Koenig[2] is one rather complete discussion. Summarizing briefly the conclusions stated by the author as well as those of some other researchers, the following principles seem to be proved.

The acid solubility of lead-containing frits increases with an increase in boric oxide and alkalies contained therein, but more so with the former. The soda content influences the solubility slightly more than the potassia. Both alumina and silica tend to decrease the solubility. Zinc, barium, and calcium oxides are increasingly effective in decreasing the lead solubility in the order given, but none is as effective as silica and alumina. Other useful deterrents are beryllia, titania, and zirconia, but these have not been employed generally. Magnesia is reported to be practically without effect.

Petrik[3] recommended the use of two frits, one containing all the lead oxide with no alkali or boric acid and the second frit containing these, but no lead. Thereby, the solution of lead from the glaze batch will be greatly reduced. Koenig concurs, saying, "this is most highly recommended."

Currier[4] worked out a precise method for determining the lead solubility of frits. He prepared and used a set of simple frits containing 60% to 65% of PbO, 30% to 35% of SiO_2, and 0.12% to 8.25% of Al_2O_3. He leached these with a 0.50% hydrochloric acid solution at 40° C. There was a crude correlation between the lead extracted and the Al_2O_3 content of the frit as shown in figure 9.5.

A great variety of frit compositions is available, having correspondingly wide differences in usefulness. Four lead-silica frits with total lead contents, lead solubility (of particles of the frit through 150-mesh and remaining on 200-mesh sieves), and melting characteristics as taken from Koenig[2] are shown in table 9.2.

Lead-aluminum silicates have been studied by numerous investigators. Lu[5] has offered the following as the formula of the deformation eutectic of the system:

$$PbO:0.254Al_2O_3:1.91SiO_2$$

Koenig[2] prepared a frit of this composition and reported that the initial formation of the glass appears at 730° C; complete fusion is at 770° C; at 1,150° C viscosity is comparable to that of a light oil. It is about sixfold more resistant to acid than the bisilicate. In fritting conduct, degree of viscosity, and nonsolubility, it is superior to the bisilicate and other silicates mentioned above.

Crawling on one edge of two-fired wall tile was traced to excessive B_2O_3 solubility in a frit.[6] The tile setter was so constructed that in drying most of the glaze moisture was removed from one edge of the sprayed tile with the result that a concentration of any soluble salts would be present along this edge. The trouble was not visible on dried tile, but crawling was experienced on fired tile along this exposed edge.

The frit showed a B_2O_3 solubility of 0.245%. A similar frit, having

Table 9.2. $PbO-SiO_2$ frits and their lead solubilities.[2]

Frits	Total % PbO	Percent of total PbO dissolved	Melting temps ° C. Initial glass	Melting temps ° C. Complete fusion
Lead orthosilicate, $2PbO \cdot SiO_2$	81.82	96.01	–	764
Lead monosilicate, $PbO \cdot SiO_2$	73.15	50.35	700	765
Lead bisilicate, $PbO \cdot 2SiO_2$	60.02	9.67	700	890
Lead trisilicate $PbO \cdot 3SiO_2$	51.36	43.57	–	–

Table 9.3. Experimental frits and their solubility[6]

Frit No.	K_2O	*CaO*	*PbO*	Al_2O_3	B_2O_3	SiO_2	*Soluble* B_2O_3*, %*
A	0.250	0.376	0.374	0.187	0.875	1.741	0.245
1	0.250	0.376	0.374	0.187	0.875	2.000	0.168
2	0.250	0.376	0.374	0.187	0.875	2.500	0.126
3	0.250	0.376	0.374	0.187	0.700	1.741	0.140
4	0.250	0.376	0.374	0.250	0.875	1.741	0.123
5	0.250	0.376	0.374	0.300	0.875	1.741	0.096
6	0.250	0.376	0.374	0.200	0.500	2.000	0.046
7	0.250	0.376	0.374	0.200	0.400	2.000	0.032

a B_2O_3 solubility of only 0.032%, was used and the crawling disappeared. The crawling could be made to reappear by adding H_3BO_3 to the glaze batch.

A family of experimental glazes in which the Al_2O_3, SiO_2 and B_2O_3 were varied, resulted in B_2O_3 solubility as shown in table 9.3.

Koenig[2] found that the fineness of the frit increased the solubility, but there was no compensating improvement in the texture of the finished glaze. The best results were to be had only after careful adjustment of the milling on the basis of systematic trials.

Lead Release Investigation

Because of the isolated instances of lead intoxication resulting from the use of improperly formulated or improperly fired lead glazes, The United States Potters Association of East Liverpool, Ohio, and International Lead Zinc Research Organization, Inc., New York, N.Y., jointly commissioned and sponsored a research program to develop sound data on the proper formulation and firing temperatures required to minimize the release of lead from lead-containing glazes. A manual[7] was published which established the following facts:

1. Dinnerware glazes showed very low lead release.
2. Lead release was less than 0.5 PPM.
3. Typical commercial stains did not increase solubility.
4. Direct addition of copper oxide was detrimental, especially in low-temperature glazes.
5. Opacifiers did not promote lead release and in some cases aided insolubility of lead.
6. Alkali oxides and earth oxides did not effect solubility of lead. An increase of B_2O_3 increased release. ZnO did not increase release.
7. In lead silicate-base low-temperature glazes (cone 07), small single

alkali oxide additions increased lead release as follows: Li_2O least, Na_2O intermediate, and K_2O most. Mixtures increased the release at a lower rate.

8. In a cone 03 glaze ($PbO \cdot 1.5SiO_2$ base), increasing Al_2O_3 lowered the lead release, B_2O_3 increased lead release and ZrO_2 additions increased acid resistance.
9. A cone 4–5 dinnerware glaze with 0.10PPM release showed 0.06PPM release after the eighth test. A cone 05 glaze containing CuO showed progressive decrease in repeated tests.
10. Lead release increased with glaze thickness, decreased with longer firing time, decreased with higher temperatures. Differences in 4–5 cone dinnerware glazes were inconclusive, being so small. In low-temperature glazes the differences were measurable.

"The base glaze used in the above-referenced work[7] is of interest since it was typical of the clear glaze used on commercial hotel china. The base glaze, given below, was the average composition of five different commercial hotel china glazes.

$0.066K_2O$		
$0.179Na_2O$	$0.340Al_2O_3$	$3.369SiO_2$
$0.261PbO$	$0.314B_2O_3$	
$0.494CaO$		

All of the above base glaze composition was fritted except the necessary mol. equivalent of Al_2O_3 and SiO_2 to provide a ten percent (10%) mill addition. This glaze was then applied on hotel china bisque cups and fired to cone 5 in a commercial glost fire. The lead release from this glaze and from commercial glazes on cups from two hotel china producers, using the standard test, is given in table 9.4. As might have been expected from earlier data, the lead release from this clear cone 5 glaze and from the two commercial hotel china glazes was very low."

Table 9.5,[8] which gives the empirical formula and weight percentage formula of six cone 06 acid-resistant glazes, is of interest to potters of artware and to hobbyists.

Table 9.4. Lead release from base glaze and two commercial hotel china (HC) glazes[7]

Glaze	*Lead PPM*	
	Individual data	*Average*
Base glaze (from text)	0.18,0.14	0.16
Commercial HC glaze 1	0.31,0.24,0.27	0.27
Commercial HC glaze 2	0.12,0.08,0.05	0.08

Note: HC = hotel china

Table 9.5. Cone 06 acid-resistant glazes (90% frit and 10% kaolin)[8]

	Empirical Formula of Glaze							
	Na_2O	CaO	SrO	PbO	Al_2O_3	B_2O_3	SiO_2	ZrO_2
1	0.05	0.06	–	0.89	0.27	0.15	2.58	0.01
2	0.10	0.14	–	0.76	0.27	0.32	2.69	0.02
3	0.05	0.07	0.22	0.72	0.27	0.24	2.68	0.01
4	0.16	0.21	–	0.63	0.28	0.49	2.80	0.03
5	0.10	0.13	0.14	0.62	0.27	0.36	2.65	0.02
6	0.16	0.20	0.08	0.56	0.27	0.51	2.78	0.03
	Weight Percent Formula of Glaze							
1	0.78	0.93	–	49.53	6.96	2.71	38.83	0.25
2	1.61	1.92	–	42.69	7.03	5.55	40.67	0.52
3	0.81	0.96	5.78	40.51	7.11	4.22	40.34	0.26
4	2.49	2.94	–	35.71	7.11	8.54	42.61	0.80
5	1.64	1.96	3.89	36.47	7.13	6.63	41.74	0.53
6	2.51	2.97	1.97	32.31	7.14	9.12	43.17	0.81

Note: While all of these glazes are clear, numbers 1, 2, and 3 develop a slight yellowish cast. Formulations 4, 5 and 6 are clear and colorless.

Proportion of Frit to Be Used

The general rules governing the composition of the frit have been given, but there still remains the important problem of apportioning the mill batch. This is a matter of considerable consequence, since experience has shown that glazes of the same ultimate chemical composition, made with the same materials and fired under similar conditions, may give results which vary from excellent to useless. They may be clear or opaque, glossy or matt, free from or filled with bubbles and blisters, all depending upon the correct selection and division of the materials. Mellor[9] was of the opinion that the proportion of the frit in the mill batch should be such that the glaze shall have completed its action on the body at the same time that the surface has attained its best gloss, because unnecessarily prolonged firing will diminish the lead content by volatilization and consequently diminish the gloss. Steger[10] found that variations in the apportioning of the glaze materials between the frit and the raw mill batch may result in differences in the stresses existing between the body and the glaze of the magnitude of 100%. Also, the rate of change of these stresses with varying temperatures will be different. Of course, such differences may be expected to cause crazing. A high frit content may make the glaze less sensitive to temperature differences in the glost kiln than does a low frit content.[11] The former causes the glaze to become fluid at a lower temperature without being unduly so as the temperature rises. On the other hand, it is easier to make emergency corrections in the mill if the frit does not constitute a very large proportion of the mix.

Calcium

The division of the lime content between the frit and the mill batch deserves careful consideration. Its useful function in diminishing the solubility of the frit has been mentioned; however, glazes containing very easily soluble frits are more difficult to keep in suspension during storing or aging because of the increased tendency to settle and, therefore, require more frequent agitation to insure homogeneity. On the other hand, if its solubility is very slightly increased, i.e., if it has a higher pH value, the glaze may settle to the degree that it is difficult to bring it back to a proper resuspension.[1] The experience of the glaze maker is analogous to that of the makers of vitreous enamels for metals, since it has been reported by Andrews[12] and Harrison[13] that the change in the consistency of slips which alter during storing is a function of the solubility of the frit therein, and that the change is greater in one containing a frit of high water solubility. The problem is quite involved because not only the lime and other alkaline earths but also alkalies and boric acid are dissolved from frits, and each has an important role in any particular case. The fineness of the frit, the temperature of storage, and the time are also important factors.

Another important item entering into the consideration of the division of the lime content between the frit and the mill batch is the possible corrosive action on the refractories (crucibles and linings) with which the frit materials are in contact during its fusion. The effect of the corrosive action of a number of frits is shown graphically[1] by figure 9.6. The compositions of these frits is shown in figure 9.4. The attack on the refractories was very noticeable when the sum of the moles of soda and lime was equal to or greater than the moles of silica. It is to be expected that the soda will be more active than the lime, and has so been reported, but the latter seems to be more active when the silica content was low, but less effective than the soda in reacting with large amounts of the silica. To prevent excessive corrosion of the refractory linings, the silica content of the frit should exceed 1.5 mol. equivalent. The fluidity of the frit (fig. 9.7) is a function of the composition and an important factor in corrosion.

The relatively lower density of precipitated calcium carbonate makes it an excellent deterrent to the settling of the suspended particles of the glaze slip; moreover, its solubility and alkaline character tend to correct

Figure 9.6. Crucible corrosion.[1]

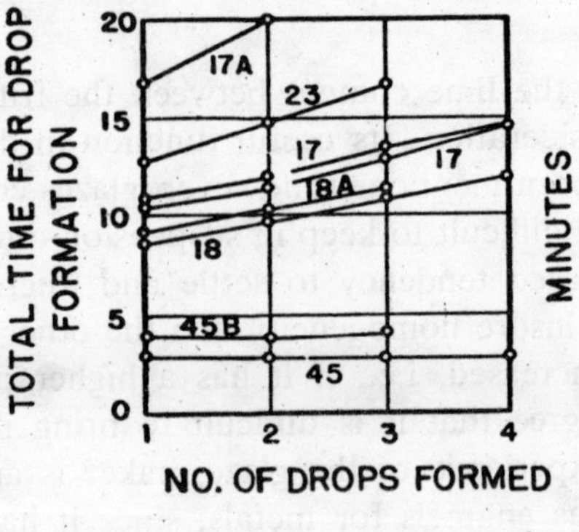

Figure 9.7. Relative fluidity of certain frits as shown by the formation of drops.[1]

acidity and consequent flocculation. The presence of some unfritted lime in the glaze batch is recommended as a good protection against the harmful effects of the oxides of sulfur present in the kiln gases during firing. However, as previously stated, the reaction of large quantities of the lime with silica is described as slow, which probably means that the temperature must be higher and the time longer. In any case, dull edges, loss of gloss, opacity, and pinholes may mar the glaze[14] if the amount of lime is excessive.

Barium

It is reasonable to expect that the use of barium carbonate is subject to similar restrictions. Steger[15] considered barium as second to lead in action as a fluxing agent and it conducts itself so in glasses and glazes. In the latter case, it is used in the frit of low-temperature compositions with very satisfactory results, and the same is true also of medium and high temperatures. When used unfritted, there is a strong tendency to produce dull or matt textures unless the composition is carefully chosen. The strong corrosive action of barium glasses on the refractory crucibles and pots is a well-known and significant illustration of the element's fluxing action. The toxic action of some of the barium compounds used by the potter is an excellent reason for introducing them as components of frits. Used under proper conditions, the barium enhances the gloss of the glaze.

The above listed rules and citations may be compared with the formulas of the frits given in table 9.6 and the range of compositions in table 9.7.[1] The latter have been compiled from the extensive literature published in books and various ceramic journals.

Although we do not have before us the mill additions for these sepa-

Table 9.6. Commercial frit compositions (molecular equivalents)[1]

No.	*Na_2O*	*K_2O*	*CaO*	*PbO*	*B_2O_3*	*Al_2O_3*	*SiO_2*
1	0.05	0.09	0.76	0.10	0.67	0.09	1.80
2	0.239	[illegible]	0.536	–	0.478	0.226	2.48
3	0.081	0.050	0.767	0.107	0.710	0.095	1.93
4	0.053	0.065	0.493	0.390	0.737	0.099	2.005
5	0.065	0.043	0.810	0.083	1.117	0.076	1.599
6	0.061	0.089	0.573	0.278	0.372	0.144	1.931
7	0.072	0.037	0.785	0.107	0.677	0.081	2.185
8	0.279	0.023	0.699	–	0.548	0.242	2.372
9	0.279	0.010	0.382	0.329	2.31	0.295	7.53
10	0.081	0.049	0.763	0.109	0.710	0.095	1.713
11	0.284	0.017	0.699	–	0.549	0.298	2.54
12	0.27	0.04	0.69	–	0.54	0.27	2.53
13	0.360	0.088	0.552	–	4.691	0.160	6.265
17	0.194	0.033	0.194	0.580	0.230	0.065	2.44
				MgO			
14	0.365	0.067	0.477	0.091	1.000	0.149	3.000
15	0.278	0.023	0.699		0.547	0.274	2.56
16	0.267	0.027	0.680	0.010	0.545	0.266	2.576

rate compositions, there is sufficient evidence that the compounding of frits and the proportioning of the mill additions have been and seemingly remain fruitful topics for study. Under special and limited circumstances, all the glaze batch may have to be fritted, but normally enough raw clay, preferably of the light color ball-clay type, and the excess of the flint above that needed in the frit, together with portions of easily floating materials such as whiting, zinc oxide, etc., are reserved for the mill addition. Nearly a century ago Purdy and Fox[16] stated that "there was neither law nor general custom in this matter." They adopted, in the research described, the practice of incorporating in the frit (1) all of the alkaline salts including feldspar; (2) all the boracic acid and borax; (3) all but 0.05 equivalents of the required clay; (4) all but 0.10 of the total calcium oxide; (5) all

Table 9.7. Range of compositions of frits expressed as molecular equivalents[1]

Base	*Neutral*	*Acid*
0.08–0.96 Na_2O		
0.00–0.43 K_2O		
0.18–0.90 CaO	0.00–1.50 B_2O_3	0.08–6.40 SiO_2
0.00–0.01 MgO*	0.00–0.64 Al_2O_3	0.00–0.41 SnO_2
0.00–0.17 BaO		
0.00–0.78 PbO		

*Impurity.

of the free aluminum oxide; (6) only sufficient silica to maintain the required oxygen ratio. Further, they concluded that the frit should constitute at least 50% by weight of the glaze. At a somewhat earlier date, Kerl[17] made the following statement:

> "It is most important that all the lead as well as the calcium carbonate and soluble constituents of the glaze with the amount of sand necessary for the formation of a bisilicate (without reference to the boric acid) are melted together and the necessary feldspar and kaolin as well as the remainder of the sand are ground with the frit. The quantity of the raw materials shall, however, at the most, be 20% in order that the glaze may be easily fusible. With more than 20% raw material, one fuses the excess of the mass with the frit."

Another ceramist of wide experience, Dr. W. Pukall,[18] prescribes the following practice in the distribution of the glaze materials between the frit and the mill batch:

> "The frit contains, besides silica, alumina, lime, magnesia, all those constituents of the batch which are separately soluble in water, as well as boric acid. . . . For the mill addition, about 20% of the batch should be retained, that is, not included in the frit. Those insoluble materials which not only remain in suspension in water best and longest, but also dissolve readily in the frit at a low temperature, are selected . . . . The others, especially the lime materials like marble, chalk, calcite, are not easily soluble (in the fusion) at kiln temperatures below cone 02*a* (1,060° C, or equiv. to the Orton Standard cone 04/03 temperature interval). Therefore, these substances are, when practicable, not included in the mill additions, and seldom left unfritted."

The desirability of including the lead compounds in the frit batch has been stated. On the other hand, the presence of unfritted lead compounds in the mill batch aids in the solution of the free calcium carbonate, whereas the lead in the fritted condition is not so effective.

Functions of the Oxides

With one exception, the oxides used in fritted glazes and their functions are the same as in the unfritted (omitting vapor glazes) and that exception is boric oxide. It is possible to introduce boric oxide into a glaze in the form of a water insoluble mineral borate, such as colemanite, a calcium borate. Of course, fritting of all or part of a glaze batch, free from boric oxide or borates, may be necessary if other water soluble constituents must be used. Boric oxide rivals lead oxide in its influence upon the fusing conduct, the strong solvent action upon other oxides, and the optical properties and mechanical properties. With its use, it is possible to prepare glazes for the minimum practicable temperatures, e.g., cone 015, at this time. In the allied field of vitreous enamels, it is almost indispensable for the low temperatures used. While it is little used in glazes designed for the upper temperature levels, yet it is not without importance in some special cases. The use of borax as a flux in glass was known in Babylonia and the technique of frits was known in Egypt and elsewhere very early.

Boron is a glass former and its chemical conduct, in general, is analogous to that of silicon; consequently the position of the oxide in the ceramic formula was formerly associated with the silica. The essential differences, as Seger[19] saw them, were an increase in fusibility and an increase in cloudiness (opalescence) with large replacements of silica by boric oxide. Some years later Purdy and Fox[16] pointed out the similarity of conduct, in some important details, between boric oxide and alumina in glazes. This was supported by Binns[20] and especially by Singer.[21] The latter cited these important facts as substantiating the similarity:

1. The substitution of boric oxide for molecular equivalents of alumina in matt glazes does not change the textural character of the glaze, although it lowers the maturing temperature.
2. Both alumina and boric oxide alter the turquoise blue color of alkaline glazes containing copper in the same manner, changing it to a dirty greenish blue.
3. The color of cobalt-blue glazes is intensified through the replacement of half of the cobalt by alumina; the substitution of boric oxide is more effective.

Other interesting citations were made in support of his views. At this time, there is no general agreement regarding the location of the boric oxide in the ceramic formula, but the American practice inclines towards Binns' suggestion that it should be considered as more closely related to the sesquioxide or amphoteric status. When so placed, the calculation of the ratio of bases to silica in useful glazes causes them to fall within the prescribed bisilicate and trisilicate position as they should. The observation made by Purdy and Fox,[16] that an important function of boric oxide, like alumina, is to prevent devitrification, points out another resemblance.

The effects of the individual RO oxides are not different in the fritted from that observed in the unfritted glaze, but the amounts and choice of the alkalies are extended to promote fusibility with or without the use of lead oxide or boric oxide. The importance of this is realized in the development of colored glazes and the use of over and underglaze decoration. This greater freedom is exhibited in the wider ranges of the oxides of magnesium and barium used in some kinds of borosilicate glazes.

Attention[22] has recently been directed to the value of strontium oxide as a component of the borosilicate glazes. Since increasing the number of the RO group members usually has the effect of improving the mechanical properties, i.e., strength, elasticity, etc., also lowering the fusion temperature and extending the maturing range, the addition of strontia may be expected to be of value. While the complete replacement of the CaO is considered as impracticable, a partial replacement in the frit batch decreased the deformation temperature, water solubility, and the viscosity, but increased the acid solubility. There was little change in the thermal expansion. The replacement of the lead oxide by the strontia had the contrary effects as well as increasing the thermal expansion. The acid solubility was decreased. The substitution of strontia for zinc acted in a manner similar to lead but in a lesser degree, excepting that the viscosity and the water solubility were decreased. Strontia is particularly effective in leadless and low-lead glazes, and glazes maturing at low temperatures.

Swift[23] has found that the fluxing of strontia in low-temperature fusing borosilicate glasses is superior as compared with the influence of baria and lead oxide, if the alumina content is low and a relatively large amount of fluorspar is used. This condition he attributes to the high solubility of the fluorides in the strontia glasses—then the two fluxes act to form very fusible melts. In the presence of lead the fluoride is less soluble and therefore less effective. The combined effect of lead oxide plus a small quantity of fluorspar is less than the action of strontia plus a greater quantity of fluorspar in solution. Glasses containing barium oxide are intermediate in fluoride solubility and in fusibility. A substitution of strontia for lead oxide in low-temperature borosilicate glasses may either decrease the fusibility, if the fluorspar is low and the alumina is high, or increase the fusibility, if the alumina is low and the fluorspar is moderately high.

Alumina, Boric Oxide, and Silica

An inspection of the formulas of fritted borosilicate glazes reported here and in other literature reveals wide variations of alumina, boric oxide, and silica and no apparent significant relationship between any two or three oxides. Purdy and Fox,[16] using a specific RO group, observed a similarity of conduct between the effects of the alumina and the boric oxide with respect to crazing and devitrification and deduced certain conclusions, referred to further on. Binns[20] sought to clarify the matter by attributing amphoteric properties to the boron and therefore placing the oxide with the alumina in the molecular equivalent formula. Stull and Radcliffe,[24] using only one RO composition in their experiments, obtained results which led them to propose that the "clear," opalescent, and crazing tendencies of the glazes will depend respectively upon the existence of the boric oxide as combined, present in a "solid solution," or uncombined. Since the term solid solution has an entirely different connotation and since the present conception of a glaze does not recognize the existence of chemical compounds, as such, in the glaze, their conclusions appear to be untenable.

Alumina increments increase the viscosity and the maturing temperature; although Purdy and Fox[16] observed that the effect was not of the same order below 0.25 mol. equiv. They found, also, that the largest index of refraction, hence gloss, was had when the alumina was 0.20 mol. equiv. or more. The alumina content has a marked influence upon the amount and character of the crazing, generally decreasing the fault. The glazes having less than 0.10–0.20 equiv. alumina most vigorously attacked the body (a porous white tile).

Purdy and Fox, using one RO composition, found that the longest heat ranges were had with compositions in which the ratio of SiO_2 to B_2O_3 varied as 1 to 0.17 to 0.25. An examination of the published compositions as compiled in table 9.8 shows that the variations are somewhat greater, but we do not know the variabilities of the heat ranges of the individual compositions. The ratios of the Al_2O_3 to the SiO_2 of the compositions in the same tables vary from 1:7 to 1:19, and the most frequent ratio is about 1:10. The OR, i.e., oxygen ratio, was considered at one time to have considerable significance in the critical analysis of the conduct of glaze compositions. The calculation of this ratio is as follows:

$$\frac{2y + 3z}{3x + 1} = \text{oxygen ratio}$$

where y = mol. equiv. of SiO_2, z = mol. equiv. of B_2O_3, x = mol. equiv. of A_2O_3, and 1 = total equiv. of bases as oxides.

The ratio was originally devised for convenience in classifying compounds of the silicates. The attempt to apply the same procedure to the study of glazes was illogical for two reasons, at least: first, glazes are not chemical compounds in the true sense, nor are chemical compounds present as such (excepting adventitious material, such as undissolved particles of crystalline silica, or crystalline separations); second, the indiscriminate grouping of any and all basic oxides as unity cancels the profound effect of such variations. This latter is contrary to some of the most important principles governing the compounding of glazes. However irrational the oxygen ratio is, it may be of interest to point out that the oxygen ratios of workable glazes vary for the most part between 1:3 and 1:4 when the boric oxide is grouped with the silica. Purdy and Fox found the OR of their glazes having the widest heat ranges to fall between 2 and 4.

Figure 9.8. Dinnerware is glazed with fritted lead glazes. *Left,* is an example of semiporcelain. *Right,* are pieces of vitrified, translucent china.

Fritted Glaze Compositions

Lead-Bearing

Frit is used for all kinds of glazing applications. Some of the more familiar products that employ frit in the glazes are dinnerware (fig. 9.8) and artwares (fig. 9.9). The use of frit in glaze compositions permits a greater choice of constituents in kinds and amounts, which in turn allows the use of a much greater range of temperatures. To illustrate this flexibility, appropriate ranges of compositions are shown in table 9.8 for various firing temperature ranges. They represent a generalized view of possibilities.

Purdy and Fox[16] made an extensive study of glaze compositions falling within the following range:

$0.126Na_2O$		
$0.124K_2O$	$0.10–0.45Al_2O_3$	$0.95–5.288SiO_2$
$0.500CaO$	$0.0–0.9614B_2O_3$	
$0.250PbO$		

The glazes were applied, by dipping, on white tile of the following composition: ball clay, 40; china clay, 40; Cornwall stone, 20; flint, 22.5, in parts by weight, respectively. The glazed pieces were fired in a laboratory kiln at cones 010 to 10 inclusive. The duration of the firing was 12 hours for the lowest cone numbers and 18 to 24 hours for higher temperatures.

A few of the compositions which are reported by the investigators

Figure 9.9. Figures in a Belleek body are made with fritted lead glazes and overglaze decorations.

Table 9.8. Approximate ranges of compositions of fritted glazes

	Molecular equivalents		
	For cones 010 to 06	*For cones 05 to 01*	*For cones 1 to 6*
PbO	0.25 to 0.70	0.25 to 0.50	0.20 to 0.50
K_2O	0.00 to 0.40	0.00 to 0.30	0.00 to 0.20
Na_2O	0.00 to 0.40	0.00 to 0.30	0.00 to 0.20
CaO	0.00 to 0.30	0.00 to 0.40	0.00 to 0.50
SrO	0.00 to 0.30	0.00 to 0.40	0.00 to 0.50
BaO	0.00 to 0.10	0.00 to 0.20	0.00 to 0.20
MgO	0.00 to 0.05	0.00 to 0.20	0.00 to 0.20
ZnO	0.00 to 0.15	0.00 to 0.20	0.00 to 0.20
Al_2O_3	0.10 to 0.25	0.15 to 0.30	0.15 to 0.40
B_2O_3	0.15 to 0.60	0.15 to 0.55	0.15 to 0.50
SiO_2	1.50 to 2.50	1.50 to 3.00	2.00 to 5.00

as satisfactory at the cones indicated are given in table 9.9. The RO group is the same in each case as previously indicated directly above.

Koenig[2] carried out a study of the properties and conduct of fifty-four lead-containing frits and seventeen leadless frits when introduced into typical fritted glazes such as are used at this time on American white earthenwares. This standard was:

$$\begin{matrix} 0.43CaO & & \\ 0.26PbO & 0.27Al_2O_3 & 2.60SiO_2 \\ 0.12K_2O & 0.31B_2O_3 & \\ 0.06Na_2O & & \\ 0.13ZnO & & \end{matrix}$$

Table 9.8. Range of firing for fritted glaze compositions[16]

Alumina	*Boric oxide*	*Silica*	*Good at cones*
0.10	0.26	1.55	05 to 10 incl.
0.10	0.47	1.89	05 to 10 incl.
0.15	0.29	1.73	05 to 10 incl.
0.15	0.53	2.11	05 to 10 incl.
0.2	0.33	1.91	05 to 10 incl.
0.2	0.55	2.18	05 to 10 incl.
0.25	0.60	2.38	05 to 10 incl.
0.25	0.40	1.59	05 to 10 incl.
0.30	0.26	1.51	05 to 10 incl.
0.30	0.45	2.65	1 to 10 incl.
0.35	0.37	1.49	010 to 5 incl.
0.35	0.65	2.61	1 to 10 incl.
0.40	0.40	1.60	1 to 5 incl.
0.40	0.70	2.80	1 to 10 incl.

Table 9.10. Compounding of a fritted earthenware glaze by Koenig.[2] (Batches in parts by weight.)

Frit			
0.26 PbO			
0.1182 CaO	$0.3087\ B_2O_3$	$1.655\ SiO_2$	
$0.056\ K_2O$	$0.0945\ Al_2O_3$		
$0.0385\ Na_2O$			
Combining weight, 202.85			
Frit Batch			
Red lead			26.27
Whiting			5.23
Connecticut feldspar			22.74
Boric acid			16.88
Flint			28.88
Mill Batch			
Frit			62.3
Whiting			9.58
No. Carolina pottery no. 1 feldspar			11.43
Connecticut glaze feldspar			2.99
Zinc oxide			3.25
English china clay			7.13
Flint			3.32
Percent fritted content in the glaze formula, 62.3			
Percent lead solubility			
Of frit, 1.99			
Of lead content, 8.59			
Specific gravity of the glaze slip used (25° C), 1.465–1.500			

Several of the glazes were applied on earthenware bodies of varying compositions and physical properties and were fired in plant kilns at cone temperatures of 01 to 5 inclusive. One of these compositions[2] which proved to be generally satisfactory was compounded as shown in table 9.10.

An example of a glaze having the same ultimate ceramic formula as that developed in table 9.10, but compounded of two frits, is shown in table 9.11, as developed by Koenig.[2] In this composition, one frit (*a*) is highly insoluble lead-containing. The frit (*b*) is leadless. This division is based on the observation of Petrik[25] that the presence of alkalies or borax in a lead frit increased its solubility.

Leadless Fritted Glazes

Leadless fritted glazes may be had in a wide variety of compositions (see table 9.12) and, therefore, of maturing temperatures and of adaptabil-

Table 9.11. Two-frit equivalent of the one-fire glaze of table 9.10.[2] (All empirical formulas in molecular equivalents; all batches in parts by weight)

Lead frit (a)			
$0.260\ PbO$ $0.065\ CaO$	$0.065\ Al_2O_3$	$0.65\ SiO_2$	
Combining weight,			107.34
Percent lead solubility			
Of total frit			0.95
Of lead content			1.89
Leadless frit (b)			
$0.136\ CaO$ $0.044\ K_2O$ $0.015\ Na_2O$	$0.310\ B_2O_3$ $0.019\ Al_2O_3$	$0.659\ SiO_2$	
Combining weight			75.71
Percent loss of weight in water			4.97
Percent fritted contents in glaze batch:			
Lead frit (a)			32.98
Leadless frit (b)			23.26
Total frit			56.24

Materials used in the glaze, parts by weight:

Lead frit (a)		Leadless frit (b)	
Red lead	51.62	Whiting	13.52
Whiting	5.65	Connecticut glaze feldspar	10.50
Aluminum hydrate	8.81	Pearl ash	4.50
Flint	33.92	Borax	2.50
		Boric acid	36.57
		Flint	32.40
Mill batch		Mill addition	
Lead frit (a)	32.98	Whiting	7.05
Leadless frit (b)	23.26	No. Carolina pottery feldspar	4.27
		Connecticut glaze feldspar	16.15
		Zinc oxide	3.25
		English china clay	5.08
		Flint	7.96

ity to a diversity of wares. They are of special importance in the manufacture of tableware because of the avoidance of the hazards associated with the employment of lead compounds and the toxic action of food which has been in prolonged contact with improperly compounded lead-containing glazes. During the last quarter of the previous century, Dr. Hermann Seger,[34] in discussing whiteware glazes, mentioned the concern felt by ceramists and others about the dangers accompanying the use of lead oxide. Characteristically, he undertook to remedy this condition insofar as the composition of the glaze was concerned. Summarizing the advantages of the use of lead oxide, he stresses the high indices of refraction, hence excellent gloss, the transparency, and the beauty of the effects obtained by the addition of coloring oxides. He concludes by stating that: "The lead oxide without doubt is the metallic oxide most suited for the

Table 9.12. Leadless glaze compositions

Glaze No.	K_2O	Na_2O	CaO	BaO	MgO	ZnO	SrO	Al_2O_3	B_2O_3	SiO_2	Cone
1[26]	0.20	0.30	0.20	0.30	–	–	–	0.20	0.60	2.20	010
*2[26]	0.30	0.23	0.27	–	–	–	0.30	0.30	0.46	3.00	010
3[27]	0.25	0.27	0.13	0.07	0.28	–	–	0.69	1.92	3.93	09
4[28]	0.15	–	0.80	–	0.05	–	–	0.15	0.80	0.90	09
5[28]	0.38	0.21	0.20	0.21	–	–	–	0.41	0.34	3.34	07
6[29]	0.13	0.25	0.38	–	0.18	0.08	–	0.26	0.50	2.50	07
7[30]	0.25	0.25	–	0.50	–	–	–	0.20	0.60	2.40	06
8[28]	0.25	0.15	0.60	–	–	–	–	0.40	1.00	3.50	05
9[31]	0.224	0.148	0.56	–	–	–	–	0.55	0.94	3.41	02
10[32]	0.25	0.25	0.20	0.30	–	–	–	0.40	0.50	3.20	5
11[22]	0.07	0.13	0.45	–	0.05	Li_2O 0.05	0.25	0.28	0.28	2.80	4–5
12[27]	0.25	0.25	0.50	–	–	–	–	0.40	0.50	3.20	4
13[22]	0.04	0.14	0.27	0.05	0.09	Li_2O 0.10	0.31	0.26	0.36	2.70	4–5
14[33]	0.20	–	0.40	0.05	0.05	ZnO 0.30	–	0.50	0.10	4.00	6

*"Very satisfactory for pink colors, using a suitable stain."

production of glazes." Any attempt to produce similar desirable results without the use of lead oxide has proved to be a difficult technical problem.

Lead oxide is a low-temperature flux reacting readily with silica, alumina, etc., and it forms melts of low viscosities and strong solvent power. Leadless frits react much more slowly, larger quantities are required to have a similar effect, and the glazes, lacking the requisite fluidity, are slower in planning, i.e., liberating enclosed bubbles. Blisters form and the defects of the surface are less easily healed and obscured. A further benefit of lead oxide's more favorable viscosity conduct is the lengthened firing range of lead glazes whereby the risk of overfiring is definitely less. Further, the period of accommodation of the glaze to the body is such as to reduce the formation of stresses which, together with the greater elasticity, lessen the development of strains in the glaze and crazing. The higher content of alkalies necessary to produce the desired fusibility in the absence of lead is accompanied with some inconveniences, since they tend to raise the coefficient of expansion and thereby cause crazing; they facilitate the development of crystals; and they react with sulfur oxides in kiln gases to cause dimming and scumming of the surface. Differences in the effects produced by the same coloring oxides may be anticipated whether they are used in underglaze, overglaze, or inglaze decorations when lead is replaced by alkalies.

Seger[19] undertook to develop a leadless glaze suitable for whiteware and reported that the following compositions gave good results below the melting temperature of gold (1,063° C):

$0.5KNaO$	$0.1Al_2O_3$	$2.7SiO_2$
$0.5CaO$	$0.5B_2O_3$	
$0.3K_2O$	$0.8Al_2O_3$	$5.4SiO_2$
$0.3Na_2O$	$1.0B_2O_3$	
$0.4CaO$		
$0.2K_2O$	$0.5Al_2O_3$	$4.0SiO_2$
$0.8CaO$	$1.0B_2O_3$	

The highly alkaline glazes are better suited for the more siliceous bodies, and the highly calcareous are better adapted to the more aluminous compositions.

A series[35] of glaze compositions lying within these limits was applied on a vitreous sanitary-ware body and fired at cones 7 and 9 in laboratory and commercial kilns. These glaze compositions were as follows:

$0.4\text{–}0.6K_2O$	$0.1\text{–}0.7Al_2O_3$	$3\text{–}7SiO_2$
$0.0\text{–}0.3ZnO$	$0.1\text{–}0.5B_2O_3$	
$0.4\text{–}0.6CaO$		

The best results were had with:

0.2–0.6K_2O	0.5–0.6Al_2O_3	5.0SiO_2
0.8–0.4CaO	0.5B_2O_3	

Dr. Mellor[36] offered the following composition as the best type of leadless glaze for earthenware available at that time.

0.45$KNaO$	0.55Al_2O_3	3.5SiO_2
0.54CaO	1.20B_2O_3	
0.01MgO		

Montgomery[37] reports that at cone 3, when applied on a nonabsorbent body (hotelware), this composition yielded a bright, smooth glaze, but it reacted badly with the underglaze colors used. The pinks and yellows were spoiled, the blue flowed, and, in general, where thickly applied there was a tendency to drain off sloping surfaces and become full of bubbles.

Berdel[38] gives the following range of compositions suited for use between cones 01 and 7:

0.2–0.5$KNaO$		
0.0–0.2MgO	0.3–0.5Al_2O_3	3.5–4.5SiO_2
0.0–0.1ZnO	0.3–0.5B_2O_3	
about 0.5CaO		

or, barium-containing:

0.2–0.5$KNaO$		
0.0–0.3CaO	0.3–0.5Al_2O_3	3.5–4.5SiO_2
0.0–0.1MgO	0.3–0.5B_2O_3	
0.0–0.1ZnO		
0.3–0.5BaO		

For the range between cones 09 and 03 he suggests using:

0.1–0.8Na_2O		
0.0–0.5K_2O	0.2–0.6Al_2O_3	1.5–5.0SiO_2
0.0–0.5CaO	0.4–1.0B_2O_3	
0.0–0.4MgO		
0.0–0.2ZnO		

or, barium-containing:

0.0–0.5$KNaO$		
0.2–0.8BaO	0.1–0.4Al_2O_3	2.0–3.5SiO_2
0.0–0.2ZnO	0.2–0.5B_2O_3	
0.0–0.5CaO		

Figure 9.10. Floor and wall tile in pastel colored glazes. These are usually the fritted lead type.

Colored Fritted Glazes

The production of colored fritted glazes has a much wider scope than is possible in any other type because of (1) the greater choice of kinds and amounts of the bases, (2) the wider heat range, (3) the significant effect of the boric oxide, (4) the omission of the lead if necessary, and

(5) the use of greater amounts of the alkalies, if desired. In all cases the results obtained will be dependent upon the manipulation of these factors. If lead oxide is an important member of the bases, the colors obtained with the various oxides will be similar to those had with the raw lead glazes subject, in some cases, to the modifying effects of the boric oxide. In the leadless glazes, notable variations from the above colors may be had. Floor and wall tile of the type shown in figure 9.10 is the most widespread example of colored fritted glazes.

Brown

Manganese oxide will produce claret browns in leadless and lead-containing alkaline glazes in the presence of alumina and boric oxide. Ferric oxide in quantities of 3%, 5%, and 6% produces browns which are improved by the presence of boric oxide and alumina in lead-containing compositions. The color is strengthened by the presence of barium oxide. More color oxide is needed in the leadless glazes. Zinc oxide is said to give a better color tone with a range from brownish-yellow to chocolate. Nickel oxide will yield a straw-brown color in all glazes containing lead. The alkaline glazes will give grey colors with low concentration of the nickel, but the larger amounts and increases in the content of alumina or boric oxides produce browns. The color may be intensified by substituting strontium for calcium, barium for strontium, potassium for lithium. The maximum amount of nickel oxide used is about 2%. The brown and buff shades are sensitive to variations of temperature.

Tan

Tan colors were produced by Holscher[39] using nickel oxide in some leadless borosilicate glazes containing 0.35 equivalents or more (preferably 0.45 equivalents) of calcium oxide, while the barium oxide should not be over 0.2 equivalents and the sum of the barium and magnesium oxides not over 0.3 equivalents.

Blue

Cobalt compounds are the usual source of blue colors in all variations of glaze compositions and throughout the entire firing range. The shades of blue may be altered by the choice of the bases, the amounts of the cobalt compounds employed, and by the presence of certain other elements which may be used accidentally or intentionally. It is known that the colors of some modern glazes and glasses are not identical with antique products, in some cases, for this reason. This has been noted in the results obtained with the use of old recipes for preparation of colors employing the more highly purified materials available today. Thus Mellor[40] suggests that the Chinese cobalt blues may contain very small quantities of nickel oxides in addition to the known content of manganese oxide. Minute traces of elements are not always sought nor identified in routine analyses. The presence of lead produces the warmer tones, approaching the ultramarine, as the concentration increases. The leadless glazes are colder in tone and lighter in shade. Appreciable differences are effected by the presence of magnesia and zinc. The influence of the latter is said to be variable. Plusch[41] reports that a high zinc content (in a terra cotta glaze) produces a violet shade, and lesser quantities give a cold blue.

A blue green (turquoise color) is obtained in leadless glazes in the absence of alumina. The amount of copper oxide required varies between 5% and 10%. The color is destroyed by temperatures above 1,100° C, sometimes at 1,000° C.

Yellow

Sodium uranate, the commercial uranium oxide, will produce yellow colors in glazes containing a high content of sodium and barium, a medium content of lime and zinc oxides. The presence of lead and boric oxide impairs the color somewhat, the former more than the latter. Boric oxide as such or as borax gives a greenish tinge. The amount of the U_2O_3 used will be from 0.003 molecular equivalents upwards.

Orange

Orange colored glazes may be had with the use of a sufficiently high content of "uranium oxide" (up to 6% to 10%) added to glaze compositions containing high lead and zinc, low alkalies and alkaline earths. Bismuth and cadmium intensify or darken the color in cone 07 glazes. Five percent of tin oxide in the presence of 6% to 8% of the uranate is said to give a brownish orange. The molecular equivalents of the U_2O_3 used for the maximum color will be of the order of 0.05.

Red

Fiery red glazes may be obtained by using compositions of the iron aventurine type, i.e., containing little else but alkalies, lead oxide, boric oxide, silica, and, of course, the iron oxide. The temperature must be low and the firing done under oxidizing conditions.

Chromium oxide in company with tin oxide calcined together with noncoloring compounds, or chromium and tin oxides in a glaze composition, will form various shades of red. Lead-containing glazes give satisfactory results. Some leadless glazes, high in lime and boric oxide, destroy the color. Relatively high lime and low alumina in the color stain, with a high proportion of lime in the glaze, may develop milkiness in the glaze or scumming.[42] Increasing the lime in the glaze makes the color more crimson and stable at the temperatures of cone 6 and above. Increasing silica tends to make the glaze more violet or bloodred, and, in the presence of boric oxide, it maintains the color. An excess of alumina tends to alter the pink to a green. Zinc oxide may replace lead oxide up to 0.15 equivalent without detriment; barium oxide may be satisfactorily used in a limited amount (0.2–0.3 equivalents) if lead is present. In either case a scummy surface may form. Strontium produces a brighter and more fusible glaze than barium with a stronger action on the color. Magnesium, even in quantities as small as 0.05 equivalents, is harmful to the color, i.e., destructive.[43]

Green

Copper oxide used in alkaline glazes produces the greenish-blue, or turquoise, color. If lead is present, the color is definitely a green which varies greatly in intensity as the concentration is increased. In a borosilicate glaze containing also zinc, lime, and the alkalies, the color is lightened by increasing the boric oxide content. Chromium oxide differs strikingly from copper oxide in being little soluble in glaze fusions; consequently, the glazes in which it is present are opaque, lacking the characteristic transparency accompanying the use of copper oxide. Moreover, chromium oxide is very refractory. In lead-containing glazes the colors vary from yellowish-green to green which is given a brownish tint by alumina; magnesia seems to improve the green; barium and lime tend to produce orange tones. Bright greens may be had in leadless glazes which alumina makes yellowish. The presence of zinc oxide is inadvisable. The Victoria green may be produced with the aid of calcium fluoride. Boric oxide does not interfere if the lime content is high and the former oxide should not be less in molecular equivalents than the alumina.

Nickel will produce greens in borosilicate lead glazes, according to the experience of Holscher.[39] The barium, magnesia, and zinc oxides may not be present in excess amounts of the order of 0.2 mol. equivalents.

Table 9.13. Physical characteristics of borosilicate glazes[44,45]

Glaze No. of table 9.14	*Coefficient of expansion* $(a \times 10^{-8})$	*Modulus of elasticity*	*Beginning of annealing, ° C*	*Critical zone, ° C*		*Beginning of softening, ° C*
				Beginning	*End*	
1	694	6,200	340	390	470	480
2	623	6,500	360	430	530	550
3	943	6,810	380	440	530	560
4	642	5,730	350	420	530	550
5	847	6,620	370	460	530	550
6	625	5,900	350	460	540	560
7	846	6,790	480	530	550	600

Zirconium oxide substituted for tin oxide in a chrome-tin pink composition is said to yield a yellowish chrome-green color.

Physical Data Pertaining to Borosilicate Glazes

The exact determination of the fundamental physical properties of glazes has been an extremely valuable contribution to the knowledge of these fusions. Progress has been slow because the technique is difficult and time consuming; the apparatus required is elaborate and expensive; and skillful, trained observers are necessary. The data which is thus being accumulated will eventually remove the making of glazes from an empirical art to an exact science. The following data (table 9.13) are illustrative of the valuable but limited information now available. It has particular significance in dealing with the problems of crazing and shivering.

The molecular compositions of the glazes whose properties are shown in table 9.13 are given in table 9.14. These have been calculated from the percentage compositions reported by Steger.[44,45]

Table 9.14. Empirical formulas of borosilicate glazes having physical properties as tabulated in table 9.13[44,45]

Glaze no.	*PbO*	K_2O	Na_2O	*CaO*	*MgO*	*ZnO*	Al_2O_3	B_2O_3	SiO_2
1	0.35	0.20	0.25	0.20	–	–	0.28	0.50	2.10
2	0.36	0.06	0.16	0.42	–	–	0.29	0.59	2.75
3	–	0.25	0.30	0.45	–	–	0.30	0.60	2.30
						BaO			
4	–	0.27	0.25	0.13	0.28	0.07	0.69	1.29	3.93
5	0.20	0.30	0.25	0.25	–	–	0.35	0.30	3.00
6	0.21	0.14	0.25	0.40	–	–	0.45	0.62	3.93
7	–	0.25	0.25	0.50	–	–	0.40	0.50	3.20

References

1. Parmelee, C. W. and Lyons, K. C. 1934. A study of some frit compositions. *J. Am. Ceram. Soc.* 17:60.
2. Koenig, J. H. 1937. Lead frits and fritted glazes. Bull. No. 95, Engineering Expt. Sta., Ohio State Univ.
3. Petrik, L. 1914. The lead question in ceramic industries. *Sprech.* 47:1.
4. Currier, Arthur E. 1947. Standard method for determining leachability of lead from lead frits. *J. Am. Ceram. Soc.* 30(11):335–38.
5. Lu, K. C. 1926. A deformation study of various alumino-silicates and borosilicates. *J. Am. Ceram. Soc.* 9:29.
6. Kywult, E. Z. and Thornton, Paul E. 1956. Effect of soluble boric acid in a frit upon glazes. *Bull. Am. Ceram. Soc.,* 35(6):234–35.
7. International Lead Zinc Research Organization. *ILZRO Manual—Ceramics. Lead glazes for dinnerware.*
8. Lead Industries Association, Inc. 1971. *Facts about lead glazes for art potters and hobbyists.*
9. Mellor, J. W. 1912–13. The behavior of some glazes in the glost oven. *Trans. Engl. Ceram. Soc.* 12:1.
10. Steger, W. 1931. On the relation of stresses in glazed ware to the distribution of glaze constituents. *Ber. Deut. Keram. Ges.* 12:43.
11. 1923. The effect of the frit content of the glaze on crazing. *Sprechsaal* 56:243.
12. Andrews, A. I. 1935. *Enamels.* Champaign: Twin City Printing Co., p 257.
13. Harrison, W. N. 1927. Vitreous enamel slips and their control. *J. Am. Ceram. Soc.* 10:970.
14. Steger, op. cit., ref. 10.
15. Seger, H. A. 1902. Whiteware glazes. *Collected writings.* Vol. 2. Easton, Pa.: Chemical Publishing Co., p 594.
16. Purdy, R. C. and Fox, H. B. 1907. Fritted glazes. *Trans. Am. Ceram. Soc.* 9:95.
17. Kerl, B. 1907. *Handbuch der gesammten Tonwaarenindustrie.* Braunschweig, p 1149.
18. Pukall, W. 1912. *Keramischen Rechnen.* 4th ed. Breslau, p 81.
19. Seger, H. 1902. Glazes free from lead. *Collected writings.* Vol. 1. Easton, Pa.: Chemical Publishing Co., p 453.
20. Binns, C. F. 1908. The function of boron in the glaze formula. *Trans. Am. Ceram. Soc.* 10:158.
21. Singer, F. G. 1910. Position of boron in the glaze formula. *Trans. Am. Ceram. Soc.* 12:676.
22. McCutchen, Earl S. 1944. Strontia and its properties in glazes. *J. Am. Ceram. Soc.* 27:233.
23. Swift, H. R. 1945. Factors influencing fluxing action of various oxides in low temperature borosilicate glasses. *J. Am. Ceram. Soc.* 28:33.
24. Stull, R. T. and Radcliffe, B. S. 1910. Opalescence and the function of B_2O_3 in the glaze. *Trans. Am. Ceram. Soc.* 12:129

25. Petrik, L. 1914. The lead question in ceramic industries. *Sprechsaal* 47:1.
26. Berge, A. 1914. Contributions from the Royal Ceramic School at Bunzlau. *Sprech.* 47:98, 113.
27. Steger, W. 1927. *Ber. Deut. Keram. Ges.* 8:31.
28. Steger, W. 1937. *Ber. Deut. Keram. Rund.* 45:337.
29. Dorfner, J. 1915. The lead problem. *Sprech.* 47:390.
30. Hecht, Hermann. 1923. *Lehrbuch der Keramik*, p 217.
31. Shah, C. P. 1917/18. *Trans. Engl. Ceram. Soc.* 17:106.
32. Berdel, E. 1929. *Einfaches chemisches Praktikum.* 2d ed. Aufl. Koburg, Vols. 5 and 6, p 43.
33. Watts, A. S. 1927. *J. Am. Ceram. Soc.* 10:148.
34. Seger, H. A. 1902. Glazes free from lead. *Collected writings.* Vol. 1. Easton, Pa.: Chemical Publishing Co. p 459.
35. Parmelee, C. W. and Williams, Geo. A. 1916. Fritted leadless glazes for sanitary ware. *Trans. Am. Ceram. Soc.* 18:812.
36. Mellor, J. W. 1912/13. Behavior of some glazes in the glost oven. *Trans. Engl. Ceram. Soc.* 12:1.
37. Montgomery, E. T. 1913. Some leadless glazes maturing at about 1,100° C. Tech. Paper No. 31, Bur. Std. (U.S.) p 19.
38. Berdel, E. 1929. Einfaches chemisches Praktikum. 5th ed. Vol. 5 and 6. Aufl. Koburg. Quoted by Funk, W. 1933. *Rohstoffe der Feinkeramik.* Berlin, pp 260–261.
39. Holscher, H. H. 1929. Some lead borosilicate glazes containing nickel oxide. *J. Am. Ceram. Soc.* 12:111.
40. Mellor, J. W. 1937. Cobalt and nickel colors. *Trans. Engl. Ceram. Soc.* 36:1.
41. Plusch, H. A. 1908. Discussion of article by Bryan, M. L., Action of chromium oxide in glazes containing zinc. *Trans. Am. Ceram. Soc.* 10:131.
42. Mellor, J. W. 1936–37. Chemistry of the chrome-tin colors. *Trans. Engl. Ceram. Soc.* 36:16.
43. Ramsden, C. E. 1912–13. A study of chromium red glazes. *Trans. Engl. Ceram. Soc.* 12:239.
44. Steger, W. 1919. On the elastic modulus of whiteware glazes. *Keram. Rundschau* 27:313.
45. Steger, W. 1927. Heat expansion and annealing temperature of glazes. *Ber. Deut. Keram. Ges.* 8:24.

10

Raw Lead Glazes

Raw lead glazes are unfritted compositions in which lead oxide is an important, or the only, member of the RO group. They are cheap, brilliant, and suitable for a great variety of wares and are fired at widely different cone temperatures—cone 015 and lower to cone 6 or even cone 8. The usual range is cone 05 to cone 2. An extensive variety of colors may be produced by the introduction of the proper oxides or pigments and many interesting variations of these may be had by altering the amount and kind of the colorless bases used. Some colors are peculiar to lead glazes only. The disadvantages of the use of lead glazes are: (1) the glazes as a class are less resistant to abrasion than most other types, (2) some are easily affected by the atmospheric gases, (3) crazing is common but not unavoidable, and (4) incorrectly balanced glazes can be sufficiently attacked by weak acid solutions present in fruit juices, beverages, etc., so as to make the latter dangerous to the health of the users.

Uses

Lead glazes find wide usage from artware, such as in figure 10.1, to highly sophisticated technical applications. They are applied on bodies in the leather-hard, bone-dry, or biscuit condition and on many kinds of wares: art pottery, structural products (roofing tile, brick, etc.), wall tile, cooking ware, sanitary ware, etc. Such glazes have been used for centuries because lead minerals are widely distributed on the earth's surface, the methods of recovery from the ores and the preparation of its compounds are simple, these compounds are cheap, can be used in a variety of proportions, and the resulting glazes are pleasant in appearance.

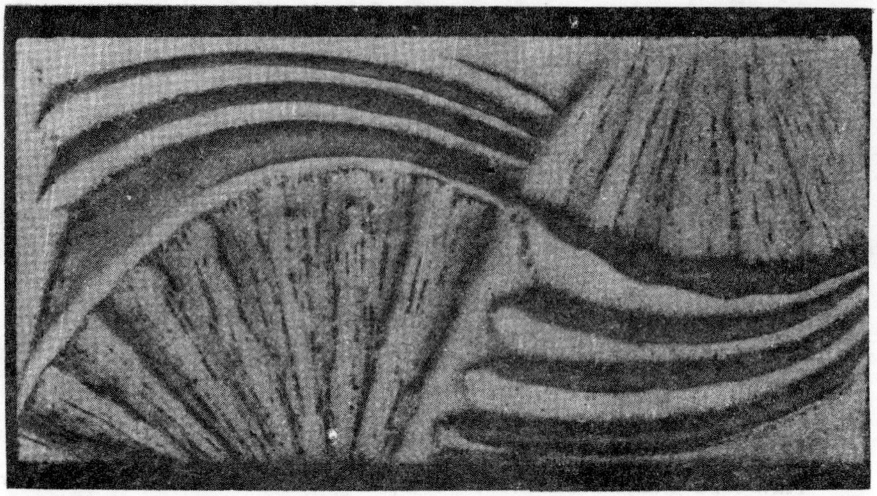

Figure 10.1. Double glazing with two different colored glazes for effect. Top glaze must mature and be fluid enough to give running effect.

Antiquity of the Lead Glaze

Lucas[1] wrote that the earliest example known to him of faience coated with a lead silicate glaze can be dated as of the Twenty Second Dynasty (of Egyptian chronology, i.e., 975–945 B.C.). The faience referred to by Lucas was a body containing upwards of 85% to 90% of powdered silica bonded by a glassy flux. Collie[2] found that a lead silicate glaze colored green with copper oxide has been traced back to the Eleventh Egyptian Dynasty (4000–3000 B.C.). According to the same writer, lead glazes were used by the Chinese until soft feldspathic compositions were introduced. Early in the thirteenth century the use of lead glazes reappeared. Shards coated with lead glazes, traceable to the first century B.C., have been found on the sites of Alexandria, Tarsus in Asia Minor, and in the Allier district of Gaul. During the Ptolemaic times (ca 332 to ca 30 B.C.) they were extensively used in Egypt and the Near East as is evident in the "Ptolemaic green" (apple green) for the production of which lead must be present with iron oxide colorant.

The compositions vary widely because the uses and necessarily the temperatures of firing differ so much with the great variety of wares. Examples of simple formulas are:

$$1PbO:1.5SiO_2$$
$$1PbO:0.1Al_2O_3:2SiO_2$$

These simple compositions give inferior results as compared with the more complex forms which contain, besides lead, one or more of the alkalies, alkaline earths, also zinc, with alumina and silica. The range of compositions is approximately:

$$\begin{array}{l} 0.3\text{–}0.7PbO \\ 0.1\text{–}0.4CaO \\ 0.0\text{–}0.4SrO : 0.1\text{–}0.35Al_2O_3 : 0.7\text{–}3.5SiO_2 \\ 0.0\text{–}0.1BaO \\ 0.0\text{–}0.1MgO \\ 0.0\text{–}0.3ZnO \end{array}$$

Opacifiers such as tin or zirconium oxides are sometimes used.

Components

Lead

A wide choice of the lead compounds is possible. Galena, mineral sulfide of lead, has been used for centuries on crude pottery. Simple methods of application are dusting the finely ground mineral on the damp piece, or rolling the damp piece in the powder. This material is suitable for crude wares only. The materials more frequently employed are white lead, the basic carbonate of lead [$2PbCO_3 \cdot Pb(OH)_2$]; litharge, lead monoxide (PbO); red lead, minium (Pb_3O_4); and artificial lead silicates. White lead was first preferred because of its relative purity and slow rate of settling in water suspensions. The fumed oxides, both yellow (PbO) and red (Pb_3O_4), are used. Slips having the same viscosity made of these fumed oxides have specific gravities in this order: the fumed red oxide the lowest, next the yellow, and the white lead the highest.

Watts[3] concluded: (1) greater fusibility was obtained by using the monoxide; (2) the texture of the finished glaze varied with the choice of material—litharge gave a glassy finish, white lead a pinhole texture; and (3) glazes containing white lead "dusted" readily, fused minium (red lead, Pb_3O_4) but slightly, and fused litharge not at all.

The *advantages* of lead as a glaze constituent are:

1. the wide range in the amount of lead which may be used
2. the ready fusibility of its silicates and alumino-silicates
3. the instability of its carbonates
4. the relative insolubility in water of the available lead compounds
5. the low viscosity and low surface tension of its fused compound,

6. the relative economy of its use (considering its fusing powers, it is the cheapest flux.)
7. the unique color effects it produces (lead silicate fusions are excellent solvents for color oxides.)
8. wide maturing range
9. high gloss and refractive index

The *disadvantages* in using lead are:

1. Raw leads are poisonous. Continued contact with the raw material or with raw glazes is harmful to the operator unless care is exercised.
2. Lead compounds have relatively high vapor pressures, consequently volatilize freely so that wares, thus coated, must be enclosed in a suitable container during firing to prevent impoverishment of the glaze and loss of gloss.
3. The glazes are easily scratched and frequently harmfully affected by atmospheric gases which cause a filmy coating to form on the surface after prolonged exposure at room temperature.
4. It tends to give a yellowish tint.
5. Incorrectly proportioned glazes may be susceptible to chemical attack by fruit and vegetable juices, and foods stored in such containers may in time become unsafe to use.

The lead oxide content may constitute the entire RO group or fall as low as 0.30 equivalents, the minimum practicable for the ordinary range of temperature. Lead alone gives yellowish glazes; the more RO members, the more nearly colorless they will be. Glazes very high in lead attack the body vigorously, dissolving material, and forming a nonhomogeneous mass which will blister and buckle. The use of a very thick coat in such a case is advisable. For practical use, the limits of variation of the PbO are approximately 0.7 and 0.4 equivalents.

Calcium

Calcium is introduced as whiting (the carbonate), precipitated carbonate, dolomite (the double carbonate of calcium and magnesium), and small quantities are brought in by the feldspars. The practical range is approximately 0.10–0.40 equivalents, but the amount used varies widely. Cone 012 seems to be the lowest at which its presence is desirable. An excess makes the glaze cloudy and refractory. Calcium oxide sometimes reacts with the oxides of sulfur in the kiln gases, forming a scummy coating on the matured surface.

Magnesium

Magnesium is introduced as the heavy carbonate, as dolomite, and as talc. It may be used in quantities not much exceeding 0.1 equivalents, since larger amounts increase refractoriness and give rise to faults of a serious character. It has a profound influence upon the development of certain colors which also may be said, in greater or lesser degree, of the other members of the RO group.

Barium

Barium is usually introduced as the precipitated carbonate. It functions best as an ingredient in matt glazes or in glazes subject to long glost heat treatment, otherwise it reacts so slowly that only immature or matt textures are likely to develop. The amounts used may vary widely: the usual limit is 0.1 equivalent, but using 0.3 equivalent, it is possible to develop a glossy glaze at cone 4, providing the other components are properly balanced.

Strontium

Strontium compounds have been used with marked advantage in the borosilicate glazes,[4,5] and it may be expected that similar results may be had in the raw lead compositions. Briefly, one expects to find that its substitution for calcium will lower the softening point and increase the fluidity of the melted glaze. The replacement of zinc will have little effect upon the fusibility but will raise the thermal expansion somewhat. If substituted for lead it will usually make the glaze more refractory, decrease the fluidity, and slightly increase the thermal expansion.

Zinc

Zinc oxide used in limited amounts develops a brilliant gloss, fusibility, a wider heat range, and physical properties which diminish crazing. In small amounts it may replace equivalent quantities of lead oxide, thus decreasing slightly the yellowish color of high lead glazes without lessening the fluidity of the melt. It functions best at cone 1 and above and must be present in amounts greater than 0.15 equivalent to give opacity.

Purdy[6] found that "zinc oxide is not necessary in raw lead glazes unless to counteract crazing in the more fluid of those which are relatively high in lead and low in alumina." He recommends that it is best to keep the ratio of ZnO to CaO not more than 1:1 and generally 1:2 or 1:3.

Alkali-free Glazes

Alkalies are generally part of the composition of raw lead glazes but they are not indispensable. Numerous examples are cited in literature, and the compositions lying within the range given below were found by Parmelee and Horak[7] to give interesting, glossy, and matt textures throughout the range of cones 03 to 6.

$0.4\text{–}0.6PbO$		
$0.2\text{–}0.3CaO$	$0.1\text{–}0.35Al_2O_3$	$0.7\text{–}1.8SiO_2$
$0.0\text{–}0.3BaO$		
$0.0\text{–}0.3ZnO$		

Alkali Content

The alkalies are introduced as feldspar or Cornwall stone, usually the former. Therefore the alkali content is limited in part by the alumina content. In feldspar glazes, the total alkalies may be as high as 0.3 equivalents but seldom exceed 0.15 equivalents. In glazes containing Cornwall stone this may be 0.1 equivalents but generally is as low as 0.05 equivalents. Crazing is liable to occur in glazes containing high alkali content with a corresponding reduction of alkaline earths.

Substitutions of Bases

Cannan[8] studied the replacement of lead oxide by alkalies, alkaline earths, and zinc oxide in the general formula

$$RO:0.2Al_2O_3:2.0SiO_2$$

throughout the heat range of cones 04–02. Replacements of lead oxide were made successively as single, double, triple, and quadruple substitutions. He reached these conclusions, among others: barium oxide was the least useful of all the oxides, in any proportion; the workable replacement of the lead oxide, with the exception of the baryta, lies between 0.15 and 0.2 equivalents of each; the more oxides substituted, the less lead is required and the better the glaze. Magnesia, contrary to expectations, could be substituted in larger amounts and gave satisfactory results in every combination tried. These conclusions have been found somewhat modified when other alumina-silica contents are used.

Table 10.1 shows the effects upon fusibility of the substitutions of molecular equivalent amounts of bases customarily used when replacing lead oxide.

Alumina Content

Alumina may be introduced in the form of Cornwall stone, feldspar, clay, cryolite, aluminum oxide, or aluminum hydroxide.

Cornwall stone is said to be of special value in the production of col-

Table 10.1. Effects of substitutions in the RO group on the fusing temperature of raw lead glazes[9]

	Empirical formula		*Maturing cone*
1.	0.3 Na_2O / 0.7 PbO	+ 0.1 Al_2O_3 + 2 SiO_2	019
2.	0.3 K_2O / 0.7 PbO	+ 0.1 Al_2O_3 + 2 SiO_2	016–017
3.	0.3 BaO / 0.7 PbO	+ 0.1 Al_2O_3 + 2 SiO_2	015–016
4.	0.3 CaO / 0.7 PbO	+ 0.1 Al_2O_3 + 2 SiO_2	015
5.	0.3 MgO / 0.7 PbO	+ 0.1 Al_2O_3 + 2 SiO_2	013–014

ored glazes, giving better results than may be obtained with feldspar. Attempts to substitute the calculated equivalents of clay, feldspar, and flint for Cornwall stone, even upon the basis of chemical analysis, are not entirely satisfactory.

The alumina content of raw lead glazes containing 0.1–0.25 equivalents of alkalies introduced as feldspar usually varies from 0.1–0.35 equivalents, depending upon the other sources of the alumina, such as clay.

Alumina-silica

The relative as well as the absolute amounts of the alumina and the silica influence the molten viscosity, the refractoriness, and the texture to an important degree. The alumina–silica ratios vary extremely widely for glazes of the same RO members and the same maturing temperatures—from $Al_2O_3:7SiO_2$ to 1:13 or 15—for glossy glazes. Within a stated range of RO composition specific ratios may be used with advantage. The most frequent ratios used lie between 1:7 and 1:11. Formerly, alumina–silica

Table 10.2. Thermal effects of increasing the silica content[9]

	Empirical formula	*Maturing temp. cone*
1.	PbO + 0.1 Al_2O_3 + 1.50 SiO_2	018–019
2.	PbO + 0.1 Al_2O_3 + 1.75 SiO_2	018
3.	PbO + 0.1 Al_2O_3 + 2.00 SiO_2	017
4.	PbO + 0.1 Al_2O_3 + 2.25 SiO_2	016
5.	PbO + 0.1 Al_2O_3 + 2.50 SiO_2	016–015
6.	PbO + 0.1 Al_2O_3 + 2.75 SiO_2	015–016
7.	PbO + 0.1 Al_2O_3 + 3.00 SiO_2	014–013

ratios were considered very important, but better acquaintance with equilibria conditions indicates that the fundamental relationships are to be found in such fields.

Table 10.2 shows the thermal effects of additions of small increments of silica to the base composition $PbO \cdot 0.1Al_2O_3 \cdot 1.5SiO_2$.

Oxygen Ratio

The oxygen ratio is the numerical ratio between the sum of the oxygen of the acid forming elements (SiO_2, B_2O_3) and the sum of the oxygen of the base forming elements (RO, R_2O_3). In former years this relationship had a considerable use in the critical study of glaze compositions and conduct. Thus, Fickes[10] has reported that he found the safest range of ratios was between the limits 1:15 and 1:2. These conclusions were drawn from a study of glazes having the general formulas of $RO:0.2Al_2O_3:2.0SiO_2$. He explicitly records his conclusion that "for each combination of RO elements composing the fluxing base of a glaze, the limits within which good glazes can be produced will depend upon its fluxing power."

Heat Range

In general, the alumina–silica content and ratio may be useful factors in controlling the heat range of glazes of a definite field. For example, Staley[11] found that glossy glazes of the compositions shown in table 10.3 were good throughout the range of cones indicated.

Quite a different series, containing no alkalies, was examined by

Table 10.3. Empirical formulas of some raw lead glazes showing the influence of composition on heat range[11]

K_2O	PbO	CaO	Al_2O_3	SiO_2
Glazes good at cones 02, 4, and 8				
0.1	0.9	0.0	0.1	1.3
0.1	0.8	0.1	0.1	1.3
0.1	0.7	0.2	0.1	1.3
0.1	0.9	0.0	0.2	1.6
0.1	0.8	0.1	0.2	1.6
0.1	0.7	0.2	0.2	1.6
Glazes good at cones 4 and 8				
0.1	0.9	0.0	0.3	1.9
0.1	0.8	0.1	0.3	1.9
0.1	0.7	0.2	0.3	1.9
0.1	0.6	0.3	0.3	1.9

Parmelee and Horak;[7] they found that, when fired at cones 03, 2, 4, and 6, all of these glazes gave good matt and glossy textures at all temperatures, irrespective of the RO content, providing that the alumina–silica amounts and ratios were suitable. The choice and amounts of the RO members have an undoubted influence upon the development of good textures. For example, those containing PbO–CaO–ZnO gave a much larger number of glossy glazes than a series with the same amount of PbO and BaO in place of ZnO. The latter series contained several good matts, the former scarcely any. The particular form of the material chosen to introduce a given constituent will be a significant factor in some cases. This is probably best illustrated by the comparison, reported by some experimenters, between the action of alumina introduced as clay, feldspar, and aluminium hydrate.

In general, it may be said that in any group of glazes having similar maturing temperatures, those members possessing the maximum heat ranges will contain the highest content of lead oxide, the largest number of members of the RO group, and the amounts of alumina and silica needed to form the maximum amount of eutectics.

Lead Glazes — Compositions

The lead glazes in common use are so complex in the numbers of constituent oxides that equilibria studies have not been made nor can they be until new techniques are discovered suitable for the purpose. Some of the simpler systems have been investigated, and a few of those of particular interest will be referred to here. In the system $PbO–SiO_2$, an eutectic lies between $2PbO \cdot SiO_2$ and $PbO \cdot SiO_2$ at 84.6% PbO–15.4% SiO_2. The liquidus temperature is $715° \pm 10°$ C.[12]

There are a number of equilibrium diagrams containing information directly related to lead glazes. Fourteen systems are contained in *Phase diagrams for ceramists,*[13] enumerated as follows:

Pb–O	$PbO–Nb_2O_5$
$Pb–Al_2O_3$	$PbO–P_2O_5$
$PbO–Al_2O_3–SiO_2$	$PbO–P_2O_5–SiO_2$
$PbO–As_2O_3$	$PbO–SiO_2$
$PbO–Bi_2O_3$	$PbO–SnO_2$
$PbO–B_2O_3–MoO_3$	$PbO–V_2O_5$
$PbO–CrO_3$	PbO_2

Eutectics of $PbO–SiO_2$ are of much importance to glaze makers accustomed to use, as necessary, a fritted lead oxide–silica glass as a medium for softening a glaze mixture. Such a mixture has been known to the glaze

Table 10.4. Lead-alumina-silica eutectics[14]

No.	Composition PbO	Al_2O_3	SiO_2	Liquidus temperature
	%	%	%	°C
1	94	6	–	865
2	70.7	1.0	29.3	725
3	82.6	1.4	16.0	695
4	84.6	2.2	13.2	704
5	89.8	1.2	9.0	694
6	93.1	1.1	5.8	695
7	91.2	5.2	3.6	764

maker as "Rocaille Flux" but no information is at hand that it is compounded according to eutectic proportions.

An examination of the study of part of the $PbO–Al_2O_3–SiO_2$ system reported by Geller and Bunting[14] is interesting. The eutectic compositions are given in table 10.4. Examples of similar simple, crude glazes are: $PbO:SiO_2$ for about 900° C, equivalent to about cone 010 and $PbO:2.5SiO_2$ for about 980° C, equivalent to about cone 08.

The lead oxide–silica compositions, or any composition, will attack the body more or less and dissolve from it alumina, silica, lime, and other components. A glaze used on a red body and therefore colored by the solution of a small amount of ferric oxide from the same is:

$$PbO \quad 0.09Al_2O_3 \quad 1.4SiO_2$$
$$0.03Fe_2O_3$$

This glaze will mature at about 954° C, i.e., cones 08–07.

However, such uncontrolled results are crude and unsatisfactory. The addition of alumina to the batch in the form of clay assists in keeping the slip mixture in suspension, promotes adhesion, controls the viscosity of the fusion, and thereby insures a more uniform coating.

In order to improve the mechanical properties of the glaze slip to facilitate dipping and adhesion; to widen the heat range; to alter its thermal expansion, elasticity, and optical properties; to obtain a more nearly colorless glaze; or to obtain specific effects with the use of a particular colorant, the number and the choice of the bases used are subject to wide variations. The net result is much diversity in compositions, ranging from the simple types mentioned to those which are very complex.

The work of Cannan[8] has been cited. His conclusion was that the workable replacement of lead oxide by the ordinary bases is limited in amount to 0.15 or 0.2 molecular equivalents of any single one and barium oxide was found unusable. In the light of more recent published results,

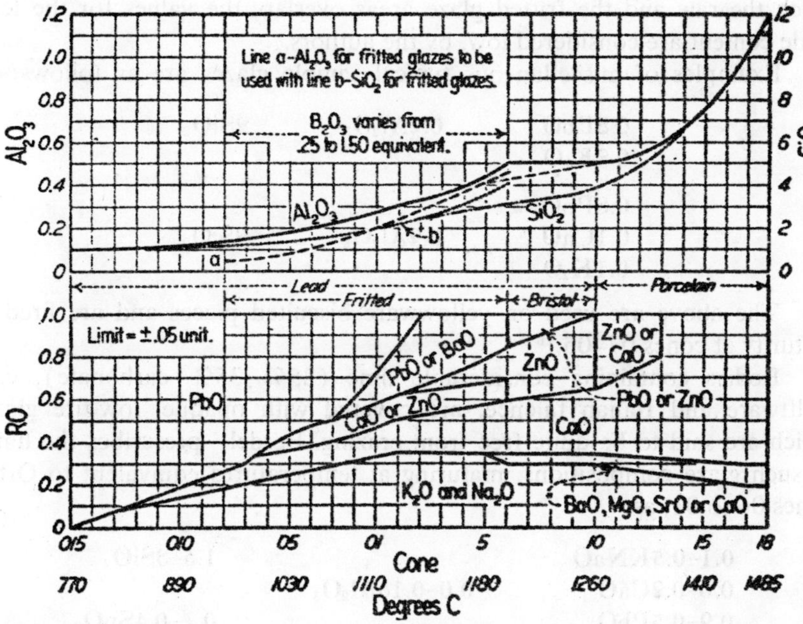

Figure 10.2. Limits in molecular equivalents found in principal types of glazes.[15]

it seems proper to infer that his conclusions should be limited to the conditions of his experiments. This is illustrated in figure 10.2. which was compiled by Holscher[15] from compositions available by 1930 and used in commercial practice. In reading the values of silica or alumina appropriate for any cone temperature, selected on the abscissa, follow the vertical line to the intersection of either the SiO_2 or the Al_2O_3 graphs and obtain the respective values from the proper ordinates. The molecular equivalents of the bases for a particular temperature may be had by tracing the vertical line at the temperature until it intersects the graph for a particular base or the area set apart for the same, then reading the value or values in equivalents on the ordinate at the left side. Of course, these readings must be made within the "lead" portion of figure 10.2.

The authors direct attention to the entry of the calcium oxide into the glaze composition at about cone 012, while zinc oxide may replace a part of the calcium oxide as low as cone 07. Zinc oxide "very definitely" comes into the formula at cone 1. The area labeled "PbO or BaO" is to be considered all lead oxide if raw lead glazes are being studied. The BaO is inserted in case fritted glazes are being planned, since the two oxides act very similarly under such a condition. In the temperature range within which the raw and the fritted glaze areas overlap, the values for the lead oxide content are considered low, by the authors.

Examples of miscellaneous typical sample glazes are as follows:

$$\begin{matrix} 0.8PbO \\ 0.2K_2O \end{matrix} \quad 0.2Al_2O_3 \quad 2SiO_2$$

$$\begin{matrix} 0.8PbO \\ 0.1CaO \\ 0.1K_2O \end{matrix} \quad 0.2Al_2O_3 \quad 2SiO_2$$

The above are used on yellowware biscuited pieces and are fired to maturity at cones 07–05.[16]

Bodies containing considerable lime (25%–35% carbonate), e.g., Delftware and Italian faience, are covered with opaque, low-fire glazes which are said to be quite free from crazing. Berdel[17] prescribes the limits of such glaze compositions, maturing at temperatures equivalent to Orton cones 06 to 01, as:

$$\begin{matrix} 0.1\text{–}0.5KNaO \\ 0.0\text{–}0.2CaO \\ 0.9\text{–}0.5PbO \end{matrix} \quad 0.0\text{–}0.15Al_2O_3 \quad \begin{matrix} 1.5\text{–}3SiO_2 \\ \\ 0.2\text{–}0.4SnO_2 \end{matrix}$$

It is obvious that the use of the maximum amount of KNaO will necessitate the use of a frit. Where possible, it is desirable to introduce the maximum amount of potash as it enhances the opacity and whiteness.

The same type of ware may be covered with either of these glazes:[18]

$$\left.\begin{matrix} 0.78PbO \\ 0.22CaO \end{matrix}\right\} \quad 0.29Al_2O_3 \quad \begin{matrix} 2.60SiO_2 \\ 0.29SnO_2 \end{matrix}$$

Table 10.5. Glossy raw lead compositions

No.	*Cone*	*PbO*	*K_2O*	*CaO*	*BaO*	*MgO*	*ZnO*	*Al_2O_3*	*SiO_2*
1[21]	09	0.90	0.10	–	–	–	–	0.10	1.50
*2[22]	08	0.85	0.05	0.10	–	–	–	0.10	1.20
3[23]	06	0.60	0.15	0.25	–	–	–	0.20	1.60
†4[24]	04	0.70	0.10	0.20	–	–	–	0.20	1.60
5[25]	02	0.60	0.10	0.15	–	–	0.15	0.15	1.50
6[26]	01	0.60	0.20	0.20	–	–	–	0.25	2.00
7[27]	1	0.35	0.20	0.30	–	–	0.15	0.25	1.75
8[28]	2	0.40	0.20	0.30	–	–	0.10	0.35	2.65
9[29]	3	0.48	0.12	0.40	–	–	–	0.32	2.12
10[25]	4	0.25	0.20	0.35	–	–	0.20	0.25	2.00
11[30]	6	0.19	0.16	0.40	–	–	0.25	0.19	2.03
‡12[31]	8	0.50	–	0.30	–	–	0.20	0.20	1.60

*Good from cones 08 to 02. † Good from cones 05 to 03. ‡ "Developed well at cone 3, better at cone 8."

$$\left.\begin{matrix}0.78PbO\\0.22K_2O\end{matrix}\right\} \quad 0.21Al_2O_3 \quad \begin{matrix}4.30SiO_2\\0.49SnO_2\end{matrix}$$

Binns[19] mentions these compositions:

PbO	0.7	0.7	0.5
CaO	0.3	0.3	0.3
ZnO	—	—	0.2
K_2O	—	—	—
Al_2O_3	0.1	0.26	0.2
SiO_2	1.3	1.78	1.6
cone	3	3	3–8

Orton[20] suggested the following composition as a satisfactory bright glaze on brick fired in commercial kilns between cones 2 and 6:

$$\begin{matrix}0.4PbO\\0.2K_2O\\0.2CaO\\0.2ZnO\end{matrix} \quad 0.35Al_2O_3 \quad 2.56SiO_2$$

A tin-enamel suitable for use on biscuit over an engobe[16] was given as:

$$\begin{matrix}0.18K_2O\\0.30CaO\\0.52PbO\end{matrix} \quad 0.27Al_2O_3 \quad 2.52SiO_2$$

(Add 11.42% of SnO_2)

Some glossy raw lead glaze compositions and their maturing temperatures are summarized in table 10.5.

Matt Glazes

The low gloss or lustre of a matt or dull glaze is due to the refraction and diffusion of the light rays reflected from a surface which has been chemically corroded or mechanically abraded, or from undissolved materials, crystals, or inert particles, suspended in a glassy matrix. In some cases mattness has been attributed also to roughening of the surface by shrinkage during the cooling of a molten glaze. There are no generally accepted specifications describing an ideal matt surface or such variants as semimatt, semigloss, dull immature, and other similar terms which are found in literature.

Very rarely have the optical characteristics of matt glazes reported in literature accompanied information regarding composition, firing conduct, and other necessary data. This regrettable lack renders the evaluation of the results of most published reports very unsatisfactory and is a possible explanation of disappointing results sometimes achieved by other experimenters attempting to repeat the experiments.

Mattness due to immaturity and the presence of undissolved material may be distinguished from the cryptocrystalline type by the microscopic examination of a thin section, particularly if it is cut at right angles to the face of contact with the body. Also, a cryptocrystalline matt drawn from the kiln at maturity and cooled quickly will be a clear glass; whereas a companion sample left in the kiln to cool slowly will develop mattness. A glaze which is matt because of immaturity or because of suspended undissolved particles will not be a clear glass at maturity irrespective of the cooling treatment. The desirable matt texture is not rough to the touch and dirt rubbed on by the fingers may be wiped off easily. This is not true of textures accompanying immaturity or the presence of undissolved particles.

Several phases nave been identified as present in and responsible for matt textures of glazes. Some of these are anorthite ($CaO \cdot Al_2O_3 \cdot 2SiO_2$), tridymite ($SiO_2$), mullite ($3Al_2O_3 \cdot 2SiO_2$), wollastonite ($CaO \cdot SiO_2$), and celsian ($BaO \cdot Al_2O_3 \cdot 2SiO_2$). A lead silicate has been reported but not described. Other compounds are present, undoubtedly. It has been suggested that mullite is one of the first compounds to be formed and may be the one most commonly present. It is the common practice to increase the alumina content of a glossy glaze in order to produce a matt. This was first reported in literature by Binns[32] who pointed out that the excess of alumina required for this purpose depends upon the kinds and amounts of the bases and the amount of the silica.

Attempts to oversimplify the technique of mattness by relating it solely to the alumina-silica ratio can be successful only within a limited composition range since the phenomenon is primarily that of saturation with a crystallizable and crystallizing compound, or the presence of much insoluble material. Naturally time and temperature are very important factors. To these we may add the contribution by the body constituents, which may be very considerable after prolonged firing.

The firing and the cooling schedule will often be the explanation of good and also poor results in the same kiln or in different operations. If a certain composition is to be fired at a higher temperature or cooled for a longer period, it is a common practice to increase the alumina content moderately. With the foregoing reservations in mind it is useful to know that the ratio of alumina to silica very frequently falls within the range of 1:3 to 1:5.48, but good matts are possible outside of those limits.

Examples of raw lead matt glaze compositions are given in table 10.6.

Table 10.6. Empirical formulas of some raw lead matt glazes.

No.	*Cone*	*PbO*	K_2O	*CaO*	*BaO*	*MgO*	*ZnO*	Al_2O_3	SiO_2
1[33]	010	0.80	0.10	0.10	–	–	–	0.17	1.00
2[24]	08	0.80	0.05	0.15	–	–	–	0.12	1.08
3[34]	06	0.65	0.15	0.20	–	–	–	0.20	1.20
*4[35]	04	0.58	0.22	0.20	–	–	–	0.35	1.60
5[36]	02	0.50	0.17	0.08	0.25	–	–	0.33	2.00
†6[33]	1	0.60	0.15	0.25	–	–	–	0.35	1.30
7[37]	2	0.35	0.20	0.45	–	–	–	0.29	1.87
‡8[36]	4	0.55	0.15	0.30	–	–	–	0.35	1.68
9[7]	6	0.40	–	0.30	0.30	–	–	0.30	1.60

*Good from cone 05 to cone 4. † Good from cone 04 to cone 1. ‡ Good from cone 02 to cone 4.

The compositions were selected so as to include compositions maturing from cone 010 up to cone 6. By and large, these glazes would fit ordinary pottery bodies or semivitreous whiteware (semiporcelain) bodies.

Colored Lead Glazes

Colored raw lead glazes continue to be most widely used, from earliest times to the present. One example of colored raw lead glazes is shown in figure 10.3.

There are two mechanisms for coloring raw lead glazes: solution colors and suspended pigments. By solution colors is meant that the color is derived from oxides which dissolve in the glaze to form colored ion species completely soluble and a part of the glass matrix. The other mechanism for color development is the dispersion or distribution within the glaze matrix of nonglass crystalline pigments and pigment aggregates. For solution colors, only those oxides that dissolve in the matrix to give colored ions are used. For pigment colors, crystalline oxides, pigments, or stains are used that do not dissolve in the glaze matrix.

Weyl[38] thoroughly analyzed the whole matter of colors in glass due to dissolved ions. A digest of some of his analysis of the subject is of value and is presented here.

The origin of color in manganese-containing glasses is due to absorption of the Mn^{3+} ion which is influenced by ionic surroundings. The large weak ionic neighbors, such as K or Na, result in minimal electrical perturbing influences and shift colors to shorter wavelengths, i.e., from red to blue. Small, strong ions, such as Mg, have the opposite effect. Another way of regarding the phenomena is that, when more of the Mn^{3+} act as network formers, the color is shifted toward the blue.

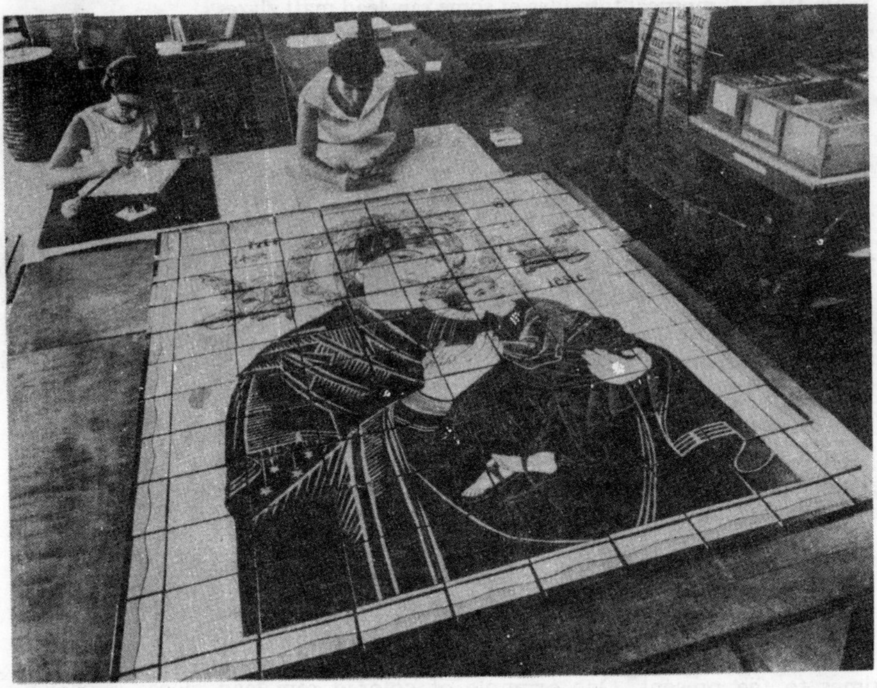

Figure 10.3. Religious tile mural coated with majolica glazes containing lead and color. They are either fritted or raw.

Divalent manganese ions will produce only yellow or brown colors which yield green or orange fluorescence. In the familiar manganese purple glasses, only a very small portion of the manganese is in the trivalent state.

Chromium in the trivalent form yields green glasses, the hue depending on the nature of the neighboring ions. When conditions permit the existence of hexavalent chromium, a yellow glass is obtained. For example, arsenic and antimony favor the trivalent state, while alkalies promote the hexavalent state. In glasses low in silica and high in RO, the tendency is to produce glasses resembling the color of the crystalline chromate. For example, barium = orange yellow, strontium = pale yellow, calcium = yellow, magnesium = orange, lead = orange to red.

The oxidation-reduction behavior of vanadium resembles that of chromium in its tendency to form anions and cations and to yield various colors. They may be colorless, yellow, brown, green, or even gray. The colorless glasses occur in extremely basic and highly oxidizing compositions. The yellowish-brown colors appear in acid glasses, where there is a tendency to form polyvanadate molecules. The vanadium greens are due to vanadic ions. Sulfur reduces the vanadium to the tetravalent state to produce blue glass.

Copper also can result in various colors. In the presence of reducing agents and at very high temperatures, cuprous ions and even copper atoms may be formed. This is the case in copper ruby and aventurine glazes. Divalent copper, when dissolved in silicate glass, forms color centers of different coordination to yield deep blue, light blue, green, and even brown.

In copper ruby, the first step is the reduction to the cuprous ion, which exists at high temperature, in solution. On cooling and striking, the cupric ion decomposes to copper atoms. During striking, these atoms are thrown out of solution to yield copper particles of various sizes and consequently of various colors.

Glasses high in lead or titania tend to give rise to green colors. At the other extreme, high soda glasses develop turquoise blue.

Although pink, red, blue, and green cobalt colors have been observed in glasses, the familiar cobalt blue always appears except under very unusual conditions. Nickel, like cobalt, forms only divalent ions, but nickel-bearing glasses vary over the visible spectrum, depending on composition, namely in the RO and R_2O members. These colors, while sensitive to glaze composition, are not influenced by furnace atmosphere or the presence of oxides or reducing agents.

Uranium oxide has been extensively used in glazes as a colorant. Uranium is amphoteric. Under normal or oxidizing conditions, the hexavalent UO_3 state is stable. When reduced, the yellow UO_3 changes to black uranous uranate, U_3O_8, as in black uranium glazes. Uranyl ions form in acidic compositions, but uranates or uranate molecules tend to exist in basic compositions.

Molybdenum as MoO_3 gives rise to opacity, being of low solubility in glazes. If reduced, typically a blue results.

The rare earth oxides produce colors usually characterized by sharp absorption spectra. Base compositions have a minor effect on color. Neodymium glasses usually are pink and praseodymium green.

Solution Colors

Colored lead glazes based on solution colors may be made in great variety because many oxides are available for producing color in silicate melts. All of the oxides shown in table 10.7, and some others, may be used, excepting only those few cases of very refractory oxides and extremely low-temperature melts. For example, chrome oxide is not suitable for use in producing greens in glazes maturing below cone 05, because

Table 10.7. Molecular equivalents of color oxides used in matt and glossy glazes[39]

	Raw lead glazes (bright) by Purdy		*Matt glazes by Gibson*			
Coloring oxide	*Commercial limits in equivalents*		*Commercial limits in equivalents*		*Possible limits in equivalents*	
CuO	0.05	0.125	0.03	0.15	0.005	0.18
CoO	0.002	0.06	0.002	0.08	0.001	0.10
MnO_2	0.03	0.15	0.02	0.20	0.010	0.25
Fe_2O_3	0.01	0.05	0.01	0.05	0.005	0.10
Cr_2O_3	0.01	0.05	–	–	–	–
NiO_2	0.01	0.05	0.01	0.10	0.010	0.10
U_2O_3	0.002	0.008	0.002	0.009	0.002	0.01

the oxide has slight solubility, if any, and the glaze must be relatively high in bases and low in silica, which conditions are unfavorable for the development of a good green color. The use of a very refractory color base such as the chrome-alumina pink would be impracticable, obviously.

Table 10.7 shows the oxides commonly used and the practicable molecular equivalents. The production of the colors is controlled by the choice of coloring oxides, the amounts and kinds of the RO members, the amounts of the alumina and silica, and the temperature of firing.

Green

Copper Oxide. This oxide is readily soluble in lead glazes producing a transparent green color which is susceptible to the kind and amount of the other bases present and the temperature. Apparently it volatilizes more readily from lead-containing glazes than other types. Walker[40] reports the effects of various oxides upon the development of greens, using copper as follows: calcium oxide, in any allowable quantity (at cones 02 to 2) had no effect upon the color; zinc oxide made the color more brilliant and more variations of shades were had; potassium oxide produces yellowish shades of green and this is true also of sodium oxide; baria and magnesia have specific effects. If potassium oxide is used with zinc oxide, the color will deepen as the former is replaced by zinc oxide. Other investigators have reported that calcia aids and magnesia diminishes the intensity of the green color. Ramsden[41] found that the solubility of the oxide in glazes melting below 1,100° C varied from 3% to 8%. This may be increased by raising the silica content, decreasing the alumina (avoiding devitrification), and increasing the alkali content at the expense of the lead oxide. If the lead oxide exceeds 0.7 mol. equiv., a small portion may be replaced with zinc oxide or magnesia. An excess of clay or copper oxide in the composition and firing above 1,100° C gives a browner shade. The author is of the opinion that calcium and barium oxides have little influence on the green color.

CHROMIUM OXIDE. Whereas the relatively easy solubility of the copper oxide in lead silicate fusions gives transparent greens, the less soluble chromium oxide—seldom greater[11] than 1% below 1,100° C—yields opaque glazes. When the amount of the oxide is so low as to be dissolved, the color will be yellowish-green. The color is made browner by aluminum, zinc, and barium oxides, also by tin oxide which later, under favorable conditions, gives pinkish to red. Calcia may be expected to give yellowish or orange tones but the evidence seems to be contradictory.

NICKEL OXIDE. The solubility of nickel oxide in silicate fusions is not greater than 1% to 3% at temperatures below 1,100° C. The lead oxide should be less than 0.7 mol. equiv., and may be replaced in part by zinc oxide. A green may be had by the use of nickel oxide with magnesium oxide as RO members in a lead[42] or a leadless[43] glaze.

COBALT-URANIUM. A green may be had by blending the oxides of cobalt and uranium in a stain. In order to insure the absence of specks, the nitrates may be mixed in the approximate proportions of 4 or 5 parts of the uranium nitrate to 1 part of the cobalt nitrate. These are added to a frit or calcine.

Yellow, Orange, Cream, Tan, and Buffs

FERRIC OXIDE. Ferric oxide may be used in lead silicate glazes to produce a weak yellow, tans, and buff. It was much used by the Chinese during the seventh century of the present era and subsequently to give yellows.

URANIUM OXIDE. Colors ranging from a light yellow to a deep orange may be had with uranium oxide, according to the amount used and the bases present. About 10% of sodium uranate is needed for the deepest color. The alkaline earths do not affect the color; the alkalies, including lithia, lighten the color. Ivory-colored shades may be produced by the addition of 6% tin oxide and 1% to 2% of sodium uranate to a lead glaze containing zinc oxide.[44]

MOLYBDENUM OXIDE. Molybdenum oxide will give yellow which varies in intensity according to the amount used, 2% to 10%. Barrett[37] considers it a strong coloring agent. The composition reported as giving satisfactory yellows was a typical raw lead glaze—having PbO, CaO, and K_2O—fired at cones 02–2.

RUTILE. Cream color may be had by the addition of rutile, with or without tin oxide, to lead glaze.[45] (See formula batch for cone 05.)

Brown

MANGANESE OXIDE. The solubility of manganese oxide varies from about 1% to 4% in lead containing glazes[46] fired at 1,100° C or lower. An increased temperature is accompanied by a greater solubility with some loss of quality of the color, which will be a claret brown. Alumina favors the development of the color but should be kept low. Zinc oxide, lime, and silica promote the formation of the pinker shades. Manganese oxide shows a tendency to volatilize and is quite sensitive to the presence of sulfur oxides in the kiln gases which form a thin film, dulling the gloss.

IRON OXIDES. The solubility of ferric oxide in glazes varies from 3% to 14% at temperatures up to 1,100° C.[46] Lowering the lime, zinc oxide, and alumina and raising the amount of lead oxide increases the solubility. Raising the temperature has the same effect but impoverishes the color. The color is improved by the presence of alumina, clay, and barium oxide. Magnesia diminishes the color.

NICKEL OXIDE. The color obtained by using nickel oxide in lead-containing glazes is strongly influenced by the other bases present. It is most commonly some shade of brown, varying from straw to purplish. The colors are likely to be variable. Holscher,[15] using a simple leadless glaze and successively substituting zinc oxide, lime, barium oxide, and magnesia, obtained blue, tan, browns, and green.

CHROMIUM OXIDE. Magnesia,[47] zinc oxide, and alumina tend to produce fawns, tans, and brownish shades when chromium oxide is used with them in lead glazes.

Blue

COBALT OXIDE. Cobalt oxide is relatively easily soluble in lead-containing glazes. It has very high tinctorial power and is somewhat susceptible to the influence of the choice of the alkalies and alkaline earths present, but not to the extent that is true in the leadless types.

NICKEL OXIDE. A slate blue and a "good" blue have been reported by experimenters who used lead oxide and zinc oxide or lead oxide, zinc oxide, and alkalies in simple glaze compositions maturing at cones 1 to 3.

Red

IRON OXIDE. Red colors may be had in highly siliceous, lead-containing glazes when the alkalies are high and lime (and the other alkaline earths) is not present. Geijbeek[48] has given the following example:

$0.70K_2O$	$1.17Al_2O_3$	$5.47SiO_2$
$0.20Na_2O$	$0.05Fe_2O_3$	
$0.10PbO$		

It is quite evident that a portion of this composition must be fritted.

URANIUM OXIDE. Uranium oxide is a realiable reagent for producing reds at temperatures up to cone 04 and only occasionally higher. Cordt[49] states that the lead and silica content should be high; zinc oxide is not harmful to the color and may be useful in producing a matt texture, but not more than 1% should be used and it should be introduced in the mill batch; little kaolin may be added, but no whiting, if it can be avoided, and no boric acid.

Four raw lead glazes colored by uranium are given in table 10.8. In the "Materials as oxides" column, uranium is listed as U_2O_3. The oxide just as well could be UO_2 or a sodium-uranium oxide complex frequently called sodium uranate. Uranium no longer is much used. It is strongly radioactive and to some degree has been outlawed. However, grades of "depleted" uranium oxides now are available that are reputed to be radiation-free and "harmless."

The batches of glazes no. 1 and no. 2 of table 10.8 are given in table 10.9.

Table 10.8. Raw lead glazes colored by uranium oxide

Components, as oxides	*Composition in molecular equivalents**			
	No. 1[50] Semi-matt cone 07	*No. 2[50] Glossy cone 03*	*No. 3[45] Bright cone 6–7*	*No. 4[51] Bright cone 04*
PbO	0.93	0.94	0.90	0.80
K_2O	0.07	0.03		0.12
Na_2O			0.10	
ZnO		0.03		0.07
Al_2O_3	0.13	0.156		0.12
U_2O_3			0.20	
"Uranium oxide"*	21%	24%		20%
SiO_2	1.17	1.37	2.00	1.33
SnO_2		0.02		

*The part of the compositions listed as "uranium oxide" is added to the batch of all other ingredients in the amounts indicated, in weight percent of the total batch.

Table 10.9. Batch weights for glazes No. 1 and No. 2 of table 10.8

Batch Materials	Amounts, parts by weight: Glaze No. 1 Total batch	Glaze No. 2 Frit batch	Glaze No. 2 Mill batch
Frit			100
Red lead	60	140	
Feldspar	11	12	
Flint	21	45	2
Kaolin		4	
Zinc oxide			1
Uranium oxide	22		27
Tin oxide		2	

Nonsolution Colors

Coral-red glazes have a distinctive color, sometimes compared to that of sealing wax, that gives them a highly decorative value. They are of technical interest because the color is developed by the reaction of chromium oxide and the RO member. The coral red is a reaction of $PbO + Cr_2O_3$ to form lead chromate crystals. Variation in shade is produced by substituting some BaO or CaO or ZnO for some of the PbO. The high content of lead necessary and other restrictions of the composition limit their use to firing temperatures of cones 013 to 05, rarely higher.

The optimum Cr_2O_3 content in high lead chrome glazes lies at about 4.5% to 5%. The reddishness and firing temperature increases with alumina, but SiO_2 opposes the development of red colors. As the silica (acidity) increases, the red disappears and green becomes the stable color. The glazes usually are crystalline, and the crystal development in the glaze surface gives interesting artistic effects. As long as the red color persists, crazing does not appear.

According to Dietzel,[51] the surface tension of molten red chromium

Table 10.10. Typical lead chromate coral-red glazes

Glaze No.	RO	R_2O_3	RO_2	Firing temp, °C
1[52]	1.0 PbO	0.10 Al_2O_3 0.05 Cr_2O_3	0.70 SiO_2	950
2[53]	0.9 PbO 0.1 CaO	0.20 Al_2O_3 0.10 Cr_2O_3	0.70 SiO_2	950
3[53]	0.88 PbO 0.05 K_2O 0.06 Na_2O	0.10 Al_2O_3 0.05 Cr_2O_3	1.30 SiO_2	945

lead glazes is extremely low. Such glazes diffuse into adjacent colorless glazes to a greater extent than any other colored glaze; the high spreading tendency was attributed by Dietzel to its surface tension effect. The chromate ions (CrO_3) decrease the surface tension so much that lead glaze containing them cannot maintain a contact edge between it and other types of glaze. The chromate state also contributes to lowered density and to high vapor pressure. There is a low binding force between Pb^{++} and $(CrO_4)^{--}$ that is responsible for the low surface tension of glasses containing Pb CrO_4. The anions $(SO_4)^{--}$ and $(VO_4)^{--}$ behave in the same fashion as does the chromate $(CrO_4)^{--}$ anions.

Dietzel postulated that a glaze with 3.2% of CrO_3 would have a surface tension of 19 dynes per cm lower than the corresponding Cr-free glaze at 900° C.

The composition of the RO group varies approximately as follows, in molecular equivalents; lead oxide from 1.0 to about 0.7; the alkalies, of which soda is said to be best, may be as much as 0.3 equivalent but 0.1 is more usual; lithia may be useful but opinions differ; calcium oxide has been recommended as the one base other than lead oxide which is essential, but the amount should not exceed one quarter of the total bases, 0.1 mol. equiv. or less is the usual amount; barium oxide may be used but not in excess of 0.05 mol. equiv.; zinc oxide in amount not exceeding one fourth of the lime brightens the gloss; magnesia may impair the brilliancy, even if used in very small quantities.

The permissible amount of alumina will be between 0.1 and 0.3 mol. equiv. and depends chiefly upon the content of silica, but the nature of the RO group is important. The silica content will be found to vary between 0.5 and 1.3 mol. equiv. The chromium oxide (Cr_2O_3) functions as an acid and varies from 0.05 to 0.3 with 0.1 mol. equiv. most frequently used. Prolonged or high fire will impair or destroy the scarlet and yield a green color.

Some typical formulas of coral-red glaze compositions are given in table 10.10. There are many suitable variations from these compositions.

References

1. Lucas, A. 1936. Glazed ware in Egypt, India, and Mesopotamia. *J. of Egyptian Archaeology* 22:141.
2. Collie, J. N. 1915–16. Notes on some Chinese glazes on pottery and porcelain. *Trans. Engl. Ceram. Soc.* 15:160.
3. Watts, A. S. 1915. Oxides of lead versus carbonate of lead in glazes. *Trans. Am. Ceram. Soc.* 17:474.
4. Clark, J. D. 1944. Strontia as a ceramic-glaze oxide. Foote Prints 16:9.

5. McCutchen, E. S. 1944. Strontia and its properties in glazes. *J. Am. Ceram. Soc.* 27:233.
6. Purdy, R. C. 1911. Raw lead glazes. *Pottery and Glass.* 6(8):31.
7. Parmelee, C. W. and Horak, W. 1934. The microstructure of some raw lead matt glazes. *J. Am. Ceram. Soc.* 17:67.
8. Cannan, W. 1901. A new glaze flux. *Trans. Am. Ceram. Soc.* 3:113.
9. 1916. *Sprechsaal Kalendar,* p. 34.
10. Fickes, W. M. 1901. Permissible variation in the silica and alumina contents of raw lead glazes. *Trans. Am. Ceram. Soc.* 3:82.
11. Staley, H. F. 1913. A study of the relations between fusibility and heat range in glazes. *Trans. Am. Ceram. Soc.* 15:694.
12. Cooper, H. C., Shaw, L. I., and Loomis, N. E. 1909. *Am. J. Sci.* 42(4):461 as given by Hall, F. P., and Insley, H. 1933. *J. Am. Cer. Soc.* 16:494.
13. Levin, Ernest M., Robbins, Carl R. and McMurdie, Howard R. 1964. *Phase diagrams for ceramists.* Columbus, Ohio: American Ceramic Society.
14. Geller, R. F. and Bunting, E. N. 1943. Report on the systems lead oxide-alumina and lead oxide-alumina-silica, *J. Res. Natl. Bur. Std.* (U.S.) 31:255.
15. Holscher, H. H. and Watts, A. S. 1931. A graphical representation of the molecular formulas of ceramic glazes. *J. Am. Ceram. Soc.* 14:583.
16. Langenbeck, K. 1895. *Chemistry of pottery.* Easton, Pa.: Chemical Publishing Co., p 71.
17. Berdel, E. 1929. *Einfaches chemisches Praktikum.* 5th ed. Vol. 6. Koburg, p 27.
18. Funk, W. 1933. *Rohstoffe der Feinkeramik.* Berlin, p 251.
19. Binns, C. F. 1900. Monosilicate glazes. *Trans. Am. Ceram. Soc.* 2:151.
20. Orton, Edward, Jr. 1908. A study of a type of matt glaze maturing at cone 2–4. *Trans. Am. Ceram. Soc.* 10:547.
21. Berge, A. 1913. Report from the Royal Bunzlau Ceramic School. *Sprech.* 46:125,140.
22. Worcester, W. G. and Orton, E., Jr. 1910. The manufacture of roofing tiles. *Ohio State Geological Survey.* Bull. 11:423.
23. Binns, C. F. 1910. *The potters craft.* London: Constable and Co., p 131.
24. Stull, R. T. Communication.
25. Watts, A. S. 1915. Oxide of lead versus carbonate of lead in glazes. *Trans. Am. Ceram. Soc.* 17:474.
26. Worcester and Orton, op. cit., ref. 22, p 424.
27. Binns, op. cit., ref. 23, p 132.
28. Dept. of Ceramic Engineering, Univ. of Illinois.
29. Staley, H. F. and Hewitt, L. C. 1917. The cost of raw lead glazes. *Trans. Am. Ceram. Soc.* 19:659.
30. Weelans, C. 1907. Bodies and glazes. *Trans. Am. Ceram. Soc.* 9:483.
31. Binns, C. F. 1900. Monosilicate glazes. *Trans. Am. Ceram. Soc.* 2:151.
32. Binns, C. F. 1903. The development of the matt glaze. *Trans. Am. Ceram. Soc.* 5:50.

33. Montgomery, E. T. and Tefft, C. F. 1914. Roofing tile slips and glazes. *Trans. Am. Ceram. Soc.* 16:144.
34. Communication.
35. Purdy, R. C. 1912. Matt glazes. *Trans. Am. Ceram. Soc.* 14:671.
36. Heubach, A. R. 1913. Notes on the cause of mattness in glazes. *Trans. Am. Ceram. Soc.* 15:591.
37. Barrett, W. E. 1925. Glazes colored by molybdenum. *J. Am. Ceram. Soc.* 8:306.
38. Weyl, W. A. 1944. Colored glasses: 2, Color of glasses produced by various coloring ions (continued). *J. Soc. Glass Tech.* 28(128):158–266T.
39. Gibson, Millard F. 1910. Color series for matt glazes at cone 2–4. *Trans. Am. Ceram. Soc.* 12:533.
40. Walker, F. W. 1902. Notes on the development of greens from cupric oxide in glazes. *Trans. Am. Ceram. Soc.* 4:278.
41. Ramsden, C. E. 1907–8. Solubilities of metallic oxides in glazes. *Trans. Engl. Ceram. Soc.* 7:21.
42. Wicks, H. and Mellor, J. W. 1913–14. Nickel in glaze colors. *Trans. Engl. Ceram. Soc.* 13:61.
43. Holscher, H. H. 1929. Some leadless borosilicate glazes containing nickel oxide. *J. Am. Ceram. Soc.* 12:111.
44. Kautz, K. 1934. The effect of glaze composition upon colors produced by sodium uranate. *J. Am. Ceram. Soc.* 17:8.
45. 1938. Unusual pink and maroon glazes by the use of colemanite. *Cer. Ind.* 31(9):42.
46. Ramsden, C. E. 1905. Solubilities of metallic oxides in glazes. *Trans. Engl. Ceram. Soc.* 5:18.
47. Minton, R. H. 1914. The effect of variation of RO elements upon chromium oxide as a coloring agent in a matt glaze," *Trans. Am. Ceram. Soc.* 16:248.
48. Geijbeek, S. 1899. Red glazes at high temperatures. *Trans. Am. Ceram. Soc.* 1:56.
49. Cordt, F. W. 1933. Production of red glazes. *Cer. Ind.* 21:172.
50. Binns and Lyttle. 1920. *J. Am. Ceram. Soc.* 3:913.
51. Dietzel, A. 1949. Chromium red colored glazes. *Mitt. Deut. Keram. Ges.* 1:1244, 2:15–21.
52. Berge, A. 1911. Red chrome glazes. *Sprech.* 44:581.
53. Binns, C. F. and Craig, E. 1927. A chromium red glaze. *J. Am. Ceram. Soc.* 10:73.

11

Engobes, Slips, Underslips, and Terra Sigillata

An engobe or slip is a coating or decoration of a mixture of clays, fluxes, pigments, and nonplastics that is applied on a ceramic body to form a color smoothly covering all surface defects and coarse particles. An essential difference between a glaze and an engobe or underslip is the greater amount of glassy phase in the former. Engobes may be white, the most common, clay colors, or artificially colored. If a glaze is applied on the engobe, the latter may be called an underslip. These are usually made with white firing clays in order to provide a suitable base upon which delicately colored glazes may be used without suffering harm from contact with iron-bearing and other objectionable minerals.

Engobes are used on a wide variety of wares ranging from pottery to structural materials. Many kinds of wares containing large quantities of fine grog, such as architectural terra cotta, and enameled brick are coated with glazes, and these glazes are frequently colored in delicate shades. In order to attain the requisite perfection of surface on the ware and to preserve the colors, the engobe layer is applied as a smooth white intermediate layer (underslip). The requirements for building brick and roofing tile are less rigorous; therefore slip coats, without a glaze, may be used in order to improve the surface texture and color of one or more faces of the wares. Such coatings may be prepared from a body clay or more complex mixtures. Engobes are applied on pottery as a part of the decorative scheme or as an intermediate coating for the reasons already stated. Vitreous, i.e., vitrified, slips are used extensively in lieu of glazes since they afford the same protection against the weather as the full glaze and they may be colored and otherwise handled to simulate the texture and appearance of natural stone or other designs of the ceramist.

The use of the engobe has been traced to very remote ages and all stages of culture in many parts of the world. Neolithic pottery,[1] dating about 3000 B.C., decorated with red, black, and white slips—not glazed—has been found in Eastern Asia. According to Leisner,[2] Egyptian potters, during the Twelfth Dynasty (2160–1788 B.C.), used engobes which were 0.5 mm to 2.5 mm in thickness. These were varied in color, and the technique had been so skillfully perfected that the color used was selected to enhance or modify that produced by the covering glaze. For example, a yellowish underslip was used under a blue glaze so as to obtain a particular greenish shade as the final total effect. In another example cited, two shades of blue were had under different areas of the same blue glaze by using a white engobe under those portions where a lighter shade was desired. This furnished a contrasting light-colored pattern on a darker blue background.

Pottery[3] relics from Corinth, Greece, have been found decorated with designs painted thereon with slip. These are attributed to a period earlier than the sixth century B.C., when the process was revived.

Castor[3] ware made in Britain during the Roman occupancy has a white paste body covered with a dark-colored slip. A style of decoration now known as "barbotine" or "enbarbotine," which is done by applying the engobe thickly and modeling it to form a pattern in relief, is believed by Walters[3] to have been originated at an early period in Gaul or Germany.

Requirements

Engobes should be physically homogeneous to the extent of having a fine texture which is not slimy to the feel. The control of the particle size is of considerable importance as will be shown later. The colloidally dispersed portion has an important role in determining the duration and the completeness of the suspension of the slip and the dispersoids are responsible for the adhesion of the slip to the surface of the ware prior to and during the firing. An excess will cause high shrinkage during drying and firing, but behavior and even the amounts of dispersoids present are susceptible of control by the use of electrolytes.

The presence of mineral particles such as the oxides and carbonate of iron, pyrites, the carbonate of lime, the double carbonate of lime, and magnesia (dolomite)—naming the most common sorts—if coarser than 80-mesh in size, will cause popping, specking, staining, or pitting, according to their nature. These impurities may be expected to accompany the use of common clays employed as bases for engobes; such materials must be purified by "washing," i.e., levigating and grinding. These defects are not experienced in the use of white engobes since they are uniformly prepared from commercial materials which have been selected and purified—except ball clay. This material will be discussed later.

The drying and the firing shrinkages of engobes must be moderate and in agreement with those of the body on which they are applied. However, slips and bodies, when fired separately, may and usually do show slightly different shrinkages. In such cases the strength and the elasticity of the slip must be sufficient to permit the formation of a firm bond between the two members.

The drying shrinkage of the engobe applied on a biscuited body should be negligible since the latter will not shrink, whereas an engobe applied on a body in the "leather hard" condition must shrink in proportion to the change taking place in the same. The body, being much thicker, is much stronger than the thinner slip coat so the latter must be sufficiently elastic to compensate for the difference. If the difference is too great or the slip does not adhere properly, the slip will crack and probably peel off.

The drying and firing shrinkages of the engobe may be measured on test pieces prepared for the purpose by casting them in a plaster mold designed for this purpose. A suitable mold would be a block of plaster having in one face a rectangular depression large enough to form a cast test piece approximately six inches long, one inch wide, and one inch deep. Reference marks can be made, suitably spaced, on the interior face of the mold so that they will be repeated on the cast test piece. The shrinkage of the dry cast test piece is determined by comparison of the distance between the reference points in the mold and on the dry test piece. The firing shrinkages may be measured by using the same test piece and noting the changes occurring after the desired thermal treatment in the kiln. However, McDowell[1] doubts the value of the test.

Materials

Clays suitable for use as engobes after simple preparation are not abundant, but many common clays may be rendered suitable without much trouble, assuming, of course, that in any given case the clay fires to a satisfactory color. An essential step in the preparation is the removal of all coarse particles. It is thoroughly blunged and the slip is passed through an 80-mesh or finer lawn. The coarse residue is discarded. A ball mill is commonly used for a combined blunging and grinding effect. This is indispensable if the material is hard. In this case also the slip must be lawned. If the batches are small the blunging operation may be done in a small receptacle by hand stirring; but very convenient, inexpensive, electrically operated stirrers which are rapid and efficient and available in a wide variety of sizes may be had.

Usually it is necessary to add fluxes, nonplastics, and even coloring agents to the local clays just as is done in the ordinary procedure of making engobes from white firing clays. Where it is possible to use the body clay as the base, certain advantages are claimed for the practice, namely, better adhesion in the unfired state and better fit during the drying and firing shrinkages. Finely ground calcined clay, or clay and fluxes, may be useful to correct drying shrinkage.

For reasons already noted, most of the underslips and vitreous slips are compounded of white firing clays to which are added pigments and fluxes to promote vitrification and nonplastics to regulate the drying and firing shrinkages. Engobes may be divided into "standard" underslips and vitreous slips. Both may be colored or white. The ancients and primitive peoples of all times have not usually been sufficiently familiar with ceramic technology to use vitreous slips. Engobes were used by them for decoration, as, for example, wares made by the Pueblo Indians. Notable exceptions to the foregoing were the use by the Egyptians of underslips and the red and black slipped ware of the Romans and the Greeks, particularly the terra sigillata, which were vitreous coatings.

White underslips resemble white earthenware bodies in composition, appearance, and physical characteristics. The vitreous slips are porcellanic and consequently nonabsorbent; therefore, a glaze coating is neither needed nor used. They are frequently colored and more frequently treated so as to simulate the color and texture of rocks used in stone masonry, even to the reproductions of the specks and mottling such as seen on granite. Underslips are sometimes designed to become nonabsorbent when coated with a glaze in order to prevent staining of the ware due to the passage of water through cracks or chipping of the glaze.

Clays

The clays used in the engobes, except for local materials, are of three different kinds: the primary kaolins or china clays, the sedimentary kaolins, and ball clays. The proper choice and proportioning of these clays are necessary to produce engobes having these properties:

1. the desired whiteness
2. a good covering power, thus hiding the body and its defects
3. a satisfactory consistency, so that the nonplastic ingredients will be held

Table 11.1. Clay content of underslips to fit green, dry or bisque bodies[5]

Underbody to be coated	*Clay content of slip, kinds and amounts percent by wt.*	
	China clay	Ball clay
I scuit	15 to 25	10
Leather-hard	25 to 65	10
Bone-dry	15 to 25	10

in suspension for long periods of time, and the slip can be applied without difficulty

4. good adhesive properties to make the slip stick firmly to the ware when dried, otherwise the surface will be scratched or marred by the necessary handling during the unfired stage

The choice of clays, aside from color and refractoriness, is governed at the present time by empirical considerations. The essential differences are dependent, in fact, upon the coarser particles, their sizes, shapes, and distribution, and upon the amount and kinds of colloids present. With the accumulation of more scientific data and the proper interpretation of that now available, the preparation of engobes will become simpler and more dependable.

The amounts and kinds of clays used in the underslips must be regulated according to the condition of the ware upon which they are to be applied. Bodies in the leather-hard condition contain a relatively high shrinkage water content and consequently are subject to a correspondingly large change during drying. Bodies in the plastic condition, which are sometimes slip coated, contain more water and shrink more. At the other extreme is the bisque ware which has neither drying nor firing shrinkage. The bone-dry body is an intermediate condition between the leather-hard and the biscuit body. In table 11.1 are shown the variation limits of china clay content—when the ball clay was constant at 10%—as reported by Stull.[5]

BALL CLAY is a usual but not indispensable component of engobes. The amount used obviously will be influenced by its characteristics. Even the best of clays will show variations between different shipments so it is well to use at least two or more different ball clays in the slip so as to minimize these differences. For engobes to be applied on biscuit, 5% to 7% of ball clay is sufficient; for the leather-hard body, from 10% to 13% may be used, although the higher figure may produce an objectionable color, especially if the English ball clays are used.

Ball clays are strong, flexible, and adhesive and they vitrify at relatively low temperatures (cone 5 to cone 10), and have high drying and firing shrinkages. Engobes made with different ball clays will show important differences in covering pits and small cavities on the surface of the ware.[6] Schurecht and McMahon[7] found that certain ball clays cause more blistering than others when used in underslips. Calcining and finely grinding part of the ball clay is a useful expedient to avoid some of the difficulties mentioned and yet have the advantage of the low temperature vitrifying conduct. Too low a temperature of calcination (800° C) was found by McDowell[4] to be a possible source of pinholes due to the excessive porosity. Calcined ball clay ground to 200-mesh weakened the slip and caused cracking.[8] This result would normally accompany use of an excessive amount.

PRIMARY KAOLINS OR CHINA CLAYS are important constituents in engobes and are generally used because of their whiteness and refractoriness when fired. Their plasticity, adhesiveness, and shrinkages, both drying and firing, are low. Careful selection of the clays used is important.

SEDIMENTARY KAOLINS are intermediate in their properties between ball clays and primary kaolins. Their colors, when fired, are inferior to primary kaolins and superior to those of the ball clays. The shrinkages are of the same order as those of the ball clays. The floating properties, adhesiveness, and strength approach but do not equal those of the ball clays. Their vitrification conduct is similar to that of the kaolins.

Fluxes

Since all engobes are sintered or vitrified to a greater or lesser degree—some completely so, e.g., vitreous slips—fluxes are essential ingredients. Even the natural clay engobes must be modified sometimes with small additions of lead oxide, etc. The more complex engobe is "softened" by the addition of feldspar, Cornwall stone, whiting (calcium carbonate), marble, or chalk. Magnesium carbonate, barium carbonate, bone ash, zinc oxide, mica, and lead oxide are some of the other materials which have been employed to a limited extent.

FELDSPAR is most widely used in this country and in continental Europe. In England, where Cornwall stone occurs in commercial quantities, naturally that is the usual fluxing agent. Many ceramists in the United States believe that it possesses unique advantages; therefore, it is found included in many formulas. In general, the amount used of either of these two minerals, singly or combined, may be as high as 30% or even 50%. The higher the amount, the greater the degree of vitrification. The larger amounts (30% or above at cone 7) of Cornwall stone may be accompanied by the appearance of blistering and crazing. Stull[5] expressed the opinion that the substitution of Cornwall stone for feldspar (a soda type feldspar) diminished the amount of crazing, cracking, and flaking. Wilson[8] substituted a similar feldspar for Cornwall stone in a vitreous slip composition and observed a graying of the color and more gloss. These effects were the results of the more complete vitrification which permitted the color of the body to appear or allowed the slip to react with iron oxides contained therein to the detriment of the engobe. When a harder or less fusible feldspar of the potash type was substituted the vitrification and the associated physical changes were diminished.

Calcium Carbonate, sometimes loosely referred to as "lime," is a powerful accessory flux and in the presence of feldspathic materials is likely to be of special service in the vitreous slip compositions, in amounts of the order of 1% or 2%. In the nonvitreous engobe the amount of calcium carbonate may be raised to 10% without accompanying difficulties, if the clay content is more than 40%. An investigator states, "A clay content of the engobe of more than 40% requires a feldspar content of more than 15% to cause vitrification at cone 9, unless 1% of lime (i.e., calcium carbonate) is present." Less clay and more feldspar give earlier and more complete vitrification and crazing will occur if the latter exceeds 45%. According to Davis and Lathrop,[10] the clay content for good vitreous slips, at cones 4 and 5, lies between 30% and 50%. A low clay content will be accompanied by crazing.

Flint, when used, is employed as a nonplastic, a refractory, and as a whitening agent because it markedly improves the color. There are differences of opinion as to its desirability in either the nonvitreous engobe or vitreous slip. The objectors say that it should be omitted entirely or carefully limited in use, otherwise it will cause crazing. On the other hand, numerous recipes may be found in print which propose considerable quantities of this material.

Magnesium Carbonate and other magnesium compounds do not appear to have been used much as engobe constituents. Strontium compounds may be expected to act like calcium. Specific data concerning the conduct of barium compounds in slips is not available, but its successful use in vitreous bodies suggests interesting possibilities. The action of barium oxide (less than 5%) in some bodies has been found comparable to an equivalent of the same moles of lead oxide.

Calcium Sulfate

Many English and some American recipes for engobes specify plaster of Paris (the hemihydrated calcium sulfate) as one of the ingredients. It has been claimed that it not only acts as a flux but also has a bleaching action on the iron content introduced by the clays. Calcium sulfate has a considerable solubility in water and may be expected to act as an electrolyte in the slip, thickening its consistency. A much more serious fault is roughening, scumming, and blistering of the glazes applied on top of the slip. Calcium sulfate is not recommended.

Chlorite Mica

Wilson[8] found that the addition of 10% to 15% chlorite mica to a vitreous slip composition strengthened it and darkened the color of the slip. McDowell[11] reported that it increased the porosity.

Sodium Carbonate

One percent of the weight of the dry batch of sodium carbonate (anhydrous) is very generally added to the engobe to promote the adhesion of the same to the body. The explanation usually made assumed that the sodium carbonate crystallizes during the drying and thereby creates a stronger bond. Sodium borate or sodium silicate are similarly used.

Compositions

The selection of an engobe composition suited for a particular use must finally be dependent upon trials conducted with the body and mate-

Table 11.2. Range of composition for underslips for a fire-clay grog body[9]

Constituents	*Range*
Potash feldspar	20% to 45%
Flint, French pebble	10% to 40%
English china clay	30% to 60%
Calcium carbonate	0 to 10%

Table 11.3. Limits for vitreous slips for clay-grog bodies[10]

Constituents	*Range*
Cornwall stone	25% to 50%
Feldspar	0 to 35%
Clay	25% to 55%
English china clay	
English ball clay	
"Ivory fat"	
Flint	0 to 10%

rials, also the firing conditions which are in use. However, there is much information available concerning the experiences of many investigators which may serve as useful guides. A brief compilation of such data is given in tables 11.2, 11.3, and 11.4.

A range of compositions[9] for underslips for a fire-clay grog body, one fire at about cone 9, long duration, i.e., several days, is given in table 11.2.

Davis and Lathrop[10] gave in table 11.3 the limits for vitreous slips to be used on clay-grog bodies (architectural terra cotta) matured at cones 4–5 after several days' firing.

Wilson[12] gave the compositions in table 11.4 as typical underslips for use on architectural terra cotta bodies at cones 3–7. In this table, underslip no. 1 was useful on bodies difficult to cover. The high clay content, particularly if about one-half English ball clay is used, gave a very tenacious coating. The plastic, dry, and fired properties of each of these underslips can be varied considerably by the use of different clays and feldspar or by the use of Cornwall stone to replace the feldspar.

Table 11.5 lists compositions of several underslips used by Stull[5] on bodies made of 25% to 75% of plastic fireclay and 75% to 25% of nonplastics. The slips were applied by dipping on the samples of the biscuit, leather-hard, and bone-dry conditions and the firing was done at cones 3 to 8 with good results.

One common engobe[13] used on terra cotta was a regular buff terra

Table 11.4. Typical underslip formulae for terra cotta bodies[12]

Constituents	*1*	*2*	*3*	*4*
Clays	80%	40%	45%	57.3%
Whiting	8	5	–	8.2
Flint	12	35	10	20.5
Feldspar	–	20	–	14.0
Cornwall stone	–	–	45	–

Table 11.5. Stull's limits for good engobes[5]

Underslips	*On biscuit body (%)*	*On leather-hard body (%)*	*On bone-dry body (%)*
M. G. R. English china clay	15–25	25–65	15–25
English Cornwall stone	25–55	5–50	25–55
Ohio flint	15–50	0–45	20–50
Pike's No. 20 English ball clay	10	10	10
Sodium carbonate	1	1	1
North Carolina kaolin	15–25	55–65	15–25
English Cornwall stone	15–55	5–25	25–45
Ohio flint	15–50	0–30	25–40
Pike's No. 20 English ball clay	10	10	10
Sodium carbonate	1	1	1
North Carolina kaolin	15–25	55–65	
Brandywine feldspar	15–55	5–30	
Ohio flint	15–50	0–30	
Pike's No. 20 English ball clay	10	10	
Sodium carbonate	1	1	

cotta clay which had been milled and screened similar to a glaze. This was applied at a dry thickness of 0.008 in. on a dry body. Although the shrinkages of the engobe and body were widely different since the body contained 45% of grog, the engobe fitted the body very well, probably due to the thin application used. If this engobe were applied thicker, it would undoubtedly check, due to the differences in shrinkage.

Preparation

A well-prepared slip must be completely in suspension and must remain so for many hours. It must be homogeneous, free from coarse particles, lumps, and air or gas bubbles. It should not gel unless it is to be applied by painting. The consistency should be suitable for the method of application used and the condition of the body upon which it is to be applied. Assuming that the nonplastic materials employed in the batch are of standard purity and fineness, the mixing operation is simply a process of incorporating them with the clay and water to make a homogeneous suspension. This may be done either in a blunger or a ball mill, depending upon whether simple mixing or combined grinding and mixing is required.

The preferred practice is to carefully wet-mill the slip mixture to achieve the proper fineness and consistency for application. The milled engobe must be free of gas bubbles and coarse particles. One technique giving good results is to wet-mill the nonplastics and stain to suitable fineness, then add the clay and perform the final milling and preparation of the slip. If the batch ingredients are purchased in a specified preground condition, the slip could be prepared by blunging or at most a minimum of ball mill time. The best practice is to vacuum-blunge the slip or at least allow it to stand to self-de-air.

The engobe should be prepared exactly to a constant and specific value of density. With this constant the consistency may be fixed by careful additions of electrolytes.

Magnetic Separator

After the slip has been prepared as described, it is passed over magnets to remove any particles of iron which may be present, and then is poured through a fine lawn.

De-airing

The slip dissolves and mechanically entraps air, which subsequently may be the cause of blisters and pinholes, during the course of the preparation. It is important, therefore, to get rid of this potential source of trouble as soon as possible. The quickest method is the use of a partial vacuum above the surface of the slip in a closed vessel, slowly agitating the slip during the process. G. W. Lapp[14] has described a process and the equipment for the de-airing of a body slip which are suited for use with an engobe. The blunged slip is made to flow as a thin layer down the inside wall of a closed cylinder while the maximum vacuum is maintained, limited only by the boiling point of the slip. An old method, seldom used now although of recognized merit, is the practice of boiling the slip. Good vacuum blungers are available commercially.

Aging can be used to de-gas slips, which is done by storing the slip for a week or more at a fairly constant temperature of 80° to 90° F. The slip becomes smoother and stronger. Fermentation may be prevented or stopped by the addition of small amounts of carbolic acid or a soluble phenolate—e.g., sodium phenolate—methyl salicylate (oil of wintergreen), and other bactericides. Slips should not be stored in old wooden barrels or tanks, which themselves may undergo similar changes, unless they have been given a good coating of creosote. Neither should engobes be stored in newly made concrete tanks because of the slight but important reactions which may ensue.

THE DENSITY of the slip will be controlled according to its composition and the method of application, i.e., whether it is to be painted, sprayed, or dipped. It will range from a density of 1.350 for a slip without alkali electrolyte used for "wet spraying" to a density of 1.520 for a vitreous slip containing alkali electrolyte. A thin slip may be applied uniformly and rapidly, but it needs frequent stirring to prevent settling; moreover, careful attention is needed to insure that the application is thick enough to completely cover the surface of the ware. On the other hand, a thick slip settles only slowly; the coverage is good, but the thicker coat is much more likely to develop cracks in drying and firing. The consistency is controlled primarily by the amount of water used in the mixing of the batch, but the final adjustment is done by the use of electrolytes.

In general, it may be stated that small quantities of the carbonates of sodium and potassium reagents "thin" the slip. On the other hand, small quantities of humic, sulfuric, and hydrochloric acids, also aluminum chloride, borax, aluminum sulfate, calcium chloride, ammonium chloride, etc. will "stiffen" the slip, i.e., increase the viscosity. The effects to be expected by the addition of alkali or acid in general may be predicted, but the complexity of the engobe composition may result in side reactions which will alter the final results. For example, magnesium and sodium sulfates may be expected to cause a thickening of the slip; on the contrary they will also, under some circumstances, thin the slip.

Batch components are in a very finely divided condition and therefore are susceptible to solution, in a greater or less degree, if subjected to prolonged contact with water. This is accelerated by heat and, in some cases, by the presence of carbon dioxide. Potter's flint, the clay minerals, i.e., the aluminum silicates, and some of the other materials are scarcely affected, but the feldspars are quite sensitive to attack by water and after standing a few hours will yield enough alkalies to alter the viscosity of the slip. The soluble organic and inorganic compounds present in clays and in the water used in the batch are very important factors whose effects are better known than understood.

The profound effect of small amounts of certain electrolytes upon the consistency is illustrated by their effect upon pottery casting bodies similar in composition to engobes. A typical body slip containing 50% to 60% water will weigh about 30 ounces to the pint. After addition of 0.2% to 0.3% (of the dry weight) of certain electrolytes, the same fluidity may be had in a slip containing only 30% of water and weighing as much as 36 ounces to the pint.

The greater fluidity of the slip brought about by the addition of small amounts of appropriate electrolytes (alkalies) facilitates the escape of the mechanically held gases. Also, the lower water content required for the necessary fluidity decreases the degree of surface soaking when the ware is brought into contact with the slip. The drying shrinkage decreases with the lower water content.

Table 11.6. Clay slip specifications for the preparation of slips and engobes of high clay content*

Requirements	*High-clay slips*	*Low-clay slips (standard finishes and underslips)*
Consistency		
ounces, per quart	41.0 to 42.1	44.0 to 51.0
specific gravity	1.23 to 1.26	1.32 to 1.53
Baumé (degrees)	27.2 to 30.00	35.1 to 50.00
Dry thickness (inches)	0.009 to 0.011	0.009 to 0.011
Coverage (sq ft) by 1 lb of slip	4.61	2.72
Slip required (lbs) for 1 sq ft	0.217	0.368

*Communicated to C. W. Parmelee by H. G. Schurecht

Specification[13] for preparation and application of high-clay slip and engobes in the terra cotta industry are summarized in table 11.6.

Application

Before the engobe is applied, care must be taken to remove all dust and foreign matter which has accumulated on the surface of the ware. This is done by dusting or brushing the dry surface, by the use of a damp sponge, by using a light air blast, or by use of a vacuum cleaning apparatus. In special cases the ware is gently rubbed with a fine emery or sand paper and the dust is then carefully removed. The choice of procedure will depend upon the condition of the ware, i.e., whether it is biscuit, plastic, leather-hard, or bone-dry.

The engobe may be applied by one of the following methods:

1. by pouring the slip over the ware; by dipping the ware into the slip; by filling the ware with slip and promptly emptying out the excess
2. by painting with a brush
3. by spraying or atomizing the slip onto the ware
4. by automatically spreading a veneer coat on the ware

Dipping and Pouring, as usually handled, do not require special equipment but are slow, costly in time and labor, and wasteful of material. The control of the thickness of application is largely a matter of judgment. The introduction of mechanical dipping equipment has removed most of these objections. It is obvious that these methods are adapted only to the smaller pieces of ware and are impractical for the larger pieces or for those with special modeling or decoration.

Stull[5] described the dipping of a brick as a rhythmic operation, progressing as follows: (1) The edge of the brick is brought in contact with the slip, (2) the brick is given a gentle rocking motion so that the slip is washed across the face, (3) without interrupting the rhythm or removing the brick from contact with the slip the operation is reversed and, finally, (4) the brick is removed in a manner to permit the excess of the slip to drain off a corner of the surface.

PAINTING is done with brushes in the conventional manner. This very ancient skill was originally used for the decoration of wares with simple designs of straight or curved lines assembled in geometrical, symbolical, or random patterns. With the development of the more refined cultures, there followed a greater diversity and intricacy of technique, which, in the case of the Romans and especially the Greeks, rivals the best produced in the later centuries. Many examples of this superior art have been found by archaeologists in the southwestern United States, the countries of the Mediterranean Basin, and in some parts of Asia. The more primitive peoples in almost all habitable parts of the world, in the past as well as the present, have made and do make many interesting examples.

A round paint brush, about one and one-half or two inches in diameter, having short bristles, is used for spreading the first two coats of the thick slip over the coarse body. The strokes are made back and forth, crosswise and circular, so that the slip is spread in a thin uniform layer, filling up all the pores and imperfections of the surface. By the thorough working of the brush, the air in the larger pores or blebs at the surface can be displaced by the slip, thus preventing the possibility of the later escape and consequent formation of pinholes and blisters. Drying of the first coat will require from a few hours to a day, depending on the room temperature, the humidity, and the air circulation about the piece of ware. The application of the second coat will be made with the same brush and will be dried for the same period as the first. The subsequent coatings will be painted on with a brush having long black bristles which can be more easily seen and removed if they loosen and remain in the slip coat on the ware, later causing defects in the engobe and glaze coat when fired.

According to German practice the fifth or last coat, while still soft, is carefully "slicked" with a flat folded pad of doeskin or chamois. When the engobe is no longer sticky, it is polished with the bare hand. An alternative method permits the last coat to dry undisturbed which gives a hard surface because of the use of gelatin or glue in the composition of the slip. The rough streaky surface left by the brush strokes must be removed by the careful use of sandpaper. Since the number of slip coats may be as many as five or even seven and the total final thickness will be from one-twentieth to one-tenth of an inch, it is helpful to color each separate slip coat with a different soluble dyestuff in order to make the progress of the application of each coat more readily seen with respect to its coverage. Also, it is of great assistance during the sandpapering operation.

PREPARATION OF ADHESIVES. The preparation of the glue or gelatin for use in the slip varies somewhat in detail with different ceramists, but the procedure is about as follows: a good grade of the material which has been proved to be suited to the purpose is selected and weighed (from ½ oz to ¾ oz according to its strength), and soaked in 10 times its weight of water until it is completely softened; when this has been done, the mixture is heated carefully to avoid scorching or burning. A double boiler is the safest utensil to use for the purpose. The mixture is stirred into a thin fluid, free from lumps, and then passed through a coarse lawn if necessary. One pint of the fluid will be mixed with 20 times that quantity of engobe. The whole mixture must be stirred vigorously to a uniform consistency. It will be very stiff at first, but continued stirring will make it thin enough to pass through an 80-mesh lawn. The higher the temperature of the slip and the higher the ball clay content, the more glue or gelatin will be required. The engobe can be more easily applied if the ball-clay content is kept low. The finished engobe should be stored in a refrigerator with the temperature between freezing and 45° F. It will become pasty, even livery, which is most satisfactory for use.

There are several adhesives, other than gelatin and glue, which are available for use as outlined more fully in chapters 3, 4, and 5.

Spraying is done by an atomizer, which projects the droplets of the slip on the surface of the ware. The method is rapid, efficient, economical, and peculiarly useful for coating large pieces, also for ware whose design or decorations would otherwise require painting because of complexity. Spraying is well adapted to the automatic coating of brick and smaller wares. Small pieces are supported on a conveyor belt during the operation, which greatly facilitates the production.

Uniformity in the coating of smaller pieces is readily had by rotating or otherwise moving the wares in the field of one or more fixed sprayers. Since the larger pieces are not so readily manipulated, the spray gun is attached at the end of a flexible hose held by the operator, and the ware is supported on a turntable which is rotated at his convenience. The thin stream of spray is quickly swept across the face of the ware in parallel bands, overlapping at their margins. The movement is first to the right and then to the left.

WET AND DRY SPRAYING. Wilson[12] describes two spraying techniques which are called "wet spraying" and "dry spraying." The first is used with slips which do not flow or heal themselves readily in the kiln, merely forming a smooth vitreous surface—the "vitreous slip." It must contain enough water (slip density 1.350) and be sprayed at such a rate that it forms, temporarily, a smooth, watery coating. After the spray coat has become sufficiently firm so that the light touch of the finger does not mar the surface, another coating is applied so that the spray traverses the surface at right angles to the preceding paths of travel. Too heavy an application will leave puddles on the flat surfaces, depressed areas will be flooded, and "runs" will form on the vertical faces. Too thin an engobe coat will be darkened in color by the body underneath. It is almost impossible to obtain a satisfactory white when the engobe is applied on a dark-colored body.

Commenting on greater difficulty of securing satisfactory results when spraying ornamental work and internal angles, Wilson[12] says:

> "In attempting to get the slip or glaze into a depression, an excess will be added to the surrounding surfaces. Hence it is best to spray the ornamental features first and make certain that the depressions have at least a medium coat. If too much is added, blow them out with air alone. The piece can be treated as an ashlar in succeeding coats and the high points of the ornament alone considered. It is better that the internal angles have a thin coating than a thick one."

The engobe intended for "dry spraying" is prepared with aggregated materials, such as calcined clay, calcined zinc oxide, etc., and electrolytes are added; therefore, less water is required to maintain the same fluidity. A suitable adhesive, such as gum tragacanth, dextrin, gelatin, etc., must be used since the spray is, in a sense, deposited as a dust which would scatter widely. The engobe, therefore, dries rapidly with little shrinkage and negligible cracking, especially in the angles, which otherwise are difficult to cover properly.

Wilson's[12] directions for "dry spraying" on the underslip are:

> ". . . blow the slip swiftly over the entire piece, filling all the body imperfections, minute cracks, and ornamental angles. Shut off the slip, hold the nozzle close to the surface and blow it dry, removing all the excess slip from the internal angles and cavities. This puts a coating of slip all over the surface and helps avoid the pink spots of the thin coatings. To tone up the piece the ashlar surfaces and the exposed portions of the ornament may need an additional coating. This can be applied immediately with the gun held at a distance. Care should be taken to avoid wetting the internal angles at this time."

VENEERING is an automatic application of slip coating about one-sixteenth of an inch thick on a bar of plastic clay as it issues from the die of a stiff-mud brick machine. Several patents have been issued for devices for accomplishing this object. The slip has the consistency of a soft plastic body.

Defects

Flaking—Shelling—Peeling—Shivering

Unfortunately, the first three terms are used interchangeably with the last; although the causes, the time and manner of occurrence, and the appearances are not alike. The characteristics of the first three are similar, since the slip (or glaze) separates from the body. Shivering is a term which has long been used by ceramists for the defect in which the glaze and the body, although firmly bonded together by fire, yield to the internal stresses and fragments of the body, with the glaze attached, spall or split off. If the ware has a thin wall of weak strength, the whole piece may disintegrate into a pile of shards.

On the other hand, the terms flaking, shelling, and peeling may be reserved properly to describe the separation of flakes of a slip (or glaze) without the rupture of the body. Flaking may take place before or during the firing operation. Shivering takes place in the kiln after firing, during the cooling period—after a lapse of a considerable time following the firing. It is very generally agreed among ceramists that shivering is due primarily to stresses in the body and in the superimposed slip or glaze or both, and to stresses caused by significant differences in their respective thermal expansions, which result in the rupture. On the other hand, flaking is due to the breaking of the bond between the body and the slip, because of the lack of proper adhesion between the two layers. This failure may take place before going into the kiln or during the firing operation.

Causes of Flaking. There are many possible causes for flaking, of which the seven discussed here are the most common:

1. The effect of freezing upon absorbent underslips which have become wetted by exposure to the weather. Therefore, enameled brick and architectural terra cotta are best protected by the use of vitreous slips with or without the glaze coat.

2. The surface of the ware was dusty or oily when the engobe was applied.

3. There has been an accumulation of soluble salts as a scum on the surface of the ware. These salts may have originated in the clays, the grog in the body, or in the water used. The remedy is to render harmless these soluble sulfates—the common cause of the trouble. The addition of about

0.2% of barium carbonate to the body is required with most terra cotta and bull-nose enamel brick.

The physics or chemistry involved in the action of a deposit of soluble salts on the surface of clay ware—as affecting the adhesion or the lack of adhesion of the engobe—is not, at present, well understood and quite contrary opinions have been expressed by different ceramists. Ashley,[15] discussing causes of the lack of adhesion of glazes, includes deposits of soluble salts and states that this fault may be corrected by the use of adhesives. He also states correction may be accomplished by "coagulating the sol (which is in a way equivalent to adding adhesives) by such coagulants as borax in excess, sodium carbonate in excess, plaster of Paris, sal soda (2%), magnesium sulfate, or boric acid." Since hydrated calcium sulfate is the most abundant constituent of the soluble salts present in clays, according to this dictum, it should be useful rather than harmful, and plaster of Paris is recommended and used in the English practice to prevent flaking. However, it is objectionable for the reasons previously mentioned.

Kirkpatrick, Arnold, and Geiger[16] hold that Ashley's opinion that the coagulated gels act as adhesives should be modified. They hold that differences in shrinkages of the two layers and the possible result of crystallization or formation of products of reactions must be considered. It should be noted that Kirkpatrick and associates were experimenting with a rather complex enamel composition and their conclusions would not necessarily apply to the simpler engobe. However, there is sufficient similarity to permit speculation.

Peeling, observed on a vitreous slip applied by spraying, was attributed by Wilson[17] to the concentration of soluble salts on small particles of grog imbedded at the surface, or on an edge or irregularity. He suggests the following explanation: The first coat dries smoothly, but as the second and the other coats are applied with a water finish, an elastic film is stretched over the surface. This slip coat film is weakened by the soluble salts acting as electrolytes and the pull of the surface tension causes a break in the film. The broken portion lifts up as a small tongue. This defect is seldom experienced unless the vitreous slip is covered with a glaze coat.

4. If the shrinkages of the engobe and the body are in agreement, the problem of adhesion and therefore flaking will be minimized. Unequal shrinkages of the body and the engobe will create stresses which will rupture the bond between the two layers with the consequent cracking and peeling. Too low shrinkage of the slip is a more likely cause of trouble than too high shrinkage. Contributory causes are the lack of mechanical strength and elasticity of the slip. The body constitutes such a large mass relative to the slip coat that the latter has to yield when serious stresses develop.

In all problems of the adjustment of the slip to the body, much depends upon the condition of the latter, whether it is biscuit, leather-hard, bone-dry, or plastic. The first named will have neither drying nor firing shrinkages, the last will have the maximum. The gross adjustment of the fit is made by the proper proportioning of the nonplastic content—the nonshrinking constituents—against the plastics—the shrinking constituents. The plastics are the clays—kaolins or china clays, secondary kaolins, and ball clays. The first named have the least shrinkage and adhesive power; the ball clays have the greatest; and the secondary kaolins are intermediate. The ultimate regulation of the shrinkages will be made by the careful selection and proportioning of these different types of clays. Further consideration must be given to the differences between individual clays of each class.

Slips containing a high proportion of nonplastics, or ground too finely, or containing too much kaolin or china clay have low adhesive power, low mechanical strength, and low shrinkage; therefore, they will flake readily. On the other hand, slips with secondary kaolins and ball clays have better adhesion and are stronger and more flexible, but the higher shrinkages may offset these advantages and cause cracking and flaking. The remedies for these troubles are to be found, obviously, in the proper selection of the kind and quantities of the clays used.

Differences in the rates of shrinkage of the slip and the body upon which it is applied are factors in causing flaking. This may be true during the firing but not during the drying operation.

5. Painting of the slip coat, containing gelatin, on a slip coat or a body which is not thoroughly dry will be followed by peeling, according to Shaw.[9]

6. Too thick a coat of the engobe is likely to flake. This may follow the application by painting if the slip does not spread easily under the brush.

7. Steaming of the ware in the kiln during the water-smoking period of the firing may be a cause of peeling.

The role of free silica and siliceous clays in causing shivering, peeling, flaking, and shelling has been extensively discussed in ceramic literature, but unfortunately no distinction has been made between the different terms and this apparently has added to the confusion. Shivering, as previously defined, connotes the spalling of the slip (and glaze) coat from the body, carrying with it substantial portions of the body. Flaking, shelling, or peeling results in separation of the slip (and glaze) layer quite cleanly from the body. Because of the unfortunate misuse of terms, it is difficult to interpret some of the literature pertaining to these matters. However, all writers concede that soluble salts are the frequent cause of shelling, peeling, and flaking; it is assumed that the same writers will agree that the presence of excessive amounts of free silica or siliceous clays in the body is the usual cause of shivering, per se. Carruthers[18] considered the presence of considerable finely ground grog of a siliceous nature as an agent contributory to shivering. To correct this trouble due to siliceous material, he recommended the addition of: (*a*) Feldspar or rock having a similar composition that acts as a flux; and (*b*) coarse silica or grog, making the body more open.

Cracking

Cracking of the engobe may occur prior to or as a result of firing. Some of the causes of cracking are listed here.

1. Excessive shrinkage due to:
   a) Too much plastic material. To correct this condition, reduce the total amount of clay or replace some of the ball clay with china clay or kaolin. Substitute calcined ball clay for some of the raw, but this should not be ground too finely since cracking would accompany the use of the material if ground to pass a 200-mesh lawn.
   b) Too thick an application of the engobe. Cracking results because of the larger amount of water present in the thick layer and the correspondingly greater shrinkage during drying.
   c) The use of materials which are too finely ground. Excessive milling of the slip will result in batches with too large an amount of water, too high shrinkage, and decreased strength. Further, prolonged grinding will increase the content of the soluble matter—particularly the alkalies—which will definitely increase the shrinkage; therefore, many ceramists prefer blunging, rather than milling engobes. Griffen[19] has expressed the opinion that "the soluble fluxes used in glazes for the wet dipping soak into the body and cause the face to shrink more than the balance, resulting in cracking." Many ceramists have observed that small amounts of alkalies (of the order of 0.1% sodium hydroxide, for example) will have this effect on some clays. On the other hand, relatively large amounts (1%) of sodium carbonate, borax, and the silicate of soda are recommended as useful to prevent cracking.
   d) The excessive use of gum or glue.
2. Slips that lack the necessary strength to withstand the stresses due to shrinkage. Here contributory factors to the formation of cracks are:
   a) Too large proportion of nonplastics. To correct this, increase the total clay content, adding more ball clay at the expense of the kaolin.
   b) A nonplastic portion that is too finely ground.
   c) Ware design producing unequal or excessive thickness of the engobe. An example is the common difficulty of obtaining a satisfactory

coating over internal angles. Wilson[8] found that the addition of chlorite mica (10% to 15%) and asbestos (3%) strengthened the slip so that such angles were properly filled, but practical difficulties in spraying were experienced.

3. The texture and the condition of the ware and the method of finishing. Engobes on bodies containing too coarse grog or poor distribution of the different sizes of grog will crack. Wilson[8] reports that grog sizes coarser than 65-mesh are liable to cause trouble; and Davis[20] found that 20- to 30-mesh and finer gave a good surface, but that those coarser as well as the 10-mesh to dust (inclusive) caused cracking.

   A surface in the leather-hard condition is the easiest to finish to a polished condition. Grogged bodies, even though the particles be as fine as the 65-mesh, will be liable to crack as the proportion of the grog is increased. Naturally the coarser grog will cause more trouble. During the drying the clay shrinks but the grog particles do not; consequently there is a movement of the clay from contact with the grog so that those grains at or immediately below the surface are exposed. Wetting or otherwise disturbing the surface produces small rupture planes. If the body is too dry and a tool is dragged across the surface, some grog particles are dislodged. Even though the movement is slight and may be disguised by further working of the surface by the tool, the bond has been broken and the cracks may be reopened easily during the subsequent drying and firing.

4. Too rapid drying of the engobe coated ware. Cracks which develop in the ware during drying will appear in the engobe.
5. Cracks developing in the body during firing which will appear in the engobe.
6. The swelling and bursting of concretionary or certain oxidizable minerals during the firing which will rupture the engobe. An example is the mineral marcasite, one of the sulfides of iron, which oxidizes readily in the presence of moisture even at atmospheric temperatures and more rapidly as the temperature rises. With the oxidation, the volume of the particle increases very considerably.
7. Shrinkage during sintering. Coarsely ground fat clays or mixtures used for engobes not only cause hairline cracks during drying but may sinter earlier than the body and the accompanying high shrinkage will result in cracks appearing in the biscuit fire. Such engobes adhere firmly to the body, but sealing may appear after the glost fire.

CROWFOOTING. Crow's foot or checking is a variation of cracking. It is so called because of the resemblance of the defect to the pattern of a bird track. Crowfooting is probably the most common defect which occurs on standard finishes used on terra cotta. It is often caused by improper body and slip compositions and also by poor finishing.

Davis and Lathrop[21] report that they were unable to find any composition of vitreous slip (in their investigations) which would be free from this fault. It was more pronounced with an increase of clay, but worse with a high feldspar than with Cornwall stone. This difference they attribute to the free flint present in the latter.

Reducing the size of grog will tend to prevent crowfooting. Using plastic clays in the body in place of lean clays may also prevent this trouble. Omitting finishing, as much as possible, after the body has been pressed, tends to overcome crowfooting. Finishing the body after it has become too dry is a frequent cause. Using a water brush for finishing is another. Often times rolling the clay well before pressing will overcome this trouble.

Crowfooting has also been corrected by substituting ivory fat clay for as high as 50% of the clay used in standard finishes. Bedminster clay has also been used in a similar manner. The addition of about 5% coarse mica to such finishes also overcame this trouble. This defect has also been overcome by adding coarse sand to the slip. Also, the substitution of English china clay for Georgia kaolin or ball clay tends to prevent this trouble.

Pinholes and Blisters

The appearance of pinholes or blisters in an engobe may occur before or after firing. If before, they will be observed during or soon after application of the slip to the body.

The sources or causes of these defects may be traced to: (1) Composition of the slip; (2) preparation of the slip; (3) application of the slip; and the (4) firing technique.

Effects of Composition

Powdered materials such as are used in compounding slips contain large volumes of air, filling the voids as well as adhering to the individual grains. The water used in the mixing also contains a considerable quantity of air dissolved as well as held in suspension as minute bubbles. Consequently these gases, as well as those churned into the slip during the violent agitation of the milling operation, constitute an important source of the defects which we call pinholes and, in aggravated form, blisters. Fortunately, if slips are put aside to stand quietly at a suitable temperature, about 70° F, a great part of the gases will escape. Gentle agitation of the slip, avoiding any whipping or beating, will assist in freeing them. Degassing the slip in a partial vacuum as previously described is helpful.

Easily decomposable salts, such as the carbonate of lime, will liberate carbon dioxide if free acids are present in the batch. This is scarcely likely to occur in ordinary circumstances. At kiln temperatures a number of similar reactions take place which are frequent causes for pinholes.

Effects of Preparation

Besides the sources mentioned, there is the evolution of a considerable volume of gas as the product of fermentation accompanying the aging of slips. The violent churning action of the ball-milling not only incorporates large volumes of air in the slip, but the rise of temperature, frequently observed, will promote chemical reactions which may liberate gases. For this and other reasons previously mentioned, blunging is preferred to milling by some ceramists. Thick slips entrap gas bubbles more readily than thin slips and, therefore, are a frequent source of trouble. The advantages of the use of "thinning" electrolytes are apparent; the gas bubbles escape more easily and less water is present in the slip, but it remains suitably fluid.

Effects of Application

The adhering to the surface of the ware of air adsorbed on the surface of dust particles and also filling the spaces between them is a source of gas bubbles in the slip; consequently, all dust must be removed from the ware before it is coated with the engobe. This may be done with a cloth, a brush, by suction, or air blast. Sometimes the ware is scrubbed with a wet brush.

Pinholes are formed if the slip is applied to ware which is too dry and too porous. This is frequently true of biscuit ware and is conspicuously true of grogged ware. When the engobe comes in contact with the ware, water is absorbed and air is forced out of the cavities on and below the surface. The pinholes do not appear until the "water-gloss" of the surface begins to disappear, then the air bubbles break through. In the case of wares which contain much grog and are matured in one fire, the defect may be avoided by painting the slip (containing an adhesive) in successive thin coats.

Wilson,[12] discussing wet spraying of architectural terra cotta, says: "If a coating is allowed to dry to whiteness and then another application is made, air bubbles from the pore spaces of the dry coating will emerge as blisters in the wet second coat. The harmfulness of these will vary with flowing and healing qualities of the superior coating in the kiln." Schurecht and McMahon[22] report: "If the successive coats of underslip or glaze are sprayed as soon as the wet sheen disappears from the previous coat, no blistering will develop, but if the intervals between coats are increased to five or ten minutes, excessive blistering may occur."

Further they report, "The structure of the body influences spraying defects. Fine grained plastic bodies produce more blistering than coarse-grained, short bodies."

McMahon[23] has found that "The ability of underslips or engobes to cover open cavities may vary widely according to the type and the amount of the plastic clay used." Also, he found that "Underslips sprayed over the surface of coal particles, after firing, may remain as a thin shell over cavities formed by burning out of the coal. These usually become broken in handling or in service, yielding small surface cavities with the appearance of popping."

If bricks or similar small wares are to be engobed on a flat surface by dipping, the entire surface should not be brought in contact with the slip in one operation since air bubbles will usually be entrapped. The correct procedure is to introduce only an edge of the brick in the slip, then give the piece a rocking motion so that the slip is washed across the face of the piece.

Effects of Firing

If an engobe fits the body properly during the drying period and adheres firmly during the low-temperature firing, but at a higher temperature separates from the body, due to the higher shrinkage of the latter, the engobe will shrivel together. To correct this fault a flux, such as feldspar, frit, or whiting, should be added to the engobe; or the body composition may be altered.

Crazing

The defect known as crazing is defined as a defect of the fired engobe, made evident by hairlines, singly or in a network, penetrating the surface. The causes are several and include: lack of agreement of the expansion coefficients of the engobe and the body, low mechanical strength (particularly tensile strength), and low modulus of elasticity of the engobe. Crazing appears only in the fired glaze and engobe, but not the body, and is due to the greater thermal expansion of the glaze, or slip or both, than of the body. Cracking differs from crazing by appearing in the unfired ware also, and by the involvement of the body in the failure if the piece has been fired.

Crazing may be avoided or corrected by the careful selection of the raw materials on the basis of their chemical composition, their particle size, and their mineralogical character. Both cracking and crazing may result from rapid temperature changes during the cooling period and even after the warm ware is taken out of the kiln. Crazing may appear days, weeks, or months after the removal of the ware from the kiln and complete cooling.

Stull[5] has stated the causes and remedies for crazing as follows:

Causes	Remedies
Slips too high in flint.	Reduce flint and increase clay, feldspar or Cornwall stone.
Slips too high in feldspar or Cornwall stone.	Reduce feldspar or Cornwall stone and increase clay.
With feldspar as a flux; burning slips at too high temperatures.	Reduce burning temperature.
With Cornwall stone as a flux; burning slips at too low a temperature.	Increase burning temperature.

Respecting the influence of flint on crazing, other writers[11,21] agree with Stull regarding its objectionable action, particularly in vitreous slips. On the other hand, numerous engobe compositions have been published containing flint, i.e., silica, in a wide variety of proportions.

Davis and Lathrop,[10] discussing the composition of vitreous slips, state that Cornwall stone is beneficial in preventing crazing if used in quantities less than 50%. They place the safe maximum limit of the feldspar as "35% and perhaps higher." Wilson[12] is in agreement.

Stull, Hill,[24] and Davis and Lathrop agree that an increase in clay decreases the crazing. Similar results were obtained by McDowell,[11] who also experimented with vitreous slips. Compositions containing high clay resisted "moisture crazing." ("Moisture crazing" is crazing due to volume changes in the ware after prolonged exposure to atmospheric conditions or steam under pressure.)

Davis and Lathrop found that crazing is associated with a low clay content in a vitreous slip and good vitrification could be had, at cones 4–5, only when the clay content was held between the limits of 30% and 50%.

Schurecht and Pole,[25] using the ring test for measuring strains in glazes, have shown that slips under high compression (short of the shivering point) are more resistant to moisture crazing or that type of crazing which develops after long exposure to weather.

McDowell,[11] using a similar method, reached these conclusions: (1) The vitreous slips having a high clay content were under high compression and resistant to moisture crazing; (2) additions of mica slightly lowered the compression; (3) additions of zinc oxide lowered the compression and caused crazing; and (4) additions of whiting had little effect on compression.

Colored Slips

White, cream and buff, reds and browns, and black-colored slips may be had by using natural clays fired under suitable conditions and to the required temperatures. By the addition of properly chosen oxides and other compounds to white firing clays, a very extensive palette may be contrived. The use of natural clays to produce colored engobes has been familiar to primitive peoples from the earliest times, and the more complicated technique of using white clays and colored oxides is many thousand years old.

The most important of the natural slips are the low-temperature sintering, iron-rich clays, which will give weak and strong, clear reds in an oxidizing fire. In a reducing fire, which is most effective if held at about 600° C, the color may be darkened through reds to browns to blacks. If sufficient manganese is present or added the color is intensified within the range of brown to black, but it will be dull. Clays rich in lime and with a moderate amount of iron oxide will give greenish yellow tones.

Commercial Stains

The stains most popular in engobes were listed by Coulter[26] as follows:

YELLOW. The best yellow stains for engobes are tin-vanadium yellows. Zirconium-vanadium yellows are weaker pigments and lead-antimony colors are not stable at the higher temperatures.

ORANGE AND BUFF. Blends of chrome-iron-zinc stains with chrome-alumina or manganese-alumina pinks made good orange colors. These are brightest in the presence of zinc oxide.

PINK AND MAROON. Delicate pink shades from manganese-alumina stains are popular in engobes. Chrome-tin crimsons are obtained in engobes but high concentration of the stain and high CaO content in the engobe are required.

BLUE. Cobalt-base stains are almost exclusively used for blue. For matts, cobalt-alumina stains are preferred and cobalt-silica colors are better in brighter textures.

TURQUOISE. Zirconium-vanadium stains form the basis of most of the turquoise engobes. A range of colors from blue to chartreuse is obtained by blending tin-vanadium yellows with zirconium-vanadium stains. Satisfactory blue-green engobes are derived with cobalt chrome stains.

GREEN. Stains based on Cr_2O_3 are used in engobes. The colors are stable, whereas copper lacks stability and diffuses out of the engobe into the glaze and tends to burn out at high temperatures.

GRAY. Blue-gray and dove-gray engobes can be achieved with tin-antimony stains. These commercial stains were quoted by Coulter[26] as being satisfactory for engobes to temperatures through cone 11. As in all work with colors, proper care and consistent practice is required to achieve ideal constancy in shades. Detectable variations in shades occur due to fluctuations in thickness of 0.001 inch. Temperature differentials in firing should be kept to within as narrow limits as practical to insure perfect constancy in shades. Color can vary due to the type of crank and to the type of crank spray used. It is important to exercise good control in the glost firing as well as in the bisque.

In addition to these types of commercial stains there are other effective ones on the market. New and improved stains continue to be developed and introduced.

It is well to be familiar with effects and colors to be derived from the more elementary colorants such as simple oxides and their blends. Some of these behavior patterns are given in the following paragraphs.

Oxide Colorants

Attempts to enrich the color of naturally red firing clays, for use as engobes, by the addition of the oxide of iron, copperas, or other iron compounds almost always give unsatisfactory results. McVay and Parmelee[27] studied the effects of the introduction of sundry iron compounds into engobes of varying clay-flint-feldspar proportions and arrived at the following conclusions:

a. The most satisfactory method for adding iron oxide is to precipitate the iron in the engobe as the hydroxide, $FeCl_3 + 3NH_4OH \rightarrow Fe(OH)_3 + 3NH_4Cl$, because uniform colors are obtained. The dispersion of the iron oxide is not so great as with naturally occurring clays, but the results are satisfactory.

b. Unusual effects are procured by using a silica gel in which ferric hydroxide had been precipitated because orchid shades are obtained which are unlike colors produced by any other method.

c. Direct addition of commercial red iron oxide causes specks due to the large particle size of the ferric oxide.

d. Very dark gray colors are obtained in certain engobes with a moderate feldspar content, although the iron oxide is in the ferric form. The effect is due to the crystal growth of the hematite. Where commercial iron oxide is added to engobes with a high feldspar content, fairly satisfactory red colors are obtained.

e. With calcined mixtures of co-precipitated aluminum and ferric hydroxides, those with a high iron content produce grays, while those with a high alumina content give buff colors. These differences are due to the colors of the individual calcines and not to the total amount of iron present, since this is kept constant.

f. The composition of the engobes is one of the important factors in the production of colors, and these colors depend to a marked extent upon the fineness of division of the particles, and upon the fusibility of the feldspar. It has been shown that coarse-grained clays, like North Carolina kaolin, give a more intense color than fine-grained clays of the Florida type and that ground potter's flint gives a lighter color than the commercial product when like amounts of iron hydroxide are precipitated in them and the mixtures are calcined.

g. To obtain buff colors, a high clay content is advisable; if browns are desired the quartz content should be high and for good red colors the feldspar content should be about 60%.

Improving Whiteness

The color of the usual white engobe will be dependent, in a large measure, upon the amount of flint and the amount of ball clay present. The kaolin or china clay content can always be employed to improve the whiteness, assuming that good grades are used. The ball clay content in excess of 10% will be harmful to the purity of the color, according to its quality. In order to correct the off-shade of the engobe intended to be a good white, either alone or under a glaze, it is a frequent practice to add 0.01% to 0.02% of cobalt oxide (CoO) to the slip. It is said that small amounts of zinc oxide, magnesia, and lime are useful whitening materials.

High- and Low-fire Colorants

Colored engobes are produced in great and pleasing varieties by the judicious use of certain oxides or other chemical compounds. The results will be dependent upon the coloring agents used, the composition of the slip, the mode of introduction of the coloring agents, the temperature and the character of the firing, and the composition of the glaze coat, if any. The most pleasing results are those which are had by careful blending of two or more of the different colors. The coloring agents may be divided into two groups: those suitable for the higher temperature range, i.e., cone 6 or above, and those reliable only at the lower temperature range. There are even some shades which may be had only at temperatures of the order of cone 05 and lower. The duration of the firing is an important item. It should also be remembered that the introduction of some coloring agents may have a disturbing effect upon the maturing conduct of the slip. In general, the introduction of more than 8% of a coloring oxide—particularly of the high temperature group—should be compensated by a corresponding decrease in the total refractory constituents. Further, some adhesive must be added, otherwise the engobe may dust off.

The basic oxides used to produce colored engobes are listed below.

blue: cobalt oxide; 2% for light color, 10% for dark
green: chromium oxide; 5% for light color, 20% for dark
grey, greyish green, and loam: nickel oxide; 2% for light color, 10% for dark
brown: manganese dioxide; 5% for light color, 20% for dark
red, pink, brownish: iron oxide; 5% for light color, 15% for dark. (The color will be variable, being susceptible to the effect of composition, particle size, and kiln atmosphere.)
yellow, amber: uranium oxide; 5% for the light color, 10% for the darker. (It is expensive.)
black: This may be obtained by strong reduction of the iron present

Table 11.7. Examples of three clays that produced successful terra sigillata coatings[31]

	*Amounts, weight %**		
Oxide	*No. 1*	*No. 2*	*No. 3*
SiO_2	62.2	62.0	54.1
Al_2O_3	17.2	23.8	26.3
Fe_2O_3	6.8	0.8	3.3
TiO_2	1.1	1.3	1.2
CaO	0.4	0.1	0.7
MgO	1.5	T	0.2
Na_2O	0.1	0.4	4.3
K_2O	3.7	1.2	0.6
Illite	major	some	–
Kaolinite	present	major	mainly
Quartz	present	present	present
Muscovite	–	–	minor

*Loss on ignition brings the total to 100.

(10%), or by using a calcine made of 20% cobalt oxide, 20% manganese dioxide, and 10% chromium oxide.

red, pink: a calcine made with the oxide of chromium, whiting, and a small amount of tin oxide will give pinks and red superior to those had with iron oxide and more dependable.

The above colors may be had at temperatures below cone 6 by the use of the reagents listed. In addition, copper oxide may be used to produce greens, and antimony will give excellent yellows, but only at low temperature.

Variations in color may be due to a variety of causes, for example: (*a*) variations in thickness of engobe coat; (*b*) variations in kiln temperature; (*c*) the slip may be under- or over-fired; (*d*) if glazed, the coat may be too thick or fired too long; (*e*) the glaze may attack the engobe too freely; (*f*) the action of sulfur oxide in kiln gases; and (*g*) the reduction by kiln gases.

Terra Sigillata

Terra sigillata is antique pottery of Roman origin made with a vitrified red-brown glossy clay coating. The fine-grained dense material makes a beautiful lustrous finish. The coatings have been referred to as "terra sigillata." This antique finish has been revised and the coatings cannot be classified as an engobe or a glaze. Because the coatings are so very thin, the shrinkages of the glaze and the substrate body need not be closely matched and are of minor significance. The half-glossy coatings are from 5 microns to 15 microns (about 0.2 mil to 0.6 mil) in thickness. These are made from very fine clay, made into a slip, applied to the body, and fired.

Schumann[28] described modern techniques for the preparation of terra sigillata. He coated clay wares with coatings made from the same clay as that in the body and/or other clays. He added water to bring the specific gravity to about 1.2 or lower in the presence of an effective deflocculant. He allowed the suspension to set for times calculated for particles coarser than 1 micron (by Stoke's law) to settle from the top of the column to the bottom. The fraction in suspension was drawn off and used as the coating either at the concentration as separated or after concentration.

It was stated by Prins de Jong[29] and by Amberg[30] that clays making good terra sigillata were composed primarily of micalike minerals such as illite and sericite.

It seems evident that the unique[31] gloss is caused mainly by the plate structure and shape of the materials making up the coating. The superposed parallel platelets during firing are sintered and cemented so as to form oriented edges and configurations of in situ glass-formation and residual crystalline phases. From this point of view, illite, sericite, and clays with strong flake structures make good terra sigillata, but montmorillonite minerals have not been successful.

Illite clays have been very successful. Some kaolinitic clays also have been used with success. Using this type of material and the dispersed suspensions containing only particles less than 1 micron, successful coatings develop when fired in the range of 900° to 1,000° C.

Examples of clays that have been successfully used are shown in table 11.7.

Terra sigillatas can be produced from various clays by following a procedure similar to that outlined below. Take materials in the following proportions: Clay material, 19.9%; distilled water, 80.0%; sodium hexameta phosphate, 0.1%. This batch should be milled in a ball mill for 4 hours, then transferred to tall settling containers and allowed to settle about 20 hours (or a time calculated for particles of 1 micron to settle). After the settling period, the liquid portion is removed, transferred to suitable trays, and evaporated to dryness. The settled portion can be diluted again and resettled to get another portion.

The suspended fraction need not be dried, but can be made to a specific gravity of 1.15 to 1.20 and used. If it is dried down, the dried fraction should be mixed with distilled water and ball-milled again.

Using the dried supernate fraction, the composition and procedure may be as follows: Dried terra sigillata + color oxide, 30%; distilled water, 70%. Make to specific gravity of 1.15–1.20; then add enough Calgon to ball mill to disperse. Various color oxides can be added, using 3%–5% of body stain or oxides of Cr, Co, Mn, etc.

The coating can be applied by spraying or dipping and should be applied to a thickness of 0.004 in. to 0.005 in. The body should be clean and smooth. The coatings mature to a vitreous state without sticking when glazed surfaces are in contact but not weighted. Fire to 1,080° C–1,150° C. The fired coatings are impervious, of good sheen and good texture, and do not craze.

Terra Nigra

Some black pottery, called "terra nigra," has been excavated from ancient Roman settlements near Heidelberg, Germany. Denninger and Ebinger[32] fired some samples of these to 1,000° C in an oxidizing atmosphere and the black disappeared. The reddish underbody then was evident, as was a yellowish surface layer. The black "terra nigra" was duplicated experimentally by adding powdered charcoal to a clay mix used for a glaze and firing in a bed of charcoal. The same method could be used to produce copper reds.

References

1. Bishop, C. W. 1940. Beginnings of civilization in Eastern Asia. *Antiquity*. 14:301; 1941. *Cer. Abst.* 20:3.
2. Leisner, reference given by Lucas, A. 1934. *Ancient Egyptian materials and industries*. 2d ed. London, p 104.
3. Walters, H. B. 1905. *History of ancient pottery*. Vol. 2. London, p 224.
4. McDowell, S. J. 1933. Terra cotta slip coatings. *J. Am. Ceram. Soc.* 16:134.
5. Stull, R. T. 1910. Notes on the manufacture of enamel brick with some investigations on enamel brick slips. *Trans. Am. Ceram. Soc.* 12:711.
6. McMahon, J. F. 1938. The ability of some underslips and glazes to cover surface imperfections. *Bull. Am. Ceram. Soc.* 17:5.
7. Schurecht, H. G. and McMahon, J. F. 1937. Influence of the composition of underslips, glazes, and bodies upon blistering and other glaze defects. *J. Am. Ceram. Soc.* 20:344–348.
8. Wilson, H. 1920. Notes on terra cotta slips with reference to the use of asbestos and chlorite mica. *J. Am. Ceram. Soc.* 3:114.
9. Shaw, J. B. 1913. A process of making sanitary ware. *Trans. Am. Ceram. Soc.* 15:467.
10. Davis, H. E. and Lathrop, J. S. 1925. Study of slips for standard finish terra cotta. *J. Am. Ceram. Soc.* 8:23.
11. McDowell, S. J. 1933. Terra cotta slip coatings. *J. Am. Ceram. Soc.* 16:134.
12. Wilson, H. E. 1923. *Architectural terra cotta*. Privately published.
13. Schurecht, H. G. Communication.
14. Lapp, G. W. 1928. The vacuum slip process of removing air from clay bodies. *J. Am. Ceram. Soc.* 11:61.
15. Ashley, H. E. 1914. Technical control of the colloidal matter of clays. Tech. paper. *Bur. Std.* (U.S.) No. 23.
16. Kirkpatrick, F. A., Arnold, H. C., and Geiger, C. F. 1916. An attempt to fit enamels to plastic clay bodies. *Trans. Am. Ceram. Soc.* 18:139.
17. Wilson, H. 1917. Note on the pinholing and peeling on terra cotta. *Trans. Am. Ceram. Soc.* 19:209.
18. Carruthers, J. L. 1922. Notes on the shivering of terra cotta. *J. Am. Ceram. Soc.* 5:518.
19. Griffen, H. R. 1896. *Clays, glazes, and enamels*. Indianapolis: T. A. Randall and Co., p 43.
20. Davis, H. E. 1920. The effect of the size of the grog grain in a terra cotta body. *J. Am. Ceram. Soc.* 3:641.

21. Davis, H. E. and Lathrop, J. S. 1925. A study of standard finish terra cotta (cone 4–5). *J. Am. Ceram. Soc.* 8:23.
22. Schurecht, H. G. and McMahon, J. F. 1937. Influence of the composition of underslips, glazes, and bodies on blistering and other glaze defects. *J. Am. Ceram. Soc.* 20:344.
23. McMahon, J. F. 1938. The ability of some underslips and glazes to cover surface imperfections. *Bull. Am. Ceram. Soc.* 17:5.
24. Hill, E. C. 1928. Some experiments on terra cotta slips. *J. Am. Ceram. Soc.* 11:260.
25. Schurecht, H. G. and Pole, G. R. 1930. Method of measuring strains between glazes and ceramic bodies. *J. Am. Ceram. Soc.* 13:369
26. Coulter, William G. 1954. Color series: 6, How to prepare and apply engobes and body stains. *Ceram. Ind.* 62(3):76–77.
27. McVay, T. N. and Parmelee, C. W. 1937. Effect of iron and its compounds on the color and properties of ceramic engobes and materials. *J. Am. Ceram. Soc.* 20:336.
28. Schumann, Theodore. *Schutte A.-G. für Ionindustrie.* German Patent 626, 112, Feb 29, 1936.
29. Prins de Jong, E. F. and Rijkens, A. J. 1946. Surface decoration on terra sigillata and on Greek black-painted vases. *Bull. Am. Ceram. Soc.* 25(1):5–7.
30. Amberg, C. R. 1948. Terra sigillata, forgotten finish. *Ceram. Ind.* 51(6):77,90,92,94.
31. Coffin, L. B. 1958. Colored terra sigillata coatings for building materials. *Bull. Amer. Ceram. Soc.* 37(10):446–47.
32. Denninger, E. and Ebinger, H. 1952. Experiments on the duplication of "terra nigra" and the firing of reduction glazes on charcoal. *Ber. Deut. Keram. Ges. u. Ber. Deut. Emailfachleute* 29(12):411–12.

12

Underglaze and Overglaze Colors

The decoration on pottery, china, earthenware, and porcelain may be applied on the glazed ware or on the body and covered by the glaze. The terms overglaze and underglaze colors clearly indicate the different uses made of them for decoration. The reagents are the same to a considerable degree, but the preparation, application, and conditions of firing differ notably. Overglaze colors are matured on surfaces of glazes at approximately red heat. Consequently they are but little or not at all affected by the composition of the glazes. On the other hand, underglaze colors must produce the desired effects at the maximum temperature required to develop the covering glaze. The colors must successfully resist the high temperature, corrosive solution, and diffusive effects of the covering glaze during its firing treatment.

The overglaze color or stain is commonly incorporated in a low-fusing frit that will bond it firmly to the glaze on which it is fired. Another function of the flux is to make the color as glossy as the glaze. The underglaze colors may or may not be mixed with a frit, but must be made sufficiently refractory and inert to serve the purpose desired. This end may be attained by calcining the mixture rather than fritting it. Underglaze colors, their preparation, and associated problems were well understood long ago and were discussed by Dr. Seger.[1] Much progress has been made since the time of Seger. New colors, materials and processes have been developed.

Underglaze decorations are applied directly to the bisque body. This distinguishes them from engobe decoration, which is the application of color directly to the unfired body to be covered with glaze.

Underglaze Work

Use Requirements

Underglaze colors normally are used under earthenware, chinaware, and porcelain glazes, maturing from cone 06 to cone 14. The choice of colors diminishes as the firing temperature increases. The most limited choice of colors is that for use under porcelain glazes, maturing generally from cone 9 to 14. A large selection of colors is found to be stable under earthenware or low-temperature glazes maturing in the general range of cone 06 to cone 1. For this class of glazes, the destructive mechanism is more likely to be due to the easily fusible and highly corrosive fluxes in the glazes than to temperature, per se. The presence of strong fluxes is likely to attack the underglaze colors, tending to dissolve them and leading to the smudging of edges and outlines. Consequently, for this type of glaze, great care must be exercised in the selection of colors and in securing precisions and uniformity in firing.

A more favorable condition exists for a class of glazes maturing from about cone 2 to 6. Typical of this class are American Chinaware glazes. The range of colors is entirely adequate. The base glaze contains few harsh fluxes and the firing temperature is moderate. The glaze is of high viscosity, preventing running, and does not promote excessive solution or diffusion. Consequently the outlines remain fixed and sharp without fading or smudging. This is true in cases where the underglaze colors and the cover-glaze both have been developed and selected with care.

Critical Variables

The successful use of underglaze colors depends on the observance of some critical details. These are outlined as follows:

1. Maturing temperature of the cover glaze; the more brilliant colors are to be had at temperatures below cone 6. Blues, grays, and blacks predominate at or above cone 12 but it is possible to produce clear pinks, crimsons, yellows, lilacs, and browns to cone 18 and above.
2. The composition and thickness of the glaze; a fritted glaze is relatively concentrated and much of the chemical work has been completed in the preparation of the frit; this lessens the potential attack on the colors and the degree of color migration will largely be controlled by diffusion. Thick applications of glaze contribute to smudging and the solvent action of glazes is much diminished in thin glazes. Some glaze components are particularly damaging to selected stains and colors. Likewise, some colors are best used in the presence of certain glaze components. Cer-

tain glaze components must be avoided in contact with certain color oxides.

3. The composition, physical condition, and temperature of preparation of the color base or stain; in many instances, the higher the temperature of the calcination, the richer and more durable the color. A color base containing zinc oxide or other rather volatile constituents cannot be calcined at as high a temperature as one of a more refractory nature. Fine grinding of the calcined color base, its thorough purification of soluble salts by washing, and recalcination is the practice commonly employed in order to insure purity of color and freedom from harmful soluble salts. The condition of the atmosphere during the calcining process must be controlled to insure good results.

THERMAL EXPANSION CHARACTERISTICS. Expansion coefficients of the underglaze stain should conform closely to those of the glaze and the body to achieve good glaze fit.

A casual consideration of the above items should impress the reader with the great importance of close attention to detail in the preparation, as well as the use, of underglaze colors. Owing to the numerous difficulties to be surmounted and the need for much experience and expert knowledge, the commercial preparation of these colors has been left largely to those individuals or firms which specialize in this field. The ceramist should acquaint himself thoroughly with the characteristics of colors to be used, whatever their source. This commonly is done by applying them in differing thicknesses on trial pieces of the body and subjecting these to the normal hardening-on firing. These samples then are coated with the glaze (or glazes) used and fired at the different temperature levels likely to be had in the factory kilns.

Preparation

Underglaze colors or stains may be grouped in two classes, insofar as their physical form is concerned: (1) Soluble coloring compounds and (2) insoluble, or solid, coloring compounds.

SOLUBLE UNDERGLAZE TECHNIQUE. The soluble salts used are those of cobalt, iron, manganese, etc., and hydrochloric, nitric, acetic, oxalic, and other suitable acids. Preference is given to those which are easily decomposable by low temperatures. The salts are dissolved in glycerine unless its solvent action is too slow or too limited, then water or some other appropriate reagent is used. Those having only slight solubility in glycerine may be dissolved in water to which a measured quantity of glycerine is added and the whole evaporated to a syrupy consistency. More glycerine is added to dilute to the desired strength. Since the solutions will be colorless or only faintly colored, appropriate aniline dyes are added to facilitate the identification of the surfaces upon which the salt solutions may be applied. After careful drying of each application, successive coatings of color may be made to build up the desired tone. Before the glaze coat is applied over the colors the decorated piece must be heated strongly enough to drive out any free water and to dissociate decomposable compounds. An oxidizing atmosphere and carefully controlled temperature are required.

The soluble colors are more delicate, although weak, and particularly suited for flat decorations and will give only one tone, no matter how thickly applied, unless the decorated ware is subjected to a high temperature before the second application of color is made.[2] The colors readily spread on the soft and porous ware. If certain parts of an area to be decorated by spraying or painting are not to be covered with a coat of the soluble underglaze, it may be protected by a "reserve," which may be a mixture of a refractory, such as kaolin, with an adhesive material, e.g., dextrin. Such a coating is readily removed after the hardening-on firing. The character of the overglaze and the temperature of maturity of the glaze will have important influence upon the tone or even the color obtained. An important advantage of the use of soluble salts is the economical and efficient use of color in very small quantities.

Pukall[3] has proposed the saturation of more or less refractory, porous, and easily pulverized bodies with solutions of metallic salts, igniting at a high temperature, and applying. He found that alumina, silica, and zinc-alumina gave good absorption bodies.

Some of the typical soluble salt recipes are as follows:[4]

Blue: 100 g. of cobalt acetate are dissolved in 700 cc of glycerine and concentrated by heating carefully, and finally enough glycerine is added to make up to the original volume.

Chrome green: 300 g. of chrome-alum are dissolved in water; 700 cc of glycerine are added and the whole is concentrated by heating until the volume is again 300 cc. Sufficient glycerine is then added to make the total volume 1,000 cc.

Brown: 10 g. of uranium nitrate are dissolved in 20 cc of glycerine.

Rose: About 10% of a colloidal dispersion of gold, such as is used for bright gold, is suspended in a convenient medium, such as glycerine, for application.

INSOLUBLE UNDERGLAZE COLOR. The insoluble underglaze color body consists of a pigmentary oxide or mixture of oxides, sometimes named stains, frequently, a flux to bind the color to the body surface; accessory materials to serve as diluents, modifiers of the color; and refractories to control the fusibility as may be needed. After the underglaze color is applied on the biscuit ware it is "hardened-on" by firing to about a red heat; then the ware is coated with glaze which is matured at the temperature necessary. It is highly important that the absorption of the hardened-on color should be approximately the same as that of the body so that the glaze coating will be uniform over all. It is therefore important that the glaze "wets" the underglaze decoration properly and that no cracks develop at any stage. The thermal expansion conduct of the underglaze and the coverglaze should not differ greatly.

Decorating Methods *

Five different techniques are in use for applying underglaze colors, the technique selected being based upon the effects desired, the pattern and material used. The following methods are used: (1) Lining and hand painting; (2) printing; (3) spraying; (4) decalcomania; and (5) stamping.

In order to apply the colors, they must be mixed with a decorating medium or vehicle. The general requirements of a medium are that it be—

a. conducive to rapid application;
b. capable of being hardened-on;
c. burn off readily in the hardening-on or glost firing;
d. must leave the color intact and undisturbed;
e. may be of either the water base or oil base type.

HAND PAINTING AND LINING. Hand painting and lining is widely used on chinaware and on artware. It is an inexpensive process and capable of high production. The pigments or stains are mixed with natural balsam or fir resins worked up on a flat glass plate with a spatula. High turpentine makes for fast application but applies a low density deposit, and if too dilute will lead to poor durability of color.

Good practice is to establish the best pigment-to-oil ratio and control this without deviation. For underglaze preparations, blends of pine oil, balsam of fir, and xylene make a good medium. The function of pine oil is to retard drying-out. Xylene is widely employed as a thinner instead of turpentine, because it does not thicken with aging. The usual proportions are in the range of 60% by weight of oil to 40% of pigment, which are mixed together in a burr mill. It is important that the stain be *thoroughly* dried before grinding with the oil.

Some stains, notably high-zinc pigments, may tend to settle from suspension. This usually is overcome by adding about 2% of soya lecithin or an acrylic resin to lower the surface tension of the vehicle and achieve improved pigment wettability.

*For underglaze screen printing, see waterfall glazing on page 149.

For thin bands, the color is applied with a brush, but spraying is used for the application of bands ¼-inch wide or more. After lining or banding, the applied color must be completely dried for a period of 8 to 24 hours to prevent the formation of pock marks and surface irregularities. The medium must then be burned off slowly on a fixed schedule with good ventilation. The dried decoration must be firmly attached to the bisque and the cover glaze must cover the decoration evenly and smoothly.

Hand painting follows the same procedure as lining, except that the decorations frequently are hardened-on by firing to 1,350° F before the cover glaze is applied. This process usually is used with porous bisque such as semiporcelain. They may utilize either water or oil as vehicles. The water-base mediums are made of glycerine and water mixtures.

PRINTING. The application of decorations by a printing technique has its preferred areas for production. In general the basic operations are: (*a*) preparation of the "ink," or oil-color mixture; (*b*) making the printing pattern; (*c*) application of the design to the ware.

A wide variety of satisfactory printing and squeegee oils are available. The vehicle must be of high viscosity, like heat-boiled linseed oil. It must wet the pattern evenly and be transferred perfectly to the ware. Usually the "ink" must be made by blending with the color in a heated roller mill. The heat is necessary because the high viscosity required for printing is too high for color-vehicle mixing.

There are a number of variations and innovations in the process of making and applying the pattern. One typical method is to engrave a copper plate or cylinder. The ink is applied to the engraved plate and the excess scraped off with a sharp blade or other scraper. At this stage, the ink usually is heated to about 150° F. The engraved cylinder with its engraved recesses filled with "ink" would be rolled over a sheet of thin paper, thus transferring the design to the paper. This pattern then is placed face-down on the ware and rubbed down with a stiff brush. The ware then is wetted with water and the paper sponged off, leaving the pattern on the ware. After the design has been dried, the cover glaze can be applied.

The major problems in printing are: (*a*) Color bleeding; (*b*) imperfect transference to the ware; (*c*) poor transference to the paper; (*d*) color workability less than optimum; and (*e*) color scumming.

The control of these factors is involved with materials selections, materials control, processing control, and the skill and care of the operators.

SPRAYING. This method for the application of decoration has an area of imminent applicability. There is continued effort and activity to extend the process of spray decoration to more mechanized production. It has great flexibility and by clever masking techniques all types of designs have been applied. In addition, some things can be done by spraying that are not so easily achieved otherwise, as for example, spattered colors, combinations of solid colors with speckled colors, and fade-out colors. The concepts and applications of stencils are endless.

The spraying process, in general, is now used for high-speed, mechanized, less expensive production. Unfortunately, however, the process still is expensive for complicated and multicolored designs. To accomplish this requires several operations and precision mechanization for superimposing a series of masking templates. It also tends to be wasteful of color.

Where spraying is employed, the slip may be either water- or oil-based. Light-bodied mixtures of turpentine, linseed oil, and varnish are conventionally employed. The vehicle (medium) is mixed with the pigments by ball-milling. Where water is used, a thickener and binder such as gum arabic or other water-dispersable gum are employed.

Natural gums are commonly preferred for wide bands and the like. The color is evenly sprayed, dried, and a mask representing the design is superimposed on the ware; an overcoating of clear lacquer is applied, then again thoroughly dried. The ware then is immersed in water and the color not covered with lacquer is removed. Frequently no mask at all is used, which eliminates the washing step.

It is usually required to harden-on sprayed decorations by firing to 1,350° F. It is possible to cover sprayed colors without hardening-on if the right binder and adhesive are used in the cover glaze to prevent crawling. This is not always so easy for slips used in automatic spray machines.

Decalcomania. This process has been discussed in chapter 5. This is the most widely applied decorating method used for underglazes. In this process, the decal is applied by a slide-off decal process or by a fully automated machine and fired immediately to 1,300° F. In the case of underglaze decals, the application is the same and the ware is glazed before firing to glost temperatures.

The most likely defects characteristic of overglaze decal process are: (*a*) Specks; (*b*) blisters; (*c*) color rolling; and (*d*) color scumming. Defects in underglaze decals are: (*a*) Fading from overfire; (*b*) running from fluid glaze.

These and other defects are discussed in chapter 17.

Stamping. The application of decorations to ceramic ware by printing has intriguing possibilities for low-cost mechanized decorations. There are obvious difficulties that are continually being improved upon with ingenious innovations. Rubber stamping still is not too widely applied as a primary decorating process.

The stamping mixture is prepared with a heat-boiled varnish and ground to a homogeneous "ink" with the underglaze color in a pebble mill. The mixture is taken from the mill and thoroughly smoothed by rolling out on a smooth glass plate.

The stamp, usually of rubber, is mounted on a sponge backing. This is pressed against the color plate to pick up the color. The stamp, carrying color, then is placed against the ware.

There are several possible variations of the direct printing technique. In one method, the color pattern is silk-screened upon a rubber bladder which then is inflated against the ware. This has possibilities for decorating the inside of ware or concave shapes.

Several difficulties or problems are to be associated with printing. Among them are the following.

a. variations in the uniformity of color spreading on the plate
b. variations of pick-up by the stamp
c. possibilities of stamp smudging
d. difficulties in the mechanization of fine-detail and multicolored designs
e. achieving and maintaining optimum working properties of the ink

SCREENING. This method has advantages and disadvantages. It has been discussed in chapter 5. Regardless of the technique or the colors used, all underglaze colors must be finely ground. The decorating paste must be prepared and maintained at optimum consistency. The underglaze colors as well as the cover glazes must be carefully formulated to produce the desired results. The vehicle must be selected and controlled with equal care. The cover glaze must be controlled in thickness to about 0.004 ± 0.001 in.

Color Bodies

The amount of fluxing or diluting agents added varies widely—a total of possibly 20% to 30%. Hegemann[4] states that the porcelain colors are prepared by mixing with about one-third of finely ground body. Seger[1] recommends for use on whiteware the mixture of the color with 20% of the glaze or hydrous boric acid. In the latter case, the mixture is ignited at 1,000° C or above, ground finely, washed carefully, dried, and again ground finely.

As diluents and refractories the reagents most frequently used are: alumina, kaolin, and finely ground biscuit. The category of true fluxing agents may include the glaze, feldspar, and frit used in the glaze or specially compounded, boric oxide, zinc oxide, and others. The coloring agents, diluents, refractories, and fluxes are thoroughly mixed and finely ground, calcined, ground, carefully levigated (washed), and again calcined and ground. The cycle of calcining, grinding, and washing may be repeated several times.

The underglaze color composites must be mixed with some suitable medium to permit their application to the ceramic bodies they are to decorate. Because the method of application may be any one of those common to the ceramic industry, i.e., painting, stamping, printing, screen process, etc., the medium will be selected which is appropriate to the condition of the ware and the method of application. If the body is porous, the colors may be ground with water to form a paste. If the body is highly absorbent, prior wetting will facilitate the application. Considerable skill is required and the decoration, when dry, is easily marred by any light accidental contact or careless handling.

The use of a 25% solution of gum arabic in water with a little glycerine will permit more delicate brushwork, and it may be possible to apply the decoration on the top of a background wash. The use of a medium containing too much gum may result in the formation of blisters during the firing. Sodium silicate solution is sometimes used. Glycerine alone or diluted with water is a convenient medium to use and ware so decorated does not always require a hardening-on firing. If the ware is quite absorbent, a more concentrated glycerine solution may be used. The medium most frequently employed commercially is a rectified oil of turpentine with a little linseed oil. The colors suspended in this may be applied thickly without fear of subsequent blistering. However, firing-on the color at a dull red heat is required to eliminate completely the oil before the glaze coat is applied. Vitreous bodies do not require the use of the oil medium; consequently, other mediums may be used and the hardening-on fire avoided.

The use of specially prepared colored crayons for decorating a ceramic surface has been proposed[5] and is employed. These crayons are prepared by binding the color body and any other necessary constituents with a bonding medium, adding water to make the mass plastic, and forming the same into convenient cylindrical pieces which are ready for use after drying. When color is applied by the use of these crayons, it may be sprayed with a fixative—a solution of gum in water—which will protect the decoration from harm due to careless handling prior to firing.

The selection of the composition, the thickness of application, and the conditions of firing the glaze which covers the colors, are very important details and have important influences on the ultimate results. In general, a glaze which comes to maturity quickly and therefore requires a glost fire of only short duration is desired. A prolonged heat treatment may cause the glaze coating to flow on inclined surfaces and thereby distort the decoration. To minimize the tendency to flow, the use of properly balanced glaze formulation is recommended. Those bases which are harmful to underglaze colors impair the transparency of the glaze or alter its other physical properties and are to be avoided.

A balanced glaze is the objective of the ceramist; for example, zinc oxide harms the beauty of the greens had with chromium, but there are instances of the successful use of cover glazes containing this element. Both calcium oxide and zinc oxide may lessen the transparency of the cover glaze, but both of these elements are common component glazes. Lead oxide has a vigorous chemical action in maturing glazes, but it gives brilliancy, transparency, and fusibility. Objections to the use of baryta, magnesia, and almost all the other elements have been reported. The balanced glaze is one which serves its purpose because of the usefulness of its components, selected and apportioned according to known limitations.

It is quite obvious that the color of the overglaze, if any, will alter the appearance of the underglaze. A light blue glaze applied over a yellow underglaze will make the latter appear greenish, or the same glaze applied over a manganese color will produce a purple where the two are in contact.

Underglaze Colors

BLUE: COLOR OXIDES. Cobalt is not the only source of blue in ceramic underglaze colors, but it is the strongest, most durable, and most widely used. It may be used at all temperatures through those employed for porcelain glazes. With certain modifiers, it can yield all shades from delicate pastels to intense clear blue. Cobalt may form "solution colors," due to the cobalt ion in silicate glass, when it behaves as an RO member, or an insoluble pigment as with cobalt aluminate. Its coloring power is so great that it frequently is introduced into a frit which serves as a diluent, thus furnishing a convenient means for exact control of the color to insure uniformity and consistency in the finished decoration.

Cobalt oxide, like the oxides of manganese, iron, and some other elements, has the ability to alter its state of oxidation during heating, and subsequently liberate part of the oxygen when the temperature goes above certain limits. This liberated gas may be the cause of the formation of seeds and bubbles in the viscous melt and these may remain entrapped in the cooled glaze. By combining these oxides with alumina to form a spinel at high temperature and by employing the spinel as the medium for the introduction of the cobalt, this defect may be avoided. The spinel is resistant to reducing conditions.

Some of the modifiers commonly employed in the compositions of cobalt colors, whether overglaze, underglaze, or even inglaze, are as follows:

a. Alumina promotes the formation of clear, dark blue color and a high stability if prepared as a spinel.
b. Nickel may be used as a "shading agent" to give a greyish or softer tone. This is also true of the presence of very small amounts of iron and manganese which is considered the explanation of the pleasing qualities of the blue decorations of antique Oriental and European wares; the early potters did not have available the pure cobalt materials so readily accessible today.
c. Zinc oxide tends to produce blue greens, light blues, and violet blues. Boric oxide and phosphoric oxide cause the formation of the violet tones. Uranium shades or tones the cobalt color in a manner similar to nickel.
d. Silica and high temperatures develop the darker blue color.
e. Titanium oxide may be used with small amounts of cobalt to obtain a light blue green.

The effects of the glaze composition on underglaze colors may be briefly summarized as follows: Good blue underglaze colors may be had without difficulty under leadless glazes, especially those high in alumina; whereas glazes high in lead and boric acid, alone or together, attack the colors more or less vigorously, depending upon the temperatures and the compositions. Alkalies enhance the beauty of the tone, but they are vigorous solvents and, under favorable conditions for attack, alter the color shade towards an ultramarine, which action is hastened by the prolongation of the heat treatment. High proportions of the alkaline earths in the glaze are said to cause or to accelerate chemical reactions between the underglaze color and the glaze.

BLUE: PREPARED STAINS. The following are the main blue stains used in underglaze colors: Cobalt-alumina, cobalt-silica, and zirconium-vanadium blue.

The cobalt stains are the ones most commonly employed. Because of the potent coloring and migratory effects of cobalt ions in solution in silicate melts, cobalt stains must be carefully handled. This poses no problem when reasonable care is practiced. Straight cobalt-silica, and modifiers such as zirconium, tin and zinc oxides, exert influences on the color.

Cobalt-alumina, basically a spinel of cobalt aluminate, is the most refractory of the cobalt colors and would be highly desirable in underglaze colors, but it is too refractory for most underglaze colors except for some mats. It is so inert that a good bond with the body is impossible to achieve except for very high firing temperatures. This can be cured by adding a flux to the stain, but the cobalt-silica color then is obtained which is different from the cobalt-alumina color.

Zirconium-vanadium colors are very stable and versatile. These stains must be extremely fine in particle size to be used in underglaze colors. They are extremely refractory and require the use of a strong flux to mature them to the body and prevent flaking. These stains are rapidly gaining in popularity as underglaze colors.

Copper dissolves too easily in the glaze and tends to burn-out badly and is scarcely used in underglaze colors.

GREEN: COLOR OXIDES. The chief green coloring agent for underglaze use is chromium because of its refractoriness and high tinctorial power. Copper may be used at low or some of the medium temperatures, but it is highly soluble and diffuses readily in the glaze and, sometimes, into the body. Copper enters into the formation of silicates, but the chromium does not, or only to a slight extent. Consequently, the colors containing the former are transparent while the latter are opaque.

A clear green color may be had with chromium by the presence of the alkaline earths—lime, baryta, and magnesia—especially calcium fluoride, which promotes the formation of Victoria green. A little alumina with the chromium oxide is said to lighten the color and a very little zinc oxide yields a grey green, but too much gives a dirty neutral color. A small amount of cobalt oxide enlivens the green, and iron oxide or manganese oxide in small amounts makes a brownish shade. Reducing conditions in the preparation of the underglaze (chromium) green and in the firing assist in the production of better color. High silica content of the color of the glaze also is helpful.

The underglaze green containing chromium is quite sensitive to the nature of the glaze composition and to variations of the temperature and atmosphere of the glost fire. If the content of the calcium oxide in the glaze is high, the boric oxide content will not harm the color,[6] but it has been asserted that the amount of the boric oxide should always be less than the alumina.

The Victoria-green color is rather more sensitive to the effect of the cover glaze than the other very commonly used underglaze colors, viz. chrome-tin-pink. In general, baryta is regarded as too active chemically and therefore harmful; a high boric oxide content in the glaze is favorable but where it exceeds the molecular equivalents of the alumina present, it will darken the Victoria green. If the reverse is true, the color alters toward the browns. These remarks apply to glazes for whiteware fired at cones 4–5.[7]

Table 12.1. Green color bases[7]

Constituents	*Amounts, parts by wt.* Seger-green	Victoria-green
Potassium bicarbonate	36	36
Flint	20	20
Whiting	20	20
Fluorspar	20	12
Calcium chloride, fused		12

The compositions of two green color bases frequently mentioned in ceramic literature are given in table 12.1.

The bichromate and the calcium chloride are dissolved in water, but the other three ingredients are thoroughly mixed by grinding dry. This powder then is dispersed in the solution of the salts to a stiff paste. This paste is thoroughly mixed and homogenized, then dried and calcined at around 800° F, and is followed by leaching the soluble matter from the powdered calcine. This product then is calcined at about cone 1, ground to a fine powder, and is ready to use.

Jacob,[7] referring to the color compositions of table 12.1, pointed out that the good Victoria green was readily discolored if employed under glaze (*a*) of table 12.2, but less readily discolored under glaze (*b*) of the same table.

GREEN: PREPARED STAINS. Prepared underglaze green stains are available commercially. The most widely used greens are based on Cr_2O_3. These are quite stable except in the presence of zinc and perhaps SnO_2. The Victoria green is, as indicated in the preceding section, high in calcium and is a difficult underglaze color to control. It not only requires a high lime glaze, but is sensitive to zinc, and to high concentrations of lead and B_2O_3. It is strongly influenced by firing temperature and to its position in the kiln. These problems are the price paid to secure the brightest of all underglaze colors.

Very satisfactory replacements for the old Victoria green are coming about as a result of blends of zirconium-vanadium with tin-vanadium

Table 12.2. Glazes used by Jacob[7] to cover the Victoria green of table 12.1.

Glazes	*Molecular equivalents* PbO	CaO	KNaO	Al_2O_3	B_2O_3	SiO_2
(a)	0.40	0.25–0.40	0.20–0.30	0.22–0.35	0.30–0.42	2.42–3.15
(b)	0.40	0.45	0.15	0.25	0.03–0.20	2.30–2.80

Table 12.3. Range of batch weights for the preparation of Naples yellows[9]

Constituents	*Parts by weight*
Lead nitrate or super oxide	132.4–331.0
Calcium stannate ($CaO \cdot SnO_2$)	123.6–000.0
Calcined alumina	10.2– 30.6
Antimony oxide	57.6–144.0

stains. Other blends are uranium yellow with cobalt blue. Moss green shades develop with praseodymium phosphate. A patent has been issued covering combinations of BeO with Cr_2O_3 especially suited to a very high temperature use.

YELLOW: COLOR OXIDES. Yellows may be had by the use of various reagents, particularly at low temperatures, but the problem of producing good shades above approximately cone 1 is not so readily solved. The principal reagents for the development of yellow underglaze and overglaze colors are: lead antimonate, titanates, uranates, cadmium and sulfur, cadmium and selenium, and vanadium and tin. Tungsten and molybdenum have been reported as producing yellows at high temperatures.[8]

The range of composition of the underglaze Naples yellow, which is the trade name for the lead antimonates, is given by Berdel[9] as:

0.4–1.0PbO	$0.1–0.3Al_2O_3$	$0.2–0.5Sb_2O_3$
0.6–0.0CaO		$0.6–0.0SnO_2$

The limits of the batch weights for these Naples yellows are shown in table 12.3. Common salt is added to the batch in the proportion of about one-half the weight and the whole is calcined under oxidizing conditions at about 800–900° C and washed. An orange color may be had by adding 0.15–0.3 equiv. Fe_2O_3.

The use of lead antimonate for underglaze yellows has been reported by various ceramists. Berdel[9] states that it may not be recommended for application under whiteware glaze fired between cones 3 and 6, but other ceramists[10] found usable, but not very satisfactory, antimony colors which were a little better under lead-containing than under leadless glazes.

Rutile, with some iron oxide and zinc oxide, withstands much higher temperatures, but the color is not so bright as is the case with the antimonate. Berdel[9] gives the limits for the compositions of desirable colors as follows:

1.0–0.8ZnO	$1.0TiO_2$
$0.0–0.2Fe_2O_3$	

The color is usable as an underglaze pigment if fired in an oxidizing fire at temperatures of cones 7 to 9. By the addition of other oxides, browns and olive greens may be had.

Uranium was used for the purest transparent colors on and under the glaze. Its high cost and some other restrictions limit its use. It may be used up to cone 11 but must be fired with a strongly oxidizing fire. For underglaze colors for porcelain, it may be prepared without calcining by mixing and grinding the following batch,[11] in weight %: Pegmatite, 30; kaolin, 35; and calcium uranate, 35.

Another formula[12] for use under a porcelain glaze is given in table 12.4.

YELLOW: STAINS. Lead-antimony yellow stain long has been in use for lower temperature glazes. It is best at cone 06 and can be used somewhat higher, but is completely unstable at cone 4.

The modern tin-vanadium yellows are completely reliable through cone 12. The color requires a strong flux to make it smooth down effectively under the glaze. Lead bisilicate is effective for that purpose and also brightens the color. These colors are stable at higher temperatures also where strong fluxing is not required. Praseodymium yellows can be used up to cone 12. Some ceramists believe these yellows are good at high temperatures and some report some fading.

There are other yellow stains, but unfortunately they are not satisfactory as underglaze colors. Zirconium-vanadium stains can be used, but not under lead glazes as well as tin-vanadium.

REDS AND PINKS: COLOR OXIDES. No simple or elementary oxides or colorants suitable for underglaze color applications are known. The production of good reds is one of the difficult problems for the ceramist. Deep pure red is not available for high fire. Iron oxide is regarded as unsatisfac-

Table 12.4. Compositions for frit and color batch of a uranium-bearing underglaze green color base[12]

Frit		*Color batch*	
Materials	*Parts by wt.*	*Materials*	*Parts by wt.*
Ammonium uranate	20	Frit	20
Manganese dioxide	2	Glaze	34
Calcium carbonate	105	Kaolin	48
Porcelain glaze	80		

tory for underglaze, although its employment on the New Porcelain of Sèvres was reported by Franchet.[11] Some of the reasons for widespread distrust of iron oxide (Fe_2O_3) as a basis for red underglaze color are as follows:

a. The source and method of preparation of Fe_2O_3 has a strong influence upon its color, which makes it very difficult to prepare as a dependable color.
b. The color is sensitive to glaze composition, firing temperature, details and condition of the calcination, particle size and particle shape.
c. The oxygen content, hence the color, varies with the temperature of heating and the presence and activity of reducing agents.
d. Ferrous oxide is a strong base (RO) and ferrous ions in solution in silicate melts do not produce red.

Reds and Pinks: stains and special preparations. Red and pink underglaze colors are restricted to the following: (*a*) Chrome-tin, (*b*) chrome-alumina, (*c*) manganese-alumina, (*d*) zirconium-iron, and (*e*) gold preparation.

The most dependable reds for underglaze above cone 9 are those produced with gold, manganese-alumina (not lightfast), and chrome-tin. Chrome-tin stains are the most widely used underglaze reds. With them colors from maroon through pink and violet are achieved. The possible colors are reds, maroons, pinks, lilacs, and related hues. None of these can be described as brilliant or firey. Chrome-tin pink colors are sensitive to firing conditions, and particularly so in the form of print and decal. They require a covering glaze high in lime, being less stable in contact with others. Too much lime, however, will destroy the pink color and a minimum calcium content in the stain leads to violet and lilac shades.

Chrome-tin stains are produced in different colors by varying their composition. So the ultimate color effect achieved with chrome-tin stains in underglazes depends first on the composition of the stain, but may be modified some by the cover glaze composition.

Even small amounts of BaO and of MgO in the covering glaze have been reported as harmful[7,13] to the development of chrome-tin colors. Barium oxide is said to be harmful in the presence of B_2O_3, but it acts favorably toward the development of color in glaze high in lime. At least 0.40 equivalent of CaO is required in whiteware glazes maturing at cones 4–5, according to Jacob.[7] When the CaO is 0.40 equivalent, the B_2O_3 may be 0.10. If the CaO is 0.45, the B_2O_3 may be 0.20.

Gold stains are strong and reliable. It once was the only reliable source for pink or ruby shades. It is expensive, hence has been extensively replaced by other stains.

Unique flesh and salmon shades are derived from chrome-alumina stains. If these stains are attacked or dissolved by the cover glaze a green discoloration could appear, depending upon the degree of corrosion of the stain. Under suitable and reasonable conditions this would not occur. Chrome-alumina stains have excellent potential and by and large have either been overlooked or underrated. They suffer from the problem of excessive refractioners and may be hard to bond to the body. However, they can be fluxed sufficiently to prevent flaking without destroying the color.

Red-brown colors can be derived from the newer manganese-alumina stains. The earlier stains were reported as not lightfast, but some progress has been made here. The stains are stable over a wide temperature range but the composition of the base glaze is very important. The most advanced manganese-alumina pinks require a zincless glaze high in Al_2O_3 to develop a clean pink. This stain can be blended with most stable stains, and in general holds promise for wider application.

BROWN: FROM SIMPLE OXIDES. Browns can be obtained by mixing Cr_2O_3 and iron compounds with the addition of modifiers such as ZnO, MnO, WO_3, NiO, U_3O_8, Sb_2O_5, TiO_2, and Al_2O_3. Manganese oxide, like some other oxides, will change its valence or state or oxidation during heating to liberate or combine with oxygen, depending upon conditions. In general, like iron oxides, oxygen is liberated at the higher temperatures. This has been known to be the cause of the formation of seeds, bubbles, and even blisters. This reaction may be avoided by mixing the manganese oxide with alumina and strongly igniting and using this calcine as the source of the color. Phosphoric acid or tin oxide may be substituted for the alumina in such a calcine. The range of composition for red browns and for the medium and high temperatures is given by Berdel[14] as follows:

$0.2–0.7Cr_2O_3$	$1–2ZnO$
$0.8–0.3Fe_2O_3$	

Too much zinc oxide will make the color base less resistant to the action of the cover glaze. Alumina may be added, not to exceed 0.5 equiv., to lighten the color but this also will weaken the stability. Darker browns may be had by replacing part of the ferric oxide with manganese oxide, using the larger equivalents of chromium oxide and doubling the quantity of the zinc oxide. The presence of chromium oxide gives the color furnished by the iron oxide greater stability. Iron oxide used alone in underglaze colors is subject to chemical attack and diffusion except in very fusible glazes.

The chemical composition of the cover glaze is extremely important, more so than the temperature. Glazes low in alumina have the greater solvent action. Assuming that the coloring agents may be chromites, aluminates, or ferrites, the first mentioned compounds are much more resistant then the other two, but the chromites are susceptible to ready attack in highly plumbiferous glazes which contain little alumina.[15] The ingredients are well-mixed, dry, calcined at a strong heat—cone 9 or better since the higher temperature gives the more durable color base—washed, dried, and finely ground.

A light yellow brown may be had by the addition of antimony oxide to a chrome-iron-alumina-zinc mixture. To this is added a portion of the lightly fired porcelain body and the whole mixture is calcined at cone 10.[16]

Turtle-brown—a clear, fiery brown—color may be had by using the oxides of iron, manganese, uranium, and tungsten. A light yellow brown may be had by the use of antimony oxide together with chrome-iron-alumina-zinc mixture. Nickel oxide is used as a shading agent in some of the color bases but it has the characteristic of diffusing into the body similarly to the conduct of copper.

Adderley[17] made a comprehensive study of varying proportions of china clay and zinc oxide and a mixture of equal parts of Fe_2O_3 and Cr_2O_3. The best results were had under leadless glazes.

BROWN: COMMERCIAL STAINS. Chrome-iron-zinc stains are used to yield all shades of brown underglaze colors. There are a variety of shades and colors of these brown stains for underglaze. The stains are quite stable except in the presence of zinc. High calcium glazes tend to attack printed colors.

Unfortunately, stains bearing manganese tend to be corroded by the overglaze and manganese-iron stains have not proven to be sufficiently stable as underglaze colors.

BLACK AND GRAY COLORS: SIMPLE OXIDES. Blacks and grays may be had by the use of two or more compounds of high tinctorial power, such as the oxides of iron, cobalt, manganese, chromium, and nickel. Nickel, copper, and some other oxides are occasionally employed with the stronger colorants. It is the object of the ceramist to proportion the oxides so as to produce the quality of black color desired, e.g., a pure black is had by the careful balancing of the components so that no single member may predominate.

Blacks of superior quality may be had by the use of platinum and other members of the group of the so-called "noble metals." Molybdenum and uranium compounds will yield blacks when fired in a reducing atmosphere at high temperatures (cone 6 and above). The gray shades are obtained by diluting blacks with the body mixture—fired or unfired—by diluting with the glaze, or by applying the color thinly. Berdel[9] gives the limits in mol. equiv. for blacks suitable for faience, fired at cones 09–05, and up to cones 9 and 10, under oxidizing conditions as:

0.3–0.6Cr_2O_3	0.2–0.5CoO
0.4–0.3Fe_2O_3	0–0.2NiO
0.3–0.1Mn_2O_3	

The multiple character of the composition of the blacks introduces a problem since the individual members may, and usually do, react differently with the individual constituents of the covering glaze. Part of the success of producing a good black lies in the judicious choice of the latter. The following composition in parts by weight is described[18] as a "fair approximation to an underglaze black (no perfect black is ever attained)": Cobalt oxide, 31.0; chromic oxide, 7.0; ferric oxide, 36.2; manganese oxide, 12.0; nickel oxide, 12.8.

Black and Gray Colors: commercial stains. This is perhaps the most difficult of all colors to achieve in an underglaze. The problems are basically twofold: (*a*) the stain may not be a true black and (*b*) the blue from cobalt or other shades from other component oxides tend to dissolve and separate out to create fuzzy edges, or lead to fading. Where they can be used, stains based on high purity, finely ground chromite ($FeO \cdot Cr_2O_3$) are used. A number of high grade black stains are available from manufacturers and distributors of ceramic stains.

Orange. The only satisfactory underglaze orange colors are the chrome-iron-zinc type of stains. These stains usually contain about 40% of ZnO. Such stains have some tendency to "dry-up" the covering glaze or make a little mat area in the covering glaze. These colors are a little difficult to keep in suspension in the oil vehicles. By and large, however, these stains are dependable and reliable and are quite stable. The colors derived from the chrome-zinc-iron stains are in the burnt-orange shades and have a suggestion of a smokey tint.

Blue Green. Some stable underglaze colors classed as blue green are derived from cobalt-chrome stains. This family of colors is stable, but, as with other cobalt-base stains, there is the possibility of the diffusion of the cobalt blue into the clear cover glaze. In poorly balanced and formulated stains or cover glazes, the color can run.

WHITE. For underglaze work, tin oxide remains the best pigment. The prepared stain will contain calcined SnO_2 and will contain sufficient flux to securely bond it to the body. The other opacifiers are deficient in one way or another. For example, zircon opacifiers generally are not quite white enough and their covering power is not so good as is the SnO_2. However, some of the new superfine zirconium silicates of exceptionally high purity may have promise. The SnO_2 white is a blue white compared to a yellow white for zircon.

Fading of Decalcomania Colors

Underglaze decalcomania can go off-color during firing. That is called color-fading. The possible causes can be enumerated as follows: (*a*) Diffusion of color into glaze, (*b*) diffusion of color into body, (*c*) reaction of color with glaze, (*d*) reaction of color with body, (*e*) reaction of color with kiln atmosphere.

Generally no physical solution of color oxides in the glaze takes place until the maturing temperature of the glaze is reached. Even then no solution is generally experienced unless the glaze becomes excessively fluid. The physical and chemical characteristics of the covering glaze is largely responsible for the stability of conventional underglaze colors. The colors are shown on the basis of their stability under conventional glazes. Glazes, in turn, must be selected on the basis of their suitability as overglazes.

Some types of colors cannot be used. For example, solution colors such as cobalt oxide are likely to spread. Components in the glaze that lower surface tension become important in color spreading. A glaze or its variation originated by Mayer[19] forms the basis of most American vitrified dinnerware glazes. This glaze was reputed to be satisfactory even for shades of brown, green, blue, and black, normally difficult colors. This glaze was probably used as a basis for the selection of many of the earlier underglaze colors. This glaze, fired at cone 3, was:

$0.253PbO$		
$0.053K_2O$	$0.281Al_2O_3$	$2.07SiO_2$
$0.203Na_2O$	$0.385B_2O_3$	
$0.491CaO$		

The frit was:

$0.031K_2O$	$0.271Al_2O_3$	$2.547SiO_2$
$0.273Na_2O$	$0.546B_2O_3$	
$0.696CaO$		

Mayer used 60% of frit and believed that the flowing of color could be "entirely obviated by using more frit in the glaze." This generalization has been challenged by Svec[20] and others. Svec said that a glaze too high in frit tends to attack and cause colors to run. In addition, he commented as follows:

> "Faded colors may be the result of an insufficient amount of color in the color-oil mix, or too thin an application of color. Overfiring will cause fading because the glaze at high temperature will attack the color. Colors compounded in such a manner that they contain too much flux will run. Some colors, such as cobalt will usually run under any circumstances because cobalt will not combine with the other ingredients of the color to form a permanent compound. Special firing care must be practiced in the use of cobalt-containing colors."

A review of the literature discloses some detailed comments on some specific types of colors. Some of them are reviewed here.

DECALCOMANIA: CHROME-TIN COLORS. Chrome-tin colors are best under glazes high in CaO. Among the authors who have concluded this are: Mayer,[19] Jones,[21] Hull,[22,23] Rogers and Mellor,[24] Ramsden,[25,26] and Mellor.[27]

High B_2O_3 tends to shift chrome-tin colors toward purple tints, according to Singer[28] and others.[22,23,26,27] Glazes high in Al_2O_3 are detrimental to chrome-tin colors.[26,28] Too much PbO can completely destroy chrome-tin colors, but some is beneficial and improves the color.[22,23,25,26] High SiO_2 has been said to improve the color,[23,26] but the color is seriously damaged by MgO.[13]

DECALCOMANIA COLORS: CHROMIUM GREEN. Zinc oxide, of course, tends to form browns with chromium because of the formation of zinc chromate spinel.[29,30,31,32,33,34]

Higher silica improves the chrome-greens.[6]

Cr_2O_3 is not damaged by reducing atmospheres, and it has even been reported to be favorable by Mellor,[6] but he said that B_2O_3 in excess was hard on chrome greens. Again, MgO has been reported to be unfavorable to chrome-green colors.[13]

DECALCOMANIA COLORS: COBALT. Cobalt colors are stabilized and brightened by Al_2O_3.[28,35,36]

Strong fluxes, such as PbO, B_2O_3, and alkalies are detrimental to cobalt blue in underglaze colors, making the colors run and causing fuzzy boundaries,[35,36] but ZnO improves the tone of cobalt colors.[36] Alkaline earths generally are without much influence, but when too high, tend to fade them.

DECALCOMANIA COLORS: CHROME-IRON BROWN. Raw lead glazes seriously attack chrome-iron stains,[17] and MgO as well as ZnO are deleterious.

As a result of extensive recent work, Donahey and Russell[37] were able to summarize the causes of and recommendations for improvement of color-fading of underglaze colors in chinaware. Their summary is reproduced here in the following list.

Direct cause of fading	*Indirect cause*	*Recommendations*
Melt formation at low temperature or excessive amount of initial melt causing solution of colors.	Excessive frit content.	Decrease frit content.
	Low-melting frit.	Higher-melting frit.
	Raw lead used.	Frit all of the lead.
	Too much PbO, B_2O_3, or KNaO.	Replace all or part of PbO with SrO; reduce B_2O_3 and KNaO.
Chemical alteration by glaze composition.	Alteration by ZnO, MgO, SnO_2, or Al_2O_3.	Exclude MgO, ZnO, SnO_2.
Low viscosity of maturing glaze.	Improve chemical composition of glaze.	Increase SiO_2; reduce B_2O_3; reduce Na_2O; increase CaO; increase SrO; reduce PbO.
	Fast glost fire.	Slow-up glost schedule.
Glost fire schedule incorrect.	Excessive solution of color.	Reduce soaking time.
	Long firing schedule necessitated by high surface tension of glaze.	Decrease Al_2O_3; raise B_2O_3; substitute K_2O for Na_2O.
	Volitilazition of color.	Adjust rate of firing.
Deficiency of color-supporting oxide.	Low free whiting in glaze batch.	Include 10% or more of whiting in glaze batch.
Reaction with kiln atmosphere.	Reducing atmosphere.	Provide oxidizing atmosphere.

Overglaze Work

Overglaze Colors

Overglaze colors are applied on the surface of the fired glaze to which they adhere by fusion after being heated to sufficiently high temperature. If heated beyond the limits for the decoration, sharpness of the pattern will be lost by boundary diffusion. The temperature and the manner of firing are distinctive. It is quite low, about cone 015 to 017, and the time is of short duration. A special furnace of the muffle type with excellent ventilation is required. It is essential to completely free the applied decoration of decomposing and decomposable organic adhesives and vehicles. It also is essential to protect the colors from contact with harmful gases, dust, soot, etc. The term "muffle colors" is frequently applied to overglaze colors.

The dinnerware industry is responsible for the major production of overglaze work. In that industry, overglaze decorations are applied by banding, stamping, decalcomania, silk-screening, spraying, and ground lay. Decalcomania is by far the most widely used technique of them all. Banding is also widely used, particularly with gold and platinum decorations.

As compared to underglaze decorations, overglaze has the advantage of a much wider selection of bright colors. This is made possible by the firing temperature of only 1,250° to 1,450° F. Another advantage of overglaze is the much sharper detail than that of underglaze. The disadvantage of overglaze is its vulnerability to chemical and physical damage, being directly exposed to these agencies.

The application of color decorations directly onto the unfired clay body, or on an unfired glaze or enamel applied directly to unfired bodies, has been practiced from ancient times.[38] The Chinese, Persians, Italians of the Renaissance and later, the old Delft potters, and those of Nevers, France, painted decorations on unfired glaze and enamel coatings.

REQUIREMENTS. There are some requirements that must be met by overglaze colors or stains in order for them to be of practical use. These are outlined as follows:

a. All of the color bodies used in any decorative scheme on a piece of ware and, in fact, on all of the ware subjected to any single firing should mature uniformly and satisfactorily at the temperature of the operation. This is not usually easily done because considerable differences are commonly observed in most of the colors used.

b. The color bodies must have approximately the same, or up to 10% lower, thermal expansion characteristics as the surface on which they are fired. Apparently, the metallic decorations—gold, platinum and silver decorations—are exceptions, presumably because of the ductility of the metal and because of the extreme thinness of these films.

c. The flux used should develop a firm, fused bond between the color and the surface on which the color is applied. The brilliance and textured appearance, when matured, should be in harmony with the purpose of the decoration.

d. The fired decoration should meet reasonable requirements of the service for which it is intended. There should be adequate resistance to abrasion, chemical attack by food acids and alkaline detergents, and hot water.

FLUXES. The overglaze color body consists of (*a*) the flux; (*b*) the stain, pigment or decorating material; and (*c*) diluents, possibly of refractory nature, if required.

Fluxes for glass enamels are in a little different category than overglaze fluxes and are best presented (later in this chapter) under the heading of "Glass Enamels."

The fluxes that function as cementing agents to bind the pigments to the surface on which they are applied and fired are essentially soft glasses whose compositions are selected with regard to their fusibility—about 600° to 800° C—and, of equal importance, their suitability to assist in the development of the desired color. Also of great importance are the influence of the flux compositions on the solution or suspension of the color body, the development of the desired brilliancy or mattness of the texture, the resistance of the color body to erosion or corrosion in use, and the proper thermal expansion adjustment to the glaze on which the color body is applied.

The composition of the fluxes should always be chosen to facilitate the purposes mentioned. This is done, usually, with the use of a very few oxides. These are: lead oxide, usually; boric oxide or borax, soda, potassa, and silica, generally; alkaline earths, seldom; and alumina, rarely. Other elements are not often used and then only to serve some special purpose, e.g., a coloring agent or an accessory constituent. An example is the use of antimony in the following compositions of a Naples yellow[39] for porcelain:

$$0.9PbO:0.1K_2O:0.1Sb_2O_3:0.6SiO_2$$

The color may be made darker by the addition of 0.05 mol. equiv. of ferric oxide or lightened to a citron yellow by the addition of 1.0 mol. equiv. boric oxide.

Examples of flux compositions for use with colors are shown in table 12.5.[40] They were recommended for the following colors:

No. 1. An ordinary gray flux which is useful for the cobalt blues and certain reds prepared from iron oxide.
No. 2. Useful for a variety of colors, particularly yellows, pale brown, red colors from iron oxide, and grays.
No. 3. For green colors prepared with chromium compounds and with mixtures of cobalt and chrome yellows.
No. 4. This flux is suited for the carmine and light purple obtained by the use of gold.
No. 5. This flux was recommended for dark purple prepared with gold.
No. 6. For very delicate water green, very pale bottle green, and a turquoise bluish green.

Table 12.5. Batches for the preparation of fluxes for overglaze colors[40]

	Amounts, parts by weight					
Materials	*No. 1*	*No. 2*	*No. 3*	*No. 4*	*No. 5*	*No. 6*
Flint	25 to 20	16	70 to 73	34	15	35
Red lead	.75 to 80	61	10 to 18	12	38	
Borax				58		
Boric acid		23	20 to 9		50	65

Fluxes free from B_2O_3 cannot contain much silica because they become too refractory. Berdel[14] recommended them for porous bodies and believed that silica taken from the body by the flux forms an intermediate, elastic layer. The possible range of molecular equivalents of such fluxes he gave as follows:

$$0.8\text{–}1.0\text{PbO} : 0.0\text{–}0.1\text{BaO} : 0.0\text{–}0.1\text{CaO} : 0.1\text{–}0.5\text{SiO}_2$$

Some boric-oxide–containing fluxes for the same approximate range of temperatures—600° to 800° C—are given in table 12.6.

The proportions of the color to be mixed with the flux will vary from 10% to 50%, depending upon the strength of the color desired and the brilliancy or dullness. If a matt color is the goal, the ratio may be of the order of 1 : 1, or additions of 5% to 20% of kaolin or aluminum hydroxide may be made to the mill batch of flux and color.

FORMULATIONS. Commercial stains usually are employed for the preparation of the decorating bodies. The ceramist may prepare his own colors, pigments, or stains and his own frit for fluxing. Regardless of the source of the stains and fluxes the decorating bodies usually are prepared in-house.

The stains and the low-temperature fluxes are weighed out in accordance with an established batch formula and wet-milled. The formulation will be such that the color body (mixture of color and flux) when fired in the decorating kiln will bond tightly to the glaze. It should mature

Table 12.6. Empirical formula (in molecular equivalents) of B_2O_3-bearing fluxes for maturing in the range of 600°C to 800°C[9]

PbO	*K_2O*	*Na_2O*	*CaO*	*BaO*	*B_2O_3*	*Al_2O_3*	*SiO_2*
0.5–0.9	0.5–0.0	0.0–0.5			0.5–1.5	–	1.0–2.5
0.5–0.9	0.5–0.0	0.0–0.5	0.0–0.1	0.0–0.1	0.5–1.0	–	1.0–2.0
0.5–0.9	0.5–0.0	0.0–0.5	0.0–0.1	0.0–0.1	0.8–1.0	0–0.1	1.0–2.0
1.0	–	–	–	–	0.5–1.5	–	1.0–2.5

to the proper degree of gloss and not cause the pattern to become blurred. The general requirements were outlined in this chapter under the headings of "Overglaze Colors" and "Requirements."

DECORATING METHODS. More overglaze decoration is done with decalcomania than any other technique. The decals almost always are purchased from a decal manufacturer. The method of manufacturing and applying overglaze decals is the same as that for underglaze decals. Gold is one of the critical decal colors and tends to blister if not fired precisely. Purples and maroons also are tricky.

The banding technique for overglaze decoration is about the same as previously described for underglaze work. The color must be very finely ground and thoroughly blended with a vehicle of turpentine and fat oil, or fat oil-xylene-pine oil solution. Banding is done some with colors, but most of it is for applying fine lines of precious metal, such as gold and platinum. The preferred gold is the liquid gold resinate. To the liquid resinate as purchased, a flux, usually bismuth subnitrate, may be added. When some rhodium is substituted for gold in the formula, the fired gold is converted from a red to a yellow cast.

Stamping is used some with overglaze. The general techniques closely follow those described in the section on underglazes.

Spraying and groundlay are not used much for overglaze work. They are used for covering wide areas in solid colors which is better and more cheaply done by underglaze or engobe methods. The technique as used in overglaze work consists of brushing or spraying tacky oil on the surface to be decorated, then applying the color to the tacky oil by dusting. This is then smoothed out by patting down with a cloth pad to smooth it out. Needless to say, only great skill could succeed in applying layers of uniform thickness and color.

The silk-screen process is widely used for applying decorations to glass, and is discussed under the heading of "Glass Enamels." The screening technique is gaining some favor for application of decorations to glazed surfaces.

OVERGLAZE COLOR BODIES: SELECTION OF PIGMENTS. Most overglaze decoration work is done with commercially prepared stains. The fluxes may or may not be prepared in-house. There are occasions for the development and preparation of colors and stains in-house. The constitution and methods of preparation of stains and colors is treated at length in a separate chapter. The discussion on color bodies immediately to follow presents information and discussions intended to outline the behavior patterns of various color materials and the general concepts of color bodies.

In general, the stains and pigments used for overglaze work and their various modifications are those discussed under colored raw and fritted glazes. All of the stains used in underglaze colors and many others are used in onglaze formulations. Among the types that can be used for onglaze but not for underglaze are those based on or containing cadmium, sulfur, selenium, and some of the rare and costly elements.

In general, overglaze colors have the advantage of other types of decoration in the number of colors and colorants available. The choice of the flux is critical in order to develop the required resistance to mechanical wear and to corrosion by food acids and alkaline detergents.

OVERGLAZE COLORS: BLUE. Cobalt oxide is the basis for almost all blues used in overglaze decorations. Many modifications may be had by the use of sundry oxides mentioned in the discussion on the preparation of underglaze blue colors. Good commercial stains in various shades and hues are based on (*a*) cobalt-silica, (*b*) cobalt-alumina, and (*c*) zirconium-vanadium.

Cobalt oxide is such a powerful colorant that it is rarely used alone. It is calcined or fritted with other oxides to act as dilutents or modifiers of its intensity to alter the hue. This makes a stain. Such preparations also tend to eliminate specks caused by accidental occurrence of small particles of the very strong oxide.

As an alternative to grinding the color base to the necessary degree of fineness, a salt of cobalt may be dissolved in water with an aluminum soluble salt and the two bases precipitated by the addition of a calculated amount of a solution of sodium carbonate or ammonia. This precipitate must be thoroughly washed before drying and calcining. Other soluble chromophores may be coprecipitated and various modifiers—salts of zinc, magnesia, etc.—may be added or substituted for the alumina. This method is also practical for mixture of arsenates, phosphates, and other compounds occasionally used to modify the cobalt color.

An example of the use of the arsenate, introduced in a dry mixture, is the blue of Sèvres,[11] as follows (in weight percent): Silica sand (flint), 24; feldspar, 5; minium, 32; sodium carbonate, 5; borax, 20; arsenate of cobalt, 14. Fusibility may be modified by altering the amounts of silica and lead. The whole composition is fused and finely ground.

OVERGLAZE COLORS: REDS AND PINKS. The available overglaze reds include the chrome-tin-pinks and the preparations made from iron oxide with the use of such modifiers as calcia, magnesia, baryta, zinc oxide, and gold. The preparation and characteristics of these reds have been discussed. The peculiarly suitable reds for the overglaze decoration include the following: coral-red, cadmium-selenium, and cadmium sulfoselenide compounds. Ruby glass—either gold or copper—may be used, but chrome-alumina and manganese-alumina chromophores are too refractory.

The coral-red is a basic lead chromate which may be prepared in the wet way by precipitation from a lead acetate solution through the addition of a solution of potassium bichromate. The precipitate of chrome yellow pigment thus formed is converted into the basic chromate by boiling in a strong solution of soda. This chromate is collected, washed, dried, and mixed with an equivalent quantity of an easily fusible lead-containing flux. Similar color may be had in the dry way by the fusion of chrome oxide in a plumbiferous, alkaline flux.

The muffle temperature for firing this overglaze color should be limited to about 800° C, and the duration of the firing short. Otherwise the color body will dissolve silica and boric oxide from the surface of the glaze and the resulting yellow neutral chromate forms will be followed, if the time and temperature permit, by the appearance of a green color indicating the replacement of the chromic acid by silica and boric oxide.

Cadmium red is said to be a mixed crystal, $CdS/CdSe$,[41] and its composition may vary within wide limits with considerable range of color. The cadmium red is unstable at temperatures above about cones 015–010 and dependable only under short duration of heating. Thin applications of the color as overglaze are quite susceptible of variations, but satisfactory results may be had by the use of thick coatings of color and care in the firing. A plumbiferous flux is necessary and this is stabilized by the presence of cadmium to prevent the impoverishment of the color by excessive volatilization during the firing in the muffle; 80% to 90% of flux is used with 20% to 10% of color. The large use is in the decalcomania, banding, and lining.

A whole series of reds may be had by the use of gold in the form of the purple of Cassius which is prepared from the trichloride of the metal. A number of methods of preparation in the wet way have been described in the literature, and it is possible to make the color by the dry method by fusing the metals gold, silver, and tin in borax to form an homogeneous alloy. The borax is removed by solution in water; the silver is dissolved by treatment with dilute nitric acid and the residuum will be the gold purple.[42] In the preparation by either wet or dry methods care must be taken to remove all trace of nitric acid from the purple of Cassius.

Gold purples may be prepared also by precipitating the metal from a solution of gold trichloride upon magnesia or alumina. The precipitate is washed, dried, and calcined at a red heat.

Iron oxide is used for overglaze reds but the preparation of reliably uniform shades is difficult because the fineness of grind and the temperature of the calcination must be very closely controlled. A wide variety of shades may be had by the introduction of small quantities of alumina, calcia, magnesia, zinc, and other oxides. The colors may be easily prepared by the coprecipitation of soluble salts of iron and other bases. These are carefully washed, dried, and calcined. Iron pigments, made by calcining natural minerals, e.g., hematite, ochres, umbers, siennas, clays, etc., do not yield uniform colors.

OVERGLAZE COLORS: YELLOW. The pigments available for making yellows include a satisfactorily wide range, both in quality of tone and in price. The list includes: uranium compounds, ferric oxide, rutile or titanium and iron oxides, lead antimonate (Naples yellow), potassium antimonate, lead chromate (chrome yellow), and silver oxide. Some of the above pigments and their preparation have been discussed under underglaze colors.

Henry[43] recently summarized the availability and composition of ceramic colors. In the case of yellows, there are now in general use at least a half-dozen types of yellows.

Naples yellow is prepared from the oxides of lead and antimony to form the yellow compound, lead antimoniate. Shades of yellow ranging from lemon yellow to orange yellow may be had by use, in its preparation, of one or more of the modifiers: ZnO, SnO_2, CaO, Al_2O_3 and Fe_2O_3. These all are suited for overglaze work and are stable to conventional decorating temperatures. Naples yellow cannot be mixed with other colors. This color also requires a high lead flux.

Cadmium sulfide yellow is a strong pigment and is used in glass enamels and low-temperature artware glazes.

Stains prepared by calcining mixtures of the oxides of titanium, antimony and chromium yield a very stable series of colors. The colors range from yellow to ivory. They are entirely stable through, and well above, decorating temperatures.

To these stains can be added a fourth type: tin-vanadium yellows. Excellent clear lemon yellows are produced by the calcination of oxides of tin and vanadium. Shade variations are achieved by modifiers such as Al_2O_3 and TiO_2. This is an excellent stain and is stable and is even used as a ceramic body stain where relatively high temperatures are used. They are expensive stains and work directed toward developing cheaper ones led to the development of the newest type of yellow stain, zirconium-vanadium.

Zirconium-vanadium yellows are cheaper than the Sn-V type and although less stable than the Sn-V stains, are entirely stable in the overglaze range. These require careful control in use but are entirely practical. These stains still are under active investigation and new developments still are to be anticipated.

Uranium compounds formed the base of the best yellows before the Second World War. These yellows were transparent and require the presence of an opacifier. Uranium generally has been restricted to atomic-energy use. It is further restricted because of its strong radiation activity. Grades low in radiation, called "depleted" uranium, now are available. Uranium compounds produce glasses that fluoresce in ultraviolet light to a greenish-yellow color.

Silver makes very handsome yellows. One way it may be prepared is by the preparation of silver oxide from the nitrate or silver chloride mixed with a flux. Silver salts are sensitive to sunlight, and in the use of the chloride sunlight should be avoided.

OVERGLAZE COLORS: ORANGE. In addition to the orange shades available through the use of the "yellow" stains outlined in the preceding paragraphs, the best orange is through the use of chrome-iron-zinc types of stains. These are burnt-orange shades and require high concentrations of flux to prevent "dryness."

OVERGLAZE COLORS: BROWN. Stains of the ZnO-Cr_2O_3-Fe_2O_3 type are brown. The presence of manganese darkens the brown. A wide variety of yellow browns are achieved by varying the ratio of the Cr:Zn:Fe and by adding Al_2O_3. No single oxide has been used to produce reliable brown.

A general formula for red browns is as follows:[14]

$$0.2\text{–}0.7Cr_2O_3 \qquad 1\text{–}2ZnO$$
$$0.8\text{–}0.3Fe_2O_3$$

OVERGLAZE COLORS: VIOLET. Violet may be had by the use of small amounts of carefully prepared manganese oxide. It must be carefully protected against organic matter during preparation, storage, and application. The firing must be strictly oxidizing.

The addition of a small amount of cobalt oxide to purple of Cassius furnishes a superior violet.

Good violets are prepared commercially by modifying chrome-tin pigments with cobalt.

OVERGLAZE COLORS: GREEN. Copper oxide has a limited use in overglaze colors. It yields clean colors ranging from turquoise to green, depending on the composition of the flux. Alkaline fluxes yield transparent turquoise while normal flux compositions give transparent green glasses.

Chromium oxide is the usual basis for the production of an opaque green overglaze color. It is very refractory and generally stable but sensitive to the effect of contact with strongly alkaline fusions that may cause a scumming of the color. The influence of other bases on chromium oxide in fusions has been described in the discussion of underglaze colors. Variations in tone may be had by blending with cobalt compounds, Naples yellow, and cadmium yellows. Mixtures containing these yellows are sensitive to milling and firing conditions. An excessive amount of Cr_2O_3 in an overglaze body may result in the separation of a surface film due to segregation. Solutions of the chrome base in high lead, low silica, (basic) bases may be expected to lead to red, orange, or yellows.

Clean Victoria green stains are made by combining Cr_2O_3 with CaO and SiO_2 by calcination. Greens also are produced by blending a blue green or a blue with Naples yellow or with tin-vanadium yellow. Opaque greens are derived from blends of zirconium-vanadium turquoise and tin-vanadium yellows.

Uranium oxide and cobalt oxide will produce a stable green. Praseodymium phosphate is reported as useful for producing a transparent, delicate green.

Copper oxide is less desirable and reliable as a coloring agent than Cr_2O_3. It is sensitive to reducing gases in firing. Additions of antimony and iron oxides produce a yellow green. In the absence of lead, high alkalies cause the formation of bluish-green colors. Copper greens are stable in the presence of both ZnO and SnO_2 and both are incompatible in chromium-base greens.

OVERGLAZE COLORS: BLACK. Combinations of CoO, Cr_2O_3, Fe_2O_3, and MnO form the basis of some black stains. Among these are very stable, intense blacks. There are two types of cobalt-free blacks. One suitable for overglaze is prepared from Cr_2O_3 and CuO. Another black stain is the result of calcining mixtures of Cr_2O_3, Fe_2O_3, and MnO_2, but these tend to be brown blacks. A widely used black is basically chromite, $FeO \cdot Cr_2O_3$. A striking peculiarity of the complex blacks is their sensitivity to the solvent action of glazes and fluxes which exert a selective action, i.e., some components of the color body may be selectively attacked. This is not always obvious in overglazes. The most stable of these are the chromite base blacks.

Platinum and iridium are expensive but yield superior blacks.

OVERGLAZE COLORS: GRAY. There are stains that are gray, per se. There are others that are diluted blacks. Finely divided platinum metal yields an excellent gray. Grays may be had by applying the black thinly or by diluting the black with an opacifier.

OVERGLAZE COLORS: WHITE. Tin oxide is the principal material added to the flux to make a white. A special grade of zircon of extreme finess holds promise. Most other opacifiers are not white enough.

Lusters

Luster is a film-like coating of metal or metallic oxide matured on the surface of the glaze after a special composition has been applied and fired at a low temperature, between 600° and 800° C. These coatings may have a metallic, nacreous, or iridescent sheen. The metallic lusters obtained with silver and the noble metals may closely resemble the effects obtained with the same metals by gilding, silvering, or platinizing; however, the thickness of the true luster is very much less than that obtained by the latter technique. Further, the true luster is prepared as a resinate which is dissolved in an essential oil, e.g., turpentine, oil of lavender, and others, and applied. The preparation of metallized coatings may or may not entail this step.

Luster decoration probably originated in Egypt and was carried from there into Persia. The knowledge of it was spread by the Moors through Africa into Spain and then into Italy. The earliest examples of it are from the site of Phages, which was once the capital of the Persian Empire and was destroyed in the 13th century. The practice of firing gold on pottery, unknown to the great potters of the Middle Ages, was first used in Europe about the middle of the 18th century. A pottery at Vincennes, France, was the first European factory to use it extensively.

Simeon Shaw[44] states that the practice of using finely divided gold precipitated from solution was employed by the Staffordshire potteries in the last decade of the 18th century. In Spain and Italy, according to Franchet,[11] metallic lusters have been used without interruption since about the fourth century. The work of Carocci of Gubbio, 1860, stimulated a revival of interest in Italy. In France, the manufacture of lusters was renewed in 1876 by Besnard. He followed the practice described by writers of the 17th and 18th centuries.

Zsnolnay of Pics, Hungary, has been noted for the production of the ruby stain copper luster and also for designs based on Byzantine, Persian, and Indian motifs in lusters in blue, purple, brown, and white. Since 1900 Zsnolnay's ware has deteriorated, showing a garish display of red copper-stained, bright, metallic luster.[45] Brianchlon of Paris invented bismuth luster in 1856. According to his patent, a certain nitrate of bismuth dissolved in balsam of sulfur, coated on white glaze, and fired at a very low red heat in a muffle with a good draft for ventilation, will yield nacreous luster. Copper and silver luster earthenware were first produced at Staffordshire,

Leeds and Sunderland, and Swansea during the latter part of the 18th century.

Lusters are commonly classified as: *Colorless,* i.e., they have an iridescence but no fixed color. They are prepared by the use of alumina, lead, zinc, and bismuth; and *colored,* those which have fixed color shades and hues. These are prepared by the use of:

Cadmium—yellowish red	Copper—brownish red
Iron—lustrous red, light brown, golden	Manganese—brown
Uranium—greenish yellow	Chromium with lead—yellow
Nickel—light brown	Gold—reddish tones
Cobalt—brown	Platinum—silvery white

Also mixtures of two or more of the above

There are two methods for the preparation of the lusters, the wet and the dry. In both cases the resinate of a metal is prepared which is dissolved in oil of lavender or turpentine.

The procedure for the wet method begins with the sodium-resinate, or soda-resin soap, which is easily prepared by adding powdered pine resin to a strong soda lye and boiling until no more resin is dissolved and the frothing ceases, indicating that the reaction is completed. The liquid is diluted and reboiled, cooled, and decanted from the settlings. A solution of the metallic salt—either chloride or nitrate—is added to the resin soap solution and the precipitate is separated, washed, and dried. Many of these resinates deteriorate if exposed in a damp condition to the light.

The dry method of preparation, in its simplest form, is conducted by melting resin at a moderate temperature and slowly stirring into it the metallic salt. The resinate will be very viscous and must be thinned by the gradual addition of oil of lavender or turpentine. Hainbach[12] described the preparation of some lusters by the dry method as stated in the paragraphs that follow.

Bismuth luster is prepared as a resinate; for example, 10 parts of crystallized bismuth nitrate, 75 parts of lavender oil, 30 parts of resin. When the latter is melted, the temperature is raised slightly and the nitrate added in small portions with active stirring. When the mixture turns brown, the lavender oil is added slowly. The mixture is allowed to stand quietly until all undissolved particles have settled. The liquid is decanted and ready to use.

Zinc luster is prepared by compounding 1 part of zinc acetate with $2\frac{1}{2}$ parts of resin and dissolving in warm oil of lavender.

Lead luster is prepared by compounding 1 part of lead acetate melted with 3 parts of resin and dissolving in oil of lavender.

Noble metal lusters are prepared as resinates or by the use of sulfur balsam as previously described. The proportion of bismuth flux added has a strong influence upon the results; for example, 1 part of gold to 5 parts of bismuth will produce a coppery sheen, whereas if the ratio is 1:2 to 3 a bluish-violet shade with a golden sheen will result. Higher concentrations of gold may give blue to purple to rose to rose red. The lusters may be applied by painting, spraying, or stamping. When they are fired, the organic constituents are destroyed, leaving the metal components, which are present in a very finely divided form, fused to the surface of the glaze by the action of the bismuth.

Hegemann,[4] Hainbach,[42] and many others have published much detailed information regarding the preparation and use of lusters. Hegemann has given the following information regarding the developing of a superior luster on porcelain: The piece of ware, previously coated with a vitrifiable color (*schmelzfarben*), is painted or sprayed with bismuth oxide. After drying the ware is fired in a muffle at about 920° C. Then it is coated with a purple luster composition containing gold and tin and fired again at a low temperature, 600° to 700° C. The bright purple-violet object will next be covered uniformly with a uranium-bismuth-gold luster composition and fired carefully in a muffle to 790° C. Too high a temperature will cause the luster coat to sink into the bismuth flux. The uranium-bismuth gold luster is prepared by mixing 20 parts, by weight, with 10 of bismuth luster and 1 part of bright gold. The uranium luster is prepared, in the dry way, by heating 6 g of uranium oxide with 30 g of dammar resin. The product is dissolved in 100 g of the oil of lavender, filtered in the hot condition, and cooled. The bismuth luster is prepared by fusing 6 g of bismuth subnitrate with 30 g of dammar resin and diluting with the oil of lavender. Since not all of the resin will be dissolved, the hot liquid is allowed to stand until it is clear and then it is decanted.

Resinates of the metals can be prepared by adding 500 g of any of the following salts to a solution of 1 kg of soda resinate dissolved in 21 kg of water: iron chloride, copper sulfate, chrome alum, uranium nitrate, manganese sulfate, cobalt sulfate, or the sugar of lead (lead acetate).

Much information has been published in the literature previously referred to, as well as in ceramic journals, regarding the composition and preparation of lusters. A few[14,42] are given as examples.

Red luster is prepared from iron resinate, 3 parts; bismuth resinate, 1 part dissolved in rosemary oil; or iron resinate dissolved in the oil.

Lemon-yellow luster is prepared from 1 part of chromium resinate and 2 or 3 parts of bismuth resinate dissolved in rosemary (or lavender) oil, or 1 part of chromium resinate dissolved in 3 parts oil, or 1 part of uranium resinate dissolved in 2 parts of rosemary oil and 0.3 part of benzol.

Gray-brown luster is prepared from manganese resinate 3 parts, bismuth resinate 1 part dissolved in the oil.

Bronze luster is prepared from chromium resinate 1 part and 3 parts of lead resinate dissolved in the oil.

Franchet[11] makes a distinction between the lusters obtained under oxidizing firing conditions and the surface effects had under reducing conditions (*reflets metalliques*) and protests the confusion of the two. This distinction does not seem to be made by other ceramists although it is a distinction of interest since the techniques of firing are notably different. He observes that the most ancient of the lustered ware known to us was made under reducing conditions. It is noteworthy that the recognition of bismuth as a metal distinct from silver was not made until about 1529 A.D. Prior to that time it was regarded as impure silver.

Here are 3 modern examples of the compositions, in percent by weight, used for obtaining lusters under reducing conditions: (*a*) carbonate of copper, 30 and red ocher, 70; (*b*) carbonate of copper, 28, carbonate of silver, 2, and red ocher, 70; (*c*) carbonate of silver, 3, subnitrate of bismuth, 12, and red ocher, 85. These components are ground together, a solution of gum arabic, gum tragacanth, or similar adhesive is added—the ancient formulas specify vinegar—and the mixtures are painted or otherwise applied on the fired glaze. The early European application of lusters was made on faience (or majolica) ware. Since the typical metallic reflectance was dependent upon the effect of reducing firing conditions at low temperatures, 650° C, the glaze was a kind which matured at about cones 07 to 08 (945° to 970° C). This reduction may be obtained by firing in a muffle capable of being closed tightly. After the low red heat is attained, the firing is stopped and illuminating gas, wood shavings, coarse grasses, naphthalene or tarry materials, even sugar, is introduced into the chamber with the ware. The muffle is tightly closed for a half hour or much longer, depending upon the tightness of the muffle, the reducing agent, the temperature, and the compositions. Draw trials are useful to determine the progress of the reduction.

By painting the luster on the glaze, it is possible to place designs where desired. If one wishes to obtain metallic reflectance by incorporating the essential metals in the glaze mixture itself, it is possible to do so, as shown in the following compositions for metallic luster given by Franchet.[11]

The *base glaze* (to be fused, quenched, and ground) consists of the following, in percent by weight: silica, 45; red lead, 41; boric acid, 8; and potassium carbonate, 6. The batch, in parts by weight, consists of base glaze, 100; zinc oxide, 1; tin oxide, 1; silver carbonate, 0.5; and copper oxide (CuO), 3.

The nature of the supporting glaze is of importance; either lead or alkaline glazes may be used. The use of SnO_2 is not recommended in glazes on which this luster is to be applied, because of the bad effects of reduction of the SnO_2 on color.

Burgos luster is a transparent film having a peculiar red sheen. It is prepared by adding a colorless bismuth luster to a gold luster of suitable color.

Cantharides luster is so named because its characteristic golden yellow has bluish or greenish colorations similar to those of the cantharides beetle wing. It is prepared by adding a small quantity of bismuth and silver chloride to a lead glaze and firing in a reducing atmosphere.

Glass Enamels

Glass enamels form a special class of overglaze decoration. Glass enamels are used to decorate glassware items such as bottles, dinnerware, tumblers, lightbulbs, and the like. These are not colored glasses but designs applied on the surface of glasswares and bonded by firing. They are overglazes in every sense except that they are applied over glass instead of over glaze.

In constitution, glass enamels consist of a low-fusing glass or frit into which has been incorporated up to 10% of stain or pigment.

Perhaps the most critical feature of glass enamels is their resistance to attack by mild acids and alkaline detergent solutions. It is absolutely essential, however, that no unfavorable stresses develop at or near the interface of the fired-on decoration. This will develop due to an unfavorable thermal expansion match between the base and the applied enamel. If the thermal expansion of the applied layer is higher than that of the glass the system will be mechanically weakened and could even be spontaneously fractured. The system is mechanically stable, even strengthened, when the expansion coefficient of the coating is up to 10% lower than the glass base. Expansion differences much greater than that may again create mechanical unstability.

Another, but equally important, source of interfacial stress is due to unfavorable ion diffusion from the enamel flux into the glass base. For example, lithium can readily diffuse from an enamel containing it into a nonlithium bearing substrate glass. This diffusion can cause a major change in the expansion coefficient of the substrate and create unfavorable or even disastrous interfacial stress. There are obviously numerous possibilities for such exchanges, some being favorable, and some not.

COMPOSITION. Fluxes for glass enamels closely resemble those used with overglaze decorations. They usually are lead borosilicate glasses having thermal expansions closely resembling those of the glasses. A flux for glass colors, having coefficient of mean linear thermal expansion = 90 × 10^{-} /° C and fusing at 620° C, was patented by Ray Andrews.[46] This enamel has fair chemical stability and is not subject to damage by reducing agents or sulfides. This enamel is unusual because it is lead-free.

The ceramic formula was:

0.650ZnO		$0.314SiO_2$
$0.101Li_2O$	$0.0Al_2O_3$	$0.072F_2$
0.072CaO	$0.305B_2O_3$	$0.141TiO_2$
$0.177Na_2O$		

Maturing temperature—cone 020.

Lead-bearing vitrifiable fluxes are more usual. One such is contained in a British patent.[47] The composition was given, in weight percent, as: PbO, 64.9; SiO_2, 26.2; B_2O_3, 5.2; and Na_2O, 3.7. This corresponds to the ceramic formula:

0.83PbO	$0.213B_2O_3$	$1.24SiO_2$
$0.17Na_2O$		

The enamel was made from 95.5% of this flux plus 4.5% of opacifier. To make a vitrifiable enamel for overglaze the flux needs to be of lower expansion, which could be obtained by raising the SiO_2 and adding Al_2O_3.

An acid-resistant glass enamel was described in a patent by Andrews and Murray.[48] This enamel was adjusted in fusibility to fire onto and fit soda-lime-glass, having an expansion coefficient a little higher than would be suitable for most glazed ceramic ware. The composition, when converted to the empirical ceramic formula, was:

0.616PbO		$1.19SiO_2$
0.066CdO	$0.305B_2O_3$	$0.152TiO_2$
$0.186Na_2O$		$0.135ZrO_2$
$0.132Li_2O$		

It should be observed that this formula is too low in SiO_2 and Al_2O_3 to meet the requirements of a conventional glaze. It was claimed that the acid resistance could be increased by firing the glass enamel onto glass in a steam atmosphere, a process not recommended for glazes. When fired in air to around 1,200° F, the lead solubility was 5 PPM, compared to 2 PPM of lead when fired in steam.

Titania frequently is used as a part of the frit formula to increase chemical resistance. Because most of the vitrifiable glass-enamel frits are lead-bearing, a balance between TiO_2 and PbO must be found that gives required acid resistance without developing a yellow color. To obtain the acid resistance from TiO_2 it must be put into solution in the molten frit. The tendency then, except for specialized circumstances, is to have the formation of lead titanate, a yellow color.

When added to the mill and ground with the frit, TiO_2 acts as an opacifier, and gives a very satisfactory white color, but adds nothing to chemical durability. The stain additions, however, usually supply the required opacity and additional opacifier is not required and serves only to dull the color.

COLORS. All of the colors suitable for overglaze work and described under that heading are applicable to glass enamels. Some colored frits are especially prepared for glass enamels. These include those to be used with the cadmium-selenium colors. For these colors some cadmium is smelted into the frit. The purpose of this is to prevent the formation of lead sulfide from the lead component in the flux and the sulfide component of the color. The formation of lead sulfide (black) would destroy the intended bright red color.

PREPARATION AND APPLICATION

Tumbler and Bottle Colors. The silk-screening technique is almost standard. The decoration is done by automatic machines. This, of course, requires the use of a very special color body, developed and controlled to function perfectly under the mechanized automated conditions. The powdered colors and the squeegee oils can be purchased already mixed or may be purchased separately and mixed in-house.

Multicolor decorations are common. Only one color is applied at a time, and it is thoroughly dried or "set" before the next is printed. By the use of hot thermoplastic oil mediums, rapid two-color applications are done. With this system, the stain-oil mixture or color body is so formulated that it is hard at room temperature but becomes soft and "screenable" at about 180° F. The color "sets" on the ware only an instant after its deposition there, and the second color, prepared for "cold" screening, can be applied straight away.

With cylindrical objects, such as tumblers and bottles, the mechanism may be one of rolling. For flat ware the screen is put into contact with the ware and an automatic circular-motion squeegee rubs the color through the screen.

Colors on Tableware. Glass tableware in large volume is decorated with glass enamels. This is done almost exclusively by automatic spraying. The color slip is prepared in ball mills, using a vehicle or medium composed of a solution of water, alcohol, and glycol, and, when necessary, thickening and suspending agents. Most dinnerware colors are sprayed solid over large areas ideal for spraying. Some decorations are not in solid colors but in more delicate designs. These and other instances call for mediums prepared from oil and turpentine, as in overglaze work.

For dinnerware, it is imperative to make sure that unfavorable interfacial stresses do not develop between enamel and glaze. If the enamel is even slightly higher in thermal expansion than the base glass, the ware will be disastrously weakened and can even cause breakage. It is particularly critical in tableware because the coatings are applied solid over large areas. In addition, tableware is expected to endure reasonably rough service for extended periods of time.

Another difference between enamels for tableware and for bottles is the requirement for chemical durability. Tableware absolutely must withstand long and repeated contact with food acids and hot alkaline detergents. From the health standpoint, the fluxes must be low in the release of lead and, for that matter, any other toxic component. This is conventionally tested by long periods of boiling in acetic acid solutions. The lead release should not exceed 5 PPM if it is to be used in the dispensing or preparation of food.

Light Bulb Markings. Light bulbs and other types of lighting units are marked by spraying of glass enamel. The enamel is applied in very thin deposits that must have adequate opacity to form good identification markings. Most application is to coat the glass to diffuse the light and reduce glare without appreciable reduction in transmission. The colors are produced in glossy and in mat surfaces. The chemical durability problem here is to prevent damage from atmospheric gases such as water vapor, sulfuric acid, or sulfide gases. Here again, the problem is not so much with development or selection of colors as it is with the flux or enamel base.

References

1. Seger, H. A. 1902. Underglaze colors and their preparation. *Collected writings.* Vol. 2. Easton, Pa.: The Chemical Publishing Co., p 658.
2. Rhead, F. H. 1922. Painting in underglaze colors on the biscuit. *J. Am. Ceram. Soc.* 5:376.
3. Pukall, W. 1912. New porcelain hard fire colors. *Sprechsaal* 45:211.
4. Hegemann, H. 1938. *Die Herstellung des Porzellans.* 2d ed. revised by F. Dettmer. Berlin, p 120.
5. Smith, K. E. and Stevens, W. 1932. Further work in the experimentation and application of underglaze color crayons. *J. Am. Ceram. Soc.* 15:630.

6. Mellor, J. W. 1937. Discoloration of chrome-green colors. *Trans. Engl. Ceram. Soc.* 36:28.
7. Jacob, K. 1915. The influence of whiteware glaze composition upon the development of under-glaze colors. *Sprechsaal* 48:98,107.
8. Hertwig, T. 1903. New yellow hard fire colors. *Sprechsaal* 36:1845.
9. Berdel, E. 1911. *Einfaches chemisches Praktikum.* Vol. 5 and 6. Coburg, p 63.
10. Chambers, A. and Rigg, J. F. 1925–26. Notes on antimony yellows. *Trans. Engl. Ceram. Soc.* 25:101.
11. Franchet, L. 1911. *La fabrication industrielle des emaux et couleurs ceramiques.* Paris, p 102.
12. Hegemann, op. cit., ref. 4, p 192.
13. Shah, C. P. 1917–18. The effect of magnesium glazes on underglaze colors. *Trans. Engl. Ceram. Soc.* 17:106.
14. Berdel, op. cit., ref. 9, p 61.
15. Rieke, R. and Paetsch, W. 1922. The constitution of some ceramic coloring materials. *Ber. Deut. Ker. Ges.* 3:147. also: 1921. The solubility of coloring metal oxides in china glazes. *Ber. Deut. Ker. Ges.* 2:77.
16. 1905. Brown colored bodies for underglaze colors. *Sprechsaal* 38:557.
17. Adderley, J. R. 1915–16. Studies on the brown colors. *Trans. Engl. Ceram. Soc.* 15:133.
18. Meir, G. E. and Mellor, J. W. 1937. The ferric oxide colors. *Trans. Engl. Ceram. Soc.* 36:31.
19. Mayer, Ernst. 1899. Notes on the production of underglaze colors. *Trans. Am. Ceram. Soc.* 1:56–61.
20. Svec, J. J. 1946. *Pottery production processes.* Chicago, Ill.: Industrial Publications, Inc.
21. Jones, R. H. 1901–1902. Crimson glazes. *Trans. Engl. Ceram. Soc.* 1:3–8.
22. Hull, W. A. 1902. The constitution of chromium-tin pink. *Trans. Am. Ceram. Soc.* 4:230–54.
23. Hull, W. A. 1904. Chrome-tin pink—A further discussion. *Trans. Am. Ceram. Soc.* 6:148–54.
24. Rogers, J. and Mellor, J. W. 1904–1905. Notes on the crimson chromium tin glaze. *Trans. Engl. Ceram. Soc.* 4:66.
25. Ramsden, C. E. 1911–1912. Notes on chromium red glaze. *Trans. Engl. Ceram. Soc.* 11:196–203.
26. Ramsden, C. E. 1912–13. A study of chromium red glaze. *Trans. Engl. Ceram. Soc.* 12:239–60.
27. Mellor, J. W. 1937. Chemistry of chrome-tin colors. *Trans. Engl. Ceram. Soc.* 26(1):16–27.
28. Singer, F. G. 1910. Concerning the position of boron in the glaze formula. *Trans. Am. Ceram. Soc.* 12:676–70.
29. Bryan, M. L. 1908. Action of chromium oxide in glazes containing zinc. *Trans. Am. Ceram. Soc.* 10:124–32.
30. Pence, F. K. 1913. Effect of zinc in underglaze colors containing chromium. *Trans. Am. Ceram. Soc.* 15:118–24.

31. Mayer, Ernst 1914. A comparison between English and American glaze practice. *Trans. Am. Ceram. Soc.* 16:307–10.
32. Minton, R. H. 1915. The influence of some unusual zinc compounds in a chrome green glaze. *Trans. Am. Ceram. Soc.* 17:667–71.
33. Wilson, Hewitt. 1918. Cobalt-uranium green glaze for terra cotta. *J. Am. Ceram. Soc.* 1(4):238–46.
34. Anon. 1968. Materials for ceramic processing. *Ceramic Industry,* 90(1): 130.
35. Hollinghead, A. D., Turner, J., and Mellor, J. W. 1914. Cobalt and nickel colors. *Trans. Engl. Ceram. Soc.* 14:167–22.
36. Mellor, J. W. 1937. Cobalt and nickel colors. *Trans. Engl. Ceram. Soc.* 36(1):1–9.
37. Donahey, John W. and Russell, Ralston, Jr. 1950. Color fading of underglaze decalcomania. *J. Am. Ceram. Soc.* 33(9):283–290.
38. Rhead, F. H. 1922. The Italian majolica process and printing over tin enamels. *Bull. Am. Ceram. Soc.* 1:177.
39. Berge, A. 1914. *Keramisches Praktikum.* Halle a.S., p 83.
40. Hainbach, R. 1924. *Pottery decorating.* 2d rev. Eng. ed. London: Scott, Greenwood & Son, p 152–4.
41. Stuckert, L. 1935. "Cadmium yellow and cadmium red as pigments in the silicate industry. *Farben-Ztg.* Nos. 1 and 3; abst. in 1936. *Glashutte* 66(25):421; 1934. *Farben-Ztg.* 39:36,61.
42. Hainbach, op. cit., ref. 40, p 167.
43. Henry, Paul. 1957. Chemicals used in the manufacture of ceramic colors. *Bull. Am. Ceram. Soc.* 36(11):431 32.
44. Shaw, S. 1900. *History of the Staffordshire potteries.* London: Scott, Greenwood & Son, p 229.
45. Burton, W. 1907. Lustre ware. *J. Soc. Arts* 55:756.
46. Andrews, Ray, *Flux.* U.S. Patent 2,482,533, Sept 20, 1949.
47. Johnson, Matthey & Co. Ltd., and F. E. Kerridge. *Vitrifiable enamels for decorating glass.* British Patent 634,356, Jan 25, 1950.
48. Andrews, Ray and Murray, Robert S. *Method of improving acid resistance of glass colors.* U.S. Patent 2724,662, Nov 22, 1955.

13
Color Development

The matrix in ceramic glazes is composed of silicate glass. There are two main mechanisms for coloring in glazes: (1) inclusions or mixtures of microscopic colored solid particles of pigments or stains, and (2) color development in and an integral part of the glass matrix, but not necessarily part of the fundamental silicate structure. The latter can be subdivided into two types: (*a*) those in which the color is derived from soluble colored ions forming part of the fundamental silicate structure and (*b*) those which are colloids distributed throughout the glass. Therefore, there are two types of colored glasses, per se, without added pigments, the "solution" or ionic type and the "nucleated colloid" type.

Coloring Ions in Glass

Structural and Atomic Considerations

Silicate glasses fundamentally are built of a random network of SiO_4 tetrahedra that shares oxygens to build a structure resembling that of crystalline silica, such as quartz. Due to high viscosity, the polymerization in cooling remains more like that of the liquid state than the orderly crystalline state. This would be an overly simplified description of vitreous silica, frequently referred to as "fused quartz." With this as a base solvent various cations such as Na^+ or Ca^{2+} occupy spaces in the random silica polymers. Thus, the cations appear to be surrounded by (SiO_4) polymers. The amphoteric elements, such as B, Al, and P, when not in excess become substituted for some Si in the silica network. All of the cations are present as dissolved ions in this network.

Some of the cations give rise to solution color in glass. This includes ions of the transition elements. A number of these ions are able to adapt to different degrees of coordination, depending on their size and their potential. In the molten state, equilibrium is established with respect to the number of oxygens shared by the dissolved color ion. This depends upon the glass composition (competition for oxygens surrounding the silicons and held tight by them), ambient oxygen pressure, the temperature, and the rate of cooling. Some or all of these factors influence the color produced by the colored ions.

Some examples of the development of color by dissolved color oxides are to follow. The entire subject requires detailed discussion that need not be done here. An excellent monograph on the subject by Weyl[1] is often quoted as the most authoritative work on the subject. Sufficient is given here to form a basis for a realization of the different mechanisms for color development in glazes.

Colored Glasses

COBALT COLORS. Cobalt makes blue glasses. The Co^{2+} ion in special circumstances can produce a range of colors in glasses from pink to blue. Even green glasses have been made with cobalt.

Blue glass is obtained when Co^{2+} ions are surrounded by 4 oxygens. Pink results when the Co^{2+} ions are surrounded by 6 or more oxygens, each being farther from the cobalt than when in the coordination that favors blue. This will occur in high alkali glasses and as the sodium is reduced the color changes from pink to blue.

The odd green cobalt glass was produced in melts containing some iodine (I^-) ions. This was explained by Yates[2] as being due to an I^- being substituted for O^{2-} in the glass structure. The iodine is easily deformed and tends to form covalent rather than ionic links with Co^{2+}.

NICKEL COLORS. At glaze temperature, nickel has only one valence, Ni^{2+}. The color produced due to nickel ions in solution in glass depends upon the polarization as determined by the number of oxygen ions surrounding it, the distance from them, and the influence of other cations on these factors. The influence of glass composition on the color of nickel glasses is explained in terms of the competition with other cations to be surrounded by structural oxygens. Studies on simple nickel-bearing R_2O–SiO_2 glasses in which R_2O was Li, Na, K, and Rb showed systematic changes in color. In the Rb_2O glasses the nickel could obtain a four-fold coordination in the network and a violet color resulted. With Li_2O–SiO_2 glasses nickel ions could exist only as network modifiers, not being able to successfully compete for oxygens. The resulting color was yellow. In the whole series from Rb to Li there was a continuous shift in colors from violet to yellow, depending upon the size of the alkali cation.

The presence of Zn^{2+} notably influences the colors due to Ni^{2+}. Zinc and nickel ions are similar in size and field strength; that results in close competition for available O^{2-}.

CHROMIUM. When Cr_2O_3 dissolves in glass it produces green. It has very low solubility in glass, but the Cr^{3+} ion is an extremely strong colorant. The color imparted by chromium ions depends upon the equilibrium between Cr^{3+} and Cr^{6+}. The trivalent form is commonly the one present and the ion is small and strong and usually occupies a network modifying position in the structure, producing green. In glasses very low in SiO_2 and high in RO, the Cr^{6+} state prevails, leading to yellows and orange, depending upon the nature of the associated cations.

MANGANESE. Manganese ions in solution in glass can be either divalent or trivalent. The state of oxidation of the system determines the valency that will prevail. The characteristic color due to trivalent manganese in solution is intense violet, but the color is strongly dependent upon the concentration and species of other cations making up the glaze composition. The important factor again is the sharing of available oxygen between manganese and other RO members. By substituting a series of alkali ions of different size in a base glass, it develops that the larger the ionic radius of the cation, the bluer the color. A similar kind of change occurs with divalent cations, but is not so pronounced.

Divalent (Mn^{2+}) manganese makes a straw or weak brown color. Manganese is in the divalent form in almost all normal glazes fired in air. But the color imparted by divalent manganese is weak and it takes only a little of the potent trivalent manganese to influence the color. With manganese, the state of oxidation can be a more influential factor on color than the associated cation species. Things or materials that influence the equilibrium between divalent and trivalent manganese consequently profoundly influence color.

IRON COLORS. Iron ions in glass may be ferrous, or ferric, but usually both. Ferrous iron in glass is a very strong blue colorant, but ferric iron produces reddish colors. Ferric ions (Fe^{3+}) as a network former with a four-fold coordination produce a brownish color. When the same ferric ions are in six-fold coordination and are a network modifier, a weak yellow pink appears.

The familiar color of silicate melts contaminated by a little iron is blue green. This is due to the combined effects of Fe^{3+} and Fe^{2+}. The degree of oxidation of iron itself is strongly influenced by temperature. The equilibrium continually shifts to the ferrous form as the temperature is raised above about 1,000° C. The color also is shifted by compositional effects that shift the balance in the demand by the cations present for the available oxygen-sharing. A wide variety of colors and shades is possible from minor amounts of iron present. It is so hard to control that it is rarely used as an intentional colorant.

Colloidal Colors

Copper Reds

Copper red, Sang de Boeuf, oxblood, rouge flambé, flambé reds, and ruby all are terms that have been applied to a distinctive red glaze first produced in China during the Sung dynasty. The color was due to colloidal metallic copper formed and dispersed in situ in glazes containing copper and fired under reducing conditions. Original glazes were colored porcelain glazes, and subsequent copper reds have been prepared in several glaze types.

Ebelman and Salvitat were the first Europeans to prepare a copper red glaze. They analyzed chips from a Chinese vase, obtaining the following analysis: SiO_2, 73.9; Al_2O_3, 6; Fe_2O_3, 2.10; CaO, 7.30; K_2O, 3.00; Na_2O, 3.10; and CuO, 4.60. In the usual glaze empirical terms, this is:

0.484CaO		
$0.118K_2O$	$0.213Al_2O_3$	$4.53SiO_2$
$0.185Na_2O$	$0.049Fe_2O_3$	
0.213CuO		

According to Franchet in volume 44 of *Sprechsaal,* early copper ruby glazes contained around 3% of CuO, 8% of SnO_2, and 10% of PbO. According to Reuter-Brocks,[3] red glazes resembling the 15th century Chinese copper reds were prepared in Europe in 1883. His base composition was:

0.75PbO	$0.20Al_2O_3$	$2.20SiO_2$
0.25CaO	$0.35B_2O_3$	

to which he added 0.30 CuO and 0.6 SnO_2. The glaze was fired at cone 05 (1,040° C) in a reducing atmosphere. Excessive smoke with soot settling on the glaze was used. Later, reducing and oxidizing periods were used until the firing was finished. The ware was cooled slowly.

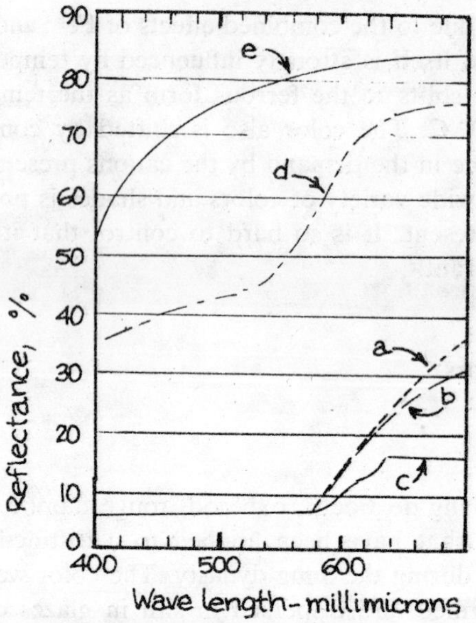

Figure 13.1. Spectrophotometer curves. (a) Glaze with 0.8% of Cu, (b) glaze with 2.4% of Cu, (c) cuprous oxide in medium of same refractive index as glass, (d) burnished copper plate, and (e) copper-free glaze on tile.[10]

Glazes said to resemble the copper reds (rouge flambé) of the period from 960–1279 in China were described by Albonetti.[4] These were copper reds of which the following fritted glaze is an example. The empirical formula of the frit was:

$0.347K_2O$	$0.011Al_2O_3$	$1.086SiO_2$
$0.322Na_2O$	$1.042B_2O_3$	
$0.331CaO$		

The glaze recipe, using the preceding frit, was as follows in weight percent: Frit, 36; high potassium feldspar, 59; tin oxide, 3.5; copper oxide (CuO), 1.4. The glaze was fired under reducing conditions.

Chinese copper-red glazes (Sang de Boeuf, blood red) were described by Hetherington.[5] He used colloidal metallic copper with the assistance of iron and tin oxides fired in a reducing atmosphere. The extremely fine copper gave a yellow color.

Ganzenmuller[6] referred to copper ruby glass as having been made in Egyptian antiquity, in which modern scientific examination has revealed the presence of Cu_2O. Porcelain was made in China during the period 1426–1435 having brilliant copper-red underglaze decorations. Copper-red porcelain glazes continue to be produced in China at the present time. There are many museum specimens made during the time from 1661–1672.

CONSTITUTION OF GLAZES. Mellor[7] published a comprehensive review of the chemistry of the formation of copper reds in 1936, which he characterized as "more dogmatic than demonstrative."

Beyersdorfer,[8] employing electron microscope techniques, in 1951 found octahedral crystals, 10–30 mμ in diameter, in good red glazes. When the size increased by an order of magnitude (100 mμ to 300 mμ) the glazes had the characteristic "livery" appearance. In earlier work, Beyersdorfer[9] studied ruby glasses to observe their striking behavior and to establish the striking temperature for gold, copper, and selenium He found the mechanism to be based on the growth of the respective metallic crystalloids depended upon the mobility of the metals in the glass. The larger atoms had lower mobilities than the smaller ones so the striking temperature was higher.

Byersdorfer[9] observed that in gold ruby, cubic particles were developed having sizes in the range of 120 to 150 Angstrom units. In copper ruby, the particles were more densely situated than the particles in gold ruby, making for the more dense color.

Where gold ruby was made with an addition of a silver component along with the gold, the silver particles strike before the gold particles, giving the color a yellowish cast.

When the particles grow to macroscopic size, aventurines result. Such large crystals are possible only when the diffusion halo around the growing crystal can continue to be supplied with metal by diffusion from the parent glass. In copper aventurine, the diffusion halos are readily observed with an electron microscope.

The subject of copper-red glazes was treated scientifically by Brown

Table 13.1. Empirical formulas of five copper ruby glaze compositions[10]

Constituents	*1*[11]	*2*[10]	*3*[12]	*4*[12]	*5*[13]
K_2O	0.059	0.500	–	0.25	0.20
Na_2O	0.433	–	–	0.25	0.43
CaO	0.263	0.500	0.30	–	0.17
BaO	–	–	–	0.50	–
PbO	0.245	–	0.70	–	0.20
Al_2O_3	0.365	0.100	0.15	0.15	0.15
B_2O_3	0.525	1.000	0.40	0.50	1.00
SiO_2	2.000	2.500	2.10	2.30	2.50
SnO_2	0.040	–	0.02	0.15	0.13
Cu,%	0.30	0.60	0.15	3.0	3.0
Mat. temp. (cone)	07	06	05	05	05

and Norton.[10] They presented spectrophotometer curves of the reflective intensity plotted against wavelength for two copper ruby glazes having different concentrations of copper, a mixture of Cu_2O in oil, a polished copper plate, and a copper-free glaze. Norton's[10] curves are shown in figure 13.1.

In his studies, Norton used the five glazes with compositions and sources as tabulated in table 13.1. The best copper ruby was obtained with glaze no. 3, but most of his experiments were based on composition no. 1.

REDUCTION TECHNIQUES. Norton[10] tried some different degrees of reduction as shown in table 13.2. He concluded that strong reducing agents such as hydrogen promoted too rapid growth of copper particles. The result was the formation of black instead of red. Carbon monoxide seemed to favor the proper growth rate of copper crystalloids to yield good reds.

The reduction can be achieved by using reducing reagents as a part of the glaze batch and firing in an oxidizing atmosphere. The literature contains some references to the use of finely powdered SiC in the batch with varying degrees of success. Internal reducing agents have successfully been used, such as powdered silicon, antimony sulfide, and molybdenum sulfide. Any material that will be sufficiently resistant to oxidation to retain sufficient reducing powers by the time the glaze sinters to a gas-tight system holds promise.

STRIKING. In order to produce the red, a process known as striking is required. This accomplishes two things: formation of copper nuclei and growth from the nuclei to the required size of crystallites. Norton[10] favors the practice of forming of Cu nuclei at the maturing temperature, followed by rapid cooling to room temperature. By subsequent heat treatment at an appropriate temperature, the nuclei will grow into little crystallites of the right size to give reds. Schematic curves of nucleation and crystallization are shown in figures 6.22, 6.27, 6.28, 13.2 and 13.3. Some actual data are plotted in figures 6.25 and 6.26. Time and temperature conditions for nucleation and crystallization are shown in all of these illustrations.

Table 13.2. Some experimental firing atmospheres and resulting colors[10]

Gas	*Results*
$N_2 + 0.3\% H_2$	A few pink spots
$CO_2 + 0.3\% H_2$	No reds; black or green
$N_2 + 4.0\% CO$	Good reds
$CO_2 + 0.3\% H_2 + xH_2O$	Good reds

Note: x means varying

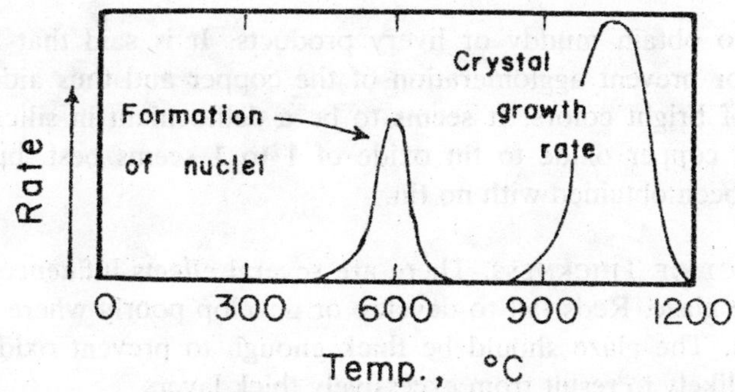

Figure 13.2 Type of material requiring controlled conditions for striking.[10]

Figures 13.2 and 13.3 were constructed by Norton[10] specifically for some copper red glazes.

When the curves for nuclei rate formation and crystal growth overlap, as in figure 13.3, a condition favorable for spontaneous striking can occur, and controlled crystallization would not be possible. When the curves for formation of nuclei and for crystal growth rate are separated, as in figure 13.2, spontaneous crystallization cannot occur.

Influence of Glaze Compositions on Color. Good reds can be obtained with a wide range of base glaze compositions and the color development is relatively independent of them. Reds develop with as little as 0.1% of Cu and up to more than 5%. With lowest copper content the most brilliant reds are developed but they require very careful control in firing. With higher copper content, less careful heat treatment control is required, but the shades tend to be muddy.

Tin oxide promotes the development of bright colors and reduces the

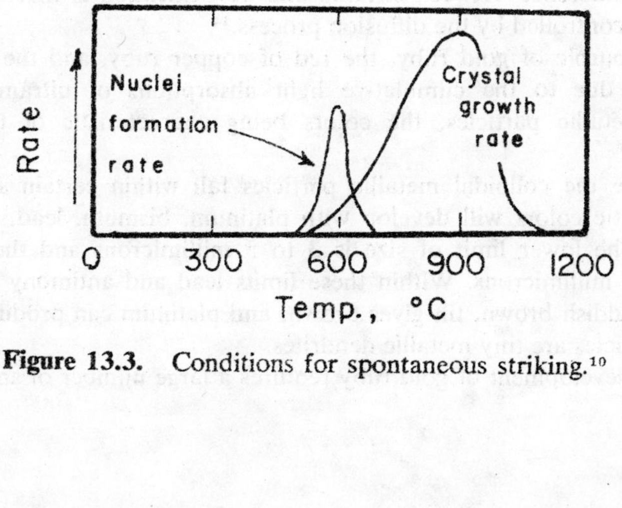

Figure 13.3. Conditions for spontaneous striking.[10]

tendency to obtain muddy or livery products. It is said that SnO_2 tends to retard or prevent agglomeration of the copper and thus aids in the attainment of bright colors. It seems to be a deflocculant in silicate fusions. A ratio of copper oxide to tin oxide of 1 to 1 seems best, but excellent reds have been obtained with no tin.

EFFECT OF THICKNESS. There are several effects influenced by thickness of the glaze. Reds fail to develop or develop poorly where the coating is too thin. The glaze should be thick enough to prevent oxidation. Dull colors are likely to result from excessively thick layers.

The reduction may be achieved in any of several ways with internal reducing agents or with reducing gaseous atmospheres.

Pyrophysical Behavior of Gold, Silver, and Copper in Silicate Melts

Gold ruby, silver in glasses, silver staining, copper ruby, and copper staining all owe their color to finely dispersed metallic particles. The solubility of metals, per se, in glass approaches nil, the major solubility being of metallic ions. The stability of Au^+, Ag^+, Cu^+ and Cu^{2+}, and all of the precious metal ions decreases with increasing temperature, so appreciable amounts of silver, gold, and platinum metals cannot be kept in solution. As shown by Weyl,[14] the solubility of metal in glass is greatly influenced by the presence of certain components, notably tin, bismuth, and lead.

Weyl pointed out that stannous or stannic ions in glass tend to associate with metal atoms so as to contribute to an increased solubility of the metal in glass. This is the function of tin in gold ruby glasses. Also, once a tiny metal crystal is formed, it adsorbs stannous ions to provide a barrier to further growth and thus tends to stabilize the colloidal subdivision.

The difference between striking and devitrification is that the rate of striking is controlled by the diffusion process.[14]

The purple of gold ruby, the red of copper ruby, and the yellow of silver are due to the cumulative light absorptions of ultramicroscopic opaque metallic particles, the colors being characteristic of the metals concerned.

Where the colloidal metallic particles fall within certain size limits, characteristic colors will develop with platinum, bismuth, lead, antimony, and tin. The lower limit of size is 3 to 5 millimicrons and the upper is 70 to 100 millimicrons. Within these limits lead and antimony give gray, bismuth reddish brown, tin gives brown, and platinum can produce a pink. These particles are tiny metallic dendrites.

The development of gold ruby requires a large number of small nuclei and the smaller and more numerous the nuclei the better the ruby. Factors in the development of the ruby color are the rates of (1) nucleus formation, (2) crystal growth, and (3) coagulation and recrystallization. In general, a lower striking temperature favors better ruby development.

Silver also becomes more soluble in glasses containing lead, bismuth, or tin, and slightly reducing conditions favor the development of more metallic silver. In silver staining, silver ions replace sodium ions in a base exchange process. The migration of silver into glass is facilitated by using a carrier, such as kaolin, to hold the displaced sodium ions and thus favor continued migration of silver into glass. To induce travel or diffusion of silver further into glass, heat treatment is effective. Minor constituents in the glass, such as As, Sb, or Fe have a very great influence on silver staining.

Copper staining of glass is similar to silver staining except that here the major ingredients rather than the minor constituents are of paramount influence.

Coloration of Glasses by Gold, Silver, and Copper

DEVELOPMENT OF GOLD RUBY GLASS. The color development in gold ruby *glasses* has been a subject of interest and investigation for a long time. For example, Rose[15] surmised that metallic gold was dissolved at high temperature by molten glass to form a gold silicate that was colorless. As the glass cooled, he postulated that gold silicate dissociated to form, as one product, a colored gold oxide. By around 1900, Zsigmondy[16] found that gold ruby glasses contained dispersed particles approximately 4 to 6 millimicrons in diameter. There have been a large number of investigations into the subject of which those cited are typical.[17–26]

It has been concluded that gold ions from a gold oxide dissolve in molten glass at glass-melting temperatures. The glass will remain colorless, while the gold, as ions, remains in solution. When conditions, such as reduction, occur that form atomic (metal) gold, the characteristic colorations can develop. The resulting color will depend upon the distribution and particle sizes of the precipitated gold. The presence of such compounds as those of tin and bismuth act as reducing agents at low temperature to convert gold ions to gold atoms. Without reducing agents the glasses remain essentially colorless. The reduction may be achieved photochemically as described by Stookey.[27]

The principles that apply to gold glasses also are applicable to silver and copper glasses.

In the composition of gold ruby glass the essential ingredients are gold, one or more compounds of polyvalent elements, and an oxidizing agent, such as nitrate. Of the polyvalent elements including Sn, Sb, As, Bi, Pb, Se, Te, etc., the best are Se and Te. Compounds of these elements may induce ruby development when the other elements fail to do so. Gold ruby develops best in glasses high in alkali, but lead glasses seem to yield better rubies than nonlead.

COPPER COLORS. To achieve copper ruby, it is essential that the batch contain a suitable copper compound, one or more of the polyvalent elements listed under gold ruby, and a mild reducing agent. Additional reduction usually is employed by means of a reducing gaseous atmospheric environment. Copper ruby cannot be expected to form if the copper reagents have been too highly oxidized, because cupric ions cannot be reduced to the atomic state by heat treatment alone, and greens and blues result from copper ions. Excessive reduction, though, produces massive metallic copper in the melting of the glass and the result to be expected would be muddy brown colors. What is required is an intermediate degree of reduction, not too strong and not too mild, that will yield a colorless product that can be struck to ruby by proper lower temperature heat treatment. In the absence of the auxilliary polyvalent ions the color will be green, or poor amber if highly reduced.

Under usual circumstances, the Cu^{2+} ion is stable, but the lower oxidation states Cu^{+} and Cu^{0} are formed and prevail, depending upon the degree of reduction from the environment. Colors from copper in glass resemble those from aqueous solutions of cupric ions producing blue in most glasses. Greenish blue is due to the simultaneous presence of Cu^{2+} and Cu^{+}. No color is obtained when all of the copper is Cu^{+}. On the other hand, Cu^{0}, copper atoms, when present as very small particles and well dispersed (colloidal), impart the well-known copper ruby.

Under favorable circumstances, copper can activate luminescent properties in glass. By means of electron paramagnetic resonance measurements, Karapetyan[28] showed that divalent ions produced absorption bands peaking at 800 and 880 $m\mu$ and was not fluorescent; but after reduction with carbon the absorption peaks disappeared and became fluorescent under ultraviolet radiation, which Karapetyan was able to show was due to monovalent copper. Upon further reduction and heat treatment the red color characteristic of dispersed colloidal copper crystals appeared.

SILVER COLORS. In silver-bearing glasses, the silver can exist as the colorless Ag^{+} ion, atomic (metallic) silver Ag^{0}, and silver crystals $(Ag^{0})_r$. No color is produced by Ag^{+} or Ag^{0} but the latter will show a strong white fluorescence when irradiated with ultraviolet light. The $(Ag^{0})_r$ does not luminesce but produces a yellow or an amber color in the glass. Thermal dissociation of silver ions in silicate glasses occurs readily. If the concentration exceeds about 0.1% this dissociation occurs during the melting process. In general, it has proved impossible to maintain a sufficiently high degree of oxidation to prevent some atomic silver from forming at concentrations exceeding 0.1% to 0.2% of Ag. This Ag then proceeds to start to form crystallite aggregates $(Ag^0)_x$, even in rapidly cooled glass. Once silver atoms are formed, atomic silver may disperse rapidly under heat treatment from the metal vapor. Silver in glass is sufficiently easily reduced that glass only slightly warmer than room temperature can be reduced to the luminescent state by exposure to hydrogen.

Silver yellow glazes are produced under conditions similar to those used for gold ruby. Cloudy ambers are derived from the use of too much silver or too much reduction. It takes about one order of magnitude more of silver to produce yellow glazes than of gold for gold ruby.

General Considerations about the Formation of Reduced Metal and Clear Colored Glazes

In working with gold, copper, and silver glazes, some compositions will show reduced metal in varying proportions, and some will be struck to clear colored glazes. Perhaps some even will be clear but could be heat treated to produce color, while still others would not be colored even by additional heat treatment. The factors controlling these behaviors are: (*a*) the degree and state of oxidation (and reduction) of the glaze during its firing and (*b*) the concentrations of Au, Cu, or Ag in the batch. High concentrations and strong reduction leads to metal precipitation, while low concentrations and strongly oxidizing conditions operate to prevent atomic or metal precipitation.

With glasses it is usual to bring out the color by striking, a mild reheating process. Glazes generally must be so structured and handled that they automatically strike during the initial cooling in the glost burn.

Strike temperatures depend on a number of factors including the kind and amount of polyvalent catalyst, base glaze composition, and viscosity characteristics. The warming-in temperatures and the temperatures for making the colors disappear in general are reversible and roughly are categorized as shown in table 13.3.

Colors Due to Platinum, Palladium, and Rhodium in Glass

Rindone and Rhoads[29] discussed the coloring effects from elements of the platinum group. The following two paragraphs were taken from their paper.

Table 13.3. Examples of heat-treatments causing colors in silver-, copper-, and gold-glazes to appear, disappear and reappear.

Element	Temperature, °C	
	Color forms	*Color disappears*
Silver	400–500	600–700
Copper	600–700	800
Gold	600–700	1,150–1,200

Metals can exist in three different states in glasses. They may be colored or colorless as ions, depending on the metal. They may exist as atoms and produce no color but may fluoresce when exposed to appropriate radiations. The atoms may coalesce, or form atom-groups of tiny metallic particles that produce colors, the color varying with the size of the metallic particles or groups.

There are many examples. Copper in silicate melts may exist as Cu^{+}, Cu^{2+} and elemental Cu^{0}. The copper ions produce colors characteristic to the state of the equilibrium between the two valence states. The colors range from green to blue depending on the characteristics of the glass in which they are a part. The copper atoms when dissolved or dispersed as individual atoms do not produce color. When the copper forms aggregates of colloidal copper or metallic crystals copper-ruby is formed. As the aggregate or crystallite grows to larger sizes, livery or muddy colors result. It appears that platinum, rhodium, and palladium in alkali silicate, borate, and phosphate glasses exist either in ionic or in dispersed metal states. The gray color is due to colloidal or dispersed metal, but the ionic colors could not be changed by heat treatment. The colors produced in glasses by metals of the platinum group are summarized in table 13.4.

Colors Produced in Silicate Melts by Members of the Cd-S-Se System

True reds are produced in silicate melts by copper ruby, uranium-bearing compounds, and the family of Cd-S-Se pigments. Other colors in the red family are gold ruby, Fe_2O_3, chrome-tin-pink stains, chrome-

Table 13.4. Colors produced in simple glasses by platinum, palladium, and rhodium[29]

Glass type	Alkali silicates	Alkali borates	Alkali phosphates
Platinum	gray	gray	gray yellow
Palladium	yellow	yellow	yellow brown
Rhodium	yellowish	yellow	yellow amber

alumina pinks and a few others. Selenium ruby is the most widely produced clear ruby glass. The selenium-based stains are used as pigments in low-temperature glazes and in overglaze colors. There is some good information concerning selenium glasses which is of indirect value and perhaps of direct interest to those concerned with colored glazes.

There are two separate mechanisms of color formation in this system. One is the pigment type, in which crystals and solid solutions of CdS and CdSe are responsible for the color. Another mechanism of color development is directly analogous to the color formation in copper and gold ruby. The pigment type of color development will be discussed in the chapter on stains.

General Requirements for Selenium Ruby Glasses. To obtain good selenium ruby glasses, some minor elements commonly are required in addition to the well-known major ingredients. For glasses, among these are ZnO, fluorine, phosphate, and minute amounts of copper or nickel oxide. The function of these minor constituents is to provide nuclei[30] for the cadmium sulfoselenide which requires a lower temperature for its formation. Owing to the extreme unsolubility of copper and nickel sulfide in silicate melts, these compounds form at high temperature to provide exnuclei. Phosphate, as from bone ash and fluorine as well, produce extremely low solubility phosphates, fluorides and fluophosphates, especially of calcium and aluminum. Although present in amounts too small to produce noticeable opacity, the mechanism is the same. The presence of these phases provides nuclei for the formation of the selenium-bearing phase during the striking process.

Cadmium sulfoselenide does not exist[30] at glass-melting temperatures and in strikable glasses, the dissociated components exist in solution in the silicate melt. Fluorine in the silicate melt facilitates diffusion and ionic and molecular movement; the higher field-strength ions (divalent and trivalent, e.g., Ca, Mg, or Al) retard such mobility. Fluroides increase low-temperature mobility and speed up striking.

The chief function of zinc oxide is to help in the retention of sulfur and selenium.

Alkali sulfoferrite and selenoferrite produce a red-brown color in glasses containing strong reducing agents, such as carbon, silicon, or the like. This can account for the intense color of some glasses containing only small concentrations of cadmium sulfoselenide.

The color of selenium ruby is related to the basis glass composition as well as to the colorants and manufacturing conditions. For example, as pointed out by Lamin and Rabinovich,[31] the best reds require the presence of zinc oxide. It was shown by them that the finest and most

Table 13.5. The influence of Se, CdS, and Si on the "selenium ruby" colors[32]

Additives and amounts wt %			
Selenium	*Cadmium sulfide*	*Silicon*	*Color*
1.0	0.6	–	Weak yellow
1.0	0.6	0.025	Greenish yellow
1.0	0.6	0.05	Light yellow
1.0	0.6	0.10	Intense yellow orange
1.0	0.6	0.20	Ruby, orange cast
1.0	1.0	–	Light yellowish green
1.0	1.0	0.05	Light green
1.0	1.0	0.10	Yellow
1.0	1.0	0.20	Orange
1.0	1.0	0.25	Red orange
1.0	0.4	0.10	Weak red, orange cast
1.0	0.4	0.20	Brilliant red
1.2	0.4	0.10	Brilliant red
1.2	0.4	0.20	Brilliant red
1.2	–	0.20	Brown
0.7	0.6	0.20	Orange red
0.9	0.6	0.20	Red with orange cast
1.1	0.6	0.20	Red
1.3	0.6	0.20	Red
1.2	–	0.10	Reddish brown

stable colors were obtained in glasses with about 2% of CaO, 8% of Na_2O and 11% of ZnO.

PROPORTIONS OF Se, CdS, AND Si. Glasses containing various proportions of Se, CdS, and silicon metal were prepared by Pelikan.[32] The glass was of the following composition:

$$\begin{matrix} 0.623Na_2O & \\ 0.079K_2O & 3.30SiO_2 \\ 0.300CaO & \end{matrix}$$

It was melted at 1,400° C and annealed at 560° C. The colors obtained with the varying additions were as shown in table 13.5.

Important factors influencing the colors of selenium ruby glasses were studied by Pavlish and Austin.[33] They used a batch calculated to yield: Silica, 72.8%; alumina, 2.5%; calcium oxide, 6.4%; magnesia, 4.2%; sodium oxide, 12.6%; and potassium oxide, 1.5%.

The retention of selenium is a problem. Selenium boils at 688° C. It is readily oxidized to selenium dioxide which has a higher vapor pressure, subliming at temperatures as low as about 300° C. It is advisable, therefore, to prevent the oxidation of selenium, sulfur, and cadmium. This can be done by the presence of reducing agents in the glass batch or by partially reducing conditions in the furnace gases.

Selenium retention can be greatly improved by the use of reducing agents in the batch. Retention of selenium then depends on (1) the amount of selenium in the batch, (2) kind and amount of reducing agents, and (3) the manner of adding cadmium, e.g., the retention is greater when metallic cadmium is added than when cadmium sulfide is used.

The retention of cadmium also is a problem since it also can be lost by vaporization. The conditions most favorable for the retention of cadmium are favorable for the loss of selenium. High retention of cadmium requires the presence of oxidation agents, such as nitrates or arsenic pentoxide. It, therefore, is necessary to balance the reducing agent in such a way as to obtain an optimum result. Metallic silicon seems to be among the more effective reducing agents.

COLORS OTHER THAN RED. Selenium has been extensively used to produce red and pink glasses and low-temperature glazes. Some other colors are possible, but only a limited amount has been published on the

Table 13.6. Some colors in glasses containing selenium, cadmium sulfide and silicon[33]

	Colorants			*Oxide added (%)*		*Reducing agent (%)*	
Color	*Se (%)*	*Cd (%)*	*CdS (%)*				
Ruby	0.35		0.35			Calcium boride	0.23
Ruby	0.25	0.30				Silicon	0.055
Ruby	0.35		0.35	$NaNO_3$	0.05	Silicon	0.18
Amber	0.25			$Fe_2(C_2O_4)_3$	0.10	Silicon	0.10
Topaz	0.10			Bi_2O_3	0.10	Silicon	0.035
Yellow	0.25			As_2O_3	0.10	Silicon	0.10
Yellow	0.25			Bi_2O_3	0.10	Silicon	0.15
Yellow	0.25	0.30				Silicon	0.035
Yellow	0.10			Sb_2O_3	0.10	Silicon	0.035
Pink	0.25			TiO_2	0.10	Silicon	0.025
Pink	0.25						
Pink	0.10			MnO_2	0.10		
Pink	0.25			Ce_2O_3	0.10		
Pink	0.25			As_2O_3	0.10		
Emerald	0.20			Cr_2O_3	0.20	Silicon	0.035
Green	0.25			Cr_2O_3	0.10	Silicon	0.10
Tan	0.25			SnO	0.10	Silicon	0.10
Orange	0.35		0.60			Silicon	0.125
Orange	0.35		0.35	$NaNO_3$	0.25	Silicon	0.125
Brown	0.20			NiO	0.10	Silicon	0.035
Brown	0.10			Bi_2O_3	0.10	Silicon	0.05
Brown	0.20			Ag_2O	0.20	Silicon	0.07
Brown	0.20		0.20			CaSi	0.73
Black	0.25			Cu_2O	0.10	Silicon	0.05
Black	0.25			Cu_2O	0.10	Silicon	0.10
Black	0.25			Co_2O_3	0.10	Silicon	0.15

possible colors. Selenium, it is known, will combine with other metals to form colored selenides. Often, there may be a similarity in the colors of the sulfides and the corresponding selenides.

Black glass was prepared by Austin and Sullivan[34] by using selenium with cobalt, nickel, or iron. Black glasses also were prepared with relatively low concentration of colorants using either copper or cobalt together with selenium, in conjunction with elemental silicon as a reducing agent. Some of the glasses, at low concentrations of colorants, were dichroic. Selenium yellow glasses result from admixtures of arsenic, bismuth, or antimony oxides with selenium. Emerald green can be produced by using 0.2% of selenium with an equal amount of Cr_2O_3 and using 0.035% of silicon. Various colors and shades in glass are possible as illustrated in table 13.6.

References

1. Weyl, W. A. 1945. Colored glasses. *J. Society of Glass Technology.* 29(135):291–389.
2. Yates, D. J. 1959. The development of colour in glass. *Trans. Brit. Ceram. Soc.* 53(10):573–88.
3. Reuter-Brocks, Eike. 1970. Copper-red glazes. *Europaische Tonind.* 2(7):169–70.
4. Albonetti, Franco. 1955. Flambé reds. *Faenza* 51(5):117–22.
5. Hetherington, A. L. 1950. Chinese ceramic glazes. *Proc. Roy. Inst. Gt. Brit.* 34 Pt. 3(156):424–26.
6. Ganzenmuller, W. 1939. Colored glass with the changing times. *Glashutte* 69(45):761–64; (46):774–75; (47):786–88; *Ceram. Abst.* 1940. 19(5):109.
7. Mellor, J. W. 1936. Chemistry of Chinese copper-red glazes, 1–2. *Trans. Engl. Ceram. Soc.* 35(8):364–78; (11):478–91.
8. Beyersdorfer, Kurt. 1951. Elektronenmikroskopische Untersuchungen an Rubingläsern (Investigation of ruby glasses with the electron microscope). *Sprechsaal* 84(10):186–80.
9. Beyersdorfer, P. 1950. Red striking colors in glass-adventurine. *Glashutte* 76(9):129–32.
10. Brown, S. F. and Norton, F. N. 1959. Constitution of copper-red glazes. *J. Am. Ceram. Soc.* 42(11): 499–503.
11. Harden, C. M. 1936. Red glazes and underglaze red by reduction. *J. Am. Ceram. Soc.* 19(1):26–28.
12. Breitenfeldt, Eberhard. 1936. Experiments on copper-red glazes. *Keram. Rundschau* 37:393–94.
13. Cordt, F. W. 1933. Suggestions for production of red glazes. *Ceram. Ind.* 21(4):172–75; translated and reprinted from 1933. *Keram. Rundschau* 41(24):307–10.

14. Weyl, W. A. 1945. Colored glasses: 4, Colors produced by metals. *J. Soc. Glass Tech.* 29(135):291–389T.
15. Rose, H. 1848. *Dinglers Polytech. J.* 107:129.
16. Zsigmondy, Richard. 1909. *Colloids and the ultramicroscope.* Translated by Jerome Alexander. New York: John Wiley & Sons, Inc.
17. Zsigmondy, R. *Composition for ruby glass.* U.S. Patent 703,512, July 1, 1902.
18. Lange, B. 1930. Coloration and genesis of gold ruby and sapphire glasses. No. 1. Kaiser-Wilhelm Inst. Silikatforsch. *Berlin-Dahlem* 3:5–16.
19. Silverman, Alexander. 1931. Colloids in glass, in *Colloid chemistry.* Vol. 3. New York, N.Y.: Chemical Catalog Co., Inc. pp 283–88.
20. Badger, A. E., Weyl, W., and Rudow, H. 1939. Effect of heat-treatment on color of gold ruby glass. *Glass Ind.* 20(11):407–14.
21. Truby, H. A. *Method and batch for making colored glass.* U.S. Patent 2,237 042, April 1, 1941.
22. Veazie, F. M. and Weyl, W. A. 1942. Effect of tin in gold ruby glass. *J. Am. Ceram. Soc.* 25(10):280–81.
23. Dietzel, A. 1945. Dimming of glasses colored by metal colloids. *Z. Elektrochem.* 51(1,2):32–37.
24. Weyl, op. cit., ref. 14.
25. Bachman, G. S., Fischer, R. B., and Badger, A. E. 1946. Observation of gold particles in glass with the electron microscope. *Glass Ind.* 27(8):399,416,418,422.
26. Stookey, S. D. 1949. Coloration of glass by gold, silver and copper. *J. Am. Ceram. Soc.* 32(8):246–49.
27. Stookey, S. D. 1949. Photosensitive glass. *Ind. Eng. Chem.* 41(4):856–61.
28. Karapetyan, G. O. 1961. Luminescence of copper activated glasses. *Izv. Akad. Nauk. SSSR Ser. Fiz.* 25(4):539–41.
29. Rindone, G. E. and Rhoads, J. L. 1956. The colors of platinum, palladium and rhodium in simple glasses. *J. Am. Ceram. Soc.* 39(5):173–80.
30. Shively, R. R., Jr. and Weyl, W. A. 1947. Functions of minor constituents in commercial selenium ruby batch. *J. Am. Ceram. Soc.* 30(10):311–14.
31. Lamin, B. A. and Rabinovich, I. A. 1948. Manufacture of selenium ruby. *Legkaya Prom.* 8(12):10–11.
32. Pelikan, A. 1949. Selenium ruby. *Sklarske Rozhledy* 25(4–5):63–67.
33. Pavlish, A. E. and Austin, C. R. 1947. Selenium-ruby and other glasses colored by selenium. *J. Am. Ceram. Soc.* 30(1):1–11.
34. Austin, C. R. and Sullivan, J. D. 1942. Selenium black glass. *J. Am. Ceram. Soc.* 25(5):128–29.

14

Ceramic Stains

The glaze ceramist is coming more and more to depend upon prepared pigments, called stains, for the preparation of colored glazes. Just a few decades ago the ceramist prepared his colored glazes by including one or more of the dozen colored oxides into his glaze formula to develop his colors. The oxides and salts of the following were his source for coloring materials: cadmium, chromium, cobalt, copper, gold, iron, manganese, nickel, platinum, silver, titanium, uranium, and vanadium. He still is dependent upon these elements for color, but most of his colors now are in the form of preprepared pigments, called stains, or ceramic colors.

Ceramic stains usually are prepared by blending appropriate raw materials by: (*a*) dry mixing, (*b*) wet milling, or (*c*) by preparing a slurry or slip from the powdered reagents. Wet milling is preferred. This requires the steps of filtering, dehydration, and drying. Slush mixing, using lower water content, is fast and cheap. Dry mixing is entirely satisfactory and, for some batches, the only choice. Regardless of the initial mixing method, the mixed dry powders usually are micronized prior to calcining. In other cases, the lumps taken from the dryer can be directly calcined.

The calcining process is critical as to temperature, time, draft, atmosphere, and the crucibles. The volume, weight, and density of packing of the batch for calcining also must be closely controlled, because they have an important influence on the final color. When possible, it is preferable to use a soft calcine. Some stains, however, must be calcined into a dense, hard clinker-like product. By way of summary, the following factors are critical to the proper preparation of a stain·

a. raw material: its type, quality, purity, density, and uniformity
b. method and effectiveness of mixing, milling, and blending

c. weight, volume, density, porosity, and uniformity of packing of stain batch for calcination
d. calcining parameters—temperature, time, atmosphere, draft, type of fuel, and type of crucible
e. particle size and particle shape of the calcined stain
f. testing, grading, controlling, and blending of final stain

Ceramic pigments in general were classified by Evans[1] on the basis of their crystal structure. On that basis, there are two broad categories: compounds and solid solutions. Possible and existing disorder in the structure can explain possible and existing color development. The heat-treatment, or more properly the sintering of the batch reagents is for the purpose of achieving these states through high-temperature or solid state chemical reactions.

Chrome-Alumina Pinks

There is a continuous series of solid solutions of Al_2O_3 and Cr_2O_3. When a small amount of Al is replaced by Cr in the high-temperature phase (corundum) of Al_2O_3, the well-known ruby is obtained. Chrome-alumina pinks are essentially very small particles of synthetic ruby. The pyrochemical and pyrophysical properties of alumina pink stain are identical to those of alumina or corundum of the same particle size.

These stains develop strong pink shades through cone 11. They are also used to develop browns and tans in underglaze decorations. These stains are of a high order of stability and can be used for a wide range of shades.

The color tones are influenced some by the composition of the base glaze. A generalization in this regard is that best tones are obtained in glazes high in Al_2O_3 and in ZnO but low in CaO.

Chrome-alumina pinks have been used a long time, but not discussed much in the literature. Arthur Watts was the first to write about them.[2] He obtained a pink by calcining a mixture of 82.3% of alumina and 17.7% of Cr_2O_3. He obtained a good stain with several calcined compositions containing Al_2O_3 and Cr_2O_3. For example, Al_2O_3, 87.64%; Cr_2O_3, 7.06%; and B_2O_3, 5.30%; or Al_2O_3, 87.3%; Cr_2O_3, 8.7%; and ZnO, 10.0%.

Chrome-alumina pinks were reviewed by Hawks,[3] who said that commercially these stains date back to 1930. They began to be marketed by color companies in 1939. Hawks, in summarizing chrome-alumina stains, said the glaze should be lime-free and low in PbO and B_2O_3, but high in ZnO and Al_2O_3. Fluid glazes are not desirable; rather relatively viscous ones are recommended. Now Cr_2O_3 in the presence of zinc tends to form zinc chromate spinels, a strong brown. So sufficient ZnO is necessary to balance the glaze and in addition prevent Cr_2O_3 from stealing zinc from the Cr_2O_3–ZnO–Al_2O_3 pink stain. The glaze also must have sufficient Al_2O_3 to retard the tendency of the Al_2O_3 of the stain from dissolving in the glaze. The chrome-alumina pink stain is prepared with Al_2O_3 as the carrier.

Hawks reported that, by using various base glaze compositions, a wide palette, ranging from grays to pinks, is produced. Heat treatment definitely influences the shade obtained. Lower temperatures generally produce shades with the higher yellow component. With overfired ware, bluer shades develop.

This stain is sensitive to the composition of the RO members of the glaze. In a typical glaze, added CaO caused some deterioration of the pink, but BaO resulted in a pronounced deterioration. The addition of SrO tended to increase the yellow component of the color, as did MgO.

The strongest pinks appeared with about 8% of ZnO, but Li_2O tended to decrease the pink; and with 10% of lithium silicate a tan resulted. B_2O_3 is deleterious, but high Al_2O_3 is essential.

Chrome-alumina pink stains were studied by Rao,[4] who observed the effects of ZnO, SiO_2, B_2O_3, CaO, and MgO. Some good Cr–Al stains were obtained by calcining at 1,300° C with 3% of potassium dichromate. Dark rose pink resulted from 20% Al_2O_3, 40% ZnO, and 40% B_2O_3. The same color was obtained from 20% Al_2O_3, 40% ZnO, 20% B_2O_3, and 17% SiO_2. A brick-red stain was derived from Al_2O_3, 60%; CaO, 20%; and B_2O_3, 20%. The CaO functions only as a mineralizing constituent and thus deepens the color. As the calcination temperatures were increased, the color deepened, being optimum at 1,450° C. The calcination temperature was lowered by PbO and thus deepened the color.

Chrome-Cobalt Blue Greens

Green and blue-green stains are derived from calcined combinations of Cr_2O_3–CoO–Al_2O_3. A wide variety of shades and tones are possible from this system. The stains are applicable in either zinc-bearing or zincless glazes. It is interesting that although tin oxide must be avoided in most Cr_2O_3-bearing glazes it can be used with the better chrome-cobalt blue-green stains. These stains, however, when diluted or weakened develop a dirty gray color.

The colors are quite stable, both as to firing temperature and as to glaze composition. However, in keeping with most cobalt-base colors, the cobalt blue will separate from the green, and run, in poorly formulated or excessively fluid glazes.

The cobalt-blue greens are derived by calcining mixtures rich in Cr_2O_3 and low in CoO. As the Cr_2O_3 is decreased and the CoO is increased, the colors shift from green blue-green to blue blue-greens. These stains are satisfactory for blending with the popular yellow stains: Naples yellow, praseodymium yellow, tin-vanadium yellow, or zirconium-vanadium yellow. These blends produce stable greens. This type of coloring was discussed by Henry,[5] who also cautioned that low percentages of the blue-green stains create dirty gray colors.

Blue to green cobalt base pigments may be prepared by the reaction of preferred mixtures of CoO, Al_2O_3, and TiO_2 at 700° to 1,100° C, as described by Chrest, Rummery, Richards, and Roseman.[6]

Chrome Green

Chromium trioxide is a strong stable color and is widely used as a green pigment, not only in ceramics, but elsewhere. It has perhaps the lowest solubility and the strongest coloring power in silicate glasses of any oxide. In glazes it is used in amounts usually in the range of 1% to 5%. Straight Cr_2O_3 has a definite tendency to fume or volatilize some during firing, to be absorbed by, or deposited on, furnace refractories and adjacent ware. The vapor pressure is low and the vaporization rate is minute, but the extraordinarily strong tinting power requires that even this be watched. One result is that the vapors can cause pink tints on glazes containing SnO_2. Another is the tendency to form brown colors in zinc-bearing glazes.

Cr_2O_3 can be used straight, and produce strong greens, but seldom is. When strongly calcined with Al_2O_3, a solid solution could be formed that is red; academically, ruby. Cr_2O_3–SiO_2 forms fairly stable calcines, but there is no compound in the system, or liquid either, for that matter, until very near the melting point of SiO_2. Nevertheless, such calcines can be used with greater success than with raw Cr_2O_3.

The stronger greens are derived from calcined mixtures of Cr_2O_3, Co_3O_4 and Al_2O_3. The green shades have a minimum cobalt content. There is but little color difference among chrome-green stains. The tinting power is considerable, and they have good hiding power, even without an auxillary opacifier. Base glazes must be free of ZnO and are best with high CaO. The colors are stable through the porcelain glaze range.

Brown and Tan Colorants

Browns basically are derived from iron, nickel, manganese, and chromium, and their combinations with other materials. Zinc chromite, formed from the reaction of ZnO and Cr_2O_3, yields a strong, intense brown. This color formation was discussed by Minton in 1915.[7]

Ochers, umbers, and other natural earthy materials high in iron oxides or complex hydrated compounds of iron, and perhaps manganese, are common sources for brown pigments. Natural rutile and illmenite are iron-bearing titania minerals extensively used. Natural minerals and ores composed predominately of iron chromite make practical brown pigments. Natural low-fusion clays, volcanic tufts, and similar materials, such as slip clays, have long had an important role as brown colorants for glazes.[8]

From chemical and mineralogical points of view, nickel oxide has considerable potential as a glaze colorant. It does have a tendency to be sensitive to glaze composition, preparation, firing time, temperature, and atmosphere. There remains a good potential for such colors for artware, but commercial and industrial applications require greater stability than is afforded by the direct use of nickel oxide. Marquis and Carpenter,[9] commenting on this, quoted Wicks and Mellor:[10]

"Most of the nickel browns, drabs, fawns, and buff colors are unstable and can be reproduced by other more reliable means."

The well-known brown or mahogany glazes on high voltage insulators, stoneware-ovenware, and some artware are based on iron-manganese colors, and have been widely used. The literature is replete with references to it, such as by Fuller and Watts.[8] Sometimes glazes containing manganese develop a bluish metallic sheen in the form of thin surface films or "scum." This has been attributed by Montgomery[11] to the effects of volatilization and vaporization of manganese. The direct use of MnO_2 as such in glazes is limited because of possible variable coloration results. It is very useful as a minor additive to color compositions to be made into stains by calcination or to be combined by sintering with other components.

Chrome-Iron-Tin Stains

Still another type of tan stain is the Cr–Fe–Sn. In this stain the yellow component is replaced by red. This type of stain is based on calcined mixtures of Cr_2O_3–Fe_2O_3–SnO_2. These tan stains seem to be more stable than their parent, Cr–Fe–Zn. They are used for beige shades and are blended with chrome-alumina pinks to produce coral shades. These stains are not very sensitive to components in the matrix glaze, except that the glaze should contain at least 5% of ZnO. In this stain, the yellow component increases in zinc-bearing glazes as Fe_2O_3 is substituted for Cr_2O_3.[9]

Chrome-Iron-Zinc Browns

The chrome-iron-zinc system, according to Marquis and Carpenter,[9] forms the basis for tans and browns having a high degree of uniformity and stability. Stains of this system are a popular and reliable source for commercial brown coloring.

These authors discussed Cr–Fe–Zn stains and their use in some detail.[9] Because most users purchase commercially prepared stains, the average ceramist has only a limited need of a detailed knowledge of how to make stains. It is useful to know something of the physics, chemistry, and techniques of its use.

Marquis and Carpenter outlined the basic principles of changes in color of Cr–Fe–Zn browns resulting from their chemical composition. In summary these are:

a. With significant increases in the chromium and decrease in ZnO, the colors will grade into shades of green in zincless glazes and become grayer or yellower in zinc-bearing bases.
b. The addition of MnO_2 in the manufacture of the stains reduces the reddish cast in all glazes, making them yellower and grayer.
c. The presence of nickel in the stain makes darker shades.
d. The incorporation of some Al_2O_3 in the Cr–Fe–Zn stain forms a new type (Cr–Fe–Zn–Al) and is livelier and brighter due to an increase in Al_2O_3 at the expense of ZnO.

In the matrix glaze, the components of SiO_2, B_2O_3, K_2O, Na_2O, and PbO have little influence on the shades produced. The browns are, however, modified by the presence of ZnO, Al_2O_3, ZrO_2, and SnO_2. The stain is effective in proportions ranging from 0.5% to 10% in glazes opacified with zircon. At least 2% is required in clear glazes. The optimum coverage is achieved at glaze thicknesses of 10 mils to 15 mils.

Chrome-Tin Pink

The red base with the widest heat range of usefulness is generally known by the term chrome-tin pink. The term is indicative of two of the essential components. The possible colors are reds, maroons, pinks, lilacs, and related hues. None of these can be described as brilliant or fiery.

An explanation of the color formation, as proposed by Petrik[12] many years ago and generally accepted, was, namely, that it is caused by the deposition of very finely divided (aerosol) chromic oxide on the stannic oxide particles and the remarkable range of colors is due to variations in particle size, caused by the dispersing action of some reagent present. This may be analogous to the many colors which may be observed in glass colored by the presence of colloidally dispersed gold—the variation being due to the difference in the size of the gold particles formed by the heat treatment.

Kerstan[13] concluded that the red color from Cr_2O_3 in contact with SnO_2 is due to a modification of calcium stannate in a manner entirely analogous to ruby formation in corundum in glass tank blocks. This he attributed to isolated CrO_6 groups entering the corundum structure surrounded by AlO_6 coordination. The CrO_6 group can remain as an independant group up to about 8% of Cr_2O_3, after which it is unstable and the color changes to green.

When SnO_2 is present, small quantities of Cr_2O_3 create a pink cast. The gas atmosphere is important, the pink being suppressed in a reducing atmosphere. Halogens, especially fluorides, tend to eliminate the pink. CaO stabilizes the pink, apparently forming a calcium stannate that stabilizes the CrO_6 coordination.

Bose[14] said that when Cr_2O_3 is sufficiently finely divided, it appears crimson. He applied very thin layers of Cr_2O_3 onto the surfaces of SnO_2 and to Al_2O_3 and obtained pink colors.

An alternative explanation is the formation of solid solutions by the reaction of the chromium oxide and other material. Herold[15] studied color strains of this type both microscopically and by X-ray diffraction methods. He concluded that the red color is due to the stabilization of the colloidal chromium oxide on the calcium stannate present and that the violet colors are attributable to the stabilizing action of the tin oxide. The resistance of these colors to the destructive action of most glazes is due to the highly stabilized colloidal system which is quite insoluble. However, if too much colloidal matter is present, instability may develop.

The procedure used by Bose[16] to produce chrome-tin pink stains was to blend SnO_2, $CaCO_3$, and SiO_2 with 3% of potassium dichromate. After wet-grinding the batch, he dried it and calcined at 1,200° C. The powdered calcines were washed with water until the leachings were colorless. The resulting colors were dependent upon composition and varied from ivory to light green to lilac to pink to red. Best pinks were with 20% to 60% of SnO_2 and 20% to 40% of CaO. Silica from small amounts up to as high as 40% helped to brighten the colors.

Bose[16] prepared a chrome-tin pink stain suitable for underglaze colors having the following composition CaO, 23.32; SnO_2, 31.45; SiO_2, 41.64; PbO, 2.69; and Cr_2O_3 (as lead chromate or Cr_2O_3), 0.9. This mixture was calcined at 1,200° C and then thoroughly washed.

A variation of the chrome-tin pink stain was developed by Jamieson.[17]

This was prepared by calcining zircon, SnO_2, $CaCO_3$, and potassium dichromate at 1,100° to 1,400° C. According to Ikegaki[18] chrome-tin pink stains should be prepared by calcining mixtures of $CaO–SnO_2–SiO_2–Cr_2O_3$ at cones 9–10. The CaO content should not exceed 25% and CaO/SnO_2 should equal one. The Cr_2O_3 may be derived from $K_2Cr_2O_7$ or from Cr_2O_3 with the same results, but the amount should be in the range of 1.5% to 3%. The addition of 5% of borax to the batch before calcination helps to stabilize the colors.

A recipe for a pure pink red, published many years ago by Seger[19] and frequently referred to, is, in parts by weight: Pure, calcined tin oxide, 50; whiting or some form of commercially pure calcium carbonate, 25; and flint, 18.

These materials are ground together, then treated with a hot saturated solution of 3 parts of potassium bichromate and 4 parts of borax. The mass is dried, mixed intimately, and ignited strongly under oxidizing conditions. The calcine is finely ground and washed.

Berdel[20] has given the range of composition for the chrome-tin-pink color as follows:

0–1Na_2O	0–2B_2O_3	0–2SiO_2
0–1CaO		1–6SnO_2

In general, the presence of the calcium content gives the color a greater stability and a more fiery red color. Too much calcium oxide will destroy the pink color and a smaller quantity will develop violet and lilac shades. The lilac shades are not as stable at the high fire (porcelain) temperatures as the compositions containing greater calcium oxide.

Hurd[21] summarized chrome-tin colors at a symposium on ceramic colors. In this presentation, he stated that historians agree that chrome-tin colors date back to approximately the 13th century. Hurd pointed out that the color actually is due to tin oxide particles being coated with thin layers of chromic oxide. Chrome oxide vapors are deposited on SnO_2, which serves as a mordant. This makes a good mordant because it has a very low degree of solubility in nearly all glazes.

In practice, the color of the stain varies with the ratio of Cr_2O_3 to SnO_2, as illustrated in figure 14.1. Another essential component is CaO, which may comprise as much as 25% of the weight of the stain. Other ingredients also are used, as shown by the typical examples of table 14.1.

The reactive batch ingredients are thoroughly mixed and calcined at 2,300° to 2,400° F. It is required that the atmosphere be oxidizing. The mature stains are stable in air to temperatures as high as their original calcination.

In his review, Hurd[21] noted that SrO in the glaze is harmful to the

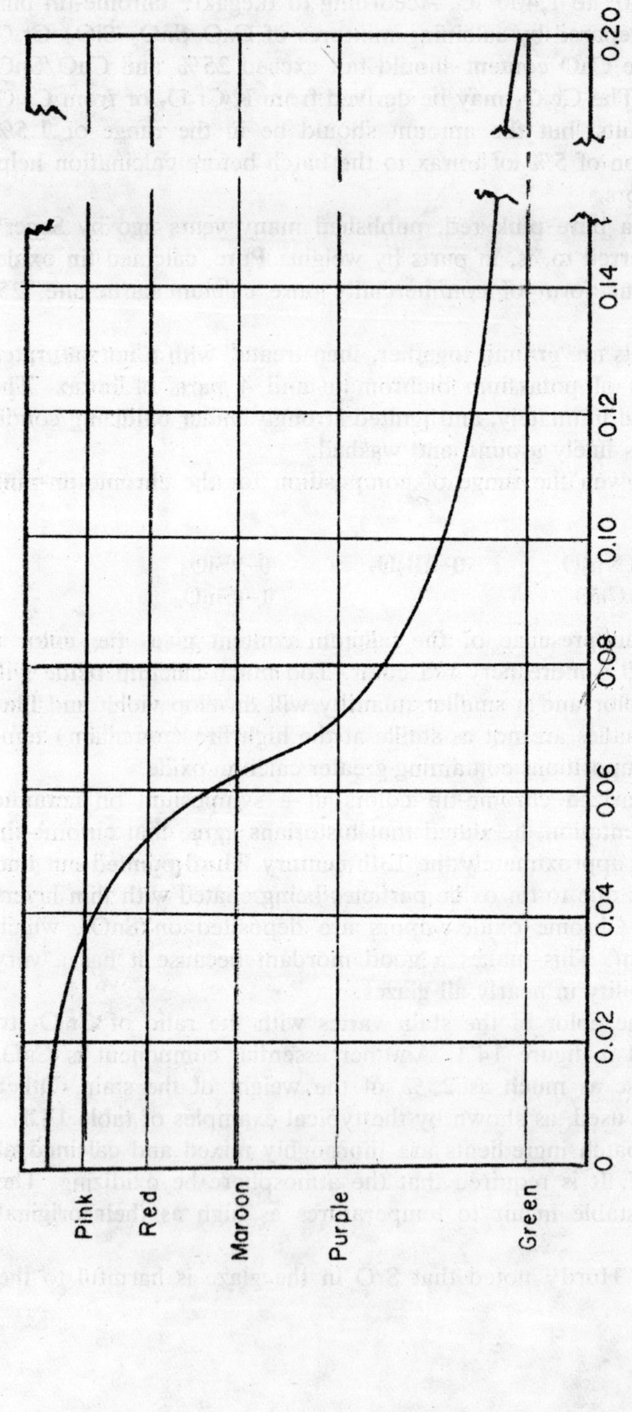

Figure 14.1. Schematic of the relation of $Cr_2O_3:SnO_2$ ratio to colors of chrome-tin pinks. Data after Hurd.[21]

Table 14.1. Examples of compositions (wt %) of some chrome-tin stains[21]

Oxide	*Pink*	*Bluish pink*	*Violet*
SnO_2	57.69	78.97	92.51
CaO	16.15	15.78	–
SiO_2	20.76	–	–
Cr_2O_3	1.79	1.75	0.43
K_2O	1.10	1.08	–
Na_2O	0.70	0.73	–
B_2O_3	1.73	1.69	5.18
PbO	–	–	0.96
Co_3O_4	–		0.92

stains, and that alkalies must be held at a minimum to avoid their solvent action. B_2O_3 is in much the same category in that regard.

The pink color can be damaged by the presence of ZnO in the glaze[22] and destroyed in glazes containing P_2O_5, Sb_2O_5, or sodium antimonate. This stain also is unstable in the presence of MgO. As with all tin-based stains, reducing conditions are lethal and the red can be completely destroyed, leaving only the white from SnO_2. Any reducing contaminants such as SiC, C, Fe, or metallic particles will destroy the color in the area of the contaminant. Zinc and aluminum are other materials that would lead to white specks.

Alumina and silica both have stabilizing influences and appear to reduce the solvent or bleaching action of deleterious constituents. They tend to counteract the solvent action of B_2O_3. Calcium oxide in the glaze also tends to counteract the ill effects of B_2O_3, particularly when the ratio of $CaO:B_2O_3$ can be at least 3:1.

Maroons are derived from stains having a favorable ratio of $CaO:SnO_2$ (see fig. 14.1) and in glazes essentially free of opacifier. This requires about 10% of stain and many glazes can tolerate concentrations as high as 20% without losing gloss.

Chrome-tins are reputed to be stable up to cone 12. However, it is difficult to control the shade of pastel pinks, and good temperature control is required with these pigments, as it is with others. When overfiring, leading to lighter shades is a problem, the addition of 1% or 2% or SnO_2 has been useful.

These stains are, and have for a long time, been very popular and form the basis of most moderate and high temperature reds and pinks.

Tumanov and Filippova[23] reinvestigated chrome-tin pink stains by replacing CaO successively with each other possible RO; by replacing SnO_2 with TiO_2 and ZrO_2; and SiO_2 with ZrO_2, TiO_2, and P_2O_5. They found nothing new of importance.

The fundamental reason for the color development in chrome-tin

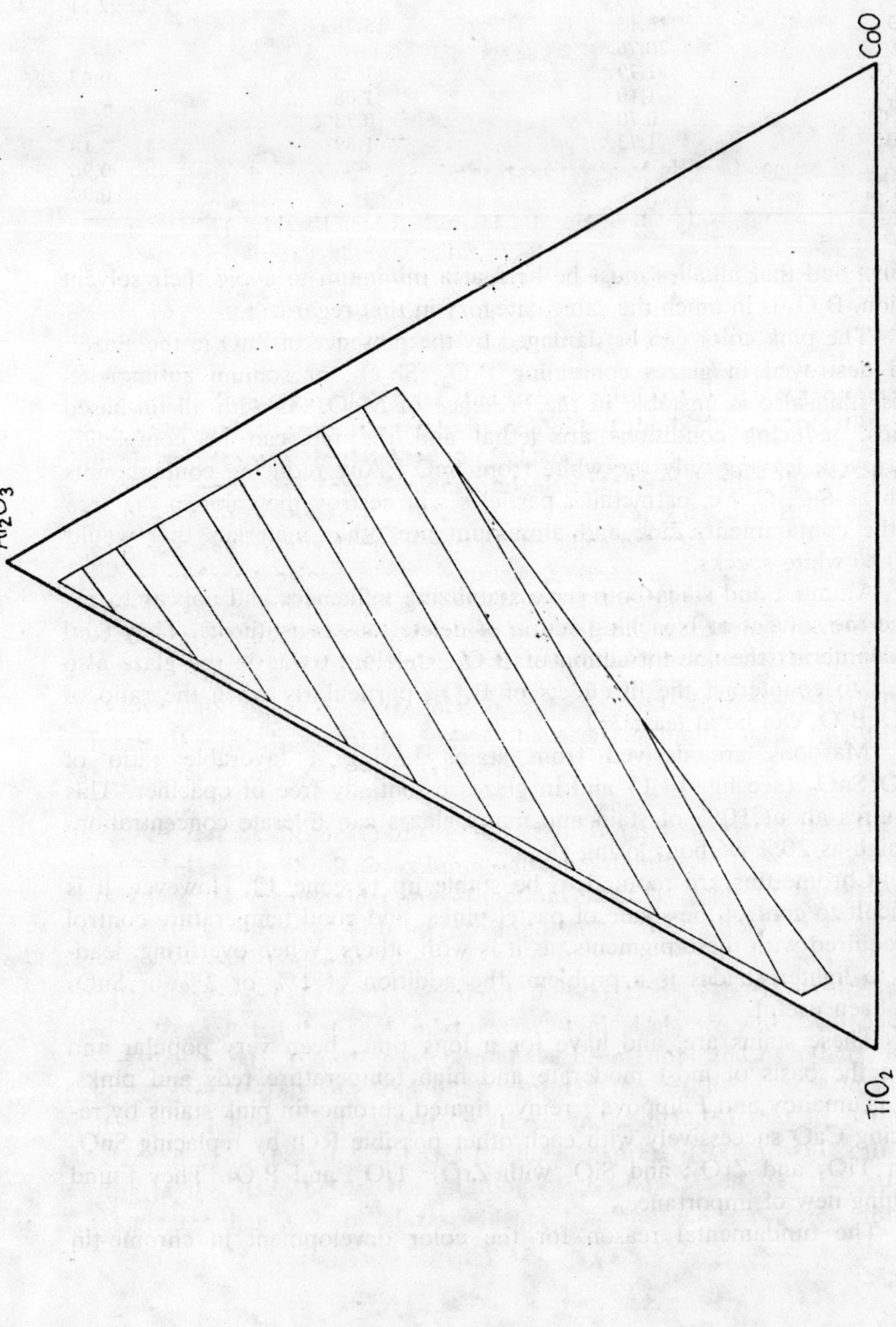

Figure 14.2. Area of compositions for stains in the system cobalt-alumina-titania.[6]

pinks was further studied by Tumanov and Filippova.[24] Their objective was to settle the old controversy of whether the color is due to thin film deposits of Cr_2O_3 or to chromium ions in the SnO_2 lattice. Their evidence still was inconclusive and they postulated that pinks have a crystal structure resembling that of sphene ($CaTiSiO_5$). The best color was developed in the composition: $0.4CaO \cdot 0.2SnO_2 \cdot 0.4SiO_2$ with 0.0023 mole of Cr_2O_3.

There seems to be a continuous series of solid solutions between chrome-tin pink and sphene ($CaO \cdot TiO_2 \cdot SiO_2$) according to Kato and Kanaoka.[25] This was observed in a series from sphene ($CaO \cdot TiO_2 \cdot SiO_2$) and a chrome tin base $CaO \cdot SnO_2 \cdot SiO_2$. It was concluded that the chrome-tin pink base is similar in structure to sphene, and that chrome-tin pink is a tin sphene stained by a small amount of chromium.

Using a fixed Cr_2O_3 content and a starting base of $CaO \cdot SnO_2 \cdot SiO_2$, part of the CaO was successively replaced by MgO, ZnO, CdO, PbO, SrO and BaO. All of these gave about the same reddish purple color with modest deviations characteristic of the RO replacement.[26]

Chrome-Tin-Cobalt

Orchid, lilac, violet, and purple shades are developed by including some cobalt in a chrome-tin base. A composition given as typical by Hurd[21] is as follows: SnO_2, 92.51; B_2O_3, 5.18; PbO, 0.96; Cr_2O_3, 0.43; Co_2O_3, 0.92, in weight percent, respectively. The stains are calcined to 2,300° to 2,400° F and can be stable to those temperatures. These stains should be used in high lime, low zinc glazes. The matrix glaze, ideally, should contain some SnO_2 in addition to the regular zircon opacifier.

Cobalt–Alumina–Titania

Stains ranging in color from green to blue, composed of CoO, Al_2O_3, and TiO_2 were patented by Chrest, Rummery, et al.[6] The field of compositions as indicated in figure 14.2 were mixed, calcined at 700° to 1,100° C, and ground to controlled particle size gradings.

Cobalt Blue

Cobalt in glazes makes blue, with only very minor exceptions. It is effective in almost any glaze from low-fire 010 glazes to high-fire porcelain. They are solution colors and not much affected by glaze compositions or firing atmosphere. However, where strong reduction persists, an iridescent film, on rare occasions, might develop.

Cobalt usually is used in prepared, calcined stains instead of direct additions of the oxide. The best vehicle may be Al_2O_3, which seems to strengthen and extend the blue. A well-balanced and well-calcined cobalt-alumina-silica stain performs well even in reducing conditions. Another disadvantage of using raw cobalt oxide is its tendency to throw small bubbles at high temperatures due to release of oxygen.

Cobalt stains can be used with any opacifier. Because cobalt is a solution color, opacifiers usually are used to provide good coverage. Zirconium opacifiers are preferred over all, because the presence or pick-up of chromium when tin is used will lead to a little lavender shade. Where there is no such danger, SnO_2 gives a softer hue.

Zinc oxide makes particularly good colors with cobalt. The most vivid blues, according to Mason,[27] are developed in the presence of ZnO. Very strong blues are obtained with stains of the cobalt-zinc and silicate variety. Mason[27] states that purple glazes should not contain zinc. Purples are based on the use of 80%–90% of chrome-tin crimson stain with 10% to 20% of a zinc-free cobalt blue stain. Mason[27] cautions that in using strong colors such as cobalt, variations in shades can result from sloppy weighing. Where a small portion of a strong stain is mixed with a large portion of opacifier, a small error in weighing can shift the shade. He advises that a larger portion of a weaker stain and less opacifier would be better formulation.

Another caution to use with cobalt stains is to carefully control the particle size reduction during grinding. He also advises that high quality scoops should be provided and each scoop reserved for a particular pigment. The scoop preferably should be smooth stainless steel, free of crevices, recesses, and cracks. There are obvious disadvantages to tin or wooden scoops.

Stewart[28] reported that more blue shades are used in glass enamels than any other color. The blue stains most commonly used are prepared by calcining mixtures of cobalt oxide with Al_2O_3, SiO_2, MgO, and ZnO. The stains should be prepared and calcined to promote a thorough degree of chemical reaction among the stain components.

The strong "royal blue" used since ancient times is $CoO–SiO_2$. It is a very strong color and is influenced in shade by the presence of BaO or ZnO. It is useful at all temperatures. Cobalt-silica stains are purplish blue.

Cobalt-silica-zinc ($CoO–SiO_2–ZnO$) stains contain about 40% of CoO and are strong dark blue, similar in hue to $CoO–SiO_2$ stains. They are said to be a little more resistant to running than those without ZnO.

The replacement of SiO_2 with Al_2O_3 gives a typical cobalt aluminate shade. This is a very strong stain but it is refractory. Straight cobalt-silica stains are easily dissolved by the glaze, whereas Co–Al blues are much more stable and have a highly desirable color. It is too refractory to form a bond with the body so cannot be used as an underglaze color. The cobalt aluminate colors do not have the strong purple shade typical of the silicate cobalts. Alumina may be the best vehicle for cobalt colors.

A highly stable pastel blue, $CoO–Al_2O_3–ZnO$, contains around 5% of cobalt. The cobalt-alumina-silica-zinc ($CoO–Al_2O_3–SiO_2–ZnO$) type of stain is a pale blue with only about 2% of Co_3O_4. The blue stain $CoO–Al_2O_3–SiO_2–SnO_2$ is popular in sanitary ware and contains about 20% of cobalt, making it a medium cobalt blue color. A well-balanced, well-calcined cobalt-alumina-silica stain performs well under a wide variety of conditions.

Cobalt Black

The usual black stains are produced by calcining a combination of the oxides of cobalt, chromium, and manganese. This combination yields a stable, neutral black color. A bluish black, used extensively, is prepared with a mixture of the oxides of cobalt, iron, and manganese, eliminating the Cr_2O_3. The cobalt-bearing black stains are satisfactory for either zincless or zinc-bearing glazes. The black stains are good through cone 11.

Cobalt-free Blacks

These were developed as a result of cobalt restrictions during World War II. There are two types of cobalt-free black stains. One for lower temperature service is prepared from a mixture of the oxides of chromium and copper, properly blended and calcined. These stains are restricted to applications not exceeding about 1,700° F.

The other type of cobalt-free black is based on the oxides of chromium and iron, or chromium, iron, and manganese. Some of the better ones approach $FeO \cdot Cr_2O_3$ in composition. They are stable through cone 12 but are restricted to zinc-free base glazes. In zinc-bearing glazes, the color becomes tan to brown.

Copper Turquoise

Copper-based stains furnish clean colors ranging from turquoise to green. A highly alkaline zincless glaze is required for the turquoise and the maximum firing temperature is from cone 1 to cone 5. Copper is not used much, since it lacks high temperature stability.

Copper oxide, CuO, acts as a strong flux in glazes, going into solution to form a part of the glass structure. The Cu^{++} ion makes green glazes, except in those very high in alkalies, where the color is turquoise blue.

Henry[5] pointed out that good green stains are prepared by calcining CuO with ZnO. Copper green glazes will be transparent unless an opacifier is used, but none of them interferes with copper green. Because copper tends to burn out at high temperatures, particularly at edges and thin places, it is not recommended for temperatures in excess of 2,200° F. The vaporization of copper, even though it has higher volatility at high temperatures than Cr_2O_3, does not create much of a contamination problem because of its weak coloring power.

Gold Pinks

Characteristic shades of rose, lavender, and purple are obtained with gold colors that are not obtained in any other way. Using delicate and precise techniques, gold-bearing organic preparations in conjunction with SnO_2 and Al_2O_3, good gold-color relies on the deposition of thin layers of gold on the SnO_2 or Al_2O_3 to give pigments of the desired shade. These colors mainly are used in overglaze decorations. They are very strong and are mixed with frit to extend the gold pigment and improve the accuracy in weigh-out. The colors are typified by the roses in floral overglaze decorations. The shade and tint are only slightly sensitive to heat treatment. The higher the firing temperature, the less is the blue component in the gold red color.

A whole series of reds may be had by the use of gold in the form of the purple of Cassius which is prepared from the trichloride of the metal. A number of methods of preparation in the wet way have been described in the literature, and it is possible to make the color by the dry method by fusing the metals gold, silver, and tin in borax to form an homogeneous alloy. The borax is removed by solution in water; the silver is dissolved by treatment with dilute nitric acid and the residuum will be the gold purple.[29] In the preparation by either wet or dry methods care must be taken to remove all trace of nitric acid from the purple of Cassius.

Gold purples may be prepared also by precipitating the metal from a solution of gold trichloride upon magnesia or alumina. The precipitate is washed, dried, and calcined at a red heat.

Purple of Cassius long has been a reliable stain for producing red, pink, and ruby. According to Kato,[30] it can be prepared from gold salts by the reducing action of hydrazine or hydroquinone followed by the coagulation of that sol. Coagulation agents may be (*a*) stannic ammonium chloride, (*b*) zirconyl chloride, (*c*) ceric ammonium nitrate, or (*d*) bismuth nitrate. The purpose of the coagulating reagents was to hydrolyze the solution and form a gold-bearing precipitate. When (*a*) or (*c*) is used, hydrolysis is immediate, but with reagents (*b*) or (*d*) coagulation does not occur until the system is acidified with sulfuric acid.

The color of the purple of Cassius depends largely upon the choice of the flux and the coagulators. Coagulation reagents (*a*) and (*b*) give reddish purple, (*c*) a bluish tint, and (*d*) a purple tint to the final gold color.

Kato[31] said that a better reddish hue is obtained due to the addition of little silver to the starting compositions. An excess, however, causes a yellow cast. This may partially be circumvented by adding SnO_2, ZrO_2 or Al_2O_3 to the flux comprised of $PbO–KNaO–B_2O_3–SiO_2$.

Lead Yellows

LEAD CHROMATE. Lead chromate makes a very bright yellow color, up to about cone 08. Above that the compound dissociates and the green Cr_2O_3 becomes the dominating coloring agent. A theoretical composition is $7PbO \cdot 2CrO_3$. This compound melts at 854° C and decomposes at 830° C. A pigment, generally known as chrome yellow or Leipzig yellow, has the composition $PbO \cdot CrO_3$ and decomposes at 600° C. A basic lead chromate, $2PbO \cdot CrO_3$, red in color, called American vermillion, Chinese scarlet, and chrome red, is basic lead chromate and widely used for anti-corrosive base coats for steel. In the system $PbO–PbO \cdot CrO_3$ there are four binary compounds; all have congruent melting points in the range of 815° to 920° C.[32]

LEAD ANTIMONY YELLOW. Naples yellow has as its essential ingredients the oxides of lead and antimony. Varying shades from lemon yellow to orange yellow are obtained by varying the proportions of lead oxide and antimony oxide and by adding modifying oxides. Chief among the modifying oxides are: ZnO, SnO_2, CaO, Fe_2O_3, Al_2O_3, and TiO_2 (chrome-titanium yellow).

Naples yellow is a lively color and is stable to cone 04. Under particularly favorable circumstances it can be used as high as cone 02. These stains are used in any type of low-firing glazes but are brightest when used in high lead, zinc-bearing glazes.

King[33] modified a lead antimoniate stain with CeO_2 and Al_2O_3 to improve the high temperature stability. The calcined stain was comprised of the following: PbO, 1 mole; Sb_2O_5, 1 mole; CeO_2, 1% to 15%; and Al_2O_3, 1.5% to 15%.

Antimony yellow stains for ceramic applications always include, in addition to the lead and antimony oxides, one or more secondary oxides. Chief among these are ZnO, CeO_2, Al_2O_3, Fe_2O_3, and SnO_2. In a typical stain described by Kato and Kanaoka[34] the molar proportions were

$2PbO + 1Sb_2O_5 + 1(ZnO, Al_2O_3$ and/or $Fe_2O_3)$. Where CaO or SnO_2 were used, they were used in smaller proportions than the above. Antimony yellow is comprised of solid solutions of the pyrochlore structure regardless of composition.

Binary Manganese Colors

Manganese-alumina pink stains have been in commercial production for some time. They are good for overglaze, in-glaze, and underglaze. A recent innovation was patented by Eugen Meyer-Simon and Herbert Mann.[35] The batch compositions and some critical constants are given in table 14.2.

These are strong pink shades and are stable to cone 12. The stability of this color depends upon the components in the matrix glaze. To get a clean color, a high alumina, zinc-free glaze is required. The stain is obtained by calcining mixtures of MnO_2 or $MnCO_3$ with Al_2O_3 or $Al_2O_3 \cdot 3HO$. Minor additions of alkali and alkaline earth salts with or without lead salts are used as mineralizers. The calcination is done at 700° to 1,350° C in an oxidizing atmosphere.

Rich brown stains are produced by roasting preferred proportions of manganese and iron-bearing reagents. The color closely resembles the brown color of Albany slip.

Selenium Colors

Bright red, yellow and orange colors can be obtained by using cadmium-sulfur-selenium compositions useful at firing temperatures nominally not exceeding cone 010. These are widely used in art glazes. Cadmium sulfosemenide pigments are most successful when used in glazes specifically designed for their use. Lead oxide has a tendency to react with these pigments and because of this, some effort from time to time has been directed toward the development of suitable lead-free bases. None of the leadless frits, however, have yet proved entirely satisfactory. The use of about 5% of CdO either in the frit or as a mill addition greatly buffers these glazes and renders them satisfactory. Sometimes as little as 1% or 2% of mill-added CdO will bring satisfactory results.

Draft or ventilation in the kiln is important to the development of consistent Cd–S–Se glazes. This probably is largely due to the need to remove the organic vehicles used in the decorating of artware. It is very important to maintain good ventilation in the range generally called the water-smoking zone (300°–500° F). Lack of good draft leads to some decomposition of the pigments and to formation of a brown black or even a dirty translucent gray. This can happen even on a part or patch of a

Table 14.2. Batch composition and critical properties of four manganese-alumina pink stains.[35]

	Percent by wt.			
Example number	*1*	*2*	*3*	*4*
$MnCO_3$	11.49	11.49	11.49	–
MnO_2	–	–	–	19.79
$Al(OH)_3$	271.28	404.40	671.95	683.65
Moles of Al_2O_3 per mole of MnO	17.4	25.9	43.1	43.8
NaF	8.42	15.4	8.31	14.22
NaCl	–	21.82	–	–
$CaCl_2$	7.50	–	7.47	–
$CaCO_3$	–	–	–	10.25
Moles of mineralizers per mole of MnO	1.7	3.7	1.7	2.7
Firing temp, deg C	1050	1050	1050	1050
Color intensity in glaze	strong	strong	med. strong	strong

glazed surface, the discoloration being cured when adequate ventilation is supplied.

CONSTITUTION AND COLOR OF PIGMENTS. True red colors are produced in silicate melts by copper ruby, uranium-bearing compounds, and the family of Cd–S–Se pigments. Other colors in the red family are gold ruby, Fe_2O_3, chrome-tin-pink stains, chrome-alumina pinks, and a few other rare occurrences.

Eroles and Friedberg[36] showed that cadmium sulfide and cadmium selenide form a continuous solid solution series of the substitutional type. The colors of different solid solutions are shown in table 14.3.

PREPARATION. Yamauchi and Endo[37] examined some cadmium-selenium reds and found them to be constituted of solid solutions of alpha (CdS and CdSe). An increase in the concentration of CdSe in the solid

Table 14.3. Colors of CdS-CdSe solid solutions[36]

Compositions, mole %		
CdSe	*CdS*	*Colors*
12.6	87.4	Orange
20.0	80.0	Orange red
36.0	64.0	Light red
43.0	57.0	Dark red
49.0	51.0	Maroon
54.0	45.5	Dark maroon

solution lead to a darkening of the color. The colors were prepared as follows:

$$CdCO_3 + S + 2\ Se \text{ roasted 15 min at } 550°C$$

or

$$CdCO_3 + S + 14\% \text{ to } 20\% \text{ of Se, 20 min at } 450°–650°\ C$$

Both gave good reds.

HIGHER-TEMPERATURE STAINS. Cadmium-selenium pigments are fairly stable up to 1,700° or 1,800° F and relatively insoluble in aqueous and organic solvents; some colors ranging from orange to dark red were developed by Kenworthy, Goda, and Golland.[38] Mixtures of CdS, Se, and a secondary component of a clay, fuller's earth or diatomaceous earth, were calcined at 1,100° F for 1¼ to 3½ hours. A typical composition was reported as 1.25 to 9 parts of CdS, one part of Se and 10% to 40% of the earthy component.

Spinels

One family of pigments and stains is based on colored spinels. These are very stable and have the general formula of $RO \cdot R_2O_3$. The RO member may be MgO, ZnO, NiO, CoO, CdO, MnO, or FeO. The sesquioxide may be Cr_2O_3, Al_2O_3, or Fe_2O_3. Well-known examples of spinels are $FeO \cdot Fe_2O_3$ or Fe_3O_4 (magnetite), which is black, and $FeO \cdot Cr_2O_3$ chromite, also black. Examples of some of the colors among common spinels are:

$NiO \cdot Cr_2O_3$—a moss green	$CdO \cdot Cr_2O_3$—a light green
$NiO \cdot Al_2O_3$—a sky blue	$FeO \cdot Al_2O_3$—ocher yellow
$MgO \cdot Fe_2O_3$—Indian red	$CdO \cdot Fe_2O_3$—reddish brown

PREPARATION. One method sometimes used for the preparation of spinel colors is to mix soluble reagent salts, such as sulfates, nitrates, etc. in solution in stochiometric proportions to form the desired $RO \cdot R_2O_3$. These would be precipitated with ammonia, washed, dried, and calcined. A method that may be preferred is to thoroughly mix and grind the oxides or their salts, then consolidate into crucibles and calcine to form the spinels by solid state reaction. The calcined product then is carefully ground (and, if necessary, washed) to a predetermined particle size distribution.

BLACKS. There are two major types of black stains. They are (*a*) calcined mixtures of dark-colored oxides with cobalt oxide and (*b*) chrome-iron blacks. The chrome-iron stains are useful only in zinc-free glazes, but the better cobalt-bearing stains work in either zincless or zinc-bearing glazes.

The development of a surface scum having a metallic sheen on glaze surfaces may be a common development accompanying the use of black stains. This is most prevalent in highly fluxed, corrosive glazes. It is not prevalent in well-balanced glazes, the sensitivity to kiln gases being characteristic of improperly adjusted glaze compositions.

The most common and widely used black stains are basically spinels, with cubic structures of composition, $RO \cdot R_2O_3$. Chromite, $FeO \cdot Cr_2O_3$ and magnetite, $FeO \cdot Fe_2O_3$ are examples. The complex blacks usually have multiple RO and R_2O_3 species.

UNCONVENTIONAL SPINELS. The spinel structure forms a very large family, indeed. Some of them that have been prepared and used as ceramic pigments were described by Yamaguchi, et al.[39] Some of these and their colors are listed in table 14.4. There are others.

One reason for interest in spinels as pigments is that, as a class, they are highly stable, mechanically, chemically, and pyrochemically. Spinels are hard and not too reactive. A very wide range of colors is possible. They have, as a class, high coefficients of thermal expansion. Although spinels usually are thought of as binary compounds, they are by no means restricted to that. Very many spinels are polycomponent in composition.

Brilliant pigments having a spinel structure were found in the systems $CoO–MgO–TiO_2–SnO_2$, $NiO–ZnO–TiO_2–SnO_2$, $CoO–NiO–ZnO–TiO_2–SnO_2$ and $CoO–ZnO–Al_2O_3–Cr_2O_3$ by Ohtsuka.[40]

In the CoO–MgO titanium-tin system, brilliant colors ranging in hue from greenish blue to blue were found. In the second and third systems,

Table 14.4. Colors of unconventional spinels[39]

System	*Color*
$CoO\text{-}MgO\text{-}Al_2O_3$	blue
$CoO\text{-}NiO\text{-}MgO\text{-}Al_2O_3$	blue
$NiO \cdot Al_2O_3$	blue
$CuO \cdot Al_2O_3$	brown; blue above 1,100° C
$CoO \cdot MgO \cdot 2Cr_2O_3$	green
$CoO \cdot NiO \cdot 2Cr_2O_3$	green
$CoO \cdot ZnO \cdot 2Cr_2O_3$	green
$CoO \cdot 3MgO \cdot 2Cr_2O_3 \cdot 2Al_2O_3$	green
$NiO\text{-}CoO\text{-}MgO\text{-}SnO_2$	blue; unstable
$NiO\text{-}CoO\text{-}ZnO\text{-}SnO_2$	green
$ZnO\text{-}Cr_2O_3\text{-}Al_2O_3$	pink
$MgO\text{-}Cr_2O_3\text{-}Al_2O_3$	brown; unstable

yellow greens to bluish greens existed. In the fourth system, greens predominated in high Cr_2O_3 and blues in the high CoO compositions.

Gray Stains

Of the several possible sources for gray glazes the most common gray stains are: Zirconium–cobalt–nickel; tin–cobalt–nickel; and tin–antimony. Gray also is prepared by mixing opacifiers with chromite. In times past, gray glazes were prepared by adding simple oxides or even platinum powder to glaze batches.

COBALT-BEARING GRAY STAINS. Many commercial gray stains contain cobalt. Because zinc oxide intensifies the blue from cobalt, these stains could not be used for gray colors in zinc-bearing glazes. However, if the ZnO content is less than 3–4%, satisfactory grays can be obtained. In a similar way, because PbO is such a powerful flux, there is a tendency for the glaze to dissolve or decompose the stains. In case the stain contains a component that produces strong solution colors, such as nickel or cobalt, the resulting color will show a tendency toward brown or blue. All strong fluxes have this tendency, such as KNaO and B_2O_3. At high temperature, BaO, SrO, and CaO are similarly reactive but the effects are milder than those of PbO or the alkalies. These statements do not apply to normally well-balanced glazes, but are applicable where these corrosive components are unusually high.

Votava[41] pointed out that in zinc-titanium glazes, it is particularly difficult to prepare stable gray glazes. He reported that pyrochemical reactions between cobalt and titania yield an unstable greenish product.

TIN-ANTIMONY. For low-to-medium firing-temperature glazes, tin-antimony gray stains are useful. These are only used in opaque glazes and SnO_2 seems the preferable choice.

Pastel gray shades are difficult to develop and to control. There is a tendency to use strong pigments and dilute them with opacifiers. Although more expensive, it is technically preferable to use a larger proportion of a lighter colored stain. It usually requires the order of 10% or so of good opacifier and very long milling times.

DILUTED BLACKS. Gray glazes can be prepared from black stains by incorporating small quantities of it along with adequate opacification.

MOLYBDENUM-ALUMINUM. A gray pigment can be made by calcining at 1,300° C a mixture of $92.4Al(OH)_3$, 30ZnO, and 13.6 parts of

$(NH_4)_2MoO_4$. These pigments and their preparation were described in a French patent.[42]

ZIRCONIUM GRAYS. Zirconium grays and their preparation were described in a patent by John Olby.[43] Silica and zirconia in equal molar proportions, together with secondary reagents of alkali halides and a cobalt salt, were mixed and heated at 650° to 1,150° C. After being calcined, the products were thoroughly leached to remove water soluble salts.

CHROME-IRON. Excellent black and gray stains are derived from the simple chrome-iron system. The resulting stains are highly stable and result in a minimum of defects such as metallic scum, eggshelling, and pinholes. Chromite blacks have a tendency to show a brownish cast in sunlight. Zinc oxide in the matrix glaze also has a tendency to create brown.

Tin–vanadium yellows

There are two common types of tin-vanadium yellow.[44] The weaker one is a reaction product of essentially SnO_2 and V_2O_5. When a small amount of pure TiO_2 is added, the lemon yellow of the first type is replaced by a stronger yellow with an increase in the red component.

During the earlier history of tin-vanadium stains, their use sometimes was accompanied by defects in the glaze called dimples and welts. These defects were caused by unreacted vanadium oxide. Long ago, through more thorough reactions and leaching to remove soluble matter, this disadvantage became a thing of the past.

Lemon-yellow colors are produced in all types of glazes with tin-vanadium stains. This type of stain is sensitive to particle size and can be damaged by overgrinding. They are sensitive to reducing atmospheres. The suppliers recommend that tin-vanadium stains not be used in glazes containing Cr_2O_3 but they are stable in contact with chrome-iron-zinc browns and chrome-alumina pinks, particularly in glazes containing zinc and magnesium. The development of the chrome-tin pink blush is inhibited by the presence of both zinc and magnesium and by glazes fairly fluid at maturity.

The color of a tin-vanadium stain is compared[44] with that of tin-vanadium-titanium and with praseodymium-zirconium yellows in figure 14.3.

Zirconia-base Stains

WITHOUT SILICA. A zirconia-silver pink was developed by Illiff.[45] The batches for compounding the stain contained 20 to 90 parts of decompos-

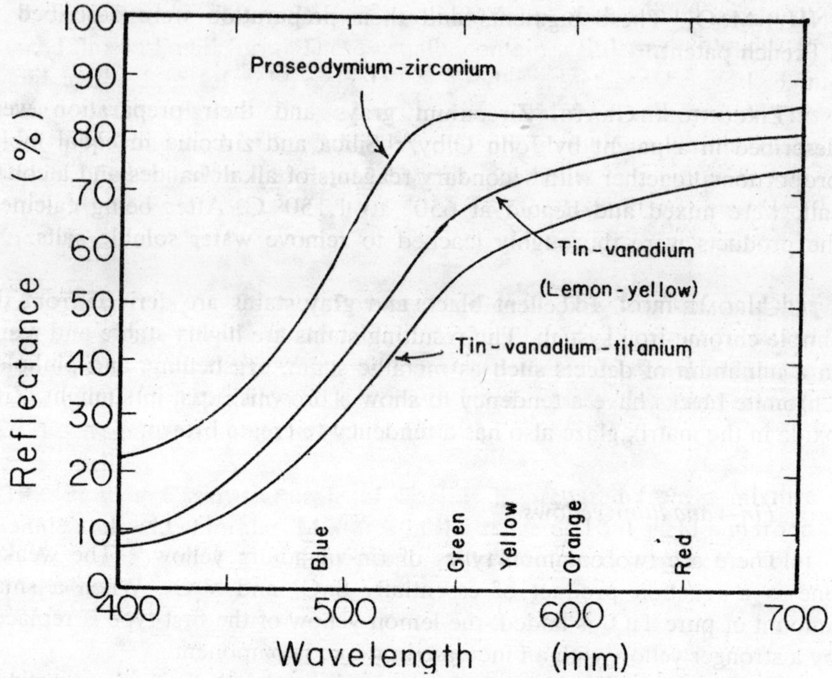

Figure 14.3. Tin-vanadium and praseodymium yellow stains.[44]

able zirconium salts, such as hydrates, carbonates, acetates, etc., 0.2 to 10 parts of silver-bearing salts and 7 to 50% of ammonium or zirconium fluoride.

Zirconia (ZrO_2), V_2O_5, and TiO_2, when combined in preferred proportions, result in rich brown stains. These pigments are described by King and Tesar[46] as developing good yellow colors when used as a pigment in ceramic bodies.

The incorporation of indium into the zirconium-vanadium type of stain, which produced indium orange, was initiated by Weyl.[47] He modified a zircon-vanadium stain with In and Y and mixtures of them. The preferred compositional ranges in terms of component oxides were 90.4% to 95% ZrO_2, 3.1% to 7.0% V_2O_5, and 0.1% to 1.6% of In_2O_3 or Y_2O_3. The calcining temperature was in the range of 1,250° to 1,375° C in a neutral or weakly reducing atmosphere. The colors developed were tannish yellow but better results were to be had with the indium than the yttrium. These stains differ from most other zirconium stains. In these, large proportions of free silica are to be avoided. The stronger yellows result from the use of high purity ZrO_2. A strong orange yellow was derived from the calcination of: 94% ZrO_2, 5% NH_4VO_3, and 1% of In_2O_3.

Mixtures of ZrO_2 and V_2O_5 without silica, heated to 1,000° C result in powders that vary from unreacted mixtures of ZrO_2 and V_2O_5 to complete conversion to zirconium pyrovanadate. The characteristic blue or green does not materialize. Good ivory to yellow stains were prepared by Earl,[48] however at 2,550° F.

Stains ranging in color from ivory through yellow were prepared by J. A. Earl, who applied for a patent on Aug. 23, 1944, that was granted March 23, 1948. Mixtures of 80% to 99% pure ZrO_2 with 1 to 20 parts of ammonium metavanodate were calcined at about 2,550° F. A few weeks later, a patent on zirconium-vanadium stains was issued to Seabright.[49] Seabright's stains were green and blue. The green pigments were obtained in the following composition ranges, in parts by weight:

55–80ZrO_2
3–17V_2O_5
55–10SiO_2

} The mixed reagents were calcined at 700°–900°C for 1 to 8 hours.

Blue pigments are prepared from the same materials to which has been added 0.5% to 5% of alkali, preferably as the fluoride.

Some typical compositions as given by Seabright and Draker[50] are shown in table 14.5. These are nominal compositions for zirconium yellow compared with zircon blue and zirconium-indium orange. Comparison of their spectrophotometer curves are given in figure 14.3.

Marquis and Carpenter[51] introduced an innovation on zirconium-iron pink. They prepared a thorough mixture of ZrO_2 (98% purity, 1 to 6 micron) 50% to 75%; minus 325 mesh SiO_2, 13% to 40%; alkali silicofluoride mineralizer, 2% to 10%; and Fe_2O_3, 2.5% to 25%.

ZIRCONIA-SILICA-VANADIA BASE. In 1948, Seabright[49,52] disclosed the discovery of zirconium-vanadium blue pigments. This has proven to be

Table 14.5. Nominal components in zirconium-vanadium stains[50]

Components	*Blue**	*Yellow*	*Orange**
Zirconium oxide	62.0	95.0	94.0
Silica	30.0	–	–
Ammonium vanadate	5.0	5.0	5.0
Sodium fluoride	3.0	–	–
Indium oxide	–	–	1.0
Other elements	0.0–2.0	0.0–5.0	0.0–5.0
Calcining temp °C	750–900	1200–1400	1200–1400
Mean diameters of particles of stain, μ	2.5	2.5	2.5
Leached to remove soluble vanadium	yes	yes	yes

*Harshaw patent

one of the most significant contributions to color technology in several decades.

At the outset, Seabright established that the base of the pigment was $ZrO_2 \cdot SiO_2$. This phase resulted from the pyrochemical reaction of the starting zirconia- and silica-bearing reagents. He also knew that the reaction product of $ZrO_2 + SiO_2$ in the presence of a few percent of V_2O_5 was green. If soda or potash were present, the calcined product was blue.

The production and use of zirconium-vanadium pigments has become widespread, indeed, as have research investigations on the system. Some details relating to the origin of the blue color remain unexplained. Booth and Peel[53] did show that the valence of the vanadium was plus four. Nothing was established regarding its location in the lattice nor concerning the possible existence and placement of V^{3+} or V^{5+}. The critical role of alkali halides, such as NaF, also remained obscure. It was theoretically possible for V^{4+}, with its ionic radius of 0.63, to occupy a silicon or a zirconium site, or to be present interstitially.

The high temperature reactions in the system ZrO_2–SiO_2–V_2O_5 were studied by Cini,[54,55] Matkovich and Corbett,[56] and by Tudo and Tridot.[57]

These people showed that a reaction took place between V_2O_5 and ZrO_2 as low as 730° C, which in turn combined with silica to form zircon, occluding some vanadium in the lattice. Several additives besides V_2O_5 were shown to have varying degrees of effectiveness. Tudo and Tridot[57] found a new blue phase in the V-O system: $VO_2 \cdot V_2O_5$. The valency and polarization in this phase may have similar valencies, coordinations, and polarizations to that found in blue zircon-vanadium pigments.

Demiray, Nath, and Hummel[58] concluded that V^{4+} is solely responsible for the color. They also confirmed the existence of V^{4+} in the ZrO_8 position in the zircon structure. They further concluded: (*a*) "Flux additions increased the solubility and thermal stability of V^{4+} in zircon but did not affect valence and coordination," and (*b*) ". . . V^{4+} is possibly the only oxidation state of vanadium occurring in zircon-vanadium blue."

Zirconium-vanadium Greens. Seabright[49,52] prepared green stains by calcining mixtures of ZrO_2, SiO_2, V_2O_5, and some auxilliary reagents. The broad ranges cited in the patent were 35% to 80% ZrO_2, 55% to 10% SiO_2, and 3% to 17% of V_2O_5. The mixtures were calcined at 700° to 900° C. When 0.5% to 5% of alkali, preferably as the fluoride, was added to the above mixture, the resulting pigment was blue. These colors could not be prepared by the reaction of zircon ($ZrO_2 \cdot SiO_2$) and a vanadium salt.

Greens result from the calcination of ZrO_2 and V_2O_5 in the presence of silica. With no silica the color is yellow. True greens develop with higher concentrations of SiO_2 until the turquoise shades develop. Zirconium-vanadium greens are good for pastel shades. They are stable with respect to firing temperature, glaze composition, and firing atmosphere. They may be successfully blended with other stable stains such as tin-vanadium yellow.

When appropriate mixtures of ZrO_2, SiO_2 and V_2O_5 are heated to at least 730° C, a green product is formed. By X-ray diffraction, it can be established that the reaction product is zircon, with some vanadium in the lattice. When the reaction is essentially complete, the pattern may show zircon and free V_2O_5 only. The excess V_2O_5 can be removed by leaching with water and, as the free vanadium oxide is washed out, the color slowly changes from green to light blue. Pure zircon is colorless, but the vanadium-bearing leached product is blue. The X-ray diffraction pattern of the blue stain shows only zircon with the spacings similar to those for zircon, but differing slightly in size. The optimum proportion of V_2O_5 is about 4% or in the range of 3%–5% of V_2O_5 and 97%–95% of $ZrO_2 \cdot SiO_2$.

Upon prolonged heating the vanadium-bearing zircon slowly rejects V_2O_5 to eventually yield zircon + V_2O_5. The green color appears to result from a mixture of vanadium, zircon, and a yellow V_2O_5 component.

ZIRCONIUM-VANADIUM TURQUOISE. The calcination of mixtures of ZrO_2, SiO_2, and V_2O_3 produce turquoise-zircon when all of the vanadium is present in the tetravalent form and green zircon when part of the vanadium is pentavalent (according to Marchesini and Ramos.[59] The tetravalent form is encouraged by the presence of sodium fluoride. The lattice spacings in both green and turquoise zircon are smaller than in pure zircon. It appears, from this, that vanadium replaces zirconium in the zircon structure.

ZIRCONIUM-VANADIUM BLUE. Blue pigments were prepared by Seabright[60] by calcining zirconia–silica–vanadium reagents in the absence of oxygen at 600° to 1,000° C. Under these circumstances, blues were secured within the following limits of composition: 30% to 80% ZrO_2, 10% to 55% SiO_2, 1% to 12% V_2O_5, 0.25% to 8% KNaO, 0.25% to 5% F_2 and 0.25% to 8% Cl_2 or Br_2.

Zirconium-vanadium blues also were prepared by Kato[61] by sintering the following mixture at 1,100° C: ZrO_2, 60 parts, SiO_2, 40 parts; NH_4VO_3, 10 parts; and NaCl, 10 parts. The calcined product was found to be zircon ($ZrO_2 \cdot SiO_2$) with V in solid solution. Kato observed that V_2O_5 is an excellent catalyst-mineralizer for the solid state reaction of $ZrO_2 + SiO_2 \rightarrow ZrO_2 \cdot SiO_2$. In addition, he found it essential in the formation of the blue solid solutions to have present as secondary reagents alkali carbonates, halides or sulfates, and especially alkali borates or phosphates.

These secondary reagents seemed to be essential to the development of the required solid solutions by low-temperature sintering. When Na_2CO_3 is used, a true blue color is developed, but NaCl gives a Turkish blue or greenish blue.

Blue and pink pigments were prepared by Gascon[62] by calcining a mixture of one mole of sodium silico zirconate, one mole of zirconium sulfate, and silica plus coloring and mineralizing agents. He found sodium sulfate in excess to be an effective mineralizer. These reagents, when well mixed, were calcined at 900° C, followed by thorough washing with water to remove the excess sodium sulfate.

Excellent blue pigments were obtained when:

$$\frac{(NH_4)V_2O_5}{ZrO_2 + SiO_2} = 1.5\% \text{ to } 2.5\%$$

Pink stains resulted when:

$$\frac{FeSO_4}{ZrO_2 + SiO_2} = 10\% \text{ to } 15\%$$

and calcined in the presence of a halogen.

MISCELLANEOUS Zr-V STAINS. A variety of Zr-V stains have been prepared. They include: (*a*) zirconium-vanadium, (*b*) hafnium-vanadium, (*c*) zirconium-vanadium with secondary P_2O_5, (*d*) zirconium-vanadium with secondary MnO_2, (*e*) zirconium-vanadium stains in which the vanadium is replaced by Mn, Cr, Pr, and terbium, and stains based on zirconium and chromium with a variety of secondary elements. These have been reviewed by Booth and Peel[53] along with the effects of glaze composition on the colors imported by these stains.

A field of stains developed by Morris and Tesar[63] consisted essentially of the oxides of Zr, Sn, Si, and V. The broad scope of effective proportions was as follows: ZrO_2, 30 to 85; SiO_2, 10 to 65; SnO_2, 5 to 50, and V_2O_5, 1 to 5 percent respectively. When calcined in the range of 1,275° to 1,375° C good green pigments developed; temperatures less than 1,275° C resulted in increased bluish cast, but a yellowish cast developed with calcination temperatures in excess of 1,375° C. One typical starting formulation was ZrO_2, 52.3; SnO_2, 23.8; SiO_2, 19.0; and NH_4VO_3, 4.9 parts by weight respectively. When used in a zincless matrix, this pigment produced a green glaze.

Another variation was patented by Jamieson.[64] In addition to the usual reagents, she incorporated the oxides of Zn, Fe, Sn, Cr, and Al.

A wide variety of starting reagents has been used in the preparation of vanadium-zirconium stains. For example, Olby[65] used the following:

ZrO_2, silica, ammonium vanadate, sodium fluoride, and water soluble phosphate. His objective was to try to insure complete conversion of the ZrO_2 and SiO_2 into the compound $ZrO_2 \cdot SiO_2$, having in interstitial solution sufficient vanadium to produce colored zircon.

Pink pigments were prepared by Gascon[66] from a batch composed of basic zirconium phosphate, ferrous phosphate, sodium silica zirconate, and silica. Ferrous sulfate in a proportion calculated to yield 7 weight percent of iron was recommended. The batch was calcined at 700° to 950° C and residual sodium sulfate removed by leaching with water.

Zirconium-iron pink stains were discussed in a paper by John Ray[67] particularly in regard to their behavior in various base glazes. He advised that the stains are stable in glazes opacified with either ZnO or zircon. The ZrFe stains may be blended with other stains with reasonably predictable results.

Iron zirconium coral pinks were added to the zirconium-based stains by Seabright.[68] In constitution, the stain was zircon ($ZrO_2 \cdot SiO_2$), with Fe in the lattice. The color was produced from ZrO_2 and SiO_2 reagents reacting in the solid state to form zircon. In terms of component oxides, the calcined stains of interest were in the following range of proportions, in weight percentage: 30 to 80, ZrO_2; 15 to 55, SiO_2; and 0.25 to 25, Fe_2O_3. In the reacted stain, about 40% of the oxides were in the form of zircon ($ZrO_2 \cdot SiO_2$), containing around 0.25% of iron oxide in solid solution.

The stain may be extensively modified by using fluorides as illustrated by one patented by Olby.[69] He made it by calcining mixtures of the following, in parts by weight, with ZrO_2: 48.8 to 50 SiO_2 and 1.8 to 9 NaF with 0.5 to 10 CrF_3, 1.0 to 15 FeF_3, 5 to 20 CeF_3, 5 to 20 NdF_3, 0.5 to 15 TbF_3, or 5 to 20 ErF_3.

PRASEODYMIUM YELLOW. Seabright[70] developed a new yellow pigment containing praseodymium as a critical ingredient. As described in his patent, the broad limits of composition were: ZrO_2, 35–80; Pr_6O_{11}, 0.5 to 10; SiO_2, 10 to 55; KNaO, 0.25 to 8; F_2, 0.25 to 3; and halides, other than F_2, 0.025 to 8 in weight percentages.

Praseodymium yellow stains are produced by adding about 5% of praseodymium oxide to an equal molar mixture of ZrO_2 and SiO_2 (in the proportions of zircon). When the mixture is calcined, zircon, containing a dispersion of Pr_6O_{11}, is the result. It is something like the zirconium-vanadium turquoise, except praseodymium oxide is present instead of vanadium. With praseodymium, the yellow color is not sensitive to the $ZrO_2:SiO_2$ ratio. A peculiarity of this stain is that, in glazes, the intensity of color increases with concentration up to about 5% and further addition does not influence the color.

This stain is expensive; not only is praseodymium oxide costly, but the ZrO_2 used must be of high purity.

The praseodymium colors are cleaner and brighter than the Sn-V yellows[44] and as pigments are about equivalent in strength. The colors are compared in figure 14.3. The praseodymium stains are useful in a very wide variety of glazes ranging from cone 02 to cone 12 and are not as sensitive to reducing gases as the tin stains. No trouble has been reported as to deleterious effects of particular glaze components.

The stain should be used with zircon. Its presence seems to greatly reduce any tendency of the stain to dissolve. Two percent to 3% of zircon is helpful but still more does not lend further stability. Zinc oxide can be used to increase stability in the absence of zircon.

Weber[71] obtained a patent on a process for preparing a praseodymium yellow stain. He mixed very fine zircon powder with less than about 1% of a sodium salt and calcined the mixture at about 1,000° ± 100° C. To the powdered calcined product he added water to form a slurry. A praseodymium reagent, such as Pr_6O_{11}, was incorporated into the slurry and the alkali component neutralized with a mineral acid, causing it to stiffen. The stain then was formed by calcining this mixture at 850°–1,300° C.

Zirconium-praseodymium yellow pigments in a silica-free system were described in a patent issued in 1961 to Seabright.[72,74] The pigments were prepared from constituents capable of yielding the following oxide components in the following proportions: ZrO_2, 99.9 to 30; Pr_6O_{11}, 0.1 to 10.0, in parts by weight.

A new stain based on the presence of praseodymium and cerium oxides in a zirconium base was invented by Bruneau.[73] The broad limits of composition were given in weight percentage, as: 35 to 80ZrO_2, 10 to 55SiO_2, 0.5 to 10 praseodymium oxide, and 0.25 to 10 cerium oxide.

CHARACTERISTICS OF ZIRCONIA-BASE STAINS. Seabright and Draker,[74] using newer stains based on zirconia, showed it is possible through blending of only three stains to obtain a wide range of colors and tints in glazes. With three base end-member stains, turquoise, yellow and coral, all shades were possible except pink, chocolate, navy blue, and dark green. An example of the colors obtained by Seabright and Draker is shown in figure 14.4. The stains used were vanadium-zirconium-silica (turquoise), iron-zirconia silica (coral), and two yellows: the new praseodymium yellow stain and an older vanadium-zirconia yellow. The praseodymium yellow and the iron coral both were completely stable and compatible with the vanadium yellow and the turquoise, and with one another. The stains also were satisfactory in a zinc-bearing leadless glaze fired at 1,130° C, a lead-

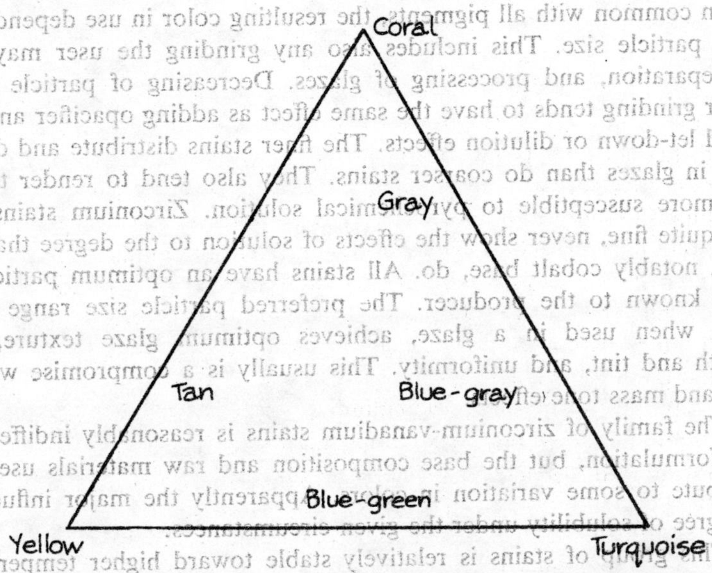

Figure 14.4. Colors in glaze produced by triaxial blends.[74]

bearing zinc glaze at 1,130° C, a high-lime–high-zinc–high-titania textured floor tile glaze for cone 1, and a mat glaze, slow-fire–long-hold at 1,180° C.

The original turquoise blue has been improved tc widen its range and to produce stronger pigments. The presently available zirconium-vanadium yellows produce stronger and cleaner shades than the earlier introductions. A lively bright lemon yellow, employing praseodymium, is among the very best and stable stains. Also commercially available is the bright indium orange. Nominal compositions published by Seabright and Draker[50,74] are given in table 14.5.

Vanadium-zirconium turquoise blues differ in color from cobalt blues. They are greenish in cast; cobalt colors have a characteristic reddish tone. Turquoise blues vary in hue depending on their composition and technique of preparation. Two common variants are the type of ZrO_2 used and the proportions of vanadium present.

If the silica is eliminated or curtailed, the green does not develop and the yellow is obtained. Various hues in this system can be achieved by controlled amounts of TiO_2, SiO_2, Al_2O_3, and B_2O_3. The zirconium-vanadium yellows should not be confused with another family of yellows based on SnO_2–V_2O_5. The tin-base colors are likely to be the stronger pigments in glazes and the tin colors are somewhat different. The indium orange of Harshaw is a modification of the zirconium-vanadium yellow, but is much darker.

In common with all pigments, the resulting color in use depends some on its particle size. This includes also any grinding the user may do in his preparation, and processing of glazes. Decreasing of particle size or further grinding tends to have the same effect as adding opacifier and tends toward let-down or dilution effects. The finer stains distribute and disperse better in glazes than do coarser stains. They also tend to render the pigment more susceptible to pyrochemical solution. Zirconium stains, even when quite fine, never show the effects of solution to the degree that some colors, notably cobalt base, do. All stains have an optimum particle size range, known to the producer. The preferred particle size range is that which, when used in a glaze, achieves optimum glaze texture, color strength and tint, and uniformity. This usually is a compromise with let-down and mass tone effects.

The family of zirconium-vanadium stains is reasonably indifferent to glaze formulation, but the base composition and raw materials used both contribute to some variation in colors. Apparently the major influence is the degree of solubility under the given circumstances.

This group of stains is relatively stable toward higher temperatures, but they all show some fading or color change due to varying times and temperatures of heat treatment. For precise color and shade control, firing should be controlled within narrow limits. Each stain will be found to have a certain degree of stability for a given color or shade. The use of opacifier-additions as a part of the glaze formulation acts to broaden the range and level out differences between different stains. All of these stains are applicable to conventional glazes firing to cone 12 and above.

In general, zirconium-base stains are stable toward variations in kiln atmospheres. They stand up well both in oxidizing and reducing conditions. In this respect they differ from tin-vanadium yellows that will fade completely in reducing atmospheres.

It should be emphasized that white opacifiers are pigments, and their presence, amounts, variations, and effectiveness change the overall color just as much as do the colored pigments. Each type and kind of opacifier has its own influence on the appearance of colored glazes. This must be determined by trial.

References

1. Evans, W. D. J. 1968. Ceramic pigments—a structural approach. *Trans. Brit. Ceram. Soc.* 67(9):397–419.
2. Watts, A. S. 1911. Notes on chrome-alumina colors. *Trans. Am. Ceram. Soc.* 13:301–5.

3. Hawks, Ralph L. 1961. Chrome-alumina pink at various temperatures. *Bull. Am. Ceram. Soc.* 40(1):7–8.
4. Rao, N. S. Gopala. 1958. Chrome alumina pink ceramic colors. *Central Glass & Ceram. Research Inst. Bull.* (*India*) 5(1):25–28; 1960. *Ceram. Abstr.* Jan.: 10b.
5. Henry, Paul. 1961. Ceramic green colors for whiteware glazes. *Bull. Am. Ceram. Soc.* 40(1):9–10.
6. Chrest, Roy W., Rummery, Frank O., Richards, J. Dudley, and Roseman, Reuben. *Inorganic blue to green pigments and process for making them.* U.S. Patent 3,079,269, Feb. 26, 1963.
7. Minton, R. H. 1915. The influence of some unusual zinc compounds in a chrome green glaze. *Trans. Am. Ceram. Soc.* 17:667–71.
8. Fuller, R. B. and Watts, A. S. 1943. Duplication of chrome-brown electrical porcelain glazes with nonessential materials. *J. Am. Ceram. Soc.* 26(12): 414.
9. Marquis, John E. and Carpenter, Robert E. 1961. Plant control problems with whiteware glazes containing brown and tan stains. *Bull. Am. Ceram. Soc.* 40(1):19–24.
10. Wicks, H. and Mellor, J. W. 1913–14. Nickel in-glaze colours, 1. *Trans. Engl. Ceram. Soc.* 13:61–66.
11. Montgomery, E. T. and Kruson, I. A. 1914. Colored porcelain glazes at cone 10. *Trans. Am. Ceram. Soc.* 16:347–63.
12. Petrik, L. 1894. Constitution of chrome-tin pink. *Sprechsaal* 27:360.
13. Kerstan, W. 1951. Red staining of tin glazes. *Ber. Deut. Keram. Ges. u. Ver. Deut. Emailfachleute* 28(11):634–42.
14. Bose, H. N. 1948. Note on chrome-tin-pink color. *Trans. Indian Ceram. Soc.* 7(1):28–31.
15. Herold, P. G. 1939. Mineralogical investigation of chrome-tin pinks as ceramic stains. *Bull. Missouri School of Mines and Metallurgy.* 13(2).
16. Bose, H. N. 1949. Note on chrome-tin-pink color. *Ceram. Age* 53(1): 17, 29.
17. Jamieson, Helen D. *Pigments.* U.S. Patent 3,053,685 Sept 11, 1962· 1963. *Cer. Abstr.* Jan:18j.
18. Iegaki, Toshio. 1948. Chromium colors. *Bull. Govt. Research. Inst. Ceramics* (*Kyoto*) 2(2):31–34.
19. Seger, H. A. 1902. *Underglaze colors and their preparation. Collected writings.* Vol. 2. Easton, Pa.: The Chemical Publishing Co., p 663.
20. Berdel, E. 1911. *Einfaches chemisches Praktikum.* Vol. 5 and 6. Coburg, p 61.
21. Hurd, Burgess M. 1961. Chrome-tin pinks and maroons. *Bull. Am. Ceram. Soc.* 40(1):11–12.
22. Mellor, J. W. 1936–37. The chemistry of the chrome-tin colours. *Trans. Engl. Ceram. Soc.* 36(1):16–27.
23. Tumanov, S. G. and Filippova, E. A. 1968. Preparation of variously colored pigments of the pink series. *Steklo Keram.* 25(10):24–27; 1970. *Ceram. Abstr.*, Feb:436.

24. Tumanov, S. G. and Filippova, E. A. 1968. Conditions for forming pink pigments and their structure. *Steklo i Keram.* 25(4):37–39.

25. Kato, Etsuzo and Kanaoka, Shigeto. 1958. Chrome-tin pinks: 1, Constituent minerals. *Nagoya Kogyo Gijutsu Shikensho Hokoku* 7(2):151–54; 1962. *Cer. Abstr.* Jan: 11*i*.

26. Ibid. 1960. Ref. 25, 9(8):147–51.

27. Mason, Ronald K. 1961. Use of cobalt colors in glazes. *Bull. Am. Ceram. Soc.* 40(1):5–6.

28. Stewart, J. A. 1968. Blues and greens over 50% of the color spectrum. *Glass Ind.* 49(8):447,458.

29. Hainbach. R. 1924. *Pottery decorating.* 2d ed. London: Scott, Greenwood and Son, p 167.

30. Kato, Etsuzo. 1950. Gold colors: 1, Preparation of purple of Cassius. *Bull. Govt. Research Inst. Ceramics (Kyoto)* 4(2):1–3.

31. Kato, Etsuzo. 1951. Gold colors: 2, Effect of addition of silver. Ibid. 5(1):12–15.

32. Levin, Ernst M., Robbins, Carl, and McMurdie, Howard F. 1964. *Phase diagrams for ceramists.* Columbus, Ohio: American Ceramic Society, Inc.

33. King, Burnham W. and Tesar, Adolph O. *Ceramic pigments.* U.S. Patent 2552,795, May 15, 1951.

34. Kato, Etsuzo and Kanaoka, Shigeto. 1965. Chemical and mineral composition of antimony yellow: 1, Preparation of antimony yellow. *Nagoya Kogyo Gijutsu Shikensho Hokoku* 14(8):315–20. 1966. *Ceram. Abstr.* April:102d.

35. Meyer-Simon, Eugen and Mann, Herbert. *(Deutsche Gold-und Silber Scheidensalt Vonmals Roessler), Manganese and aluminum containing pink pigments for glazes and underglazes.* U.S. Patent 3,330,678, July 11, 1967.

36. Eroles, A. J. and Friedberg, A. L. 1965. Color and structural character of CdS–CdSe pigments. *J. Am. Ceram. Soc.* 48(5):223–27.

37. Yamauchi, Toshiyoshi and Endo Yukio. 1952. Cadmium-selenium red: 1. *J. Ceram. Assoc. Japan* 60(676):417–21.

38. Kenworthy, Orville O., Goda, Ernest H., and Golland, Jack. *Pigment and method of producing.* U.S. Patent 2,523,119, Sept 19, 1950; 1951. *Cer. Abstr.* May:81i.

39. Yamaguchi, Goro, Tanabe, Hiroshi, and Tomiura, Koji. 1954. Research on spinel pigments. *J. Ceram. Assoc. Japan* 62(693):191–96.

40. Ohtsuka, Atsushi. 1962. Pigments of titanium-tin and aluminum-chromium spinels. *Yogyo Kyokai Shi* 70(796):110–13. 1966. *Ceram. Abstr.* May:139i.

41. Votava, Werner F. 1961. Gray and black stains in whiteware glazes. *Bull. Am. Ceram. Soc.* 40(1):17–18.

42. Soc. des Usines Chimiques Rhone-Poulenc. *New gray coloring agents for ceramics and enamels.* French Patent 955,646, Jan. 16, 1950; 1951. *Ceram. Abstr.* Oct:183C.

43. Olby, John K. *Method of preparing zirconium silicate ceramic stains.*

U.S. Patent 3,261,286, July 19, 1966; 1966. *Ceram. Abstr.* Sept:242c; also U.S. Patent 3,257,221, June 21, 1966.
44. Ray, E. H., Carnahan, T. D., and Sullivan, R. M. 1961. Tin-vanadium yellows and praseodymium yellows. *Bull. Am. Ceram. Soc.* 40(1):13–16.
45. Illiff, Frederic K. *Silver-zirconia pink*. U.S. Patent 3,046,151, July 24, 1962.
46. King, Burnham W. and Tesar, Adolph O. *Ceramic pigments*. U.S. Patent 2,623,833, December 30, 1952.
47. Weyl, Woldemar. *Ceramic pigment.* U.S. Patent 2,875,086, Feb 24, 1959. 1959. *Ceram. Abstr.* July:185g.
48. Earl, J. A. (Vitro Manufacturing Co.) *Making ceramic stains*. U.S. Patent 2,438,335, March 23, 1948.
49. Seabright, C. A. (Harshaw Chemical Co.) *Ceramic pigments*. U.S. Patent 2,441,447, May 11, 1948; 1948. *Ceram. Abstr.* Sept:208a.
50. Seabright, C. A. and Draker, H. C. 1961. Ceramic stains from zirconium and vanadium oxides. *Bull. Am. Ceram. Soc.* 40(1):1–4.
51. Marquis, John E. and Carpenter, Robert E. *Pink ceramic stains and process.* U.S. Patent 3,189,475, June 15, 1965.
52. Harshaw Chemical Co. *Ceramic pigments*. Brit. Patent 625,448, July 13, 1949; 1950. *Ceram. Abstr.* Sept:1869.
53. Booth, F. T. and Peel, G. N. 1962. Preparation and properties of some zirconium stains. *Trans. Brit. Ceram. Soc.* 61:359–400.
54. Cini, L. 1961. Reactions between SiO_2, ZrO_2, V_2O_5 their relations to the formation of pigments. *Ceramica (Florence)* 16 (11):60–62.
55. Cini, L. and Passalacqua, V. 1963. SiO_2–ZrO_2–V_2O_5 pigment. Effect of NaF on the formation of Turkish blue. *Chim. Ind. (Milan)* 45(9):345–46.
56. Matkovich, V. I. and Corbett, P. M. 1961. Formation of zircon from zirconium dioxide and silicon dioxide in the presence of vanadium pentoxide. *J. Am. Ceram. Soc.* 44(3):128–30.
57. Tudo, Joseph and Tridot, Gabriel. 1965. Vanadium-oxygen system—existence of a new phase with composition VO_2. *Compt. Rend.* 261(15) (Groupe 8):2911–14.
58. Demiray, Temel, Nath, D. K., and Hummel, F. A. 1970. Zircon-vanadium blue pigment. *J. Am. Ceram. Soc.* 53(1):1–4.
59. Marchesini, L. and Ramos, E. 1964. Structure of green and turquoise blue pigments containing vanadium. *Vetro Silicati* 8(8):5–9; 1965. *Ceram. Abstr.* Nov:17*d*.
60. Seabright, Clarence A. *Blue pigments.* U.S. Patent 3,025,178, March 13, 1962.
61. Kato, Etsuzo. 1961. Ceramic pigments. *Keram. F.* 13(11):617–22; 1962. *Ceram. Abstr.* May:123*i*.
62. Gascon, Joseph. *Preparation of colored ceramic pigments based on synthetic zircon.* U.S. Patent 3,528,835, Sept 15, 1970.
63. Morris, William C. and Tesar, Adolph O. *Ceramic pigments.* U.S. Patent 2,875,085, Feb 24, 1959; 1959. *Ceram. Abstr.* July:185*d*.
64. Jamieson, Helen D. *Pigments.* U.S. Patent 3,046,150, July 24, 1962.

65. Olby, John K. *Pigments.* U.S. Patent 3,058,838, Oct. 16, 1962; 1963. *Ceram. Abstr.* March:84*f*.
66. Gascon, Joseph. *Production of zirconium-based ceramic pigments containing iron.* U.S. Patent 3,528,834, Sept 15, 1970.
67. Ray, John M. 1963. Technology of zirconium iron pink stains. *J. Am. Ceram. Soc.* 32:83–88.
68. Seabright, Clarence A. *Iron ceramic pigment.* U.S. Patent 3,166,430, Jan 19, 1965.
69. Olby, John K. Zirconium stain for ceramic glazes. U.S. Patent 3,171,753, March 2, 1965.
70. Seabright, Clarence A. *Yellow pigments.* U.S. Patent 3,012,898, Dec 12, 1961.
71. Weber, Horst. *Process for the production of zirconium-praseodymium yellow pigments.* U.S. Patent 3,510,332, May 5, 1970.
72. Seabright, Clarence A. *Yellow ceramic pigments.* U.S. Patent 2,992,123, July 11, 1961.
73. Bruneau, Jean P. *Praseodymium-cerium yellow.* U.S. Patent 3,168,410, Feb 2, 1965. 1965. *Ceram. Abstr.* April:117*f*.
74. Seabright, C. A. and Draker, H. C. 1962. Triaxial color blending. *Bull. Am. Ceram. Soc.* 41(2):100–101.

15

Unconventional Glazes

There are cases for which glazes cannot be provided by conventional means. Glazes for some glass-ceramics, low-expansion bodies such as those based on beta spodumene or cordierite, are examples. Still another area is that of providing durable glazes with exceptionally low maturing temperatures. These problems were recognized many years ago and some suggestions for their solution offered.[1] Since that time, progress has been made in pyrochemistry and pyrophysics. The problems and approaches outlined by Harman still exist, but means for their practical implementation now are at hand. The development of unconventional glazing techniques has been slow. This is due mainly to general unfamiliarity with the principles involved and their potentialities. It is the purpose of this chapter to point out areas where these principles might be applied.

Glaze-Fit Problems

Glaze fit basically is dependent upon the nature and magnitude of stresses that develop during initial cooling due to differences in strain between the glaze layer and the substrate body. In the classical case, the body is a polycrystalline or polyphase composite having a definite and predictable reversible thermal expansion behavior. The conventional glaze layer is visualized as congealing during initial cooling to a glass or predominately glass-like substance. The glaze consequently has a reversible thermal expansion behavior identical to or closely resembling that of glass.

The importance of this is that there are no glasses possible with thermal expansion coefficient low enough to match that of low-expansion bodies. About the best that can be done with conventional approaches is to glaze successfully high-firing porcelains having coefficients of thermal expansion of the order of 25×10^{-7} per ° C. Among glasses, those with the lowest expansion coefficients invariably have high melting temperatures. A familiar example is fused silica having a coefficient of expansion of 5.5×10^{-7} per ° C, and a melting temperature of 1713° C (around 4000° F).

In summary, ceramic bodies readily are available with expansion coefficients far below those of any possible glass. The technique of loading glass with low-expansion crystalline inclusions to produce low-expansion glazes, although helpful, has not solved the problem.

Because it is impossible, though conventional approaches, to prepare glazes for low-expansion bodies, or moderate to low expansion glazes with low firing temperatures, different techniques are required. The development and use of such approaches requires a knowledge and application of details not normally regarded as of primary importance to the practice of conventional glaze technology.

New unconventional glazes may be based on the exploitation of one or more of the following general concepts: (a) The various recognized critical points of glass in terms of viscosity as shown in table 15.1. Some of these are indicated on the thermal dilation curve in figure 15.1; (b) the pyrophysical and pyrochemical nature of some important crystal phases, especially those having unusually low coefficients of thermal expansion, and (c) microscopic and submicroscopic phase separation in glasses, and the principles concerned with glass-ceramics.

Basis-Considerations for New Developments

There is an increasing demand for glazes and glaze-like coatings that cannot be fulfilled by the application of conventional glaze concepts. On the basis of newer information and concepts, glazes now are produced that were impossible only a few years ago. Some of these are discussed in a subsequent section in this chapter.

The purpose in the present section is to briefly outline some concepts of the type that could be used in approaches for the development of new unconventional glazes. The systems $MgO–Al_2O_3–SiO_2$ and $Li_2O–Al_2O_3–SiO_2$ have been extensively investigated and contain interesting crystal and glass phases that are useful. The potentialities of liquid-liquid separation and of nucleated crystallization are of primary importance.

The preparation of nucleated glasses has been developed to a considerable degree, but not very much has been done as yet to use the concept

Table 15.1. Recognized critical temperatures in the thermal history of glasses

Symbol	*Point*	*Viscosity, poise*
T_s	Lower annealing or strain-release temperature	$10^{14.5}$
T_g	Transformation temperature	$10^{13.3}$
T_u	Upper annealing temperature	10^{13}
T_d	Dilatometer softening point	10^{11}–10^{12}
T_L	Littleton softening point	4.5×10^7
T_s	Sintering point	10^6
T_f	Flow point	10^5
T_w	Glass-working viscosity	10^4
T_m	Melting viscosity	10^3–10^2

in glaze development. It is a purpose here to encourage the glaze ceramist to become familiar with these concepts and literature.

Many will find it useful to touch on some pertinent characteristics of the $MgO–Al_2O_3–SiO_2$ and $Li_2O–Al_2O_3–SiO_2$ systems and on nucleated glasses. Following that, some practical examples of nucleated glazes are given.

Rankin and Merwin[2] were the first to describe synthetic cordierite

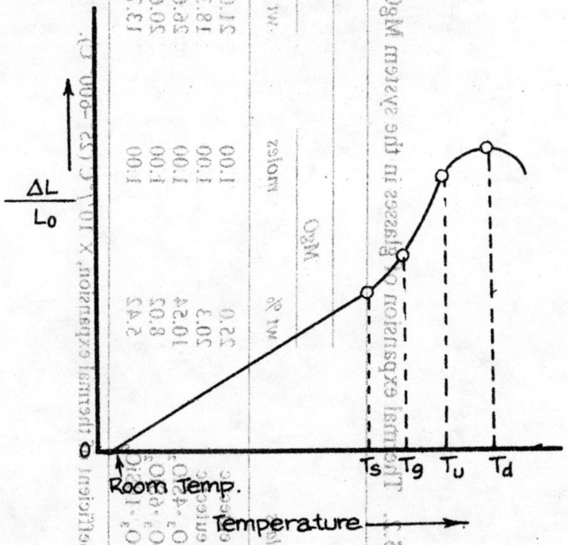

Figure 15.1. Critical points shown on thermal expansion ($\Delta L/L_0$) curve. For meaning of symbols, see table 15.1.

Table 15.2. Thermal expansion of glasses in the system $MgO–Al_2O_3–SiO_2$[5]

Glass	Composition						Expansivity*
	MgO		Al_2O_3		SiO_2		
	wt %	moles	wt %	moles	wt %	moles	
1,030° C eutectic	25.0	1.00	21.0	0.414	54.0	1.450	51.3
1,345° C eutectic	20.3	1.00	18.3	0.357	61.4	2.03	43.1
$MgO \cdot Al_2O_3 \cdot 4SiO_2$	10.54	1.00	26.65	1.00	62.81	4.00	33.1
$MgO \cdot Al_2O_3 \cdot 6SiO_2$	8.02	1.00	20.68	1.00	71.70	6.00	27.1
$MgO \cdot Al_2O_3 \cdot 10SiO_2$	5.42	1.00	13.72	1.00	80.86	10.00	20.2

*Mean coefficient of thermal expansion, × 10^7/°C (25°–600° C).

($2MgO \cdot 2Al_2O_3 \cdot 5SiO_2$), which melts incongruently at 1,470° C into glass and mullite. Three polymorphic forms of it have been reported,[2,3] two stable (β, α) and one metastable form (μ). Cordierite has unusually low thermal expansion coefficients. Singer[4] developed a cordierite body having a thermal expansion coefficient of 5.3×10^{-7} per ° C for the range 0° to 200° C.

The natural mineral is the high temperature (α) form, but the stable β (low temperature) phase can be formed under hydrothermal conditions from glass. The high temperature form develops from solid state reactions of batch materials and from the devitrification of glass between 1,050° and 1,460° C.[3] The metastable μ form can be obtained by heating powdered glass for many hours at 800° to 900° C. The β and μ phases invert to the α-form in the range above 830° C.

Hummel[3] measured the coefficient of thermal expansion of μ-cordierite as 47.2×10^{-7} and the α-form as 24.7×10^{-7} for the range 25° to 1,000° C.

The compositions and thermal expansions of some glasses in the MgO–Al_2O_3–SiO_2 system are summarized in table 15.2. The behavior of these materials is such that they could function as conventional glazes of the porcelain type. When extensively crystallized they might be considered for the development of nucleated glass-ceramic type of coatings. The prospects for success are limited.

Lithium–Alumina–Silica

Spodumene ($Li_2O \cdot Al_2O_3 \cdot 4SiO_2$) crystals when heated above 700° C sluggishly invert to beta-spodumene. The high temperature form has a very low thermal expansion.[6] There is a complete series of metastable solid solutions between β-spodumene and μ-cordierite at lower temperatures. There is only limited solid solution between cordierite and spodumene at high temperatures.

Solid solutions of the high quartz structure can be crystallized from some glasses. Roy[7] described a complete solid solution between $Li_2O \cdot Al_2O_3 \cdot 2SiO_2$ and SiO_2, all having the beta- (high) quartz structure. High-quartz type of solid solutions also occur in the $MgO \cdot Al_2O_3 \cdot nSiO_2$ and $Li_2O \cdot Al_2O_3 \cdot nSiO$ systems. These were studied by Ray and Muchow[8] in some detail. The phases fell into a group of compounds referred to as "stuffed derivatives of the silica structures" by Buerger.[9] These include high quartz solid solutions of $Li_2O \cdot Al_2O_3 \cdot nSiO_2$ (where $n \gtrless 2$); keatite solid solutions, $Li_2O \cdot Al_2O_3 \cdot nSiO_2$ (where $n > 3.5$). A keatite solid solution series includes the beta-spodumene phase.

A number of glasses were prepared by Ray and Muchow,[8] then heat

Table 15.3. Solid solution phases from thermally crystallized glasses in the system $(Li_2O, MgO) \cdot Al_2O_3 \cdot n\ SiO_2$.[8]

Composition, moles Li_2O	MgO	Al_2O_3	SiO_2	*Temp. (°C)*	*Time (Hrs.)*	*Phases developed*
1.0		1.0	2.0	650	64	High quartz ss†, glass
1.0		1.0	2.0	1,100	16	High quartz ss†, Li spinel (tr.)
1.0		1.0	3.0	750	16	High quartz ss†
1.0		1.0	3.0	1,200	16	High quartz ss†, α alumina
1.0		1.0	3.8	1,000	16	High quartz ss†, Keatite ss*
1.0		1.0	3.8	1,275	16	Keatite ss*
1.0		1.0	5.7	800	1	High quartz ss†, Keatite ss*
1.0		1.0	5.7	800	96	Keatite ss*
0.8	0.2	1.0	2.0	1,100	16	High quartz ss‡, spinel
0.8	0.2	1.0	4.0	1,000	1	Keatite ss**
0.4	0.6	1.0	2.0	900	1	High quartz ss‡, cordierite
0.4	0.6	1.0	2.0	1,000	1	Cordierite, high quartz ss‡
0.4	0.6	1.0	3.0	1,000	1	Cordierite, Keatite**, high quartz‡
0.4	0.6	1.0	4.0	900	1	Quartz ss
0.4	0.6	1.0	4.0	1,100	16	Cordierite, Keatite ss**
0.4	0.6	1.0	5.0	900	1	High quartz, Keatite ss**
0.4	0.6	1.0	5.0	1,100	16	Cordierite, Keatite ss**

Phase compositions

†High quartz ss = $Li_2O \cdot Al_2O_3 \cdot nSiO_2$ (where $n \gtrless 2$)

‡High quartz ss = $(Li_2O, MgO) \cdot Al_2O_3 \cdot nSiO_2$ (where $n \geqslant 2$)

*Keatite ss = $Li_2O \cdot Al_2O_3 \cdot nSiO_2$ (where $n > 3.5$)

**Keatite ss = $(Li_2O, MgO) \cdot Al_2O_3 \cdot nSiO_2$ (where $n > 3.5$)

Cordierite = $2MgO \cdot 2Al_2O_3 \cdot 5SiO_2$

treated to promote their crystallization. The stuffed quartz solid solutions resulting from specified heat treatments of these glasses are summarized in table 15.3.

The thermal expansion of glasses composed of Li_2O, Al_2O_3, and SiO_2 were measured and published by Brackbill, McKinstry and Hummel.[10] Typical thermal expansions of glasses in the system are shown in table 15.4. These simple glasses are not, in general, advocated for direct use as glazes. The thermal expansion data are useful in considerations relating to the preparation of special glazes. Note that the thermal expansion of the 1:1:8 composition in glass form is about 43×10^{-7}. Compare this with the low, even large negative values for the same composition in crystalline form, e.g., petalite bodies.

Nucleated Glass-Ceramics

The phenomenon of nucleation and its relationship to phase separation long has been appreciated. It usually has been studiously avoided in conventional glass wares. There are exceptions. The precipitation of minor

Table 15.4. Thermal expansions of Li_2O–Al_2O_3–SiO_2 glasses.[10]

Glass Composition	Li_2O		Al_2O_3		SiO_2		Expansivity*
	wt. %	moles	wt. %	moles	wt. %	moles	
$Li_2O \cdot Al_2O_3 \cdot 2SiO_2$	11.8	1.0	40.5	1.0	47.7	2.0	$76.0 \times 10^{-7}/°C$
$Li_2O \cdot Al_2O_3 \cdot 4SiO_2$	8.0	1.0	27.4	1.0	64.6	4.0	66.6
$Li_2O \cdot Al_2O_3 \cdot 6SiO_2$	6.1	1.0	20.7	1.0	73.2	6.0	52.5
$Li_2O \cdot Al_2O_3 \cdot 8SiO_2$	4.9	1.0	16.6	1.0	78.5	8.0	43.6
$Li_2O \cdot Al_2O_3 \cdot 10SiO_2$	4.1	1.0	13.9	1.0	82.0	10.0	39.3

*Mean coefficient of linear thermal expansion for the range 30° to 500°C.

Table 15.5. Composition of Corning's glass no. 9608[24]

Oxide	*% by wt*
SiO_2	69.5
Al_2O_3	17.8
MgO	2.8
Li_2O	2.5
TiO_2	4.75
ZrO_2	0.25
ZnO	1.0
Na_2O	0.4
As_2O_3	1.0

ingredients to form opacity or color are examples. Fluoride and phosphate opals are examples. Others are gold, copper, and cadmium sulfoselemides to form red glass. In glazes, nucleation has been useful in the development of colors, opacity, and macroscopic crystals (crystal glazes).

A new twist to an old process recently has been introduced. Stookey[11] introduced the practice of fabricating glass articles that later could be crystallized into fine-grained glass-ceramics having exceptional properties. Most of the subsequent developments in this field have dealt with high-crystal-content bodies. Only recently has the concept been considered as a basis for special glaze development.

The development of new products on the basis of nucleated phase separation was initiated by Stookey.[12] Since his original contribution, a variety of kinds of crystals have been caused to separate, by nucleation, from various glasses.[13,14]

Liquid-liquid separation has been discussed in detail by Goldstein,[15] Ohlberg,[16] and Cahn and Charles.[17] Composition investigations in the system Na_2O–Al_2O_3–SiO_2 by Kivlighn[18] and Na_2O–BaO–Al_2O_3–SiO_2 by MacDowell[19] have further contributed. In addition, the use of titania as a nucleating agent or as a catalyst to cause crystallization in sodium-alumina-silica glasses has been dealt with by Kivlighn[18] and by MacDowell.[19]

Surfaces of glass have been put into compression by exchanging lithium ions for sodium ions in some glasses above their annealing temperatures as discussed by Hood and Stookey.[20] Low-expansion surfaces have been achieved by causing the crystallization of low-expansion crystals in glass surfaces. Examples of this have been given by Olcott and Stookey[21] and by Garfinkle, Rothermel and Stookey.[22] Methods of strengthening of glass surfaces have been reviewed by Stookey.[23]

It is common that two or more crystal species will separate from a glass due to heat treatments. The separate phases nearly always have their own conditions as to temperature and time for crystallizing. This was well

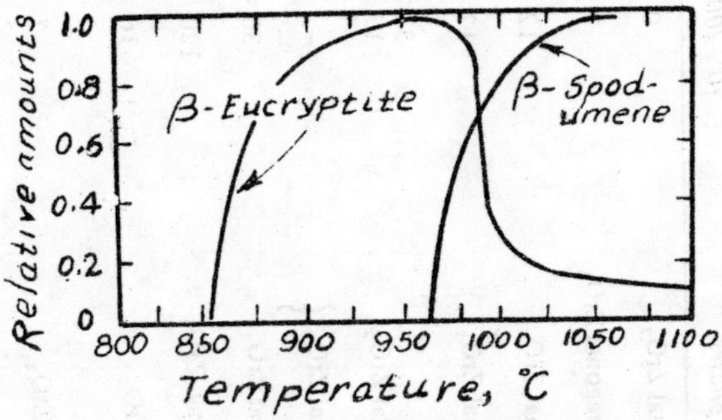

Figure 15.2. Phases appearing when the glass of table 15.5 was reheated, and their relative proportions.[24]

illustrated by Dohfrty, Lee and Davis[24] with a proprietary glass of table 15.5, with results as shown in figure 15.2.

Beta-eucryptite began to appear around 850° C and continued until 925° C. At that temperature the eucryptite started to diminish and beta-spodumene appeared. By 1,050° C, the transformation was essentially stabilized. The titania, in the form of rutile (not shown), appeared in minor quantities around 1,050° C.

Glasses of the same composition as that of table 15.5, except for having up to 2.5% of titania, were prepared.[24] When treated in the same manner as the first example, the glasses containing 0 to 2.0% of TiO_2 developed crystals at the surface but none in the interior of the glass. The sample containing 2.5% of TiO_2 crystallized within the volume, but those lower in TiO_2 did not.

The authors[24] were able to conclude that, in the glasses with more

Table 15.6. Stuffed β-quartz-type glass-ceramic compositions.[25]

	Parts by weight of indicated oxides								
No.	*SiO_2*	*Al_2O_3*	*MgO*	*ZnO*	*Li_2O*	*ZrO_2*	*TiO_2*	*As_2O_5*	*Total*
1	75	18	3	–	4	4	–	–	104
2	70.5	21	4	2	2.5	4	–	0.5	104.5
3	70	22	6	–	2	5	–	–	105
4	65	25	10	–	–	10	–	–	110
5	74	19.5	4.5	–	2	4	0.5	–	104.5
6	70	18	–	10	2	6	–	–	106
7	60	29	11	–	–	–	9	–	109
8	55	32	13	–	–	–	10	–	110
9	73	19.5	–	4	3.5	3.5	1	1	105.5

Table 15.7. Some types and characteristics of products resulting from nucleated crystallization[25]

Comp. No. in Table 15.6	Heat Treatment: Temp. °C	Heat Treatment: Time Hr.	Results of crystallization: Appearance	Results of crystallization: Fracture	Results of crystallization: Crystal phases	Linear thermal exp. coeff. × 10^7/°C (0°–300° C)
1	780	4	Transparent, colorless	Glassy	β - quartz ss, tetragonal ZrO_2	0
1	825	4				
1	800	4	White	Cherty	β - spodumene ss, tetragonal ZrO_2	7
1	850	6				
2	780	4	Transparent	Waxy	β - quartz ss, tetragonal ZrO_2	12
2	830	4				
2	850	4	White, transparent	Cherty	β - quartz ss, tetragonal ZrO_2	12
2	905	4				
3	830	4	Transparent, colorless	Glassy	tetragonal ZrO_2	32
3	800	4	Transparent, colorless	Waxy	β - quartz ss, tetragonal ZrO_2	19
3	880	4				
3	980	4	White	Cherty	{β - quartz ss, tetragonal ZrO_2, spinel, β - spodumene}	—
3	1,140	4				—
4	880	4	Transparent, colorless	Cherty	β - quartz ss, tetragonal ZrO_2	30
4	960	4				
4	800	4	White	Cherty	α - quartz, spinel, tetrag. ZrO_2	120
4	1,100	6				
5	780	4	Transparent, colorless	Glassy	β - quartz ss, tetrag. ZrO_2	16
5	830	4				
5	900	4				
6	810	6	Translucent	Waxy	β - quartz, tetragonal ZrO_2	-7
6	850	6				
6	800	6	White	Cherty	α - quartz, spinel, tetrag. ZrO_2	127
6	910	6				
6	905	6	White	Sugary	Cristobalite, spinel, ZrO_2	—
6	1,035	6				
7	800	4	Blue, transparent	Glassy	β - quartz, magnesium titanate	—
7	880	1				

7	800	4	Blue, transparent	Glassy	α - and β - quartz, magnesium titanate	–
7	900	0.25				
7	800	4	Bluish	Cherty	β - quartz ss, magnesium titanate	–
7	900	4				
7	800	4	Bluish	Cherty	α - quartz, spinel, $MgO \cdot 2TiO_2$	–
7	1,000	1.5				
7	800	4	White	Cherty	Cordierite, α - quartz, spinel, rutile	–
7	1,100	2.5				
8	800	4	Blue, transparent	Waxy	β - quartz ss, $MgO \cdot 2TiO_2$	40
8	880	4				
8	800	4	Blue	Cherty	α - quartz, spinel, sapphirine, $MgO \cdot 2TiO_2$	95
8	880	4				
8	1,000	4				
9	800	4	Transparent, pale yellow	Glassy	β - quartz ss, tetragonal ZrO_2	-12
9	860	4				
9	500	4	White	Cherty	β - spodumene, spinel, ZrO_2	4

than 2.5% of TiO_2, liquid-liquid phase separation was on a scale of about 50 Å. When reheated, a phase believed to be $Al_2O_3 \cdot 2TiO_2$ formed, which also had a particle size of about 50 Å. As the reheating continued to higher temperatures, the aluminum titanate phase nucleated β-eucryptite crystals. They in turn inverted to β-spodumene at appropriate temperature ranges. It was believed that the original aluminum titanate nucleii eventually decomposed into TiO_2 and residual Al_2O_3 as demanded by the equilibrium.

GLAZES BY NUCLEATED CRYSTALLIZATION. Since the discovery by Stookey that fine-grained crystals can be precipitated in glass in a controlled manner to yield products otherwise not possible, this has held promise also of producing glazes not otherwise possible. Most glasses in the system $MgO \cdot Al_2O_3$–$Li_2O \cdot Al_2O_3$–SiO_2 can be made to precipitate metastable β-quartz solid solution. These quartz solid solutions are commonly referred to as stuffed β-quartz.[25] Either transparent or opaque products are possible from compositions of table 15.6 containing about 70% of SiO_2. The transparent glasses may contain one or more stuffed β-quartz phases of exceptionally small particle size. Thermal expansion coefficients from quite low, even negative, to higher values are shown in table 15.7.

Generally the values may lie in the range from -20 to $+50 \times 10^{-7}/°$ C. The thermal stability of these products is highly variable. Stuffed-quartz products can be strengthened by ion exchange to yield modulus of rupture values exceeding 150,000 psi.

Most of the stuffed β-quartz glass-ceramics composites can be strengthened by ion exchange. This has been done by Beall et al.[25] with fused salt baths. Using a molten potassium salt, the exchange $K^+ \rightleftarrows Li^+$ was effective. In a fused lithium salt, $2\ Li^+ \rightleftarrows Mg^{2+}$ was productive in greatly increasing the flexural strength.

Alkali exchange results in surface compression because of a crowding mechanism. The reaction was achieved[25] by immersing the glass-ceramic in a salt bath of 52% KCl + 48% of K_2SO_4 and holding it at 500°–700° C for several hours. Favorable $2Li^+ \rightleftarrows Mg^{2+}$ exchange was achieved on magnesium-bearing β-quartz glass-ceramics. Li_2SO_4 containing minor additions of K_2SO_4 held at 800°–900° C was best.

Low-expansion, Low-firing Nucleated Glazes

Bismuth-bearing Glazes

The same principles that are applied to the preparation of glass-ceramics by nucleation and crystallization can form the basis for low tem-

Table 15.8. Five low-expansion, nucleated glazes and respective expansion coefficient values.[26]

No.	Parts by weight of indicated oxides								Coeff. of therm. exp. × 10^7/°C
	SiO_2	B_2O_3	Al_2O_3	Li_2O	TiO_2	Bi_2O_3	CdO	PbO	
1	61.8	5.7	20.6	6.7	5.2				10.7
2	53.9	0.9	23.9	7.9	6.0	7.5			10.6
3	54.7	0.9	24.3	8.1	1.5	7.6	3.0		−23.7
4	53.0	0.9	23.5	7.8	1.5	7.4	2.9	3.0	−5.5
5	52.3	0.9	23.2	7.7	1.4	7.2	2.9	4.4	−14.9

perature, low-expansion glazes and enamels. Kosiorek and Loughman[26] described some coatings for glass-ceramics to be glost-fired at 2,000° F and having very low coefficients of linear thermal expansion. The reported values ranged from 10×10^{-7}/° C to negative values as low as -24×10^{-7}/° C.

Examples of compositions and respective thermal expansion values are shown in table 15.8. To make glazes from these compositions, they were mixed and melted into homogeneous glasses at 1540° C, then powdered and made into slurries. Organic floating agents were used to prevent possible interference with nucleation and crystallization that might result from inorganic suspension agents. The resulting slips were used to coat the substrate bodies, and the coated bodies then were heat-treated to produce the desired glazed finished product. The critical heat-treatment schedule required to induce nucleation and subsequent crystallization and a glossy finish was as follows:

Temperature, °F	*Time periods*	*Function*
At 2000	for 20 minutes	Development of gloss
2000 to 900	in 15 minutes	Cool and quench
At 900	for 1 hour	Nucleation
900 to 975	in ½ hour	Start of crystallization
975 to 1050	in ½ hour	Crystallization
1050 to 1125	in ½ hour	Crystallization
1125 to 1200	in ½ hour	Crystallization
1200 to 1275	in ½ hour	Crystallization
1275 to 1350	in ½ hour	Crystallization
1350 to 1425	in ½ hour	Crystallization
1425 to 1500	in ½ hour	Crystallization
1500 to 1600	in ½ hour	Crystallization
at 1600	for 2 hours	Crystallization
Cool to room temperature		Finished article

The presence of Bi_2O_3 and CdO results in reduced molten viscosity, improved nucleation, and crystallization and could be used to control the desired thermal expansion behavior.

By this unconventional technique, low-expansion, low-fusing glazes can be prepared from crystallizable glasses and applied in the conventional manner, but they must be fired with a special schedule. The compositions first are melted into homogeneous glasses and quenched. These melted products differ from the conventional frits in that the quenched product must be a homogeneous glass, which is not a requirement for the usual glaze frit.

Examples of compositions that form crystallizable glasses of the type to be considered as potential unconventional glazes are shown in table 15.9. To make glazes, these glasses would be melted, ground, and made into slips. After being applied as glaze coatings, the ware then would be heat-treated according to a predetermined schedule. During the heat-treating process, very minute crystallites of beta-spodumene would be precipitated, thus forming coatings with mean expansion coefficients in the range of 13×10^{-7} per °C to 20×10^{-7} per °C. The compositions are from Wolf and Kosiorek[27] who fired these at 1,700 to 1,800° F on glass-ceramics according to the following schedule:

1. Heated at 1,700 to 1,800° F to develop a glossy surface.
2. Cooled to 900° F in 30 minutes or less.
3. Temperature maintained at 900° F for 1 hour.
4. Temperature raised from 900° F to 1600° F in 1 hour.
5. Temperature maintained at 1600° F for 3 hours.
6. Cooled to room temperature in 3 hours.

Bismuth-free Glazes

Two nucleatable glasses, taken from Smith,[28] and shown in table 15.10 are capable of being processed into low-thermal expansion glass-ceramics. Glazes to fit low-expansion bodies might be prepared by coating low-expansion ware with slips made of these glasses. The ware would be heated to a temperature above the liquidus temperature, cooled rapidly below the nucleating temperature, then reheated to nucleate and crystallize. The heat-treatment schedule used by Smith to transform the glasses of table 15.10 into glass-ceramics was as follows:

1. Heated from 1,100° F to 1,200° F at 145° F per hour.
2. Heated from 1,200° F to 1,300° F at 25° F per hour.
3. Heated from 1,300° F to 1,600° F at 50° F per hour.
4. Heated from 1,600° F to 1,950° F at 145° F per hour.

Table 15.9. Crystallizable glazes to mature at 1800° F with coefficients of linear thermal expansion of 13 to 20 × 10^{-7}/°C.[27]

	Parts by weight (%) of indicated oxides						Coeff. of lin. therm. expansion
No.	*SiO_2*	*B_2O_3*	*Al_2O_3*	*Li_2O*	*TiO_2*	*Bi_2O_3*	*(× 10^7 /°C)*
1	59.19	13.37	11.14	7.94	4.18	4.18	13.4
2	58.69	13.15	12.52	7.04	4.69	3.91	19.7
3	56.05	12.56	16.44	6.73	4.48	3.74	14.4
4	59.35	12.46	13.35	6.68	4.45	3.71	16.2
5	59.52	13.33	12.70	5.72	4.76	3.97	13.9
6	60.49	11.29	12.90	6.45	4.84	4.03	15.1

5. Temperature maintained at 1,950° F for 1 hour.
6. Cooled at 400° F per hour.

Other compositions suitable for glass-ceramics as shown in table 15.11 were developed by Ellis.[29] He used these as coatings in the form of slips prepared from the ground glass mixed with squeegee oil and silk-screened onto the substrate. One of the heat-treating cycles found to be effective was the following: heated for 2 hours at 1,300° F, plus 1 hour at 1,500° F followed by finishing at 1,550° F for 1 hour. The glazes were of good gloss and they were deep reddish in color.

High-expansion Glaze, Low-expansion Substrate

Favorable Volume Changes Due to Crystallization

Glazes can be so constituted that, during crystallization, the specific volume of the glaze is being increased, thus opposing volume-decreases due to reversible thermal expansion. Such a system was reported by Harman[1] several years ago. One such glaze was of the following composition:

$0.12K_2O$		
$0.48PbO$	$0.18Al_2O_3$	$1.80SiO_2$
$0.25BaO$		
$0.15ZnO$		

A typical example of the stress variation during the cooling of a glaze of this kind is shown in figure 15.3. The viscosity of the cooling glaze becomes high enough at the "strain point" to permit development of initial tensile stress. As cooling continues, crystallization starts and the small ten-

Table 15.10. Two nucleatable glasses that can make glass-ceramics.[28]

No.	SiO_2	Al_2O_3	MgO	Li_2O	ZrO_2	TiO_2	F_2	P_2O_5	Na_2O	Sb_2O_5	Liquid-us temp., °C	Log 4 viscosity, °C	Anneal-ing temp., °C	Smelt-ing temp., °C	Coeff. of lin. therm. expansion per °C × 10^7
	Oxides and their percent by wt.														
1	7.12	17.0	4.3	3.2	1.3	1.8	0.14	0.6	0.5		1289	1308	653	1593	18.9*
2	71.6	16.9	3.0	3.5	1.5	1.5		1.0	0.6	0.4	1340	1337	651	1593	11.0*

*Expansion coefficients after nucleating and crystallizing.

Table 15.11. Low-expansion, low-temperature glazes for glass-ceramics.[29]

No.	Composition, mole % Li_2O	Cu_2O	Fe_2O_3	Al_2O_3	SiO_2	Melting point, °C	Glassy edge, °C	Coeff. of lin. therm. expansion $\times 10^7/°C$* (0° to 300° C)
6	19.00	12.49	2.23	8.07	60.40	929	871	20.4*
7	14.48	7.91	1.71	6.21	69.69	936	920	16.9
8	21.12	11.45	2.48	8.91	56.02	932	889	23.1

***Note:** Coefficient of expansion = $20.4 \times 10^{-7}/°C$, but the number appearing in the tables is $20.4 \times 10^7 = 20.4 \times 10^{-7}$. The coefficients of expansion, being $n \times 10^{-7}$, have been multiplied by 10^7 to simplify their tabulation.

sile stress is wiped out and a larger compressive stress develops. On continued cooling, the volume contraction due to reversible thermal expansion reduces the compression built up by crystallization. In a well-balanced glaze, an appreciable residual stress will remain.

The principal crystal phase was hyalophane (orthoclase with celsian in solid solution). This phase has a higher specific volume than the mother

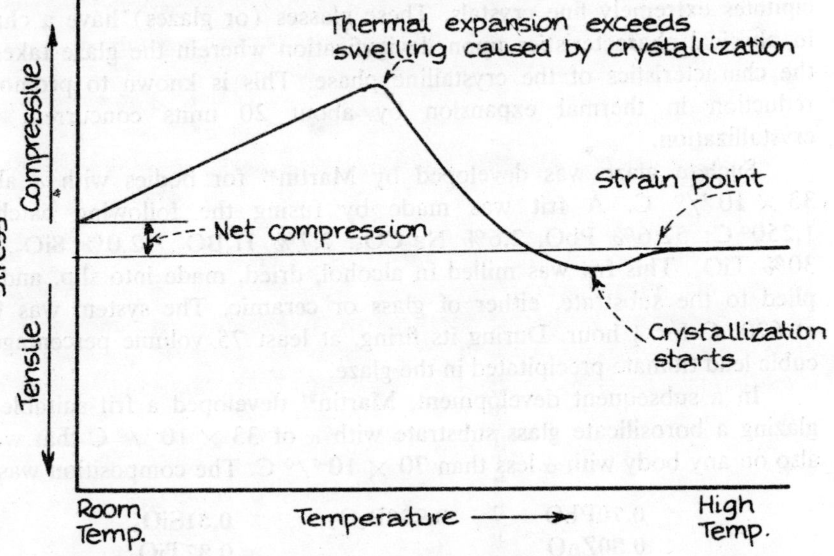

Figure 15.3. Typical example of stress variation during the cooling of a glaze undergoing expansion due to crystallization.[1]

liquid from which it separated. The glaze fits a whiteware body if allowed to crystallize, but will craze if no crystals are allowed to form.

A similar type of glaze has the following empirical formula:

0.4613PbO		
0.1636MnO	$0.055Al_2O_3$	$0.4904SiO_2$
0.2683CuO		
0.1063CoO		

It will fit semivitreous whiteware bodies or a cordierite body as well. The reversible expansion coefficient is $73 \times 10^{-7}/°$ C.

Effects of Inhibited Interfacial Reaction with Nucleatable Glaze

The expansion match between the glaze and its substrate, is not sharply critical under special circumstances. This seems to be the case with glazes that do not react appreciably with the substrate. One way[30] to accomplish this is to use a low-melting frit that devitrifies immediately upon reaching its maturing temperature. Thermally devitrifiable sealing glasses crystallize as soon as they start to soften and bond. This inhibits interfacial reaction and provides a crystal phase separating concurrently with maturing of the glaze. This development must be of the nucleated type that precipitates extremely fine crystals. These glasses (or glazes) have a change in physical characteristics upon devitrification wherein the glaze takes on the characteristics of the crystalline phase. This is known to promote a reduction in thermal expansion by about 20 units concurrent with crystallization.

Such a glaze was developed by Martin[30] for bodies with α about $33 \times 10^{-7}/°$ C. A frit was made by fusing the following batch at 1,250° C: 52.6% PbO, 2.6% Na_2CO_3, 2.7% H_3BO_3, 12.0% SiO_2, and 30% TiO_2. This frit was milled in alcohol, dried, made into slip, and applied to the substrate, either of glass or ceramic. The system was fired at 620° C for ½ hour. During its firing, at least 75 volume percentage of cubic lead titanate precipitated in the glaze.

In a subsequent development, Martin[31] developed a frit suitable for glazing a borosilicate glass substrate with α of $33 \times 10^{-7}/°$ C that works also on any body with α less than $70 \times 10^{-7}/°$ C. The composition was:

0.70PbO	$0.266B_2O_3$	$0.31SiO_2$
0.30ZnO		$0.37TiO_2$

This had a reversible expansion coefficient of $46 \times 10^{-7}/°$ C, but even when applied to a body with $\alpha = 33 \times 10^{-7}$ there was no loss in strength or crazing. When fired for ½ hour at 620° C, fine crystals of lead titanate separated. One percent of powdered lead titanate added to the glaze slip as a seed helped to control the devitrification.

Martin[31] defined a thermally devitrifiable sealing glass as one "capable of forming a vitreous seal, such as a glaze on the surface of a preformed body." During the formation of the seal it undergoes "a thermally induced, nucleated type of crystallization by further heating at, or near the sealing temperature." In the process, "the glass separates into a crystal phase and a glassy phase, the former being in the form of relatively fine crystals uniformally dispersed." This provides "a material of essentially uniform physical characteristics ordinarily differing from those of the original glass." This differs from opal glass in the amounts and types of crystals.

Utilizing Great Differences in Expansion between Glaze and Body

Under conventional circumstances and with conventional ceramic bodies and glazes, maximum strength in the composite occurs when the expansion coefficient of the glaze is around 10% to 20% lower than that of the body. Harold Bopp[32] and his associates found that some glass-ceramics can gain advantages from glazes having up to 60% lower expansion than the substrate body.

They postulated that it is possible to utilize these great differences in expansion with high-strength, highly homogeneous glass-ceramic sub-

Table 15.12. Influence of glazing on the strength of a glass-ceramic.[32]

	Glass-Ceramic Underbody	*Glaze*
Composition, wt. %		
SiO_2	50.0	47.7
Al_2O_3	26.1	7.4
B_2O_3		9.8
TiO_2	4.5	
Na_2O		4.0
K_2O	17.2	1.0
MgO	2.2	
CaO		8.2
PbO		21.1
ZrO_2		0.8
Softening point, °C		702
Annealing point, °C		549
Coef. lin. expansion × 10^7/°C	120	65.3
Modulus of rupture, psi		
Before glazing	13,000	
After glazing	35,000	
Firing	see text	see text

Table 15.13. A glass-ceramic and its heat-treating schedule.[33]

Composition wt. %		*Schedule for nucleating and crystallization*
SiO_2	70.7	1,100° to 1,200°F at 145°F / hr.
Al_2O_3	16.8	1,200° to 1,300°F at 25°F / hr.
Li_2O	3.4	1,300° to 1,600°F at 55°F / hr.
TiO_2	1.8	1,600° to 1,950°F at 145°F / hr.
ZrO_2	1.3	1,950° F for 1 hour
MgO	3.9	Cool to room temp. at 400°F / hr.
P_2O_5	1.4	
Na_2O	0.5	Coefficient of thermal expansion of the final crystallized glass-ceramic = $14 \times 10^{-7}/°C$
As_2O_3	0.1	
F_2	0.09	

strates. In these underbodies, the crystals are very tiny and uniform in size and distribution, and are of inherently high tensile strength. They believe also that an interfacial layer between substrate and glaze that is advantageous, can develop. One of the advantages of the interfacial layer is to distribute the shearing stress at the interface over a relatively thick zone, extending into the substrate as well as into the glaze.

Bopp, et al.[32] found that expansion differences of at least 30% were

Table 15.14. Five unconventional glazes used on glass-ceramics*,[33]

Oxide, wt %	*1*	*2*	*3*	*4*	*5*
SiO_2	25.0	25.1	27.1	16.1	8.5
B_2O_3	10.8	3.6	3.4	10.5	8.5
Al_2O_3	6.0	0.5	0.4	5.2	2.0
Fe_2O_3	1.2	–	–	–	2.2
Cr_2O_3	0.2	12.3	0.8	17.2	1.2
TiO_2	0.2	4.7	1.1	–	11.0
ZrO_2	14.5	2.8	1.5	–	–
V_2O_5	0.2	–	–	–	–
SnO_2	1.3	–	–	–	–
MoO_3	0.2	–	–	–	–
CoO	0.2	1.2	–	4.1	0.4
PbO	39.1	44.9	48.5	38.8	54.3
NiO	0.7	–	–	–	–
MnO	–	–	0.7	2.8	–
BaO	–	0.7	1.4	–	1.0
CuO	–	–	4.6	0.2	–
ZnO	–	–	–	2.6	3.9
Na_2O	–	3.1	2.6	–	–
K_2O	–	0.1	0.1	0.8	–
Li_2O	0.4	–	–	0.4	–
CdO	–	–	–	–	6.7

*These glazes have expansion coefficients in the range of 75 to $100 \times 10^{-7}/°C$. They fit glass-ceramic substrates having coefficients of thermal expansion as low as $25 \times 10^{-7}/°C$.

required to double the strength. The compositions of the underbody glass-ceramic and a glaze for it, are shown in table 15.12. The body was prepared by melting to a glass, fabricating a glass article from it, and then crystallizing it by the following process: heat to 800° C at 5° C per min, hold 4 hr, and cool.

The glaze was prepared as 94% glass and 6% kaolin in slip form. The coating was applied to a thickness of 5 to 12 mils and fired at 5° C per min to 1,060° C and held 1 to 2 hours. As shown in table 15.12, the expansion of the body was 120×10^{-7} and that of the glaze, 65×10^{-7}. The glaze increased the flexural strength from 13,000 psi to 35,000 psi.

Unconventional Glazes for Glass-ceramics

A glass-ceramic composition along with heat-treatment schedules to nucleate and crystallize it are shown in table 15.13. Medert[33] decorated this type of substrate with a clear low-fusing glaze having a higher expansion than the substrate. He postulated that crazing was avoided because of the formation of a diffusion-developed layer favorable to good interfacial bonding. Some of the glazes, with expansions in the range of 75 to

Table 15.15. Nucleated glass-ceramics and glazes for them.[34]

	Glass-ceramic to be glazed			*Glazes for glass-ceramic*			
	1	*2*	*3*	*A*	*B*	*C*	*D*
Composition (wt. %)							
SiO_2	50	50	50	50	50	50	44
Al_2O_3	33	30	34	5	5	5	5
B_2O_3				10	10	10	10
Na_2O	17	20	16	7	7	10	7
K_2O				2	5	5	2
ZnO	2						
MgO		6		2			2
BaO			6				
PbO				24	21	18	24
CaO					2	2	6
TiO_2	3	3	3				
ZrO_2	1	2	2				
Coefficient of expansion, α							
$\alpha \times 10^7/°C$ of body	118	125	115				
$\alpha \times 10^7/°C$ of glaze	68.7	68.7	68.7	68.7			
(α body − α glaze) = difference, $\times 10^7$	42	45	41				

Note: Coefficients of linear thermal expansion values are designated as α, and are reduced from $n \times 10^{-7}$ to n by multiplying by 10^7 for convenience of tabulating.

100, are given in table 15.14. These glazes can be fired up to 1,950° F, but not higher.

Glazes for Bodies with Extremely High Thermal Expansions

Glass-ceramic bodies having reversible thermal expansions in the range of $120 \times 10^{-7}/°$ C were greatly strengthened with a glaze having an expansion less than 70×10^{-7}. Some glass-ceramic underbodies, and glazes for them, are shown in table 15.15 as published by Tashiro, Wadi, Vamanaka and Tani.[34] The glaze was melted as a glass, ground, made into slip, applied to the underbody, and fired at 1,100° C for 2 hours.

The glass-ceramics were made by melting and quenching the glass, then heat treating to nucleate and crystallize. The glass was heated at 750° C for 2 hours, raised to 1,000° C at 5° C per min and held 2 hours, then cooled to room temperature.

Devitrified Solder Glasses with Low Expansions

Coatings of very low thermal expansion, based on devitrified solder glasses, were developed by Mills.[35] When crystallized, these coatings contained beta-spodumene or beta-eucriptite as the primary crystalline phase. The coefficients of expansion, after crystallizing, were in the range of minus 5 to plus $30 \times 10^{-7}/°$ C. The compositions were in the following range: 12% to 23% PbO, 4% to 11% B_2O_3, 4% to 6% Li_2O, 14% to 19% Al_2O_3, and 39% to 50% of SiO_2.

References

1. Harman, C. G. 1944. Suggestions for solution of difficult glaze-fit problems. *J. Am. Ceram. Soc.* 27(8):231–33.
2. Rankin, G. A. and Merwin, H. E. 1918. The ternary system $MgO–Al_2O_3–SiO_2$. *Am. J. Sci.* 45(4):301–35.
3. Karkhanavaia, M. D. and Hummel, F. A. 1953. The polymorphism of cordierite. *J. Am. Ceram. Soc.* 36(12)389–92.
4. Singer, Felix. 1929. New stoneware bodies: 1, Composition. *Ber. Deut. Keram. Ges.* 10(6):269–71.
5. Hummel, F. A. and Reid, H. W. 1951. Thermal expansion of some glasses in the system $MgO–Al_2O_3–SiO_2$. *J. Am. Ceram. Soc.* 34(10):319–21.
6. Hummel, F. A. 1951. Thermal-expansion properties of some synthetic lithia minerals. *J. Am. Ceram. Soc.* 34(8):235–39.
7. Roy, R. 1959. Silica O, a new common form of silica. *Z. Krist.* 111(3):185–99.

8. Ray, Satyabrata and Muchow, G. M. 1968. High quartz solid solution phases from thermally crystallized glasses of composition (Li_2O, MgO) · $Al_2O_3 \cdot nSiO_2$.
9. Buerger, J. M. 1954. Stuffed derivatives of the silica structure. *Am. Mineralogist* 39(7–8):600–14.
10. Brackbill, C. E., McKinstry, H. A., and Hummel, F. A. 1951. Thermal expansion of some glasses in the system Li_2O–Al_2O_3–SiO_2. *J. Am. Ceram. Soc.* 34(4):107–9.
11. Stookey, S. D. 1959. Catalyzed crystallization of glass in theory and practice. *Glastech. Ber.* 32(5):1–8; 1961. *Ceram. Abstr.* May:123*h*.
12. Stookey, S. D. 1959. Catalyzed crystallization of glass in theory and practice. *Ind. Eng. Chem.* 51(7):805–808.
13. McMillan, P. W. 1964. *Glass ceramics*. New York: Academic Press, Inc.
14. Porai-Koshits, E. A. ed. 1964. *Structure of glass*. Vol. 3. Translated from the Russian by Consultants Bureau, New York.
15. Goldstein, Martin. 1965. Light scattering and spinoidal decomposition in glasses. *J. Am. Ceram. Soc.* 48(3):126–30.
16. Ohlberg, S. M., Hammel, J. J., and Golob, H. R. 1965. Phenomenology in noncrystalline microphase separation in glass. *J. Am. Ceram. Soc.* 48(4):178–80.
17. Cahn, J. W. and Charles, R. J. 1965. Initial stages of phase separation in glasses. *Phys. Chem. Glasses* 6(5):181–91.
18. Kivlighn, H. D. *Method of making semicrystalline ceramic bodies and the composition thereof*. U.S. Patent 3,146,114, Aug 25, 1964.
19. MacDowell, J. F. *Glass-ceramic bodies and method of making them*. U.S. Patent 3,201,266, Aug 17, 1965.
20. Hood, H. P. and Stookey, S. D. *Method of making a glass article of high mechanical strength and article made thereby*. U.S. Patent 2,779,136, Jan 29, 1957.
21. Olcott, J. S. and Stookey, S. D. 1962. in *Advances in glass technology*. New York: Plenum Press, pp 400–403.
22. Garfinkle, M. M., Rothermel, D. M., and Stookey, S. D. 1962. *Advances in glass technology*. New York: Plenum Press, pp 404–411.
23. Stookey, S. D. In Zackay, V. F., ed. 1965. *High-strength materials*. New York: John Wiley & Sons, Inc., pp. 669–81.
24. Dohfrty, P. E., Lee, D. W., and Davis, R. S. 1967. Direct observations of the crystallization of Li_2O–Al_2O_3–SiO_2 glasses containing TiO_2. *J. Am. Ceram. Soc.* 50(2):77–81.
25. Beall, G. H., Karstetter, B. R., and Rittler, H. L. 1967. Crystallization and chemical strengthening of stuffed β-quartz glass ceramics. *J. Am. Ceram. Soc.* 50(4):181–90.
26. Kosiorek, Raymond and Loughman, John I. *Crystallizable enamels for glass-ceramics*. U.S. Patent 3,463,647, Aug 26, 1969.
27. Wolf, William F. and Kosiorek, Raymond. *Crystallizable enamels for glass ceramics*. U.S. Patent 3,428,466, Feb 18, 1969.
28. Smith, William E. *Glass composition and method and product*. U.S. Patent 3,380,818, April 30, 1968.

29. Ellis, James Leslie. *Glass-compositions*. U.S. Patent 3,459,569, Aug 5, 1969.
30. Martin, Francis W. *Crystalline glazed ceramic containing lead titanate crystals and method*. U.S. Patent 3,405,003, Oct 8, 1968.
31. Martin, Francis W. *Method for glazing*. U.S. Patent 3,488,216, Jan 6, 1970.
32. Bopp, Harold, Megles, John E., and Morrison, Joseph W. *Method of glazing semicrystalline glass-ceramic articles and resultant intermediate layer containing composite*. U.S. Patent 3,384,508, May 1, 1968.
33. Medert, Warren C. *Art of decorating glass-ceramic substrate*. U.S. Patent 3,418,156, Dec. 24, 1968.
34. Tashiro, M., Wadi, M., Vamanaka, T., and Tani, K. *Method of strengthening* Na_2O–Al_2O_3–SiO_2 *glass ceramics with leaded glaze and product*. U.S. Patent 3,473,937, Oct 21, 1969.
35. Mills, Walter H. *Crystallizable lead borosilicate compositions for use as low thermal expansion devitrifying solder glasses or coatings*. U.S. Patent 3,503,763, March 31, 1970.

16

Glazes for Various Applications

Artware

Aventurine Glazes

Aventurine glazes are transparent glasses containing thin, plate-like crystals or spangles suspended in the glassy matrix. These reflect the incident light so as to produce a glittering or sparkling appearance. The name, aventurine, is used to describe the glazes because of the general similarity in appearance to the minerals, aventurine quartz and a feldspar, both of which contain small platelike crystals of hematite.

The production of the aventurine appearance in glass melts was well known, apparently, before systematic methods of producing similar effects in glazes were attempted.

Iron is the element which has been used most frequently in vitreous melts for the purpose, but chromium does very well. Although copper gives good results in glass, there do not appear to be any references to its use in glazes. Uranium aventurines are referred to fairly frequently in the literature and may be made with little difficulty.

A typical lead glaze is capable of dissolving 6% and more of ferric oxide, depending upon the temperature of fusion. If slow cooling follows, a separation of the excess will take place. If the excess is large, a rough surface, formed by the abundant coarse crystals, will be the result, or perhaps a scummy effect. If care is exercised in selecting the correct composition and heat treatment, fine crystals suspended in the glassy matrix will appear. The habit of the crystals will depend upon these conditions and possibly upon the influence of other components present.

Ferruginous bodies are preferred for the application of the iron aventurine glazes, but others may be used. The use of an underslip containing abundant ferric oxide as the intermediate layer on a nonferruginous body has been reported as of little value.

The compositions of iron aventurine glazes which have been discussed[1,2,3] represent a considerable range of compositions as feasible throughout wide temperature limits. The firing conditions, particularly the manner of cooling, are of very great importance. Summing up the information briefly as it pertains to the limits of the glazes studied:

1. Soda may be the only base used and the amount has an important influence on the extent and size of the crystal growth. Potash seems to be much less useful and lithia is reported as useful by some investigators, but not so by others. Lead oxide is frequently used and it is the experience of some ceramists that the decrease of the lead and the increase of the soda content will increase the crystallization, but there may be a lessening of the gloss. Lime may be present even up to 0.4 equivalent, depending upon the maturing temperature. It is the least useful of the bases mentioned for the promotion of the crystallization.
2. In general the alumina content should be as low as is consistent with the proper viscosity of the glaze to prevent excessive flow. As much as 0.2 equivalent may be used. It is absent in some glazes.
3. Boric oxide is commonly present in amounts necessary for the desired maturity, which in turn is dependent upon other constituents. The amount will be comparable to compositions of other than aventurine glazes.
4. The amount of the ferric oxide may vary from 0.20 equivalent to 0.85 equivalent.
5. The silica content will be chosen to permit the desired maturity under the conditions fostered by the active fluxes present.

GLAZE COMPOSITIONS. A few compositions which have yielded interesting iron aventurine glazes are the following:

1.[4]	$0.15K_2O$	$0.15Al_2O_3$	$1.59SiO_2$	Cone 010
	$0.08CaO$	$0.07Fe_2O_3$		
	$0.77PbO$			

Apply on ground color consisting of finely ground chrome oxide or iron chromate.

2.[5]	$0.4Na_2O$	$0.03Al_2O_3$		
	$0.46PbO$		$2.1SiO_2$	Cone 09
	$0.14FeO$	$0.32B_2O_3$		

Frit Composition

$0.5Na_2O$

		$0.4B_2O_3$	$2.0SiO_2$	
	$0.4PbO$			
3.[5]	$0.9Na_2O$	$0.05Al_2O_3$		
		$2.00B_2O_3$	$6.0SiO_2$	
	$0.1BaO$	$0.85Fe_2O_3$		Cone 07

Frit the entire batch. Add gum and apply thickly.

4.[2]		$0.15Al_2O_3$		
	$1.0Na_2O$	$1.25B_2O_3$	$7.0SiO_2$	Cone 1
		$0.75Fe_2O_3$		

This composition was entirely fritted.

5.[5]	$0.10K_2O$			
	$0.15Na_2O$	$0.22Al_2O_3$		
	$0.25CaO$		$2.3SiO_2$	Cone 2
	$0.35PbO$	$0.30B_2O_3$		
	$0.15FeO$			

Frit Composition

	$0.2K_2O$		
	$0.3Na_2O$	$0.2Al_2O_3$	
	$0.2CaO$		$2.0SiO_2$
	$0.2PbO$	$0.6B_2O_3$	
	$0.1FeO$		

6.[5]	$0.9Na_2O$	$0.15Al_2O_3$		
		$2.0B_2O_3$	$6.0SiO_2$	Cone 4
	$0.1BaO$	$0.95Fe_2O_3$		

This composition was entirely fritted.

7.[1]	$0.4Na_2O$	$0.05Al_2O_3$		
		$0.25B_2O_3$	$2.4–4.2SiO_2$	Cone 4
	$0.6PbO$	0.12 to 0.81 Fe_2O_3		

The Frit

	$0.57Na_2O$	$0.375B_2O_3$	
			$2.5SiO_2$
	$0.43PbO$	$0.17Fe_2O_3$	

Copper aventurine glasses have been made for many centuries but a corresponding glaze does not appear to have been developed or, if so, there is no reference to it in the technical literature. Chrome aventurine glazes have been discussed to some extent. Haldeman[3] has given a brief resume of earlier literature as well as a report on his own studies, which had to do with the substitution of the chromium oxide for part of the ferric oxide. He obtained a wide range of color variation from clear green to

Figure 16.1. *Left,* glazes used with paints for decorative effects. *Right,* crackle glazes used for decorative effects.

brown and from matt to isolated crystalline flitters suspended in the matrix. Kondo[6] has described his experiments with fritted glaze compositions into which chrome oxide was introduced. He gives the following composition as the best for a chrome aventurine at cone 5a (Standard Orton Cone 5):

$0.25K_2O$		
$0.25Na_2O$	$0.05Al_2O_3$	$1.65SiO_2$
$0.50CaO$	0.02 to $0.10Cr_2O_3$	$0.60B_2O_3$

Uranium aventurine glazes have been discussed to a slight extent by Koerner[7] and by others. Examples of decorative glazes are shown in figure 16.1.

Flowing, Running, Marbled, Streaked, and Shaded Glazes

Special surface effects are obtained by applying on the finish of a prefired glaze a coating of a more fusible glaze which flows, during the second firing, over the surface of the first coating. The flowing glaze is applied thickly and only on the rim and shoulder of the ware. The shape of the piece should be chosen with consideration of the final effect desired. Usually dextrine or some suitable thickener is added to the slip of the second coat and the application may be made by painting or pouring. Since the primary purpose of the technique is to decorate, coloring agents are added to the foundation glaze as well as to the second coat. These should be selected to produce a pleasing harmony or contrast. The final effect may be greatly enhanced by the addition of 5% of tin oxide.

If the flowing glaze contains titanium oxide or rutile, crystals will frequently develop during the cooling with very pleasing effect. Care must be taken not to hasten the cooling period. The use of 8% to 15% of copper oxide, manganese oxide, or cobalt oxide, etc., produces interesting results. The beauty and brilliance of the crystal separations are enhanced by the addition of small quantities of the oxides of tungsten, molybdenum, and especially from 0.2% to 2% of vanadium pentoxide.[8]

In order to prepare flowing glazes for use on porcelain, the composition of the base glaze may be altered for use as the coating glaze by reducing the amount of alumina as much as 7% and reducing the silica content by two equivalents and substituting one-half of that amount as boric oxide. The presence of the latter will correct any tendency to craze due to the diminished alumina content.

Iridescent Glazes

Iridescence is a surface phenomenon developed by chemical or mechanical means or by both operating together. Antique glass excavated after centuries of burial in the ground, exposed to the attack of the mineralized water present; modern glass if improperly prepared and weathered; some of the resinate lusters influenced by the firing conditions; and some glazes fired in an atmosphere charged with acid fumes or even subjected to them after maturity and at room temperatures—all these furnish good examples of iridescence. The optical effect is due to the interference of the light rays refracted and reflected from two glaze surfaces separated by a few wavelengths of distance. A glaze layer of uniform thickness reflects uniform color, whereas mother of pearl or a diffraction grating breaks the white light into its component wavelengths. Some of these are visible to us as color and some are annulled by interference.

In order to produce an irised effect, a glaze of a suitable composition is matured in the usual manner and later subjected to an atmosphere of acid fumes in a muffle heated to about 700° C. Franchet[9] recommended the use of tin chloride as preferable to titanium chloride. The former he mixed with about 10 times its weight of whiting in order to retard the decomposition. This he placed in a receptacle on the floor of the muffle and he carefully maintained the temperature as uniform as possible. When the maximum iridescence was attained as shown by a draw trial, the tray containing the salts was withdrawn and the temperature raised somewhat (820° C) in order to fix the irisation more certainly. He found that the glazes containing lead were less beautiful than those that were leadless.

Watkins[10] studied the irisation of a series of glazes containing potassa, soda, calcia, lead oxide, boric oxide, and silica, varying the last four. The irising mixture was, in parts by weight: barium nitrate, 2; strontium nitrate, 1; stannic chloride, 3; bismuth nitrate, 0.5; sulfur, 1.

Tile glazed at cone 10 were placed in a small electric furnace and heated to a temperature of 700° C. The above mixture was strewn on the floor of the furnace at that temperature. The furnace was then shut off and the contents allowed to cool. An excess of bismuth nitrate blackened the objects, obscuring the irising. If the temperature was too low the effect produced was faint. The glazes became matt if heated too strongly or if too much of the salts were used. His conclusions were as follows:

1. Glazes with a medium or low acid content gave the best effects.
2. High lead and low lime gave the better results.
3. Glazes having a low acid content, that is boric acid to silica ratios of 1:2 or 1:2.5 were favored.

Crystalline Glazes

Crystalline glazes are characterized by notable separations of crystals, either microscopic or macroscopic, suspended within the glaze or on the surface, and sometimes growing above the latter. Isolated crystalline particles originating in the raw materials of the batch and remaining undissolved are accidental and not to be included in this category.

Crystalline glazes may be classified as macrocrystalline and microcrystalline. Macrocrystalline are those in which the crystals are large enough to be readily distinguished by the naked eye. There are two kinds:

a. Aventurine glazes where the crystals are sufficiently large and separated so as to be easily observed as minute scales or flitters suspended below the surface of the glaze; or, they may be very small and so numerous and oriented as to reflect light rays from the internal surfaces of the suspended crystals, producing an effect similar to the mineral, catseye.
b. Crystalline glazes (the typical crystalline glaze) where the surface may be covered completely or partially with well-developed individual crystals (some, perhaps, projecting above); or where the crystals may be below the surface, immersed in the glassy matrix. The crystals are usually in clusters, frequently covering considerable areas.

Microcrystalline are those in which the crystals are not individually visible except under magnification. The typical example is the matt glaze. This has a surface which, in the best examples, has the soft, pleasing appearance of a glimmering, resinous luster similar to that exhibited by jade and chert. Less satisfactory surfaces are semiglossy, dull and greasy.

The systematic development of crystalline glazes is practiced to achieve textural variations departing from the smooth glossy, glassy surface of the typical glaze. The result may be a matt, semimatt, or interesting geometrical patterns due to the separation of fine to large individual crys-

Figure 16.2. *Left,* reduced copper glaze producing a distinct red with green streaking. *Right,* high index of refraction and thick application produce a butterfat glaze effect.

tals having the characteristics of the compound which has crystallized. These may be colored by the addition of ceramic color oxides. Frequently the colorless crystal appears imbedded in a colored magma. Since glaze layers are thin, the crystalline forms most successfully employed are needlelike, platy, or finely granular. Two examples of crystal glazes are shown in figure 16.2.

Aventurine glazes were made in the Orient many centuries ago. The first scientific discussion of the preparation of macrocrystalline glazes seems to have been made by Ebelman about 1847–52. They were produced at Sèvres during the last quarter of the 19th century and the government-operated porcelain factories at Copenhagen and Berlin soon afterward successfully undertook the manufacture. In the United States, the Rookwood factory exhibited, at the Columbian Exposition of 1893, superior specimens of crystalline glaze decorated vases, which elicited the favorable mention of eminent European ceramists.

The development of the crystalline glaze depends upon: (*a*) The chemical character and the physical properties of the solvent glaze, or magma; (*b*) the basic oxide used to form the silicate which saturates the magma and eventually appears as the crystalline compound during the cooling; (*c*) the temperature and the duration of the firing; and (*d*) the time-temperature cooling period.

The nature of the glaze (which is to act as the magma) is important chiefly because it must serve as a solvent for the silicates which are later separated during the cooling and because its physical properties, notably the viscosity during that period, must be favorable to the growth of the crystals. This is shown by the widely different types of glazes in which zinc silicate, for example, may be induced to crystallize. The reaction of the glaze and the body, insofar as the solution from the latter is concerned, may be important in some instances since a fundamental relation is thereby disturbed. This is illustrated by the occurrence in some cases of crystals in the glaze-body interface.

Crystalline glazes may be prepared by introducing the necessary materials in the raw glaze batch, by fritting a portion of the batch containing the crystallizing agent, and by applying on the surface of a fired glaze a mixture containing the crystallizer either raw or as a frit, then completing the operation in a kiln. Since this latter coat is, by nature, very fluid during the firing, interesting decorative patterns may result from the mottling or streaking of the running coat. Some materials, notably rutile, may be sprayed or dusted on the damp glaze coat, before firing, to develop other interesting effects.

Stull[11] made the following observations concerning the composition of crystalline glazes:

a. The strongest crystalline tendencies are given to glazes by those chemical elements of the low atomic weights whose oxides go to make up the RO, such as Li, Mg, Ca, Mn, Fe, Zn.

b. Those metals of high atomic weight, such as Ba, Pb, etc. seem to be unfavorable to crystallization.

c. Those elements of higher atomic weight whose oxides make the acid portion of the glaze, such as Si, Ti, P, etc., produce the best crystallizing agents, while those of less atomic weight, such as B, impart fluidity to a glaze which is detrimental to crystallization.

d. The introduction of the R_2O_3 materially assists crystallization in some cases, while it may be detrimental in others.

RO groups having only a few members give good results and, theoretically, the more complex should be less favorable because they tend to form the more glassy melts; however, numerous examples of such have been reported as giving satisfactory results.

Bases Used in Crystalline Glazes. The oxides most commonly used to form macrocrystals are zinc, titanium, and iron. Zinc forms large fan-like separations which have been identified as willemite ($2ZnO \cdot SiO_2$). Purdy and Krehbiel[12] found that the proportion of zinc oxide to alkali which was most conducive to crystallization lay within these limits: 0.3 to 0.6ZnO and 0.7 to 0.4KNaO. Soda was the more conducive to crystallizations and the crystals were larger and more pleasing. Crystalline glazes may be had by adding zinc oxides to borosilicate compositions. Kondo[13] found the following composition was the best of a series studied by him at cone 12: $0.2K_2O$ and 0.8ZnO with $2.0SiO_2$ and $0.2B_2O_3$. It seems to be immaterial whether the zinc oxide is added to the raw batch or introduced in a frit, and Hainbach[14] reported that it was the practice at the Royal Pottery at Copenhagen to apply a mixture of silica and zinc oxide upon the surface of a matured glaze and refire. Porst,[15] using draw trials for studying the firing conduct of a cone 8 crystalline glaze, found that the range of formation of crystals was from 750° to 1,050° C. Schwartz,[16] using a similar technique and a cone 6 crystalline glaze composition, found crystals separating at 500° C.

Titanite ($CaO \cdot TiO_2 \cdot SiO_2$) forms readily as small, acicular (needle-like) crystals. Frequently they are so small and numerous as to give the glaze a mattlike texture. This compound forms more readily than willemite and may be developed with it in the same glaze coating. Some investigators report that it is undesirable to introduce the titanium oxide or the rutile in a frit.

Other metals found to yield interesting results include: bismuth, which gives best results in a "neutral" or basic glaze; manganese, which is said, by Purdy, to give better results with zinc than may be had with zinc-alkali or zinc-titanium. Copper, manganese, cobalt, and manganese with zinc give better crystals than zinc with alkali or titanium. Tungsten, molybdenum, and vanadium in small amounts promote the formation of crystals by other agents. Molybdenum is especially useful. Kondo[17] says that a calcium silicate separates as crystals in cone 14 glazes but magnesia is more effective. Koerner[7] reports that bismuth, because of its strongly basic nature, is disposed to form crystalline compounds with uranic acid; a neutral or basic glaze is most favorable. Lithium facilitates the formation of crystals and may be introduced as the carbonate or in other convenient forms.

Alumina. Alumina influences the viscosity of the molten glaze importantly, and its presence controls the rate of formation of the crystals, their size, the flowing of the glaze coating, and its heat range. Alumina can hinder or prevent the formation of crystals so it is understandable why it is absent from many formulae, or present in small amounts. Worcester,[18] using a borosilicate composition, compared the effects of alumina introduced into the batch in these forms: raw clay, alumina fritted with the batch, feldspar fritted in the batch, and clay fritted in the batch. Raw clay was the best because of its mechanical properties in the glaze slip and the wider heat range in maturing during firing.

COMPOSITIONS. Some compositions from various sources that have been used successfully to produce crystalline glazes are listed in table 16.1. Included in the tabulation are various types. There are high lead, moderate lead, and leadless. All but one contain ZnO. Five are free of TiO_2. In all cases the silica is low, an essential requirement. The firing temperatures cover the range from cone 010 to cone 12. Crystal glazes are possible both below and above these limits. No compositions in the table contain Li_2O. When Li_2O is substituted for other alkalies, the crystallizing tendency is greatly enhanced. With direct substitutions, there is a marked increase in both the number and total quantity of crystals developed.

FIRING. A wide choice of compositions may be used for crystalline glazes having a correspondingly wide range of maturing temperatures. The rate of rise of temperature does not require any different control than ordinarily used, but the rate of cooling should be regulated with respect to the formation of the crystal nuclei and the rate of growth of the individual crystals formed therefrom. For each different crystalline glaze composition, there is a time-temperature zone of maximum rate of growth. Accordingly, the cooling of the kiln should be adjusted to this rate. If the cooling is too rapid in this zone, either there will not be any visible crystals or they will be small, possibly forming a matt texture. Unduly prolonged cooling may yield coarse crystals and a roughened glaze surface. According to Norton,[27] nuclei form so rapidly in crystalline glaze melts that a high temperature and fluidity are needed to limit the numbers. As the temperature is gradually lowered in passing through the zone of crystallization, the undissolved nuclei grow into visible crystals whose size will depend upon their chemical nature and habit. The same investigator has developed a technique of "seeding" the molten magma with "nuclei formers," which, possibly, alter the viscosity of the immediate area of contact and thereby promote crystal growth. The seeding agent will depend upon the nature of the magma. In one instance he used sodium carbonate, calcium carbonate, and zinc oxide; in another, powdered silica was successful. This technique is not new.

KILN PRACTICE. Because high fluidity is the common character of crystalline glaze magmas during the latter stage of the firing, they flow freely on inclined or vertical surfaces; therefore choice of a glaze should

Table 16.1 Empirical formulas of a variety of crystal glazes

No.	PbO	K_2O	Na_2O	CaO	BaO	MgO	CuO	ZnO	SnO_2	CoO	Al_2O_3	B_2O_3	Cr_2O_3	SiO_2	TiO_2	Cone
1[19]	1.0	–	–	–	–	–	–	–	0.08	–	0.05	–	0.12	0.50	–	010
2[20]	–	0.075	0.075	0.150	–	–	0.0145	0.70	–	–	–	0.225	–	1.375	–	02
*3[12]	–	0.105	0.189	0.029	0.052	–	–	0.625	–	–	0.045	0.378	–	1.805	–	2
4[21]	–	–	0.30	0.05	–	–	–	0.65	–	–	0.05	0.30	–	1.8	0.2	3
5[22]	0.5	–	–	0.2	–	–	–	0.3	–	–	0.2	–	–	1.8	0.4	7
6[22]	0.5	0.1	–	0.2	–	–	–	0.2	–	–	0.1	–	–	2.0	0.5	7
†7[23]	–	–	0.33	–	–	–	–	0.67	–	–	–	–	–	1.80	0.30	7–9
8[5]	–	–	0.33	–	–	–	–	0.67	–	–	–	–	–	1.80	0.30	7
9[24]	–	0.086	0.067	–	–	0.067	0.11	0.67	–	–	0.03	0.135	–	0.922	0.037	8
10[25]	–	0.235	0.0513	0.088	0.0513	–	–	0.575	–	–	0.162	–	–	1.70	0.202	9
**11[26]	–	0.16	–	0.31	0.02	0.43	–	0.08	–	–	0.24	–	–	2.20	–	10
12[13]	–	0.2	–	–	–	–	–	0.8	–	–	–	0.2	–	2.0	–	12

*The authors produced crystalline glazes using widely differing compositions and temperatures.
†Cobalt, copper, manganese, nickel, and iron were successively introduced.
**Extensive study of colors produced with the use of various oxides.

Table 16.2. Empirical formulas of some artware glazes

Code No.	*1*[28]	*2*[28]	*3*[28]	*4*[28]	*5*[29]	*6*[30]	*7*[31]	*8*[32]
Feature	Red-ware	Lead	Mat	Mat	Low-temp.	Soft	Lead-less	Pb & B free
Cone	05	05	05	05	012	022	04	08
Na_2O	–	–	–	–	0.346	0.215	–	0.38
K_2O	0.15	–	–	0.17	0.135	–	0.26	0.13
MgO	–	–	–	–	–	0.06	–	–
CaO	0.08	–	–	0.45	0.055	–	0.41	0.04
SrO	–	–	–	–	–	–	–	–
BaO	–	–	–	–	0.065	–	0.06	0.20
PbO	0.77	1.00	1.00	0.38	–	0.785	–	–
ZnO	–	–	–	–	0.264	–	0.21	0.25
B_2O_3	–	–	–	–	–	–	0.41	–
Fe_2O_3	0.07	0.03	–	–	–	–	–	–
Al_2O_3	0.15	–	0.35	0.35	0.15	–	0.40	0.10
Bi_2O_3	–	–	–	–	–	0.01	–	–
TiO_2	–	–	–	–	0.076	–	–	0.10
SiO_2	1.59	1.40	1.60	1.38	3.28	1.25	1.80	2.83
Body	Red	Red	–	–	Faience		Lime-silica	Earthenware

be made with this fact in mind. Some crystal patterns are more pleasing on broad surfaces than on narrow-necked, columnar types of pottery wares. The high fluidity is often the cause of the destruction of the piece of ware, because the accumulation of glaze at the base of the piece binds the same to the support and, when cooling, solidifies the mass. Attempts to part the two ordinarily result in the destruction of the ware. This may be avoided by placing the ware on a layer of china clay of appropriate thickness or using a short cylindrical support made of a soft clay body which may easily be removed later by an abrasive wheel.

The total number of glazes used on artware is tremendous. A few unusual ones are given in table 16.2.

Glazes for Alumina Bodies

The problems associated with the glazing of alumina bodies were discussed by Schramm,[33] Luks,[34] and others. There are problems peculiar to the glazing of alumina. This is well understood by those who have had to develop such glazes. Not much has been published on the subject, however.

Bisque ware can be glazed at low temperatures with no particular difficulty. One-fire glazes for alumina bodies, however, prove to be more difficult. The mutual chemical activity of the body and glaze ingredients

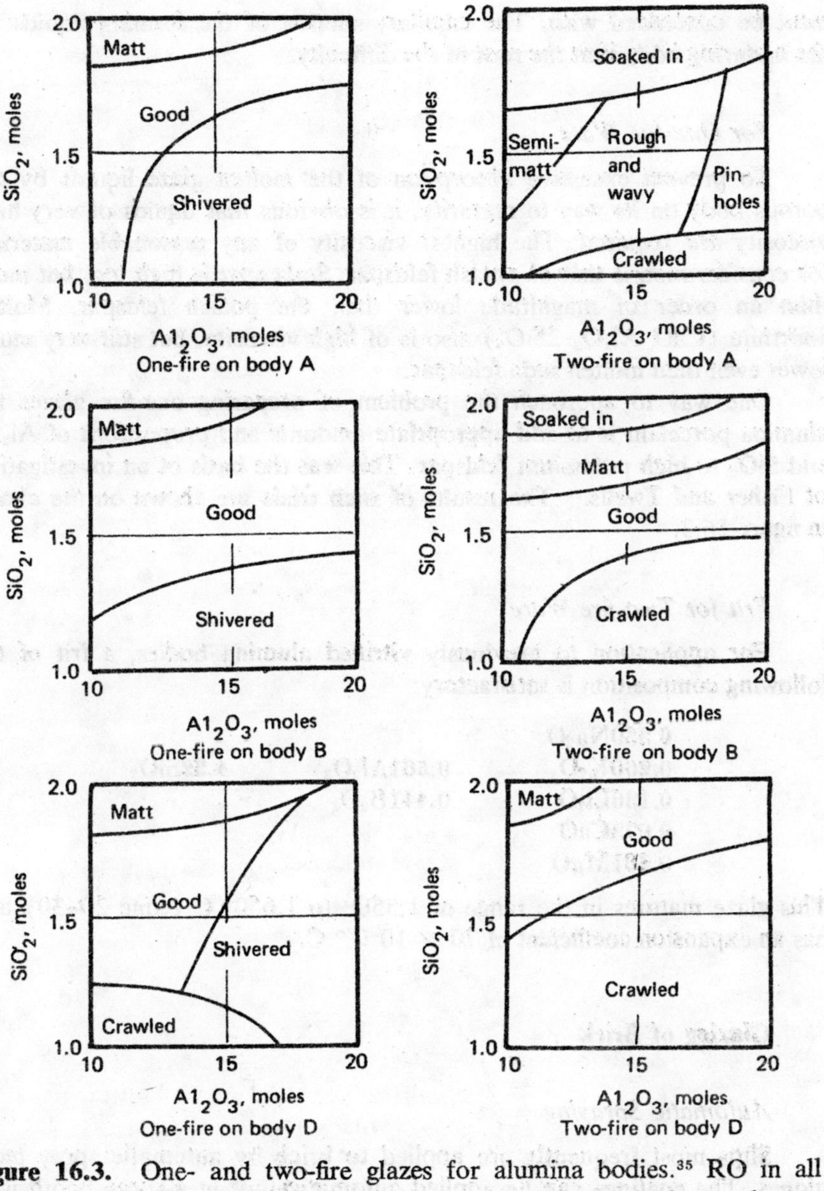

Figure 16.3. One- and two-fire glazes for alumina bodies.[35] RO in all cases is $0.75K_2O$, $0.25Na_2O$, with Al_2O_3 and SiO_2 variable as shown:

Body	*Alumina*	*Talc*	*Dolomite*	*Clay*
A	84	8	8	0
B	84	3	3	10
D	60	5	5	30

must be contended with. The capillary suction of the forming liquids by the maturing body is at the root of the difficulty.

For One-fire Ware

To prevent excessive absorption of the molten glaze liquids by the porous body on its way to maturity, it is obvious that liquids of very high viscosity are required. The highest viscosity of any reasonable materials for consideration is that of potash feldspar. Soda spar is high too, but more than an order of magnitude lower than the potash feldspar. Molten anorthite ($CaO \cdot Al_2O_3 \cdot 2SiO_2$) also is of high viscosity, but still very much lower even than molten soda feldspar.

One way to approach the problem of preparing one-fire glazes for alumina porcelain is to add appropriate amounts and proportions of Al_2O_3 and SiO_2 to high potassium feldspar. This was the basis of an investigation of Fisher and Twells.[35] The results of such trials are shown on the charts in figure 16.3.

Frit for Two-fire Ware

For application to previously vitrified alumina bodies, a frit of the following composition is satisfactory:

$0.330Na_2O$		
$0.260K_2O$	$0.561Al_2O_3$	$4.32SiO_2$
$0.136Li_2O$	$0.441B_2O_3$	
$0.073CaO$		
$0.201MgO$		

This glaze matures in the range of 1,550° to 1,650° C (cone 20–30) and has an expansion coefficient of $70 \times 10^{-7}/°$ C.

Glazing of Brick

Automatic Spraying

Slips most frequently are applied to brick by automatic spray techniques. The coatings can be applied automatically[36] in a spray booth with some mechanized spray guns, exhaust fans and stack, and a pump or pressure tank to supply the guns. To this should be added conveyors; preheating and after-drying facilities; proper guns, properly located, and a suitable number of guns; and arrangements for recirculating, reusing, or disposing of overspray.

There is a choice to make as to whether to apply the glaze to the wet column, dry column, or fired ware. All have their advantages. It is easier to do a good job of glazing on a dry column than on the wet, mainly because of the presence of crumbs, chips, and rough edges from the cutter.

Roller

Another practical method of application is by means of a roller. The chief problems are feeding the roller and cleaning the ware or of crumbs from the cutter. For the roller method the rheological properties of the slip are of paramount importance and must be controlled within narrow limits. Also it is not easy to coat vertical surfaces with a roller. The main advantage is its extreme simplicity.

Dry Coatings

Procedures for applying dry coatings are mainly of the sandblasting and the dusting and rolling type. In the second type the material is dusted on the surface of a wet column with a vibrator or chute, then pressed into the surface with a series of loaded rollers. This can do a satisfactory job on a horizontal surface, but the difficulty comes on the vertical.

Glaze Composition Considerations

Basically, glazes for structural claywares are made from feldspar, flint, clay, whiting, wollastonite, zinc oxide, lead oxide, barium carbonate, talc, zircon, and, perhaps, frit. Titanium oxides usually are avoided because of their tendency to promote crystallization and because of possible undesirable color effects. Tin oxide is expensive, and prone to discolor. Volatile components, including Sb, As, and F, are too unstable. Zircon makes good opacifiers.

For bright glazes, a ratio of silica to alumina of from 9 to 11 is required. Matt glazes occur when the SiO_2 to Al_2O_3 ratio lies in the range of 7 to 9. When the KNaO content exceeds about 0.20 equivalents, pinholes may result because of excessive reactivity of these fluxes.

Another factor to consider with some claywares is the chemical stability of the various possible sulfates. Some sulfates, for example those of calcium and magnesium, are easily formed from kiln gases and are difficult, if not impossible, to completely decompose. Their presence at high temperature will lead to blistering and or scumming. Sodium sulfate, for example, definitely will lead to defective glazes. Where kiln gases contain appreciable sulfur oxides, there are two possible courses for action: (*a*) Keep the furnace gases dry, to avoid forming H_2SO_4 in the kiln atmosphere, and (*b*) choose only those glaze components that either do not form sulfates or form sulfates that spontaneously decompose before the glaze reaches maturity.

Firing

In the firing of clays containing carbon and sulfides, the carbon should be burned out first, so the sulfides can be oxidized. Even though all of the carbon is removed at the proper stage, some sulfide from pyrite still would remain. This last portion of sulfur must be removed before the effects of sulfates can be eliminated.

For glazed structural ware the clay should all be finer than 16 mesh and, if possible, finer than 35 mesh. The fine grind influences pyrite popping, but has little influence on oxidation.

The ware should be thoroughly dry before it is placed in the kiln. It is imperative that no moisture be allowed to condense, even in the preheating areas. Glazes start to seal before oxidation has been fully accomplished. When the glaze starts to become impervious, remaining oxidizable matter will be trapped.

Glazes for Electrical Products

For Thin-film Substrates

Alumina ceramics are used as substrates for tantalum thin-film circuitry. Because the as-fired surface is too rough, a glaze is used to obtain

Table 16.3. Glazes for thin film ceramic substrates for electronic circuits[37]

Composition number	*1*	*2*	*3*	*4*	*5*	*6*	*7*
Composition, moles							
CaO	0.4000	0.454	–	0.194	0.325	0.418	0.435
BaO	0.1455	0.165	0.525	0.423	0.354	0.305	0.297
PbO	0.360	0.313	0.362	0.291	0.244	0.210	0.204
K_2O	0.0945	0.067	0.117	0.092	0.077	0.067	0.065
Al_2O_3	0.350	0.250	0.421	0.340	0.284	0.245	0.238
B_2O_3	0.642	0.228	0.775	0.466	0.261	0.112	–
Bi_2O_3	0.096	0.034	0.104	0.084	0.062	0.060	0.059
As_2O_3	0.0124	0.009	0.015	0.012	0.010	0.009	0.085
SiO_2	2.98	2.12	3.60	2.90	2.49	2.09	2.03
TiO_2	0.1117	0.079	0.068	0.054	0.045	0.039	0.028
Expansivity*	54.1	64.7	59.6	63.0	66.0	69.9	78.6
Softening point, °C	650	655	610	630	650	670	700
Firing temp., °C	1,080	1,200	1,200	1,200	1,200	1,200	1,200

*Coefficient of mean linear thermal expansion, per °C, × 10^7 (25° to 525° C)

the required smooth finish. The glaze is required to provide a clean, smooth, bubble-free surface. It should be less than 0.003 inch thick. The waviness, including the meniscus area, should be less than 0.001 inch.[37] The glaze must be essentially chemically inert to the anodizing bath and have an insulation resistance of more than 10^{10} ohms at 250° C. Finally, the glaze must fit with some compression but not enough to cause the thin underbody to warp. Di Marcello, Treptow, and Baker[37] developed glazes meeting these requirements. Several of their compositions are given in table 16.3.

The glazes were ground to pass 325 mesh, then binders were added and the slips were ground an additional 4 hours. The ideal thickness of the fired glaze was 0.0008 to 0.0016 inch.

For Thick-film Microelectronics

Microelectronics is an expanding technology in which conductors, resistors, and capacitors are prepared in the form of ceramic glazes fired onto special ceramic bodies or substrates. This specialty has developed rapidly since about 1950. Prior to that, most analogous coatings were designed and applied for decorative purposes.

The electronics industry has developed a great potential for special resistive, capacitative, and conductive glazes.[38] This general field has come to be termed "thick-film" technology. The materials, processes, and techniques are essentially ceramic in nature. Usually the films, coatings, or glazes are applied to thin and to small ceramic body substrates. Conventional as well as specialized techniques are used for applying the glazes. The most common techniques are spraying, doctor-blade spreading, printing, rolling, silk-screening, and transfer tape.

Many designs and configurations, requiring various types of electrical characteristics, are needed. One of the more common types of product is ceramic capacitors. The form may be sheets, plates, tubes, discs, or rods. These must have conductive terminals applied to them. Resistor-capacitor networks to form complete circuit modules also are common. Transistors, diodes, capacitors, and inductors in combination are applied to the ceramic substrate. Such combinations are not strictly a glaze problem, but rather a hybrid with other technologies.

There are three general categories of thick-film glazes. They are conductors, resistors, and capacitors.

Conductors

These are the "lead wires" of thick-film microelectronics. In addition to their function as electrical conductors, they must possess the attributes that make it possible to apply them to substrates, to bond to the substrates, and to have good solderability. In addition, the conductors, when applied, must have good bondability to other components in the circuit.

The typical conductors are glass or glaze filled with 75% to 90% of finely powdered metal. Usually the metal is comprised of gold, silver, platinum, or palladium. The frit or glass portion usually is of the $PbO–B_2O_3–SiO_2$ type. The glass is selected to have a thermal expansion compatible with the metal powder and to furnish a fired conductor that will "fit" the substrate. This means a slight compression, but not enough to cause warpage in the substrate.

Resistors

Dispersed conductive particles in glass applied and fired to the substrate furnishes the required resistive or conductive glaze. To do this with the control required for printed resistors, however, is difficult. The problem of utilizing powdered conductors dispersed in glassy binders presents difficulties not only because of poor resistance-temperature relationships, but especially because of the critical relationship of the resistivity of the composite to the concentration of the conductive powder.

It was shown by Auerbach[39] that the resistivity of composites of conductors and insulators can change by an order of magnitude over a very narrow range of concentration. Much of this difficulty was alleviated by D'Andrea[40] by using palladium as/or with another conductor in glaze resistors.

The resistors are prepared from a powdered borosilicate glass, usually lead borosilicate. With the glass is mixed palladium and/or palladium oxide with silver. The glass or frit is selected to fit the substrate and to fire at the desired temperature, usually at 600° to 750° C in air.

During firing, some of the palladium will alloy with silver, but some is oxidized to PdO in the temperature range 300° to 400° C. Hoffman[41] showed that the PdO starts to decompose to Pd and $\frac{1}{2}O_2$ at around 700° C. Auda and Schneider[38] enumerated the conditions that inhibit the oxidation of palladium as: (*a*) the PdO diffusion barrier on grains of Pd, (*b*) encapsulation effects of the sintered and sintering Pd-Ag alloy and the glass base, and (*c*) the short heating and holding periods.

TEMPERATURE COEFFICIENT OF RESISTANCE (TCR). There is an increase in TCR with temperature in Pd-Ag thick-film resistors. Some examples taken from Hoffman[41] are shown in tables 16.4 and 16.5.

The fit or strain in the glaze influences its resistance and the TCR. By trial, the optimum compression in the glaze can be established.

Table 16.4. Effect of adding silver to a palladium-bearing lead borosilicate resistor glaze[41]

Silver added, %	*Resistivity, ohm/sq./mil*	*TCR (ppm/°C) at 25° to 105° C*	*Noise db/decade*
0	200,000	+1720	+22
10	7,300	+ 440	+12
20	400	+ 380	+ 4
30	20	+ 175	− 8
40	0.5	+ 320	− 4

Another parameter to be controlled is the voltage coefficient of resistance (VCR). Some thick-film glazes are sensitive to applied voltage. Auda and Schneider[38] in a published review suggested that part of the VCR may be due to a TCR because of local temperature-rise during testing. There are at least these three other functions to consider: (*a*) resistivity, (*b*) terminal resistance, and (*c*) geometry.

One of the more recent compositions for resistor glazes was the subject of a patent by Mulligan and Murphy.[42] A typical composition, of a resistor enamel was: 55% of a palladium-silver mixture composed of 56% of palladium and 44% of silver; 40% of a lead borosilicate frit; and 5% of kaolin, by weight, respectively. This glaze, when applied to the substrate, was fired at 825° C.

Table 16.5. TCR and expansivity of silver-bearing lead borosilicate resistor glazes[41]

Composition, %		*TCR (ppm/°C)*		*Thermal expansion coefficient*
PbO-B_2O_3-SiO_2 frit	*Precious metal*	*(25° to 105°C)*	*(25° to 75°C)*	*× 10^7/° C (0°-300°C)*
100	0	+160	+ 50	75
70	30 Pd-Ag	+240	− 80	76
60	40 Pd-Ag	+300	−250	82
40	60 Pd-Ag	+320	−320	85
10	90 Pd-Ag			89
0	100 Pd-Ag			168
0	100 Ag			170[45]
0	100 Pd			110

Note: The thermal expansion of 100% frit = 75×10^{-7}/°C; for 70% frit, $\alpha = 76 \times 10^{-7}$/°C. In order to simplify the tabulation to simply 75, 76, 82, etc., the thermal expansion data, 75×10^{-7}, 76×10^{-7}, 82×10^{-7}, etc. were multiplied by 10^7, e.g.: $75 \times 10^{-7} \times 10^7 = 75$, hence all of the numbers in the column have been multiplied by 10^7.

Semiconductive Porcelain Glazes

Electrically conductive glazes and coatings sometimes applied on high voltage porcelain insulators should have the following attributes:[43]

a. uniformly reproducible characteristics
b. not sensitive to changes in percentages of glaze ingredients
c. compatible with conventional insulator glazes
d. not sensitive to normal variations in firing atmosphere
e. relatively constant resistance as a coating within a normal range of thickness-variations

Conductive glazes for high voltage electrical insulators can be made by mixing base porcelain glazes with combinations of such oxides as Fe_2O_3, NiO, CoO, or spinel solid solutions.[44] In this manner, the resulting network of conducting crystals in the glaze matrix can produce glazes with the desired level of conductivity.

Glazes for high voltage porcelains are too numerous to be detailed here. A recent disclosure by Horton[43] is typical. He used a mixture of: Fe_2O_3, 70%–95%; Cr_2O_3, 1.9%–1.2%; and TiO_2, 0.8%–15%.

This mixture was admixed with 30% to 70% of the regular glaze, applied to the unfired insulator, and fired along with regular porcelain insulators. An alternative method of achieving a good semiconductive high-voltage glaze as proposed by Horton[43] was the following:

(*A*)

Semiconductive coating applied to raw insulator by spraying to 5 mils thickness and covered by the cover glaze

Feldspar	14.3%
Ball clay	11.0%
Flint	11.9%
Whiting	12.7%
Cr_2O_3	3.2%
Fe_2O_3	43.8%
TiO_2	3.1%

(*B*)

Cover glaze applied over (*A*) and fired at 2,300° F

Feldspar	18.5%
Clay	22.6%
Flint	34.2%
Whiting	19.2%
Glaze stain	5.0%
Fe_2O_3	0.5%

A multilayer, nonlinear, semiconducting coating for high-tension porcelain insulators was described by Smothers.[46] Below the surface glaze and adjacent to the insulator, but not necessarily touching it, he used a semiconducting layer to provide the required conductivity. Between the glaze and the semiconducting layer he used a barrier to prevent their interaction. This was to prevent discoloration of the insulator, to prevent spurious oxidation of the semiconducting ingredients, and to guard against blistering.

A representative composition in percent by weight was: Silicon carbide powder, 65%; bentonite, 10%; feldspar, 10%; flint, 7.5%; and high strength ball clay, 7.5%.

This was mixed with 140 pounds of water per 100 pounds of solids and milled for 6 hours. The mixture was applied to the insulator by dipping or spraying and covered with a barrier coat such as the following: 35 feldspar, 15 flint, and 50 clay in percent, respectively. The regular glaze goes over this. The semiconductive coating should be 0.004 to 0.010 inch thick and should provide 10 megohms per square. The whole system was covered by the regular insulator glaze. Examples of regular glazes may be illustrated as follows:

Example (a)

$0.09K_2O$		
$0.04Na_2O$	$0.43Al_2O_3$	$4.12SiO_2$
$0.48CaO$	$0.08Fe_2O_3$	
$0.14MgO$		
$0.17MnO$		

Example (b)

$0.10K_2O$		
$0.06Na_2O$	$0.54Al_2O_3$	$3.81SiO_2$
$0.60CaO$		
$0.24MgO$		

Conductive Glasses and Coatings

A sophisticated field of conventional glazes is that of precision glaze resistors. An early ancestor of such items was carbon or graphite particles dispersed in resin binders and applied to suitable substrates by painting, spraying, or stencilling. Other ancestors comprising part of the evolution were metal films deposited by evaporation and by sputtering on ceramic substrates. Coming still closer to ceramic glaze coatings were those produced by the thermal decomposition of metallo-organic compounds on glass substrates.

Earlier ceramic glazes having resistivities of 0.1 to 45 megohms were prepared by dispersing Fe_3O_4 (added as Fe_2O_3) in the glaze.[47]

These were rather crude glazes, being composed of feldspar (or Cornwall stone), quartz, and up to 40% of Fe_2O_3. They were of interest for high-voltage line insulators. Some of the glazes developed poor or only fair gloss. These resistors all had the negative temperature coefficients as is typical of oxide resistors.

Huttar[48] and others prepared resistors by suspending powdered conductors in frit and applying this to bodies. He used up to 25% of silver and 0 to 25% of CuO plus a high concentration of Cu_2O and 10% to 25% of frit. These resistors were not very smooth and were hard to control.

With mixtures of conductors and insulators, very small changes in the degree of concentration of the solids is likely to change the resistivity of the composite by an order of magnitude or more. This has been a major deterrent to the development of precision glaze resistors. The use of palladium was advocated by D'Andrea[40] as a means to greatly improve this condition.

Good precision resistors were developed by Hoffman,[41] using powdered palladium and silver dispersed in a PbO–B_2O_3–SiO_2 frit. When palladium powder alone was used the fired glazes had useful resistivity over the range from 33% to 70% by weight of metal. Mixtures of silver and palladium were even less sensitive to compositional changes. Glaze resistor compositions were prepared to furnish resistance values ranging from 1 to 20,000 ohms per square per mil.

The fit of the conducting glaze to the body substrate is of importance. It affects the temperature coefficient of resistance and the noise level. The fit of the suspended metal to the matrix glass as well as the bond between the two is of considerable significance, for the same reasons.

CONDUCTING GLASSES. The mechanism of electrical conduction in oxide glasses below their softening points generally has been considered to be ionic. The principal charge carriers then would be alkali ions. Stansworth and associates[49] found certain vanadate glasses to be electronic conductors. Other alkali-free glasses in the V_2O_5–P_2O_5 system were found to be electronic conductors by Munakata,[50] according to Mackenzie,[51] who also prepared additional electronically conducting glasses. He reviewed the general principles involved, prepared some phosphate and vanadate glasses, and found them to conduct electronically. Mackenzie also quoted McMillan[52] as having reported that some aluminosilicate glasses, for example, $MnO \cdot Al_2O_3 \cdot SiO_2$ showed predominately electronic conduction. Mackenzie concluded that it appears certain that the preparation of all types of semiconducting oxide glasses is possible. To what extent this is possible and the possible future development of stable semiconducting glazes remain an intriguing challenge.

SEMICONDUCTING GLASSES. Glasses are conventionally termed semiconducting when volume resistivities are less than 10^9 ohm-cm at 25° C.

Electronic conductivity in glasses is known. Vitreous selenium has electronic conductivity as do vitreous selenides and tellurides, to some degree. Glasses in the system P_2O_5–V_2O_5[53] are semiconductors, as are some

Table 16.6. Semiconducting glasses in the V_2O_5-P_2O_5-GeO_2 system[56]

No.	*Mole %* GeO_2	P_4O_{10}	V_2O_5	*Softening temp. °C**	$\alpha \times 10^7$*** (25° to 300°C)*	*Dielectric constant (1MC)*	*Tan δ × 10^3*
4		60	40	705	58	9.0	79
5		50	50	595	60	9.5	69
7		30	70		69	10.0	109
8		20	80	403	82	17.0	170
15	60		40		91	14.5	27
16	80		20	580		8.3	24
17	90		10	622	72	7.0	18
20	50	50			60	6.1	16
26	30	30	40	572	67	9.6	69
27	25	25	50	500	70	11.3	137
28	20	20	60	416	76	12.2	187
29	15	15	70	349	90	14.9	348
33	45	10	45		86	10.5	141
35	25	50	25	728	57		
41	60	20	20	641	70	8.4	20
30	10	10	80	294	115	19.9	1000
31	5	5	90				
32	25	25	50				

*Softening temperature is that where viscosity = Log η = 7.65

**The coefficient of thermal expansion tabulated has been multiplied by 10^7 to eliminate repeated tabulation of 10^{-7}

in the system BaO–V_2O_5–P_2O_5 that were reported by Baynton[49] to be *n*-type. Other vanadate glasses, including those in the systems V_2O_5–P_2O_5–WO_3 and –PbO were investigated by Kitaigorodskii and Karpechenko.[54] Electronic conductivity was discussed by Weyl[55] and others.

In general, the above glasses readily devitrify unless quenched rapidly and have little, if any, practical value as conducting glazes. It was found by Janakirama-Rao[56] that remarkably improved thermal stability and electrical conductivity was to be obtained in the system P_2O_5–V_2O_5–GeO_2. Many of these glasses have thermal expansion coefficients suitable to fit ceramic body substrates, as shown in table 16.6. Softening points of these glasses also are in the range usual for glazes, as shown in the same table. Resistivities of some of these glasses are plotted in figure 16.4.

Coatings for Electrical Devices

A United States patent no. 3,441,422 described coatings for semiconductors and diodes as:

$0.988ZnO$	$0.44B_2O_3$	$0.224SiO_2$
$0.012PbO$	$0.0215Sb_2O_5$	$0.022CeO_2$

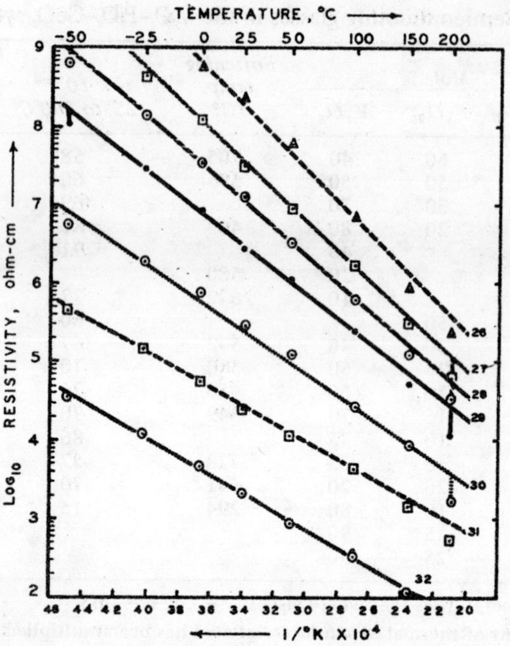

Figure 16.4. Resistivities of glasses in the system V_2O_5–P_2O_5–GeO_2[56] for compositions from table 16.4.

Table 16.7. Effect of the addition of fluorides on the dissipation factor of low-loss glassy dielectrics[58]

Specimen No.	*Fluoride added* (X)*	*Crystallization temp., °C*	*Sintering temp., °C*	*Dissipation factor at 1 KC* at 20°C	*Dissipation factor at 1 KC* at 125°C
0	none	690	680	0.00180	0.07840
1	NaF	665	630	0.00080	0.00482
2	KF	660	645	0.00052	0.00461
3	PbF_2	530	645	0.00035	0.00148
4	BaF_2	645	670	0.00046	0.00720

Reference composition		*Substituted composition*	
0.470 PbO	1.35 SiO_2	0.430 PbO	1.238 SiO_2
0.083 SrO		0.075 SrO	
0.153 MgO		0.140 MgO	
0.0588 Li_2O		0.0538 Li_2O	
0.0588 Na_2O		0.0538 Na_2O	
0.1764 K_2O		0.1610 K_2O	
		*0.086 *X*F or *X*F_2	

***The fluoride added (*X*) is used in the substituted composition as indicated by *X*F or *X*F_2**

The coating was reported to have a softening point of 635° C, liquidus temperature of 1,030° to 1,075° C, and expansion coefficient of 44.5 to $44.8 \times 10^{-7}/°$ C. The dielectric constant was 8.1 and dissipation factor at room temperature was 0.00145.

A composition was developed by Graff[57] as a coating. The characteristics of this coating were: electrical resistivity, 13.1 to 13.3 $\log_{10}$ ohm-cm at 250° C; dissipation factor of 0.00138 to 0.00145 at room temp. The coating was thermally devitrifiable at 750° to 800° C in one hour. The composition (in wt %) was: 60 ZnO, 23–25 B_2O_3, 3 CeO_2, 0.1 Bi_2O_3, 2–3 PbO, 0.5 Sb_2O_5, and 9.4 to 10.5 SiO_2.

Other glasses and crystallizable glasses were described by Hayakawa and associates.[58] The electrical properties of the coatings will vary with crystallinity, if present. The resistivity and dissipation factors of some glasses as affected by sintering and crystallization are shown in tables 16.7 and 16.8. A partial substitution of PbF_2 for RO members was effective. Additions of B_2O_3 were helpful in suppressing crystallization.

Sewer Pipe Glazes

The composition and properties of sewer pipe bodies vary so widely that glazes must be tailored for each body. Where possible, it is desirable to prepare these from locally available clays and materials. Successful

Table 16.8. Effect of B_2O_3 additions to a dielectric glass[58]

Additions of B_2O_3 in moles of B_2O_3 per mole of glaze	*Crystallization temp °C*	*Sintering temp °C*	*Crystallization tendency, arbitrary units*	*Volume resistivity at 200° C, ohm-cm*
0	530	645	35.0	2.4×10^{11}
0.0215	540	630	30.8	7.8×10^{11}
0.0645	543	625	14.0	2.0×10^{12}
0.1075	546	620	7.8	3.0×10^{12}
0.1505	550	610	Amorp.	3.6×10^{12}
0.2150	550	610	Amorp.	3.4×10^{12}

Base formula

0.430PbO		
0.075SrO		
0.140MgO		
0.0538Li_2O	0–0.215B_2O_3	1.238SiO_2
0.0538Na_2O		
0.1610K_2O		
0.086PbF_2		

Table 16.9. Chemical analysis of natural materials of possible value in sewer pipe glazes[62] (in wt. %)

	Black scoria	Red scoria	Andesitic pumice	Alluvial clay
SiO_2	54.48	53.72	60.56	57.60
Al_2O_3	20.13	20.97	17.70	19.50
FeO	2.60	0.71	—	—
Fe_2O_3	5.15	6.44	3.93	5.07
TiO_2	—	—	—	0.41
CaO	6.03	6.53	4.74	2.89
MgO	4.35	4.11	1.94	1.22
K_2O	4.10	3.06	} 4.84	} 2.00
Na_2O	2.66	3.86		
L.O.I.	0.69	0.65	6.29	10.77

sewer pipe glazes have been prepared from natural volcanic ash and similar materials by many workers.[59–66]

Conventional materials with or without the use of local materials have found more favor in the U.S than abroad. Examples are by Koenig,[67] Stull and Johnson,[68] and by Wilson and Koenig.[69]

A slip glaze maturing at 2,000° F to a glossy finish was developed by Bauleke.[70] It was of the following composition:

Glaze			*Batch, wt%*	
$0.188K_2O$			volcanic ash	65
$0.111Na_2O$	$0.366Al_2O_3$		siliceous clay	16
$0.559CaO$	$0.023Fe_2O_3$	$4.438SiO_2$	wollastonite	16
$0.142ZnO$			zinc oxide	3

The use of fusible natural materials for sewer pipe glazes was discussed by Knizek.[62] Typical compositions of some fusible earthy materials

Table 16.10. Some sewer pipe glazes from natural volcanic materials in Mexico[62]

	Parts by weight					
Composition no.	1	2	3	4	5	6
Pumice	50	—	60	50	—	—
Scoria	—	50	—	—	50	50
Alluvial clay	50	20	—	20	40	—
Feldspar	—	30	40	30	10	50
Borax	3	3	2	4	—	—
Litharge	—	—	—	—	2	4
Total batch	103	103	102	104	102	104

Note: Glaze set at 60% of solids with sp. gr. of 1.50; applied at 0.6 grams per sq cm; fired to cone 6.

are given in table 16.9. The composition of some sewer pipe glazes using such materials are tabulated in table 16.10. The glazes of table 16.10 were set at 60% of solids, giving a specific gravity of 1.56. The application was at the rate of 20 grams per square foot and fired at cone 6.

Salt glazes in textures from matt to glossy and of uniform and speckled colors were prepared by Fliess.[71] He used two techniques. In one process, the conventional salt glaze technique was employed, using a mixture of NaCl with $MnCl_2$ or $CeCl_2$ to give violet or yellow, respectively. In an alternative method, the clay body was coated with a colored frit, then the salt glaze deposited over this to give any color or texture.

Vitrifiable Enamels

Solder Glasses

A class of compositions known as solder glasses has potential use as enamels for decorating, low-temperature fluxes for glass enamels, electrical ceramics, encapsulation, or fluxes for colors. Solder glasses are almost always applied as powders, either dry or in suspension. If two pieces of glass or ceramics are to be stuck together, each part would be coated with a suitable layer. This is usually a layer about 0.005 inch thick, but in special applications it may be very much thicker. Where used as a base for ceramic colors the thickness is dictated by the applicable art. Some pertinent data from Gallup and Dingwall[72] on flux-glasses in the system $PbO–B_2O_3–SiO_2$ are given in table 16.11 and figures 16.5, 16.6, and 16.7. These figures clearly show how viscosity, annealing temperature, and thermal expansion behavior vary with temperature.

Table 16.11. Thermal expansion of some flux-glass compositions in the system $PbO–B_2O_3–SiO_2$[72]

Composition, wt. %			*Mean coefficient of linear thermal expansion × 10⁷ /°C**
PbO	*B_2O_3*	*SiO_2*	*(30° to 300° C)*
71.3		28.7	74
84.7		15.3	108
76.2	23.8		93
82.7	17.3		108
88.0	12.0		124
72.0	14.0	14.0	85
85.0	7.5	7.5	117

*The correct values for thermal expansion are to be obtained by multiplying the tabulated numbers by 10^{-7}

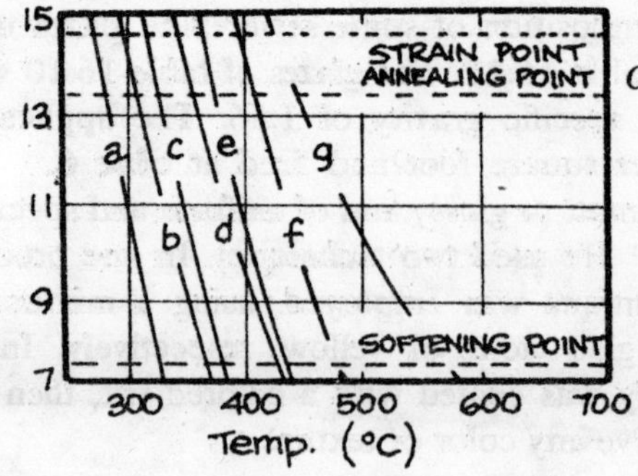

Legend

Curve	PbO	B_2O_3	SiO_2
a	88	12	—
b	85	7.5	7.5
c	82.7	17.3	—
d	84.7	—	15.3
e	76.2	23.8	—
f	72	14	14

Figure 16.5. Viscosity-temperature curves for glasses in the system $PbO–B_2O_3–SiO_2$.[72]

Vitrifiable Enamels

An example of a vitrifiable enamel based on the $PbO–B_2O_3–SiO_2$ system, from Kerridge,[73] was composed of 95.5% of frit and 4.5% of MoO_3. The frit composition, in weight percent, was: PbO, 64.9; SiO_2, 26.2; B_2O_3, 5.2; and NaO, 3.7, respectively.

Crystallizable Enamels

The glazing of ceramic materials by means of thermally devitrifiable glass was the subject of a patent by Martin.[74] He used a sealing glass frit which he applied as a glaze. The coating of frit was heated to form a glaze and caused to crystallize after the glaze had been fused. Martin's glass

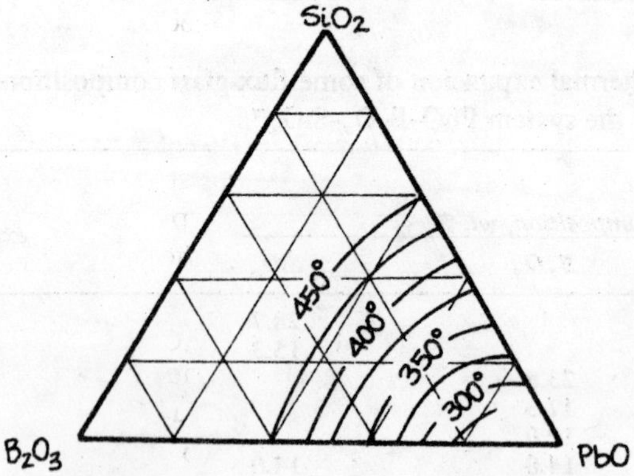

Figure 16.6. Lines of equal annealing temperature (viscosity of $10^{13.4}$ poises) for lead borosilicate glasses.[72]

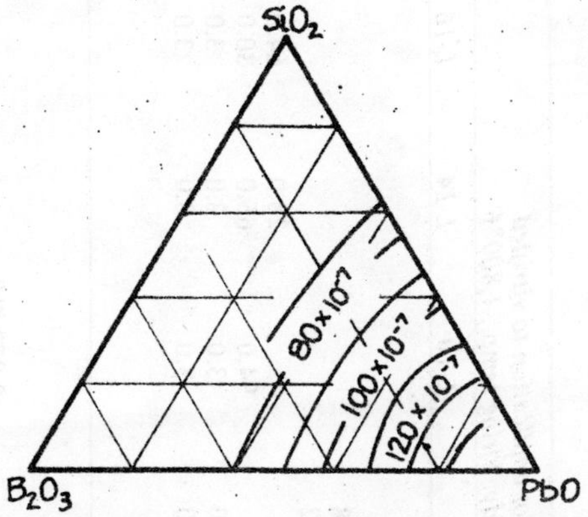

Figure 16.7. Lines of equal thermal expansion for lead borosilicate glasses.[72] Numbers on curves are mean coefficients for the range 20° to 300° C.[72]

devitrified to a composite with a thermal expansion coefficient of less than 70×10^{-7} per °C. The firing temperature was low enough to use as a glaze for borosilicate glassware.

Decorative glazing compositions for low-expansion vitreous bodies were disclosed by Petticrew.[75] The glazes were designed to fit glass-ceramic bodies having expansion coefficients of less than 25×10^{-7} per °C. Glasses of compositions shown in table 16.12 were fused, water-quenched, ground, and made into slips. The underbody was coated by dipping, spraying, or silk-screening. The firing was conducted as follows:

1. Heated rapidly to 1,100° F
2. 1,100° to 1,200° F at 145° F/hr.
3. 1,200° to 1,300° F at 25° F/hr.
4. 1,300° to 1,600° F at 50° F/hr.
5. 1,600° to 1,950° F at 145° F/hr.
6. Maintained at 1,950° F for 1 hr.
7. Cooled at rate of 400° F/hr.

Table 16.12. Glazes for glass-ceramic bodies having thermal expansions of 25×10^{-7}/° C or less[75]

Oxide	*No. 1 (%)*	*No. 2 (%)*	*No. 3 (%)*	*No. 4 (%)*	*No. 5 (%)*
SiO_2	73.97	70.0	70.0	70.0	70.0
Al_2O_3	9.59	–	–	–	2.0
Li_2O	14.41	–	5.0	–	3.0
Co_3O_4	2.0	0.5	0.5	0.5	1.0
B_2O_3	–	24.5	24.5	24.5	24.0
MgO	–	5.0	–	–	–
Na_2O	–	–	–	5.0	–

Table 16.13. Recipes for two types of steatite glazes: for raw bodies and for vitrified bodies[76]

Glaze recipe, % by weight									
	For application to raw body Maturing temp., Cone 10½					*For application to vitrified body. Firing temp., 1,800°F*			
Number	*H9*	*H10*	*H42*	*H85*	*Number*	*L-9*	*L-10*	*L-14*	*L-16*
Potash feldspar	50.0	44.0	45.4	45.0					
Nepheline syenite		35.0							
Spodumene	20.0				Frit GL-6*	43.8			
California talc	12.0	15.0			Frit GL-8*	50.2			
Whiting	5.0		14.7	19.0	Frit GL-7*			28.0	64.0
Flint			23.0	22.0	Frit GL-5*		94.0	66.0	30.0
Miss. M. & D. clay	10.0	6.0	5.9	13.8	Bentonite	3.0	3.0	3.0	3.0
Zinc oxide			1.0		Fla. kaolin	3.0	3.0	3.0	3.0
Zircon			5.0						
Lead bisilicate	3.0								

*Frit compositions

GL-5	0.81 PbO, 0.19 Na_2O	0.041 Al_2O_3, 1.774 B_2O_3	3.372 SiO_2
GL-6	1.00 PbO	1.631 B_2O_3	3.014 SiO_2
GL-7	1.00 PbO	0.238 B_2O_3	0.780 SiO_2
GL-8	1.00 PbO	0.254 Al_2O_3	1.91 SiO_2

Glazes for Steatite Bodies

Low-loss steatite bodies have relatively high expansion coefficients and are fired at critical temperatures in the range of cones 10 to 12. The electrical properties of the glazes are of primary interest and for that reason glazes with little or no alkali are preferred. The glazes may be of the once-fired or twice-fired type. Examples of both were published by Theiss[76] and their compositions are given in table 16.13. Nonsilicate glazes containing up to 73.9% of P_2O_5 were developed by Gebler.[77] They were said to be stable and lower in dielectric losses than conventional silica-bearing glazes. The glazes contained ZnO, PbO, and BeO with Al_2O_3 and P_2O_5. They were fritted at 2,300° F and fired as glazes in the range of 1,500° to 1,600° F.

Bloor[78] computed the empirical ceramic formulas for Gebler's glazes and they are shown in table 16.14.

Glazes for Zircon Bodies

The thermal expansion of zircon bodies is low, making for difficult glaze-fit problems. The coefficient of between 40 and $50 \times 10^{-7}/°$ C is compensated somewhat by the refractory nature of the porcelain, making it possible to use some of the more refractory porcelain glazes. Glazes high in MgO have been the more popular. Two formulae were cited by Bloor[78] from Luttrell[79] and from Van Gordon.[80] These were:

0.65MgO		
0.15CaO	$0.58Al_2O_3$	$5.4–5.9SiO_2$
$0.13K_2O$		
$0.07Na_2O$		

0.56MgO		
0.26CaO	$0.57Al_2O_3$	$5.15SiO_2$
$0.12K_2O$		$0.25ZrO_2$
$0.06Na_2O$		

A satisfactory conventional glaze for a zircon porcelain, having a mean coefficient of thermal expansion of $43.6 \times 10^{-7}/°$ C, was described by Luttrell[79] for cone 9 to 11, as·

$0.09Na_2O$		
$0.14K_2O$	$0.42Al_2O_3$	$4.21SiO_2$
0.17CaO	$0.18B_2O_3$	$0.69ZrO_2$
0.49MgO		
0.12ZnO		

Table 16.14. Calculated molecular formulae of Gebler's glazes[77,78] for zircon bodies.

No.	ZnO	PbO	BeO	Al_2O_3	P_2O_5	Bi_2O_3	Ce_2O_3	TiO_2
1	0.25	0.08	0.67	0.41	1.56	–	–	–
2	0.25	0.08	0.67	0.31	1.69	–	–	–
3	0.21	0.09	0.70	0.31	1.74	–	–	–
4	0.19	0.07	0.74	0.28	1.54	–	–	–
5	0.21	0.09	0.70	0.22	1.23	–	–	–
6	0.21	0.09	0.70	0.16	0.91	–	–	–
7	0.21	0.09	0.70	0.12	0.69	–	–	–
8	0.24	0.08	0.68	0.43	2.39	0.05	–	–
9	0.24	0.08	0.68	0.43	2.39	–	0.03	–
10	0.24	0.08	0.68	0.43	2.39	–	–	0.06

The batch composition in weight percentage was: Buckingham feldspar, 15.9; whiting, 1.4; talc, 13.3; zinc oxide, 2.1; Florida kaolin, 15.6; flint, 17.0; frit, 8.3; and zircon opacifier, 26.4. The frit in weight percentage was: SiO_2, 23.4; B_2O_3, 32.5; Na_2O, 14.6; CaO, 15.0; and ZrO_2, 14.5.

The high MgO content of this glaze promotes both gloss and craze resistance. The MgO is about 0.25 equivalents higher than would be acceptable for conventional clear bright porcelain or Bristol glazes fired at cone 10. Note that the alkalies are low and the $SiO_2:Al_2O_3$ ratio is about 10:1. This ratio has an important influence on finish and texture. Most of the ZrO_2 separates as zircon, thus contributing to the required low expansion. The use of B_2O_3 in this type of glaze is limited to no more than 0.2 equivalents before damage results to the finish and texture.

Glazes for high zircon bodies firing in the range of cones 11–14 and having expansion coefficients of $43 \times 10^{-7}/°$ C (25°–700° C) as developed by Van Gordon[80] were in the following range:

0.20KNaO		
0.15–0.25CaO	0.6–0.7Al_2O_3	9–11SiO_2
0.55–0.65MgO		

Batch for selected glaze had the following composition in weight percentage; Potash feldspar, 22.70; whiting, 1.60; talc, 17.00; kaolin, 20.80; flint, 26.52; and zircon, 11.38.

Glazes for Cordierite Bodies

Conventional glazes for cordierite bodies have not been very successful. The approaches discussed in the chapter on unconventional glazes are recommended. Mixtures based on petalite have been reportedly successful.

Table 16.15. Three types of bodies and their glazes used by Orth[82] in fast-fired wall tile (single-fire)

	Talc body (wt. %)	*Wollastonite body (wt. %)*	*Fritted body (wt. %)*
Talc	70	55	58
Wollastonite		55	5
Ball clay	30	30	30
Flint		15	
Frit (E, table 16.17)			7
Glaze used	A of table 16.16	A of table 16.16	B of table 16.16

Semimatt glazes were obtained by Theiss,[81] using slips of the same body containing an admixture of coloring oxides. A dark brown matt glaze with an expansion coefficient of $28 \times 10^{-7}/°$ C was obtained, but the texture was not very good. A smooth semimatt glaze was prepared from talc, ball clay, boric oxide, and coloring oxides to yield the following ultimate chemical analysis: 52.0, SiO_2; 13.5, Al_2O_3; 15.5, MgO; 3.2, B_2O_3; 9.0, Fe_2O_3; and 6.5, Cr_2O_3. These were one-fire glazes, being applied to the raw body.

Wall Tile

The variety of wall-tile bodies is exceeded only by the variety of glazes used on wall tile. There is no typical tile glaze.

Fast-fire Glazes

A study was made by Orth[82] on the rapid firing of wall tile. Three different types of bodies—talc, wollastonite, and fritted bodies—were used with two glazes, all of which are summarized in tables 16.15, 16.16, and 16.17. It was concluded that the fast-fire process potentially is applicable to all types of materials for cycles even as fast as 10 minutes.

Orth noted that the thermal expansion of bodies varied in a predictable manner with the firing treatment. The thermal expansion of bodies tends to decrease with the time of firing. Consequently, glaze fit becomes a critical factor. This can easily be adjusted through formulation.

In fast-firing, glaze-body reactions at the interface are less extensive than for the longer burns. This also must be compensated for through glaze formulation.

Table 16.16. Two glazes used by Orth[82] on fast-fired experimental wall tile

	Glaze A (wt. %)	Glaze B (wt. %)
Frit C, table 16.17	19.5	
Frit D, table 16.17		88.0
Feldspar	28.4	
Flint	8.7	
Clay	8.9	3.0
Zinc oxide	9.6	
Wollastonite	14.3	
Barium carbonate	1.0	
Opacifier	9.6	9.0

It is considered to be desirable to use a high frit or even a totally fritted glaze for fast firing. Best results often are obtained by using two frits: a hard and a soft one. The soft frit should amount to about $\frac{1}{3}$ of the total glaze batch.

Fast-fire glazes, of course, have been with us a long time. Porcelain enamels, jewelry enamels, and glass enamels always have been fired in minutes, rather than hours. Fast-firing glazes must be developed for a specific body and fired under specifically controlled conditions.

As compared to standard slow-cycle operations, fast-firing glazes introduce different behavior patterns. The differences may be summarized as follows:

a. Reduced interfacial reactions between body and glaze with a resulting reduction in defects due to that cause.
b. Greater consistency in colors.
c. Greater uniformity of firing.
d. Less smoothing of glazed surface due to glost firing; the fired glaze surface contours closely resemble the as-sprayed surface; this requires greater care as to glaze application.

Table 16.17. Three frit compositions used by Orth in the preparation of fast-firing wall tile glazes[82]

	Frit C (wt. %)	Frit D (wt. %)	Frit E (wt. %)
K_2O	0.3		1.7
Na_2O	8.5	3.6	14.7
CaO	17.0	4.5	0.1
PbO		31.0	
Al_2O_3	5.0	3.4	3.6
B_2O_3	18.7	13.0	28.9
SiO_2	50.0	43.5	51.0
ZrO_2		1.0	

Table 16.18. Examples of crystalline and textured glazes[83]

Glaze composition

	Amounts (% by weight)		
	Cone 01-2	*Cone 01-2*	*Cone 4-5*
Frit P-1733	49.5	27.2	40.5
Frit P-926		20.8	
Kaolin	9.0	8.5	9.0
Zinc oxide	10.8	14.0	10.8
Fluorspar	11.7	9.5	11.7
Opacifier (zircon)	13.5	20.0	13.5
Alumina	5.5		5.5
Silica			9.0

Frit compositions

	Amounts (% by wt.)	
	P-1733	*P-926*
K_2O		0.3
Na_2O	9.4	8.5
CaO	4.2	17.0
ZnO	15.5	5.0
Al_2O_3		18.7
B_2O_3	30.2	50.5
SiO_2	40.7	

e. Electrolytes and consistency-controlling additives usually are necessary in order to develop and maintain smooth glaze application.

f. Fast-firing results in lower thermal expansion in most bodies than conventional slow cycles. This means that fast-fire glazes must be of lower expansion than those used on the same body under slow schedules. Glaze-fit problems can arise due to variations in firing heat treatment and in variations in the reactivity of body ingredients.

g. Glazes should be as high in frit as is practical.

h. New and brighter shades of colors can be produced because of greater kiln control and uniformity.

Textured or Crystalline Glazes

Hard, or "crystal" glazes have become popular for tile to be used on floors. Their abrasion resistance makes them very durable as floor tile. The surface characteristics also add to their decorative value for wall tile as well as glazed flooring tile.

These glazes are somewhat sensitive as to the body type and texture and to firing treatment. They are particularly sensitive as to batch ingredi-

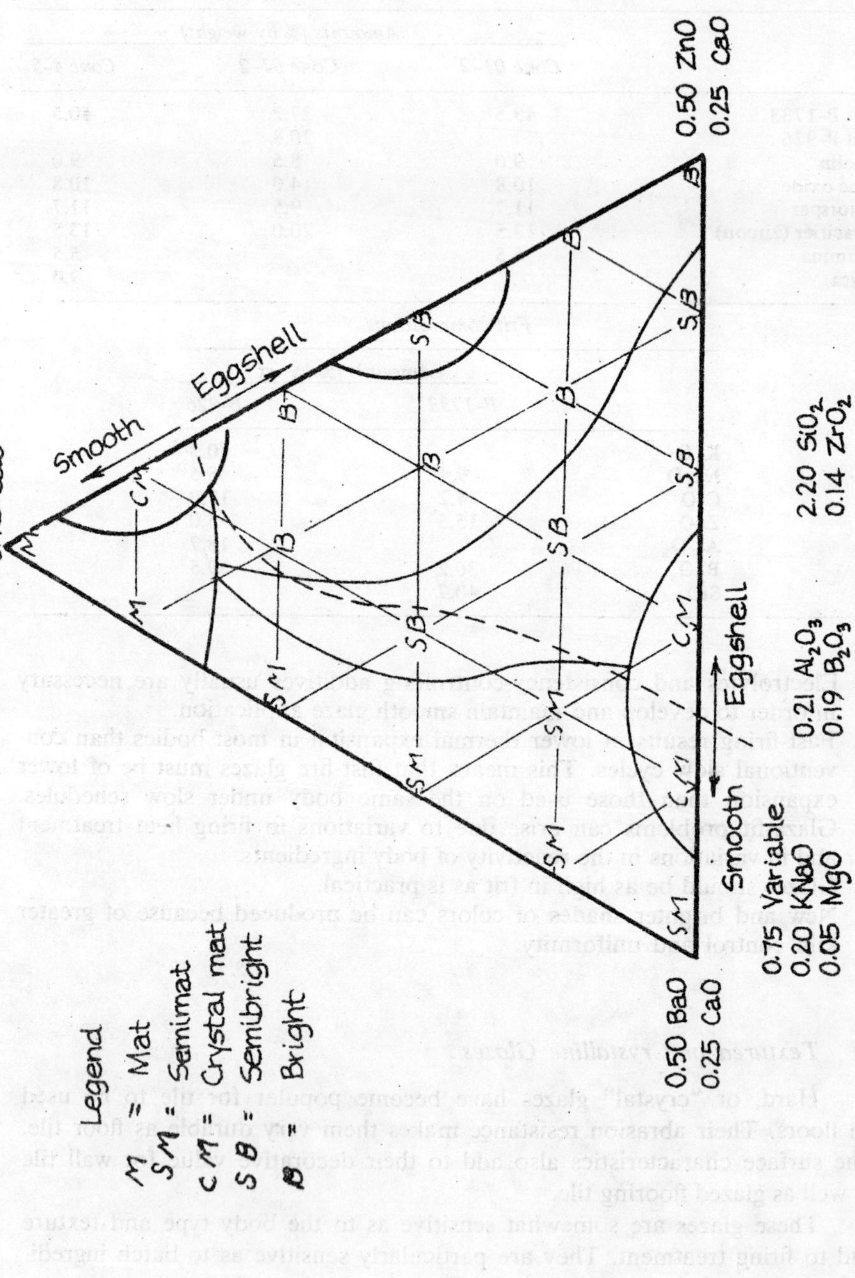

Figure 16.8. Leadless opaque cone 04 glazes.[84]

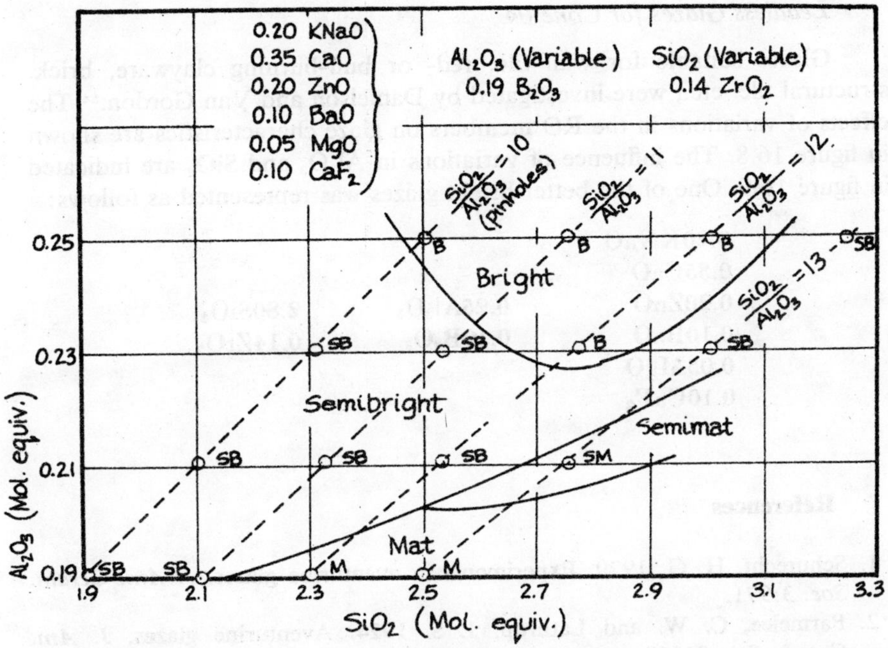

Figure 16.9. Influence of Al_2O_3 and SiO_2 variations in cone 04 leadless glazes.[84]

ents and the physical degree of fineness of the materials, as well as to the mill-addition portion.

Examples of satisfactory glaze formulae for talc-based wall tile are given in table 16.18. These widely used compositions were originated by Pemco, Baltimore, Md.[83] These glazes are effective when made according to the recipes given. They cannot reliably be prepared solely on the basis of their empirical formulas.

It is possible to prepare textured glazes for various maturing temperatures, say from cone 06 to cone 6. They may be lead-bearing or lead-free, zinc-bearing or zinc-free. The common feature is low silica and low Al_2O_3. It is quite characteristic that these textured glazes be richer than usual in zircon and quite high in CaF_2.

The glazes are applied fairly heavy—thirty to forty thousandths of an inch. Two-coat glazes have been developed and used some but are now largely abandoned. The two-coat glazes were harder to control than the types shown in table 16.18.

Leadless Glazes for Cone 04

Glazes suitable for wall tile, red- or buff-burning clayware, brick, structural tile, etc., were investigated by Danielson and Van Gordon.[84] The effects of variations in the RO members on glaze characteristics are shown in figure 16.8. The influence of variations in Al_2O_3 and SiO_2 are indicated in figure 16.9. One of the better bright glazes was represented as follows:

0.20KNaO		
0.35CaO		
0.20ZnO	$0.25Al_2O_3$	$2.80SiO_2$
0.10BaO	$0.19B_2O_3$	$0.14ZrO_2$
0.05MgO		
$0.10CaF_2$		

References

1. Schurecht, H. G. 1920. Experiments in aventurine glazes. *J. Am. Ceram. Soc.* 3:971.
2. Parmelee, C. W. and Lathrop, J. S. 1924. Aventurine glazes. *J. Am. Ceram. Soc.* 7:567.
3. Haldeman, V. K. 1924. Aventurine glazes. *J. Am. Cer. Soc.* 7:824.
4. Langenbeck, Karl. *Chemistry of pottery,* p 63.
5. Dept. Ceram. Eng., Univ. of Illinois.
6. Kondo, S., 1925. Chrome Aventurine glaze. *The Tokio Higher Technical School Bull.* 3:13; 1926. *Ceram. Abstr.* 5:3.
7. Koerner, J. 1908. New crystalline glazes. *Trans. Am. Ceram. Soc.* 10:61.
8. Pukall, W. 1908. Crystalline glazes. *Sprechsaal* 41:519.
9. Franchet, L. 1911. La fabrication industrielle des emaux et couleurs. Paris: *Ceramiques,* p 122.
10. Watkins, R. T. 1922. The degree to which different glaze compositions take vapor lusters. *J. Am. Ceram. Soc.* 5:28.
11. Stull, R. T. 1904. Notes on the production of crystalline glazes. *Trans. Am. Ceram. Soc.* 6:186.
12. Purdy, R. C. and Krehbiel, J. F. 1907. Crystalline glazes. *Trans. Am. Ceram. Soc.* 9:319.
13. Kondo, S. 1925. Zinc crystal glazes. *J. Jap. Ceram. Assoc.* 33:165; 1928. *Ceram. Abstr.* 7:125.
14. Hainbach, R. 1924. *Pottery decorating.* 2d ed. London: Scott, Greenwood and Son, p 91.
15. Porst, E. 1932. Unpublished data, Dept. of Ceram. Eng., University of Illinois.
16. Schwartz, J. 1932. Unpublished data, Dept. of Ceram. Eng., University of Illinois.

17. Kondo, S. 1925. Manganese crystal glazes. *J. Jap. Ceram. Assoc.* 33:387; 1928. *Ceram. Abstr.* 7:127.
18. Worcester, W. G. 1908. The function of alumina in a crystalline glaze. *Trans. Am. Ceram. Soc.* 10:450.
19. Stull, R. T. University of Illinois Ceramic Eng. Dept.
20. Riddle, F. H. 1906. A few facts concerning the so-called zinc silicate crystals. *Trans. Am. Ceram. Soc.* 8:336.
21. Rand, C. C. and Schurecht, H. G. 1914. A type of crystalline glaze at cone 3. *Trans. Am. Ceram. Soc.* 16:342.
22. Pukall, W. 1908. My experience with crystal glazes. *Trans. Am. Ceram. Soc.* 10:183.
23. Kraner, H. M. 1924. Colors in a zinc silicate glaze. *J. Am. Ceram. Soc.* 7:868.
24. Wolf, Jos. 1913. The use of zinc oxide in the ceramic industries with special reference to the manufacture of glazes. *Sprech.* 46:237,256.
25. Norton, F. H. 1937. Control of crystalline glazes. *J. Am. Ceram. Soc.* 20:217.
26. Thiemecke, H. W. Notes on a cone 10 raw crystal glaze. *J. Am. Ceram. Soc.* 17:359.
27. Norton, F. H. 1937. Control of crystalline glazes. *J. Am. Ceram. Soc.* 20:217.
28. Cox, Paul E. 1948. Low temperature glazes. *Ceram. Age* 51(2):78,81.
29. German Patent No. 942,797.
30. German Patent No. 945,498.
31. Zielke, Gottfried. 1955. Development of a transparent lead-free boron glaze for a Segar cone 05a to 03a. *Sprechsaal* 88(20):444–47; (21):475–77; (22):493–95; (23):514–16; (24):536–38.
32. Claudette, A. F. M. *Glazing earthenware and glaze therefor*. U.S. Patent 2,498,912, Feb 28, 1950.
33. Schramm, Edward. 1938. Problems in whiteware glazes. *Bull. Am. Ceram. Soc.* 17(11):436–40.
34. Luks, D. W. 1956. Aluminum oxide ceramics: III, How to finish Al_2O_3 ceramics. *Ceram. Ind.* 67(2):97–99.
35. Fisher, Eugene and Twells, Robert. 1957. High-temperature glazing of alumina bodies. *J. Am. Ceram. Soc.* 40(11):385–388.
36. Verba, R. J. 1958. Automatic application of special brick coatings. *Bull. Am. Ceram. Soc.* 37(8):364–65.
37. Di Marcello, F. V., Treptow, A. W., and Baker, L. A. 1968. Glaze for ceramic substrates for thin films. *Bull. Am. Ceram. Soc.* 47(5):511–16.
38. Auda, D. and Schneider, M. 1968. Ceramic glazes for thick film microelectronics. *Bull. Am. Ceram. Soc.* 47(6):565–68.
39. Auerbach, Rudolph. 1949. Electrical conductivity of solid dispersoids. *Kolloid-Z.* 112:60–66.
40. D'Andrea, J. B. (E.I. du Pont de Nemours & Co.) *Ceramic composition and article*. U.S. Patent 2,924,540 Feb 9, 1960; 1960. *Ceram. Abstr.* July:264*b*.

41. Hoffman, L. C. 1963. Precision glaze resistors. *Bull. Am. Ceram. Soc.* 42(6):490–93.
42. Mulligan, W. A. and Murphy, R. A. *Vitreous enamel resistor composition and resistor made therefrom.* U.S. Patent 3,441,516, April 29, 1969.
43. Horton, Paul B. *Ceramic electrical insulator having a semiconducting glaze coating.* U.S. Patent 2,797,175, June 25, 1957.
44. Vose, W. *Electrically conductive ceramic composition.* Canadian Patent 458,118, July 12, 1949.
45. American Society for Metals. *Metals handbook.* 8th ed. 1961. New York: Reinhold Publishing Corp.
46. Smothers, William J. *Coated insulator.* U.S. Patent 3,389,214, June 18, 1948.
47. Forrest, J. S. 1947. The electrical properties of semiconductive ceramic glazes. *J. Sci. Instruments* 24(8):211–17; 1950. *Ceram. Abstr.* Feb:28*i*.
48. Huttar, Daniel E. (E. I. Du Pont de Nemours & Co.) U.S. Patent 2,837,487, June 3, 1958.
49. Baynton, P. L., Rawson, H., and Stansworth, J. E. 1957. Semiconducting properties of some vanadate glasses. *J. Electrochem. Soc.* 104:237–40.
50. Munakata, M. 1960. Electrical conductivity of high vanadium phosphate glass. *Solid-State Electron.* 1:159–63.
51. Mackenzie, J. D. 1964. Semiconducting oxide glasses; general principle for preparation. *J. Amer. Ceram. Soc.* 47(5):211–14.
52. McMillan, P. W. Preparation and properties of glasses containing major proportions of certain transition metal oxides, in *Advances in glass technology*—Technical papers of the Sixth International Congress on Glass, July, 1962, Washington, D.C. 1962. New York: Plenum Press, pp 333–473; 1962. *Ceram. Abstr.* Sept:227*i*.
53. Denton, E. P., Rawson, H., and Stanworth, J. E. 1954. Vanadate glasses. *Nature* 173(4413):1030–32.
54. Kitaigorodskii, I. I. and Karpenchenko, V. G. 1960. Synthesis and investigation of certain vanadium glasses. *Glass Ceram.* (*USSR*) (English Translation) 15(9):294–97.
55. Weyl, W. A. *Electrical conductivity of glasses.* Unclassified document No. 5685/ATI/125271, Wright-Patterson Air Force Base, Ohio, July, 1956.
56. Janakirama-Rao, B. H. V. 1965. Structure and mechanism of conduction of semiconductor glasses. *J. Am. Ceram. Soc.* 48(6):311–19.
57. Graff, William A. *Coating glasses for electrical devices.* U.S. Patent 3,441,422, April 29, 1969.
58. Mikoda, M., Kuroda, T., and Hayakawa, S. 1968. Preparation and electrical properties of a low-loss dielectric. *Bull. Am. Ceram. Soc.* 47(5): 474–76.
59. Chernashkin, I. T. 1958. Low temperature glaze based on volcanic ash. *Steklo i Keram.* 15(9):35–37; 1959. *Ceram. Abstr.* (1):11*f*.
60. Fain, I. A. 1958. New glaze formula for ceramic (sewer) pipe, *Steklo i Keram* 15(5):36–37; 1958. *Ceram. Abstr.* Sept:235*j*.

61. Gotlib, I. M. and Kordonskaya, R. K. 1956. Glaze for sewer pipe made from easily fusible clays. *Steklo i. Keram.* 13(3):23–25; 1959. *Ceram. Abstr.* June:158*b*.
62. Knizek, I. O. 1956. Development of sewer pipe glazes from volcanic materials. *Bull. Am. Ceram. Soc.* 35(10):399–401.
63. Manvelyan, M. G., Pogosyan, R. P., and Ter-Karapetyan, S. A. 1956. Glazed ware from tuff. *Steklo i Keram.* 13(1):16–17; 1959. *Ceram. Abstr.* June:162*b*.
64. Panchenko, D. M. 1959. Easily fusible glaze for sewer pipe. *Steklo i Keram.* 16(4):43–44; 1959. *Ceram. Abstr.* Sept:235*j*.
65. Plotnikov, L. A. 1951. Low melting glaze for sewer pipe. *Stekl i Keram.* 8(11):18–19; 1953. *Ceram. Abstr.* July:121*b*.
66. Zaitseva, M. I. 1952. Ceramic sewer pipe from low melting clay and lead-free glazes. *Steklo i Keram.* 9(2):12–13; 1953. *Ceram. Abstr.* Oct:176*d*.
67. Koenig, J. H. 1956. *Lead in the ceramic industry*. Sect. 8. New York: Lead Industries Association.
68. Stull, R. T. and Johnson, P. V. 1942. Low-cost glazes for structural clay products. *Bur. Std.* Circ. c 436; 1942. *Ceram. Abstr.* 21(7):144.
69. Wilson, R. C. and Koenig, C. J. 1958. Sewer pipe glazes containing nepheline syenite. *J. Am. Ceram. Soc.* 27:56–73. 1959. *Ceram. Abstr.* Jan:11c.
70. Bauleke, M. P. 1960. Sewer pipe glaze from Kansas volcanic ash. *Bull. Am. Ceram. Soc.* 39(11):680–81.
71. Fliess, H. 1969. Colored salt glazes. *Keram.* 21(5):310–11.
72. Gallup, John and Dingwall, A. G. F. 1957. Properties of low-temperature solder glasses. *Bull. Am. Ceram. Soc.* 36(2):47–51.
73. Kerridge, Frank Enoch. *Vitrifiable enamels for the decoration of glass and method of making.* U.S. Patent 2,557,545, June 19, 1951.
74. Martin, Francis W. *Method for glazing.* U.S. Patent 3,488,216, Jan 6, 1970.
75. Petticrew, Richard W. Glazing compositions and process. U.S. Patent 3,532,524, Oct 6, 1970.
76. Theiss, L. E. 1946. Steatite glazes. *J. Am. Cer. Soc.* 19(9):84–86.
77. Gebler, Kenneth A. 1951. P_2O_5 glazes for steatite. *Ceram. Age* 58(3): 15–17.
78. Bloor, E. C. 1956. Glaze composition, glass structural theory and its application to glazes. *Trans. Brit. Ceram. Soc.* 55(10):631–660.
79. Luttrell, Carolyn Banks. 1949. Glazes for zircon porcelains. *J. Am. Ceram. Soc.* 32(10):327–32.
80. Van Gordon, D. V. 1951. High-fire opaque glazes for zircon bodies. *J. Am. Ceram. Soc.* 34(2):33–38.
81. Theiss, L. E. 1943. Vitrified cordierite bodies. *J. Am. Ceram. Soc.* 26(3):99–102.
82. Orth, William H. 1967. Effect of firing rate on physical properties of wall tile. *Bull. Am. Ceram. Soc.* 46(9):841–44.

83. *Suggested glaze batches. Crystalline and textured glazes.* Technical Bulletin #5013. Baltimore, Md.: Pemco (now Glidden-Durkee Div., Pemco Products, SCM Corp).
84. Danielson, R. R. and van Gordon, D. V. 1950. Leadless opaque glazes at cone 04. *J. Am. Ceram. Soc.* 33(11):323–327.

17

Glaze Defects

The general appearance of blisters and pinholes is clearly indicated by the titles, so description is not necessary. Eggshell refers to a glaze surface more or less marred by minute depressions which appear as though they had been made by the point of a very fine needle. The fault is more common with the harder, less fusible glazes, e.g., the porcelain type, which are very viscous at maturing temperatures, whereas the softer glazes, maturing at the lower temperatures, are sufficiently fluid at maturity to heal these defects.

All of these faults have a similar origin, namely the presence of gas blebs in the glaze from the early sintering period until maturity. A fired body or glaze will retain considerable amounts of gases whose presence is not easily detected. Some of the gas is dissolved just as air is dissolved in water; some is contained in minute pores in the body—seeds or bubbles in the glaze. Some gas is adsorbed on the surface of the body, to be released under favorable conditions of temperature. The minute seeds and blebs below the surface of the glaze do not worry the potter if they are few and inconspicuous. However, they may give rise to the appearance of "cutlery marks" on tableware in use or, if present on chemical or electrical wares, they may be objectionable for technical reasons.

The origins of the gases causing these defects are many. They mav be traced to the materials, preparation, forming, finishing, and firing of the bodies; or to the materials, preparation, application, and firing of the glazes. Explanation of the physical causes must be sought in such phenomena as solution, dissolution, chemical reactions, viscosity, surface tension, etc.

Most defects, however, originate from causes other than gases and bubbles. Variations in uniformity of application result in color variations, waviness, roughness, or even crawling. Impurities or foreign matter in glaze materials, overfiring, underfiring, careless handling, glaze-runs, spots, and a number of other defects are familiar.

Defects Originating before Firing

Defects Associated with the Unfired Body

Blistering and pinholes appear when glazes are applied to green, unfired clayware. Certain defects may be traced to body conditions or body behavior, which are outlined as follows:

a. Insufficient blunging; body is not homogeneous.
b. Introduction of air into slip through faulty operation of the slip pump.
c. Poor pugging.
d. Molds, if casting is done, that are too dry or too hot.
e. Too much water used in finishing the piece.
f. Ware that is too hard when fettled.
g. Dust or oil on the surface of the ware.
h. Air entrapped in small cavities in the surface and not displaced during the dipping.
i. Failure to soak very porous ware in water before coating with the glaze slip.
j. Temperature disparity between ware and glaze. Ware having a rough surface, and the glaze slip for coating it, should be at approximately the same temperature before bringing together. If the glaze is much warmer, the air entrapped on the surface will expand and form a bubble in the coating.
k. Slow application. An unfired body which remains too long in contact with the glaze slip will absorb too freely and pimples may form. This is more frequently the case with dry bodies but is also true of others. The general remedies, besides quick application and proper temperature control, include the use of more nonplastics and less plastic clay in the body.
l. Soluble salts concentrated on the surface edges, rims, or raised ornaments of a clay body. Wilson[1] found that such an accumulation resulted in the concentration of sulfates on particles of grog. This weakened the coating of underslip at those points, and the high surface tension of the same, when wetted by the application of the glaze, causes a contraction about the particles of grog, leaving an air pocket. The decomposition of the sulfates liberates gas with the formation of seeds, etc.

Wilson recommends the addition of barium carbonate, chloride, or fluoride to the body to render the soluble sulfates harmless, and gum tragacanth to the glaze and underslip. This addition increases the strength of the underslip and glaze sufficiently to withstand the pressure of the gases present. He found that lightly sandpapering the body (architectural terra cotta) to remove the accumulation of salts was useful.

m. The structure of an unfired body. Fine grain bodies containing much plastic materials are more prone to cause blisters than the coarser, clay-grogged mixtures.[2] Blistering is almost as frequent when glazes are sprayed on biscuit body as on the unfired.

Gases causing pinholes and blisters may originate in the glaze slip, from the following sources:

a. Fermentation of organic mátter naturally present in the batch as, for example, with some ball clays, and introduced accidentally in the raw materials. The addition to the glaze slip of organic adhesives, such as gum arabic, gum tragacanth, glue, etc., will prove a fertile source of trouble unless prevented by the use of a few drops of carbolic acid or some phenol derivative, the oil of wintergreen, formaldehyde, etc.

b. Chemical decomposition of carbonates, etc., while the slip is in storage.

c. Insufficient or overlong storage of the glaze slip, especially in a warm place. This may lead to the accumulation of gases from the causes enumerated above. If the period is short and the slip is too viscous, the air entrapped during the milling or blunging will not be sufficiently removed. Thorough but not violent agitation can be had by properly designed stirrers.

d. Saturation of thin-wall ware with water during the dipping or spraying operations.

e. Flat dipping, entrapping air between the glaze slip and the piece of ware.

f. Too violent spraying. This may break the adhesion of the glaze coat to the underslip or body and pinholes, blisters, and bare spots may develop.

g. Too long an interval between application of successive coats. If the application of underslip or glaze is timed to follow the disappearance of the wet sheen of the preceding application, no blistering will develop. Delay of, say, 5 or 10 minutes will be followed by very bad blistering.

h. The amount and kind of the ball clay content, the thickness of the underslip, its permeability by water, and the fineness of grain. All are important factors influencing pinholing and blistering.[2]

i. The differential shrinkage of a very thick glaze coat. This has been assigned as a cause of blistering.[3]

j. Too fine grinding of the glaze.

k. The rising through the glaze coat of small tongues of underslip on an architectural terra cotta body. This has been known to leave a pinhole.

Table 17.1. Analysis of gas in glasses[4]

	Measured in volumes		
	Oxygen	Carbon dioxide	Nitrogen
Barium flint glass	83.0	27.0	less than 1.0
Thermometer glass	4.5	10.0	3.0
Borosilicate glass	6.0	5.0	6.0

Defects Originating during Firing

Fluid melts of silicate mixtures contain considerable volumes of gases unless removed by special heat treatment. For this reason, in the manufacture of commercial glass, a period of soaking heat, following melting, is maintained to rid the batch of gas bubbles. Certain chemicals are added to facilitate the action and, in special cases, mechanical stirring is employed. This is called the fining or planing period. Glaze coatings are very thin and do not require as prolonged planing as commercial glass, but they must pass through a similar experience.

High- and Low-temperature Glazes

The more fluid the glaze at maturity, the more readily and completely the gases escape; the higher temperature glazes are more viscous and neither plane as readily nor heal the surface pinholes left by the escaping gases as smoothly as lower temperature glazes. In either case underfiring may leave blisters or the craters of those which have burst. Overfiring may be accompanied by the fresh evolution of seeds, bubbles, or blisters caused by renewed chemical action in the glaze or between the glaze and the body. The higher temperature will decrease the viscosity of the glaze and expand and thereby increase the buoyancy of the gas bubbles, which rise more rapidly and sweep many of the smaller bubbles along.

Gases in Solution

The evidence of the presence of gases in glasses (or glazes) is not limited to those which may be seen, since considerable may be present in solution. Using special methods gases have been extracted from commercial glasses, measured, and identified as shown in table 17.1.

Washburn[4] and his associates, who investigated the phenomena, concluded that these gases had been held in solution in these commercial glasses. Other investigators have extracted water vapor from several types of glasses while those glasses made from batches containing sulfates have yielded carbon dioxide, oxygen, and sulfur dioxide. The kind and quantity of the gases extracted were found to be dependent upon the temperature and the nature of the furnace atmosphere during the melting as well as the composition of the raw batch. Glazes have not, as yet, been so exhaustively studied, but there is every reason to believe that similar results will be discovered when that is done.

Besides the furnace (i.e., kiln) atmosphere, which must be a relatively limited source of the gases found in glazes, there are other much more prolific sources.

Gases are retained in the interstices between the particles of the glaze batch and adsorbed on the surfaces. Blakely[5] observed that bubbles are formed from such conditions at about 900° C in a borosilicate glaze.

Chemical Decomposition

The carbonates of the alkaline earths and other metals, the nitrates, sulfides, hydrates, sulfates, fluorides (notably present in Cornwall stone), and the oxides of some metals may decompose.

Watts[6] found that bubbles were less frequently present in glazes made with the fumed oxides of lead than with white lead because the latter liberated large volumes of gases at such times and temperatures during the fusion of the glaze coat as to form bubbles, seeds, and pinholes. Metallic lead, present as an impurity, and zinc oxide, a frequently used glaze constituent, volatilize readily and may cause pinholes. Several of the color oxides, notably those of iron, manganese, cobalt, and nickel, have the property during firing of forming more complex oxides which subsequently decompose at higher temperatures and liberate the excess oxygen as bubbles. Coarse particles of decomposable compounds are particularly liable to cause trouble. Pieces of plaster from worn molds are potential trouble makers.

The decomposition of many carbonates in contact with finely divided silica takes place more readily and at lower temperatures than if alone, and may facilitate the escape of other gases. On the other hand, most sulfates remain unaffected until sintering has advanced to fusion, and the oxides of sulfur are entrapped in the viscous melt from which they escape only with difficulty, frequently forming blisters and worse.

Feldspars may and do contain gases dissolved or mechanically held which are a potential cause of trouble. Frits which are improperly constructed may take up water subsequent to their fusion and later, during or after fusion on the ware, the water vapor may be liberated as seeds or bubbles. By increasing slightly the amount of china clay added to the mill batch, the glaze during early sintering will remain porous long enough to facilitate the escape of the vapor as well as other gases.

Particles of organic matter—coal, soot, lignitic material from the ball clays, material accidentally falling into the glaze slip during its preparation, e.g., bits of paper, string, etc.—if not consumed during the firing before sintering, may become entrapped in the fused glaze, oxidizing later during more favorable conditions.

When this happens, the carbon oxides form gas bubbles, and, finally, pinholes. If the blisters on a porcelain glaze are greyish or black, they indicate that the reducing conditions—characteristic of the technique of firing hard porcelain according to the European method—have been too prolonged or too severe. In ordinary kiln firing practice, the presence of smoke, soot, or coal particles indicate poor kiln design or firing.

Viscosity

The importance of the viscosity of the glaze in relation to these faults has been mentioned. Knollman[7] found that a glaze which gave trouble apparently due to sulphates formed during watersmoking, was corrected by modifying the composition so as to make it more fluid at the necessary firing temperature. A softer feldspar was used and the glaze was applied more thinly. A higher temperature or longer fire would probably have served.

It has been observed that a difficulty of the kind described above has been noted in kilns containing vitreous sanitary ware, whereas the same glaze fired in mixed kilns of vitreous and solid porcelain did not show this fault. There may be several equally satisfactory explanations. One is that the effect of the greater mass of wares in the latter instance would be to store up a greater quantity of heat without an apparent change in the pyrometric temperature. This lag in heating and, of course, in cooling would be equivalent to a soaking heat and a longer period for the glaze to liberate gases. Or the slower firing rate of a mixed kiln, as compared with a kiln of thinner ware, would facilitate the escape of the gases.

Sulfur-bearing Gases

Prolific sources of the oxides of sulfur are the gases of combustion during the firing operations. The sulfur gases lag in their flow through the kiln chamber and the unfused or partly fused glazes dissolve or react with these gases. Sulfates of lime and other bases are formed and retained until the higher temperatures are reached, when they decompose and yield gas bubbles, blisters, a dry and dull matt or, in very bad cases, a shriveled surface.

Sulfuring takes place most readily during the watersmoking period of the firing when the kiln is relatively cold and moisture from the ware as well as the water vapor from the fuel saturates the atmosphere and condenses on the ware. Slow watersmoking due to poor fuel, faulty methods of firing, poor kiln design, and even improper drainage of the flues and area on which the kiln is placed are important contributory causes.

All colored glazes are susceptible to injury by the sulfur gases which impair their beauty. Many of those containing manganese develop a film-like coating readily discernible but extremely thin. This characteristic appearance provides a convenient "telltale" to detect the presence of sulfur gases. Albany slip is another convenient medium for testing the kiln conditions and many generations of potters have utilized it for the purpose by smearing it on the surface of draw trials which are removed from the kiln from time to time. Unfortunately the harm has been done to the ware by the time these trial pieces are withdrawn, but it is not irreparable since careful finishing fires, with an atmosphere free from the sulfur gases, will probably restore the glossy appearance of the glaze surface.

Firing Schedules

Too slow watersmoking accompanied by strongly reducing conditions results in the deposition of carbon particles in the unfused glaze.

If this condition continues the carbon particles penetrate deeply and the fusion of the layer accompanying the rising temperature locks the particles in the surface and the glaze has a grey or black color. This effect is very pronounced when lead or copper is present in the glaze. Thorough oxidation, if not too late, restores the glaze to its proper appearance but the trace of carbon may remain in solution, giving it a faintly ivory color. It is reasonable to expect that the glaze in a molten condition will dissolve more or less of the reducing gases even without showing the presence of carbon particles. This is particularly true of the softer glazes such as used on wall tile, many kinds of artware, and table ware. Such glazed wares, although apparently satisfactory when they come from the kiln, may show numerous minute gas bubbles when subsequently refired even at very low temperatures. An especially troublesome defect of this kind is known to the potters as "spit out."

While a reducing condition, if improperly controlled, may be a cause of serious trouble, it is also true that the sulfates present may be rendered harmless by a careful reduction to sulfites, which are readily decomposed at low temperatures, the gases freed, and dissipated.

Soluble Salts

Most clay mixtures contain soluble salts, with the sulfates of the alkalies and alkali earths predominating.

These salts will concentrate on the surface, especially at the corners, edges, and on raised ornaments. The glaze naturally reacts with them and gases are liberated. The common remedy for this fault is the addition of sufficient amounts of barium carbonate, chloride, or fluoride to render the sulfates insoluble.

The use of color oxides containing sulfate impurities, the inadequate calcination of frits and stains which contain decomposable compounds, and the insufficient washing of calcines are all possible causes of pinholes.

Crawling, Ruckling, Beading

Crawling, also known as ruckling, butterfly, rolling, and curdling, is a defect displayed by the matured glaze although it may originate in the prefire or in the firing stages. It is characterized by bare areas on the ware, small or relatively large, which the glaze, when fused, has failed to cover. The margin of the glaze coat bordering on the unglazed area, whether a crack or patch, is frequently thickened as though it had contracted (crawled) while in the fused condition; moreover, it is smoothly rounded.

The term butterfly refers to the larger thickened patch which sometimes appears as though a small portion of the glaze had folded back on itself. Curdling and rolling are good descriptive terms for characteristic appearances, and "parting cracks" describes very well the frequently observed mild form of the fault. Beading is the extreme type. In this case the glaze may withdraw in small patches or even form small beads, resembling drops of water on a hot plate.

The fundamental physical causes, singly or collectively, of crawling and related defects are:

1. Shrinkages—drying and firing
2. Adhesion (interfacial tension) or its absence in the unfired state
3. Interfacial reactions in the fired stage
4. Viscosity of the maturing glaze
5. Surface tension of the maturing glaze

Contributory causes of such defects are:

1. Chemical composition of the glaze
2. Physical condition of the glaze—fineness of grind, use of frit
3. Physical condition of the body—shrinkage, texture, vitrification
4. Firing duration, temperature, atmosphere
5. Thickness of application

Shrinkage

Significant differences between the shrinkages of the body and the glaze during the drying and the firing stages will cause the formation of cracks in the latter. If the molten glaze is highly viscous, as is notably the case of the Bristol type, the break cannot be repaired by flowing of the melt as will frequently happen with raw lead compositions. Moreover, the surface tension, which is high in Bristol glazes, will cause the coating to withdraw along the edge of the crack. Some of the causes for the excessive shrinkage are:

1. The use of the wrong kind and amount of clay.
2. Excessive grinding of the glaze batch will increase the amount of soluble salts derived from the feldspar or frit, if any is used. In turn, these soluble salts may influence the conduct of the clay in the glaze batch. For this reason overground glazes, if left undisturbed for a little time, may settle as a cementlike mass. Prolonged grinding may cause the hydration of some part of a frit batch. The release of the water during the firing may cause blistering or pinholes.
3. Glaze constituents which contract unduly at high temperatures, e.g., zinc oxide and minerals which decrepitate, e.g., certain calcium borates, may cause trouble. Calcining the zinc oxide is advisable. Wollastonite and bone ash are said to act like the zinc oxide.
4. Too thick an application of the glaze slip.
5. Glazes sweated by contact with a stagnant or slow moving, moisture-laden atmosphere during the watersmoking period (especially if the kiln flues are wet) will absorb moisture, swell, and later contract as the kiln atmosphere becomes hotter and drier. Setting the ware too damp or closing the saggers too tightly, particularly if the ware is placed in the green condition, will contribute to this condition. But if the early stage of the firing of the kiln is too rapid, the moisture in the glaze coat may be driven out at a rate which will weaken the layer as well as its bond with the body.
6. Green bodies containing considerable quantities of coarse nonplastics, e.g., architectural terra cotta, are difficult to coat with a smooth glaze because of the irregular shrinkages localized about individual particles of grog. Strains, originating during the drying and the early firing, may cause small cracks which will extend through the underslip and the glaze coat during the firing. Glazes having high fluidity and low surface tension may cover and fill small cracks, but the Bristol type with its high surface tension and high viscosity will crawl. It is a function of the underslip to provide a smooth, strong, elastic layer which minimizes or prevents the irregularities of shrinkages from affecting the properties of the glaze coat.
7. The body, if it has not been well prepared and lacks homogeneity, may be at fault. This may be true of green and biscuit wares.

Imperfect Bond

An imperfect bond between the glaze and the body or underslip is a frequent cause of crawling. Some of the reasons for the failure are:

1. The surface of the ware may be smeared with oil, grease, or some water repellent.
2. Dust may have accumulated on the surface of the biscuit or bone-dry ware. A loose, dust-like underglaze decoration may prevent a proper bond.
3. Damp areas of a clay body or biscuit, or hard-fired areas of a biscuit interfere with the bond. This is true of any relatively chemically inactive portion which is not "wetted" by the molten glaze or only slowly, e.g., and underglaze decoration, a bit of refractory grog. Small areas on cast pieces where the first impact of the casting slip on the face of the mold has taken place apparently fire more densely than the surrounding surface, thus giving rise to the formation of crawling, ruckling, or butterfly. The "springing-off" of the glaze from some underglaze colors, notably pinks, cobalt blues, and chrome greens, is attributed to their "dryness." They may lack sufficient flux or may not have been well prepared and washed to remove sulfates or other soluble salts. It has been reported that slips used for casting a body may not contain more than 0.2% electrolyte without interfering with the adherence of the glaze to the biscuit.
4. Improper firing of the biscuit may leave the ware too absorbent and it will, therefore, take on too thick a coat of the glaze slip, which will develop shrinkage cracks. Or overfiring of the biscuit may prevent proper adhesion unless a suitable change is made in the kind or amount of clay in the glaze batch or unless adhesives are used.
5. Glazes which have been allowed to stand for several hours or days will frequently crawl. The change is chemical in nature and will be hastened by warmth and, possibly, bacterial action. In the case of the last named agent, light is known to be an important factor. Presumably electrolytes are liberated by the solvent action of water on the finely ground feldspar and other batch material, including many frits. The condition may be corrected by drying the batch, bringing it into a slip condition, and using without delay. The correction of the pH of the glaze slip which has been stored by the careful addition of acetic, hydrochloric, or some other unobjectionable acid is practical.

The fundamental cause of the difficulties listed under 1 to 5, inclusive, is the inadequate adjustment of the interfacial tension of glaze to the body wherever crawling appears. Lampman[8] studied the conduct of several glazes on certain bodies and found that the maturing temperature of the same glaze may vary as much as four cones, apparently determined by the interfacial (the wetting) conduct. It is for the same reason, probably, that the angle of joining of two surfaces is frequently the location of parting cracks, and the coating of raised ornamental decorations is troublesome. In ascribing to interfacial tension an important function in crawling of glazes, due regard must be had for the importance of surface tension and the viscosity of the glaze melt. Just what role the presence of soluble salt deposits on the surface of unfired wares may have on the glaze coat seems to depend upon conditions not at present fully understood, since radically different opinions have appeared in the literature.

Summary of Physical Factors

Crawling frequently is said to be due to high surface tension of the molten glaze. This is highly unlikely; in any event other factors are the more important. The kind and amount of raw clay in the glaze, the thickness of application, the degree of adhesion of the glaze film, and the strength of the unfired glaze coating all are of direct and paramount importance.

BINDERS. The floating agents, binders, gums, and adhesives become very important. Electrolytes also are important. The most common binders are gum Arabic, gum tragacanth, and starch, as well as waxes, glues, and cellulose derivatives. Molasses, brown sugar, and refined sugar in the amount of about 1% commonly are used.

Starches ferment, but there are starch products now available that are said not to. Cellulose products and synthetic polymers also have wide use. They commonly are used at 0.2% and up to 0.5%. They are useful on structural products, and will adhere even to the hard, slick surfaces.

TESTS FOR CRAWLING. Some very practical tests for crawling have been proposed by Danielson.[9] Several deep scratches are made in the surface of the green body and marks are made on the body with a wax pencil before the glaze is applied. This can give an index to the wetting qualities and to the healing properties. The use of curved test pieces with holes, and sharp concave and convex edges help reveal tendencies to tear or crawl. Different thicknesses of application also are indicative of any crawling tendencies.

A series of draw trials at 100° F intervals then are made. Crawling or cracking may appear below red heat or not until 2,000° F. In cases when the viscosity and wetting properties of the glazes are controlling features, the crawling starts with the beginning of glaze-maturing.

INITIATION OF CRAWLING. If there is excessive shrinkage, cracks may start during drying. Cracks that are due to sintering shrinkage start 300° to 400° below the finish temperature. Some glazes crack badly during the early stages of firing, then heal over as the glaze matures. The tear areas will remain visible and give the finished glaze a pebble-grained appearance.

Fine cracks at edges are incipient crawling indicators and this can be cured by materials or binder selection. Sweating of the glaze in slow-moving, moisture-laden atmospheres during the watersmoking period leads to trouble. Close setting may cause poor ventilation and lead to crawling. Localized excessive heating rates and inverted, hollow, bowl-like shapes may retard moisture removal and lead to severe cases of glaze-blistering.

Loss of Gloss

The failure of the glaze to develop the expected glossy surface may be due to any of a number of causes. Most of these are discussed under their respective headings to follow.

Sucking up of the Glaze

If the ware is very porous, especially if highly siliceous, a glaze coat—particularly of the low-temperature, highly fluid type—may be absorbed by the body and leave only a slightly glassy trace on the surface.

Volatilization

All bases used in glazes volatilize more or less; lead is the outstanding example. Ware coated with a composition containing this constituent and fired will lose the desired gloss unless the amount of the oxide is quite small or the article has been enclosed in a sagger. In the latter case the inside walls of the sagger should be given a preliminary wash of a mixture containing considerable lead oxide. It is obvious that uncoated ware in the same sagger will be fumed and show a slight sheen. The fuming of certain coloring agents may be useful or objectionable, according to the skill of the ceramist, since this is an accepted method of decoration. Rapid volatilization may be a cause of blisters.

Undissolved Material

The presence of notable amounts of undissolved material in a glaze particularly at or immediately under the surface will cause dullness or a pseudomattness. Some of the materials most commonly inactive are: silica, calcia, baryta, magnesia, tin oxide, calcium phosphate, alumina, chromium oxide, and also the spinel group.

Devitrification

Literally, devitrification means a loss of glassy characteristics and can be properly applied to the crystalline glazes having either macro- or micro-crystal development. The latter constitutes the true matt texture. It is common practice to use the term to designate such appearances as are caused by undissolved materials.[3]

To avoid one cause of devitrification, the molecular ratio of the silica to the content of bases should be normally less than 3 to 1, but a loss of gloss may accompany a smaller ratio since the choice of bases is important. This may be observed with an excessive content of lime, which fault may be corrected by increasing the silica or decreasing both. If the ratio of the silica to the alumina is low, mattness or immaturity will result. Mattness, due to high alumina, may be quite sensitive to the rate of cooling; thus a glazed surface may show bright and matt areas, or pieces of ware, not widely separated, may differ in a similar manner. The conspicuous presence of appropriate crystalline forms of silica in the glaze may be the explanation of a dull surface; however, scattered particles of quartz may be undissolved fragments—residue from the batch materials.

Wares which have become dull because of an excess of alumina frequently may be made bright by coating them with a somewhat more fusible glaze and refiring.

Dullness, or a dry surface, due to excess of the oxides of tin or zinc, may be corrected by the addition of small amounts of silica and alumina.

Steaming

Water vapor in the kiln, especially in the presence of fumes from common salt and probably other similar alkali compounds, acts as a mineralizer, and assists in devitrification.[10] Fired glazes exposed to dampness may become coated with whitish film which may be wiped off, only to return later. This is an indication that the glaze is too high in alkalies and deficient in silica.

A frit which contains much alkali, as may be the case with those prepared with barium or tin compounds, must be carefully washed to remove the excess, according to Jako.[11] Otherwise, the glaze prepared with the frit may become dull or covered with a film or crust.

Sulfur

The harmful effects of sulfates in the body, in raw materials, or in water used in preparing glazes, or the oxides of sulfur present in the kiln gases may give rise to a variety of defects; amongst these are: dullness, surface film, dryness, wrinkling, pinholes, and blistering.

Lead-free glazes are relatively high in alkalies which should be introduced as frits. If these are not sufficiently rich in alumina, silica, and boric oxide, usually they are susceptible to attack by the oxides of sulfur. The introduction of ground window and some other forms of glass is said to be open to the same objection.

Jako[11] reports that if the amount of the sulfur oxides is not too great, the addition of 8% to 15% of unfritted carbonate of lead (white lead will do) to the mill batch will readily form a harmless sulfate. This is decomposed by contact with silica at about 920° C and, presumably, the sulfur trioxide is driven off. It is possible to cause the decomposition of the sulfate compounds in the glaze and the dispersion of the sulfurous oxide by maintaining reducing conditions in the kiln before the glaze becomes molten, then finishing the firing in the normally oxidizing manner. Excessive reduction will produce smoked glazes. Carbonaceous matter, such as finely divided coal, coke, and charcoal, may be added to the batch for the same purpose as Seger[12] did in using barium sulfate in a glaze composition.

Immaturity Is an Ordinary Cause of the Lack of Gloss

If more than one glaze composition is used on ware fired in the same kiln, consideration should be given to the placing and the firing so as to create the conditions needed for each, insofar as is possible.

Sulfuring by Kiln Gases

The damage done to glazes by the presence of excessive amounts of sulfur oxides in the kiln gases is similar in many respects to that due to the introduction of sulfates in the glaze materials. The manifestations on the glaze surface are known by a variety of names which are descriptive of the fault. They are:

feathering	discoloration
mattness, dullness, starving	polka dot
blistering	airing
wrinkling	sweat marks
cutlery or knife marks	struck effects

The gases which are responsible for these faults are sulfurous (SO_2) and sulfuric (SO_3) oxides, and both may be and customarily are present in proportions which vary with the temperature, the character, and the amounts of the other gases present, notably oxygen. It is also quite probable that the clayware in the kiln, including firebrick and saggers, exercises a catalytic action of some degree, promoting the conversion of the SO_2 to the SO_3. If reducing conditions prevail in the kiln chamber or flues, sulfurous oxide will dominate. If there is a considerable excess of oxygen, the sulfuric oxide forms. During the watersmoking period of the firing it reacts with moisture to form sulfuric acid. This acid promptly attacks the basic constituents of the glaze coating to form sulfates, e.g., lead, lime, magnesia, and others not too firmly bound with silica or other acid radicals.

Any sulfites which may form are quite easily decomposed by relatively low temperatures; whereas, the sulfates are very resistant to a change. This is well illustrated by the frequent use of sodium sulfate in batches for certain kinds of commercial glass. In that case molten sulfate may separate as an immiscible liquid layer on the surface, unless suitable precautions are taken. In order to avoid this difficulty and to decompose the sulfate—thus liberating the sodium to function properly—sufficient finely divided coal is introduced in the batch as a reducing agent. Seger[12] used a similar expedient successfully in preparing a frit with barium sulfate as an ingredient.

Amount of Sulfur Compounds

The amounts of sulfur dioxide liberated by the perfect combustion of typical fuels has been reported to be as follows:[13]

A typical semibituminous coal containing 1% of sulfur is 0.081% SO_2.
A typical fuel oil containing 0.7% of sulfur is 0.04% SO_2.
A city gas containing 30.0 grains sulfur per 100 cu ft is 0.01% SO_2.

Since the sulfites are so readily decomposed, it is the sulfur trioxide which attacks the surface of the molten glaze at temperatures not much more than the "congealing point" of the glaze, according to Mellor.[14] Ortman[15] drew trial pieces, coated with a glaze, from a muffle kiln, starting at 700° C and ceasing at 875° C, when the glaze was too hard to scrape off. The chemical analyses showed the sulfur trioxide content at the minimum temperature to be 1.83%; the maximum amount was 3.37%, and there was no apparent relation between the temperature and the fluctuations in the oxide.

Doll[16] reports that dullness did not appear on glaze trials which were introduced into an oil-fired tunnel kiln at temperatures above a red heat, i.e., "1,000° to 1,200° F." The oil fuel contained, by specification, less than one-half of 1% of sulfur. Geller and Creamer[17] found that a 3% concentration of sulfur dioxide caused the glaze on hotel ware and earthenware to become dull and mattlike, but blistering and scumming did not appear until the concentration exceeded 5%; except that a glaze on a colored vitrified body blistered after exposure to a concentration of 1% to 1½% of the gas. On the other hand Watts[13] reports that the presence of 0.25% of sulfur dioxide in a small laboratory furnace produced dull patches and scumming of a tile glaze which, he suggests, may have been due in part to the influence of water vapor which was present.

The sulfates formed by reaction with the glaze during the early period of firing cause the characteristic dullness, mattness, and feathering. The last-named term is applied to the appearance of delicate, featherlike surface markings which resemble frost patterns.. It is possible to produce a matt-texture glaze by throwing sulfur or pyrites in the firebox of a kiln at the proper period of firing. The sulfates may diffuse through the glaze to attain a saturation of about 4.5% in a bisilicate and about 2% in a trisilicate composition. That is to say, a good bisilicate glaze may be caused to blister by simply increasing the silica content. The silicic oxide is a more powerful reagent at high temperatures than the sulfuric radical and displaces the same with the consequent evolution of gas.

Ortman[15] has directed attention to the probable displacement of boric oxide and to the reaction with color oxides and some fluxes with the consequent harm to the color and texture of the mature glaze. He suggests the following precautions to lessen or prevent these troubles:

a. Providing maximum possible ventilation consistent with the satisfactory progress of the kiln
b. Firing so as to avoid choking the flues with large volumes of gas
c. Maintaining adequate secondary air supply in the fire boxes
d. Maintaining adequate stack draft and oxidizing conditions throughout

These observations relate to his experience in firing architectural terra cotta in periodic muffle kilns, but they are valuable for other types of operations. To these may be added the obvious necessity of using a low-sulfur fuel. The walls of muffles are sometimes given a coat of lime wash, but the effectiveness of this will depend upon frequent renewals of the coating and the tightness of the muffle construction during firing.

Steger[18] studied a series of glazes to discover their susceptibility to the attack by furnace gases containing moisture and 20% of sulfur dioxide. The range of the compositions of the whole series and of those not affected by the gases were as shown in table 17.2.

It is fundamentally necessary to keep the content of alkali oxides and calcium oxide low; the silica content may be slight (36% to 38%) and

Table 17.2. Influence of glaze components on susceptibility of glazes to attack by furnace gases containing moisture and 20% of SO_2[18]

	Composition, wt. %	
Component oxide	*Total range*	*Not affected by the gases*
Lead	11.1 to 47.1	17 to 20
Alkalies	0.0 to 12.9	3 to 6
Calcium	1.3 to 9.0	4 to 6
Aluminum	4.0 to 11.0	4 to 8
Silicon	35.7 to 55.8	36 to 54
Boron	4.5 to 15.0	5 to 12

the boric acid may not exceed 12%. If the glaze is specially rich in alkali, the boric oxide must be increased to above 12%. Glazes rich in lime may perhaps be made more resistant to furnace gases containing sulfur by the introduction of zinc oxide. A low concentration (2%) of sulfur dioxide in an atmosphere of nitrogen harmed the glazes less than when oxygen and water vapor were present and the range of fusion was widened. When glazes have been glost fired in a stream of dry air, contact with damp air and sulfur dioxide causes surface changes such as dullness, cloudiness, and separation of salts or crystal skeletons.

The sensitivity of lead-free glazes—chosen for the lower temperatures—to the action of sulfur in kiln gases is very generally recognized. Steger[19] studied 19 glazes of this type which would mature at about cones 08 to 03. From the results he made the following recommendations: sodium and lithium oxides cannot be used, therefore borax is not available as a source of boric oxide; calcium should be substituted for those oxides; magnesium can effectively replace a part of the calcium and is believed to be better.

On the average, 15% of boric oxide is the maximum necessary with 55% of silica in the melted glaze. Chemically resistant glazes having a high content of alumina and silica and, therefore, requiring a high temperature for maturity are susceptible to attack by the oxides of sulfur under oxidizing conditions. In general, the action may be prevented or lessened by the use of reduction, properly controlled, followed by oxidizing conditions.[20]

Cutlery Marking

The metal marking or "cutlery marking" of glazes is the grayish streak left on the surface resulting from contact with a knife edge, the tines of a fork, or some other metal object. The obvious cause is the abrasive action of the glaze surface due to an abnormal roughness. Geller and Creamer[17] subjected several samples of domestic and foreign earthenware and vitrified ware to contact with various gases in an electrically heated laboratory furnace which was carefully controlled. Some of the conclusions they reached were:

1. Concentrations of SO_2 as high as 1.2% at 860° C did not produce surface markings, on any specimens tested which could be metal marked.
2. The only specimens which would take a "metal mark" were of one brand of a vitrified, relatively low-fired ware. Concentrations of 3% and 5% of sulfur dioxide were required, but no scumming or blistering was detectable macroscopically. Concentrations of 7½% and above produced a slight scum and impaired the gloss; evidence of marking could not be entirely removed by washing after an exposure to a concentration of 12½%; and the scum formed was composed, at least partly, of lead sulfate.

Cutlery marking is characteristic of all glazes containing mill-added opacifiers. Strictly kiln-fresh ware may not mark but the thin protective skin over the opacifiers soon disappears and marking can result. The best hope for opaque glazes that will not mark lies in the development of nucleated opacification.

Other Gases Causing Loss of Gloss, Pinholes, Blistering, and Discoloration

Watts[13] made an extensive study, under laboratory conditions, of the influence of the products of combustion of city gas as well as the individual constituent gases commonly present in kilns. He summarized the results in the following statement:

> A normal atmosphere almost invariably produced good glaze surfaces provided, of course, that the glaze was of satisfactory composition. Atmospheres containing a carbon monoxide produced a gray or yellowish discoloration in a white glaze and caused bubbles and roughness. The effect was still evident when the carbon monoxide present was only 2% of the furnace atmosphere. Unburned hydrocarbons may break down in a furnace atmosphere and darken a white glaze and body by the deposition of finely divided carbon. A neutral atmosphere of carbon dioxide and nitrogen was not enough to produce good glazes and was sometimes responsible for inferior ones. An oxidizing atmosphere in which 4% to 5% O_2 was present was often an aid in obtaining good glaze surfaces. Water vapor has a very harmful effect on glazes. Leadless and lead-containing, fritted, wall tile-type glazes which matured at cone O2 were studied.

The blistering of a typical semivitreous glaze in commercial production, when the factory changed its fuel from natural to manufactured gas, was attributed by McHattie and Westman[21] to one or more of the burners allowing small amounts of hydrogen and carbon monoxide to come in contact with the ware. This effect apparently could occur without visible flame impingement and after a brief exposure, at high fire, to conditions slightly on the reducing side of the theoretical neutral point. Sulfur dioxide alone could not produce the effect except at relatively high concentrations but, in the opinion of the investigators, its presence may be a necessary condition to cause blistering.

Smoking

The term "smoking"[22] is applied to a yellow, greenish-yellow, or brown discoloration due to the action of sulfur, but not to the gray to black stains caused by carbon. It develops only in a reducing atmosphere. "Sweat marks"[23] or "sulfur patches" are due to the formation of SiS_2 under reducing conditions at high temperature in the last stages of the firing operations. The sulfide has a high gravity and collects in the lowest parts of the sagger or the ware. Contact with air, particularly in the presence of moisture, causes the deposition of silica. Dettmer[24] agrees in attributing it to the formation of polysulfides.

Ortman and Watts[13,15] found that reducing conditions, particularly after the glaze is fused, may cause blistering and scumming because of "the reduction of sulfates previously absorbed and the liberation of sulfur dioxide and oxygen through the molten glaze." Lead-containing glazes are altered to gray or black by prolonged reduction.

Particles of carbon deposited in the glaze before or during sintering and protected from oxidation by being sealed in the fused coating may be a cause of specking[13,25] and one of the possible explanations of spit-out.

"Spit-out"

"Spit-out" or "spitting-out" is the effect caused by the bursting of very small bubbles at the surface of the glaze during the firing in the decorating kiln. The temperature is not sufficiently high to fuse smoothly the thin edges of the craters thus formed. The fault is frequently associated with the decalcomania decorated wares which have stood for some time in a warehouse before going into the decorating kiln, and notably true of goods stored in a place which is not quite dry. The causes of the defect are many and obscure. They have been discussed by several investigators.[26–31]

A review of the present knowledge and theories relating to the causes of the defect gives these conclusions: The defects are due to the evolution of gases which may have originated with carbonaceous material in the body or glaze; sulfates may be present in the body or glaze; the gases of the kiln atmosphere, e.g., oxides of sulfur and moisture, may be ab- or adsorbed by body or glaze; the hydrocarbon gases, sometimes present in the atmosphere of the decorating kiln, may be absorbed by the glaze to be released at a higher temperature; gases of whatever origin will be liberated from a glaze when the temperature-pressure conditions permit; moisture may be absorbed by the body if the ware is measurably porous and is stored for some time.

Flowing or Running-off of Glazes during Firing

Glazes which become too fluid during firing are prone to drain off from the more elevated portions to the lower. This condition may result in a "shading" of colored glaze coatings. To avoid this fault tile are sometimes fired in a horizontal position although vertical setting is more economical of the sagger or kiln space. If tile are set in an inclined or vertical position, that edge which shows the thickest application should be uppermost to permit the coating to become equalized.

Very fluid glazes, e.g., the crystalline type, applied on vases and similar articles will form thick accumulations about the lower portion, even practically draining off and sometimes cementing the ware to the stilt or other support upon which it rests. Attempts to separate the pieces result too frequently in the destruction of the ware. A method of dealing with this difficulty is to place the ware on a layer of fine refractory powder, such as china clay. The glaze may flow over the clay, but this excess may be removed by the aid of an abrasive wheel. If it is impracticable to rest the ware on a bed of powder, it may be supported on a short cylinder made of any refractory body, fired, and coated on the contact surface with a thin layer of china clay.

Flowing glazes are used as a means of decoration. They contain coloring materials and are rather thickly applied about the neck and shoulder of vases coated with glazes previously fired. A second fire will cause the later application to flow over the surface, producing interesting results. Easily flowing glazes which are partially or fully opaque give more uniformity of tone. The use of glazes having a tendency to flow is to be avoided in the development of underglaze decorations, for obvious reasons.

The chief causes of flowing of glazes are:

1. Too thick an application. Spraying will give more uniformity with less likelihood of irregularities such as accompany the dipping operation. Naturally the consistency and density of the glaze are important factors regulating the slip distribution, which affects the ultimate appearance of the mature glaze. An excessively thick application will increase the tendency of the molten glaze to flow on inclined surfaces.
2. Faulty glaze composition which may be altered to decrease the fluidity, when fused, by any one or more of the following changes: (*a*) decrease the content of boric oxide and increase the silica; (*b*) substitute bases having the lower molecular weights for those which are higher; and (*c*) carefully increase the alumina content, using a kaolin (or china clay) if possible, which will add silica and thus avoid altering the glossiness.

References

1. Wilson, H. 1917. Note on pinholing and peeling on terra cotta. *Trans. Am. Ceram. Soc.* 19:209.
2. Schurecht, H. G. and McMahon, J. F. 1937. Influence of the composition of underslips, glazes and bodies on blistering and other glaze defects. *J. Am. Ceram. Soc.* 20:344.
3. Schramm, E. 1938. Problems in whiteware glazes. *Bull. Am. Ceram. Soc.* 17:436.
4. Washburn, E. W., Footit, F. F., and Bunting, E. E. 1920. *Dissolved gases in glass.* Bull. No. 118. Eng. Expt. Sta. Univ. of Illinois.
5. Blakely, A. M. 1938. The life history of a glaze. 1. *J. Am. Ceram. Soc* 21:239.
6. Watts, A. S. 1915. Oxide of lead versus carbonate of lead in glazes. *Trans. Am. Ceram. Soc.* 17:474.
7. Knollman, H. J. 1915. An unusual case of pinholing of glazes. *Trans. Am. Ceram. Soc.* 17:165.
8. Lampman, C. M. 1938. The effect of different bodies on some wetting and flow characteristics of glazes. *J. Am. Ceram. Soc.* 21:252.
9. Danielson, R. R. 1954. The crawling of glazes. *Bull. Amer. Ceram. Soc.* 33(3):73–74.
10. Blumen, A. M. 1938. *Stroit. Materialy.* 12:14; 1939. *Ceram. Abstr.* 18:248.
11. Jako, G. 1926. *Keramische Fabrikationsfehler.* Coburg: p 30.
12. Seger, H. A. 1902. Whiteware glazes containing barium sulfate. *Collected writings.* Vol. 2. Easton, Pa.: Chemical Publishing Co., p 634.
13. Watts, A. P. 1931. Effect of furnace atmospheres on the quality of certain types of glazes. *J. Am. Ceram. Soc.* 14:460.

14. Mellor, J. W. 1906–1907. The sulphuring and feathering of glazes. *Trans. Engl. Ceram. Soc.* 6:71.
15. Ortman, F. B. 1920. The composition of kiln gases and their effect on terra cotta glazes and colors. *J. Am. Ceram. Soc.* 3:476.
16. Doll, C. E. 1925. Discussion on some forms of sulfuring of earthenwa-e glazes. *Bull. Am. Ceram. Soc.* 4:616.
17. Geller, R. F. and Creamer, A. S. 1931. Metal marking of whiteware glazes as influenced by sulfur and carbon in kiln atmospheres. *J. Am. Ceram. Soc.* 14:624.
18. Steger, W. 1940. Comparative tests on whiteware glazes. 3. Effect of sulfur dioxide on whiteware glazes containing lead and boron, *Ber. Deut. Keram. Ges.* 21:228; 1941. *Ceram. Abstr.* 20:149.
19. Steger, W. 1940. Lead free whiteware glazes resistant to sulfurous acid. *Ber. Deut. Keram. Ges.* 21:3; 1941. *Ceram. Abstr.* 20:120.
20. Faber, A. 1927. Extraction of sulfur dioxide from flame gases by glasses and glazes. *Gas. u. Wàsserfach.* 70:419. 1928. *Ceram. Abstr.* 7:250.
21. McHattie, K. J. W. and Westman, A. E. R. 1942. Effect of sulfur and reducing gases on a semivitreous dinnerware glaze and decalcomania decoration. *J. Am. Ceram. Soc.* 25:416.
22. Czech, J. and Kieffer, E. 1937. Testing the susceptibility of porcelain glazes to smoking. *Ber. Deut. Keram. Ges.* 18:87.
23. Kieffer, E. and Czech, J. 1938. Origin of "sweat marks" on hard porcelain. *Ber. Deut. Keram. Ges.* 19:54.
24. Detthner, F. 1927. Effects of sulfur on porcelain glazes. *Sprech.* 60:667.
25. Zimmer, W. H. 1901. Discussion of the relation between the kiln atmosphere and the color of porcelain. *Trans. Am. Ceram. Soc.* 3:216.
26. Mellor, J. W. 1935–36. Spitting of glazes in the enamel-kiln. *Trans. Engl. Ceram. Soc.* 35:355.
27. Mellor, J. W. and Moore, B. 1907–1908. The adsorption and dissolution of gases by silicates— spit-out. *Trans. Engl. Cer. Soc.* 7:1.
28. Discussion of "spit-out." 1904–1905. *Trans. Engl. Ceram. Soc.* 3:30.
29. Cowan, R. G. 1907. Spitting-out—A phenomenon of the decorating kiln. *Trans. Am. Ceram. Soc.* 9:493.
30. Bleininger, A. V. 1928. Physical factors in pottery manufacture. *Ceram. Age* 12:4.
31. Koenig, C. J. 1936. Spit-out. *J. Am. Ceram. Soc.* 19:287.

Index